CW00855352

Few studies of the history of provincial France have hitherto spanned the conventional medieval/early-modern divide, and David Potter's detailed examination of war and government in Picardy, a region of France hitherto neglected by historians, has much to say about the development of French absolutism. Picardy emerged as a province after the conquests effected by Louis XI between 1470 and 1477, but its character was profoundly shaped by the impact of Habsburg–Valois Wars between 1521 and 1559. Picardy became the most exposed frontier region of the French kingdom and suffered repeated devastations, which culminated in the 1550s. Though the province had in the main no regularly organised estates and was relatively close to the centres of royal government and power, it had to be incorporated in the kingdom by inducements to its numerous nobility and urban oligarchies. Its experience of the first period of absolutism provides an enlightening contrast with that of other, more outlying provinces: the Picard nobility was notable for the extent of its participation in the army, the court and the government of France. David Potter provides a detailed analysis of the organisation of French military power in the province and the effects of war on town and country-side, and the work concludes with Picardy about to enter a new and difficult period of civil war.

WAR AND GOVERNMENT IN THE FRENCH PROVINCES

WAR AND GOVERNMENT
IN THE FRENCH PROVINCES

Picardy 1470–1560

DAVID POTTER

Lecturer in History at the University of Kent at Canterbury

Published by the Press Syndicate of the University of Cambridge
The Pitt Building, Trumpington Street, Cambridge CB2 1RP
40 West 20th Street, New York, NY 10011–4211, USA
10 Stamford Road, Oakleigh, Victoria 3166, Australia

First published 1993

Printed in Great Britain at the University Press, Cambridge

A catalogue record for this book is available from the British Library

Library of Congress cataloguing in publication data
Potter, David, 1948–
War and government in the French provinces: Picardy, 1470–1569 /
David Potter.
p.   cm.
Includes bibliographical references (p.   )
ISBN 0 521 43189 1 (hc)
1. Picardy (France) – History. 2. France – Politics and
government – 16th century. 3. France – Military policy – History – 16th
century. 4. Nobility – France – Picardy – History – 16th century.
5. France – Boundaries – Belgium. 6. Belgium – Boundaries – France.
I. Title.
DC611.P588P68 1993
944'.26 – dc20   92–11887   CIP

ISBN 0 521 43189 1 hardback

WD

To my father,
Linley Potter

tous les livres qui sont faitz ne serviroient de riens, si ce n'estoit pour ramener à memoire les choses passées (Philippe de Commynes)

CONTENTS

ACKNOWLEDGEMENTS

The initial research for this book was funded by a generous grant from the British Academy and subsequent study aided by a series of small grants from the University of Kent at Canterbury. Thanks are due to Sir Geoffrey Elton and Professor R. J. Knecht for their encouragement over the years and to early modernist colleagues at the University of Kent, especially Peter Laven and Peter Roberts and the late and still sadly missed Gerhard Benecke. The archivists and librarians in France whose kindness and help have always been invaluable are too numerous to list but special thanks are due to M. P. Le Roy, secrétaire of the Société des Antiquaires de Picardie, Mlle A. Durieux at Compiègne and Mme M. Agache at Abbeville. Barbara Thompson and William Cottle helped my research in Paris and London in many practical ways as did my sister, Christine Harvey. The secretaries in Keynes College at Canterbury showed patience beyond the call of duty in typing the earlier drafts. The various readers of the text gave valuable advice. I must also thank Richard Fisher for his persistence and encouragement and Christine Lyall Grant for her editorial work. Finally, I must thank my wife Suzie, without whose help and forbearance it would have been impossible to revise and improve the book. Though not entirely convinced of the charms of academic history, her infectious and voracious enthusiasm for French literature, her love of stories and curiosities reminded me of the importance of historical narrative. The advice and ideas of friends, colleagues and students, though they may not have known it, were the source of much that is of value in this book. For any shortcomings, of course, I am myself responsible. D'autres en auraient pu faire un livre; mais l'histoire que je raconte ici, j'ai mis toute ma force à la vivre et ma vertu s'y est usée.

ABBREVIATIONS

AC	Archives Communales
AD	Archives Départementales
Add. MS	Additional Manuscript, British Library, London
AM	Archives Municipales
AN	Archives Nationales, Paris
ANG	*Acta Nuntiaturae Gallicae: Correspondance des Nonces en France* vols. (Rome,) see bibliography under J. Lestocquoy (ed.)
APC	*Acts of the Privy Council of England*, ed. J. Dasent, 42 vols. London (1890–1938)
BEC	*Bibliothèque de l'Ecole des Chartes*
BL	British Library, London
BM	Bibliothèque Municipale
BN	Bibliothèque Nationale, Paris
BPH	*Bulletin philologique et historique du Comité des Travaux historiques et scientifiques*
BSAB	*Bulletin de la Société académique de l'arrondissement de Boulogne-sur-Mer*
BSAP	*Bulletin de la Société des Antiquaires de Picardie*
BSA Laon	*Bulletin de la Société académique de Laon*
BSA Morinie	*Bulletin de la Société académique de la Morinie* (Saint-Omer)
BSEA	*Bulletin de la Société d'Emulation d'Abbeville*
Cab. hist.	*Cabinet historique de l'Artois et de la Picardie*
CAF	*Catalogue des Actes de François Ier* (Académie des Sciences Morales et Politiques, 10 vols. Paris, 1887–1910)

CAH	*Catalogue des actes de Henri II* (Académie des Sciences Morales et Politiques, 3 vols. so far, Paris, 1979–)
Clair.	Collection Clairambault, Bibliothèque Nationale
CDH	Collection de Documents inédits sur l'histoire de France (published originally by the *Ministère de l'Instruction publique*, continuing)
CSPF	*Calendar of State Papers, Foreign Series, of the Reign of Queen Elizabeth* 23 vols. (London, 1863–1950), first 5 vols. edited by J. Stevenson
CSPF Edward VI	*Calendar of State Papers, Foreign Series, of the Reign of Edward VI, 1547–53* ed. W. B. Turnbull (London, 1861)
CSP Spanish	*Calendar of Letters, Despatches and State Papers relating to the Negotiations Between England and Spain Preserved in the Archives at Vienna, Brussels, Simancas and Elsewhere* (covers the period down to 1558) ed. P. de Gayangos, G. Bergenroth, M. Hume *et al.*, 13 vols. (London, 1873–1954)
DBF	*Dictionnaire de biographie française* 18 vols. so far (Paris, 1933–)
EHR	*English Historical Review*
fr.	fonds français, Bibliothèque Nationale, cabinet des manuscrits
HHuStA	Vienna, Haus-, Hof- und Staatsarchiv
Inventaire sommaire . . .	Refers to the series of *Inventaires sommaires des archives départementales, municipales, communales* published uniformly but under the aegis of each town or department. Each reference, followed by the name of the department or town can be found in the bibliography, first section, Inventories and Archives, in the order of the place name.
L&P	*Letters and Papers, Foreign and Domestic, of the reign of Henry VIII* ed. J. S. Brewer, J. Gairdner and R. H. Brodie, 21 vols. (London, 1662–1932)
MC Chantilly	Musée Condé, château de Chantilly, archives de la maison de Montmorency
Michaud et Poujoulat	J. F. Michaud and J. J. F. Poujoulat, *Nouvelle collection de mémoires pour servir à l'histoire de France*
MASA	*Mémoires de l'Académie des Sciences (Lettres et Arts) d'Arras*
MSAB	*Mémoires de la Société académique de l'arrondissement de Boulogne-sur-Mer*
MSA Morinie	*Mémoires de la Société académique de la Morinie*

MSAO	*Mémoires de la Société académique de l'Oise*
MSAP	*Mémoires de la Société des Antiquaires de Picardie* including series of *Mémoires in-4to*
MSEA	*Mémoires de la Société d'Emulation d'Abbeville*
MSEC	*Mémoires de la Société d'Emulation de Cambrai*
nafr.	nouvelles acquisitions françaises (MSS of BN)
Ordonnances	*Ordonnances des Roys de France de la troisiesme race* ed. Laurière, Secousse, Vilevault, Bréquigny, Pastoret, 23 vols. (Paris, 1723–1849)
Ordonnances François Ier	*Ordonnances des Rois de France: Règne de François Ier* (Académie des Sciences Morales et Politiques) 9 vols. so far, down to 1539 (Paris, 1902–1989)
PAPS	*Proceedings of the American Philosophical Society*
PRO	Public Record Office, London
PWSFH	*Proceedings of the Western Society for French History*
p.o.	pièces originales (BN MSS, genealogical collections)
Registres, Paris	*Histoire générale de Paris. Collection de documents. Registres des délibérations du bureau de la ville de Paris.* vol. I–V, ed. A. Tuety, F. Bonnardot, P. Guérin (Paris, 1883–92)
Rés. impr.	Réserve imprimés, special collections, BN
RH	*Revue historique*
RHMC	*Revue d'histoire moderne et contemporaine*
SAP	Société des Antiquaires de Picardie (formerly Société d'Archéologie du département de la Somme), Amiens, collection of MSS
SHF	Société de l'Histoire de France
SP	State Papers, series of (PRO)
Thierry, *Tiers Etat*	A. Thierry, *Recueil des monuments inédits de l'histoire du Tiers Etat. Ière série. région du Nord* 4 vols. (Paris, CDI, 1856–70)
Gorguette, 'Thieulaine'	X. de Gorguette d'Argoeuves, 'Un livre de raison en Artois (XVIe siècle)' (Jean Thieulaine), *MSA Morinie* XXI, 139–99

NOTES ON TRANSCRIPTIONS OF
DOCUMENTS, UNITS OF MONEY,
AND MEASURES

As is well known, the use of accents was only tentatively established in printed French during the sixteenth century and is largely absent from manuscripts until late in the century. For reasons of consistency and clarity, though the spelling of all documents, printed and manuscript, has been retained in original form, accentuation has been added according to modern practice where appropriate.

The money of account used for computation was the *livre tournois* made up of 20 *sols* each worth 12 *deniers*. The *livre parisis* was not so widely used. It was a slightly larger unit (1 *sol parisis* = 15 *deniers tournois*). During the sixteenth century, the *livre tournois* fluctuated at between 9 and 10 to the pound sterling. The symbol used here is 'L' before the sum of money to avoid confusion with the £ sterling. In France, the crown had the power to regulate the 'rate' of real coins in circulation against the money of account according to its needs of the scarcity of specie. The general trend was for gold and silver coins actually to rise in value in terms of money of account, from a point at which the gold *écu*, for instance rose from roughly 30 *sols tournois* to 60 *sols*. In the main, figures are given below in money of account.

The most frequent dry measure of capacity used is the *sétier*, which in Paris was equal to 156 litres. Twelve *sétiers* were equal to one *muid*.

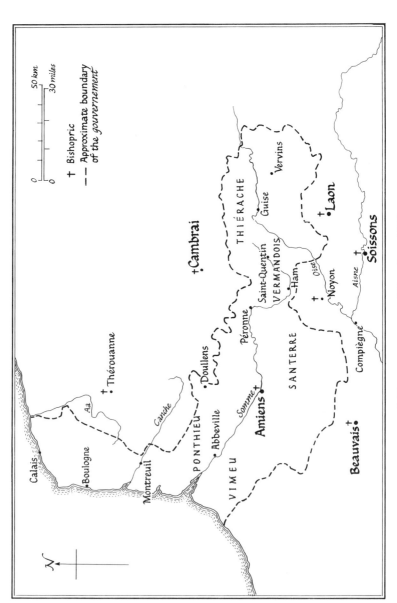

1 The *gouvernement* of Picardy, c. 1560

INTRODUCTION

In 1470, the dominant power in the region of Picardy was the Burgundian state, which then seemed to be at its zenith. By the time that Henry II of France made peace with the Habsburgs in 1559, Picardy was a clearly organised province of France, the *fidelissima Picardiae natio* whose loyalty had been reinforced by generations of war. A loosely defined and undifferentiated region had become one of the great *gouvernements* of the French kingdom and had taken its place as the French frontier with the Empire and the kingdom's first line of defence. The process by which this was achieved was not straightforward and was accompanied by generations of warfare and political adjustment, which are the themes of this study.

The history of Picardy, though a rich territory for the historian of the earlier middle ages,[1] has been largely neglected in the early modern period. American historians have begun to explore, notably, the religious history of the area and the clientage connections of the nobility during the wars of religion,[2] but the emergence of the province during the decisive period from the mid-fifteenth to the mid-sixteenth centuries is, apart from the pioneering work of Augustin Thierry and Edouard Maugis, an historiographical blank.[3] Some differences of perspective and emphasis from other regional studies may result from the nature of the sources characteristic of the century before 1560. Many of the great *pays d'états* have been studied through the sources left behind by their

---

[1] R. Fossier, *La terre et les hommes en Picardie jusqu'à la fin du XIIIᵉ siècle* (2 vols., 1968); Fossier (ed.), *Histoire de la Picardie* (1974).

[2] D. Rosenberg, 'Social Experience and Religious Choice: a Case Study of the Protestant Weavers and Woolcombers of Amiens in the XVIth century' (Yale thesis, 1978). K. Neuschel, 'The Prince of Condé and the Nobility of Picardy: a Study of the Structure of Noble Relationships in Sixteenth-Century France' (Brown Univ. thesis, 1982); Neuschel, *Word of Honor. Interpreting Noble Culture in Sixteenth-Century France* (1989).

[3] See the bibliography for the works of these scholars.

1

estates or their *parlements* in their battles with the crown. The studies by
William Beik of Languedoc, by Daniel Hickey of Dauphiné, and by Sharon
Kettering of Provence, are three obvious recent examples concentrating on
the seventeenth century.[4] Provinces closer to the centre of power have not been
so well served, while modern French historians have, until recently, been
reluctant to embark upon a reassessment of the political and administrative
history of the sixteenth century or to continue the work of Philippe Contamine
on the fourteenth and fifteenth centuries. The major studies by French
historians of the *Annales* tradition have only lately begun to turn to this
field, though at their best they integrate the history of social structures and
institutions.[5]

An exploration of the diverse sources for central and local government in
Picardy from the late fifteenth century onwards quickly revealed the pre-
eminence of war and its impact on the lives and assumptions of all the people.
Allied to this was the obvious point that the process by which the province of
Picardy took shape coincided with a period usually associated with the
tentative development of the late mediaeval *Etat de justice* into the *Etat de
finance* of the early modern period. Michel Antoine, in a fine series of studies,
has begun to reveal the extraordinary extent of administrative innovations
generated by the demands made on government in the reigns of Francis I and
Henri II.[6] One reason for viewing this period as a high point of a proto-
administrative monarchy is that, in the context of the long epoch of internal
strife from the early fourteenth to the mid-seventeenth centuries, the years from
1500 to 1560 were ones in which the political supremacy of the monarchy
went largely unchallenged. This was a stage of political development born
in the English and Burgundian struggles of the fifteenth century and further

[4] W. Beik, *Absolutism and Society in Seventeenth-Century France. State Power and Provincial Aristocracy in Languedoc* (1985); D. Hickey, *The Coming of French Absolutism; the Struggle for Tax Reform in the Province of Dauphiné, 1540–1640* (1986); S. Kettering, *Judicial Politics and Urban Revolt in Seventeenth-Century France: the Parlement of Aix, 1629–59* (1978).
[5] E.g. E. Le Roy Ladurie, *Les paysans de Languedoc* (2 vols., 1966); J. Jacquart, *La crise rurale en Ile-de-France 1550–1670* (1974); P. Deyon, *Amiens, capitale provinciale. Etude sur la société urbaine au 17ᵉ siècle* (1967). Some important provincial studies have concentrated on culture and religion: N. Lemaître, *Le Rouergue flamboyant* (1988) and C. Longeon, *Une province française à la Renaissance. La vie intellectuelle en Forez* (1975).
[6] The renewal of interest in sixteenth-century administration was begun by H. Michaud's magisterial *La grande chancellerie et les écritures royales au XVIᵉ siècle (1515–89)* (1967). M. Antoine, 'La chancellerie de France au XVIᵉ siècle' and 'L'administration centrale des finances en France du XVIᵉ au XVIIIᵉ siècle', repr. in his *Le dur métier de roi. Etudes sur la civilisation politique de la France d'Ancien Régime* (1986); Antoine, 'Genèse de l'institution des intendants', *Journal des Savants* (1982), 283–317; 'Institutions françaises en Italie sous le règne de Henri II: Gouverneurs et intendants', *Mélanges de l'Ecole française de Rome* 94 (1982), 759–818, a study of capital importance based on the du Thier papers in Moscow. On the concept of the *Etat de finance*, see B. Barbiche, 'Henri IV, Sully et la première "monarchie administrative"' in *PWSFH*, 17 (1990), 10–23.

galvanised through the demands of the Italian and Habsburg–Valois Wars of the sixteenth century. That the monarchs of the Renaissance, from Charles VIII to Henry II, were warrior kings who led their armies in the field at the head of their cavalry gave added impetus. In fact, the initial phase of 'absolutist' state-building from the mid-fifteenth to the mid-sixteenth centuries can be seen as the engagement of state power in the construction of a war machine adequate for participation in large-scale dynastic conflict.

Paradoxically, the 'guerres de magnificence' in Italy from 1494 to 1521 did little to aggravate the general fiscal burden; indeed, they provided opportunities for enrichment while keeping the negative effects of war away from French territory. The scale of military operations remained limited; the monarchy was maintaining armies of little more than 25,000 men on a semi-permanent basis in the 1490s and 1500s, the burdens substantially borne by the theatre of operations.[7] The transformation of these wars after 1521, when the Habsburg dynasty succeeded in balancing the resources of France, involved an important expansion of investment in military personnel, equipment and administration. By the end of the 1550s, the crown was forced to maintain an army of 50,000 men on the northern frontier alone for several months. The maintenance of armies on a wartime establishment for several years running inevitably generated greater taxation. Nor were the wars of that period self-financing, while for some regions, most notably Picardy, they became increasingly destructive, both in terms of enemy devastation and of the burden of army support. If military expenditure absorbed at least one-half of crown revenues in the later fifteenth century, by the 1530s there were years in which the proportion was above three-quarters.[8]

The years from, roughly, 1460 to 1560, however, were those in which the economic and demographic recovery from the calamities of the previous century, though delayed in northern France, permitted the accumulation of the surplus necessary for more extensive state activity, particularly in the field of

---

[7] F. Lot, *Recherches sur les effectifs de armées françaises des guerres d'Italie aux guerres de religion* (1962): the expeditions of 1499–1501, involving no more than about 25,000 men, virtually denuded France of troops, while total state revenues stood at only L 2.5 million in 1501. The vast disparity in military costs, estimated by the Venetian Contarini in 1492 at L 2.3m for the gendarmerie and L 3m for fortifications and military equipment while total income was L 3.6m (see L. Firpo, *Relazioni di ambasciatori veneti al Senato*, 11 vols. (1965–84), V (1978), 19–20) is to be explained not by the imposition of extra taxes, as he thought, but by the transfer of costs to Italy; see P. Chaunu, 'L'Etat' in F. Braudel and E. Labrousse (eds.), *Histoire économique et sociale de la France* (1977) I, i, 155.

[8] P. Contamine, 'Guerre, fiscalité royale et économie en France (deuxième moitié du XVᵉ siècle)', in M. Flinn (ed.), *Seventh International Economic History Congress*, II, 269. For 1536: total revenues of L 6,725,000, expenditure on *extraordinaire des guerres*, L 4,439,890; under Henri II, average global revenues, 1548–55 10 millions, average exp. on *extraordinaires* 1548–55, L 6,317,538 (figures, Clamageran, *Histoire de l'impôt* (3 vols., 1867–76) and below, p. 189 and appendix 6A).

warfare, and enabled French society to sustain an increased fiscal burden. The potential resources of the French monarchy were already the most formidable in Europe: 60–3 tonnes of fine silver p.a. in the years 1484–1515, 92–6 tonnes in 1523–43, 209 tonnes in 1547–59, though the purchasing power of such sums remained more stable. The high levels of taxation prevailing in the 1550s did not equal the purchasing power of Louis XI's revenues in 1482 (125 tonnes of silver). The rise under Francis I from 63 tonnes p.a. to 115 tonnes (183%) was almost offset by the 160 per cent rise in prices in terms of silver. The near 100 per cent rise in revenues under Henri II, however, took place at a time of more moderate inflation and is to be explained by the crown's ability to tap the resources of the clergy in that period. Over the longer term, in relation to total productivity, royal taxes rose from 18.5 per cent to 26.5 per cent from 1453 to 1482, but had sunk to 14.8 per cent in 1559. Except for the later years of Louis XI and those of Henri II, the growth in the taxation burden cannot be compared with the grotesque increases promulgated under the war finance régime of the seventeenth-century cardinal ministers, though the expansion of French society from the 1480s to the 1550s provided an increasing resource for the state.[9]

Henry Heller has argued that the fiscal burden of the monarchy was one of the factors that aggravated what he sees as the endemic social conflict between nobles and commoners that prevailed throughout the sixteenth century in France and that the magnificence of the Renaissance was built up on increasing commoner impoverishment. Though there is reason to doubt this particular explanation, his study does reopen the question of whether the idea of the 'society of orders' was so generally accepted and this has implications for the state.[10] There has been much ultimately inconclusive debate about the social configurations which permitted or encouraged the development of absolutism, much of it concentrating on the seventeenth century and influenced to a greater or lesser extent by a view of political systems of control as super-structures dependent upon social forces.[11] In this specific case: who actually benefited from the construction of the modern state? Rival interpretations,

---

[9] See P. Chaunu, 'L'Etat', in Braudel and Labrousse, *Histoire économique et sociale*, 39–45, 148–66; Morineau, in *ibid.*, I, ii, 978–81 (tables). N.B. revenue figures in terms of silver are based on the computations of A. Guéry. The feebleness of royal revenues as a proportion of productivity is stressed more recently by E. Le Roy Ladurie, *L'Etat royal de Louis XI à Henri IV, 1460–1610* (1987), 59.

[10] H. Heller, *Iron and Blood. Civil Wars in Sixteenth-Century France* (1991), 3–11, 23–7. He argues that tax increases outstripped inflation and that *crues* and *taillons* should be taken into account. Even so, it is difficult to see taxes as a major source of impoverishment except in certain special circumstances, like Dauphiné in the 1530–40s.

[11] R. Mousnier and F. Hartung, 'Quelques problèmes concernant la monarchie absolue' in *Relazione del X Congresso Internazionale di Scienze Storiche* IV (Rome, 1955), 1–55 and the discussions in the same volume. P. Anderson, *Lineages of the Absolute State* (1979 edn), 1–59, has, from a Marxist perspective, stressed the centrality of war in this process.

which see in Absolute Monarchy a channel for the increasing power of proto-capitalist urban wealth in the creation of a national market, or alternatively a device willed into being by feudal aristocracies confronted by the agrarian crisis of the fourteenth and fifteenth centuries, in order to reinforce their control of a refractory peasantry, are in themselves no more than historians' arbitrary constructs. Nor is the notion of a balance of forces which allowed the monarchy to emancipate itself from controls any more convincing; any effective state structure must involve a substantial range of interests in its survival.[12]

For this period, the problem is posed most starkly in the common assumption that Louis XI's objective was to eliminate aristocratic power by enlisting the support of the cities. The second half of Louis's reign saw, as has been pointed out, a prodigious increase in the burden of royal taxes on French society not to be paralleled until the 1550s. Despite spectacular cases of destruction of princely power, systematic study of the royal council in the period reveals that this governing institution continued to be dominated by the nobility.[13] It should not, therefore, be surprising that the apogée of this first stage of classical absolutism, customarily placed between 1520 and 1560, should see the crown continue in its role as supreme patron of the nobility and provider of the employment and opportunities created by war, or that the court had emerged as at one and the same time the most centralising and also the most aristocratic institution of the kingdom. Jean de Tillet's observation, in his *Advertissement à la noblesse*, that 'la gresse & opulence de ce Royaume, toutes les grandeurs & commoditez, retournent aux gentils-hommes', was pointed.[14] As Philippe Contamine observed, by the time of the Estates-General of 1484 the principal political objective of the French nobility was the assurance of place, salaries and pensions within the monarchical system.[15]

Part of the explanation for this may be sought in the economic position of the nobility. The collapse of seigneurial revenues in the fourteenth and fifteenth centuries is now widely accepted. The consequences in the succeeding period,

[12] N. Elias, *The Civilizing Process*, vol. II, *State Formation and Civilization* (1982), 161.

[13] On the development of this idea, B., Guénée, 'L'histoire de l'Etat en France à la fin du Moyen Age', *RH* 232 (1964), 331–60; H. Sée, *Louis XI et les villes* (1891); R. Gandilhon, *Politique économique de Louis XI* (1940) and comments in G. Zeller, 'Louis XI, la noblesse et la marchandise' in his *Aspects de la politique française* (1964), 240–53; B. Chevalier, 'La politique de Louis XI à l'égard des bonnes villes. Le cas de Tours' *Moyen Age*, 70 (1964); H. Miskimin, *Money and Power in Fifteenth-century France* (1984), 91–105 on the influence of bullion shortage on the thrust of royal policy. P.-R. Gaussin, 'Les conseillers de Louis XI', in B. Chevalier and P. Contamine (eds.), *La France de la fin du XVe siècle – Apogée et Renouveau* (1985), 123, 128.

[14] Jean de Tillet, *Advertissement envoyée à la noblesse de France* (1574 edn), fl. Biij v–ivr.

[15] P. Contamine, 'De la puissance aux privilèges' in his *La France aux XIVe et XVe siècles. Hommes, mentalités, guerre et paix* (1981), 255.

however, are not certain and wide variations have to be envisaged. The development is illustrated by the fortunes of the La Trémoille family, parlous under Louis XI, who treated it with disfavour, but resplendent by the 1530s after a generation of royal favour and employment.[16] Indeed, studies of aristocratic wealth, including that of the Bourbons in Picardy, increasingly reveal the great opportunities for restoration available to the wealthier nobility with direct access to crown patronage during the economic revival of the late fifteenth and early sixteenth centuries; reflected, too, in the emergence of sharper stratification as a result of the increasing exclusivity of the rank of *chevaliers* within the nobility.[17] For middle and lesser nobility, however, the prospects may have been more ambiguous, dependent on genealogical chance and personal ability. Here, military and administrative employment were an important supplement to income. In Picardy, the Mailly family was nearly ruined in the early sixteenth century and was rescued only by direct royal support.[18] The patterns observed by Robert Fossier for the thirteenth century, first for the vast proliferation of seigneuries in Picardy and, secondly, for the consolidation of a small number of successful lignages through astute management and links with the Capetian monarchy, are to some extent echoed in the sixteenth, as will be seen in chapter 3.[19]

Much has been made of the pronouncements of contemporary theorists

[16] G. Bois, 'Noblesse et crise des revenues seigneuriaux en France aux XIVᵉ et XVᵉ siècles: essai d'interpretation', in P. Contamine (ed.), *La Noblesse au Moyen Age* (1976), 219–33. W. A. Weary, 'La Maison de La Trémoille pendant la Renaissance: une seigneurie agrandie', in B. Chevalier and P. Contamine (eds.), *La France de la fin du XVᵉ siècle*, 197–212 and introduction, pp. 4–5, on Chabannes family. On the importance of royal subventions for one favoured member of the La Trémoille family, see P. Contamine, 'Georges de La Trémoille' in his *La France au XIVᵉ et XVᵉ siècles* II, 72.

[17] E.g. D. L. Potter, 'The Luxembourg Inheritance: the House of Bourbon and its Lands in Northern France during the Sixteenth Century', *French History* 6 (1992); M. Greengrass, 'Property and Politics in Sixteenth-Century France: the Landed Fortunes of the Constable Anne de Montmorency', *French History* 2 (1988), 371–98. P. Contamine, 'Points de vue sur la chevalerie en France à la fin du moyen âge' in *La France au XIVᵉ et XVᵉ siècles*, 259–62, 271, 283–5: the number of chevaliers contracted from around 5,000–10,000 in 1300 to around 1,000 in 1500, growing slightly to a little under 2,000 by the 1570s: see M. Orlea, *La noblesse aux Etats generaux de 1576 et de 1588* (1980), 50–67. For the numbers in Picardy, see below, ch. 4.

[18] For studies of other regions where the fortunes of the nobility in the late fifteenth and early sixteenth centuries were very mixed see: M. Le Mené, *Les campagnes angevines à la fin du moyen âge* (1982), 487–99; P. Charbonnier, *Une autre France. La seigneurie rurale en Basse-Auvergne du XIVᵉ au XVIᵉ siècle* (1980) I, 547–77, II, 830–53, 945–88, esp. 974–88: there was a strengthening of incomes in the middle range, 1488–1551, but signs of indebtedness among the small hill-country landowners. A. Ledru, *Histoire de la maison de Mailly* (1893) I, 176–81 on difficulties of Antoine de Mailly caused by expenses in the Anglo-French naval war, 1512–13.

[19] R. Fossier, *La terre et les hommes en Picardie*, II; Fossier, 'La noblesse picarde au temps de Philippe le Bel', in P. Contamine (ed.), *La noblesse au Moyen Age* (1976), 105–27, esp. 111–14, 126–7.

concerning the development of absolutism, though the differences between them may have been exaggerated, and we should be alert to the facts that not only is the use of systematic theory in the history of power too static a perspective, but also not even the most rigorous defender of royal sovereignty could countenance despotism. The point was quite effectively established by Roland Mousnier.[20] Furthermore, it hardly needs to be stressed that the very word 'absolutism' is a neologism, though public discourse was no stranger to the concepts of 'puissance absolue, de plain pouvoir, de propre mouvement' castigated by Estienne Pasquier in the mid-sixteenth century.[21] As a 'system', however, it was simply not an issue either in the province discussed in this book or in France as a whole, though the various ways in which the royal power was invoked, used, manipulated and twisted certainly were, since that power wielded military force.

The engagement of the monarchy in the Italian wars from the 1490s and the wider conflict from 1521 may well have concealed fundamental disagreements over the demands of the state, but the power of the crown to manage exterior policy was unchallenged and public discourse was dominated by those, mainly nobles and jurists, who sought to glorify external conquest or urge vigorous defence. Thus, although there is good reason to suppose that the recurrence of war, with its attendant grave effects on international commerce, contributed to the outbreaks of violent disorder in the cities (for instance at La Rochelle, Rouen and Tours in 1542 or Troyes in 1529), there is little evidence that the right of the crown to manage military and diplomatic policy could be called into question; rather, discontent was focused elsewhere. The king could not be directly blamed; instead the 'triste et misérable estat de la guerre' was conceived of as a sort of natural calamity.[22] For a province like Picardy, involved in the exportation of grain to the Low Countries – indeed a major cause of discontent – the commencement of war had at least the stabilising effect of prohibiting cross-border grain movements.[23]

---

[20] C. de Seyssel, *La Monarchie de France*, ed. J. Poujol (1961), 113–28, esp. 120; B. Basse, *La constitution de l'ancienne France* (1986), chs. x and xiii; on Bodin, see J. L. Bourgeon, 'La Fronde parlementaire à la veille de la Saint-Barthélemy', *BEC* (1990), I, 17–89, esp. p. 34; H. Lloyd, *The State, France and the Sixteenth Century* (1983), 158–60; D. Parker, 'Law, Society and the State in the Thought of Jean Bodin', *History of Political Thought* 2 (1981), 253–85. Mousnier and Hartung, see note 11.

[21] E. Pasquier, *Lettres* (Amsterdam, 1723), II, 155.

[22] AM Compiègne BB 21 fo. 56v (18 Oct. 1552). Municipal records often register the reception of news about the start of war but usually confine themselves to the resulting decisions concerning security. H. Heller, *Iron and Blood*, 27–9, on the role of war in provoking riots because of the interruption of trade.

[23] Grain exportation was prohibited both in war and in times of shortage by governors' *ordonnances*: AM Amiens AA 12 fo. 164v (1530), 165v, 167v (1531); fo. 181 (1535), 183 (1536), 191 (1538), 193 (1539), 185 (1540), 206v, 211 (1542), 222 (1547); AA fol. 10r (1552).

One reason for cooperation was the participation of urban oligarchies in the propaganda of the crown, evident in the manifestos accompanying the demands for the *taille* that sought to justify the king's actions, and also in the public ceremonial – processions, prayers, bonfires – by which the crown insisted that the *bonnes villes* participate in the triumphs and disasters of the monarchy. Michèle Fogel has shown how important the reign of Henri II was in the genesis at Paris of frequent public ceremonies, like the *Te Deum*, as supplements to the traditional intercessory processions to mark public events; the same could be said of the main towns of Picardy.[24] Less frequently, though more spectacularly, the personal presence of the king, especially at his first ceremonial entry into the towns of the province, gave a vivid opportunity for propaganda. Louis XI's entry at Amiens was staged soon after its recovery, in 1464. Charles VIII and Louis XII both delayed their *entrées* for many years, while Francis I and Henry II arrived soon after their accessions (1517 and 1547). Such events now tended to concentrate on emphasising the splendour of the crown rather than any contractual obligations between king and community, though the towns of Picardy remained attached to the 'mysteries', in the traditions of sacred drama, staged on such occasions, and placed great emphasis on the Glorious Virgin in fostering their relations with the king. The programmes of these pageants could be contradictory; on Charles VIII's entry at Abbeville in 1492 one tableau showing the annunciation called for peace while another, of the Trinity, called for the king's victory over his enemies.[25]

---

[24] E.g. Sept. 1489, *Te Deum* and procession at Amiens with a large image of the Virgin and the head of St John the Baptist, for the peace treaty with the emperor (AM Amiens AA 12 fo. 97v); from April 1509 the governor ordered weekly processions and prayers for the success of Louis XII's campaign in Italy until news of the victory (AM Péronne BB 6 fo. 196r–7r); standard phrase 'faciez rendre grâces à Dieu ensemble faire processions et feuz de joye' (on news of Marignano, *ibid.* BB 7 fo. 7); on the birth of the dauphin, April 1518 (AM Amiens AA 12 fo. 131v); on the truce of Nice, processions with relics were ordered at Compiègne and a sermon at St-Corneille 'contenant plus au long les raisons, causes et moyens desd. tresves' (AM Compiègne BB 19 fo. 3r). *Te Deum, feux de joie* and procession for the peace with England, March 1550 (AM Amiens, AA 12 fo. 230v–31r). On Paris, M. Fogel, *Les cérémonies d'information dans la France du XVIe au XVIIIe siècle* (1989), 133–88.

[25] On the royal entry ceremonial, see L. Bryant, *The King and the City in the Parisian Royal Entry Ceremony: Politics, Ritual and Art in the Renaissance* (1986); Bryant, 'The Medieval Entry Ceremony at Paris' in J. M. Bak (ed.), *Coronations* (1990); J. Brink, 'Royal Power Through Provincial Eyes: Languedoc 1515–60', *PWSFH* 10 (1982), 52–9. A certain number of royal *entrées* in Picardy have been printed: A. Ledieu, 'Entrée solonelle du roi Charles VIII à Abbeville (1493)', *Bull. archéol. du Comité des travaux hist.* 1888, I, 55–65; Ledieu, 'Entrée de la reine Eléonore d'Autriche à Abbeville le 19 décembre 1531', *BSEA* 5 (1900–2), 15ff., 33ff., F.-C. Louandre, *Histoire d'Abbeville* 2 vols. (1844–4) II, 1–17; for the entry of Francis I at Abbeville in June 1517, see *Inventaire sommaire, Abbeville*, 148; Pollet, 'L'entrée d'Henri II à Calais en 1558', *Bull. comm. Monuments hist. Pas-de-Calais* 7, v (1956), 547ff. A. Dubois, *Entrées royales et princières dans Amiens pendant les 15e et 16e siècles* (1868): Charles VIII made his entry in 1493 but Louis XII delayed his ceremonial entry as late as 1513 (AM Amiens, BB 21 fo. 177–86: provisions for the staging of 'mystères'). Francis I in June 1517

In more routine matters, after Louis XI's frenetic activity in the region, Charles VIII and Louis XII appeared only rarely, but from 1513 the royal itinerary indicates a growing royal presence in Picardy, with the king either on campaign, a tour of inspection or staying with the duke of Vendôme at La Fère. Of 662 days spent by Francis I in the province (excluding many long stays at Compiègne), there were 220 between 1515 and 1530, 442 from 1531 to 1547.[26]

The *chants royaux*, composed each year at Amiens in the competition for verses in honour of the Virgin for the confraternity of the *Puy Notre-Dame*, emphasised the duty of obedience to the king; one competitor in 1472 proclaimed:

> Voeullons huy tous de une alliance,
> Servir au noble roi de France,
>   . . .
> Car le bon roi, par industrie,
> Scet de cœur et pensée france
> Honorer la Vierge Marie.

The competition took on a special significance for the entry of Francis I and Louise of Savoy into the city in 1517. The yearly paintings commissioned for the festival had, since their inception in the mid-fifteenth century, brought the figure of the king to prominence in conjunction with that of the Virgin herself. A painting of 1519 depicts a complex allegory concerning the king's title to the Empire.[27] Earlier, around 1500, the confraternity had commissioned two tryptych side panels, now at the Cluny Museum in Paris, showing the coronations of David and Louis XII, the latter inscribed: 'Une foy, une loy, un roy'.

The French monarchy, like its Castilian counterpart, had an absolutist ideology inherited from the early mediaeval past, which invoked doctrines of Roman law in justification of its command of public policy. As an *avocat* of

---

(AM Amiens CC fo. 194v); queen Eléonore, 1531: details not preserved. Entry of Henri II at Amiens, Aug. 1547, AM Amiens, BB 25 fo. 288–92: the 'rétoriciens' Obry and Lemaire were given 'ce quy a esté faict anchienement' for staging the 'mistères' and 'istores'. On the latter, see A. de Calonne, *Histoire de ville d'Amiens* 3 vols. (1899–1906), I, 343–52, 400–1, 486–7. The *mystère* of 'Jonas sortant de la baleine' was staged for the entry of Louis XI in 1464, for Marguerite of Austria as dauphine in 1483: 'l'ancienne histoire dont jadis vint Franchion et la noble maison de France'.

26 For royal itineraries, now complete between 1461 and 1559, see Louis XI: J. Vaesen and E. Charavay, *Lettres de Louis XI*, 12 vols. (SHF, 1883–1909), XI; Charles VIII: *Bulletin philologique et historique*, 1896, 629–90; Louis XII, *ibid.*, 1972, 171–206; Francis I: *CAF* VIII, 411–548; Henri II: *CAH* III, introduction.

27 A.-M. Lecoq, *François Ier imaginaire* (1987), 325–42. The poem of 1472 was by Jean Du Bosquel, see *ibid.*, 341.

the Parlement put it in 1491, 'l'autorité du roi . . . n'est sujette aux opinions'. It may, though, be argued that this in itself was not the generator of authoritarian rule or of despotism. R. Bonney has drawn attention to the traditional distinction between the king's 'retained' and 'delegated' justice, which he sees as essential in understanding Bodin's adumbration of a theory for the growing power of royal *commissaires* in the sixteenth century.[28] Nor is absolutism synonymous with state centralisation, which could take shape within a wide range of early modern polities.[29] A useful case in point emerges from the separation of Picardy and Artois which occurred as a result of the conflicts of the late fifteenth century, discussed in chapter 1. Artois retained its estates organisation, and there is good reason to suppose that distrust of the taxation powers of the French monarchy was an important factor in the ultimate maintenance of its loyalty to Burgundy and later to the Habsburgs. Yet the compromises made by the French crown in the course of its acquisition of Picardy must raise a question over whether Picardy was more heavily taxed than Artois by the middle of the sixteenth century. The existence of estates certainly channelled a degree of political awareness and provincial loyalty but did not in itself deny the implementation of authoritarian policies.

Bonney has argued that the concept of 'centralisation' in early modern France is anachronistic, though others have pointed out that centralisation is a useful term that does not imply uniformity in a society marked by corporate privilege and regional and local autonomies.[30] There is an undoubted sense in which the changes in France and elsewhere during the sixteenth and seventeenth centuries shifted the initiative to the crown and its circle of institutions: the court, the councils and bureaucracy. The common feature in this process was the response to international conflict and military emergency, which becomes ever more exigent from the late fifteenth century onwards. The centralised monarchies of the early modern period have rightly been called

---

[28] R. Bonney, 'Bodin and the development of the French Monarchy', *TRHS* ser. 5, 40 (1990), 43–61, at 50.
[29] On absolutist ideology in Castile, see J. A. Maravall, 'The Origins of the Modern State', *Journal of World History*, 6 (1961), 789–808. By contrast, Württemberg, a classic *ständestaat*, was a highly governed polity: see D. Sabean, *Power in the Blood. Popular Culture and Village Discourse in Early Modern Germany* (1984), 12–27; while Venice, as an aristocratic oligarchy, was one of the most effectively governed early modern states, see G. Cossi and M. Knapton, *La Repubblica di Venezia nell'età moderna* (1986), part 2. The point is also made by J.-P. Genet in *Genèse de l'état moderne: bilans et perspectives* (1990), 261–81, where he argues that the 'modern state' born in the crisis of the fourteenth and fifteenth centuries and firmly anchored in the economic and political dynamism of feudalism, could give rise to a range of systems 'fortement différenciées'.
[30] R. Bonney, 'Absolutism: What's in a Name?', *French History* 1 (1987), 94; R. Mousnier, 'Centralisation et décentralisation', *XVIIe siècle* 155 (1987), 101–11; B. Barbiche, 'Henri IV, Sully et la première "monarchie administrative"', 10.

machines built for the battlefield.[31] It is, however, too seldom stressed that such machines were, as yet, extremely rickety and did not convey unchallenged rights to command.

It is often assumed that early modern governments were determined to root out rival sources of influence and authority, like assemblies of estates and great aristocratic connections, as though these were in themselves regarded as incompatible with firm rule. In fact, the process by which their roles changed was haphazard and the result of decisions which accumulated through emergencies. It was never complete during the ancien régime. The late fifteenth century saw the effective absorption of great appanages like Provence, Burgundy and Brittany into the royal domain. This did not mean that the crown was in a position to rule them directly without reference to their traditions. It did, though, inaugurate the process by which they were to be integrated in the overall political life of the French kingdom.

Debate over the extent to which the French crown 'consulted' its subjects in the sixteenth century has centred on the provincial estates and their relationship with the crown; in this period, notable provincial studies have indeed made much use of the records of such institutions and have tended to emphasise their continued vigour. The continued sense of autonomy in provinces far from the centre of royal power has become a theme of what J. Russell Major has characterised as a 'Renaissance Monarchy' basically cooperative and con-sensual in nature. Studies of certain provinces have begun to respond to Michel Antoine's call for the exploration of sixteenth-century provincial adminis-tration. In Comminges, for instance, the cooperation of the various local authorities was crucial in the effective military organisation of the region. In provinces equipped with active estates, like Dauphiné and Languedoc, they were especially quick to challenge royal military demands in the first half of the sixteenth century. It is clear, however, that even in areas like Dauphiné with powerful provincial estates, local notables had no united line to offer in response to the *démarches* of the crown in the sixteenth and early seventeenth centuries.[32] While such provincial cases are important, though, it is also

[31] P. Anderson, *Lineages of the Absolute State*, 32. The point is also reinforced by J.-P. Genet, *Genèse de l'état moderne*, 261.
[32] Cf. R. J. Knecht, *Francis I* (1982), esp. 356, 361, and J. Russell Major, *Representative Government in Early Modern France* (1980), esp. 55, and numerous other works; also H. Lloyd, *The State, France and the Sixteenth Century*; more recently, Le Roy Ladurie, *L'Etat royal de Louis XI à Henri IV* (1987), 170–80, on innovations under Henri II, and 246–63 on C. Figon's 'Arbre des Estatz', 1579. For the theme of provincial history: M. Antoine, *Le dur métier*, 327; see notable L. S. van Doren, 'War Taxation, Institutional Change and Social Conflict in Provincial France – the Royal *Taille* in Dauphiné, 1494–1559', *Proceedings of the American Philosophical Society* (hereafter *PAPS*), 121, i (1977), 70–96; van Doren, 'Military Administration and Intercommunal Relations in Dauphiné, 1494–1559', *PAPS*, 130, i (1986), 79–100. J. Brink, 'Les Etats de Languedoc: une autonomie en question', *Annales du Midi* 88

necessary to know how such demands and pressures were accommodated in regions like Picardy, closer to the centre.

In the earlier sixteenth century, the absolutist ideology of the monarchy could coexist with a degree of negotiation with local representative assemblies, as in the case of the rival claims of the estates of Rouergue, Quercy and Périgord from the 1530s to the 1550s.[33] The pressures on those negotiations came from the demands of war and the authoritarian temperaments of Francis I and Henri II. Estates viewed the world from the province outward, the crown saw the kingdom as a unity. Tension was to some extent natural, though it should also be remembered that many matters pertaining to local government were uncontroversial. The traditional picture of the lightly burdened *pays d'états* and the heavily burdened *pays d'élections* is, however, of limited use. Normandy paid around a quarter of the entire revenues of the monarchy, while Languedoc, with a similar population, paid only a third of Normandy's contribution. Among the provinces acquired in 1477, Burgundy, with estates, and Picardy, without, were both under-assessed.[34] The failure of the demand for a *recherche générale des feux* in 1491, occasioned by resentment in Normandy, is a clear enough indication of differences so irreconcilable as to render the system immobile.[35]

'Centralisation' could impinge not only on regions which had long-standing political institutions, privileges and estates but also on those, like Picardy, which had not been appanages and had only partially developed estates organisation for purposes of taxation, the *pays d'élections*. It is usually assumed that, where there were no regular meetings of the estates, there was in fact little practical limitation on the royal power, especially that to tax at will. The area within the jurisdiction of the Parlement of Paris might seem to be the one in which the crown exercised the plenitude of powers untrammelled by limitations, yet even here nothing was settled by the disputes between the crown and the Parlement in the 1520s, so clearly discussed by Roger Doucet

(1976), 287–305; Brink, 'The King's Army and the People of Languedoc, 1500–1560', *PWSFH* 14 (1986), 1–9. P. Solon, 'War and the *bonnes villes*: the Case of Narbonne, ca. 1450–1550', *PWSFH* 17 (1990), 65–73; Solon, 'Le rôle des forces armées en Comminges avant les guerres de Religion (1502–62), *Annales du Midi* 103 (1991), 19–40. D. Hickey, *The Coming of French Absolutism*, 3.

[33] J. Bousquet, *Enquête sur les commodités de Rouergue en 1552. Procès avec l'Agenais, le Quercy et le Périgord* (1969), 15–25.

[34] P. Contamine, 'Guerre, fiscalité royale et économie en France'; P. Chaunu, 'L'Etat', in Braudel and Labrousse, *Histoire économique et sociale* I, i, 148–9.

[35] A. Spont, 'Une recherche générale des feux à la fin du XVe siècle', *Annuaire-bulletin de la SHF*, 1892, 222–36: the main difficulty lay in attaining agreement on a common basis for assessing tax liability. The *brevets de taille* of November 1492 actually included expenses 'pour la recherche des feux qui se fait par tout led. royaume' in their justification, see e.g. AM Chauny BB 1 fo. 10r.

and emphasised by R. J. Knecht in his interpretation of the period. Indeed, recent work suggests that the Parlement itself, often for its own sectional interests, maintained a guerrilla war against the actions of the royal council and ministers which grew throughout the sixteenth century, rather than diminished.[36] However, beyond this point, it could be argued that the impact of royal power on the *pays d'élections*, particularly in the *ressort* of the Parlement of Paris, shows how the actual limitations on royal power were practical rather than theoretical. Even in a heavily garrisoned province like Picardy, the capacity for obstruction and immobilism was ever present, especially in a period when the administrative cadre of the monarchy was small in comparison with the later seventeenth century.[37]

Bernard Guénée's general distinction between areas of France in terms of distance and the physical possibilities of control from the centre is certainly suggestive,[38] but it should not be assumed that relative proximity to Paris obviated, for the crown, the need to persuade and to win over support, especially in the earlier part of the period covered by this study. Picardy was then still a land in contention between the rival powers of France and Burgundy and doubts about its loyalty remained well into the sixteenth century. Moreover, the fluctuating fortunes of war created changes in the frontier and consequently of political loyalties until the middle of the sixteenth century. Indeed, the very uncertainty of the frontier, only temporarily settled in 1493, was bound to generate conflict in the following century; the complexities of the problems created are explored in chapter 8. The process by which a frontier of the kingdom was 'discovered' is one of the more telling expressions of state power in the period.

It is intended to show here, particularly in chapter 1, that in Picardy, as a *pays d'élections*, the impact of royal power in this period depended on a mixture of force and the winning over, especially under Louis XI, of a wide range of local notables. Force was exercised in the demolition of the power held by the greatest feudatory of the region, the constable Louis de Luxembourg, more subtle methods in the concession of privileges both to corporate towns and the regional nobility. In subsequent generations, the process continued by the integration of the latter into the kingdom's military machine and the establishment of a complex network of relationships between the province and the

[36] R. Doucet, *Etude sur le gouvernement de François Ier dans ses rapports avec le Parlement de Paris*, 2 vols. (1921 6); J. L. Bourgeon, 'La Fronde parlementaire', 25, 30–1, 35.
[37] R. Mousnier, 'Etat numérique de la fonction publique en France' in *Le conseil du roi de Louis XII à la Revolution* (1970), 17–20, suggests a minimum figure of 4,041 *officiers*. With clerks, we may estimate 7–8,000 for the administrative 'technostructure' in 1515 (see P. Chaunu, 'L'Etat', in Braudel and Labrousse, *Histoire économique et sociale* I, i, 37).
[38] B. Guénée, 'Espace et état en la France mediévale', *Annales* (1968), 744–58.

royal court in a constant reciprocal movement of men and interests. A major aspect of this was the increased authority conferred on aristocratic provincial governors from marshal d'Esquerdes to the Bourbon dukes of Vendôme, both as commanders of armies and as provincial representatives of the crown, from the late fifteenth century onwards. In all this, war was an important catalyst.[39]

Beneath them, the administrative functions of the middle-ranking nobility were augmented, alongside professional bureaucrats or royal commissioners. Mikhael Harsgor's seminal work on the *conseil du roi* in the late fifteenth and early sixteenth centuries has thrown into relief the way in which the ideologies of absolutism served to articulate the fact of rule by those members of the middle-ranking nobility and the leaders of the *peuple gras*, whom he calls 'les maîtres du royaume', an oligarchy linked to the crown by self-interest, holding local power or office conferring the title of *conseiller du roi*. These seigneurs, warriors, lawyers and financiers may be said in one sense to be the beneficiaries of enhanced monarchical rule created by Louis XI, though the latter did not exist exclusively to promote their interests.[40] Harsgor's analysis, however, goes a long way towards explaining the readiness with which Louis XI sought to purchase support in Picardy from men like marshal d'Esquerdes, a quintessential *maître du royaume*. It is clear that, if there was an oligarchy of this sort, it represented neither a class or an order but rather a fluctuating group in a position to use the state.

If such an oligarchical structure was perpetuated into the mid-sixteenth century, its field of activity should be widened to include the royal court as well as the council and the great administrative *corps*. Chapter 3 addresses this question specifically and attempts to draw attention to the nexus of influence between the court and local aristocratic society, in a sense which is complementary with what Kristen Neuschel has told us about the complexities of clientage in the decades after 1560, though the interpretation here does not share her perspective that the early modern state should be seen as peripheral from the viewpoint of the nobility. Jonathan Dewald's discoveries about the engagement of the interests of key Norman notables in pursuit of the profits of absolute rule during the sixteenth and seventeenth centuries are to the point here.[41] The emphasis which will emerge from this particular study is that the viability of the relatively stable political order of the earlier sixteenth century

[39] R. Harding, *Anatomy of a Power Elite. The Provincial Governors of Early Modern France* (1978); M. Greengrass, 'Property and politics'.

[40] M. Harsgor, *Recherches sur le personnel du conseil du roi sous Charles VIII et Louis XII* (typescript thesis, 4 vols., 1988); Harsgor, 'Maîtres d'un royaume. Le groupe dirigeant français à la fin du XVᵉ siècle', in B. Chevalier and P. Contamine, *La France de la fin du XVᵉ siècle*, 135–46.

[41] J. Dewald, *Pont-Saint-Pierre, 1398–1789. Lordship, Community and Capitalism in Early Modern France* (1987).

should be understood in terms of the penetration of provincial society by the attractions of service and rewards in the royal 'affinity', either in terms of simple military service, or administrative and court functions. The much-discussed aristocratic *clientèle* was subsumed in this framework until the beginning of the 1560s. This is the impression in Picardy, though in some other provinces, like Auvergne, the draw of royal service, as indicated by the returns for the feudal levy, was obviously not so great in the first half of the sixteenth century.[42]

At the same time, the crown became the guarantor of urban privileges and the object of constant petitioning by town councils, whose municipal electoral independence was abridged in return for considerable fiscal concessions, which only came under severe pressure in the 1550s. Admittedly, these pressures went far towards breaking the consensus between the crown and urban society that had been another pillar of the monarchy before 1560. In its attitudes to municipal independence in the north, the crown in that period seems to have had no consistent policy except to maintain the security of a very vulnerable frontier. All this took place against a background of crippling expenditure on new fortifications. The changes, explored here in chapter 7, invoked by war policies in this period, seem in Picardy to have contained in themselves the seeds of their limitations.

That a 'province' of Picardy emerged from this period of conflict is partly explained by the construction of a superstructure of military and political control during this century, but also by the mutation of ideas concerning local loyalties which concentrated a hitherto incoherent sense of identity into a more sharply defined area. The territory known as Picardy throughout much of the middle ages covered a wide area from the Somme region northwards towards Flanders, where a distinctive dialect produced by the confrontation of Romance and Germanic tongues was spoken.[43] It was a region of diverse feudal jurisdictions, not of royal appanages, and of many small fiefs held directly of the crown as a result of the latter's acquisition in the principal counties and *châtellenies* during the late twelfth and early thirteenth centuries. Only in 1348, with the appointment of a royal *capitaine-général* 'sur les frontières de Flandre et en toute la langue picarde', does an institutional framework begin to emerge, though its boundaries remained fluid, ebbing and flowing with the fortunes of the monarchy.[44] After 1435, for instance,

---

[42] P. Charbonnier, *Une autre France* I, 919.
[43] A. Demangeon, *La Picardie et les régions voisines* (1905), 420ff.; R. Fossier (ed.), *Histoire de la Picardie*, 5–7 argues that the only possible definition for mediaeval Picardy is geographical.
[44] P. D. Abbott, *Pays et Seigneuries of France* (1981), 108–28. Demangeon, 422. Guy de Châtillon was appointed as lieutenant for the Regent 'ès partyes de Picardie, de Beauvoisis et de Vermandois' in 1359, BL Add. MS 30572 fo. 1, copy.

Beauvaisis and Senlisis were never again to be included in the province, and it was the struggles with the rulers of the Netherlands from the fifteenth century onwards which determined the shape of the ancien régime *gouvernement*, an area very different from the amorphous Picardy of the early middle ages (and also from the modern region of Somme-Oise-Aisne that bears the same name).

The development of an institutional framework for provincial life provided a definition of 'la Picardie' which was notably different from that generated by the consciousness of *pays* characteristic of the late middle ages. Demangeon pointed out that the existence of a Picard 'nation' at the University of Paris from the early thirteenth century onwards fostered a distinctive cultural awareness in the whole of northern France and the southern Low Countries, though by the early sixteenth century this must have had less meaning for the lands under Habsburg rule. However, as late as 1552, Charles Estienne, compiler of the first systematic guide to the roads of France, could include much of the southern Low Countries in what he called 'la haute Picardie', while La Morlière in the early seventeenth century even included Rethelois, Beauvaisis and Artois in his definition of Picardy. E. Lambert, in his study of provincial boundaries, argued that Picardy never had any political shape during the ancien régime. This is evidently incorrect, since the province constituted one of the great *gouvernements* of the kingdom, though the older and much wider concept of Picardy survived into the eighteenth century.[45]

Consciousness of provincial loyalty coexisted with more restricted local loyalties. Boulonnais, for instance, somewhat remote from the centre of the province (it was called a 'cul de sac' by Jean du Bellay in 1528), certainly seems to have lived a life apart. Complaints by Picard deputies at the Estates-General of 1484 against the removal of the *bailliage* of Vermandois from the *généralité* of Amiens, despite 'la conformité de mœurs et de langage que ces pays ont avec nous' and the fact that it 'retient et conserve le nom et langue de Picardie', certainly seem to indicate some sense of common identity. The same may lie behind the conference which met at Montreuil in 1500 to discuss the coinage and 'le bien du pays de Picardie'. The deputies appointed by Abbeville to attend the Estates-General of 1506 were empowered to

[45] Demangeon, 423–4. E. Bimbenet, 'La nation de Picardie à l'Université d'Orléans', *MASP* 10 (1850). B. de Mandrot (ed.), *Journal de Jean de Roye connu sous le nom de Chronique Scandaleuse* 2 vols. (1894–6), customarily describes the troops of Charles the Bold as 'Bourguignons et Picards'; C. Estienne, *Le guide des chemins de France* (1553) ed., J. Bonnerot (1936), 18. A. de Morlière, *Recueil de plusieurs nobles et illustres maisons . . . du diocèse d'Amiens* (1630), 469. E. Lambert, 'Les limites de la Picardie', *Comptes rendus et mémoires de la Société archéologique, historique et scientifique de Noyon* 34 (1972), 53–65.

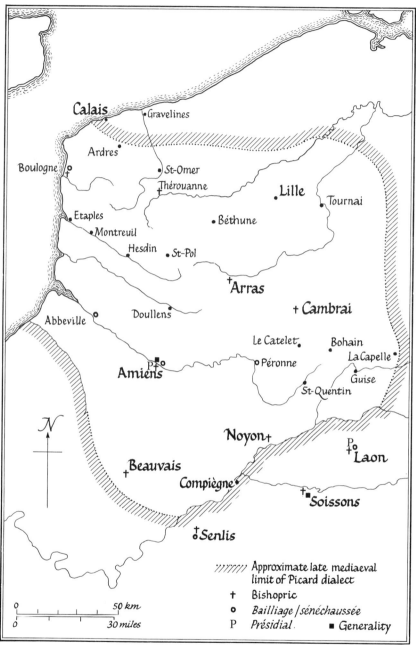

Calais
•Gravelines
Ardres•
Boulogne †o
•St-Omer
†Thérouanne
•Lille
Tournai•
Etaples•
•Béthune
•Montreuil
Hesdin• •St-Pol
†Arras
+Cambrai
Abbeville o Doullens•
Le Catelet•
Bohain•
LaCapelle•
P†•o Péronne o
Amiens
Guise
St-Quentin
N
Noyon†
P o †Laon
•Beauvais
†
Compiègne•
†•Soissons
†Senlis o

///////// Approximate late mediaeval
limit of Picard dialect
†   Bishopric
o   Bailliage / sénéchaussée
P   Présidial   ■ Generality

0
50 km
0
30 miles

2 Picardy in the wider sense

deliberate on 'le bien d'icellui (royaume), la chose publicque et de ce pays de Picardye'.[46]

Isolated remarks recorded in the earlier sixteenth century indicate that a distinctive idea of the 'pays de Picardie' was taking shape. The claims, by marshal du Biez in 1543 that 'Picards are good men to keep a hold', and by another Picard nobleman that 'nostre pais de Picardie est lieux lymitrof, aussy que sommes nation assez tost esmute', indicate the importance of military experience in all this. The new Picard legion, led by the local nobility, marched at its review in 1534 to *chants* designed to foster local loyalty by distinction from others: 'Ne desplaise aux Normands ne à leur compaignie, / Si on donne l'honneur à ceulx de Picardie.'[47] It is also possible that, as in the Netherlands, consciousness of *pays* was most strong at first among the nobility. A nobleman marrying his daughter in 1530 spoke of his son-in-law as 'bonne rasse et bonne et anchienne maison de cette Picardie' while another in 1543 was described in his obituary as 'Picard de nation, de la langue de France'. Antoine de Créqui in 1524 regretted, as 'Picard born myself' that 'my country is destroyed by the war'.[48]

Such sentiments were complemented by the dissemination of clichés and myths. Jean Molinet, who knew the region well, described Picards as 'cauteleux, fort soutilz et ingénieux', and went on to recount an old tale of their descent from the Greeks. Charles Estienne in 1552 surmised that their name came either from their use of pikes or from a Greek word meaning 'fort prompt et soubdain'. Commanders frequently commented on the readiness of the country people to defend themselves, sometimes to the irritation of authoritarian captains, one of whom, Villebon, called them in 1557 'oppiniâtre', adding 'il ne veullent [*sic*] faire chose qu'on leur commande'. Kiernan's argument that the poverty of frontier regions explains their usefulness as recruitment grounds for soldiers is only a partial explanation.[49] The Boulonnais had long enjoyed a special status, providing the crown with troops in place of

---

[46] *Ambassades en Angleterre de Jean du Bellay*, ed. V.-L. Bourrilly and P. de Vaissière (1905), 509; *Journal des Etats-Généraux de France tenus à Tours en 1484*, ed. A. Bernier, CDI (1935), 469; *Inventaire sommaire, Abbeville*, 137 (28 April 1506).

[47] *L&P* XVIII, i, no. 256; La Hargerie to Montmorency, 4 June (1531) MC Chantilly, L VII fo. 118; A. de Montaiglon, *Recueil des poésies françoises des XVᵉ et XVIᵉ siècles*, 13 vols (1855–78) I, 176–81.

[48] P. Rosenfeld, 'The Provincial Governors of the Netherlands from the Minority of Charles V to the Revolt', *Anciens Pays et Assemblées d'Etats* 17 (1959), 14–15. La Hargerie to Montmorency, 11 Aug. (1530), MC Chantilly L VIII fo. 351. P. de Cagny, *Notice historique sur le château de Suzanne-en-Santerre* (1857), 41. *L&P* IV, i, no. 735.

[49] Jean Molinet, *Chroniques*, ed. Jodogne et Doutrepont, 3 vols. (1935–7) I, 571. Charles Estienne, *La guide des chemins de France*, 16. On peasants fighting plundering soldiers, cf. *L&P* III, ii, no. 2566; Vendôme to Francis I, 16/26 Aug. 1543, BN 20521 fo. 30; Villebon to Humières, 12 Sept. 1557/3 Jan. 1558, BN fr. 3128 fo. 130, 96.

certain taxes. Indeed, the emperor Maximilian I, with some experience, wrote in 1513 that 'c'est le quartier de pays où l'on fait les meilleurs gens d'armes de France'. For the rest of the region, the presence of a large military establishment may have provided the incentive to recruitment.[50]

By contrast, the subjects of the Habsburgs on the other side of the increasingly defined frontier remained, until the mid-sixteenth century, 'the Burgundians'. Estienne Pasquier wrote later that 'en nostre jeunesse nous appellions tous les ennemis communs de France, Bourguignons, de quelque nation qu'ils fussent', but this was an exaggeration; the term applied essentially to the Low Countries. In the late fifteenth century, that devoted chronicler of the house of Burgundy, Jean Molinet, born at Desvres in the Boulonnais, could still be sentimentally attached to his 'French' origins.[51] By the middle of the sixteenth century, the Arras chronicler Jacques Genelle would still be thoroughly imbued with 'Burgundian' loyalties.[52] This point should be related to Peter Sahlins's perceptive remarks about the development of 'national' identity in the early modern period. If we look at the frontier region at the opposite end of the French kingdom, Cerdagne and Roussillon, in the seventeenth and eighteenth centuries, we find the emergence of 'French' and 'Spanish' identities springing as much from local determinants as from the imposition of state power from the centre.[53] The analogy is the emergence of 'Picardy' as a decidedly French province in its loyalties between 1470 and 1560.

The emergence of the province of Picardy through the construction of a military superstructure, then, was accompanied by the development of a degree of provincial consciousness which can hardly be compared to the fierce loyalties of Bretons or Gascons, but should not be underestimated. Nor should the very rawness of this self-image permit the supposition that the crown was at liberty to treat the province simply as a military outpost subject to its direction. The memory of the troubles of the mid-fifteenth century was too recent for that.

---

[50] Du Biez to Montmorency, 28 May 1523, BN fr. 3004 fo. 16–18. Order to 'faire sonner le tabourin avant les villaiges', 1537, *Inventaire sommaire, Amiens* II, 409. V. G. Kiernan, 'Foreign Mercenaries and Absolute Monarchy', in T. Aston (ed.), *Crisis in Europe* (1965), 120. Le Glay, *Correspondance de l'empereur Maximilien Ier*, SHF (1839), II, 153.

[51] E. Pasquier, *Recherches de France* (Amsterdam, 1723), VIII, 7. See also e.g. AM Péronne BB 7 fo. 213r ('Les bourguignons noz ennemys', 1524); G. de Lhomel, *Nouveau recueil de documents pour servir à l'histoire de Montreuil-sur-Mer* (1910), 1`55 ('ladite ville (Montreuil) est frontière et limitrophe aux Anglois et Bourguignons', 1548); BM Beauvais, Coll. Bucquet 57 p. 694 ('les bourguignons sont dans Chauny', 1552); O. Jodogne, 'Le caractère de Jean Molinet' in *La Renaissance dans les provinces du Nord*, ed. F. Lesure, CNRS (1956), 99.

[52] A. Genel (ed.), 'Les mémoires de Jacques Genelle, bourgeois d'Arras', *Revue du Nord* 51 (1969), 81, 83, 'de la desfaicte des Bourguignons' (1552).

[53] P. Sahlins, *Boundaries. The Making of France and Spain in the Pyrenees* (1989), 8–9.

By the first half of the sixteenth century, the province of Picardy was inter-sected by all sorts of overlaid jurisdictions inherited from the past and which remained a tangle until the end of the ancien régime, as in all other provinces of the kingdom. There were two episcopal cities in the province, Amiens and Thérouanne, but the province was divided between three sees, Amiens, Thérouanne and Noyon, with peripheral territory in the sees of Laon (mainly the county of Guise), Cambrai and Beauvais. From the 1490s Thérouanne was a French enclave in Artois, but held jurisdiction in the Boulonnais. The cathedral was destroyed in 1553 and the bishopric divided between Boulogne and Saint-Omer.

A Milanese traveller in 1518 noted that, for royal justice, there was, of course, no *parlement*, but that appeals went to the Parlement of Paris. The sort of regional identity fostered by a local *parlement* was therefore absent. How-ever, beneath this level came the local royal jurisdictions: the *sénéchaussées* of Boulogne (from 1477) and Ponthieu (at Abbeville), the *bailliages* of Amiens (including Montreuil) and Vermandois (with its seat outside the province at Laon but a dependency at Saint-Quentin) and the *gouvernement* of Péronne, Montdidier and Roye.[54] In 1552, a royal edict created a new layer of regional appeal courts, the *présidaux*. Amiens was the natural choice. However, Péronne now came under the *présidial* of Laon, much to the disgust of the Amiens lawyers, who wanted compensation for their loss of business during the wars. Abbeville wanted its own *présidial* but was denied this and placed under Amiens. The common factor in all these courts was their staffing by a corps of local lawyers who considered themselves representatives of royal justice, yet were drawn from the ranks of families which had established predominance in municipal politics.[55]

Royal justice, however, was only part of the picture, for it was underpinned by a complex network of seigneurial, forest and communal courts which were the tribunals of first instance for the mass of the population. Seigneurs holding high, middle and low justice and *châtelains* continued to receive the profits of justice and assure local order. At Ancre in the 1470s, the seigneurial court registered land transactions, dealt with robberies and arrested youths for disorderly conduct. The seigneurial court at Lucheux in the sixteenth

---

[54] G. Dupont-Ferrier, *Les Officiers royaux des bailliages et sénéchaussées et les institutions monarchiques locales en France à la fin du moyen âge* (Bibl. de l'école des Hautes Etudes, fasc. 145, 1902). The *ressort* of the *bailliage* of Amiens was originally much wider, but constantly on the retreat from the Low Countries from the late fifteenth century. See M. Fleury, "Le bailliage d'Amiens, son ressort et le problème des limites administratives au moyen-âge', *BEC* (1956), 56–7.

[55] AM Amiens BB 31 (29 Oct. 1557). E. Maugis, *Essai sur le recrutement et les attributions des principaux officiers . . . du bailliage d'Amiens, 1300–1600* (1906).

century was involved in much the same activity.[56] In the *bonnes villes* of Picardy, the *échevinage* usually administered high, middle and low justice. At Amiens, this was restricted by royal cognizance of certain *cas réservés*. Others, like Abbeville and Noyon, were *villes de loy* with no restriction on their jurisdiction. This in effect gave powers to fine, banish or execute offenders, even in cases involving *lèse-majeste divine* and *humaine*, though in the former case this inevitably brought conflict with the ecclesiastical courts.[57]

For royal taxation, the province was divided between the *élections* of Amiens, Abbeville, Doullens, Saint-Quentin, Péronne and Noyon, districts derived loosely from the ecclesiastical structure but now hopelessly complicated. In the course of the first half of the sixteenth century, the *généralité* of Picardy developed to coordinate them but did not extend to the whole province. Boulonnais remained an anomaly, with provincial estates but not subject to the *taille royale* in this period by special privilege stemming from the events of 1477. These developments are examined in chapter 7.

Over this heterogeneous administrative and judicial jungle, the exigencies of war built up around the governor, especially in the years from 1521 to 1559, a further superstructure of command which introduced an element of coherence. This established the governor as a provincial viceroy with a council and household officers (examined in chapter 3). For much of the period covered by this book, primacy was in the hands of the cadet family of the house of Bourbon, the dukes of Vendôme, who inherited the domains of the Luxembourg family and eventually stood next in line to the throne after the immediate royal family. The Bourbon dukes and their connections bulk large in this discussion.

The governor's military command was complemented by a corps of royal *commissaires* responsible for the specialist services of army support and fortifications (see chapter 5). As has been shown cogently by M. Antoine in his studies of French administration in Piedmont during the same period, it was this which formed the nucleus of the centralising royal administration of the seventeenth century. In the period under discussion, as has already been pointed out, many of these administrators were firmly rooted in the milieu of the lesser nobility of the province.

---

[56] For examples of registers of seigneurial justice in the period: AN Z/2 no. 1, Ancre 1477–82; AC Lucheux no. 222, 1517–20; BM Boulogne, MS 125/A, Doudeauville 1472–8.

[57] AM Péronne BB 6, *passim*. The *échevinage* of Amiens were 'juges royaux ordinaires en matière civile et criminelle', *Inventaire sommaire, Amiens* II, 352 (1543). J. Boca, *La justice criminelle de l'échevinage d'Abbeville au moyen âge (1183–1516)* (1930), 73–5, 84, for the cessation of municipal jurisdiction during the period of *franc-fête*, when the worst disorder occurred, see 85.

The population of Picardy at the start of this period was undoubtedly marked by the impact of the long-drawn-out catastrophe which had resulted from the combined effect of the Hundred Years War and the century of recurrent plague which accompanied it.[58] The demography of France before the seventeenth century is often a matter of guesswork, proceeding from extrapolations from the *Etat des paroisses et des feux* of 1328. Picardy has no reliable series of late mediaeval fiscal records of the kind available for demographers of other provinces, like Normandy.[59] Fortunately, there are for northern France a few points of illumination from which general trends can be established. If, as seems reasonable, the 1328 survey yields a population for Picardy at the height of the 'monde plein' of 600,000 souls, forming with Normandy and the Ile-de-France the most densely populated region of France,[60] the great survey of hearths conducted in 1469 by the Burgundian government, then in control of all Picardy, produces a figure of 231,500 for the province as it came to exist in the sixteenth century (including Boulonnais and Saint-Quentin).[61] These two surveys, however, based on different criteria, are not strictly comparable. More significant is the fall in the average number of households per parish from around 100 in 1328 to around 30 in 1469. It is quite clear that the social and demographic patterns of Artois and Picardy were, and remained, very similar. In terms of density, they may both be placed in the third 'zone' of W. Prévenier's demographic analysis of the Low Countries, with about 35 to the sq km (in place of 12.05 hearths in 1328) and 21–2 per cent urban

[58] A. Huguet, 'Aspects de la guerre de Cent Ans en la Picardie maritime 1400–1450', *MSAP*, vols. 48 and 50 (1941–3).
[59] G. Bois, *Crise de féodalisme* (1976), 27–42.
[60] F. Lot, 'L'Etat des paroisses et des feux de 1328', *BEC* 90 (1929), 51–107, 256–316 with comments in J. Dupâquier (ed.), *Histoire de la population française* (1988) I, 259–66. At that time the population of Picardy has been estimated at one-tenth that of the royal domain: see R. Fossier, *La terre et les hommes en Picardie*, 276–7; Fossier (ed.), *Histoire de la Picardie*, 216, argues that the decline of 1328–1469 was 'sensible' but not total. The 1328 figure may be roughly deduced as follows: the *bailliage* of Amiens with 1,144 parishes had 115,716 *feux*, but part of the later Picardy is obviously included in the vast *bailliage* of Vermandois. There were roughly 1,375 parishes in the sixteenth century *généralité* of Amiens and 1,362 in the three dioceses of Boulogne, Amiens and Noyon. We should therefore add 200 parishes to the 1,144 and attain 131,716 *feux* and 592,722 souls.
[61] AD Nord B 195, 196, 197. Returns for the Somme are printed in J. Estienne, 'Déclaration des feux de 1469' *BSAP* 34 (1931–2), 96–137. Those for the Saint-Quentin *élection*: AD Nord B 197 fo. 26v–27v and for Boulonnais in A. Bocquet, *Recherches sur la population rurale de l'Artois et du Boulonnais pendant la période bourguignonne* (1969), 124–7, and a critique of the source, 129–33. A full analysis of the survey, with a few errors, is in W. P. Blockmans *et al.*, 'Tussen crisis en welvaart: sociale veranderingen 1300–1500', *Algemene Geschiedenis der Nederlanden* IV (1980), 42–7, using a multiplier of 4.5 for towns and 5 for the country. This has been followed in my own calculations. Only roughly 1,200 parishes instead of *c*. 1,360 were counted for Picardy and Boulonnais, so the overall figure is an under-estimate.

population.[62] The fuller evidence for Artois (population in 1469, not including Boulonnais, around 180,000) indicates that, after a startlingly low level in the first decades of the fifteenth century and truly catastrophic years in the 1430s and 1440s, the population started to recover in the 1460s, with a 4 per cent growth from 1469 to 1475, severely limited by the wars after 1477.[63] The savage fall in population, however, was accompanied by higher productivity, with Picardy in the 1460s and 1470s a major exporter of grain to the Low Countries and Spain. From 1477, the grainlands of the Santerre were sending their produce instead southwards to Paris and the Ile-de-France.[64]

Provinces experienced differing rates of change and it is in the highest degree improbable that the tripling of population in the period from 1470 to 1540 that has been observed in Provence was paralleled in the north. Evidence for the towns is, at best, fragmentary. Abbeville had 3,121 hearths in 1469 (around 14,000 people) and had grown by 1517 when a traveller estimated 4,000 (perhaps around 18,000 people).[65] Amiens has no record between the *Aide pour le passage de la mer* of 1386, which registered 2,432 hearths (though this omitted clerical jurisdictions) and the intendant's report of 1698, which estimated 35,000 people. The town certainly grew economically after 1480, with the establishment of the textile industry of *saieterie*, which by the mid-sixteenth century generated employment for around two-thirds of the population. On the other hand, wars and epidemics may well have wasted much new population growth. Edouard Maugis thought that the town had grown little by the 1540s (at around 12,000–15,000), while more recent estimations have the figure fluctuating wildly around 20,000 in the first half of the sixteenth century.[66]

---

[62] W. Prévenier, 'La démographie des villes du comté de Flandre aux XIVᵉ et XVᵉ siècles', *Revue du Nord* 65 (1983), 255–75, esp. 271–2. Flanders was, of course, most densely populated at 77.9% per sq km. Total pop. for Flanders: 734,173 (see Blockmans *et al.* in *Algemene Geschiedenis* IV, 45).

[63] A. Bocquet, *Recherches*, 141–5. Artois also has a survey before and after the devastating campaign of 1475 with which to compare 1469.

[64] See the article by Sneller, trans. J. Godard in *BSAP* (1947) and R. Fossier (ed.), *Histoire de la Picardie*, 214. See also H. Duchaussoy, 'La vigne en Picardie', *MSAP* 41 and 42 (1926–8). In 1484, the crown could compensate a *fermier* of dues at Abbeville for concessions made by Louis XI to Dutch merchants importing grain from the region, see A. Bernier (ed.), *Procès-verbaux des séances du conseil de régence du roi Charles VIII* (1836), 203.

[65] On Provence, see E. Baratier, *La démographie provençale du XIIIᵉ au XVIᵉ siècles* (1961). For Abbeville: Estienne, 'Déclaration des feux', 113–14; J. R. Hale (ed.), *The Travel Journal of Antonio de Beatis* (1979), 106. For cautions on the towns, eee Lot, 'L'Etat des paroisses', 289–90, and B. Chevalier, *Les bonnes villes de France* (1982), 25–30. Abbeville had 4,131 hearths and 12,245 people in 1772 (BN Picardie 8).

[66] R. Hubscher (ed.), *Histoire d'Amiens* (1986), 122; P. Deyon, *Amiens capitale provinçiale*, 3–16, esp. 7; A. Labarre, *Le livre dans la vie amiénoise du 16me siècle* (1971), 21–4. For the 1386 survey, see A. Dubois, 'Aide de L 5975 10s 4d, dite aide ordonnée pour le passage de la mer', *MSAP*, 26 (1879), 165–259. E. Maugis, *La Saieterie à Amiens (1480–1587)* (1907);

Population figures for the countryside in the sixteenth century are sparse.
H. Neveux, in a study of a few villages of the Cambrésis, has shown a
population growth which started earlier than in Artois, around 1450, collapsed
again after 1477 but started to rise in the late 1480s. The first half of the
sixteenth century saw stagnation until 1540 (when the number of hearths was
back to its 1365 level), followed by new growth, interrupted by the wars of the
1550s, that continued into the 1570s. Pierre Deyon has revealed a sharp
increase in rents between 1530 and 1560, as well as steep increases in prices,
but primarily in years of warfare and poor harvests like the 1520s and early
1530s.[67] Though there are no overall surveys for the first half of the sixteenth
century, the figures published in the *Secret des finances de France* of 1581,
thought to be at least usable for northern France, indicate a startling contrast
with the previous century. Exact comparisons are not possible, but the three
dioceses of Boulogne, Amiens and Noyon (somewhat larger than the province)
produce the figure of 125,000 hearths, or around 560,000 people.[68] We
should probably envisage a doubling of the population between the mid-
fifteenth-century low point and 1580, most of it rural. There had been no
further growth by the time of Vauban's *Projet*, when the *généralité* of Picardy
had 520,000 people and a density of 57.4 per sq km. A survey of 1772
produced 172,533 hearths and 543,423 people, while the urban population had
fallen to 14 per cent. There were probably around 600,000 on the eve of the

Maugis, *Recherches sur les transformations du régime politique et sociale de la ville d'Amiens,
des origines de la commune à la fin du XVIe siècle* (1906), 602–7, establishes church
jurisdiction as one-sixth of the town and, in 1452–3, 450–500 hearths. Hence his figure of
12–15,000 people at that time. The population of Amiens in 1772: 8,341 hearths and 35,325
people (BN Picardie 8)

67 H. Neveux, *Vie et déclin d'une structure économique. Les grains du Cambrésis* (1980),
167–78, esp. the indices on 169 and table 401–4. The study is confined to a sample of
twenty villages, part of a series of surveys of Hainault: see M. A. Arnould, *Les dénombrements
des foyers dans le comté de Hainault* (1956). E. Le Roy Ladurie, *The French Peasantry*
(trans. 1987), 98, argues that this area experienced a smaller drop in the fifteenth century
and smaller rise in the sixteenth. P. Deyon, 'Quelques remarques sur l'évolution du
régime seigneurial en Picardie' *RHMC* 8 (1961), 270ff., uses judicial cases involving the
abbey of Corbie in the early sixteenth century, and above all his *Contribution à l'étude
des revenues fonciers en Picardie* (1967), chs. 1–4, the fermages of the *Hôtel-Dieu* of
Amiens.

68 'N. Froumenteau', *Secret des finances de France* (1581), 137–58. The difficulties of using this
source are obvious: the use of dioceses instead of *généralités* for computation. The diocese of
Boulogne at 40,700 hearths is much too large and must include part of Artois. On the other
hand, the diocese of Laon (for the county of Guise) is omitted. For commentary, see J.
Dupâquier (ed.), *Histoire de la population française* II, 52–3, 75–7, and J. B. Wood, 'The
Impact of the Wars of Religion: A View of France in 1581', *Sixteenth Century Journal* 15
(1984), 131–68. The number of parishes in Boulogne–Amiens–Noyon (the latter representing
Péronne and St-Quentin) at 1,362 is very close to the 1,375 in the *généralité* of Picardy in 1587
(excluding Noyon outside Picardy): see Lot, 'Etat des paroisses', 312; BN Picardie 112 bis fo.
51.

Revolution.[69] This seems to have been the limit of density before the agricultural and industrial revolutions. The period covered by this book, therefore, was one in which a lengthy restoration of population density was taking place, delayed and prolonged by war.

Much of the restoration must have taken place in the two decades around 1500. The limitations on productivity, however, were bound to engender a deterioration in the material conditions of life thereafter. One sign of this was that plague remained a major scourge and the early years of the sixteenth century saw a notable recrudescence of its impact.[70] All the towns of the province registered alarm at the threat of plague from early 1515 (1512–14 had been years of poor harvest, war with England and grain riots like those at Péronne in 1512), there was another attack in 1519 and a severe crisis in 1522–3.[71] The harvest failures of 1529–32 presaged another attack, which duly started in 1534, and 1545–6 and 1556–7 were years of severe dearth. These phenomena, with the dislocations of war, should caution us against envisaging a completion of the population growth in Picardy before the second half of the sixteenth century.

Bare statistics may be augmented by the impressionistic accounts of travellers in the region, which become more numerous from the late fifteenth-century journals of Jerome Munzer and the early sixteenth-century equivalents of Antonio Beatis and the anonymous Milanese of 1516–18, as well as by travel itineraries like those of Jacques le Saige (1519), Nicolas Carewe (1529) and Jean Second (1533). The picture which emerges from their accounts is of a population whose language and manners were much like those of the French-speaking Low Countries, though with idiosyncracies, especially in costume (which was a feature travellers were often careful to observe). Landscape was

---

[69] Dupâquier, *Histoire de la population française* II, 75–7. *Généralité* of Amiens at 9,049 sq km. See also the population survey of 1772 for the province of Picardy in BN Picardie 8. The urban population was then 75,726. N.B. The hearth:person ratio is this survey is 3.1 on average.

[70] Dubois, 'Les pestes ou contagions à Amiens pendant les XVᶜ, XVIᶜ et XVIIᶜ siècles', *MSAP* 23 (1873); G. Lecocq, 'Histoire de la peste à Saint-Quentin (1401–1792)', *Le Vermandois* 5 (1877), 109ff., 494ff.; C. de Marsy, 'La peste à Compiègne', *La Picardie* (1878–9), 281–300; La Fons Mélicocq, 'Péronne en temps de peste, XVIᶜ siècle', *La Picardie* 2 (1856), 506–12. AM Péronne BB 7 fo. 2, 11 (1515), fo. 86r (1519); AM Chauny BB 3 fo. 34v, BB 4, 9 April, 8 May 1523; BM Abbeville MS 378 fo. 12; A. Thierry, *Recueil de monuments historiques de l'histoire du Tiers Etat. 1ère série. Région du Nord*, 4 vols. (1850–70), II, 570.

[71] H. Heller, *Blood and Iron*, stresses the importance of riot and rebellion 1500–60 without saying much on Picardy. In October 1512, the *franc-fête* at Péronne saw grain riots against merchants who were exporting grain at a time of dearth. One of the leaders, Oudin Picquet, accused the merchant Andrieu Noiret of being a 'traistre et lui disant que s'il eust esté en beaucoup de bonnes villes passé dix ans il eust esté assommé' (AM Péronne BB 6 fo. 303r–306v). In 1530 there were riots during another period of dearth (MC Chantilly L VII fo. 118 – see ch. 4). However, the intensification of military destruction in this region seems to have made bare survival the main priority after 1530 (see ch. 6).

not generally of much interest to sixteenth-century travellers, though it was common to notice the richness of the land, with the valley of the Somme around Abbeville full of all sorts of fruit and the wide plain of the Santerre south of Amiens rich in grain and livestock. Not surprisingly for travellers, it was the state of accommodation which concerned most of them and a general consensus emerges that the inns of the region were of distinctly mixed quality.[72]

All travellers were concerned with the state of the roads. For horsemen, the *gouvernement* of Picardy, a territory of roughly 10,000 sq km, was two days' journey from east–west. The routes given by Charles Estienne in 1552 indicate that most places along the Somme were two and two-and-a-half days' journey from Paris but it took another three-and-a-half days to get to Calais from Amiens, a journey of 31 leagues by much less satisfactory roads. Nicolas Carewe in 1529 took seven days for his journey to Paris via Amiens and even the journey from Amiens to Paris via the common route through Clermont and Luzarches took three overnight stops at seven leagues a day. Ten leagues was possible, though only for a traveller in a hurry. A rider in post using the royal postal system under the *grand écuyer* could, of course, move more quickly. With a distance of 20 leagues (80 km) a day the maximum for a courier of the royal posts, news could travel from Paris to Amiens (150 km) in a minimum of two days and to Calais (300 km) in four.[73]

Of the towns, only Amiens and its cathedral, described by the Milanese of 1518 as the most beautiful in France, attracted any attention. For the rest, these travellers in the main ignored the architectural and artistic renewal which swept Picardy from the late fifteenth century and endowed it with the late gothic *flamboyant* churches which constitute the major architectural legacy of

---

[72] 'Le voyage de Hieronimus Monetarius à travers la France, 1494–5', ed. E. P. Goldschmidt, *Humanisme et Renaissance* 6 (1939), 331–3; J. R. Hale (ed.), *The Travel Journal of Antonio de Beatis*, 105–7; the anonymous Milanese, BL Add. MS 24180 fo. 15–32; G. Prévôt (ed.), 'Les Itinera de Jean Second', *Revue du Nord* 9 (1923); H. R. Duthilloeul (ed.), *Voyage de Jacques le Saige de Douai à Rome* (1851), 2; Ellis Gruffydd, *Chronicl*, ed. and trans. by M. B. Davies as 'Suffolk's Expedition to Montdidier', *Bulletin of the Faculty of Arts of Fouad I University, Cairo* 7 (1944), 6; R. J. Knecht (ed.), *The Voyage of Sir Nicolas Carewe to the Emperor Charles V in the Year 1530* (1959).

[73] C. Estienne, *La guide des chemins de France*, 16–35. See also A. Ledieu, *Voyages en Picardie d'un gentilhomme lillois à la fin du XVIIe siècle* (n.d.), 14–15. Travel times for couriers: 70–80 km a day (*Le Moyen Age* 82 (1976), 311; *Bulletin de la Commission royale d'histoire* 103 (1938), 236). The journey from Paris to London via Boulogne or Calais could be done by special messengers in as little as six days, see V.-L. Bourrilly and P. de Vaissière (eds.), *Ambassades en Angleterre de Jean du Bellay: la première ambassade (septembre 1527–février 1529)* (1905), 376–7, 459, 488, 502. On the establishment of posts in Picardy: at Péronne 1528, AM Péronne BB 7 fo. 341v; payments to the postal officials in the province, AD Pas-de-Calais 12J 196, p. 128; orders by Coligny, June 1557, BN fr. 3150 fo. 11. The *généralité* of Amiens was 9,049 sq km (of which 6,227 is the modern dep. of Somme), to which must be added the county of Guise and Thiérarche.

the period. Until 1914 there were 280 churches in the Somme (about a quarter of the total) built in this period. Many, like Montcavrel, north of Montreuil, were highly accomplished. Town churches were rebuilt on a grand scale at Montdidier (Saint-Pierre), Péronne (Saint-Jean), Poix (Saint-Denis), Roye and Auxy-le-château.[74] The great examples, like the west front of Saint-Vulfran at Abbeville (started 1488, discontinued for lack of funds in 1539) and the façade of the abbey of Saint-Riquier (rebuilt under abbé Pierre Le Prebstre in the 1470s) demonstrate how the predominantly flamboyant style of the region gradually adapted to Renaissance tastes.[75] At the chapel of the Holy Spirit at Rue (1506–14), the vaulting displays mastery of the late gothic idiom while mixing in some Italianate decoration.

However, as Pierre Heliot showed, Picardy, like Artois, remained a bastion of *flamboyant* architecture into the seventeenth century, unlike the Ile-de-France.[76] This is seen as much in civil architecture the active rebuilding of town halls in the same period: Péronne, Saint-Quentin (finished 1509), Compiègne (under Louis XII), Noyon (1485–1522) and the *bailliage* of Amiens (under Francis I).[77] Of the seigneurial architecture of the period, which as elsewhere perpetuated the traditions of the late mediaeval château with Renaissance influences, less has survived as a result of the extensive reconstructions which took place in the seventeenth century.[78]

[74] *La Picardie historique et monumentale*, 7 vols (1893–1931) and supplement in R. Rodière and P. Des Forts, *Le pays de Vimeu* (1938). G. Durand, 'Les tailleurs d'images du milieu du XVe au milieu du XVe siècle', *Bulletin monumental* 90 (1931), 333.

[75] BM Abbeville MSS 409–10, building accounts. H. Zanettacci, 'Statuaire de la façade à Saint-Vulfran d'Abbeville', *Bulletin monumental* 95 (1936), 357–67. G. Durand, *L'église de Saint-Riquier* (1933).

[76] P. Heliot, 'L'église de Hesdin et l'architecture de la Renaissance en Artois', *Bulletin monumental* 96 (1937), 488–9; G. Durand, 'Les Lannoy, Folleville et l'art italien dans le Nord de la France', *Bulletin monumental* 70 (1906), 329–404; J. Lestocquoy, 'Relations artistiques entre Arras et Amiens à la fin du XVe et au début du XVIe siècle', *BSAP* 37 (1937–8), 325–7. J. Vanuxem, 'Aspects de la sculpture dans le Nord de la France entre 1480 et 1540', in F. Lesure (ed.), *La Renaissance dans les provinces du Nord*, 159–67. H. Zanettacci, *Les ateliers picards de sculpture à la fin du moyen-âge* (1954).

[77] J. Lestocquoy, *Beffrois, Halles, Hôtels de Ville dans le Nord de la France et la Belgique* (1948), 95ff. H. Dusevel, 'Notes sur la construction et la décoration des édifices publics dans la ville d'Amiens au XVIe siècle', *La Picardie* 6 (1860).

[78] For a useful brief introduction to the evolution of late mediaeval French châteaux, see J. Guillaume, 'Le château français du milieu du XVe au début du XVIe siècle: formes et sens', in Chevalier and Contamine, *La France de la fin du XVe siècle*, 221–4 (and plates). On Picardy, and the residences of the late middle ages, see P. Héliot, 'Les demeures seigneuriales dans la région picarde au Moyen Age. Châteaux ou manoirs?', in *Recueil des travaux offerts à M. Clovis Brunel* (1955). For examples, see E. Prarond, *Notice sur Rambures* (1859); P. Seydoux, *Le château de Rambures et la guerre au XVe siècle en Picardie* (1974); R. Rodière and P. des Forts, *Le pays de Vimeu*; M. Crampon, *Picquigny: le château fort, la collégiale, la ville* (1963). The few new residences of the first half of the sixteenth century include in Vimeu Avesnes-Chaussoy, started by the Villiers de l'Isle-Adam around 1500 and Beaucamps-le-jeune, probably started by Anne de Pisseleu in 1537. Among the greater houses, the castle of

Whether there was a 'Picard school' in art during this period has been a matter of controversy but, though much of the work of the period is anonymous, it is extraordinarily accomplished. This is as much the case with the choir stalls of Amiens cathedral (finished in 1522) as with the group portraits of the confraternity of the Puy Notre-Dame, especially those of 1518–21 ascribed to the *maître d'Amiens*.[79] The quality of this work indicates that the early sixteenth century was a high point of taste and patronage at Amiens and that Picardy was no cultural backwater, confirming the vitality of intellectual life in the generation of Robert Gaguin, Lefebvre d'Etaples, Charles de Bovelles, Gerard Roussel and François Vatable, all Picards. On the other hand, we know that the Collège d'Amiens had fallen into decay by the mid-sixteenth century, probably as a result of wartime impoverishment.[80]

The general picture which emerges at the start of this study is one of a region in which the recovery from the devastations of the period of the Hundred Years War period was decidedly retarded by the struggle for control with Burgundy. The respite from war that began in the 1490s seems to have stimulated a significant recovery manifested in rebuilding and art patronage. The pause, however, was savagely interrupted by the opening of a new and more devastating generation of war after 1521.

Ham was vastly refurbished under the constable of Saint-Pol in the 1450s and 1460s: see C. Gomart, *Ham, son château, ses prisonniers* (1864), baron de La Fons Mélicocq and Lioux, 'Notice sur la ville et château de Ham', *MSAP* 2, 273ff. That of La Fère-sur-Oise became a major princely residence in the reign of Francis I: see D. L. Potter, 'The Luxembourg Inheritance', 42. See the splendid print of it in 1595 reproduced in *La Picardie* (1867), opp. p. 200. War severely damaged a large number of seigneurial residences in Picardy during the sixteenth century. On seventeenth-century rebuilding, see J. Sartre, *Châteaux 'brique et pierre' en Picardie* (1973).

[79] G. Durand, *L'art en Picardie* (1914); H. Zanettacci, *Les ateliers picards*; A. Janvier, *La vièrge du palmier* (1896); M. C. Delacroix, 'Les Puys d'Amiens, un fleuron original de la peinture gothique', *L'estampille* 105 (Jan. 1979), 32–9; A. M. Lecocq, 'Le Puy d'Amiens de 1518', *Revue de L'art* 38 (Dec. 1977), 64–74. C. Sterling, 'La peinture sur panneau picarde et son rayonnement dans le Nord de la France au XVe siècle', *Bulletin de la Société de l'histoire de l'art français*, année 1979 (1981), 7–49.

[80] A. Labarre, *Le livre dans la vie amienoise*, 16–21. Printers worked at Abbeville, 1486–7 (for instance, the sumptuous edition of Jean Boutilier's *Somme rurale* published there by P. Gerard in 1486) and at Amiens 1508–10, but neither town was able to develop an industry in the sixteenth century, though there was a lively book trade, *ibid.*, 50–60. On C. de Bovelles, Josquin des Prez *et al.* at Noyon, see L. P. Colliette, *Mémoires pour servir à l'histoire ecclésiastique, civile et militaire de la province du Vermandois* 3 vols. (1771–3), III, 137–58.

1

✚

RETURN TO ALLEGIANCE: PICARDY
AND THE FRANCO-BURGUNDIAN WARS,
1470–1493

Attached piecemeal to the French royal domain in the late twelfth and thirteenth centuries, Picardy might seem on the maps to be a region close to the centre of royal power in the later middle ages. Such an impression, however, is deceptive.[1] Though it formed no single province or appanage, the centrifugal tendencies of its nobles and the independent urban traditions of an area that had been at the centre of the early mediaeval communal movements were enough to ensure that the grip of the crown had been periodically weakened during the fourteenth-century struggles with the Plantagenets, fatally so in the fifteenth. Such interests were realigned during the late fourteenth-century 'régime of the dukes' around the Valois dukes of Burgundy.[2] For much of the fifteenth century, the region was controlled by the English or Burgundians, formally so after the Treaty of Arras in 1435 conceded the Somme towns to Philip the Good, on condition that the crown might redeem them at some future date; Boulogne and Ponthieu were ceded without condition to the male line of the Burgundian dukes.[3]

Burgundy was the dominant power in northern France from the 1420s to 1477 and became in consequence deeply embedded in the clientage networks of the local nobility. Artois, with its intimate connections with Flanders, was a

---

[1] On the absorption of Picardy into the royal domain, see R. Fossier (ed.), *Histoire de la Picardie*, 170–5. On distance and space, R.-H. Bautier, 'Recherches sur les routes de l'Europe médiévale', *BPH* (1960), 102, n. 2.
[2] R. Fossier, 'La noblesse picarde au temps de Philippe le Bel', 105; P. Contamine, 'De la puissance aux privilèges', 243–50, both in P. Contamine (ed.), *La noblesse au moyen âge*. R. Cazelles, *La société politique sous Philippe VI* (1958), and *La société politique sous Jean le Bon et Charles V* (1982), esp. 91. But see also B. Leroy, 'Autour de Charles "le Mauvais". Groupes et personnalités', *RH*, 553 (1985), 3–18.
[3] G. Dickinson, *The Congress of Arras* (1955), 164–5; E. Cosneau, *Le connétable de Richemont* (1886), 552–4, enquiry re: Somme towns, 1449; 555–6, letter of duke of Burgundy, 1435.

natural adjunct of the Burgundian state; Picardy, which in a sense stood at the crossroads between the Ile-de-France and the Low Countries, was more equivocal in its loyalties. There are signs that the Somme towns had become restive with Burgundian domination by the 1470s, but the province was being incorporated in the increasingly centralised institutions of the Burgundian state and was usually represented at the Estates-General of the ducal lands from the 1460s.[4] The newly important grain exportation trade made Picardy, and particularly the Santerre, a major supplier of the Netherlands until 1470, establishing fundamental economic links with Burgundy. Picardy and Artois shared similar patterns of social organisation in this context. The eventual frontier between France and the Low Countries was not preordained, therefore, and in some senses ripped apart an entity of growing coherence in the mid-fifteenth century.

The final expulsion of the English from France in the 1450s opened the way for a reassertion of royal power in the north, but it was not until the accession of Louis XI in 1461 that serious moves were made in this direction. Picardy, along with Artois and Flanders, had remained within the *mouvance* of the crown but increasingly subject in fact to the attenuation of royal power. The moves made by Louis XI from 1461 were not systematic, but rather the result of mistakes made and opportunities seized. Nor were they confined to the reoccupation of Picardy alone. The French crown sought, naturally, to undermine the duke of Burgundy's power wherever possible; in 1477 it was presented with an unlooked-for opportunity to annihilate Burgundian power completely. Indeed, it has been argued that the French crown sought throughout the late fifteenth and early sixteenth centuries to regain control of all the lands of its *mouvance*, including Artois and Flanders, and that only the effective resistance of the Flemish cities in 1477–8 and of Maximilian thereafter prevented this.[5] Thus, as a result of the long period of warfare and negotiation leading to the compromise peace of Senlis in 1493, it was only control of Picardy itself that the French crown regained.

In 1463, Louis XI negotiated the repurchase of the mortgaged Somme towns for 400,000 écus under the terms of the treaty of Arras and installed his own governor at Amiens, remarking to the Milanese ambassador on his entry in June 1464: 'Non vi pare che questa città sola vaglia molto meglio che li quatrocento milia scuti che ho pagato?'[6] The king's policy in his early years,

[4] R. Wellens, *Les états généraux des Pays-Bas des origines à la fin du règne de Philippe le Beau* (1972) I, 360–1.
[5] W. P. Blockmans, 'La position du comté de Flandre dans le royaume à la fin du XVᵉ siècle', in B. Chevalier and P. Contamine, *La France de la fin du XVᵉ siècle*, 71–89.
[6] Lannoy in place of Saveuses: Thierry, *Tiers Etat*, II, 285; *Dépêches des ambassadeurs milanais*, ed. B. de Mandrot and C. Samaran, 4 vols. (1916–23) II, 181.

however, in displacing so many of his father's advisers and making so many enemies, led to the collapse of his plans in the rebellion of 1465. The grandiloquently named *Ligue du Bien Public* was a coalition between Charles the Bold and the leading French princes, including Louis de Luxembourg, count of Saint-Pol, the greatest feudatory of Picardy and co-heir of the Coucy inheritance, who was in effect building up a semi-independent power base in lands straddling royal and Burgundian territory.[7] The treaty that was extracted from the king at Conflans in October 1465 registered a severe reversal of his plans for Picardy, transferring Boulogne, Ponthieu and most of the Somme towns to Burgundy in full inheritance and Péronne, Montdidier and Roye under the existing terms of the treaty of Arras. In addition, the king had to agree to the promotion of Saint-Pol as constable of France.[8]

The tortuous events of the next ten years or so illustrate Commynes's remark that no ruler was more effective in retrieving a disastrous situation than Louis XI.[9] The calamity of his imprisonment and blackmail by the duke of Burgundy at Péronne in October 1468 extracted from him a treaty which further limited royal jurisdiction in Picardy and Artois.[10] Despite this, and the added complications of Saint-Pol's double-dealing, the king held to his course of trying to undermine Burgundian power. This must be set against a background of chronic conspiracy, fear and suspicion among the princes, as well as the intervention of participants in the factional turmoil in England.[11]

---

[7] On Saint Pol's military clientage in Picardy, see J. Quicherat, 'Lettres, mémoires, instructions et autres documents relatifs à la guerre du bien public', *Mélanges historiques*, CDI, II, 207–8, 280; R. Vaughan, *Charles the Bold* (1973), 250–3.

[8] Thierry, *Tiers Etat*, II, 307; *Ordonnances*, XVI, letters of gift, 5 Oct. 1465; *Mémoires de Philippe de Commynes*, ed. B. de Mandrot, 2 vols. (1901–3), I, 88; text of treaty of Conflans, Commynes, *Mémoires*, trans. A. Scoble (London, 1885), 73–8. For Burgundy's accusation that the people of Amiens and Saint-Quentin had been 'corrompy . . . par argent et belles promesses', see Jean Molinet, *Chroniques*, ed. G. Doutrepont and O. Jodogne, 3 vols. (1935–7), ch. xviii.

[9] E.g., Commynes, *Mémoires* I, 257: 'Je luy ose bien porter ceste louenge (et ne sçay si je l'ay dict ailleurs; et quant je l'aurois dict, si vault il bien le dire deux foiz) que jamais je ne congneu si saige homme en adversité.'

[10] Commynes, *Mémoires* I, 175–81; K. Bittmann, *Ludwig XI. und Karl der Kühne* (1964), I, 289–301; R. Vaughan, *Charles the Bold*, 54–8.

[11] On the king's continuing intervention at Abbeville in 1467, see draft reply to a petition from that town, BN fr. 20490 fo. 43. On the effects of the continuing jurisdiction of the Parlement of Paris in the *bailliage* of Amiens, see comte de Marsy, 'L'exécution d'un arrêt de Parlement au XVe siècle. Adjudication du château de Raincheval et mis en possession du nouveau seigneur (1469)', *MSAP* 26 (1879), 149–64. W. S. Paravicini, 'Peur, pratiques, intelligences. Formes de l'opposition aristocratique à Louis XI d'après les interrogatoires du connétable de Saint-Pol', in B. Chevalier and P. Contamine, *La France de la fin du XVe siècle*, esp. 185–7.

The Franco-Burgundian wars, 1470–1493

The wars for the control of northern France began effectively at the end of 1470 and formed part of the struggle between Charles the Bold and his many enemies in France and the Empire, of which Louis XI was to be the ultimate beneficiary. Louis had begun by detaching Saint-Pol from the duke of Burgundy after 1468, since any move towards the reoccupation of Picardy would have to confront the power of the Luxembourg family. The government of Normandy and promises of marriage to Marie de Savoie, Louis's sister-in-law, and of the county of Guise, never effected, were enough to win over the constable.[12] Though the constable did not at first break openly with the duke, his relations with the latter deteriorated sharply after 1470 and Saint-Pol's lands in the Low Countries were confiscated, and some administered by his relatives there.[13]

Louis declared openly against Burgundy on 3 December 1470 and it may be assumed that the constable's seizure of Saint-Quentin for the king on 10 December was concerted with the handing over of Amiens to the king's lieutenant in Picardy, Dammartin, on 31 January.[14] The duke had realised the danger and prepared for the relief of Amiens, but it was too late, though his governor at Abbeville, Esquerdes, just managed to secure that town from a similar fate. Thereafter Amiens, which extracted extensive privileges for its change of loyalty, remained in royal control and became the centre of Louis's plans to recover Picardy, while Péronne and Abbeville remained secure in Burgundian power. In February 1471, the duke mounted a counter-attack, took Picquigny and beseiged Amiens, but difficulties elsewhere forced him to conclude a one-year truce in April, followed by peace talks between Ham and Péronne in May. In the diplomatic moves from September 1471 to March 1472, it is clear that such was Louis's need for peace that, in

---

[12] G. Duboscq, 'Le mariage de Charles d'Anjou comte du Maine et le comté de Guise (1431–73), *BEC* 96 (1935), 338–66. Saint-Pol himself had a hereditary claim to Guise. Royal letters-patent, 10 Dec. 1470, compensation for the count of Maine for the county of Guise and seigneurie of Novion, promised to Saint-Pol, BN fr. 20494 fo. 67, copy. For documents on Louis de Luxembourg and Guise, see MC: D 2 (1443–1512). See also L. Germain, *René II, duc de Lorraine et le comté de Guise* (1888), 27–9.

[13] Paravicini, 'Peur, pratiques', in Chevalier and Contamine, *La France de la fin du XVᵉ siècle*, 191. On the seigneurie of Lucheux and its castle, transferred to Burgundy in 1470, see AN K 71 no. 3 and D. L. Potter, 'The Luxembourg Inheritance', 38–41.

[14] At Saint-Quentin, the duke had ordered prayers in December 1470 for his delivery from a murder attempt in which he blamed Louis XI: see BN Picardie 89 fo. 300. By November 1471 a royal agent was reporting from Saint-Quentin that 'on a fort besongné à la fortiffication et emparement d'icelle', BN fr. 20485 fo. 78. Act of surrender of Amiens, signed by A. de Chabannes (Dammartin), J. Rouault, Torcy, see AM Amiens AA 5 fo. 145 (2 Feb. 1471); K. Bittmann, *Ludwig XI. und Karl der Kühne* I, 489; II, 377.

return for the duke's homage, he was willing to give up Amiens and Saint-Quentin.[15]

The duke of Burgundy, however, was anxious to return to war. The discontent of the French princes was growing and the death of the figurehead for rebellion, Charles de France, in May 1472, followed by the expiry of the truce on 15 June, provided a pretext. After burning Nesle in a notorious atrocity, Burgundy moved on to capture Montdidier and Roye, but failed before Beauvais and withdrew, burning Poix and villages around Oisemont. Gamaches, the castle of the French marshal, Joachim Rouault, was burned and the duke himself seized Saint-Valéry and Eu before moving into Normandy. Louis had been sanguine about these successes, telling Saint-Pol that the duke's gains might frighten people, but 'au regard des meschantes places, il ne gaigne rient, quant il les gaigne, et se afoyblist'.[16] For their part, French soldiers from Amiens raided villages towards Hesdin under Burgundian control, while plague-ridden and unruly Burgundian soldiers streaming back from Normandy wrought havoc everywhere before the duke concluded a winter truce at Beaurevoir.[17] The campaign of 1472 had been unusually destructive, a fact confirmed by the narrative of the Burgundian abbé of Saint-Riquier, Pierre le Prebstre, as well as by Philippe de Commynes, who noted that the burning had been unusual on both sides before this time, but became the norm afterwards.[18]

The conclusion of a Franco-Burgundian treaty at Le Crotoy on 3 October 1472 confirmed the treaties of Arras, Conflans and Péronne, but in effect maintained the status quo at the end of the fighting. The peace was extremely fragile, however, and, despite an attempted peace conference at Compiègne in December 1473, it was haunted by rumours of Burgundian plots to surprise Amiens.[19] Within France, the political situation became more grave during 1473–4. A general, though ultimately ineffective conspiracy to revive the *Bien*

---

[15] Thierry, *Tiers Etat*, II, 319–31, 336–7; Commynes, *Mémoires*, I, 181–2. K. Bittmann, *Ludwig XI. und Karl der Kühne* I, 510–11, 561–76.
[16] *Chronique de Pierre le Prestre, abbé de Saint-Riquier*, ed. G. Vasseur in *Saint-Riquier* II (1971) (hereafter Le Prestre, *Chronique*), 21–2. See also la Fons-Mélicocq, 'Guerres de Charles-le-Téméraire en Picardie', *La Picardie* 5 (1859), 225–7, based on accounts of *argentier* of Lille, on the dangers of the route from Abbeville to Auxy. Letter of constable, 17 June 1472, J. Vaesen and E. Charavay (eds.), *Lettres de Louis XI*, 12 vols. (1883–1909) V, 375. Louis XI to Saint-Pol, 20 June 1472, *ibid.*, 5–7.
[17] Le Prestre, *Chronique*, 23–5.
[18] Commynes, *Mémoires* I, 251. See also *Un manuscrit interpolé de la chronique scandaleuse*, ed. Quicherat, *BEC* 16 (1865) (hereafter, *Chronique interpolé*), 16, 436–42, on the burning of Coucy and Guise and *ibid.*, 17, 256–7.
[19] Le Prestre, *Chronique*, 32; *Inventaire sommaire, Amiens* II, 211 (10, 17 May 1473). On Compiègne conference, see Vaesen, *Lettres de Louis XI* V, 206–12. On the involvement of Saint-Pol in talks with the Burgundians, see his letters to Louis XI, Noyon, 7 Sept. (1472), BN Picardie 89 fo. 333–4 and to the officiers of Laon, Ham 27 Jan. (?1474), *ibid.*, fo. 320.

public involving Saint-Pol, Nemours, the house of Anjou and possibly Bourbon was taking shape in the aftermath of the shock and fear stemming from the destruction of the Armagnac family in 1473. From outside, the power of Burgundy, Brittany and England were drawn in.[20]

As yet, the conspiracy was undeclared but the seizure of control at Saint-Quentin by Saint-Pol in December 1473, when he replaced the royal garrison by his own men, was an important sign of trouble. At his trial, he was accused of aiming to acquire Laon, Compiègne, Noyon and Senlis as a result of his alliance with England.[21] Though it may be surmised that the Constable was aiming to secure his position as a third force in northern France and already possessed, as well as Saint-Quentin, fortresses like La Fère, Bohain and above all Ham, where he had built an immensely powerful tower, how secure was he? Commynes's judgement of his assets is worth recalling:

> Cest homme situé aux confins de ces deux princes ennemys, aiant si fortes places en ses mains, quatre cens hommes d'armes bien paiez, dont il estoit commissaire, et y mettoit qui y vouloit . . . il estoit très saige et vaillant chevalier et qui avoit beaucop, bien apparente, grand argent content: il faut bien dire que ceste tromperesse, l'avoit regardé de son mauvais visaige.[22]

Recourse to ill fortune in the explanation of political calamities was natural for Commynes.

In retrospect, the constable's power itself looks precarious. Though he had had the 400 royal *gens d'armes* since 1465 and held lucrative governorships and the *connétablie*, his properties were widely dispersed through the Low Countries and northern and eastern France. With his Low Countries domain administered by sons who remained in Burgundian service, his capacity to make use of the 'gens de son lignage' was limited. In addition, his French retinue, including key Picard lords like Moy and Genlis, was fatally easy to corrupt in the event. There is good reason to suppose that he was in a state of

[20] Mandrot, 'Jacques d'Armagnac duc de Nemours' *RH* 44 (1890), 264ff.; W. Paravicini, 'Peur, pratiques', in Chevalier and Contamine, *La France de la fin du XVᵉ siècle*, 193–6. Saint-Pol to Louis XI, Noyon, 7 Sept.: 'touchant le brevet que m'aves envoyé faisant mencion Darmaignac et de Connestable, sur mon ame ce ny entends riens et ne sçay que sest', BN Pic. 89 fo. 333 and *Revue des documents historiques* 3, 97–9. On the terror against the Armagnacs: C. Samaran, *La maison d'Armagnac au XVᵉ siècle* (1920), 162–98; on conspiracies of 1473–4, B. de Mandrot, 'Jacques d'Armagnac duc de Nemours' *RH* 44 (1890), 261–4. On fear: Mandrot, *Dépêches . . . milanais* II, 336: 'vivono con gran timore de questo Re'.
[21] K. Bittmann, *Ludwig XI. und Karl der Kühne* II, 167ff.; Vaesen, *Lettres de Louis XI* V, 209–11. Saint-Pol's justification for his action was the desire of Duras, the royal commander to 'prandre cognoissance par dessus moy'. He had placed the town in the king's hands and had guarded it well until the arrival of Duras and will continue to do so 'quelque chose qu'il vous en ait dit ne escript': Ham, 20 Nov. (1473), BN Picardie 89 fo. 243. Formal trial record: BN fr. 3869 fo. 23r (4 Dec. 1475).
[22] Commynes, *Mémoires* I, 291, and similar comments, 252.

acute anxiety throughout the period.[23] Again at his trial, he referred time after time to the doubt he was in as a result of the fact that 'ses besognes n'estoient pas bonnes en court', that 'l'on disoit que le Roy n'estoit pas content de lui', that the *grand maître* Dammartin was his enemy. He claimed that he was in doubt lest the latter attack him in Saint-Quentin and cut him to pieces.[24] His coexistence with Dammartin during the latter's period as governor in Picardy (1471–2) had been uneasy and sometimes acrimonious. His fears were exacerbated by the Bouvines agreement of 1473 whereby the king and Burgundy agreed to cooperate against him, a fate from which he saved himself momentarily by persuading the king that Burgundy had duped him.[25] Relations with the king became worse when it transpired that a meeting between them at Fargniers could only take place with Saint-Pol backed by his military retinue.[26]

The Franco-Burgundian truce expired on 1 May 1475. Though Commynes claims that Louis would have prolonged it but for Burgundian threats, the opportunities for gain were obvious, with Burgundy still obsessed by the siege of Neuss and the duke of Lorraine attacking him in Luxembourg. The king was prepared to move before the expiry and rapidly seized Tronquoy, Roye, Montdidier, Corbie and Doullens.[27] To the east, the king's new governor at Laon, Robert d'Estouteville, assembled a force to crush Burgundian outposts at Marle (a castle of the constable's) and Assis.[28] In June the admiral de Bourbon advanced towards Arras, burning the villages as he went,[29] but at the start of the following month Edward IV crossed to Calais, ready to mount his long-awaited expedition to France and take advantage of the increasing aristocratic opposition to the French king. The story of the campaign is well known: Edward, disappointed by the lack of support from the duke of

---

[23] W. Paravicini, 'Peur, pratiques', in Chevalier and Contamine, *La France de la fin du XVᵉ siècle*, 186–93; Vaesen, *Lettres de Louis XI* V, 210: 'il me semble que monseigneur de Genly a bonne voulenté, et m'a promis de gaigner monseigneur de Mouy' (21 Dec. 1473).

[24] BN fr. 3869 fo. 12r, 23r: he had assembled men at Saint-Quentin 'afin de se garder des violences que l'on disoit que monsr. le grant maistre [Dammartin] et autres vouloient faire' and the king 'voulust faire recouvrer la ville de Saint Quentin sur lui par force et qu'on le taillast en pièces dedans'.

[25] Saint-Pol to Dammartin, 11 Oct. 1472: see, *Louis XI et les villes*, 384; Commynes, *Mémoires* I, 252–4; Mandrot, 'Jacques d'Armagnac', *RH* 44, 264–5.

[26] Commynes, on the meeting at Fargniers-sur-Oise 14 May 1474, *Mémoires* I, 255–6; on Louis's suspicions and orders to Laon not to allow entry to Saint Pol's men in Dec. 1474, see magistrates of Laon to Louis XI, 18 Jan. (1475), AM Laon EE 3. The king's attempt to allay Saint-Pol's suspicions: Vaesen, *Lettres de Louis XI* V, 322 (3 Feb. 1475).

[27] Commynes, *Mémoires* I, 277; Le Prestre, *Chronique*, 36–7; L'Epinois, 'Notes extraites des archives communales de Compiègne', *BEC* 25, 124–36; bulletin of Louis's campaign, AM Compiègne, BB 4.

[28] Patent of Robert d'Estouteville, 26 April 1475, AM Laon EE 3; of his commissaire Doulcet, 10 May, *ibid.*; missives of Estouteville to Laon, 16, 21 June; Laon to Louis XI, 5 June, *ibid.*

[29] Le Prestre, *Chronique*, 37–40, esp. 38.

Burgundy, came to an agreement at Picquigny with a French king who was only too happy to buy him off (29 August).

Most significantly for the affairs of Picardy, the English invasion had finally ruined the constable of Saint-Pol. Though it might have been expected that Saint-Pol would have collaborated with his English nephew-by-marriage, when the English came before Saint-Quentin they were fired on by the men of a constable frightened to lose control of what he regarded as his last guarantee of security. He thus made another enemy, who handed over his letters to Louis XI.[30] The noose was drawing tighter. On 13 September, the king concluded another truce (this time for nine years) with Burgundy at Vervins, largely directed against Saint-Pol's independence.[31] On 14 September, the sieur de Moy occupied Saint-Quentin in the king's name. The constable, uncertain what to do, placed himself in the hands of the duke of Burgundy. The latter, anxious to deal with Lorraine and unwilling to break with Louis, handed him over for a rapid trial and execution (November–December 1475). In return for his betrayal of the constable, and under the terms of the Vervins agreement, Burgundy obtained Saint-Quentin, Ham and Bohain in *seigneurie* under the French crown.[32] Both sides gained from the constable's fall, therefore, but it should be pointed out that the destruction of the Luxembourg interest in Picardy made the French reoccupation of the region a much simpler matter.

The entire military and diplomatic framework of western Europe was over-turned by the defeat and death of Charles the Bold at Nancy on 5 January 1477. Without that event, whose consequences broke the ties of loyalty that bound many of the nobles of the region to the House of Burgundy, Louis XI's rapid reconquest of Picardy is inconceivable. Commynes later related that it had long been the king's plan to lay hands on the duke's inheritance should he outlive him, but that his insensitivity denied him more extensive gains.[33] The king's impetuosity can perhaps be explained by the vast opportunities for conquest that seemed to be opening up as far as Flanders.

---

[30] J. Calmette and G. Perinelle, *Louis XI et l'Angleterre* (1930), 190, 200. Louis had sent to warn Saint-Pol against collaborating with the English: Vaesen, *Lettres de Louis XI* V, p. 367.

[31] Commynes, *Mémoires* I, 291; text of truce: see ed. Scoble, 287–90; for resultant treaty, see R. Vaughan, *Charles the Bold*, 351. Seizure of Saint-Quentin: Molinet, *Chroniques*, ch. xviii; trial statement by Saint-Pol: 'ung nommé Alnequin de Soissons escripvit unes lettres à ung nomme la Cat de Saint-Quentin . . . lesquelles contenoit qu'il trouvast moyen de parler à ses voisins et amys, affin qu'ils meissent la ville de Saint-Quentin entre les mains du roy, et qu'il qui parle en fust osté dehors' (BN fr. 3869 fo. 11v).

[32] Letters of pardon by Charles for Saint-Quentin after the truce 'pour en jouir et les tenir par nous en tels drois comme nous faisions paravant les commencemens des présentes guerres', *Le Vermandois* 1 (1873), 428–32. These were required by the truce.

[33] Commynes, *Mémoires* I, 400–1.

Louis from the first had the advantage of surprise. Well informed at Tours by his excellent postal system, he was certain of Burgundy's death by 10 January, whereas the duchess Marie and her stepmother at Ghent were still in hope of his survival until 24 January.[34] The king made public his determination to occupy Picardy, Artois and Flanders on 19 January[35] but had already sent Torcy to Abbeville, which, with Péronne, was a linchpin of Burgundian power on the Somme. The *échevins* received him on 17 January, heard the king's promises, took the oath and expelled the garrison. All the strongholds of maritime Picardy were quickly won over, though there was a struggle at Rue.[36]

The king himself advanced with an army into the Santerre, besieged and slaughtered the garrison of Tronquoy and took Montdidier, Roye and Moreuil. At Péronne, the commander, Clary, made a show of resistance but quickly surrendered, taking the oath with twenty-one other 'chevaliers et nobles hommes de Picardie'.[37] From there, on 5 February, Louis sent to Compiègne and Reims for artillery and supplies.[38] The fall of Péronne caused widespread dismay among the Burgundians and other places began to fall. In the east, Saint-Quentin, Vervins, Saint-Gobain, Marle and Beaurevoir surrendered or were abandoned, further west Corbie and Bray changed hands.[39] The initial onslaught on the Somme had been entirely successful.

The king now turned his attention to Artois. Here, his subtle propositions to the Burgundian governor of Picardy, Philippe de Crèvecœur, sieur d'Esquerdes, proved decisive; his desertion of the Burgundian cause devastating. As Molinet put it, 'la conversion de ce chevalier plonga maint cœur en tribulacion, pource qu'il avoit esté sœuf noury en la maison de Bourgogne'.[40] Though still nervous about whether Esquerdes would go through with the bargain at the beginning of March, the king entered the *cité* of Arras on 5 March, largely by Esquerdes's doing. Lens and Béthune were then taken, while Thérouanne and the town of Arras surrendered at the end of the month. Even Hesdin, with its great and powerful castle so beloved of the Burgundian

[34] M.-A. Arnould, 'Les lendemains de Nancy dans les "Pays de par deçà"', in W. P. Blockmans (ed.), *Le privilège général et les privilèges régionaux de Marie de Bourgogne* (1985), 1–13.
[35] Vaesen, *Lettres de Louis XI* VI, 115.
[36] BN Coll. Picardie 91 fo. 175; Molinet, *Chroniques* I, 181ff.; Le Prestre, *Chronique*, 49.
[37] Molinet, *Chroniques* I, ch. xi. Commynes, *Mémoires* I, 414: Guillaume de Biche, sieur de Clary was 'homme de fort petit estat' who had been given the post of Péronne by the duke 'pour ce que sa maison appellée Clery estoit auprès'.
[38] Vaesen, *Lettres de Louis XI* VI, 122–3. Péronne was occupied 2 Feb. On the king's movements: Compiègne, 29 Jan., Noyon 30th, Falvy, 31st, Péronne and Clery until 20 Feb., see AM Compiègne BB 4 fo. 186v. For the king's frequent demands for masons, carpenters and artillery, see *ibid.*, fos. 289–396.
[39] Le Prestre, *Chronique*, 50.   [40] Molinet, *Chroniques* I, 211.

dukes, surrendered by Esquerdes's machinations.[41] From there on 7 April, Louis turned his attention to the Boulonnais: Desvres and Fiennes fell first and then Boulogne itself after a bombardment (by 20 April). Louis annexed the county by first restoring it to its claimant, La Tour d'Auvergne, then concluding an exchange with him and finally resorting to the unusual device of swearing homage himself to Notre-Dame of Boulogne in April 1478.[42]

The salient point about these events is the rapidity with which Louis was able to annexe Picardy and Artois. The explanation lies in the treason of the nobility and the disaffection of the Picard town leaders. At Boulogne, for instance, when it was rumoured that the governor would bring in English help to stave off the French threat, 'le peuple estoit fort esmeu'.[43] The Burgundian government had fallen into a state of utter confusion and, at this stage, before the arrival of Maximilian of Habsburg as duchess Marie's consort, the initiative passed to the Flemish cities and the estates. The latter, after initial negotiations with Louis XI, rallied to the duchess's cause, but only after her concession of the *Grand Privilège*, which in effect reversed the unpopular policies of Charles the Bold.[44] Moreover, the king took pains to stir up the hostility of the cities to the former ducal councillors in the form of popular disturbances. There was also substantial resistance to the French in Artois, which was widely considered a fief that should pass to Marie by hereditary right and where French rule was identified with heavier taxation. Towards the end of April, the citizens of Arras rose to throw off French control, but Louis moved swiftly to execute some leaders and expel others.[45] The garrisons of Lille, Douai and Orchies were defeated in an attempt to rescue the city, but remained in being. Indeed, the resistance of both French and Flemish Flanders stiffened through May and June 1477. In Artois, Saint-Omer and Aire continued to hold out, the former sustaining a siege through much of August

[41] On the winning over of Esquerdes, see A. Collet, 'Philippe de Crèvecœur, maréchal d'Esquerdes', *MSAB*, 28 (1917), 376–471. Vaesen, *Lettres de Louis XI* VI, 135, 148, 151. On Commynes's part in his conversion: 'on parla à aucuns, qui tost après furent bons serviteurs du roy', *Mémoires* I, 398. The best recent study is M. Harsgor, *Recherches*, II, 1077–1116. M. A. Arnould, 'Les lendemains de Nancy', in Blockmans, *Le privilège général*, 21.
[42] Molinet, *Chroniques* I, ch. xi; Commynes, *Mémoires* II, 418; Le Prestre, *Chronique*, 152–4; Vaesen, *Lettres de Louis XI* VI, 147–8. Boulogne was besieged on 12th and surrendered on 20th, see P. Héliot, 'Louis XI et le Boulonnais', *BEC* 100 (1939), 112–44. Letters-patent, 5 Jan. 1478 BN Picardie 89 fo. 327; 18 Apr. 1478, AN J 1125 no. 16.
[43] Enquiry of 8 May 1477 ordered by Esquerdes into the circumstances of the capture of Boulogne, BN fr. 20494 fo. 97–8. Cf. also *MSAB* XVII, 421.
[44] M. A. Arnould, 'Les lendemains de Nancy', 18–19, in Blockmans, *Le privilège général*; W. P. Blockmans, 'La position du comté de Flandre dans le royaume à la fin du XVe siècle', in Chevalier and Contamine, *La France de la fin du XVe siècle*, 74.
[45] C. Hirschauer, *Les états d'Artois* (1923), 215. For an account of Arras in the period, amateurish but based on the chronicle of a monk of Saint-Vaast, see Proyat, 'Louis XI à Arras', *MASA* 35 (1862), 69–122.

and, though the Flemish troops stationed at the Neuf-Fossé were defeated, Louis had to give up.[46]

In Hainault, the French king had no justifiable claim and his attack on Avesnes in June indicates his general lack of concern for legal rights in his objectives. However, there too Valenciennes proved too tough to crack.[47] At Tournai, long an isolated pocket of royal territory in Burgundian land, he was determined to assert his power, however, and managed to establish a garrison which subjected it to more than a year of disastrous raiding by Burgundian troops.[48] The arrival of Maximilian brought a new coherence to Burgundian court policy; he demanded restoration of his wife's rights and offered negotiations for the restoration of the 1475 truce. Finally, a truce was concluded at Lens on 18 September.[49]

The state of affairs prevailing at the end of 1477, then, was royal control over all Picardy, most of Artois (save Saint-Omer and Aire), and Tournai.[50] There is no reason to suppose that Louis XI had abandoned his desire to conquer Flanders or at least to stir it up against the régime of Maximilian. Nor was the latter content to acquiesce in the loss of Artois. War was therefore bound to continue over the delimitation of royal and Burgundian territory. Maximilian mounted his first major counter-attack in Hainault in the spring of 1478, though he failed to bring Louis to battle at Arras and the king failed to establish a land corridor to Tournai before the conclusion of a truce on 11 July.[51] Subsequently, Louis agreed to hand back positions he held in Hainault and Cambrésis and not to keep a garrison at Tournai.[52]

[46] W. P. Blockmans, 'La position du comté de Flandre', in Chevalier and Contamine, *La France de la Fin du XVe siècle*, 74. Le Prestre, *Chronique*, 53–4, 57–8; Vaesen, *Lettres de Louis XI* VI, 216–17.

[47] Molinet, *Chroniques* I, 196–7, 211, 215–18. A brief truce in May rapidly broke down, see Vaesen, *Lettres de Louis XI* VI, 175, 183–5.

[48] On Tournai, see Jean de Nicolay, *Kalendrier de la guerre de Tournai (1477–79)* ed. F. Hennebert, with appendices of extracts from the *registres des consaux*, in *Mémoires de la Société historique et littéraire de Tournai* 2 (1853) and 3 (1856) and L. P. Gachard, *Extraits des registres des consaux de Tournai* (1846).

[49] Text of truce; Le Prestre, *Chronique*, 60–1; T. Basin, *Histoire de Louis XI*, ed. Samaran (1972) III, 71, indicates that Maximilian was mainly attempting that winter to cut off Tournai.

[50] 'En brief toute la conté d'Artois luy fu rendu reserveez Saint Omer et Aire', Le Prestre, *Chronique*, 53–4.

[51] Maximilian's destruction of the Tournaisis and Louis XI's capture of Condé in Hainault: Basin, *Histoire de Louis XI*, III, 72. Truce, pub. 11 July 1478: Molinet, *Chroniques* I, 264. Movement of garrisons at the end of the campaign from Arras: AM Compiègne BB 5 fo. 11r (25 July). Resentment of Flemings at the truce and their continued attacks on Tournai, see Basin, *Histoire*, 71–3.

[52] Commynes, *Mémoires* II, 18–19; J. de Nicolay, *Kalendrier des guerres de Tournai*; L. P. Gachard, *Extraits des registres*, 29–32, 34–6; A. Lesort, 'Un document inédit concernant la diplomatie de Louis XI à propos de la neutralité de Tournai (1478–9)', *BEC* 62 (1901), 15–24. AN K 72 no. 19, 20.

The French possession of Thérouanne by this time, in the inimitable words of Molinet, 'grevoit la conté de Flandres aveuc le demourant d'Arthois, comme la mauvaise fenestre dont le vent françois se desgorge'.[53] Indeed, it was to remain a thorn in the side of the Low Countries until 1553. In 1479, Maximilian assembled an army at Arques with a view to recapturing it and won a set-piece battle nearby at Guinegatte against a relieving force led by Esquerdes. By October, he had the exceptionally large force of 10,000 horse and 26,000 foot at his disposal for an attack on Lillers. The French at Saint-Pol and Lillers resisted, however, and the first of his many financial crises dissolved the archduke's army.[54] Yet another short truce was concluded but it did not hold.[55] Raiding became endemic between French and Burgundian positions over the next two years, but without serious campaigns.

During 1480, Esquerdes worked to make major improvements in French military organisation by raising a new levy of French infantry to limit the king's dependence on the Swiss. At the camp of Famechon, Louis was thus able to dispose of a force of 20,000 men with new equipment, and all regularly paid.[56] It was this and pressure placed on the Burgundian government by the stimulation of discord in Flanders after the death of duchess Marie in March 1482[57] that opened a further opportunity for French pressure, the assembly of a force of 15,000 men at Blangy in March 1482 and the capture of Aire by Esquerdes in July. Resistance by Flemish troops in the event checked this move and brought a formal end to conflict at the treaty of Arras (December 1482). This aimed to settle the claim to Artois and Franche-Comté by constituting them as the dowry of Margaret of Austria on her marriage to the dauphin,[58] but it also opened the way for closer French dealings with the towns of Flanders and the renewal of royal claims to sovereignty there

---

[53] Molinet, *Chroniques* I, 301–4.
[54] *Ibid.*, I, 317. On the supply of Esquerdes's army in Sept. 1479, see AM Compiègne BB 5 fo. 67v, 68v.
[55] In Sept. 1480, the frontier garrisons were stood down and lodged at Compiègne: AM Compiègne BB 5 fo. 107–8.
[56] Harsgor, *Recherches* II, 1092; BN nafr. 7639, pp. 168–9, 303–30. In July 1482, though, Esquerdes was still in command of 'Suisses et autres gens d'armes' at Doullens, AM Compiègne BB 7 fo. 35r.
[57] W. P. Blockmans, 'La position du comté de Flandre', in Chevalier and Contamine, *La France de la fin du XVᵉ siècle*, 80.
[58] Commynes, *Mémoires* II, 3–9; Molinet, *Chroniques* I, 377–406. Esquerdes to Abbeville, Famechon, 24 Dec. (1482), BM Abbeville MS 807, dossier Esquerdes, fo. 2; to Amiens, same date, AM Amiens AA 5 fo. 211: announcing the peace. Louis XI to Estates of Abbeville, 7 Dec. 1482, BN Picardie 91; to Amiens, 21 Dec. 1482, Thierry, *Tiers Etat* II, 402–3: requiring their assent to treaty.

by the crown's confirmation of the advances made by the estates since 1477.[59]

Louis XI's death on 30 August 1483 may have prolonged the peace in that the Regency government had too much on its hands to cope with war in the Low Countries. However, not only was the personnel of the new régime little different from that of the old, but the broad lines of French ambitions to dominate Flanders remained. Of the new councillors from northern France admitted to the royal council after 1477 – including Louis de Hallewin, Jean de La Gruthuse, the Grand Bastard of Burgundy – most were Flemings rather than Picards.[60] This was reinforced by the increasing influence of marshal d'Esquerdes after 1483. Louis XI had been more generous to him than to any other of his Burgundian converts, but had kept him outside the inner circle of influential councillors. In recommending him to the Regency government, he prepared the way for an increase in his influence at court; whereas he seldom appeared in the council under Louis XI, he began to attend meetings not infrequently from August 1483 onwards and to press for the primacy of the Flanders question in French policy. His lack of earlier experience in the council may have limited his weight in argument, however.[61]

The main thrust of French policy in Flanders during 1483–5 was to support the council of regency representing the Flemish towns against Maximilian.[62] However, the latter was already planning his restoration in Flanders,while the outbreak of a new French civil war, *la guerre folle*, provided an opportunity. In May 1485, Esquerdes led a force of 500 lances and 4,000 foot via Tournai (and threatening its neutrality) towards Ghent, ostensibly to mediate between the Flemish regency council and Maximilian, but in reality to gain possession of the young archduke.[63] The attempt was a failure and Maximilian's power was

[59] W. P. Blockmans, 'La position du comté de Flandre', in Chevalier and Contamine, *La France de la fin du XVᵉ siècle*, 80–1. I. L. A. Diegerick, *Inventaire analytique et chronologique des chartes et documents appartenant à la ville d'Ypres* 4 vols. (1853–9) nos. 1097–8, 1100, 1101, 1105, 1109.

[60] P.-R. Gaussin, 'Les conseillers de Louis XI (1461–83)' in B. Chevalier and P. Contamine, *La France de la fin du XVᵉ siècle*, 123–5. On the continuity of the *conseil du roi*, cf. Harsgor, *Recherches* I.

[61] See note 41 and Harsgor, *Recherches* II, 1077–1116, 1576–1602. Gaussin, 'Les conseillers de Louis XI', in Chevalier and Contamine, *La France de la fin du XVᵉ siècle*, does not mention him, but he in fact attended for the *jussio* first on 4 May 1477, again in Sept. and Jan. 1478 (G. Espinas, *Recueil de documents relatifs à l'histoire du droit municipal en France. Artois* (1934–43) I, 443; *Ordonnances* XVIII, 296, 356; BN Picardie 89 fo. 327) but then not again until Aug. 1483.

[62] P. Pelicier, *Lettres de Charles VIII*, 5 vols. (1898–1905) I, 50–6.

[63] Gachard, *Extraits des registres*, 50–60 (delib. 6–12 May, 11 June 1485). Molinet, *Chroniques* I, 446, 445–6.

recognised on 28 June and reinforced in 1486 by his election as king of the Romans.[64]

War now continued throughout Artois, with border commanders starting in March 1486 to 'prendre bons marchans et piller le plat pays'.[65] By June 1486, Maximilian's troops had retaken Mortaigne, l'Ecluse, Honnecourt and, above all, Thérouanne, a severe blow for the French. His campaign culminated in the recapture of Lens, though, as in 1479, financial difficulties intervened and he was frustrated at Saint-Quentin. Marshals Esquerdes and Gié were thus able to contain the damage and Maximilian withdrew.[66] By May of the following year, the French admiral de Graville reported that there were no Burgundian troops between Picardy and Flanders.[67] Esquerdes thus gained his revenge by the recapture of the technically neutral place of Saint-Omer in May 1487, then in July of Thérouanne, a town, he reported 'qui destroussoit tout le pays', followed the same month by his defeat of the Burgundian army near Béthune.[68]

By the end of 1487, Maximilian was in deep trouble again; Ghent had rejected his authority in November, the other cities followed early the next year. Esquerdes was authorised to take Flanders into French protection.[69] The first months of 1488 saw Maximilian detained at Ghent and up to July 1488 French troops went unchallenged. The marshal assured Bruges that he would back it with powerful forces.[70] The year 1488 saw the influence of Esquerdes and the Flanders policy at its zenith, but it was precisely at this time that the question of Brittany began to impinge on French policy and undermine his

[64] W. P. Blockmans, 'La position du comté de Flandre', in Chevalier and Contamine, *La France*, 82.
[65] Molinet, *Chroniques* I, 519. Magistrates of Saint-Omer to Ypres, 16 March 1486: 'Sommes advertis que les Franchois sont délibérez et resolus faire et executer la guerre', in J. Diegerick, 'Quelques lettres et autres documents concernant Thérouanne et Saint-Omer (1486–1537)' *BSA Morinie* iii, 26.
[66] Molinet, *Chroniques* I, 521, 542–6; Diegerick, 'Quelques lettres', 27–30 (letters on capture of Thérouanne, 10 June 1486 and failure at Saint-Quentin). See also G. Lecocq, 'Attaque de la ville de Saint-Quentin par Frédéric de Horne', *Le Vermandois* 3 (1875), 595–7.
[67] J. C. S. Bridge, *A History of France from the Death of Louis XI* (1921) I, 267–8; P. M. Perret, *Notice biographique sur Louis Malet de Graville, amiral de France (144?–1516)* (1889).
[68] Molinet, *Chroniques* I, 557, 568, 571; Diegerick, 'Quelques lettres', 30–1 (24 May 1487). On Esquerdes's financial preparations, see his letter to Péronne, Aire, 23 Jan. 1487, AM Péronne BB 6 fo. 52r. AM Douai BB 1 fo. 72–6: news of Esquerdes's movements, June 1487. On the capture of Thérouanne: Esquerdes to Abbeville, Aire, 27 July (1487), BM Abbeville MS 807, dossier Esquerdes, fo. 1.
[69] W. P. Blockmans, 'La position du comté de Flandre', in Chevalier and Contamine, *La France de la fin du XVe siècle*, 83; I. Diegerick, 'Correspondance des magistrate d'Ypres, députés à Gand et à Bruges pendant les troubles de Flandre sous Maximilian, 1488', *Annales de la Société d'Emulation de Bruges* (1853) no. xix–xxii.
[70] Esquerdes to Bruges, Hesdin, 24 Apr. 1488, BN fr. 11590 fo. 265v; to Ypres, 2, 9 July 1488, L. P. Gachard, *Lettres inédites de Maximilien sur les affaires des Pays-Bas* 2 vols. (1851–2) I, 106–7, 108–9.

position. Esquerdes occupied the castle of Coucy, northern stronghold of the rebellious Louis d'Orléans, in 1487, on the pretext that it was in danger. Louis had withdrawn to Brittany and from this time the Breton question became more pressing, with the Breton duke Francis II appealing for help from Maximilian in February 1486 and debates in the royal council over priorities. Esquerdes argued that 'cellui de deça emportera le fait de Bretaigne, et non pas cellui de Bretaigne l'affaire de Flandres', in other words that victory in Flanders would decide the whole issue.[71] However, French policy was now indecisive. Despite Esquerdes's agreement with the estates of French Flanders in December 1488,[72] Maximilian was able to conclude an alliance with Henry VII at Dordrecht (14 February 1489) as part of a triple alliance against France.

The decision of the council was to give priority to Brittany and direct Esquerdes to delay matters in the Low Countries. Nevertheless, even with the English descent on Brittany in prospect, he arrived at Tournai in February 1489 in order to dabble in the affairs of Flanders.[73] His advice to the king was to exploit Philippe de Clèves's rebellion there, join with his 5,000 men and the troops of their Flemish towns and conquer the 'West-pays' in April–May. Otherwise, the English and Maximilian would link up and:

> vous perderez toutes les meschantes villes comme Monstrœul, Hesdin, Saint-Pol et lieux d'environ ceste lisière, parquoy la ville de Béthune, d'Aire et Thérouenne seront assiégées de pouvoir avoir vivres et Boullongne ne demourra pas en grant seureté.[74]

Esquerdes in fact led 18,000 men, with the count of Vendôme, to join the Flemings in the siege of Dixmude, a town loyal to Maximilian, but the appeal of the latter to Henry VII was enough to bring English intervention that broke the Flemish army (June 1489) before it could link up with the French, who were left to conduct a fruitless but ferocious siege of Nieupoort.[75] All

---

[71] Pelicier, *Lettres de Charles VIII*, III, p. j. iv (Esquerdes to king, 17 July 1488); Harsgor, *Recherches* II, 1094–7, studies all this in detail, though he misdates some events and ignores the 1489 campaign. See also Blockmans, 'La position du comté de Flandre', 84. 'Siège et prise du château de Coucy en 1487' *BEC* 24, 79–82; E. de Bucheré de l'Epinois, *Histoire de la ville et des sires de Coucy* (1859), 267–8.

[72] Treaty of Wavrin, 14 Dec. 1488: *Inventaire sommaire, Douai* AA 258–260, AM Douai BB 1 fo. 82–94. Molinet, *Chroniques* II, 78–86 (N.B. the original of the treaty was in the archives of Souverain-Moulin, printed in A. Collet, 'Philippe de Crèvecœur', 445–53): the treaty registered the neutrality of Lille–Douai–Orchies in the war between the estates and Maximilian.

[73] Gachard, *Extraits des registres*, 75–6.

[74] Esquerdes to Charles VIII, Auxy, 17 Mar. (1489), BN fr. 15541 fo. 49; agreement between Esquerdes and Ypres, 20 Mar. 1489, in Diegerick, *Inventaire . . . Ypres* no. 1204.

[75] Esquerdes to Compiègne, Paris, 15 May 1489, AM Compiègne BB 12 fo. 35–6 (order for transport of wine 'tant pour la provision de mon hostel que pour la furniture et advitaillement de l'armée que le Roy a ordonné (sic) estre mise desus pour aller ou pays de Flandres'); to Charles VIII, 17 March (1489), BN fr. 15541 fo. 459; Molinet, *Chroniques* II, 133–40.

this gave Maximilian enough of an advantage to break from the triple alliance with Spain and England to sign the treaty of Frankfurt with France (28 July 1489). The peace was fragile but marked a watershed in that it registered the failure, much to his disillusionment, of Esquerdes's Flanders programme.[76]

By the summer of 1490 Maximilian was, however, drifting back to his former allies.[77] The impending French threat to Brittany brought his proxy marriage to the duchess Anne in December, while the talk of Charles VIII's rejection of Margaret of Austria as his wife in favour of the Breton duchess was another cause of dispute, since the return of Margaret's dowry of Artois and Franche-Comté could now be demanded. War was delayed until 1492, however, while Maximilian dealt with the last major rebellion against his rule, that of Philippe de Clèves-Ravestein, besieged at Sluys from June to October 1492. The garrisons of Thiérache and Hainault began border raids[78] and Henry VII mounted his expedition to Boulogne, prematurely ended by the anxiety of the French court, through Esquerdes, to come to terms by restoring the English pensions (the treaty of Etaples).[79]

French power in Artois received a decisive blow when Arras was taken by the Burgundians in conjunction with its disaffected citizens (5 November 1492).[80] Despite all Esquerdes's attempts, it could not be retaken and the rival powers came to terms at last in the treaty of Senlis (23 May 1493), which brought an end to the struggle between France and Burgundy for a generation by confirming Picardy in the possession of France and Artois in that of the house of Burgundy. Opposition to the treaty was led by Esquerdes, the admiral de Graville, who feared a diminution of their influence, marshal de Gié, who obviously had interests in the north, and the duke of Orléans.[81] While it was once accepted that this treaty was the heavy price paid by France in the north

[76] Harsgor, *Recherches* II, 1097–8.
[77] See his new treaty of alliance with England, 16 September 1490. T. Rymer, *Foedera, Conventiones, Literae . . .* (1727) XII, 405–7.
[78] Molinet, *Chroniques* II, 309–21, 328.
[79] Despatch of Jacques d'Estouteville to Abbeville to resist English: BN Picardie 91 fo. 179r (10 Oct. 1492); supplies for 'l'ost et armée dud. Sr. quy de présent est au pays d'Artois pour résister à la descente que font les Angloix anciens ennemys de France': AM Compiègne BB 13 fo. 38v; letter to Esquerdes, 4 Oct. 1492 for the collection of supplies for an army to resist the English 'qui sont descenduz et passez de deçà la mer en grant nombre et excessif et en armes': *ibid.* fo. 47v.
[80] Molinet, *Chroniques* II, 337–49: 'La prise et reduction de la ville et cité d'Arras en l'en 1492', also pub. in *Archives historiques et littéraires du Nord de la France et du midi de la Belgique* (1853) ser. 1, III, 401–12.
[81] Perret, *Louis Malet de Graville*, 155–60. Publication of the treaty: Charles VIII to Esquerdes, Senlis, 23 May 1493, AM Amiens AA 5 fo. 219; Esquerdes to Amiens, St Christophe-les-Senlis, 24 May, *ibid.*, fo. 218–19; to Abbeville, same date, BM Abbeville, MS 807, doss. Esquerdes, fo. 11; to Abbeville, Lannoy, 3 June, *ibid.* fo. 12.

for the pursuit of Charles VIII's chimerical dreams in Italy, it has been convincingly argued[82] that the terms represented an acceptable compromise and preserved some advantages for France. Retention of Artois would, in any case, have been difficult to justify even had its chief city not been taken. Aire, Béthune and Hesdin were to remain in French hands until the archduke Philip's twentieth birthday in 1498, while Thérouanne and Tournai remained islands of the royal domain in Burgundian territory. However, it should be emphasised that a stable long-term frontier had not yet been fixed and that certain key problems were only delayed by the distraction of French attentions to Italy. France retained its juridical claims to Artois and Flanders and the archduke had to do homage for them in July 1499. As late as 1507, Louis XII was writing to Arras warning it not to accept Maximilian as *maimbour* for his grandson Charles V and in 1514 Marguerite of Austria warned Maximilian lucidly of the dangers in allowing the French to retain 'ccste souveraineté qu'ils prétendent'.[83]

The establishment of loyalty: the nobility of Picardy

In the years between 1463 and 1493, when the towns and nobility of Picardy were being subjected to a series of decisions on their political loyalties, the attitude of the greater and lesser nobility would prove crucial in assuring the allegiance of the region. The structure of the politically active nobility will be discussed at greater length in chapter 4 but, for the present, it is important to bear in mind that, with the exception of the count of Saint-Pol, removed in 1475, there were no overweening grandees in the province but, rather, a leadership in the hands of a group of between twelve and twenty 'lignages' all very much on the same level. This in itself may explain the extreme fragility of Saint-Pol's following.[84] It also proved relatively easy for Louis XI to win over the support of landowners who had in any case to accommodate themselves to the predominant power, those who, as Commynes noted, had 'leurs biens aux limites du roy' and were thus open to offers. Unlike his inept dismissals of 1461–3, Louis's treatment of the nobility in the 1470s was exemplary, seeking to maintain local noblemen in their existing posts as much as possible,

---

[82] Y. Labande-Mailfert, *Charles VIII et son milieu* (1975), 133–8.
[83] Molinet, *Chroniques* II, 462. J. Godefroy, *Lettres de Louis XII et du cardinal d'Amboise* (1712) I, 105; Le Glay, *Correspondance de Maximilien Ier* I, 7–8 (1507), II, 222–3 (1514): Marguerite argued that French suzerainty would allow them 'quant ils verront leur point reprendre sur nous ce que bon leur semblera'. Any agreement should not be a temporary one 'comme fut fait du temps de feu monsieur le duc Charles'. See also W. P. Blockmans, 'La position du comté de Flandre', in Chevalier and Contamine, *La France de la fin du XVe siècle*, 78.
[84] W. Paravicini, 'Peur, pratiques', in *ibid.*, 187–91.

while providing employment for many lesser gentlemen in his military household.[85]

The existing loyalties of the nobility, therefore, proved no great barrier to Louis's policy. Pierre le Prestre's patrons, the sires of Auxy, were strongly Burgundian, though family connections never allowed a clear separation of loyalties, Andrieu II de Rambures, royal *maître des eaux et forêts* in Picardy, was brother-in-law to Jean V de Créqui, *chambellan* to the duke of Burgundy and head of the wealthiest family of Hesdin. Rambures had surrendered to Burgundy in 1472 and lost his property to marshal Rouault in 1473 as a result. However, in 1475 his son Jacques was restored under the truce of Vervins and became a royal *conseiller et chambellan* and regained the *maîtrise des eaux et forêts*.[86] Rouault's family was established on a small scale as sieurs de Gamaches near Rambures on the border of Picardy and Normandy. The marshal had been Louis's chief commander in Picardy during the *Bien Public* but fell into disgrace in the 1470s. The family then reverted to a more modest role: his son Aloph held household posts under Louis XII and Francis I, his grandson Thibault was a military commander in mid-sixteenth-century Picardy.[87]

Family relationships usually left individuals divided in loyalties. Jean d'Ailly, *vidame* of Amiens, had been receiving a somewhat unreliable pension from Louis XI in the mid-1460s, was clearly a king's man by the 1470s but had married a bastard daughter of Philip the Good and so could not be entirely trusted by the suspicious Louis.[88] Charles de Rubempré, captain of Amiens in 1472, was a royalist but his brother Jean was a servant of Burgundy. The brothers Jean III and Nicolas de Mailly were *conseillers et chambellans* to duke Charles; after Nancy, Jean passed into French service and later commanded infantry under Esquerdes; though he drew closer to Maximilian after Louis XI's death he did not abandon French service.[89]

Even before 1477, individuals were being won over by inducements. We have seen how the head of the house of Moy, Colart, already *conseiller et*

[85] Commynes, *Mémoires* I, 416. See the 'Estat d'aucuns gentilzhommes de l'ostel du Roy de la nacion de Picardie' under Esquerdes's command, Oct. 1481, sixty-one names, chief of whom was Anthoine de Pronville and including Esquerdes's nephew Jean du Bois, Adam de La Hargerie, Anthoine d'Ailly and Baudrain de Marles, mostly paid at L 330. BN fr. 2906 fo. 14–15.
[86] Quicherat, 'Lettres ... du bien public', 249–51; E. Prarond, *Notice sur Rambures* (1859).
[87] For his correspondence, see Quicherat, 'Lettres ... du Bien Public', 239–40, 263–4, 266–7, 279, 281–2, 289, 294–5, 346. M. Darsy, 'Gamaches et ses seigneurs', *MSAP* 13, 99–189, XIV, 393–529. On Thibault, see below, ch. 4.
[88] Quicherat, 'Lettres ... Bien Public', 260–1, 271, 319–20 and partic. June 1465, 290–1, pointing out the dangers to his places from Burgundian troops and reminding the chancellor that his pension was delayed.
[89] A. Ledru, *Histoire de la maison de Mailly*, 3 vols. (1894) I, 161–4, 174–5, preuves, no. 403.

chambellan to Louis XI in 1474, abandoned the constable de Saint-Pol for the king's service and was instrumental in the royal recovery of Saint-Quentin in 1475. *Sénéchal* of Vermandois, captain of Saint-Quentin, *bailli* and captain of Tournai, Colart passed on Tournai to his son Jacques in 1478 on receiving the *bailliage* of Rouen. Jacques in turn received the post of *maître enquêteur et réformateur* of forests in Picardy and Normandy (1483), and both commanded companies of gendarmerie.[90] On a lesser level, the dismissal of La Hargerie from the governorship of Péronne in 1475 was probably connected with suspicions about his loyalties to Burgundy and his successor, Clary, admitted the king and took the oath with other nobles, despite having been 'nourry en la maison de Bourgoigne'.[91] Though the commander at Hesdin, Thomas, sieur de Lannoy, held out for a while, his position was undermined by the defection of his superior, Esquerdes. Louis was so impressed by the valour of his son Raoul in the defence that, in Molinet's words, after a surrender much to 'grant anoy' of the 'povre peuple', he 'compleut tant au Roy qu'i le retint en son service et lui fit de grans biens'. Raoul, later sieur de Morvilliers, served Louis well in the Hainault campaign and received a gold chain with which he was able to purchase the seigneurie of Paillart. He went on to serve both Charles VIII and Louis XII in Italy and to be *bailli* and captain of Amiens, his family well to the fore in the government of the province in the sixteenth century.[92] The Saveuse family lost out disastrously as a result of their Burgundian loyalties, particularly as a result of Charles de Saveuses's defence of Boulogne in 1477, and their lands were confiscated in favour of Torcy in that year. Nevertheless, even they had steered a slow passage back to royal favour by the end of the century.[93]

In rebuilding the power structures of the province, then, Louis XI sought in the 1470s above all to avoid making enemies. The disappearance of the constable's power had, however, left something of a void in landed society and also provided opportunities for patronage. These were most clearly seen in the staged distribution of the Luxembourg estates. As was usual under Louis XI, the lands confiscated from the Luxembourgs were shared out widely. In January 1476, those in Normandy and Champagne went to Georges de La Trémoille, Charles d'Amboise, François de Laval, Louis de Graville and Jean Blosset. In French Picardy, Jean d'Estouteville-Torcy was given Sourdon and

90 R. Rodière, *La maison de Moy*, 3 vols. (1928) II, preuves, no. 365, 421, 443, 444, 447, 448. AN K 74 no. 8; K 72 no. 58.
91 Molinet, *Chroniques* I, 184.
92 Molinet, *Chroniques* I, 186. C. Bazin, 'Description historique de l'église et des ruines du château de Folleville', *MSAP* 10 (1850), 1–92, esp. 58–9, 70–1.
93 Letter of Philippe de Saveuse, May 1465, Quicherat, 'Lettres', 282 and Vaesen, *Lettres de Louis XI* VI, 52. On Charles de Saveuse, gov. of Boulogne in 1477, see BN fr. 20494 fo. 97–8, enquiry into his contacts with the English.

Broye.[94] The lands in the Low Countries and Burgundian Picardy remained under the control of Burgundy and were enjoyed by Saint-Pol's eldest son, Jean count of Marle, until his death in 1476. In the aftermath of Nancy, Louis XI confiscated all those lands within his reach despite the claims of the heir, Pierre de Luxembourg: the county of Marle went to Pierre de Rohan, maréchal de Gié and in February 1477 he received another grant including Ham, lands around Bohain and Beaurevoir and half of Soissons. A vast collection of land including the county of Saint-Pol and its dependencies, with 2,000 fiefs and parishes, went to the influential Guy Pot. Pot was another Burgundian convert who was the brother of Philippe, a leading ducal minister, but had been Louis's *bailli* of Vermandois since 1463.[95]

The rights of legitimate heirs were never easy to ignore, though during Louis's reign they remained checked. Indeed, the king seems to have intended to divide the quarrelsome Luxembourg clan itself by winning over the constable's bastard Louis with a bishopric and his brother, Richebourg, not so much with land as with gifts and pensions: 'je n'ay aultre bien que ce qui me vient du Roy', he was to write.[96] The Luxembourg succession passed to Pierre II's daughter Marie in 1482, by which time she was married to the count of Romont, a prominent figure in the Low Countries. The treaty of Arras provided for reinstatement, but the rights of Luxembourg were challenged by those in possession. Torcy was in difficulty with his Picard vassals anyway,[97] and had to give way to the Luxembourgs in 1488. Pierre de Rohan, who remained an important figure in the government of Picardy as well as a powerful royal councillor, went on calling himself 'comte de Marle' throughout the 1480s, but eventually had to give way to the Luxembourgs.

Guy Pot had become one of the greatest landowners of Picardy as a result of Louis XI's gifts and his fall from favour in September 1484 was a signal for his enemies to gather. Romont actually obtained royal letters restoring his wife's rights to Saint-Pol, possibly by the manoeuvring of Richebourg in the council. He seems to have occupied the county, but Pot was stubborn and obtained letters in June 1485 maintaining his rights. His favour was to some extent restored in 1487, but at that point the count of Romont died and the way was open for the conclusion of the marriage between Marie de Luxembourg and François, count of Vendôme, that brought the Luxembourg inheritance into the

---

[94] *Archives d'un serviteur de Louis XI. Georges de La Trémoille, 1458–81*, ed. L. de La Trémoille (1888), 84–7; *Ordonnances* XVIII, 175; M. Harsgor, *Recherches* II, 1005.
[95] *Ordonnances* XVIII, 231; Harsgor, *Recherches* II, 1127, 1303; BN fr. 8546 fo. 1.
[96] Harsgor, *Recherches* IV, 2216–18, 2725–9; Harsgor, 'Maîtres d'un royaume' in *La France de la fin du XVᵉ siècle*, 142; D. L. Potter, 'The Luxembourg Inheritance', 26–8; 'Loys mon bastart' (BN fr. 20485 fo. 80) was later guardian of the rights of the Amboise children, beneficiaries of the dispersion of his father's estates (AN X/1A 4829 fo. 38r).
[97] AN X/1A 4823 fo. 10v.

possession of a junior branch of the royal lignage, and was, in the official view, 'faict pour le très grand bien et prouffit de nous et de nostre royaume'.[98] It detached Marie's interests to some extent from the Low Countries. In vain, Pot protested that the dukes of Bourbon and Orléans and the sire de Beaujeu had promised him that his rights would not be ignored.[99] The crown had decided on restoration and ultimately pressed Marie de Luxembourg's case.

If Louis XI had intended to insert his own men into the social elite of the province, his achievement was of short duration. A variant on this theme is represented by his treatment of Philippe de Crèvecœur, sieur d'Esquerdes. From a family originally of the Beauvaisis, Esquerdes had served the dukes of Burgundy with distinction, was related to a number of Picard families in Burgundian service (through his father-in-law Jean III d'Auxy), but after a very brief hesitation, transferred wholeheartedly to Louis XI's service in March 1477, with the consequences already noted. Molinet memorably recounted that 'la parole du roy estoit alors tant doulce et vertueuse qu'elle endormoit, comme la seraine, tous ceulx qui luy prestoyent oreilles'.[100] The change of allegiance was startlingly underlined, indeed, by Louis's confirmation (27 July 1477) of his post as lieutenant-general of Picardy and Artois, precisely the one he had held for Burgundy. Raoul de Lannoy was appointed his deputy. His hold on the *sénéchaussées* of Boulogne and Ponthieu was also renewed in May 1478, as well as town captaincies like that of Abbeville, confirmed in March 1477.[101] Though now *conseiller et chambellan*, he participated in council business only in 1477–8, and then only infrequently, since clearly his military duties on the frontier monopolised his time.[102] Attendances were more frequent during the Beaujeu regency and after his elevation as marshal in September 1483.

Esquerdes's kinsmen benefited from his favour and placed him at the centre of a network of clients and allies. Robert, bâtard de Saveuse, became *conseiller et chambellan* and captain of Amiens; his brother Antoine de Crèvecœur

[98] Beaujeu to Parlement, 29 Nov. 1488, Pelicier, *Lettres de Charles VIII* iii, p. j.; i, 254; ii, 265; AN X/1A 9319 no. 103.
[99] *Ordonnances* XX, 9, letter dated Ancenis July 1487; protest of Guy Pot and other beneficiaries, 4 Dec. 1487, AN X/1A 4829 fo. 36r–40r; decree of *chambre de conseil*, 14 Dec. 1487, X/1A 1495 fo. 26v.
[100] Commynes, *Mémoires* II, 9; Molinet, *Chroniques*, I, 211; Harsgor, *Recherches* II, 1089. The only substantial study, A. Collet, 'Philippe de Crèvecœur', 403–4, goes no farther than suggesting Esquerdes's patriotism in his conversion. See also Commynes's remark that he came over 'considérant que son nom et armes étaient deçà la Somme, près de Beauvais'. In fact, his lands were not situated there.
[101] Harsgor, *Recherches* II, 1090. Presentation at Abbeville of royal patent of March and Esquerdes's missive on the captaincy, 22 July 1477, BM Abbeville MS 807, dossier Esquerdes: G. de Saint-Rémy to exercise office; *Inventaire sommaire, Abbeville*, 122; BN Picardie 91 fo. 176.
[102] See note 61 above.

became *grand-louvetier* of France and *sénéchal* of Artois; his father-in-law's bastard, Georges d'Auxy, became a royal *maître d'hotel*. The marshal's brother-in-law, Jean de Bruges-La Gruthuse, son of the Louis de Bruges who had also deserted the Burgundian cause, later became governor of Picardy.[103] Another kinsman, however, Antoine de Craon, sieur de Domart, was not so lucky. Craon had gone over to Louis XI in 1468 and saw his property in the Low Countries confiscated. He chose badly again in 1474 when he returned to Burgundy, apparently expecting the king's overthrow by the Anglo-Burgundian alliance. He thus lost Domart and all his property in Ponthieu and died, the last of his line, in the Low Countries.[104] Esquerdes was built up as a local power mainly by the conferment of the financial advantages, pensions and emoluments accruing from his position as one of the *maîtres du royaume*. On the whole, his landed holdings in Picardy remained limited. He had concentrated on rounding out the estates bought by his mother in the Aa valley on the border of Flanders and these passed to his du Bois nephews. Without a son, however, he was unable to found a lasting powerful local dynasty.[105]

Louis de Hallewin, sieur de Piennes, another Flemish nobleman, was captured by Louis XI in 1466 and won over by pressure of imprisonment in the king's notorious cages. The subsequent confiscation of his estates near Cassel required compensation for him and his family in France, though as late as 1516 his grandson Antoine was leasing out land in Artois with the proviso that he might reoccupy it if he fell into disgrace in France.[106] Louis de Hallewin, *conseiller et chambellan* under Louis, really came into prominence under the Beaujeu regency as a leading councillor, governor of Béthune (1486), then of Péronne and finally of Picardy. In the 1490s, he was receiving L 10,000 in compensation for land lost in Flanders 'en haine de ce qu'il est demourant au party et service' of France. He was by then well established in Picardy: one of his sons held the bishopric of Amiens and daughters married into the Rambures and Ailly families.[107]

By the 1490s, it is clear that most of the important families of the province were secured in their obedience by grants of land, pensions, governorships or

[103] J. B. B. van Praet, *Recherches sur Louis de Bruges, seigneur de Gruthuyse* (1831), 71ff.
[104] A. Janvier and C. Bréard, *Etude sur Domart-les-Ponthieu* (1878), 42–5, piece just. no. xx, letter of rehabilitation by Charles the Bold, 10 Sept. 1474: 'moyennant qu'il tiendra dorénavant notre parti'.
[105] A. Collet, 'Philippe de Crèvecœur', 385–98: purchase of Elnes and Lumbres, 1482–3; Collet, 'Biographie chronologique des barons et seigneurs d'Elnes', *MSAB* 28 (1917), 477ff. The du Bois de Fiennes nephews and their descendants never held the same prominence as the marshal. Their property near Saint-Omer was repeatedly confiscated in wartime during the sixteenth century.
[106] Commynes, *Mémoires* II, 77–9; H. Dusevel, *Essai sur les archives du château de Lucheux* (1857), 12.
[107] BN fr. 26103 no. 790; BN p.o. 1468, doss. Hallewin, no. 9.

court posts, a pattern to be examined in chapter 4. Many of them, of course, held properties which straddled what was gradually emerging as a real frontier, and subsequent generations often solved this problem by splitting into separate branches or liquidating their holdings on the other side. The Luxembourg family is a case in point; the Fiennes branch remaining firmly loyal to the Habsburgs through the sixteenth century, the descendants of the constable fixed as firmly in French service. Other lignages, like the Hallwin and Barbançon, were in the same position. It is also clear that many of the leading families of the Netherlands nobility (Croy, Longueval, Brimeu) were of Picard origin.[108]

The establishment of loyalty: the towns of Picardy

The loyalty of the towns, less a question of personal choice, still involved inducements and pressure. The custom by which the crown bound new 'converts' to its 'party' (Molinet uses precisely these terms) was used to justify action against those who lapsed into Burgundian sympathies. When the count of Dammartin won over Amiens in January 1471, Torcy administered the oath to a town assembly of a thousand persons, asking them if they would be 'bons et loyaux Franchois et subges du Roy'. There followed a *Te Deum* and 'Noels'. He applied a similar oath to a town assembly at Abbeville in 1477.[109] However, when the townsmen of Saint-Riquier reverted to Burgundian allegiance in 1475, having briefly taken the oath to France, this was used as a justification to destroy the town.[110] Individuals were required to swear 'de soy maintenir en party du Roy comme bon et léal Françoys'.[111] Propaganda was essential in this process, involving the king's promulgation of an 'octroy et édict général' in favour of all Picards, Boulonnais and Artésiens who had rallied to him.[112]

Louis XI had appealed to the unpopularity of the Burgundian régime at

---

[108] M. R. Thielmans, 'Les Croy, conseillers des ducs de Bourgogne', *Bulletin de la commission royale d'histoire* 255 (1959), 1–141. The Croy also claimed descent from the Arpad dynasty of Hungary.

[109] AM Amiens BB 11 fo. 4; *Inventaire sommaire, Amiens* II, 201; BN Picardie 91 fo. 175 (copy from AM Abbeville).

[110] Le Prestre, *Chronique*, 37–9. On the importance of the oath of loyalty, see Morvilliers to habitants of Corbie, 10 June 1465, Quicherat, 'Lettres . . . bien public', 291-4.

[111] Receptions of oaths: AM Amiens AA 6 fo. 165v (Jehennin Berrille 'avoit esté avec et en la compaignie des Bourguignons . . . et s'en estoit retournant . . . priant grâce et mercy', 1471); fo. 166v ('Sire Mahieu Hareng, prestre, curé de Sarcus, qui avoit esté à Auxi . . . ou parti des Bourguignons', 1471); fo. 166v (Guillaume Lescochois, sieur d'Ais who had stayed at Abbeville); fo. 167v (Robinet Leconte, 1471); fo. 251 (Colinet Houchart, 1482).

[112] The Parlement seems to have resisted registration: *lettres de jussion*, 27 June 1480, Vaesen, *Lettres de Louis XI* VIII, 128, 215–16 (11 June).

Amiens over a military garrison as early as 1467. Edouard Maugis argued persuasively that the economic war initiated by Louis XI in October 1470, when he prohibited trade with the Low Countries, had forced the Amiénois to opt for France.[113] However, the decision was not a foregone conclusion. On 27 February Dammartin issued orders against dealings with those 'tenans party contraire au roy' and prohibited entry to those 'demourans et conversans au party du duc de Bourgongne'. Women with husbands in Burgundian territory were expelled and trade forbidden. On 19 February the town was divided into quarters to be administered by reliable men.[114] There are signs of lurking Burgundian sympathies still in December 1472 in the course of a quarrel between the royalist *maire* Clabault and Caurel of the *bailliage*, who stormed out of a meeting when his pension was suspended and hinted that 'another' would restore it.[115] Those who remained loyal to Burgundy had their property confiscated. In May 1473, for instance, Jean Malherbe, a tailor, had his house seized when he went over to the duke's service and in 1472 French soldiers had to be warned not to call the Amiénois 'vilains, traistres bourguignons'. Indeed, as late as 1481 Esquerdes, according to Molinet, was anxious to 'decepevoir le demourant des Piquars tenans le parti de Bourgoigne'.[116]

Nevertheless, the fact that Amiens, or its ruling circles including men like Antoine Clabault and Jean Lenormand, had chosen to surrender to the king's will counted much in its favour. In 1473, Louis told a deputation that he was 'bien tenus à euls, car il ne les avoit pas conquis, mais ils s'estoient conquis eus meimes en son obéissance'. In response, the *échevinage* took care in the early years to elect *maires* who would 'luy complaire et capter sa béninvolence', adopting the slogan 'si veut le roi, si veut la loi'.[117]

A substantial process of bargaining at the time of the surrender to Dammartin on 2 February 1471 seems to have underlain these arrangements. Molinet, admittedly biased, claimed that the people of Amiens had been

[113] Louis XI to Amiens, 13 April 1467, Vaesen, *Lettres de Louis XI* III, 136–8. On Louis XI's economic measures to undermine Burgundian authority at Amiens, see E. Maugis, *Essai sur le régime financier de la ville d'Amiens*, MSAP in-4to, 33 (1899), 389.
[114] AM Amiens BB 11 fo. 1r–v, 10vff.; *Inventaire sommaire* II, 202; A. Janvier, *Les Clabault, famille municipale amiénoise* (1889), 286, 289, 291, 293, 297.
[115] Janvier, *Les Clabault*, 58. On the Burgundian party at Amiens, see Maugis, *Essai sur le régime financier*, 395–6.
[116] See also the case of Caignet, 'qui estoit lors demourant avecques le seigneur de Crèvecœur lors tenant le party desdis Bourguignons', AM Amiens AA 5 fo. 195v, royal letters 17 Aug. 1476, exemption from restitution of property (*Inventaire sommaire, Amiens* I, 47). *Ibid.* II, 211; Janvier, *Les Clabault*, 103; the unruly state of the garrison: see A. Thomas, 'Jean de Salazar et le guet-apens d'Amiens (23 juillet 1471)', *BEC* 86, 122–67. Molinet, *Chroniques* I, 357.
[117] Report, 9 July 1473, *Inventaire sommaire, Amiens* II, 203; 27 May 1471, *ibid.*, II, 103; 2 April 1476, Janvier, *Les Clabault*, 130.

'corrompy . . . par argent et belles promesses'.[118] Among the powers which the king had issued for Dammartin to reduce the towns of Picardy was one to promise those towns which freely surrendered 'toutes les choses qu'il verra estre à faire pour venir à noz fins'. The actual entry of the king's lieutenant, after his threats of a siege on 31 January, and the acclamation before the town assembly, seems to have been stage-managed.[119] On 2 February, Dammartin signed a long list of demands already made by the *échevins*, which included primarily confirmation of all privileges and freedom from *tailles*. In addition the crown granted freedom of fief-holders from the feudal levy, prohibition of violence against the town, *lettres d'abolition* for all past offences, provision for those who wished to leave, a free fair yearly in September, continuation of the existing electoral process and local use of the *gabelle* on salt. In the short-term Louis agreed to certain concessions, like the use for six years of L 1200 from the *aides* for fortifications. All this was in turn ratified by the royal chancellery and registered by the Parlement on 27 April.[120]

In March 1471, Louis made further valuable concessions designed to promote fortification by conceding to the magistrates the right to vote local *aides* without specific royal *lettres d'octroi* and abolishing most of the *aides royales*. In addition, he empowered them to raise money through the issue of *rentes*, instead of local taxes which might infringe the taxation privileges of the richest bourgeois.[121] In the autumn of 1471, the king acceded to a schedule of requests concerning the town's relations with the garrison and, after initial obstruction, for the establishment of an *estaple* on wine and salt at Amiens, in fact not enacted until 1477.[122] Thereafter, royal privileges followed regularly: freedom from dues for victualling merchants and further dues for fortifications. The accounts for the latter were constantly overspent and in 1472–5 the king ordered subventions for the *généraux des finances*.[123] Louis's presence in Picardy in 1477 brought a further crop of favours, notably on the establishment of free markets as a reward for the town's loyalty and the defence of the

---

118 Molinet, *Chroniques* ch. xvii.
119 Thierry, *Tiers Etat* II, 326–7; Dammartin's promulgation on the free surrender: AM Amiens AA 5 fo. 145.
120 Thierry, *Tiers Etat* II, 323–30; AM Amiens AA 15 fo. 3v–12, read at *échevinage*, 18 Feb.: BB 11 fo. 5. On the financial privileges of Amiens, see Maugis, *Essai sur le régime financier*, 399–403.
121 Thierry, *Tiers Etat* II, 332–6; *Ordonnances* XVII, 401; AM Amiens AA 5 fo. 155 (5 April 1471); report by Coquerel, 27 May, BB 11 fo. 16v, *Inventaire sommaire* II, 203.
122 21 Oct. 1471, AM Amiens AA 5 fo. 58–9; Thierry, *Tiers Etat* II, 337–41; 9 Feb. 1477, AA 5 fo. 203v–204.
123 27 April 1471, AM Amiens BB 11 fo. 7; 17 May 1471, Thierry, *Tiers Etat* II, 42–3; 30 June 1473, AM Amiens AA 5 fo. 180v; 30 Mar. 1474 AA 3 fo. 288, Janvier, *Les Clabault*, 105; 12 Jan. 1475, AA 5 fo. 182. For further privileges to the Collège d'Amiens, see E. Maugis, *Documents inédits concernant la ville et le siège du bailliage d'Amiens* (1914) II, 249–54.

privileges of fief-holders when these were routinely threatened by the *bailliage*.[124]

Saint-Quentin, occupied a little before Amiens, was also offered inducements by the crown. As early as November 1470, Louis had written with promises should the town refuse a Burgundian garrison. The consequence was a favourable reception for Artus de Longueval and the arrival of Saint-Pol on 10 December with 200 lances to occupy the place in the king's name. Those responsible were a group of local notables led by La Cat and Alnequin, who later took a lead in handing over the town to Louis again in 1475. On 19 January, the king wrote to thank the magistrates and encourage them to repair the fortifications and subsequently issued *lettres d'abolition*, exemption from the *droit de formariage* for strangers, exemption from the *imposition foraine* and reestablished the *prévôté* as before 1435.[125]

The events of 1477 were more complex in that some of the towns occupied had initially resisted the crown and were more suspicious of its intentions. Nevertheless, bargaining had to take place. At Arras, an agreement between the estates of Artois, the town and the king provided for *de facto* recognition of Louis XI's rule in the absence of the countess Marie, in return for the king's *lettres d'abolition* for past offences against him and the confirmation of privileges. The bourgeois needed reassurance and the king wanted to 'atraire tous noz subgetz en vraye et loyalle obéissance envers nous'. The royal letters issued in March 1477 added a moratorium on taxes still owed to the Burgundian government and orders forbidding 'aucunes injurieuses parolles' about the people of Arras and Hesdin.[126] The loyalty of Arras was more dubious than that of Hesdin, though even after the first revolt of Arras the king reconfirmed its privileges. However, though he made certain concessions to Marie of Burgundy's undoubted rights to Artois, he absorbed the county into the royal domain in November 1477, and it is clear that the leaders of the town remained unreconciled. The continuing discontent prompted Louis to one of his most notorious acts of tyranny in deporting most of the leading inhabitants to other towns, repopulating Arras from elsewhere in France and ironically renaming it 'Franchise'.[127]

[124] 9 Feb. 1477, AM Amiens AA 5 fo. 204ff.; Thierry, *Tiers Etat* II, 357–8; Louis XI to Amiens, 22 May 1481, Thierry, II, 386–7; letters-close to *bailli*, same date, *ibid.*, II, 386–8.

[125] Vaesen, *Lettres de Louis XI*, IV, 162–3, 185–7, 199–200; B. de Mandrot (ed.) *Journal de Jean de Roye*; *Ordonnances* XVII, 368–70, 365; Jean Le Prince to Louis XI, 9 Nov. (1471), BN fr. 20485 fo. 78: in Saint-Quentin 'on a fort et trèsbien besongné à la fortiffication et emparement d'icelle tant ès fossez et bouleverts comme autre part'.

[126] G. Espinas, *Recueil de documents . . . Artois* I, 418–26; letters to Arras and Hesdin, *ibid*, no. 186, 187, 515; *Ordonnances* XVIII, 268, 259–62.

[127] Espinas, *Recueil de documents . . . Artois* I, 439–43 (4 May 1477). Royal provision for the restoration of the city after siege, Etréaupont, June 1477, A. Guesnon, *Inventaire des chartes de la ville d'Arras* (n.d.n.p.) no. 230, pp. 309–10. Louis XI to Amiens, 30 Jan. 1480: 'nous ne

In Picardy itself, the loyalty of the towns tended to be won by inducements rather than violence. Montreuil had surrendered to Torcy and as early as January 1477 the king confirmed its privileges and issued *lettres d'abolition*. Louis recognised an agreement reached with the town by Torcy on 21 January to allow continuation of the levies on goods raised to pay the 'composition ancienne' of L 1,000, the royal tax, and the salary of the captain. The magistrates were anxious about the economic decline of a town 'en pais stérile à deux lieues de la mer', where war and coastal silting had ruined the former prosperity of its port, cloth trade and law-courts. The upkeep of the fortifications had encumbered the town with debts. Louis's ratification of the agreement on 29 January included exemption for bourgeois fief-holders from the feudal levy in return for the town's loyalty 'en eulx réduisant libérallement et de grant vouloir en nos mains'.[128] At nearby Rue, also subject to economic decline, the king not only confirmed the privileges in February 1477 but also, in November, issued perpetual exemption from military levies in honour of the shrine of the Holy Spirit.[129]

Except for the period 1463–5 and despite contacts with the crown in the later 1460s,[130] Abbeville had long been outside direct royal control, though Burgundian rule seems to have become increasingly irksome. When Torcy appeared before the town on 17 January 1477, he bore powers to promise the king's ratification of its privileges. The *échevins* had already expelled the Burgundian garrison before Torcy's entry on 18 January and the despatch of a deputation to make certain requests to the king. The latter's response was swift; on 2 February he promulgated the usual exemption of bourgeois fief-holders from the feudal levy and on 4 February abolished a series of burdensome duties on trades and commodities. Fortifications were dealt with by a special concession of fifty oaks a year from the royal forest of Crecy.[131] On a personal

voulons pas que homme ne femme du pays demeure en la ville, sinon ceulx que avons ordonné'. (Espinas, *Recueil de documents . . . Artois* I, no. 192.) On the largely failed attempt at repopulation: A. Laroche, 'Une vengeance de Louis XI', *MASA* 37 (1865); M. Caillet, *Repeuplement de la ville d'Arras sous Louis XI: rôle de Lyon* (1908).

[128] G. de Lhomel, *Nouvel recueil de documents pour servir à l'histoire de Montreuil-sur-Mer* (1910), 44–6, 46–51, 59–60 (20 Apr. 1477); correction of letters of 29 Jan. 1477 in July 1480 in proper form: *ibid.*, 63–5.

[129] *Ordonnances* XVIII, 267–8.

[130] See the petition from Abbeville for the king to give Torcy powers to assign offices in the county of Ponthieu etc., exped. 5 Nov. 1466, with restitution of *sénéchaussée* of Ponthieu, BN fr. 20490 fo. 43, draft (the date may be a slip).

[131] R. Richard, 'Louis XI et l'échevinage d'Abbeville' *MSEA* 27 (1960), 73–5, 135, 136–7 (formerly AM AA 63, EE 31); Prarond, *Histoire d'Abbeville – Abbeville aux temps de Charles VII, des ducs de Bourgogne . . . de Louis XI, 1426–83* (1904), 324–5, 326; BN Picardie 91 fo. 175; BM Abbeville, Livre blanc, fo. 287–8; Père Ignace, *Histoire généalogique des comtes de Pontieu de maieurs de Abbeville* (1657), 374–5; *Inventaire sommaire, Abbeville*, 13. Confirm. of privileges, Feb. 1477, see Richard, 'Louis XI et l'échevinage d'Abbeville', 138–9.

level, the maire was gratified by concession of the office of *contrôleur* of the salt *grenier*, one normally incompatible with municipal office, though customary resistance overrode this. Finally, when a royal *commissaire* arrived in July to arrange the levy of the *francs archers*, a protest that 'jamais semblables archiers ne seroient mis sus en ladicte ville' quickly brought an assurance from the king that he had only meant to raise the men in the countryside of Ponthieu.[132]

At Péronne, the other chief Burgundian stronghold in 1477, it seems that agreement had been reached by 4 February. The governor, Clary, had gone to Ghent shortly before, probably to consult with the Burgundian government. There are records of presents of wine to Guy Pot in January and to two envoys from Louis, Magny and Bourel, on 28 January and again on 31 January, in company with La Hargerie, a former governor who had already gone over to the king. The royal letters confirming the privileges and issued at Falvy in February noted the town's decision to come over and take the oath to Guy Pot and promised protection to those in the town on the day of its surrender.[133] Part of the deal involved the maintenance of Clary in his position as governor and the issue of *lettres d'abolition*.[134] Whether exemption from the *taille* was involved is not so clear. The town's exemption has been dated from this time and there was certainly a deputation to court to ask for it. However, no letters have survived to confirm it other than mention of a 'mandement d'exemption' which was rapidly infringed by local tax officials.[135] Exemption from the *taille* had to wait until the end of the century, delayed as elsewhere by opposition from the *généraux des finances*. In a minor matter, on 10 February 1477 the king remitted rent owed on the royal domain in Péronne and renewed this in 1481 for a further six years.[136]

One existing grievance the king did deal with, however. The merchants of Péronne had long been harassed by customs collectors contrary to privileges issued by Philip the Good in 1427. Even before 1477, they had made use of the surviving appellate jurisdiction of the crown to rectify this but, of course, had been blocked by the Burgundian government. In July and September 1477,

[132] Prarond, *Abbeville aux temps de Charles VII*, 327–8. BM Abbeville MS 807, dossier Esquerdes, *échev.* 23 July 1477. *Inventaire sommaire, Abbeville*, 122 (28 July).
[133] AM Péronne CC 3 fo. 96r, 96v; AA 39, orig. 'Par le Roy, le sire de Beaujeu, le duc de Calabre, l'évesque d'Evreux, le Sr de Lohéac mareschal de France, de Lude, d'Argentan, Mes. Gracien Favre président de Toulouse, Raoul Pichon et autres présens, Pichon.'
[134] AM Péronne CC 3 fo. 93r.
[135] J. Dournel, *Histoire générale de Péronne* (1879), 450; AM Péronne CC 3 fo. 91v, 93r, 92r.
[136] AM Péronne AA 8 no. 5: 'Loys, Par le Roy, Briçonnet', Bonaventure, 14 Oct. 1481.

Louis ordered the *bailliage* court to confirm the privileges and to forbid customs farmers to levy dues on vehicles returning to the town on the grounds that they were against the 'utilité de tout le pays' in a town 'qui est clef de pays marchissant à l'Empire'. The royal council reaffirmed this in December and ordered the *gouverneur-bailli* not to allow royal letters to be challenged.[137]

The other major town occupied in Picardy in 1477 was Boulogne. There, as we have seen, a short siege indicated at least military resistance, though the mood of the population precluded the enlistment of help from Lord Hastings at Calais. Esquerdes, as *sénéchal*, undermined the Burgundian loyalties of Saveuse, the governor.[138] Pierre Héliot has argued, however, that Burgundian loyalties remained strong in this town which had always been subject to comital or Burgundian rule. The *ordonnance* of 1478 levying fines for 'frivoles appellations', which he interprets as seditious talk, may be a sign of this, since Burgundian rule had brought a certain peace and prosperity to the area. Though the text of the royal letters confirming privileges has not come to light, it was often referred to in confirmations which indicate that the county was freed from *taille* in return for military service.[139]

The material effects of war and division in Picardy, 1470–90

The willingness of most of the towns and landowners of Picardy to negotiate with royal representatives was prompted in part by the inconvenience and disorder stemming from the effective division of the region between France and Burgundy after 1470 and the consequent conflicting claims on loyalty. This is seen at Amiens, where the recurrence of peace talks in May and December 1471, 1474 and 1475 gave rise to fears that the town was about to be handed back to Burgundy under a peace treaty and subjected to the vengeance of those expelled in 1471. Nor did temporary truces help much, since it is clear that landowners were still unable to collect revenues on the other side of the temporary divide. The *échevinage* of Amiens specifically

[137] AM Péronne AA 20 no. 10, Noyon 9 July 1477; no. 11, Arras 20 Dec. 1477.
[138] 'Enqueste faite de iijme jour de may de par le Roy nostre Sr par commandement de mon tréshonnore et doubté seigneur monsr d'Esquerdes', BN fr. 20494 fo. 97–8; Haigneré, *MSAB* XVII (1895–6), 421.
[139] P. Héliot, 'Louis XI et le Boulonnais', *BEC* 100 (1939), 128–9. Charles VIII confirmed Louis XI's letters (noted as April 1477) in December 1483 (AN JJ 212 fo. 14v). Letters of Henri II, Feb. 1551, *MSAB* 9 (1878), 209. Molinet recounted a story from his home town of Desvres of an old woman called Minon du Molin who 'hayoit les François à mort'. Forced finally to acknowledge defeat, she only consented to proclaim: 'Vive le Roy, de par le deable!' (*Chroniques*, I, ch. xl).

complained about this in 1473 and the abbé of Saint-Riquier was unable to collect dues in France.[140]

Such problems were dealt with by the Truce of Vervins in 1475, though the terms of that agreement indicate the continued confusions resulting from the divisions of the region. In Thiérache, for instance, the county of Marle was divided; though Jean de Luxembourg was to enjoy the seigneurial revenues, taxes were to be shared between France and Burgundy. Saint-Quentin was to be restored to the duke (who would then restore Vervins and Beaulieu to their rightful owners). In the *bailliage* of Amiens, Vimeu and the *prévôtés* of Fouilloy and Beauquesne were to go to the Burgundians, though as late as May 1476 this still had not been done. The *échevinage* of Amiens claimed that to hand them over would be to leave their town virtually under siege.[141] Louis XI in the end would make no concessions. The confusion about obedience and suzerainty was also reflected in the issue of letters of pardon throughout this period. In September 1475, for instance, the duke of Burgundy had to pardon Saint-Quentin, under the terms of the Truce of Vervins, for all offences committed against him since 1470.[142]

Despite all this, the province on the eve of the Burgundian collapse was riven with conflicting territorial claims and local power depended on the control of rival fortresses. Burgundy controlled parts of the Thiérache, Péronne, Montdidier and Roye, Ponthieu and the Boulonnais; France most but not all of the *bailliage* of Amiens. In reality, the limits of French and Burgundian rule could not possibly have been clearly demarcated and it is thus not surprising that truces were difficult to maintain. The areas most afflicted by disorder as a result were those around Amiens, where a French garrison confronted the Burgundians at Abbeville and Péronne, and in the east between the Burgundians at Marle and the French at Laon.

The latter area was a prime target for foraging on both sides, as is clear from claims made by the count of Maine in 1472 for losses in his county of Guise over the previous two years. These had been such that:

---

[140] *Inventaire sommaire, Amiens* II, 203 (27 May 1477), 205 (10 Dec. 1471), 206 (1 Jan. 1472), 217 (5 Jan. 1475). Vaesen, *Lettres de Louis XI* IV, no. 303 (12 Jan. 1472); *procès-verbal*, AM Amiens BB 11 fo. 63. Commynes's description of the pro-French and pro-Burgundian interests in the town and fears of Burgundian revenge: *Mémoires* I, 172. Difficulties over obtaining rents: *Inventaire sommaire, Amiens* II, 21; Le Prestre, *Chronique*, 32–3. Royal letters unifying Amiens to the royal domain: AM Amiens AA 5 fo. 150v, *Ordonnances* XVIII, 414.

[141] Provisions concerning the division of *prévôtés*: Molinet, *Chroniques* ch. xxv. Certain of them had been transferred in a supplement to the treaty of Conflans in order to avoid 'discordz et débatz', see *Ordonnances* XVI, 366–7. *Inventaire sommaire, Amiens* II, 220 (6 May 1476).

[142] *Le Vermandois*, III (1873), 430.

à present elle est presque destruyte, car oultre la pillerie, ilz ont bruslé mes chasteaulx de Novion, d'Ircon et d'Oysy et leurs villaiges, aussi quatre autres grans et des meilleurs villaiges de lad. conté, dont en ce que me touche seulement, sans la perte de mon revenu n'en seroye relevé pour lx M fr.

This, in fact, was the sum the whole county had been valued at for purposes of exchange with Saint-Pol in 1468 and the count's purpose was to extract compensation from the king, without which, he argued, 'je ne sauroye sans vostre aide tirer avant honnestement'.[143] The state of intense insecurity in the same area emerges from the archives of Laon. An enquiry was made in September 1473 into what look like wild accusations made by a 16-year-old servant boy, Colinet Watier, against his master, a lawyer, the *procureur du roi* and the *prévôt* who, he claimed, had 'vendu et trahy ceste ville'. He had invented a wild story that the Burgundians at Marle had ladders ready to scale the walls of Laon and that all the women of the town would be locked in the market hall and burned to death. When he told the chambermaid of a priest he had once worked for, the authorities soon hauled him in for questioning.[144] Though the accusation seems bizarre, there is no doubt that the proximity of Burgundian garrisons was a source of anxiety. Early in 1474, the magistrates told Saint-Pol that the town was poor and ill-supplied 'pour les garnisons de cy entour contraire à nous'. In January 1474, they had reported that the Burgundian garrisons 'pillent et robbent chacun jour sur les pays et subjetz' of the king.[145] Under the terms of the existing truce each side appointed a *conservateur* who was to arrange restitution for infringements. Letters between Laon and the Burgundian *conservateur*, the count of Celano, show each side accusing each other, as might be expected. A *procès-verbal* drawn up by the leading villagers of Cuirieux near Pierrepont claims that, on 4 February 1474, 120 Burgundians from Marle had come and taken off 'tous les biens meubles et besteulx qu'ilz ont peu prendre'. The ducal captain at Marle responded to French complaints that the villages concerned were in the duke's 'conqueste et obéissance' and proved unwilling to negotiate on

---

[143] Charles du Maine to Louis XI, La Ferté-Bernard, 7 Dec. (1472), BN fr. 20485 fo. 80. Saint-Pol, offered the sparing of Vendeuil by Burgundy, however, in return for not garrisoning it: 'J'ay respondu que j'ayme autant qu'il la face ardoir qu'il la laisse, et que la terre ne se peut emporter' (letter to Dammartin, 25 Oct. 1472, H. de Chabannes, *Preuves pour servir à l'histoire de la maison de Chabannes* (1872–7) II, p. 362).

[144] Enquiry at Laon, 11 Sept. 1473, BN Picardie 89 fo. 311–17, orig.

[145] Saint-Pol to Laon, Ham, 26 Jan. (1474); Laon to Saint-Pol, 27 Jan. (1474), BN Picardie 89 fo. 320; Laon to Louis XI, 14/18 Jan. 1474, AM Laon EE 2 (unnumbered).

infringements, since he claimed he intended none and the process was pointless.[146]

The magistrates of Laon reported to Louis XI that the Burgundians at Marle were seeking to 'composer' French villages in their vicinity and force them to contribute supplies to their garrisons on the excuse that lawless French soldiers had made raids on their side. Should this continue, all royal territory between Laon and Marle 'est en aventure d'estre de tout destruict', and little revenge possible since the county of Marle itself was too small to provide compensation. On 21 March, they reported another major raid right up to the suburbs of the town, though on this occasion the garrison and townsmen pursued the raiders and cut them to pieces half-way back to Marle. Further protests to the Burgundian *conservateur* brought no more than bland assurances that he had no wish to infringe the truce and that the 'raid' had not abducted children for ransom, simply taken them off to be pages.[147] The disorder around Laon continued until Robert d'Estouteville took Marle and the places around it in April 1475, after the renewal of war, though his bringing in of a royal garrison of four companies of *gens d'armes* was, perversely, opposed by the town magistrates.[148]

The list of towns sacked in the province during this period tells its own story: Corbie, Montdidier, Roye, Auxy, Saint-Valéry, Eu, Gamaches. Ardres, pillaged by the Burgundians after its capture in July 1477, was to be destroyed again by the English in 1492.[149] The grim story of Saint-Riquier in 1475 is told by abbé Pierre Le Prestre. The vidame of Amiens occupied the town in the king's name in May and administered the oath; shortly afterwards, Esquerdes's men returned amidst great celebrations, but two weeks later the French were back in force and this time, as punishment, ordered a general evacuation and the complete burning of town and abbey.[150] The capture of Nesle by Charles the Bold in 1472 was widely seen as a gross abuse of the normal rules of war. The duke's savage treatment of both garrison and population, indeed, may have spurred Commynes to abandon his service at a time when his master seemed to have lost his equilibrium. Though it was claimed by the Burgundians that the

[146] Officers of Laon to Villers, 28 Jan. (1474); declaration des prinses; captain of Laon to captain of Marle, 1 Feb. (1474); *procès-verbal*, 4 Feb. (1474); Frédéric de Wytain to captain of Laon, Marle, 7 Feb. (1474); Villers to same, 7 Feb. (1474); Celano to captain of Laon, 12 Feb. (1474); Villers to same, 12 Feb. (1474), all in AM Laon EE 2, unnumbered.

[147] Officers of Laon to Louis XI, 8 Feb. 1474, 21 Mar. (1474); to *prévôt* Le Groing (*bailli* of Saint-Pierre) and M. de Fontenailles; to count of Celano, 22 Mar. (1474); Celano to Laon, Marle, 23 Mar. (1474), AM Laon EE 2.

[148] Commission of Louis XI to Pierre de Baril, 5 June 1474; clergy and officers of Laon to Louis XI, 21 June (1474); same to Genlis, 21 June, AM Laon EE 2; Community of Laon to Louis XI, 5 June (1475); Laon to Estouteville, 8 July 1475, *ibid.*, EE 3.

[149] Ardres in 1477: Le Prestre, *Chronique*, 55; in 1492: Molinet, *Chroniques* II, 331.

[150] Le Prestre, *Chronique*, 37–40.

garrison had killed a herald sent to negotiate with them, it does seem that the town had surrendered formally after sustaining several assaults. The outraged duke ordered the slaughter of the garrison and, of the civil population who took refuge in the church, the survivors recalled in an enquiry as late as 1521 that many had been killed 'tant sur les autels que ailleurs dedans icelle, tellement que la nef d'icelle église estoit plaine de sang' and the dukes had ridden into the church shouting to his men: 'enfants, vous avez fait une belle boucherie!' The town was then burned to the ground.[151]

In the area north of Abbeville under Burgundian rule until 1477, Pierre Le Prestre gives vivid testimony to the suffering. The abbot had taken refuge at Hesdin with Mme d'Auxy during the fighting of 1472. He related how in August a company of soldiers from Amiens came to take the castle at Auxy and on their withdrawal they scoured the land around and took off 'tant de biens et de prisonniers que cestoit pitié à leur partement', burned the town and the water-mill which had been burned by 'feu de meschief' only nine years before. The French went on to attack Hesdin with near success and burned a string of villages along the Canche and Authie. At Saint-Riquier itself, they wrought the usual havoc during billetting, took off the harvest and beat the peasants 'et si ny avoit homme qui en osast parler'.[152] At the end of the fighting, Le Prestre decided to return to his abbey and had himself and his valuables transported by carriage as he was suffering from gout. In the forest of Crécy, he came across Burgundian soldiers streaming back from their defeats at Eu and Saint-Valéry. Suddenly, there were cries that the French were behind them and everybody started shouting 'To the woods'. Le Prestre painfully mounted his mule and followed them and in the general confusion, nobody noticed his treasures lying unguarded at the roadside.[153]

The area around Amiens, where jurisdiction was extremely confused up to 1477, was subject to intense raiding. In the fighting of 1471, Dammartin moved against Burgundian places to the north-west of Amiens that the *échevinage* of Amiens claimed 'leur pourroient porter grands dommaiges' and one, Conty, because its lord was a 'mauvais garson'. They were burned.[154] During the same period, the village of Rumigny and others were sacked and the people fled to Normandy so that in May 1472, the farmer of tithes there complained that 'il n'avoit pu rien toucher'. In September 1472, the *échevinage* of Amiens claimed that, in the area north of the Somme where most of the property of the king, the bourgeois and the clergy lay, the peasants had fled from the pillaging

---

[151] J. Dufournet, *La vie de Philippe de Comines* (1969), 33; Le Prestre, *Chronique*, 21; *Bulletin de la SHF* I, part 2 (1834).
[152] Le Prestre, *Chronique*, 23, 25.
[153] *Ibid.*, 27–8. [154] Chabannes, *Preuves*, II, pp. 279–80.

of the French gendarmerie to Doullens and Corbie and the harvest had not been gathered.[155]

As events at Saint-Riquier showed, the year 1475 surpassed even that of 1472 for wholesale destruction. In May, the *échevinage* at Amiens had to consider what to do about the press of refugees from Corbie, Montdidier and Doullens, in the town 'à cause de ce que leurs villes avoient esté démolies, arses et abatues de par le Roy, par ce qu'elles tenoient le party contraire au Roy'. Some argued they posed a danger as enemies within the gates, others that they merited pity. At all events, the craftsmen at least were admitted and given the right to work, while their families were given the benefit of the doubt.[156] In preparing for the English invasion, the king ordered a scorched earth policy which would scour the land between the Somme, the sea and Hesdin in order to prevent a thrust into Normandy. The effects of the campaign are conveyed by the hearth surveys in Artois of that year. Whereas there had been a slight growth of population since the survey of 1469 in the hundred or so villages of the *recettes* of Arras and Hesdin covered, the number of hearths declined from 3,901 to 1,554 in the course of 1475.[157]

The destructions of 1475 were amplified in 1477, when the French king initiated another summer campaign of destruction in order to starve out cities like Lille, Douai and Valenciennes which still opposed him. Ten thousand ironically named *faucheurs* were detailed to destroy the crops in the fields before the harvest in those areas. A survey of its lands made by a religious house in Cambrai that year reported that 'les Franchois bruloient tout le pays et se faisoient fauchier les bleds verts pour affamer le pays'. At Saint-Omer near the end of the year, Pierre Le Prestre lamented the pitiful state of the 'poure peuple, car il nont peu despoullier laust passé et si nont riens ressemé pour lanée avenir'.[158]

For Picardy itself, it seems that the French reconquest, in transforming the struggle into one for the control of Artois, Flanders and Hainault, transferred the worst of the fighting into neighbouring territory. However, the effects were bound to spill over and the immediate effects were dislocating. Molinet gives a wildly lurid and mannered description of the havoc of the times, including the

---

[155] A. Janvier, *Les Clabault*, 97–8 (*échevinage*, 25 May 1472), 106–7 (petition of Amiens, 1472). During the Burgundian threat of July 1471, 'le peuple des champs s'estoit venu retraire à Amiens', *plaidoirie* in Parlement: A. Thomas, 'Jean de Salazar', 125, 135–6.

[156] *Inventaire sommaire, Amiens* II, 218 (29 May 1475). On the destruction of Montdidier and Roye, see l'Epinois, 'Notes extraites des archives communales de Compiègne', 128: 'le village de Lyhons et Chaule par ordonnance du Roy furent ars le xiije jour dudit mois de May'.

[157] Louis XI to Dammartin, 30 June 1475, Vaesen, *Lettres de Louis XI*, V, 363–7. Remission of rent for losses during the English invasion, September 1475, Janvier, *Les Clabault*, 121. A. Bocquet, *Recherches sur la population rurale de l'Artois*, 134–40.

[158] Molinet, *Chroniques* I, 219; Le Prestre, *Chronique*, 62; H. Neveux, *Vie et déclin*, 120.

crucifixion of a prisoner by the French.[159] Even in Picardy, normal processes of law enforcement would not operate. Thieves had to be released from the seigneurial prison at Ancre in 1479 'considérant et eu regard aux divisions de ces presentes guerres . . . par quoy on a esté et est journellement occupez'.[160] As the wars continued, the spread of extortion by freebooting soldiers became more difficult to control. In 1486, for instance, a band of brigands, including a priest, were tried at Chauny as 'aguetteurs de chemins, meismement qui se tenoit en pays contraire et qu'ilz estoient venu pardeça pour prendre aucuns prisonniers et les mener audit parti contraire'. Envoys from Abbeville to Hesdin in 1488 had to be escorted by Esquerdes's archers 'pour doubte des pillars'. In 1489, a soldier at Saint-Omer, Denis de Morbecque, set up at Bourbourg 'et se tenoit neutre et de la fit sy bonne guerre' against Bergues that it had to surrender.[161]

One of the worst cases of freebooting came near the end of the wars in 1492. Molinet recounts that, after the French conquest of Brittany, "pluseurs malvais garnemens rassemblez de diverses nations, sans ordonnances, gaiges ou bienfaits' banded together and on being forced out of France established themselves in the Cambrésis 'ymaginans comment se poroyent logier en seureté pour pillarder les pays voisins à l'environ'. They attacked a poorly defended Cateau-Cambrésis, claiming to be under the command of the rebellious Philippe de Clèves-Ravestein and calling themselves 'Philippus'. Negotiations took place at Saint-Quentin for their withdrawal but they stayed for seven months reducing the lands around 'en sy grant dessertion et gastine plus que jamais paravant n'avoyent fait ne Franchois ne Bourguignons'. Eventually, the archbishop of Cambrai bought them off with 4,000 *écus*. At the same time, the captain of Bouchain, nominally a Burgundian, 'composoit et taxoit les meismes villages et les villages du party de France jusqu'à Péronne'.[162]

The peace of 1493, in creating an artificial frontier region between Picardy and Artois, was an uneasy compromise that left the way open for the renewal of the

---

[159] Molinet, *Chroniques* I, 212.
[160] Register of seigneurial justice, Ancre, AN Z/2 no. 1 fo. 243 (18 Nov. 1479).
[161] V. de Beauvillé, *Recueil de documents inédits pour servir à l'histoire de la Picardie*, 4 vols. (1865–90) I, 154–6: costs of judicial enquiry at Chauny for the arrest of brigands; BM Abbeville MS 807, dossier Esquerdes, p. 24; Molinet, *Chroniques* II, 110. For depredations of soldiers in Artois against their own population, 1478, see R. Muchembled, *La violence au village. Sociabilité et comportements populaires en Artois du XVe au XVIIe siècles* (1990), 111. On border violence in 1492, see letters of remission for Colart Deutart, 5 Nov., in Ledru, *La maison de Mailly*, II, preuves, no. 421.
[162] Molinet, *Chroniques* II, 246–51. As Harsgor points out, *Recherches*, P. de Clèves, aesthete, pornographer *avant la lettre* and masochist, gravitated into French service.

64 *War and government*

dynastic struggle on a much larger scale after 1521. In political terms, the wars of 1463–93 had effectively defined the superstructure of provincial life and it was in that period, particularly under the rule of Esquerdes, that the *gouvernement* of Picardy took on its definitive shape. In the course of the fighting and the belated and lengthy struggle for the control of the province and then for the settlement of a *de facto* frontier with the Netherlands, the process of recovery which had begun in the Ile-de-France and southwards around the middle of the fifteenth century was delayed for a generation. It was only from the 1490s that the way was open for a full process of social and economic reconstruction in Picardy in the twenty-five years of uneasy peace which followed. The respite was brief; men like the later marshal of France Oudart du Biez or the governor of Péronne Jean d'Humières, who had grown to manhood in the later stages of the Burgundian wars, took military commands in the wars from the 1520s to the 1540s. Nor could the Franco-Netherlands frontier be isolated from wider international conflict in the brief wars of 1507–8 and 1513–14, when rumours of attacks served to remind the province that it was a potential war zone.[163]

The next chapter will aim to examine the political structures which had begun to bind Picardy into the French kingdom in the later fifteenth century and became firmly established in the sixteenth.

---

[163] On the war of 1507–8, see Le Glay, *Correspondance de Maximilien Ier* I, 12–75, *passim*. December 1507: warning by La Gruthuse of an attack on Péronne by troops from Maubeuge (AM Péronne BB 6 fo. 178); April 1518, arrest of three men on the charge of plotting to betray Montreuil to 'aulcuns malveillans ennemys' (*ibid.*, BB 7 fo. 58v–59v); May 1519: reports of 'grandz préparatifz et assemblées de guerre' in Flanders (*ibid.*, BB 7 fo. 80r).

2

⊕

THE PROVINCIAL GOVERNORS AND
POLITICS

In 1558, Jean d'Estouteville, sieur de Villebon and governor of Picardy, wrote to the duke of Guise that 'il n'y a gouvernement en France où il y ait plus d'affaires qu'il a icy'.[1] The importance of the *lieutenant-général du roi* in Picardy stemmed in part from the regular army stationed there and its massive augmentation in time of war. It has been suggested that this period of war tended to limit the scope of governors' powers in the interest of the crown.[2] These powers will be examined in chapter 3, but there must be some doubt on the matter, since war arguably enhanced the political and administrative competence of governors as well as of other military officials. The lengthy tenure of the post in Picardy by princes of the house of Bourbon contributed to this augmentation but also complicated it.

The post of governor was a 'charge' revocable at royal will, but this power was seldom invoked. However, the first half of the sixteenth century saw the rapid development of the post of deputy governor, appointed at first in times of emergency but later on a permanent basis. It has perhaps too easily been assumed that the deputy governors quickly eclipsed the real power of governors, often great princes preoccupied with court politics. This is not so clear from an examination of the affairs of Picardy, which reveal a continuing central role for the governors and a complex relationship with their deputies. The latter were a group of military men drawn from families of local

---

[1] Villebon to Guise, 22 March 1558, BN nafr. 21638 fo. 490–1.
[2] R. Harding, *Anatomy of a Power Elite: the Provincial Governors of Early Modern France* (1978), 21–45. For other studies of the institution in the period, see above all G. Zeller, 'Les gouverneurs de province au XVIᵉ siècle' in his *Aspects de la politique française sous l'Ancien Régime* (1964); B. Chevalier, 'Gouverneurs et gouvernements en France entre 1450 et 1520', *Behiefte der Francia*, 9 (1980), *Histoire comparée de l'administration (IVᵉ–XVIIIᵉ siècle)*, 291–307; M. Antoine, 'Institutions françaises en Italie sous le règne de Henri II: Gouverneurs et Intendants', *Mélanges de l'Ecole française de Rome*, 94 (1982), 759–818.

importance in favour at court (Créquy, Humières, Monchy) or from others influential in court politics, which had marginal connections in the province (Montmorency, Estouteville). As the Habsburg–Valois Wars continued, the tension between local influence and military necessity increased.

The general lack of precision in both early compilations and more recent works on the succession of the provincial governors results partly from the patchy survival of letters of provision.[3] One consequence has been to obscure the political circumstances in which governors were appointed and continued in their posts, so the first task must be to clarify these details. It will then be possible to go on to analyse the way in which governors acted in provincial politics.

Local influence obviously weighed heavily. In 1470, Jean d'Estouteville-Torcy had been appointed to succeed Lohéac as *lieutenant du roi* at Amiens as 'homme notable, homme de justice et homme agréable au Roy, à son noble conseil et à la ville'. The young duke of Vendôme in 1538 was appointed governor as a 'personne de maison, crédit et auctorité qui soit au peuple agréable pour en avoyr et tirer le service'. In the first half of the sixteenth century, the house of Bourbon-Vendôme, as inheritor of the influence enjoyed by the Luxembourgs in the fifteenth century, held a quasi-hereditary control of the governorship of Picardy. It was difficult not to appoint a leading provincial magnate, whose predominance would undermine obedience to a lesser appointee. Once reaching adulthood with the accession of Francis I, Marie de Luxembourg's children enjoyed a landed income which far outstripped that of any other seigneur in the province, held the status of princes of the blood and, after 1527, were next in line to the throne after the Valois. Their claims were irresistible.[4]

It took some time for this pattern to be established, though the criterion of local influence was usually paramount. Louis XI's first governor after 1477, marshal d'Esquerdes, appointed to assure the king's control, was, as we have seen, the former trusted lieutenant of Charles the Bold and closely connected with the Picard nobility. Despite the favours showered on him, it seems that he was not built up by the crown into a leading local magnate, nor did he have a son to succeed to his influence. His landed revenues, in the main derived from Artois, were lost to the Habsburgs after 1494 and his principal income was

[3] L. F. Daire, *Histoire de la ville d'Amiens*, 2 vols. (1757), 507. The lists in G. Dupont-Ferrier, *Gallia Regia*, 6 vols. (1942–66), nos. 17507–529 give only the principal governors. Those in *CAF* IX are vague and occasionally incorrect. On letters of provision, see ch. 3.

[4] *Inventaire sommaire, Amiens*, II, 204 (30 Sept. 1471), 211 (May 1473). Provisions for Antoine de Bourbon, duke of Vendôme, (10) February 1538, BN Dupuy 276 fo. 16v–17r. Note the almost exact phrase in the provisions issued on the same day for La Rochepot, Ile-de-France, BN fr. 23149, pp. 9–12, BN Dupuy 276 fo. 17–19 (Registres, Paris II, 361–2). See D. L. Potter, 'The Luxembourg Inheritance', *French History*, 6 (1992).

derived from his *état* as governor, and periodic royal subventions. This was a position not uncommon in the sixteenth century for middle-ranking governors but was never easy to sustain against the grain of local society in the long run.[5]

The Luxembourgs survived the catastrophe of 1475 by accepting royal choice of a husband for the heiress, Marie, in the person of François de Bourbon-Vendôme. Then came the appointment of Louis count of Ligny, the constable's youngest son and first cousin to Charles VIII, in succession to Esquerdes in 1494. Thereafter, the Luxembourgs or Bourbons maintained their influence in the governorship except for the period 1504–18, when the Bourbon princes were still too young for high command. During the interval, two members of interrelated Picard–Flemish families, La Gruthuse and Piennes, held the governorship. Both were former servants of Burgundy.[6] When Piennes died in December 1519, the time was ripe for Charles de Bourbon, raised to the dukedom of Vendôme and the governorship of the Ile-de-France on the accession of Francis I, to take over. Ile-de-France went to his brother François, count of Saint-Pol and, thereafter, there was to be a close relationship between appointments to the two provinces, where military administration had to be coordinated after 1521.[7]

The fact that the landed wealth of the Bourbons was based on the domain of La Fère meant that successive dukes of Vendôme would not be absentee governors and that they would have a considerable voice in the appointment of their deputies. There were sometimes tensions between them, but the authority of the Bourbon dukes could never be ignored. Dukes Charles and Antoine of Vendôme were not first-rank military commanders and so were not regularly called away to the Italian wars. In fact, analysis of their acts and

---

5 Powers from Charles the Bold, confirmed 27 July 1477, with Jean de Lannoy as lieutenant, BN fr. 9463/Clair. 63, p. 4899, *Ordonnances* XVIII, 281. In 1477, Dammartin was already Louis XI's governor at Amiens and they may have coexisted until 1478. In 1477, Torcy is also 'nostre lieutenant-général en nostre bailliage d'Amiens et ailleurs ès pays de Picardie' (Lhomel, *Nouveau Recueil*, 48) and April 1486 lieut.-gen. 'entre la rivière de Somme et de Seine' (AN X/1A 4827 fo. 153). Oct. 1480, powers for Esquerdes over all other military commanders, A. Collet, 'Philippe de Crèvecœur', *MSAB* 28 (1917), 445–6. August 1482, Esquerdes received powers 'plus étendu qu'aucun autre', BN Picardie 155 fo. 73r. On his efforts for his nephew, Antoine du Bois, 1487 and criticism of Esquerdes, see Harsgor, *Recherches* II, 1104.
6 Ligny left for the Italian wars and returned in July 1498 (AM Amiens BB 18 fo. 49v; *Inventaire sommaire* II, 281). La Gruthuse, ment. as 'lieutenant du Roy de par deçà', 1500 (*Inventaire sommaire, Amiens* II, 286), appointed full governor, 1504 (*ibid.*, 296). For the appointment of Piennes, see Louis XII to Piennes, 11 Aug. 1512, *Cab. hist.* 1892–3, 86; *Inventaire sommaire, Amiens* II, 317.
7 Patent of Vendôme for governorship of Ile-de-France, *Ordonnances, François Ier* I, p. 317. His patent for Picardie in 1520 has not survived. Death of Piennes, Dec. 1519, see Roncherolles, Jean and Louis de Hallewin to Saint-Quentin, 12 Dec. (1519), AM Saint-Quentin, liasse 151/L, 3. A. Ledieu, 'Les funérailles de Louis de Halluin', *Cab. hist.* 1892–3, 48–54. Piennes's sons were passed over though one had been governor of Péronne.

itinerary shows the predominance of Picardy and their estate of La Fère in their activities.[8] The governors appointed in their 'absence' were, therefore, usually co-adjutors rather than substitutes meant to circumvent them.

Deputy governors (or, technically, governors 'in the absence' of the *lieutenant-général du roi*) had been appointed in the fifteenth century. For much of his time, Esquerdes had been assisted by Pierre de Rohan, marshal de Gié, who, though not of Picard origin, was one of those lords who had profited from the downfall of the constable de Saint-Pol. In 1490, Raoul de Lannoy and Esquerdes's nephew, Jean du Bois, were appointed as the marshal's lieutenants in his absence 'à ce que l'on sache à qui on s'en devera adrescher', and in 1494 admiral de Graville occupied the same position briefly during Ligny's absence on the Naples expedition. When Ligny was again in Italy in 1500, La Gruthuse acted as his deputy.[9] The appointments did not become regular, however,until after the start of the wars with the emperor in 1521.

The duke of Vendôme became governor of Picardy early in 1520 and remained sole governor for two years, though the marshal de Chabannes was certainly assisting him in command of the army of Picardy in 1521, before being attached to Duprat's mission to Calais for negotiations with the emperor. His exact status, though, is unclear. The threat of an English invasion in 1522 brought about the appointment of Louis II de La Trémoille in May, though Vendôme continued active in the province. La Trémoille remained governor of Burgundy and continued to keep an eye on affairs there through his brother Georges.[10]

Narrative accounts of the campaigns of 1522 and 1523 show that La Trémoille was the principal military commander under Vendôme's aegis. It may well be that, in view of the political difficulties encountered by the duke after the treason and flight of his kinsman, the constable of Bourbon, La Trémoille took sole charge of the province. However, he left after the English campaign of 1523 and never returned, following the king to the battle of Pavia,

---

[8] See table 2.1.
[9] Gié, deputy of Artois from 1482, was in charge of Picardy in 1486 (AM Péronne, BB 6 fo. 37v). Aug. 1490, powers for Jean du Bois, sr. de Tenques and R. de Lannoy-Morvillier as deputies of Esquerdes (*ibid.*, fo. 121v). Graville, in Sept. 1494, is 'lieutenant du Roy ès marches de Picardie pour l'absence de Monsr, le conte de Liney en l'armée ou voiage de Naples' (*Inventaire sommaire, Amiens* II, 272). Auton says that Graville was out of favour with Louis XII and he was therefore disgraced in 1498. He returned to favour on the fall of Gié in 1504.
[10] H. de Chabannes, *Preuves*, I, ii, nos. 235–281 *passim*. P. Marchegay and H. Imbert, *Lettres missives originales du XVIe siècle . . . tirées des archives du duc de La Trémoille* (1881), 29, 38, 39; AN 1AP (Papiers La Trémoille, microfilm), no. 220, 626, 613 (documents from this period). *Inventaire sommaire, Cambrai*, AA 58 no. 1. Cheyne to Wolsey, 6 May 1522, *L&P* III, ii.2232; Bryon to La Fayette, 27 May (1522) BN fr. 2934 fo. 68. La Trémoille to Montmorency, 15 Dec. (1522) BN fr. 3039 fo. 42, affairs of Burgundy.

Table 2.1. *Location of the acts of the governors of Picardy*

The following table breaks down by year and place all known acts, letters missive and close, ordonnances, presence in the royal council or at the *jussio*, of the Bourbon-Vendôme governors of Picardy, 1520–55, and is based on a full itinerary derived from a collation of all known acts.

Year	Total	Picardy	La Fère etc.	At court	Elsewhere	Percentage in Picardy
1520	3	3	1			100
1521	45	45	11			100
1522	52	52	3			100
1523	9	6	5	2	1	66.6
1524	19	16	6	3		84.2
1525	22	4	4	17	1	18.2
1526	6	0	0	6		0
1527	8	2	2	6		25
1528	28	17	14	3	8	60.7
1529	15	11	4	3	1	73.3
1530	11	4	3	5	2	36.4
1531	9	9	8	0	0	100
1532	3	2	0	3	0	66.6
1533	3	1	1	2	0	33.3
1534	4	1	0	3	1	25
1535	4	2	2	2	0	50
1536	110	107	54	1	2	97.3
1537	6	2	0	4	0	33.3
1538	7	4	3	3	0	57.1
1539	1	0	0	1	0	0
1540	3	9	0	0	3	0
1541	14	11	3		3	78.6
1542	29	24	5		5	82.8
1543	14	8	5	1	5	57.2
1544	17	15	3	0	2	88.2
1545	7	3	3	0	4	42.6
1546	2	?	?	?	?	?
1547	8	?	?	5	?	?
1548	18	0	0	15	3?	0
1549	16	4	1	0	12	25
1550	3	1	0	0	2	33.3
1551	57	51	12	1	5?	89.5
1552	60	59	8	0	1?	98.3
1553	66	56	0	0	10	84.8
1554	24	20	0	0	4	83.3
1555*	14	1	0	1	12	7.1

•January–July only

where he was killed.[11] Vendôme was certainly back in active command of the province in November 1523 and so seems to have weathered the storm. He was now assisted as deputy by Antoine de Créquy, sieur de Pont-Rémy, a noted French commander in Italy who had returned to his native province by July 1522.[12]

Vendôme's position is inextricable from national politics from 1523 to 1527, especially in the extent to which it was affected by the constable's treason. We know that Bourbon had plenty of contacts in Picardy, including the governor of Boulogne, La Fayette.[13] However, though Vendôme and his brother Saint-Pol were with the constable on an expedition to revictual Thérouanne in March 1523, they were not part of his close affinity. Their lands in the Low Countries may have given them an incentive to turn against France, and Margaret of Austria certainly thought in September 1523 that Vendôme and the duke of Lorraine would support the constable, along with the captain of Saint-Quentin, Nicolas de Moy-Chin, lieutenant of Vendôme's gendarmerie company.[14]

However, these were not the days of Louis de Luxembourg and Louis XI. Bourbon fled the country in September 1523 and it may be assumed that Vendôme's being summoned to court in August was connected with the crisis and a fear that he would join his kinsman. On the other hand, the king decided to send him back from Lyon in October, and he was present in the Parlement of Paris on 5 November as well as in the following March. The year 1524 saw him active in the defence of the province, with his lieutenant, Pont-Rémy.[15]

Vendôme had evidently convinced Francis I of his reliability. When the king left for Italy in September 1524, it was reported that Vendôme had been appointed to 'keep' the frontier. From November, with Vendôme at La Fère and Pont-Rémy in charge of maritime Picardy, we have the first example of a division of responsibilities which was to become common. News of the disaster at Pavia coincided with the most inopportune death of Pont-Rémy in a

[11] S. Gunn, 'The Duke of Suffolk's March on Paris in 1523' *EHR* (1986), 496–534. M. du Bellay, *Mémoires* (SHF ed. V.-L. Bourrilly and F. Vindry, 4 vols., 1908–19) I, 300.

[12] Pont-Rémy in Italy, 1521, see *L&P* III, ii, 2378, 2776. His return to Picardy, Vendôme to La Fayette, 20 Aug. (1522) BN fr. 2888 fo. 67; Pont-Rémy to Montmorency, 3 Oct. (1522) MC, L I fo. 154. Mentions as Vendôme's lieutenant, *L&P* IV, i, 1275; R. de la Marck, sr. de Florange, *Mémoires du maréchal de Florange dit le jeune adventureux* (SHF ed. R. Goubaux and P. A. Lemoisne, 2 vols., 1913–14) II, 134. Vendôme to Péronne, 16 Feb. 1524, AM Péronne, BB 7 fo. 213v; *L&P* IV, i, 781.

[13] S. Gunn, 'The Duke of Suffolk's March on Paris'.

[14] *L&P* III, ii, 2907; III, ii, 3308; R. Rodière, *La maison de Moy*, preuves, p. 197, no. 510, p. 202, no. 533. Moy was replaced temporarily by du Lude at Saint-Quentin in 1524.

[15] *L&P* III, ii, 3533; M. du Bellay, *Mémoires* (SHF ed.) I, 279; Florange, *Mémoires* (SHF ed.) I, 299; R. Doucet, *Etude sur le gouvernement de François Ier* I, 159; AN X/1A 1526 fo. 2v–3r, 130.

skirmish at Hesdin in February 1525.[16] The resulting crisis at national and local level provides the context for understanding the position of the Bourbon-Vendômes in detail. Vendôme heard of the disaster on 7 March and quickly decided to go to Lyon to join the regent. He was under pressure from several quarters. Martin du Bellay tells us that he was asked to take on the government of the kingdom by several counsellors of the Parlement out of hatred for chancellor Duprat, but that he refused for fear of sowing discord. He was, however, given the largely honorific post of chief of the council on his arrival at Lyon.[17] There is no reason to suppose that he posed a real threat to the regent; Florange took the view that his loyalty and good sense prevented him from competing for power. The Imperial envoy de Praet, surveying the problems facing the regent in November 1525, pointed to the 'divers entendemens en ce royaulme et plusieurs gens de toutes sortes quy luy veullent du mal'. Some capable man of the highest birth was needed to overturn the existing régime, but 'ces trois frères de Vendosme' and the house of Lorraine were unlikely to do so. One reason de Praet suggested was 'la grosse obéissance estant en ce royaulme'.[18] On the other hand, it is clear that Vendôme was dissatisfied with his position at Lyon. First, as Duprat made clear to an Imperial agent in April 1525, despite his position Vendôme could do nothing 'sans l'advis et conseil de xxiv personnaiges'. He seems to have quarrelled with Lautrec over a plan of the regent to make that experienced, if unlucky, general lieutenant-general of the kingdom. He fell ill in consequence. He was also affronted that Louise and Duprat had persuaded the childless duke of Alençon (husband of Marguerite of Angoulême) to make the king's second son Orléans his heir at the expense of his sister, Vendôme's wife Françoise.[19] So, though Vendôme remained at court for much of 1525–6 and retained the governorship of Picardy, he was disgruntled. It is to this period that an undated letter from Vendôme to the king should be ascribed: 'Monseigneur, après que je vois votre Reaume en seureté et que tous vos voisins vous demende paix . . . sy vous senble que vous puisse servir en aultre lieu que ycy, il vous plaira m'en faire commandement.' This

16 *L&P* IV, i, 616, 781; M. du Bellay, *Mémoires* (SHF ed.) I, 340–4; A. Louant, ed., *Journal d'un bourgeois de Mons 1505–36* (1969), 240.
17 Vendôme to Péronne, La Fère, 7 March 1525, AM Péronne BB 7 fo. 274. He had arrived at the court near Lyon by 23 March, see AN X/1A 1527 fo. 261v. Martin du Bellay, *Mémoires*, start of book III. Fitzwilliam to Wolsey, 20 April, *L&P* IV, i, 1275.
18 Louis de Praet to Charles V, from the French court, 4 Nov. 1525, Vienna, Belgien P.A. 92, PRO 31/18/1 fo. 1436, *CSP Spanish* Supplement, p. 448.
19 Joos Lauwerens to Margaret of Austria, April 1525, PRO 31/18/1 fo. 1400 (*CSP Spanish*, Supplement, p. 438). *L&P* IV, i, 1364–5, 1401, 1464; A. Champollion-Figeac, *Captivité du roi François Ier* (1847), 624.

was at a time when English envoys could describe him as 'as frank, gentle and liberal a heart as any man'.[20]

The breach between Marguerite of Angoulême and Vendôme was deep. It was still in evidence in 1533, when she made some most uncomplimentary remarks about him to the English envoy Norfolk, alleging disloyalty, and later still in her opposition to the marriage between her daughter Jeanne and Vendôme's son Antoine in 1548. The correspondence of Jean du Bellay at court in 1530–1, *à propos* of the manoeuvres concerning the properties of the constable's sister Louise de Bourbon, princess of La Roche-sur-Yon, also makes it clear that Vendôme was still looked on with suspicion by those closest to the king.[21]

While Vendôme was absent at court, the Parlement of Paris, in the emergency of 1525, demanded a competent substitute. Pont-Rémy's brothers had replaced him in his offices as governor of Montreuil and *bailli* of Amiens. A suggestion that his young nephew, Canaples, should succeed him as governor was dismissed, since he was 'jeune homme qui n'est pas pour y savoir pourvoir'. At Lyon, Vendôme pressed for his own man in the person of his kinsman Charles de Luxembourg, count of Brienne, an important landowner on the frontier. To the Parlement's request for a governor, he replied: 'Madame a esté d'advis, et moy aussi, de y envoyer monsieur le comte de Brienne et avec luy le sieur de Torcy mon lieutenant.' As lieutenant of Vendôme's gendarmerie company, Torcy would keep an eye on the duke's interests. This decision had been taken up by 26 March and by the middle of April Brienne had taken up his post.[22] He remained in sole charge until the return of Vendôme in 1527, after which he seems to have worked harmoniously with the duke.

What the military developments of the 1520s demonstrated was that the frontier was too long and the burdens of command were frequently too great for one man to bear alone. The appointments of deputy governors were not meant to undermine the authority of the governor, even in the exceptionally dangerous political circumstances of Bourbon's treason.

The count of Brienne died at the end of 1530. On 1 May 1531, the king announced the appointment of François de Montmorency, sieur de La Rochepot, as governor in Vendôme's absence 'comme celui qui nous avons et

20 BN fr. 20648 fo. 11. *L&P* IV, ii, 4446.
21 *L&P* VI, 692, June 1533 (accusations by Marguerite that Vendôme had not done his best for Francis I in 1525 because he favoured the emperor); A. de Ruble, *Le mariage de Jeanne d'Albret* (1877), 257ff. R. Scheurer, ed., *Correspondance du cardinal Jean du Bellay*, 2 vols. (1969–73) I, 146, 148–9 (1533). Du Bellay was suspected of favouring Vendôme in the business of Louise de Bourbon's case 'pour avoir prins partie de nourriture en sa maison'.
22 AN X/1A 1527 fo. 255v; Vendôme to Parlement, 26 March 1525, *ibid.*, fo. 272v; to Péronne, 1 April 1525, AM Péronne BB 7 fo. 276v; Brienne to Parlement, 13 April, AN X/1A 1527 fo. 374–5.

congnoissons avoir autant d'affection à nous faire service que nul autre'. The appointment represented a victory for the *grand-maître* Anne de Montmorency in a period of considerable court hostility between him and the admiral Chabot de Brion, which was only just kept under control by Francis I.[23] There is, however, no reason to suppose that Vendôme found the appointment unwelcome. The voluminous correspondence between them in 1536–7 indicates a degree of tension, but no more than would be expected in the heat of active warfare. Orders by La Rochepot on garrison disposition did provoke protests to Vendôme from some towns, but these were not serious.[24] Although La Rochepot's own inheritance lay outside the province, he had held the captaincy of Beauvais, more or less a family fief, since 1519, and had subsequently acquired experience in the Italian and northern wars. In 1522, he had married one of the most important Picard heiresses of the time, Charlotte d'Humières, who brought to him the eventual reversion of the great estates of Louise de Nesle, lady of Offémont, Mello, Ancre and Bray. The death of Louise in 1530 made La Rochepot an important Picard seigneur and his marriage gave him close connections with the Humières and Créquy families. Charlotte d'Humières also had close relations with Vendôme's mother, Marie de Luxembourg.[25]

The charge of deputy governor was a much more informal one than that of his chief. When La Rochepot fell from a gallery at Corbie and broke his ankle in November 1536, he was given leave of absence by the king in a series of solicitous letters. His father-in-law Jean d'Humières had just returned from campaigning in Piedmont and the king wrote to him shortly afterwards, 'vous ayder à la conduicte de mes affaires pardelà'. This was, in effect, a temporary commission, as is shown by Humières's description of his powers 'que en l'absence de monseigneur de Vandosme je vacque et donne ordre à tout ce qui

[23] Francis I to Abbeville, 1 May 1531, BM Abbeville, MS 378 fo. 23v; orders from La Rochepot, *ibid.*, fo. 23v–24r. Scheurer, *Correspondance de Jean du Bellay* I, *passim*, 1531–3.

[24] BM Abbeville MS 378 fo. 23v–24r, deliberation of 2 May 1531 of La Rochepot's letter to M. de Huppy.

[25] For the captaincy of Beauvais, see ch. 4. Captured at Pavia and returned with messages to Parlement (AN X/1A 1527 fo. 260); sent to England, 1527 (BL Cotton, Calig. E II fo. 107); gentleman of the chamber by 1520, *bailli* of the Palais at Paris, 1532, *CAF* II, 4790. Captain of gendarmerie in 1525 (AN X/1A 1528 fo. 596r). A. du Chesne, *Histoire de la maison de Montmorency* (1624), 365–9, and *Preuves*, 266–7. On the Humières connection through Louise de Nesle: BN fr. 20618; p.o. 2031 (fr. 28515) no. 91; *dénombrement* of Ancre, 1532, AN K 560 no. 1; G. de Seillière, *Inventaire des Titres de la Baronnie de Mello* (1932), 16–17, 94–5; Offémont became a favourite residence for La Rochepot: P. Guynemer, *La seigneurie d'Offémont* (1912), 52–8. MC Chantilly GE 1 no. 42, expenses of Le Rochepot and Charlotte d'Humières on their first visit to Offémont in 1530, L 330.15s.: 'auquel temps plusieurs seigneurs et damoyselles les sont venuz voir'. Other relationships: A. Ledru, *La maison de Mailly* II, p. 276. AN K 277: record of present from Marie de Luxembourg to Mme de La Rochepot.

surviendra en ceste frontière'. Presumably, these powers lasted until La Rochepot was on his feet again in February.[26]

The years 1537 and 1538 saw a number of changes, brought about by the duke of Vendôme's death. He had seemed well enough at the start of the campaigning season but was taken ill suddenly around 17 March and died on 26 March of a 'fièvre chaude', much to the general regret. His gendarmerie company was divided on 28 March, but no immediate steps were taken to replace him as governor, as the king was present in person.[27] The duke's son, Antoine count of Marle, was still rather young for command, but his claims could not be lightly set aside. In letters of 26 and 27 March, Montmorency told his brother that opinions around the king had changed: 'et n'est délibéré led. seigneur de autrement y pourveoir pour ceste heure, mais veult que ce pendant vous pourvoyez à toutes choses et y faciez comme vous avez trèsbien faict à son contantement jusques icy'. This was a temporary solution only. At the end of March, Marguerite of Angoulême was pressing La Rochepot's case as necessary for the king's service and asked Jean du Bellay to talk to Montmorency about it.[28] On 13 May, letters of provision were issued at Corbie for La Rochepot's succession as full governor of Picardy, and shortly afterwards he received the queen of Navarre's congratulations. There had evidently been much manoeuvring behind the scenes, since Jean du Bellay reported to Humières, 'quelques menées qu'on ait sceu faire d'aulcuns endroits' against the appointment. La Rochepot's ceremonial entries were delayed until later in the year by the pressures of campaigning.[29]

---

[26] Vendôme to Montmorency, 3 Nov. (1536), BN fr. 3072 fo. 79, 7 Nov., *ibid.*, fo. 83; Montmorency to La Rochepot, 25/26 Nov. (1536), BN fr. 3008 fo. 166, 169; Francis I to La Rochepot, 27 Nov. fr. 3008 fo. 164; 10 Dec. 1536 fo. 171; Humières to Montmorency, 15 Dec. (1536), BN fr. 20502 fo. 141. For an earlier possible temporary lieutenancy of Humières under Vendôme in 1528, see R. Macquereau, *Chronique*, 1527–9, ed. J. Barrois (1841–5), 147–8, 181.

[27] M. du Bellay, *Mémoires*, Michaud et Poujoulat, 1st ser. vol. V (1836), 439; Montmorency to La Rochepot, 17, 21, 31 March 1537, BN fr. 3008 fos. 10, 17, 29; Francis I to same, 20 March, *ibid.*, fo. 15. Breton to Dubourg, 28 March 1537, AN J 968 no. 12/18: 'au regard du gouvernement de Picardye, cela n'est point encores despesché.'

[28] Montmorency to La Rochepot, 26–27 March 1537, BN fr. 3008 fo. 24, 26. F. Génin, *Lettres de Marguerite d'Angoulême, sœur de François Ier*, 2 vols. (1841–2) I, no. 137, p. 338 and p. 449; P. Jourda, ed., *Répertoire analytique et chronologique de la correspondance de Marguerite d'Angoulême, duchesse d'Alençon, reine de Navarre* (1930) nos. 665, 1108; Vendôme's brother Saint-Pol seems to have been paid as interim governor of Picardy, April–15 June 1537, see *CAF* VIII, 144, 30596. This may be a mistake of transcription for 'Piedmont' but see his letter from court, 6 July 1537 (copy, BL Add. 38028 fos. 92–3).

[29] BN fr. 23149, pp. 9–12; La Rochepot to Humières, 17 May 1537, BN fr. 3062 fo. 135: 'led. Seigneur me laisse par deçà son lieutenant général et m'a baillé ung pouvoir aussi ample qu'il est possible de faire, et vous asseure que led. Seigneur a trèsgrant contentement de moy'. Jean du Bellay to Humières, Pentecost (10 May) 1537, BL Add. 38033 fo. 37v, copy. BM Abbeville MS 347 fo. 32, 24 Sept. 1537.

The presence of a royal army in Picardy during the summer of 1537 made the formal appointment of a deputy unnecessary, though the dauphin was entitled lieutenant-general of the king's army in Picardy. Later in 1537, however, with the king's attention turned to Piedmont, he left his younger son Orléans in the north as his lieutenant-general, mainly in order to add his prestige to the real director of affairs, Jean du Bellay. The king told La Rochepot that he had appointed his son lieutenant-general in Picardy, Normandy and the Ile-de-France. Orléans's commission is dated 18 October and on that day he wrote to La Rochepot:

> Le Roy m'a ordonné de me retirer par deçà pour pourveoir avec le conseil et advis des gens de bien et bons personnaiges de [*sic*] j'auray autour de moy, à ce qu'en son absence ses ennemis ne feissent aucune entreprise suz les frontières de Bourgogne, Picardie et Champaigne.[30]

Whatever the exact terms involved, Orléans's position effectively and formally subordinated La Rochepot's lieutenancy to that of the king's son and, though the latter visited the province in November, the real power behind him was du Bellay.[31] Despite the king's expectation that his son would remain in the north during his absence, it is clear that by February he was tiring of his position. Du Bellay reported that he 'ne soubczie ne mesle plus guèrez au maniement des affaires' and that it was difficult to get him to sign anything. In fact, Orléans had asked his father to be relieved of the post in December 1537.[32]

Orléans's lieutenancy seems to have lapsed by the time the young Antoine de Bourbon, the new duke of Vendôme, received his appointment as governor of Picardy. The letters of provision for him, though unknown to the editors of the *Catalogue des actes de François Ier*, have survived in a royal secretary's formulary and indicate that they were dated the moment that La Rochepot became full governor of the Ile-de-France on 10 February 1538. This was also the day Anne de Montmorency became constable. Vendôme's letters from May indicate that he was dealing with the affairs of the province at court. News

---

[30] Orléans to La Rochepot, 18 Oct. 1537, BN fr. 3035 fo. 71; Francis I to same, 19 oct., *ibid.*, fo. 72; blank orders to obey add. to town captains and sent to La Rochepot: BN fr. 3088 fo. 57, 3058 fo. 27.

[31] Breton to La Rochepot, 5 Jan. 1537/8 BN fr. 3052 fo. 48: 'lieutenant général du Roy en Picardye en l'absence de monseigneur d'Orléans'. La Rochepot to du Bellay, 4 Nov. 1537, BN Dupuy 263 fo. 104. Orléans's ceremonial entry at Amiens, Dec. 1537, see AM Amiens CC 132 fo. 106.

[32] Francis I to Orléans, 10 Jan. 1538, BM Carpentras, MS 490 fo. 205; Orléans to Francis I, 19/21 Jan., AN J964, nos.41, 42. Du Bellay to La Rochepot, 27 Feb. (1538), BN fr. 3071 fo. 33; La Rochepot to du Bellay, 25 Jan. 1538, BN Dupuy 263 fo. 103. Francis I to Orléans, 14 Dec. 1537, G. Ribier, *Lettres et Mémoires d'Estat* 2 vols. (1666) I, 75–6, mistakenly described as addressed to the dauphin.

of the appointment came to Amiens some time before August.[33] By the time of duke Antoine's first *ordonnance* as governor of Picardy in November 1538 it is clear that La Rochepot had reverted to the position he had held under duke Charles, that of deputy governor in Picardy, while retaining the much less military post of governor of the Ile-de-France. Antoine acted in close cooperation with La Rochepot in the next few years and, though he was back at La Fère in 1538, did not make any formal entrances as governor of the province until May 1541.[34]

The constable de Montmorency, increasingly out of tune with the king's policies and subject to virulent attack by a coalition of enemies at court, was effectively removed from power in April 1541. This coincided with the emergence of Antoine de Bourbon as active governor of the province and what seems to have been the retirement of La Rochepot from the front line. Vendôme's first official tour of duty and plans for his formal entry into Amiens came during the crisis of relations with England in April 1541. His departure from court made enough stir to be reported by the Venetian ambassador, who described him as 'molto giovane ma di buonissimo credito'. The main point of his mission was to inspect the fortifications of the frontier and coordinate plans for their rebuilding that were already under way.[35]

The constable's fall and the emergence of Vendôme as an active governor seems to have been the moment that a replacement was found for La Rochepot as deputy governor. Late in June, Oudart du Biez, the governor of Boulogne, who had been increasingly active as Vendôme's co-adjutor in the frontier inspection, told the English commander at Guînes that he had been raised to the marshalship and that Michel de Barbançon, sieur de Canny, had been made 'lieutenant of all Piccardye under monsieur de Vandosme'. Canny was brother-in-law of Montmorency's arch-enemy and the king's mistress, Anne de Pisseleu, duchess of Etampes, and held the post of *chambellan* in the duke of Orléans's household. His tenure as governor is shadowy. The duke of

[33] Patent for Vendôme, Feb. 1537/8, BN Dupuy 276 fo. 15v–17v; for La Rochepot in Ile-de-France, 10 Feb. 1537/8, *ibid.*, fo. 17v–19r; printed in *Registres, Paris* II, 361–2. La Rochepot asked to leave Picardy to take up his new governorship in July (BN fr. 3088 fo. 52). He did so in Dec., see *Registres, Paris* II, 396. AM Amiens CC 132 fo. 117v. Vendôme to Francis I, 17 May 1537, Ribier, *Lettres et mémoires d'estat* I, 162–3.

[34] *Ordonn.* of Antoine de Bourbon, La Fère, 15 Nov. 1538, AM Amiens AA 12 fo. 191; Montmorency to La Rochepot, 12 Sept. 1538, BN fr. 2995 fo. 303: add. 'gouverneur de Lisle de France et lieutenant général du Roy en Picardye'. Vendôme to same, 14/16 Sept., A. Rochambeau, *Lettres d'Antoine de Bourbon et de Jeanne d'Albret* (1877) nos. 1, 2. *Inventaire sommaire, Amiens* II, 343 (19 May 1541).

[35] F. Decrue, *Anne de Montmorency, grand maître et connétable de France à la cour … du roi François Ier* (1885) 401–3. *L&P* XV, 207; Vendôme to Francis I, 17 April 1541, BN fr. 20521 fo. 34. Dandolo to Doge, 10 April 1541, BN f. it. 1715 fo. 71–2. AM Amiens BB 24 fo. 57r (19 May 1541).

Vendôme issued some form of letters of provision for him in September 1541, but little record of his activities survives and his early death in April 1543 may indicate a premature retirement from affairs.[36]

In July 1541, the duke of Vendôme received the order to retain marshal du Biez about his person for advice,[37] but it was not until December 1542 at Cognac that the king asked du Biez to act as lieutenant-general in Vendôme's absence at court, an appointment finalised on 26 December.[38] Du Biez was an elderly soldier who had begun his career under the aegis of the Créquy family, fought in Italy, and had held the governorship of Boulogne since the 1520s. He had seen great advances in his reputation in 1536–7. Once very much a client of Anne de Montmorency, he had adroitly allied himself to the new dominant court faction, dominated by the duchess of Etampes. The most important aspect of his position in this context, though, is that he was a figure whose political authority was almost entirely dependent on royal favour. His own local landed influence was relatively small.[39] The well-known revocation of the governors' powers on 21 May 1542 and the immediate reinstatement of all except the constable de Montmorency and his brother La Rochepot therefore formalised a state of affairs which already existed in Picardy.[40]

Vendôme continued to act as effective commander in the province with du Biez as his deputy during 1543 and 1544. The remodelling of governors' powers in 1542 had brought other changes, however. Vendôme had also at that time replaced La Rochepot as governor of the Ile-de-France. He thus revived the connection of his father and of his uncle Saint-Pol with that province and it made sense to have the two provinces under the same command, as many of the towns of the Ile-de-France were vital for the supply of the armies in

[36] Wallop to Council, 19 June, *L&P* XVI, 917; to Henry VIII, 30 June 1541, PRO SP1/166 fo. 69 (*L&P* XVI, 944). *CAF* IV, 217, 11998 (payment to Canny, 21 June); BN Picardie 112 bis fo. 5r (provisions, 7 Sept. 1541); BN fr. 7853 fo. 1752–9 (death 15 Apr. 1543 in *rôles* of ducal household). Peigné-Delacourt, *Histoire de l'abbaye de Nostre-Dame d'Ourscamp* (1876) incorrectly transcribes the date 'xv calendas maii . . . MV/C XLVII aetatis suae xxxvi'.
[37] Vendôme to king, 19 July 1541, BN fr. 20521 fo. 45–6. Orders, May 1541, to Marillac in England to send news to Vendôme and, in his absence, du Biez, J. Kaulek (ed.), *Correspondance politique de MM. de Castillon et de Marillac* (1885) nos. 340, 341.
[38] Du Biez to Montmorency, 6 Nov. 1542, BN fr. 20503 fo. 27: Vendôme has gone to court 'me laissant pardeçà ce pendant'. Letters-patent, 26 Dec. 1542, AM Amiens AA 12 fo. 213: Vendôme is frequently at court 'tant pour la consanguinité dont il nous actient que pour assister aux délibérations et traictemens des affaires'. Vendôme was at court for most of Dec. 1542–Jan. 1543.
[39] D. L. Potter, 'A Treason Trial in 16th Century France', *EHR* 105 (1990), 595–623; see also Potter, 'Introduction to the Correspondence of Du Biez' (unpublished).
[40] G. Zeller, 'Les gouverneurs de province au XVIe siècle', in *Aspects de la politique française sous l'Ancien Régime* (1964), 226–7. Revocation of governors' powers, 21 May 1542, BN fr. 3005 fo. 198; reinstatement, 23 May, *ibid.*, fo. 199, 200.

Picardy.[41] Such a unified command had also effectively existed under La Rochepot from 1538.

Though the duke of Vendôme was frequently in the province during the later years of Francis I, it was upon du Biez that the most continuous burden fell, and it was he who faced the onslaught of the English in 1544. After the fall of Boulogne, his enemies at court were not slow to undermine his credit with the king and underline his failure to recapture the place. It is therefore most interesting that the king's confidence held, despite a very shaky moment in February 1546 when de Taix received a temporary commission to replace him during a visit to court. Du Biez was obviously seeking to court the favour of his old patron Montmorency in these years, but the death of Francis I removed his only sure protector.[42]

On hearing of the king's death early in April 1547, du Biez wrote a series of rather desperate letters to the duke of Aumale, a favourite of the new king Henry II, and for the time being remained in his post. Almost at the start of the new reign, however, he was deprived of his post as marshal of France. On 12 April 1547, La Rochepot returned as governor of the Ile-de-France (probably with Vendôme's agreement).[43] Some time between then and June he was reinstalled as Vendôme's deputy in Picardy, since on 11 June Martin du Bellay was appointed governor in the absence of both Vendôme and La Rochepot. The latter was at that point presumably unable to take up active duties.[44] Du Bellay, already familiar with Picardy from the Boulonnais campaigns of 1544 and 1545, continued to assist La Rochepot throughout 1548 and 1549, while Gaspard de Coligny, as colonel-general of the French infantry, also played an active part.[45] The structure of the governorship had therefore become complex. For du Biez, the remaining years of his life were a torment of legal prosecution, condemnation and imprisonment, as his enemies cashed in on Henry II's antipathy to him and his association with those court figures

[41] AM Compiègne BB 20 fo. 5v (30 June 1544); fo. 13r (19 July 1544): 'gouverneur et lieutenant général pour le Roy ès pays de Picardie et Artois et gouverneur de l'Isle-de-France'. BM Beauvais, Coll. Bucquet 57, p. 587. *CAF* IX ignores this governorship.

[42] D. L. Potter, 'A Treason Trial in 16th Century France', 598, 606–9. On de Taix's commission, 5 March 1546, see *CAF* VII, 399, 25249 and *L&P* XXI, i, 262.

[43] D. L. Potter, 'A Treason Trial', 599. Vienna, HHuStA, Frankr. Varia 6 fo. 16–19 (report of 6 April); *CAH* I, p. 38 (governorship of Ile-de-France).

[44] *CAH* I no. 476 but N.B. the act for du Biez's interrogation, 13 June, still entitles him lieutenant-general of Picardy and captain of Boulogne (*ibid.* no. 495). In August 1547, La Rochepot is still called only governor of Ile-de-France (BN p.o. 2031 no. 92) but by March 1548 governor of Ile-de-France and lieutenant-general in Picardy in Vendôme's absence (*ibid.*, no. 93).

[45] On du Bellay as lieutenant, see Henri II to La Rochepot, 12, 30 Jan., 26 Feb. 1548, BN fr. 3035 fo. 86; fr. 3134 fo. 21; fr. 3035 fo. 93. He was still in post in December 1549, see L'Homel, *Nouveau Recueil*, 139.

overthrown in 1547. His son-in-law, Jacques de Coucy-Vervins, was executed in 1549.

The duke of Vendôme spent much of his time at court in the early years of Henry II, involved in negotiations for the hand of Jeanne d'Albret and the acquisition of new interests in the south-west. Inevitably, from 1548 he was drawn into the somewhat disaffected stance of the Albrets towards the French crown, though he did return to active service in Picardy between 1551 and 1554.[46] Martin du Bellay-Langey was given leave by the king in March 1550 and shortly afterwards replaced as governor in La Rochepot's absence by Jean d'Estouteville, sieur de Villebon, whose provisions were drawn up on 1 July. Villebon, another Montmorency protégé, was a Norman whose military career had brought him great experience as governor of Thérouanne and who had acquired lands around Montreuil.[47] La Rochepot was by now frail and he died in August 1551, when Coligny succeeded to the Ile-de-France and the command of Picardy remained in the hands of Vendôme and Villebon.[48]

From 1550, the command structure of the province becomes increasingly complex as a result of the appointment of purely military *lieutenants-généraux*. Villebon retained his title until the end of the reign, but was absent for periods. Most notably, he was blamed to some extent for the loss of Thérouanne in 1553 and had to be saved by Montmorency's intervention.[49] In October 1552, there was the brief appointment of the disgraced admiral, Claude d'Annebault. More notably, the king's favourite, Jacques d'Albon, sieur de Saint-André, commanded armies in the province after 1553 and periodically held the powers of lieutenant-general there. In 1553 he was first charged with putting the fortifications of Picardy in a state of defence and then in September, with

---

[46] A. de Ruble, *Antoine de Bourbon et Jeanne d'Albret*, 4 vols. (1881–6) I, 29. Vendôme was at court for the entry into Paris in 1549 (I. D. Macfarlane, *The Entry of Henri II into Paris, 16 June 1549* (1982) 63) and joined the early stages of the Boulogne campaign (François de Lorraine, duc de Guise, *Mémoires* (ed. Michaud and Poujoulat (1850) 9–10: hereafter *Mémoires de Guise*) but left for Vendôme in September (AN K 278/A fo. 81ff.). He returned to court in March 1550 and left for Picardy soon after, see Guise to Ercole II of Ferrara, BN fr. 20648 fo. 64–5.

[47] Du Bellay to Aumale, 3 March 1550. ˙ᵢN fr. 20456; Henri II to La Rochepot, 25 May 1550, BN fr. 3035 fo. 84: 'j'ay puisnaguères estably le sieur de Villebon mon lieutenant pardelà en vostre absence'. But the patent is not datcⁱ until 1 July, see P. Des Forts, *Le château de Villebon, Eure-et-Loire* (1914), 235–7 (AD Pas-de-Calais 9B 1 fo. 40–1). See also C. de La Morandière, *La maison d'Estouteville en Normandie* (1903).

[48] La Rochepot still retained his titles (BN Clair. 961 fo. 42) until his death (BN fr. 3116 p. 111). Coligny as governor of Ile-de-France: AM Compiègne BB 21 fo. 59v (6 Nov. 1552) with Jean de Lisle, sieur de Marivault, an associate of La Rochepot, as his deputy (*ibid.*, BB 22 fo. 19v).

[49] P. des Forts, *Le château de Villebon*, 31–2. His correspondence with the Humières family fades out between Sept. 1553 and 1557. For mentions of his activities as governor in that period: 29 Dec. 1553 (AM Amiens EE 323 no. 43); July 1554 (BN Clair. 961 fo. 43); 20 Sept. 1554 (Clair. 347 fo. 301); 18 Dec. 1555 (BN Cangé 62 fo. 9); 11 Feb. 1556 (AM Amiens EE 323 no. 66).

Vendôme's uncle the cardinal de Bourbon as lieutenant-general at Amiens, we find Saint-André as 'lieutenant-général au fait de guerre' throughout the province.[50] Vendôme had left for Béarn on rumours of Henri d'Albret's death and remained there until the spring of the following year.[51] Despite his return, Saint-André continued to command armies in the province and stayed as late as February 1555.[52]

A similar rôle may explain the position of another Bourbon prince, La Roche-sur-Yon, who was appointed 'lieutenant-général du Roy ès pays de Picardie, Normandie, Boullenoys et Artois' some time in June 1554, and from Rabutin's account seems to have been in command of forces at Saint-Quentin designed to ravage Artois while the main royal armies were occupied in the Ardennes. This was probably for one campaign only and he did not replace Villebon, who remained at Montreuil throughout this period.[53]

In the summer of 1555, with the death of the king of Navarre, major changes were required in the government of Picardy. In May it was rumoured that, on Navarre's death, Antoine de Bourbon would go to Guyenne and be replaced in Picardy by Saint-André. The latter indeed wrote to the city of Lyon, where he was governor, that 'je ne vouldroys, pour un meilleur gouvernement que cestui-cy, vous laisser, tant pour l'amytié que je vous porte que pour beaucoup d'autres raisons que je vous diray quelquefoys'.[54] Antoine received his patent as governor of Guyenne on 27 July; one month earlier, Gaspard de Coligny had been appointed in his place with the same powers. It may readily be surmised that his uncle, the constable, desired to consolidate the hold of the family

---

[50] Royal commission, 15 Oct. 1552: the emperor has attacked Picardie and La Fère in particular, but has seen the good order taken by 'nostre trèscher et trèsamé cousin le sieur d'Annebault admiral de France, que nous y avons estably nostre lieutenant général', AM Compiègne BB 21 fo. 54r. Annebault died at La Fère on 2 Nov. 1552, see Pierre de Bourdeille, sr. de Brantôme, *Œuvres complètes*, ed. L. Lalanne (SHF, 11 vols., 1864–82) III, 205–11.

[51] Vendôme was absent at court and then in Anjou, Jan.–March 1553. Royal commission, 9 March 1553, AM Péronne BB 9 fo. 273–4: 'nous envoyons nostre trèscher et amé cousin le sieur de Sainct André . . . en certaines villes et places de nostre frontière de Picardie'. On his involvement in the campaigns of April–July, see L. Romier, *La carrière d'un favori: Jacques d'Albon, maréchal de Saint-Andre* (1909), 93–116. On the lieutenancy of Amiens, see *Inventaire sommaire, Amiens* II, 393. The post was revived for François de Montmorency in 1557. On Saint-André's second period of lieutenancy, see *ordonnance* by him, 5 Oct. 1553 (BM Abbeville MS 378 fo. 153–4).

[52] *Mémoires de Guise*, 212. Gorguette, 'Thieulaine', 162, makes the connection with Vendôme's departure for Béarn. Vendôme spent the winter there (see A. de Ruble, *Antoine de Bourbon et Jeanne d'Albret* I, 77–8) and joined the constable's camp at Etréaupont in June 1554. Saint-André was also back in Picardy in spring 1554 (BN fr. 3128 fo. 65). In Feb. 1555, he was at Montcornet, see L. Romier, *Jacques d'Albon*.

[53] AM Péronne BB 9 fo. 344r (27 June 1554); BM Abbeville MS 378 fo. 136–7 (1 July); AM Amiens AA 14 fo. 40v (18 July 1554). F. de Rabutin, *Commentaires des guerres de la Gaule Belgique* (SHF ed., 2 vols., 1932–42); Gorguette, 'Thieulaine', 185; La Roche-sur-Yon to Guise, 12 July 1554, BN Clair. 347 fo. 255.

[54] L. Romier, *Jacques d'Albon*, p. j.xiii, p. 427 (12 May 1555).

in key provincial governorships. The Ile-de-France was becoming a Montmorency fief, earmarked for the constable's eldest son (then in Imperial captivity), and Coligny would maintain the family interest on the frontier. The day he heard of Henry d'Albret's death, the king wrote in his own hand to the constable:

> pour se que je ne sé si aves james parlé à monsieur l'amyral pour prendre le gouvernement de Picardye, et aussy quy voulut garder seluy de l'Yle-de-France, jusques à se que votre fyls fut hors de pryson, car je tousjours a fayt accroyre à tous seux quy sont après de moy que je n'en voulois fair que ung gouvernement, et me semble quy n'y aura poynt de mal que an mandyes ung mot à monsieur l'amyral, afin quy soyt averti de tout quant je luy an parleré.[55]

It would seem strange that the king should still be unaware at this point of the constable's negotiations with Coligny. It is possible that Vendôme would have liked to pass Picardy on to his brother Condé (who did not obtain the governorship until 1561), but the king seems to have been opposed at this stage and the argument that the two provinces should be commanded by the same governor was, as has already been seen, a powerful one. Villebon continued as deputy governor under Coligny.[56]

There are signs that Coligny was not entirely happy with his new position, though he was an energetic governor. He was probably aware of opposition to his appointment and manoeuvres against him at court. After his return from the truce negotiations at Brussels in 1556, he tried to resign in order to concentrate on his post as admiral, but was dissuaded by the king. On 26 August, though, he wrote to Montmorency to explain his reaction to what he took to be a cool reception on his return from Brussels:

> Vous sçavez monseigneur que la recompence de Dieu et des hommes est du tout differente de l'une et a l'autre, car celle de Dieu est après notre mort, et celle du monde durant nostre vie . . . je vous dicts ce propos pource que de ce dernier voiage je n'ay eu ny gracieuse parolle, ny aultre démonstration pour laquelle ny moy ny les aultres hommes puissions juger que le Roy aie contantement de moy.[57]

---

[55] Henry II to Péronne, 28 July 1555, AM BB 9 fo. 397; Coligny's provisions, 27 June 1555, BN Clair. 961 fo. 45; J. Shimizu, *Conflict of Loyalties: Politics and Religion in the Career of Gaspard de Coligny* (1970), 18–19; Henri II to constable, BN fr. 3122 fo. 9 (J. Delaborde, *Gaspard de Coligny, amiral de France* (3 vols., 1879–82) I, 149).

[56] Delaborde, *Coligny* I, 144; J. L. Desormeaux, *Histoire de la maison de Bourbon*, 5 vols. (1772–88) III, 241. Also, Sénarpont may have been a temporary substitute for Villebon in July 1556, see Coligny to Humières, 12/13 July 1556, BN fr. 3128 fo. 91, 92. He is entitled 'lieutenant de monsieur l'admiral au gouvernement de Picardye' in 1556, see AM Saint-Quentin, 138 no. 19, fo. 9–15.

[57] BN fr. 31222 fo. 40–41.

This sense of grievance may have been accentuated by the odd events accompanying the renewal of war in January 1557. It is often assumed that having negotiated the truce, Coligny was opposed to a renewal of war and had only reluctantly agreed to execute a royal order for a surprise attack on Douai on 6 January. There is not much evidence for this. At any rate, the coup failed and, whatever the previous policy at court, the admiral was told to maintain peace on the frontier for as long as possible and to return the spoils of the raid. Coligny's distinct annoyance is indicated by a counter-order to Humières, 'car monsieur le Connestable ny autre peut sçavoir l'estat des affaires de mon gouvernement'. Either because he had executed the raid without full authorisation or because he had done so unsuccessfully, the attitude of the court was rather cool towards him in the early months of 1557.[58] Nevertheless, the admiral remained at his post despite a sense of grievance and supervised the opening months of the war. His position exemplifies the difficulties of a governor whose landed interests were not deeply rooted in his *gouvernement* and whose position rested heavily on royal favour.

The capture of Coligny at Saint-Quentin, following the great defeat on Saint Laurence's day 1557, posed considerable problems of reorganisation in a province which was now partly occupied and subject to continuing enemy activity. Normally the deputy governor, Villebon, could have taken over Coligny's responsibilities, but the situation was grave and other provisions were essential. Villebon, at Amiens when he heard of the fall of Saint-Quentin, was told by the king to move to Corbie, which seemed next on the enemy's list. Forces there were in great disorder and he remained until late October, except for a conference held at Compiègne.[59] From a beleaguered Corbie he could not hope to keep watch on the whole frontier so, with Jean de Monchy-Sénarpont (governor of Boulogne) in command of the maritime region, we find the duke of Nevers, governor of Champagne, responsible for looking after the Picard strongholds at his end of the frontier. He may have received a formal appointment as governor of Picardy in September and was still addressed as such in November.[60]

These were temporary arrangements and a new régime of a more permanent kind was obviously needed. There had been great disarray at court at the news from Saint-Quentin, 'dont je reçoy ung ennuy et desplaisir tel que vous pouvez

---

[58] Coligny to Humières, 17 Jan. 1557, BN fr. 3125, pp. 75–6. The whole issue is thoroughly discussed in F. J. Baumgartner, *Henri II* (1987), appendix C.

[59] Villebon to Humières, 28/30 Aug. 1557, BN fr. 3128 fo. 112, 113; Henri II to same, 31 Aug. BN fr. 3134 fo. 66–7. Villebon was at Péronne in late October (BN fr. 3149 fo. 24; AM Péronne BB 10 fo. 55–6) and Compiègne again mid-November (BN fr. 3128 fo. 138).

[60] See letter to Nevers add. as 'gouverneur et lieutenant général du Roy en Champaigne et Picardye', 7 Nov. 1557, BN Cangé 62 (F 220), fo. 50; Villebon to Humières, 17 Sept. fr. 3128 fo. 136.

bien penser', as the king wrote to Humières. Further strongholds like Le Câtelet and Ham continued to fall and the king's initial plan to assemble a new field army within a month was impracticable.[61] Above all, the battle was a severe blow to the power of the Montmorencys, though this was not at first apparent as the king sent the constable's eldest son, François, to Amiens as a special lieutenant (a position similar to that held by the cardinal de Bourbon in September 1553).[62] The cardinal of Lorraine was now the only capable minister at court, and his brother the duke of Guise was being viewed increasingly as the saviour of the kingdom. He had received orders to return from Rome on 14 September and had reached Marseilles by 20 September. With the enemy operating as far as Chauny, Claude de L'Aubespine, not surprisingly, hailed the duke's arrival at court on 1 October as 'la chose dont le Roy et le royaume avoient et ont plus de besoing aux affaires qui s'offrent'. Guise was rapidly commissioned as lieutenant-general of the kingdom and all military officials subordinated to him. He may also have been appointed 'lieutenant-général pour le Roi en picardie'.[63] Town governors and officials hastened to report to him and offer their services, no doubt judging it expedient to adjust to the new régime. It was Guise who henceforth seems to have coordinated reports from the governors and captains in the province, and the secretary hitherto responsible for the correspondence of the court with Picardy, Jacques Bourdin, was attached to the duke as a kind of personal secretary of state.[64]

A conference took place at Compiègne in mid-October at which Villebon, Nevers and most of the other lesser governors of the region met the duke of Guise to explore what enterprises might be possible. No clear decision had yet been made to move against Calais, but this emerged in the subsequent consultation with the king and before the duke's return to Compiègne early in November. From about 9 November he was established there, issuing daily orders to the commanders.[65] What had emerged was a new structure of command in which Villebon and the lesser governors were responsible first to

---

[61] Henri II to Humières, 29 Aug. 1557, BN fr. 3134 fo. 64–5 (*Mémoires de Guise*, 381–2); Villebon to Humières, 12/13 Sept., BN fr. 3128 fo. 134.

[62] Villebon to Humières, 8 Sept. 1557, BN fr. 3128 fo. 129; provisions for Montmorency, 5 Sept., AM Amiens AA 14 fo. 112v. He was replaced first by Morvilliers, capt. of Amiens, *ibid.*, AA 14 fo. 115, and then by Antoine de Crussol-Tonnerre, *ibid.*, EE 323 no. 150, letter of 15 Aug. 1558.

[63] Guise to Henri II, Rome, 14 Sept. 1557, BN fr. 20645 fo. 88; L'Aubespine to Guise, 1 Oct., fr. 20529 fo. 13–14. For a document in which Guise is entitled governor of Picardy, see AD Somme B 1 fo. 4–5.

[64] For letters to Guise from captains in Picardy, Oct. 1557, see BN fr. 20529 fo. 21–2, 53, 65–6, 83–4. For letters to him from Villebon and Humières and La Mothe-Rouge on appointments and musters, see BN fr. 20470 p. 125, fr. 20529 fo. 57, 59–60.

[65] D. L. Potter, 'The Duke of Guise and the Fall of Calais', *EHR* 98 (1983), 487–9.

the duke of Guise, who now more or less controlled the state correspondence for the province. Villebon began a tour of inspection, visiting Péronne in the first half of November, attending another conference at Compiègne around 20 November and then setting off for maritime Picardy.[66]

The arrangements made for the command and administration of the province during the active campaigning of 1558 that began with the march on Calais and did not end until the conference at Cercamp in the autumn naturally reflected the confusions of the period. Guise, as lieutenant-general of the kingdom and governor of Picardy, was often present himself in the region, especially during the summer campaign. Routine matters were looked after by the military commanders under him but they were subject to the fortunes of war. At the time of Guise's arrival before Calais, Villebon was at Compiègne, the base camp for the operation, with orders from the king to look after both the landward province and the Ile-de-France. His brief from the duke included raids to give support to Chauny and to threaten the Burgundian position at Ham. On Guise's triumphal return to court in February, Villebon moved to Abbeville but went to court early in April in a vain attempt to persuade the king to give him leave of absence to go to his estates (during this time, Sénarpont, as he had before, acted as his lieutenant in maritime Picardy).[67]

Villebon's place at Compiègne was taken by François de Montmorency, already governor of the Ile-de-France and royal lieutenant at Amiens. There was need, said the king, of a

> personnage d'autorité qui soit pour y résider et avoid l'œil et pourvoir aux choses qui s'offriront par delà, non seulement pour la seureté, conservation et défence des places fortes de la frontière de Picardye et du gouvernement de l'Isle de France mais aussi du plat pays.

The king's order to Humières: 'defferez et obéissez à mond. filz en tout ce qu'il vous commandera' clearly gives Montmorency full governor's powers in Picardy.[68] Yet again, a distinction had emerged between the military needs of

---

[66] Villebon to Humières, 19 Nov. 1557 BN fr. 3128 fo. 138: 'sela faict, je m'en retourneray à l'autre bout de ce gouvernement pour veoir comme tout y porte'.

[67] Villebon to Guise, 1 Jan. 1558, BN fr. 23191 fo. 5–6; same to Humières, 3 Jan., BN fr. 3128 fo. 96; Fontaines to Guise, 2 Jan. 1558, BN fr. 23191 fo. 19. Villebon to Saint-Martin, Abbeville, 25 Feb. 1558, BN fr. 3128 fo. 97; same to Guise, 22 March, BN nafr. 21638 fo. 490: 'les affaires ne sont si grandes que monsieur de Sénarpont n'y donne bien ordre jusques à mon retour'. Henry II to Villebon, 27 March 1558, *ibid.*, fo. 45: order to tell Sénarpont of the day of his departure so he can take order 'ainsi qu'il a faict ci devant quant vous n'y avez poinct esté.' The king ordered him back in mid-April, see BN fr. 3128 fo. 139 and Des Forts, *Le château de Villebon*, p. j. no. 63. Sénarpont was *barilli* of Amiens from Jan. 1550.

[68] Henri II to Humières, 19 Feb. 1558, BN fr. 3134 fo. 54; François de Montmorency to same, 22 Feb., fr. 3116, p. 333; to Guise, 23 Feb. fr. 20471, p. 111; Guise to Montmorency, 25 Feb., *ibid.*, pp. 115–16, draft.

the landward and maritime regions of the province. Subsequently Guise's brother Aumale emerges as king's lieutenant in landward Picardy. At what point he replaced François de Montmorency is uncertain, but this had been done by May.[69] The governmental arrangements thus outlined were brusquely overturned when a raiding expedition from Calais ended in the disaster of the battle in the dunes along the coast from Gravelines. In this, almost the last fight of the Habsburg–Valois conflict, Villebon, Sénarpont and Termes, the governor of Calais, along with many other captains, fell into enemy hands. For the moment, the province was without either governor or deputy governor. The arrival of Guise and later of the king himself at Amiens, with the task of retrieving the defeat, temporarily filled the gap. Some time in August, new appointments were made to the many vacant posts, though the exact dates are uncertain. Antoine d'Alègre, baron de Meilhaud and the vidame de Chartres were at Boulogne and Calais by September. It seems likely that the replacement for Villebon, Louis Prévost, sieur de Sansac, received his provisions some time in August.[70]

Sansac's appointment was significant as a further attempt by Guise to increase his influence in the province by inserting a dependable deputy there. Sansac was not from Picardy but had acquired considerable military experience there, notably under the duke of Guise in 1549.[71] When the duke returned to court in October 1558, he left Sansac in Picardy as sole governor. The termination of his appointment is unclear. The Ferrarese ambassador noted in mid-January 1559 that Andelot, Coligny's brother, had been appointed the latter's lieutenant in Picardy having already in December been reinstated as colonel-general of the infantry in place of Monluc. He explained this by the restored influence of Montmorency, who had by now returned from captivity, and placed it in the context of a desire to undo all that Guise and his friends had

---

[69] There are no provisions for Aumale, but he was 'established' by the king in May (letter to Humières, 25 May, BN fr. 3134 fo. 90) and carried out these duties May–July, when there are eighteen despatches from him at La Fère to Humières (BN fr. 3123 *passim*).

[70] Villebon to Humières, Dunkirk, 5 July 1558, BN fr. 3128 fo. 150; Henri de Montmorency to his mother, 19 July, fr. 20500 fo. 52. Sansac to Guise, 25 Aug. 1558, fr. 20536 fo. 45–6: 'charges qui me seront par Sa Magesté, et vous, commises et ordonnées'. Sansac to Humières, 27 Oct., fr. 3128 fo. 138: 'Le Roy m'a laissé en ce pais, là où il m'a commandé demeurer pour quelque temps.' The vidame was at Calais by 21 Sept. (BN fr. 3134 fo. 49) and Meilhaud at Boulogne by 6 Nov. (fr. 23192 fo. 27), though the term of his appointment was 19 Sept. 1558 to 28 May 1559, see P. de Vaissière, *Une famille. Les d'Alègre* (1914), 30–1. He was replaced at Boulogne by another Protestant, Morvilliers.

[71] Sansac, of an illustrious Angoumois family, commanded light horse in Picardy in 1538, at Hardelot in 1548 (BN fr. 20511 fo. 16) and Abbeville in 1557. Guise ensured his appointment as lieutenant at Montdidier in Nov. 1557 (fr. 20537 fo. 33). He was particularly hated by the Protestants in 1562.

done in the previous year. However, although Sansac's correspondence ceases in April, this is the only mention of Andelot's lieutenancy and it is possible that the release of both Coligny and Villebon from captivity made his tenure a very brief one.[72]

Almost immediately on his return after the peace, Villebon was transferred, perhaps on his own request, to his native Normandy and on 20 May 1559, his fellow captive, Jean de Monchy, sieur de Sénarpont, received a formal appointment as lieutenant in Coligny's absence, a post which he had already more than once filled unofficially. Coligny continued as governor to deal with the affairs of the province, but preoccupations elsewhere precluded many visits. It was Sénarpont who was doing most of the work and receiving royal instructions.[73]

During 1559 and 1560 the governorship of Picardy became increasingly embroiled with the factional struggles which accompanied the death of Henry II and the emplacement of the Guise regime at court. In January 1560, Coligny was finally edged out of the governorship and replaced by Charles de Cossé-Brissac, the governor of Piedmont, arguably a more reliably Catholic figure. The circumstances quickly became a matter of speculation. The admiral gave the official view when informing Humières of the change:

> Il y a quelques temps que considérant que les deux charges que j'avoys estoient fort grandes pour bien pouvoir satisfaire à toutes deux, je désirois que je peusse avecques le bon plaisir du Roy me descharger du Gouvernement de Picardye.

While it is certainly true that Coligny had already expressed doubts about his position, such scruples over pluralism were by no means common in this period. Protestant partisans saw the hand of the Guise in all this but, though Brissac was certainly regarded as a Guisard, his biographer implies that Catherine de Medici was the real author of the appointment. Villars, in fact, claimed that when informed on 28 January about the offer, Brissac replied that as Coligny's resignation 'ne pourroit avoir esté faicte que par quelque occasion peu favorable', he could not accept the post. He added that he was too old and tired and had not been given the support he had needed in Piedmont.[74] On the

---

[72] L. Romier, *Les origines politiques des guerres de religion*, 2 vols. (1913–14) II, 327. Sansac's last letter, Abbeville, 2 April 1559, is to Amiens (AM Amiens AA 14 fo. 158). Guise obtained the governorship of the Dauphin for him in November 1558, see P. Courteault, *Blaise de Monluc, historien* (1908), 380. BN fr. 23192 fo. 257, 22 Nov. 1558.

[73] Sénarpont's provisions, 20 May 1559, AD Pas-de-Calais 9B 2 fo. 98v–100r. Des Forts, *Le château de Villebon*, 35, 288–9. Coligny to Amiens, Péronne, 6 June 1559, AM Amiens AA 14 fo. 163; to Humières, 29 Aug. 1559, 20 Jan. 1560, BN fr. 3128 fo. 163, 162. All other surviving despatches of the period are from Sénarpont.

[74] Coligny to Humières, 20 Jan. 1559, BN fr. 3128 fo. 162. Catherine's letter to Brissac, 28 Jan. 1560 is summarised in F. de Boyvin, baron du Villars, *Mémoires* (Michaud et Poujoulat, 1850), 363. The letter is uncollected in H. de La Ferrière, *Lettres de Catherine de Médicis*, 10 vols.

other hand, the Protestant La Planche argues that the duke of Guise, at the time of Francis II's coronation, had told Coligny that Condé wanted the governorship and that the admiral had given way in order to be cooperative. There had actually been a rumour in July 1559 that Condé would replace Coligny in Picardy as part of a general displacement of the constable's relatives. It looked like a plot to drive a wedge between Condé and Coligny.[75]

One of his biographers has argued that the admiral's policy of working with the queen mother at this time may lie behind his cooperation. Certainly, we know that Catherine told Brissac that she had pressed for his appointment, and in February 1560 it was reported that:

> Monsieur l'Admiral par bon et prudent advis a quitté et remis entre les mains du Roy le gouvernement de Picardie sans qu'il en fust pressé ny requis, et j'estime qu'il sera baillé à M. de Brissac.

The change may also be explained by Coligny's failure to obtain support from court for a project to refortify the frontier and thus restore his military reputation. Possibly all these considerations came into play at some stage.[76]

Coligny may have expected his place to be taken by Condé, the natural candidate for the succession. If so, both were surprised by the appointment of an outsider. For Catherine, Brissac's loyalty to the crown may have counted for more than his known anti-Protestant views. His main disadvantage was lack of local connections. La Place reveals that Condé had written to Catherine and the Lorraines:

> rémonstrant que ledict gouvernement avoit esté par cy-devant exercé fidèlement par ses prédécesseurs, et naguères par le roy de Navarre son frère, et dans lequel la pluspart de ses biens estoient assis.

Condé was both the senior representative of the Bourbon-Vendôme house in the north and the husband of a great Picard heiress, Léonore de Roye. He was,

---

(889–1909). Brissac's provisions, dated 31 March 1560, ment. in C. Marchand, *Charles Ier de Cossé, comte de Brissac et maréchal de France, 1507–63* (1889), 473 (after Pinard, *Chronologie historique-militaire*, 8 vols., 1760–72, II, 269–70, based on the then existing *comptes de l'extraordinaire des guerres*: suggesting that Brissac made his entry into Amiens in May). Chantonnay to Philip II, 2 Feb. 1560, *Archivo Documental Español: Negociaciones con Francia*, 9 vols. (1950–4) I, 176. A. de Ruble, *Antoine de Bourbon* II, 50–2, accepts that Guise machinations were behind the change.

75 R. de La Planche, *Histoire de l'estat de France tant de la République que de la Religion sous le règne de François II*, ed. Buchon, Panthéon Littéraire (1836), 216–17; P. de La Place, *Commentaires de l'estat de la Religion et République*, ed. Buchon (1836), 27. On rumours about Coligny, see P. Forbes, *A Full View of the Transactions in the Reign of Queen Elizabeth*, 2 vols. (1740–1) I, 159.

76 Shimizu, *Conflict of Loyalties*, 34, 38–9; Boisset Salignac to Noailles, 15 Feb. 1560, BN Clair. 961, copy. L. Paris, *Négotiations, lettres et pièces diverses relatives au règne de François II* (1841), 213–14; L. Romier, *La conjuration d'Amboise* (1923), 93–4.

however, increasingly out of sympathy with the court in 1560. La Place makes
clear that he was 'mal content du refus' that he received over the governorship.[77]

By the time Brissac had returned from Piedmont (June or July 1560), Condé
had been involved in the Conspiracy of Amboise and was under attack.
Brissac's position, however, was not easy either. At first welcomed at court,
he found the political situation complex; though on good terms with the Guise,
his first loyalty was, as Tavannes makes clear, to the queen mother. In Picardy,
the gendarmerie companies in garrison, those of Sénarpont and Bouchavannes,
were devoted to Condé. Moreover, he found himself charged with suppressing
the violence in the aftermath of the Conspiracy. There is little evidence that he
was able to make his authority felt in the province and the main burden fell on
Sénarpont. Their relationship could not have been easy and during September–
October 1560, Sénarpont seems briefly to have been replaced by Louis
d'Ognies, sieur de Chaulnes. Then in October Chaulnes was called to court,
and authority effectively was divided on an *ad hoc* basis between Sénarpont at
Abbeville and Humières at Péronne.[78]

The claims of the prince of Condé remained strong despite his unaccept-
ability to Catholics. After the death of Francis II and his release from detention,
he went first to La Fère and then returned to court where, on 15 March, he was
admitted to the council. His rehabilitation by the Parlement was proclaimed on
13 June and in August he was publicly reconciled with the Guise. Brissac's
biographer suggests that Condé held no personal grudge against Brissac for his
holding the governorship that he considered rightly his own. However, Brissac
could not hide his opposition to Protestantism at a time, in the autumn of 1561,
when its fortunes were rising.[79]

[77] C. Marchand, *Brissac*, 479; La Place, *Commentaires*, 27.
[78] G. de Saulx, sr. de Tavannes, *Mémoires* (ed. Michaud et Poujoulat 1836), 227: Brissac
'S'estoit faict sage par sa défaveur, regardant néantmoins à la Royne, qui lui fit donner le
gouvernement de Picardie refusé au prince de Condé', a memoir written of course in the later
sixteenth century by Jean de Saulx and based on his father's recollections. La Planche, *Histoire
de l'estat de France*, 364. Chantonnay's despatches of 31 Aug. and 13 Sept. 1560, *Archivo
Documental* I, p. 341, 393. For documents naming Chaulnes as governor: 20 Sept. 1560, BM
Abbeville MS 378 fo. 111r, 112r. Sénarpont was back as governor, 4 Oct. (*ibid.*, fo. 112v).
Francis II to Humières, 7 Oct. 1560, L. Paris (ed.), *Négociations . . . de François II*, 672.
[79] Duc d'Aumale, *Histoire des princes de Condé* 8 vols. (1863–96) I, 99; Marchand, *Brissac*,
485–6. Chantonnay, 28 Dec. 1560, *Archivo Documental* I, p. 518: Condé 'han llevado hacia
Picardia a Han y a otra de las terras que tiene por allí su hermano'. See also letters of Condé to
Brissac, 25 May 1558, BN fr. 20526 fo. 67; 8 July 1559, BL Add. MS 38033 fo. 387v, copy:
mentioning 'ceste bonne volunté dont vous me faites continuelle démonstration'. K. Neuschel,
The Prince of Condé and the Nobility of Picardy does not discuss the circumstances of the
appointment nor does D. F. Secousse, ed. of *Mémoires de Condé, ou Recueil pour servir à
l'Histoire de France*, 6 vols. (1743), which prints most documents on the prince's public
career.

It was at this time that Condé finally replaced Brissac as governor. On 9 October, Nicholas Throckmorton reported that:

> it is thought the prince of Conde shall be governour of Picardie, which charge the marshall Brysac had: in recompence whereof the marshall Brysac his son shall be coronell of the foettemen in Piedmont.

Throckmorton's spy at court reported the official explanation for the change as being that Brissac had been 'fort malade', but a Catholic view, that of the papal cnvoy, was that the change was 'di male consequentia'.[80] Condé's letters of provision had been made out at Saint-Germain on 3 October and appealed specifically to his hereditary claims on the governorship, and on 9 October Sénarpont was already writing of the new appointment (in a letter to the *sénéchaussée* of Boulogne) that 'nous n'en sommes petitement heureux'. By 5 October Condé was already receiving royal orders on troop movements in the province.[81]

Condé's appointment may be seen as part of a contemplated general displacement of governors who were favourable to the Guise. Though most of the proposed changes did not take effect, J. W. Thompson's view that Condé's appointment never became effective because of the outbreak of civil war is incorrect. Condé was receiving routine instructions as governor from October 1561. However, the general position of the Protestants deteriorated sharply at the end of 1561 with the formation of the 'Triumvirate'. In mid-December, Condé and Coligny were reported to be in great doubt and to have left court for Paris, though they continued influential with the regent.[82]

In mid-December, Condé warned Amiens of his imminent arrival to punish Catholic sedition in the town, under the terms of royal orders for the suppression of religious violence, and preparations were started for his reception. He also ordered the expulsion of Protestant refugees, though 'le plus

---

[80] Throckmorton to Elizabeth I, 9 Oct. 1561, PRO SP 70/31 fo. 22; report of 12 Oct. 1561, *ibid.*, fo. 40; *ANG* XIV, 368, diario, 10 Oct. 1561. Chantonnay saw the appointment as part of a concerted Protestant offensive, at first involving Andelot's succession also as marshal, see despatches of 30 Sept., 8 and 16 Oct. 1561, *Archivo Documental* II, p. 443, 478, 498.

[81] AN X/1A 8624 fo. 109: 'CHARLES, Par le Roy, la Royne sa mère, le Roy de Navarre et autres présens, Bourdin.' 'Lecta et publicata . . . ordinatione tamen facta per curiam quod dictus princeps de Condé in albo nominatus pretextu neque sub colore contentorum in dicto albo non poterit derogare seu preiudicare auctoritatibus seu preeminentiis curie neque cuicumque jurisdictioni ordinarie.' Sénarpont to *sénéchaussée* of Boulogne, 9 Oct. 1561, AD Pas-de-Calais 9B 2 fo. 206r; Charles IX to Condé, 5 Oct., *ibid.*, fo. 203.

[82] On these projected appointments of November 1561, cf. Throckmorton, 14 Nov., in *CSPF* IV, no. 659 (Grammont to Calais, Coligny to Normandy, La Roche-sur-Yon to Paris). J. W. Thompson, *The French Wars of Religion* (1957), 126. Routine instructions to Condé: 3/6 Nov. 1561 (AM Amiens AA 14 fo. 187, BB 35), 7 Nov. (AD Pas-de-Calais 9B 2 fo. 204v). *CSPF* IV, nos. 729, 735.

doulcement et modestement que faire se poulroit'.[83] However, the *échevinage* of Amiens was now deeply divided over religion and it is clear that a group of Catholic magistrates were sharply opposed to Condé. Calling themselves 'le plus sayne partie de manans et habitans', they had gone behind his back to the constable and Condé's brother the king of Navarre in order to ask for their maintenance of the traditional faith. It was a manoeuvre, the prince said, that 'j'ay trouvé estrange et prins de mauvaise part que aucuns députez venans de vostredicte ville, m'ayent tant dédaigné que de prendre aultre adresse'.[84]

Condé never managed to get to Picardy before the outbreak of fighting. The Edict of January proved the final straw for the Catholic leadership and, during that month, the prince was ill at Paris. When he was sufficiently recovered to return to court at Saint-Germain in February, he found greater hostility. He resolved to go back to Paris to see the Edict published early in March and, arriving on 16 March, the same day as the duke of Guise, cancelled his plans to go to Picardy and attended instead a mass sermon in order to encourage the reformers.[85]

The outbreak of the Religious Wars, with the massacre of Vassy and Condé's move to Orléans, changed everything. The court moved in his absence to assure its control of Amiens by remodelling the *échevinage* and, under the fiction that Condé had been detailed at Orléans against his will, appointed his brother Charles cardinal de Bourbon in his place as governor of Picardy. At the same time, the *général des finances* Estourmel displaced Morvilliers as captain of the city. The cardinal entered Amiens on 27 July and a new era of civil wars had begun.[86]

The exact circumstances in which the provincial governors were appointed must be understood before their activities can be placed in a more general context. At this stage it can be concluded that some subtle changes had occurred over the century from 1470. First, of the sixteen individuals holding the *lieutenance-général* from 1477 to 1538, nine were local lords, five were outsiders with some interest in the province and only one was a clear outsider. Of the fifteen holding the same position between 1538 and 1562, there were six local lords and nine fairly clear outsiders. This is despite the immensely strong tradition of appointing a member of the house of Bourbon-Vendôme to the

[83] Reports of 13/17 Dec. 1561 (AM Amiens BB 35 fo. 30, 32) and Thierry, *Tiers État* II, 700.
[84] Condé to Amiens, 11 Jan. 1562, AM Amiens BB 35 fo. 44 (Thierry, *Tiers État* II, 703). *Echevinage* of 29 Jan. 1562, *ibid.*, BB 35 fo. 41v.
[85] Throckmorton to Elizabeth I, 16 Feb. 1562, *CSPF* IV, no. 891; 6 March, *ibid.*, no. 924; 9/20 March, *ibid.*, no. 930, 943.
[86] Charles IX to Amiens, Vincennes, 21 July 1562, AM Amiens AA 5 fo. 327 (no text of provisions for Bourbon); provisions for Estourmel, 16 July 1562, *ibid.*, AA 5 fo. 326v. Entry of cardinal de Bourbon into Amiens, *Inventaire sommaire, Amiens* IV, 522–4; E. Saulnier, *Le rôle politique du cardinal de Bourbon* (1912), 33–4.

senior governorship. The needs of war brought a more rapid turnover in personnel as well as the more frequent appointment of deputy governors who were men of military capacity without deep local roots. One further point will be discussed in chapter 3. With few exceptions, the important middle-ranking families (Créqui, Humières, Heilly etc.) did not obtain the governorship for any significant period. Though sometimes influential at court, their field of activity was decidedly local and more concerned with the subordinate governorships.

Lastly, what role did these governors play in the royal council? Though Louis XI seems generally to have excluded his Picard and Flemish 'converts' from the active work of the council, those who owed their all to Louis XI were brought in to buttress the Beaujeu régime after 1483 and, of the governors of Picardy, Esquerdes, Gié, Graville and Piennes were all active members of the council in the two decades around 1500. By contrast, under Francis I, although the two dukes of Vendôme were members of the council and sometimes attended, they were not (except for 1525–6) members of the executive *conseil privé*, nor were any of their deputy governors. Only under Henri II, with Picardy playing an increasingly central role in military strategy, was this trend reversed, with Coligny a member of the *conseil privé* and Saint-André of the inner *conseil des affaires*.[87]

---

[87] M. Harsgor, *Recherches* I, *passim*; for presence of the dukes of Vendôme in the council: *Ordonnances, François Ier* IV, nos. 370, 397; V, 445, 495; VII, 672; VIII, 776; IX 837.

3

--- ✥ ---

THE GOVERNORS' STAFF AND
HOUSEHOLD

What was the area over which the provincial governors exercised their authority? Godard, in 1949, put the case aptly when he said that 'au cours des guerres, le mot Picardie avait pris un sense militaire, mais restait extrèmement imprécis'.[1] It was indeed military necessity which shaped the province and, in the first half of the sixteenth century, there were still enclaves and exemptions which rendered a clear geographical definition of the province difficult. By 1560, however, custom was beginning to introduce a greater degree of clarity.

In the reign of Louis XI, the governor's powers covered at first only that part of the Somme region which owed allegiance to the king of France – the 'marches de Picardie' – but the reconquests of the 1470s naturally led to an extension of that authority. In addition, new territory seems to have fallen within the governor's sphere with the acquisition of the county of Boulogne and large parts of Artois. Even though Charles VIII formally abandoned his claims to Artois in 1493, certain enclaves remained under French jurisdiction (the most important of which was Thérouanne) and for this reason the governors were still in 1560 entitled 'lieutenant-général du roi en Picardie et Artois'.[2]

The exact status of Boulogne might seem ambivalent. Later in the ancien régime, the county had a governor of its own but, throughout the sixteenth century, the *sénéchal* and governor there were always subordinated to the governor of Picardy, though until 1494 these were the same in the person of the

---

[1] J. Godard *et al.*, *Visages de la Picardie* (1967). E. Lambert, 'Les limites de la Picardie', *Société archéol., hist., et scientifique de Noyon: comptes rendus et mémoires* 34 (1972), 53–65.
[2] Sénarpont was thus entitled in 1559. An *ordonnance* by him in Jan. 1561 makes this clear (BM Abbeville, MS 378 fo. 116v). The regent of Netherlands protested against this usage, 1546. See AD Nord B944, act of opposition by Mary of Hungary to Vendôme's use of the title 'governor of Artois' in his act of homage for lands in the Netherlands.

92

marshal d'Esquerdes. A little later, Francis I clearly regarded Boulogne as part of the 'pays de Picardie' and its governor Lafayette as subordinate to M. de Piennes.[3] Later still, although du Biez as governor of Boulogne may have enjoyed a special relationship with the court, he was still responsible to the governor of Picardy and, when he himself moved to the higher position, a new governor was appointed for Boulogne in his place.[4] During the campaign for the reconquest of the county from the English in 1549, Coligny was appointed (9 Sept. 1549) lieutenant-general 'èsdites places et pais reconquis de Boulennois par nous nouvellement conquis, et que nous pourrons cy après conquérir', well before Boulogne itself was surrendered by the English. However, Coligny was specifically made governor 'en l'absence et sous l'authorité de nosdites cousins les duc de Vendosmois et le sieur de La Rochepot'.[5]

By the time of Villebon's appointment in La Rochepot's absence, however, both Vendôme and La Rochepot were declared lieutenants-general 'en Picardie et oud. pais de Boullenois'.[6] Boulonnais had therefore returned to its former status, for Villebon in 1554 was still entitled 'lieutenant-général ès pays de Picardie, Arthoys et Boullenoys'. Though Coligny's letters of provision in 1555 make no direct mention of Boulonnais, this is certainly implied, and Sénarpont's letters in 1559 specifically mention Boulonnais as part of his territory.[7]

Similar arrangements were made in 1558 for the 'nouvelle conqueste' of Calais. When Calais fell into French hands on 7 January, Paul de Termes was almost immediately appointed governor by the king during his visit of inspection. It is most likely that, although de Termes was not directly subordinated to the governor of Picardy at first, the arrangements made for Boulogne in 1549–50 were repeated. This naturally led to some uncertainty, since the military effort being poured into Calais was great and the commander of the fortress in a position of massive responsibility. Termes seems to have started to issue instructions to Jean du Biez, then governor of Ardres, and provoked Villebon, as governor of Picardy, to ask the court to rule on the

3 Francis I to La Fayette, 12 April 1516, BN fr. 3057 pp. 1–2; Louise of Savoy to La Fayette, 20 Aug./2 Dec. 1515, fr. 2934 fo. 36, 44. Francis I to La Fayette, 2 Sept. [1516], fr. 3057 p. 189, in which he refers to 'Samer au boys en mon pays de Picardie'; see also the instructions from Vendôme to La Fayette, 1521–2 in BN fr. 2934 *passim*.
4 Du Biez retained the *sénéchaussée* of Boulogne; his son-in-law Vervins became captain, 1542.
5 BN Clair. 961 fo. 40–2; J. du Bouchet, *Preuves de l'histoire de l'illustre maison de Coligny* (1662), 452–4.
6 AD Pas-de-Calais 9B 1 fo. 40–1, copy, 1 July 1550.
7 Villebon, receipt to Jacques Veau, trés. de l'ord. des guerres, 21 July 1554, BN Clair. 961 fo. 43; Coligny, *ibid.*, fo. 45, provisions of 27 June 1555; for Sénarpont, AD Pas-de-Calais 9B 2 fo. 98–100.

delimitation between himself and Termes. The duke of Guise's reply was explicit:

> quant à la demande que vois faictes si le Roy entend séparer Ardres du gouvernement de Picardye, je vous advise que non, mais il désire bien que estant si ordinairement occupé ès autres endroictz de la frontière que vous estes, le sieur de Termes, qu'il a ordonné à la garde de Calais pour ce commancement et qui est si notable et expérimenté personnaige que sçavez, ayt l'oeil par mesme moyen sur led. Ardres qui est à sa porte et est très loing de vous que vous n'y pouvez aller que avec grande incommodité.[8]

The Calais Pale therefore stood at first as somewhat separate from the *gouvernement* of Picardy, but this was an interim measure.[9]

Distance was indeed a problem for a governor based on the Somme in controlling places as far away as Calais and Boulogne. The problem had been even greater earlier in the century when the Tournaisis was still a French enclave in the Burgundian Low Countries. Yet Tournaisis was definitely within the *gouvernement*; a messenger from the duke of Vendôme in 1521 declared that his master was governor of Picardy 'soubz lequel gouvernement estoit la ville de Tournai', though the local governor was most reluctant to accept supervision and the townsmen seem to have feared direct royal interference in their affairs as likely to attract the anger of the Brussels government. Besides, some wondered, what was the point of reporting to a governor as far away as La Fère across Burgundian territory?[10]

The boundaries of the province to the east and south were gradually formed by military necessity. The Thiérache was certainly subject to the commands of the governor in the sixteenth century, though geographically remote from the main body of the province. The *bailliage* of Vermandois was only in part subject to Picardy, since the boundary of the province separated Chauny from La Fère and Laon was by the beginning of the sixteenth century part of Ile-de-France. However, its northern area included Saint-Quentin and Le Câtelet, even though the provisions for Orléans (1482), Vendôme (1515) and Saint-Pol (1519) as governors of Ile-de-France placed the *bailliage* of Vermandois under their direction, with the exception of Saint-Quentin and other enclaves 'soubs les gouverneurs des pays de Picardie et de Champaigne'.[11] Some time between

---

[8] Guise to Villebon, 27 March 1558, BN n.a. fr. 21698 fo. 46–7, draft by Bourdin.

[9] By 1562, Condé was entitled governor of 'Picardie, Arthois, Conté d'Oye, Guines et Calais', see Sécousse (ed.), *Mémoires de Condé*, III, 524 – manifesto of 5 July 1562.

[10] G. Moreau (ed.), *Le journal d'un bourgeois de Tournai* (1975), 64, 71.

[11] Powers for Louis d'Orléans as governor of Ile-de-France, Senlis, Beauvoisis et Vermandois, 4 Oct. 1483 (BN Picardie 155 fo. 40r) and for Vendôme as governor of Ile-de-France, 18 Feb. 1515 (*Ordonnances, François Ier*, I, no. 27)

1519 and 1538 this anomaly was sorted out and the classic shape of the province emerged. At any rate, the close connections which we have seen to have existed between the *gouvernements* of Picardy and Ile-de-France obviated some of the difficulties caused by conflicts of jurisdiction.

These could not always be avoided. In December 1520, shortly after relinquishing Ile-de-France to his brother Saint-Pol, Vendôme attempted to place a garrison of fifty lances in Beauvais and the magistrates protested that they were not within his government. A deputation to Saint-Pol elicited the reply 'qu'il n'y a moyen à présent mais qu'aussitost les rois il verroit Mr. de Vendosme son frere à La Fère et luy feroit entendre que cette ville est de son gouvernement et à faire desloger la garnison'.[12] Nevertheless, Vendôme returned to the charge in the following June by interfering with the town militia and again in May 1524 his attempts to send a garrison raised protests. In September 1524, the duke called a meeting at Amiens to discuss grain supplies and Beauvais only agreed to send representatives 'encore que cette ville ne soit du gouvernement de Picardie' because the estates of the cathedral chapter lay in Picardy and so were closely concerned.[13]

There were, of course, intimate social and economic links between *pays* like the Beauvaisis and the duchy of Valois and the lands to the north in the province of Picardy. Grain from the Santerre flowed into the markets of towns to the south while those towns were sometimes called upon to supply the garrisons of the frontier. Thus, in April 1524, when Vendôme was calling on the towns of his province for army supplies, he sent exactly the same demand to Compiègne. During the war of 1536–38, Vendôme levied L 600 in the election of Compiègne for emergencies.[14] Moreover, the great military command of the governor of Picardy led him to overshadow the governor of the Ile-de-France. So, when in 1536 the newly raised legionary troops got out of control and started ravaging the villages around Beauvais, they called on the duke of Vendôme to deal with the problem.[15]

There were certain anomalies within the *gouvernement* itself. Throughout the sixteenth century the *bailli-gouverneur* of Péronne, Montdidier and Roye, who was usually a member of the Humières family, held both judicial and military power in a sense which was a survival from an earlier style of government: the post had been created in 1421 as separate from the *gouvernement* of Picardy and in many respects it remained so until the mid-sixteenth

---

12 BM Beauvais, Coll. Bucquet 57, p. 425 (5 Dec. 1520); p. 426 (24 Dec.).
13 *Ibid.*, p. 430 (25 June 1521); p. 466 (17 May 1524); p. 470 (15 Sept. 1524).
14 AM Compiègne BB 17 fo. 11r; BB 19 fo. 36r.
15 BM Beauvais, Coll. Bucquet 57, p. 550 (23 Feb. 1536).

century.[16] In military matters, however, the governor of Péronne was clearly taking his orders from the governor of Picardy throughout the Habsburg– Valois Wars, and Condé in 1563 addressed him as 'vous et les autres gouverneurs . . . de mon gouvernement'.[17] In February 1568, Jacques d'Humières, in the circumstances of civil wars which placed him in opposition to the titular governor of the province, obtained letters-patent guaranteeing his independence of the governor of Picardy on the grounds that this had been the original state of affairs before Piennes, governor of Péronne, became governor of Picardy in 1512: 'au moyen du quoy depuis son trespas, les gouverneurs . . . en icelluy pays de Picardye auroient tousiours prétendu . . . une préeminence sur led. gouvernement'. This was not a case which could be sustained, however, in the long run.[18]

The sixteenth-century provincial governor held neither an *office* with precisely defined functions nor a *commission* revocable at the royal will. He had instead an *estat* or *charge* of deliberately vague competence which in practice was not easily removed. Though in times of war he would be completely preoccupied by military affairs, his powers were regulatory and sometimes judicial. There is some reason to believe that the status and personality of an individual might considerably have influenced the scope of his activities. In the 1480s, Esquerdes was seen as all-powerful in the province (he was also governor of Boulogne and Abbeville as well as *sénéchal* of Ponthieu) and Louis XI seems considerably to have extended his powers in October 1480 and August 1482.[19] Molinet, discussing events of 1486, noted that he 'lors tenoit la monarchie de Picardie en sa demaine', and reinforced this impression by adding later that he was 'lors dominant et princiant en Picardie comme ung petit roy'.[20] While allowance should be made for Molinet's curious fascination with this arch-betrayer of the house of Burgundy – he describes him elsewhere as 'triumphant en Artois comme ung César en Romme' – there is little doubt that the man described by the Venetian Contarini in 1492 as 'il primo uomo da guerra che abbia la Sua Maestà' exercised in practice vice-regal powers of a kind only slightly more extensive than those held by sixteenth-century governors.[21]

[16] On the *baillis-gouverneurs*, see G. Zeller, *Les institutions de la France au XVIᵉ siècle* (1948), 168–9. On the creation of the *gouvernement* of Péronne, Montdidier and Roye, see Cagny, *Le château de Suzanne en Santerre*, p. 45.

[17] This is clear from the correspondence of Jean and Louis d'Humières in the 1550s: and Condé to Humières, 12 April 1563, BL Egerton 17 fo. 76.

[18] Letters of Charles IX, 4 Feb. 1568, reg. in Parlement'.17 Feb. AN X¹ᴬ 8627 fo. 162.

[19] A. Collet, 'Philippe de Crèvecoeur' 445–6 (9 Oct. 1480); BN Picardie 155 fo. 36r, 3 Aug. 1482; *Gallia Regia*, no. 17525; *Ordonnances*, xviii, p. 281.

[20] J. Molinet, *Chroniques* I, 521, 552.

[21] *Ibid.*, I, 521, 552; L. Firpo (ed.), *Relazioni di ambasciatori veneti*, X, 23.

At this early stage, too, the governor still retained the archaic title of *capitaine général de Picardie*, first formulated in the fourteenth century.[22] Esquerdes often entitled himself 'lieutenant et capitaine-général d'icellui seigneur ou pays de Picardie'.[23] This was an emphasis on military command which gradually fell out of favour in official documents, but as late as the 1520s the Burgundian chronicler Macquereau could still refer to the French governor as 'capitaine-général'.[24]

The provincial governor was the king's alter ego, replacing the person of the king in his absence. This is indicated both in royal formularies and in disputes which arose when affronts were offered to the governor's person. In a council held at Abbeville in October 1522, there was discussed the matter of rivalry between Vendôme's brother Saint-Pol and Anne de Montmorency, who had recently been appointed to command in Saint-Pol's garrison of Doullens. Saint-Pol refused to leave as to do so would dishonour him. Some agreed, but Morette, a friend of Montmorency's, intervened to say that the marshal should stay in his new command. He reported to his friend: 'quelque aultre qui estoyt là m'a demandé: Monsieur de Mezières vouldriez vous bien désobeir au Lieutenant eu Roy? Je luy ay respondu: non, monsieur, mays je ne vouldroys point avoir une honte pour luy.'[25]

The high position and esteem thought to be properly due to the king's lieutenant-general is more clearly illustrated by an event reported to the Parlement of Paris by the count of Brienne in June 1525. A quarrel had arisen in Brienne's chamber at Abbeville between Ménilles, a member of Dammartin's gendarmerie company, and the sieur de Saragosse, *commissaire des guerres*. Pay was long overdue and the commissioners were quibbling over the time due to the men. Saragosse then accused Ménilles of being a looter; at this, Ménilles stepped back and laid his hand on his sword in a typical gesture of wounded honour, but Saragosse cried out: 'Monsieur, il mect la main à l'espée en vostre présence.' A general scuffle then broke out. In his sentence, promulgated on 6 June, Brienne declared that in view of 'l'oultraige à nous faicte, représentans la personne du Roy' Saragosse should be made to apologise and Ménilles be hanged.[26]

22 Enguerrand VII de Coucy had been so called in the late fourteenth century. For titularies, see *Gallia Regia*, nos. 17507–17529, which give the changes. Guy de Châtillon was just royal 'lieutenant' in Picardy, Beauvaisis and Vermandois in 1359 (see copy of his provision, BL Add. 39572 fo. 1–2).
23 G. Espinas, *Recueil de documents relatifs à l'histoire du droit municipal en France ... Artois*, i, p. 116.
24 For Macquereau, *Traité de la maison de Bourgogne*, Barrois, ed., 1841 (for 1527–29), pp. 147–8: 'le comte de Vendosme, capitainne géneralle de la Picardie'.
25 Morette to Montmorency, 1 Oct. [1522], MC Chantilly, L I, fo, 261–2.
26 AN X¹ᴬ 1528 fo. 530r–v; Vigner, *Histoire de la maison de Luxembourg* (1617), 315.

The semi-regal position of the governor was also reflected in the elaborate ceremonial undertaken on his first entry into the towns of the province. At Amiens, this seems to have been especially spectacular, involving jousts, river displays, and processions of the city armed companies with banners to the sound of drum and fife. In 1541, for Antoine de Bourbon, pavillions and tents were erected in the suburb of La Hotoie for the jousts.[27] At Abbeville in February 1520, the town voted two ponchons of wine and a ceremonial for the presentation of the keys to Charles de Bourbon 'considéré qu'il est prince du sang et lieutenant-général du Roy', and he was to be met by the town's armed companies.[28] Smaller towns put on as much display as they could. When Coligny entered Péronne on 12 July 1555:

> Sont allez audevant de luy hors des portes à cheval messieurs les gens du Roy, esleus, greniers et contrerolleurs, les sergens royaulx, les arbalestriers, archers et canoniers de la ville avec leurs enseignes, et messieurs de la ville revestuz de leurs bonnes robbes, qui l'ont attendu à la porte où ilz ont faict la harengue aud. seigneur, présentans les clefz de la ville; et, luy estans en son logis, messieurs luy ont presenté deux petites traiettes d'estain plain de vin.[29]

The formal definition of the governor's position was enshrined in the *lettres de provision* which he received on appointment. Unfortunately, these could sometimes be vague, referring to the powers as exercised by his predecessor,[30] and there is not a complete series for the sixteenth century, since such letters were not always registered by the Parlement and survival is therefore a matter of chance. Eleven such documents are preserved concerning Picardy between 1482 and 1561.[31] All, as letters-patent, began with a formal preamble explaining the reasons for the vacancy and adding some circumstantial detail such as, for La Rochepot in 1537, the status of the province; 'qu'il nous importe autant que nul autre' and therefore is in need of a 'personnage d'auctorité'.

---

[27] AM Amiens CC 97 fo. 193– (1520); CC 137, fo. 115r–v (1541): total expenses of L 230 13.6d. CC 139 fos. 138–42 gives expenses for entertainment of Vendôme in 1542 with jousts.
[28] BM Abbeville MS 378 fo. 11r; *Inventaire sommaire, Abbeville*, p. 152.
[29] AM Péronne, BB 9 fo. 396v.
[30] Thus, Coligny's letter of provision, 27 June 1555, BN Clair. 961 fo. 45.
[31] Esquerdes, 3 Aug. 1482 (BN Picardie 155 fo. 173r, analysis); Orléans, 8 Oct. 1537 (BN fr. 3029 fo. 9, ment. Pinard, *Chronologie historique-militaire* 8 vols. (1740–62) I, 193); La Rochepot, 13 May 1537 (BN fr. 23149, pp. 9–12); Antoine de Bourbon, Feb. 1538, BN Dupuy 273, fo. 16v–17v; Du Biez, 26 Dec. 1542 (AM Amiens AA 12 fo. 213); M. du Bellay, 11 June 1547 (BN fr. 3115 fo. 62–5); Coligny, for Boulonnais, 9 Sept. 1549 (BN Clair. 961 fo. 40–2); Villebon, 1 July 1550 (AD Pas-de-Calais 9B 1 fo. 40–1, printed in P. des Forts, *Le château de Villebon*, p. j. no. 17); Coligny, 27 June 1555 (BN Clair. 961 fo. 45); Sénarpont, 20 May 1559 (AD Pas-de-Calais, 9B 2 fo. 98–100, printed, des Forts, *Le château de Villebon*, p. j. no. 74); Condé, 3 Oct. 1561, AN X^1A 8624 fo. 169–71. In addition there are powers for François de Montmorency as lieut.-gen. at Amiens (AM Amiens AA 14 fo. 112v–113r, 5 Sept. 1557). It should be noted that the powers for Charles de Bourbon (1519) have not survived.

There then followed a glowing tribute to the qualities of the appointee and an outline of the powers given. For La Rochepot, these were: (1) to assemble the municipalities and direct them 'pour le faict de la police, conservacion, deffence et seureté de leurs villes', (2) to see to munitioning of the towns, (3) to raise troops beyond those sent by the king should this be necessary, (4) to control these soldiers and see that they live peaceably with the local population, listening to the complaints of the latter, (5) to change garrison dispositions as he sees fit, (6) to fix prices for provisions and enforce them by proclamation and punishment, (7) to have his expenditure audited in the Chambre des Comptes as though ordered by the king himself and, finally, a very wide power, (8) 'génerallement de faire en cette présente charge de lieutenant général tout ce qui ce peult et doit faire et tout ainsy que nous mesmes ferions et faire pourrions sy présent en personne y estions, jaçoit que le cas requist mandement plus spécial'. The king would support all such action in his name. No wonder La Rochepot described these powers as 'aussi ample qu'il est possible de le faire'.[32]

Condé's powers, October 1561, are the longest in this period, a fact explained by the fraught circumstances of his appointment and the need to overawe opposition by specific *mandement* to the Parlement, *baillis* and lesser governors to accept his authority, and to the *trésorier de l'épargne* to pay his pension and emoluments. While the preamble rehearsed 'la grandeur des insignes, trèsgrandz et mémorables services que tous ses ancestres ont faictz . . . spéciallement en la direction, maniement et administration des affaires dud. gouvernement de Picardie', the letters went on specifically to empower him to 'contenir noz bons et loyaulz subiectz . . . en l'obéissance qu'ilz nous doivent et en l'amitié, union et concorde qui est requise pour leur commun bon'. Specific powers mentioned were to convoke and instruct magistrates, listen to and deal with complaints, convoke the *ban* through the *bailliages* for local police work, allocate garrisons and troop captaincies, establish *taux de vivres*, administer military justice, keep foreigners under surveillance, appoint temporary town governors, oversee town *munitions*, check the use of the *octrois* for fortification work, and order expenditure on fortifications. The general empowering phrase used in 1537 was almost exactly repeated. The core of Condé's powers were therefore much the same as La Rochepot's in 1537, the difference lying in the political context.[33]

---

[32] La Rochepot to Humières, 17 May 1537, BN fr. 3062 fo. 135. The powers to du Biez simply say: 'pouvoir et auctorité de pourveoir et donner ordre à toutes choses quy surviendront et occureront touchant et concernant le faict dud. gouvernement', with the standard provision 'jaçoyt ce qu'il eust chose quy requist mandement plus espécial' (AM Amiens AA 12 fo. 213). The order was usually completed by an injunction to all civil and military officials to obey.

[33] Letters-patent, Saint-Germain-en-Laye, 3 October 1561, AN X^{1A} 8624 fo. 169–71.

These powers were wide but not as extensive as those sometimes conceded by the crown to great magnates in the fourteenth and fifteenth centuries. Guy de Châtillon, count of Saint-Pol as governor of Picardy in 1359 for the regent Charles, was empowered to raise troops on his own authority, appoint to offices for life and issue letters of grace in his own name.[34] The sixteenth-century powers indicate the advance in the authority of the crown since that time, but remained substantial and capable of extension in practice.

As far as the deputy governors were concerned, their powers were much the same, though usually expressed in an abbreviated form. Those given to Villebon in 1550 contained most of the military provisions of 1537, though without the expenditure clause, and a general injunction 'faire et ordonner en l'absence de nred. cousin de Vendosmois et dud. sr. de La Rochepot pour le bien, seureté et conservacion dud. pais'. The special circumstances of 1559, however, seem to have resulted in much more extensive provisions for Sénarpont. After a preliminary and very wide commission 'veoir, entendre et pourveoir aux affaires dud. gouvernement', he was given power in particular: (1) to make sure that judicial officers did their duty, (2) ensure that the king's subjects lived together in peace and obedience, (3) suppress all pillaging by vagabonds and 'mauvais garçons', making sure that the *prévôts des maréchaux* did their duty, (4) ensure that the garrisons behaved peaceably and punish all offenders, (5) change garrisons as appropriate, (6) oversee the musters, (7) examine the accounts of the *deniers communs* in the towns and (8) generally act as the king would in person. His powers, then, were somewhat more specific than usual and reflected the disorders attendant on the financial problems which the crown faced in paying its troops at the end of the period of warfare. On appointment, letters-close would also be sent out to lesser governors and town captains for them to obey the new provincial governor and 'différez et obéyssez comme . . . à ma propre personne'.[35]

The question of the governor's judicial power is a vexed one in that this is not usually spelled out in provisions, and it might be assumed that the network of royal courts precluded much interference from the governor except in cases of purely military justice administered by the *prévôts des maréchaux*. In practice this was not so. Antoine de Bourbon in 1542 issued a *mandement* to the *bailliage* of Amiens to interrogate a priest, Adrien Le Brun, in a case between the town and the bishop's *official* at Corbie. This was followed by his letters declaring the innocence of the *official* and allowing the case to be

---

[34] Copy of provisions, 14 July 1359, BL Add. 30572 fo. 1–2.
[35] Henri II to Humières, 29 June 1555, BN fr. 3134 fo. 51 (for Coligny's appointment).

transferred to the ecclesiastical courts.[36] In 1552, another priest was executed at Amiens on Vendôme's orders. Jehan Crampon and another priest were accused and convicted of the murder of M. de Sénarpont's eldest son and the duke gave the order for both interrogation and execution.[37]

Military justice under the *prévôts des maréchaux* naturally came much more clearly within the remit of the governors, as their provisions made clear. La Rochepot, for instance, authorised the *prévôt* at Montreuil, the sieur de Roussoy, to see to the case of a man who had been sentenced to death for climbing in and out of Abbeville at night. He also saw to the pursuit and arrest of one of the leaders of the 1548 rebellion in Guyenne by sending five men to Dieppe.[38]

To do all this, the governors had to have funds at their disposal and, indeed, as *ordonnateurs* of expenditure they were empowered to authorise the disbursement of funds as if by the king himself. Louis XI transferred L 27,000 to Esquerdes from the *recette* of Normandy, in March 1483 the *élection* of Gisors was levied for his expenses and in May so was the *recette-général* of Normandy.[39] By the 1530s, governors like La Rochepot were able to draw upon funds controlled by the *commissaire de l'extraordinaire des guerres* for unexpected expenses. One account has survived for 1537–8 and, although it is incomplete, there are records of expenses for journeys, gifts, salaries, rewards, wages of muster commissioners and unexpected expenses for spies totalling L 3,007 (Aug. 1537–Feb. 1538). Another *trésorier de l'extraordinaire* paid out L 200 in May 1549 alone on La Rochepot's orders, including a payment to 'aucuns espyes pour aucunement les récompenser des despenses hors de ce royaume'.[40]

In fact, governors were frequently expected to lay out their own funds and most often to engage their plate and then claim reimbursement from the crown. La Rochepot did this frequently, as did the dukes of Vendôme, and on many occasions had difficulty in getting repayment. In April 1537, chancellor Dubourg made a fuss about the bureaucratic procedures and Montmorency had to intervene on his brother's behalf so he could redeem his plate:

> si l'ordre ou serymonye n'y a esté gardée comme il se doit, me semble,
> Monsieur, qu'on ne so doit pas fort arrester à cela mais seullement

---

[36] Document mentioned in BN fr. 18959 fo. 524; letter of Vendôme, 5 Nov. 1542, BN Picardie 31.
[37] 10 March 1552, *Inventaire sommaire, Amiens*, II, p. 384 and AM Amiens CC 157 fo. 88, *Inventaire sommaire*, IV p. 496.
[38] BN fr. 26132 no. 290, May 1549 – arrest by Philippe Thiebault on La Rochepot's orders.
[39] BN fr. 20685 fo. 636; Harsgor, *Recherches* II, 1099.
[40] V. de Beauvillé, *Recueil de documents inédits concernant la Picardie*, IV, 276–80. See also BN fr. 26132 no. 290, cert. for Chambre des Comptes, 1549.

regarder que cela a esté employé en choses plusque requises . . . qui me
fait vous prier vouloir donner ordre à l'en faire rembourser, ou s'il est
besoing que le roy y meste la main, je luy en parleray.[41]

In order to supplement their income but also, in fact, to increase their local
authority, provincial governors, as has been seen, were empowered to
confiscate the property of those supporting the Habsburgs during the war.
Esquerdes made use of this power frequently during the confused times after
1477 and we find Vendôme demanding confirmation of it in 1521:

> du temps de deffunct monsieur le mareschal d'Esquerd, monsieur le grant
> maistre de Chaumont et pareillement du temps présent pour l'Ytallie, les
> gouverneurs ont eu puissance et auctorité du Roy de donner les
> confiscacions et je demande estre oy à les despartir à ceulx quy sont au
> service du maistre et que je congnois quy leur mérite. Il me samble que ma
> demande est raisonnable.[42]

What this in effect means was that the governors were able to assure first their
own compensation for war losses and then that of their reliable followers.

In the exercise of his powers, the governor (or lieutenant in his absence), was
the centre of a household and staff which was in many ways parallel to,
though of course less elaborate than, the king's household. The governor was
surrounded by a miniature court consisting of officers both civil and military
acting as gendarmerie officers, *maîtres d'hôtel*, secretaries, councillors and
below-stairs servants. This household was itinerant, naturally, but was centred
on one or two of the governor's private domains or town-houses. Jean de
Bruges-La Gruthuse, for instance, took over the sumptuous town-house at
Abbeville occupied by his brother-in-law Esquerdes, a house fine enough to
receive the royal household at the time of Louis XII's marriage in 1513.[43] In
addition, there was the 'logis du Roy' at Amiens, the permanent residence of
the king's representative.[44] Such a 'court', if so it may be called, was also
expected to keep up the pomp of the governor's position, especially on
ceremonial entries. A typical entourage of this kind is listed on the occasion
that La Rochepot went to Paris for his ceremonial entry as governor of the Ile-
de-France in December 1538. The list includes thirty-six noblemen, most

---

[41] Montmorency to Dubourg, 7 April [1537], AN J 965 no. 8[10].
[42] Vendôme to Robertet, 27 Aug. [1521] BN fr. 3060 fo. 58.
[43] This house was destroyed by fire in 1795, though a print of it survived. See Van Praet,
Recherches sur Louis de Bruges, 71.
[44] When he stayed at Amiens, duke Antoine of Vendôme often resided in the 1540s at the hôtel
du Fresnoy (AM Amiens CC 140 fo. 81v), but by 1549 it was more usual for him to stay at
the hôtel des Trois Cailloux (CC 153 fo. 97v; CC 155 fo. 90; CC 159 fo. 96) on the site of the
building later to be called the 'logis du Roi', residence of the governors of Picardy, built in
1565. This still survives in part.

of them Picards, from the Créqui, Ailly, Moreuil, Rouault and Estourmel families, with 'plusieurs autres gentilshommes en grans nombre de la maison dudict sieur de La Rochepot', many of whom were professional soldiers like captain Picquet, La Lande, Haraucourt, Senlis, Marivaulx, Dampont and Stavaye.[45]

By the middle of the sixteenth century, the armature of the governor's administration was his *conseil*. In most provinces this seldom left any institutional records which might reveal the full picture of its activity, but Michel Antoine has stressed its importance and argued that the governor, as king's representative in the province, was bound to act 'in council' on most matters and that, with specialist appointees from central government, this formed the nucleus of local administration later to develop into the intendancy.[46] In the quarrel discussed earlier concerning violence in his presence, Brienne in 1525 promulgated his sentence with the advice of lawyers in the Parlement 'pour ce que je ne veulx totallement user du conseil de pardeçà'.[47]

It is possible that the sixteenth century saw nothing entirely new here, for as far back as 1474 we find an assembly in M. de Torcy's *chambre de conseil* at Amiens of some *échevins*, the *bailli*, captain and 'autres seigneurs et gens de guerre'.[48] In the mid-sixteenth century, however, it is clear that the crown was taking much greater interest in the advice offered to governors. In May 1536 Francis I appointed a *maître des requêtes*, Ymbert de Saveuses, a local nobleman and former *bailli* of Amiens, to advise La Rochepot as 'homme de bon conseil et service . . . ès choses qui seront utilles, requises et necessaires à délibérer tant pour la fortiffication des villes et places que autres affaires occurans dud. pays'. A wider remit would be difficult to imagine. Again, in June 1537, Montmorency told La Rochepot to 'retenir' Jean d'Estourmel 'auprès de vous et vous servir de luy'.[49] These are early examples of an important development. In the military crisis of 1552, the king ordered the duke of Vendôme to call upon Villebon and Sénarpont specifically for advice.[50] In appointing Louis cardinal de Bourbon as temporary lieutenant-general at Paris

[45] *Registres, Paris*, II, 396.
[46] This has been argued most cogently by M. Antoine in 'Genèse de l'institution des intendants', *Journal des Savants* (1982), 283–317 and 'Institutions françaises en Italie sous le règne de Henri II: Gouverneurs et intendants', *Mélanges de l'Ecole française de Rome*, vol. 94 (1982), 759–818.
[47] AM X[1A] 1528 fo. 529v.
[48] AM Amiens BB 11 fo. 172, 26 July 1474, *Inventaire sommaire*, II, 216.
[49] Francis I to La Rochepot, 30 May 1536, BN fr. 3008 fo. 36; Montmorency to same, 6 June 1537, BN n.a. fr. 10227 no. 2.
[50] Instructions to M. de Contay (Louis d'Humières) 30 Oct. 1552, BN fr. 3134 fo. 1–2: as Vendôme has only Jarnac and Langey with him, he is to call on Sénarpont and Villebon 'personnes dignes et capables pour s'ayder de leur adviz et conseil'.

in June 1554, the king had named the council which was to advise him.[51] However, it is in 1562 that we see an important example for the first time in Picardy of a phenomenon amply documented by Antoine for Piedmont in the same period: namely, the attachment to the governor's council of a royal judicial official. On 20 July 1562, Cathcrine de Medici had the *conseil privé* issue a brevet for the appointment of Philibert Barjot as assistant to the cardinal Charles de Bourbon:

> le roy . . . considérant combien il est nécessaire que Monsr. le Cardinal de Bourbon, qu'il a fait son lieutenant général au gouvernement de Picardie, ait auprès de sa personne un notable personnage de judicature pour l'employer en affaires de justice qui se pourroient offrir d'heurs à autre, a commandé et ordonné à Mr Barjot, président au Grand Conseil et me. des requestes de son hostel, qu'il se transporte par devers luy pour demeurer et résider ordinairement auprès de sa personne.[52]

It was precisely this kind of appointment to the governor's council which was to develop into the intendancy.

The council was usually made up of the major captains in attendance and the governor's personal staff. In July 1521, Vendôme's council consisted of his deputy, Chabannes, the lieutenant of his gendarmerie company, Torcy, Jean d'Humières, the governor of Péronne, and 'plusieurs autres seigneurs et cappitaines estans avec luy'.[53] One of the duke's closest advisers, of course, was his brother the cardinal Louis de Bourbon, who was with the duke in 1521 and 1522 and seems to have assisted him.[54] In 1542, Antoine de Bourbon was taking the advice of 'plusieurs bons et notables personnages estans vers nous' in punishing riots.[55]

The scope of the council was informal and wide. In 1519, Vendôme promised to send 'aucun des gens de nostre conseil' to Laon to enquire into a dispute between the town and the gendarmerie.[56] In 1521, when a report from

[51] Copy of letters-patent of appointment, BL Egerton fo. 41 (naming cardinals du Bellay and Meudon, chancellor Olivier, secretary Villeroy and Nantouillet, *prévôt* of Paris and gentleman of the chamber, as his colleagues). See also Henri II to Nantouillet, Laon, 16 June 1554, Egerton 5 fo. 11: 'et pour ce que je désire qu'il soit accompaigné, conseillé et obéy par de là . . . je vous prye ne faillir à vos rendre et trouver au près de luy'; and cardinal de Bourbon to Nantouillet, Auxy-le-Château, 16 June 1554, Egerton 17 fo. 74.
[52] BN Clair. 961 fo. 48, copy: 'Brevet pour faire assister Mr le Cardinal de Bourbon Gouverneur de Picardie par Philibert Barjot, prés. au gd. con.cl. La reine mère présent, Bourdin.' Barjot was *conseiller lai* in the Parlement, 1554 (BN fr. 5128 fo. 323, 332–3).
[53] Report of 24 July 1521, BN fr. 2968 fo. 1.
[54] G. Moreau (ed.), *Journal d'un bourgeois de Tournai*, 80–1; Louis de Bourbon to La Fayette, 17 June [1522] (BN fr. 2888 fo. 55); 4 Sept. [1522] (*ibid.*, fo. 57) and 7 Sept. [1522] (*ibid.*, fo. 59).
[55] Vendôme to Amiens, 18 Nov. 1542, La Fère (AM Amiens, BB 24, Thierry, *Tiers Etat* II, 616–17).
[56] Vendôme to Laon, 8 Feb. 1519/20, La Fère, AM Laon EE 5.

a spy at Mortagne came in, the duke reported: 'J'ay mis en conseil ceste matière et ay trouvé que promptement je luy devoys accorder sa demande.'[57] In 1542, his son Antoine prohibited grain movements by 'meure delibéracion de conseil'.[58] In fact, there is reason to believe that many, if not most, of the *ordonnances* issued in the name of the governor were formulated at meetings of the *conseil*.[59] Judicial matters, above all, required 'l'advis des plus notables et apparens' before decision, as Coligny made clear in February 1557.[60]

Though such an informal body would not leave institutional records, the governors promulgated their orders through the range of instruments available to central government: letters-missive, letters-close headed 'de par le duc et pair, lieutenant général du Roy' and the more formal *ordonnance* drawn up as letters-patent, addressed either to individuals or to categories of people and involving orders of a more general or permanent kind. The drawing up of this correspondence was in the hands of the governor's secretarial staff. As with the royal chancellery, their counter-signature would authenticate the more formal documents.

Military administration, especially at times of active campaigning, vastly increased the business passing through the hands of the governors' staff. To judge by one of the governors' archives to survive for this period, that of La Rochepot (only in part), this could generate much paper: sixty-eight despatches survive addressed to him for May to mid-July 1536, and for June of 1537 there are thirty. During the campaign of the royal army in Picardy in that year, Montmorency wrote 114 despatches to the chancellor alone. Where we have the files of a campaigning royal lieutenant (as for Guise in 1558) we find at least six despatches a day going out to local commanders. Governors of Picardy corresponded with their subordinates and with the court (including the king, the principal minister like Montmorency, Chabot, Annebault and with the secretary charged with the province's affairs at the time: Robertet in the 1520s, Jean Breton in the 1530s, later still Bochetel, De L'Aubespine and, above all, Jacques Bourdin). In addition they also maintained a regular correspondence in cipher with the ambassadors in England, who usually forwarded their despatches through Vendôme or La Rochepot. What all this

---

57 Vendôme to Francis I, 22 August 1521, BN fr. 3030 fo. 1.
58 Vendôme to Amiens, 17 Nov. 1542, La Fère (AM Amiens AA 12 fo. 211).
59 For a ducal *ordonnance* clearly drawn up in council, see the sentence concerning the riot at Amiens over elections, La Fère, 15 Nov. 1542 (AM Amiens, BB 24 fo. 220r–221v): 'Veu laquel procez, nous par l'advis de plusieurs notables personnaiges de nostre conseil'.
60 Coligny to Humières, 21 Feb. 1557, BN fr. 3148, p. 51. For a reference to the *conseil* in action, see Georges de Créqui to Jean d'Humières, Paris, 2 Aug. [1537], Pichon, 'Correspondance des d'Humières', no. 81: he is to go to Amiens to see La Rochepot 'en attendant que son rapporteur soit prest à faire ses esquestes. Son conseil, en présence de M. Disque a été d'avis qu'il doit emporter la moitié de Vandeuvre.'

required was a sophisticated secretarial staff in some ways modelled on the royal secretariat.

The Bourbon dukes of Vendôme always had a number of secretaries in their service, though some were clearly more intimate with their masters than others. In the 1520s, duke Charles was served by de Chesnaye, Levain, de Parenty and de Lanzeray.[61] About the last two there is rather more information available than just their bare countersignature on ducal documents. Jean de Parenty had previously served Conti, La Gruuse and Piennes as secretary and had in some sense been inherited by Vendôme. He was certainly counter-signing his correspondence by July 1520. In October 1521, the duke was requesting his transfer from the *élection* of Doullens to that of Noyon; he was clearly a financial expert and perhaps of more use nearer to the La Fère domain.[62] After his death in late 1522, we learn, in the arrangements for the remarriage of his wife to Saint-Pol's *argentier*, that the governor of Boulogne, Lafayette, had been responsible for fixing up Parenty's marriage. His name certainly suggests an origin in the Boulonnais.[63] The tendency for the secretary of one governor to be inherited by another is confirmed by the career of Guillaume le Sueur, 'secrétaire de monseigneur' to Vendôme in 1535 and subsequently acting in this capacity for La Rochepot in 1538. It is possible that he was the Boulonnais Protestant lawyer who wrote one of the first accounts of the strange case of Martin Guerre, once he had followed Antoine de Bourbon to the south-west after 1555.[64]

Gaspard de Lanzeray was secretary to Vendôme in 1524 and also acted in this capacity for Brienne during the duke's absence at court in the crisis of 1525.[65] He was inherited by duke Antoine and is still found countersigning documents in 1552.[66] His career illustrates the kind of profits which could be reaped by a man in his position. In 1532, he is found in receipt of 14 écus from the town of Abbeville for services rendered.[67] By 1534, he was *contrôleur-*

---

[61] Counter-signatures: De Chesnaye, 18 April 1524 (AM Péronne BB 7 fo. 217v); Levain, 21 Feb. 1524 (AM Saint-Quentin liasse 151, C no. 4); Parenty, 23 March 1522 (AM Péronne BB 7 fo. 151r–v); Lanzeray, 12 Feb. 1524 (AM Saint-Quentin liasse 151, C no. 7).

[62] See his countersignature on Vendôme to Péronne, 10 July 1520 (AM Péronne BB 7 fo. 114v); Vendôme to Robertet, 1 Oct. [1521], BN fr. 3059 fo. 108.

[63] Saint-Pol to La Fayette, Abbeville, 1 Oct. [?1522] BN fr. 2888 fo. 102. See also L. E. de la G. Rosny, *Recherches généalogiques sur les comtes de Ponthieu, de Boulogne et de Guînes*, 4 vols. (1874–7) III, 1113.

[64] AN KK 277; voyages, 21 July; Beauvillé, *Recueil de documents*, IV 280 (on an expenditure *rôle*, 2 March 1538); N. Z. Davis, *The Return of Martin Guerre* (1983) 94–5. He may also have been the *contrôleur de l'extraordinaire des guerres* in 1557, see Beauvillé, 543. Compare with the 'du Chesne' who countersigns a patent of La Rochepot, 29 May 1550 (AD Pas-de-Calais 9B 1 fo. 80v) and a procl. by Vendôme, 25 May 1553 (*ibid.*, fo. 237–8).

[65] *Ordonnance* of Brienne, 1 Aug. 1525 (AM Péronne BB 7 fo. 287v), crs.

[66] *Ordonnance* of Vendôme, 15 Feb. 1552 (AD Pas-de-Calais 9B 1 fo. 160–1), crs.

[67] BM Abbeville MS 347 p. 26; also archer under Brienne, 1527, BN nafr. 8618 no. 27.

général des réparations de Picardie and in 1550 signed the muster-roll of the Saint-Quentin garrison as *contrôleur de l'extraordinaire des guerres.*[68] In the 1540s, another secretarial figure comes to prominence in the ducal household. In 1548, Gaspard de Lanzeray had his salary assigned on the duchy of Vendôme. From the domain of La Fère, the highest secretarial salary, L 500, went to Antoine Bouchet.[69] This ranked him with the ducal *chambellans* drawn from the local nobility. Bouchet was the most important secretary in the 1540s and probably drew up most of his master's secret correspondence.[70] By 1542, he held the post of *contrôleur des mortespaies de Picardie* and *maître de ouvrages* in the Boulonnais.[71] Such appointments were paralleled in the fifteenth century by the appointment of Jean de La Forge, Esquerdes's 'secretaire de l'hostel', as *receveur-général de Picardie* and of Jean de Moncheux, his servant, as *général des finances.*[72]

That Antoine Bouchet was an important figure in the ducal entourage is apparent from the administration of the Bourbon private domain at La Fère, but he was also an influential, indeed wealthy, man who could, in 1554, advance L 12,000 to Amiens, either on his own account or from his master's resources is not clear, in return for a *rente* of L 1,000. The purpose had been to use the money for urgent work on the fortifications and the loan had been contracted by special royal commission.[73] Service to the duke of Vendôme could therefore be profitable, since he took trouble to advance his secretaries' interests. In October 1548, for instance he got another of his regular secretaries, Valenciennes, the office of *maître des ports de Picardie* even before it had been definitely decided to create the post.[74]

The dukes also kept secretaries specifically assigned to look after their interests at court. Duke Charles had one Courcelles as his 'solliciteur en court' in 1524[75] and duke Antoine had Jean de Lagoutte, his 'secrétaire estant pour les

---

68 Beauvillé, *Recueil* I, 232–3; *Société acad. Laon*, 12 (1862) 345–56. Act as *contrôleur*, 1548, BN fr. 25794 no. 37.

69 AN KK 278A fo. 96–. Bouchet was also *receveur-général* of the La Fère domain.

70 See the inventory of Antoine Bouchet's papers (1581) BN fr. 18959; Bouchet's correspondence with Heilly, 15 May 1544, S.A.P. 57 no. 47. The collection of the duke's papers (1541–49) BN fr. 20521 may have been formed by him or by another ducal secretary, Victor Brodeau (see J. P. G. Blanchet, 'Recueil de lettres missives addressées à Antoine de Bourbon, 1553–62', *Bulletin de Mémoires de la Société Archéologique de la Charente*, ser. 7, vol. IV (1904–5), 29–185.

71 Beauvillé, *Recueil*, II, 208–9.

72 *Inventaire sommaire, Amiens* II, 262; E. Prarond, *Abbeville au temps de Charles VII . . . et de Louis XI*, 331. AM Amiens BB 16 fo. 262v.

73 AM Amiens CC 621 fo. 1: 'a esté constitué . . . la somme de mil Lt. de rente raceptable, au proufict de Anthoine Bouchet secrétaire de Mgr. le duc de Vendosmois'.

74 *CAH* II, no. 3767. Valenciennes had already accompanied Vendôme's brother Enghien to Italy in 1543–4 as an extra *contrôleur de l'extraordinaire* for the infantry (BN fr. 25792 no. 464).

75 Vendôme to Montmorency, 8 Aug. 1524, BN fr. 3068 fo. 31.

affaires de mond. seigneur en court'.[76] They, too, could channel favours. When, in 1544, the magistrates of Amiens needed confirmation of some offices or wished to protest against supplying German mercenaries, they applied to Lagoutte for help.[77] The reason for their influence was quite simply that they controlled the ducal papers; when a petition for a tenancy was addressed to duke Charles in 1522, Parenty minuted the response at the foot of the petition and it was signed by the duke. Without his cooperation, it could not even have reached his master.[78] When despatches arrived from the court, it was the secretary who received and opened them before reporting to his master.[79]

The governor's secretary was, not surprisingly, in an influential position to prefer suits and channel patronage. Thus, in 1536, both the secretaries of Vendôme and La Rochepot (the *bailli* of Boulogne) received two fine pieces of Amiens cloth 'pour plusieurs services que les dessusdis ont fait à ladicte ville'.[80] In 1541, an 'argentier et secrétaire' to Vendôme (probably Bouchet) received a present of 8 *écus* 'en considération des solicitudes qu'il a faictes devers mondit seigneur de Vendosme, luy estans à la court'.[81] In 1548, another secretary of Vendôme received 45s and a 'pot de vin' to bring a suit from the town of Péronne to his master's attention.[82] Routine letters and their drafting brought in a small but useful income: Langey's secretary, Guillaume Leprebtre, was paid 4 *écus* in 1550 'pour plusieurs dépêches . . . faictes pour les affaires de ladicte ville d'Amiens'[83] and later du Pré, Coligny's secretary, was paid by Saint-Quentin for engrossing *lettres d'attache* in his master's name for the town's benefit.[84]

Such servants and officers were thus of use and worth cultivating. In 1542, the town of Amiens entertained the *bailli* of Marle (Pierre de Flavigny), the

---

[76] AN KK 278A.
[77] Letters to Lagoutte, Feb. 1524, 'son secrétaire et son solliciteur au privé conseil du Roy' (*Inventaire sommaire, Amiens* II, 355) and December 1545, *ibid.*, II, 364: for Lagoutte's handling of Vendôme's business with the Duke of Guise, see La Ferrière, *Marguerite d'Angoulême . . . son livre de dépenses 1540–49*, 131. In 1545, the city of Beauvais, wishing to avoid a garrison, wrote to Antoine Bouchet 'faire souvenir' the duke of their privileges (BM Beauvais, Coll. Bucquet 57, p. 609).
[78] Document of 13 April 1521/1, BM Reims, Coll. Tarbé VIII, 50.
[79] 'qu'il avoit baillé à vostre secrétaire mais que dedans ne c'estoit trouvé les lettres . . . je vous prie mon frère vous informer . . . de vostre secrétaire si les choses sont telles'. Montmorency to La Rochepot, 27 July 1548, BN fr. 3035 fo. 101.
[80] AM Amiens CC 128 fo. 80.
[81] *Ibid.*, CC 137 fo. 104v–.   [82] AM Péronne BB 9 fo. 84v, 93r.
[83] AM Amiens CC 153 fo. 95v.
[84] AM Saint-Quentin, liasse 69 no. 55 fo. 31r: 6 *écus*. The town at the same time paid 48s to Le Gras, another of Coligny's secretaries 'pour avoir dressé une missive accordée ausd. de la ville par mond. Seigneur l'admiral adressant à monsieur le cardinal de Chastillon affin de faire oyr led. Fiallart (maître des requêtes) en son rapport' (*ibid.*, liasse 138 no. 19, fo. 16–17).

secretaries and *maîtres d'hôtel* of the duke during his stay in the town 'adfin que lesdis officiers voeullent tousjours avoyr en bonne recommandation les affaires d'icelle ville', and again paid money in 1551 'pour festoyer les secrétaires de Mgr. le duc de Vendosmois' during the entry of the queen dowager of Scotland into the town.[85]

Pierre de Flavigny, *bailli* of Marle, was an influential figure in the administration of the ducal private domain and inevitably regarded as a useful mediator. When in 1536 the town of Chauny wished to recover from the *élus* of Noyon some money raised for troops who were never employed, they sent envoys to La Fère who spoke to Flavigny. He told them to come back with the relevant documents but when they did indeed return, and Flavigny spoke to the duke, the latter would only order the despatch of the case back to the *élus*. Further problems caused Flavigny to tell the representatives 'qu'il convenoit avoir quelque homme d'auctorité pour en parler audit seigneur de Vendosme' and this man was found in the person of the vicomte de Chépoix, a ducal *chambellan*, who was going to La Fère to see the duke. Even this proved negative:

> Ledit seigneur viconte avoit parlé aud. seigneur duc touchant les deniers pour le paiement des iij[c] hommes de pied mys sus aud. Noion, qui luy avoit faict responce qu'il voulloit oyr ceulx de Noion; et n'en avoir peu avoir autre responce.[86]

By 1542, Flavigny is noted by duke Antoine as 'l'un des maîtres des requestes de nostre hostel' and is delegated by him to enquire into a quarrel between the city and chapter at Amiens.[87]

The *chambellans* and *maîtres d'hôtel* of the ducal household were used extensively by the dukes in transmitting their orders as governors. In the early 1520s, a particularly active individual in this sense was Feroand de Nédonchel, *contrôleur* of the ducal household, a gentleman of Artois who had lost his property because of the war and was a candidate for royal compensation 'veu que plusieurs fois il s'est employé à faire quelques services aud. seigneur' (i.e. the king).[88] A similar case is that of Antoine, sieur de Hammes, *chambellan* to dukes Charles and Antoine in turn. He was a descendant of an ancient family

---

[85] AM Amiens, CC 155 fo. 88 (1551).

[86] AM Chauny BB 5 fo. 198v, 198r–v, 200r. Pierre de Chépoy was *chambellan* to duke Antoine in 1549 (AN KK 278ᴬ).

[87] Vendôme to Amiens, Paris, 4 March 1542 (AM Amiens, BB 24 fo. 167r–v). In May, Flavigny is also reported making a survey of the course of the Somme, see *Inventaire summaire, Amiens* II, 348.

[88] Vendôme to Robertet, 25 Aug. 1521, BN fr. 3060 fo. 54. He was descended from Arnould, count of Guînes (La Gorgue-Rosny, *Recherches généalogiques*, 722). See also E. de Rosny, 'Liste de personnes tenant fiefs (1529)', *MSAP* VI, where he paid L 24.

which had lost its considerable property as a result of the English occupation of the Calais Pale. Having been 'retiré d'Artois pour faire service' to the king by duke Charles and assigned an income on the royal domain at Amiens, he found it impossible to obtain payment and had to be supported by the assignation of a *rente* on the Bourbon châtellenie of Vendeuil.[89]

The head of the ducal household in 1549 was Nicolas de Lavardin, sieur de Ronnay, one of the most frequently employed political agents and listed as both *conseiller* and *chambellan*. Again, he had been inherited by duke Antoine from duke Charles.[90] The same position was held by Nicolas de Bours, sieur de Gennes, listed in 1549 as 'gentilhomme de la chambre' and 'maistre de la garderobe' but by 1551 *conseiller et chambellan*. He was particularly active in Vendôme's confidential service in the mid-1540s, carrying frequent messages to court, and in 1547 received a royal grant of a house at Amiens.[91] In 1553, he performed a signal service for his master. Some at court had wished to give the duke of Bouillon the credit for revictualling Thérouanne 'maiz monsieur de Gennes a joué aussi dextrement en cest affaire comme il est possible de faire à bon serviteur' and had made sure that Vendôme's achievements were fully known.[92] Service to the Bourbons was a family affair, for his uncle was Guillaume de Bours, sieur de Saint-Michel, Vendôme's *maître d'hôtel* in 1542 and *commissaire ordinaire des montres en Picardie*, a post in which he was succeeded by his nephew, Gennes's brother Louis sieur de Monflan, in 1548. The property of the family lay in and around Auxi-le-Château.[93]

The post of *maître d'hôtel* was held by a number of individuals who were active in the governors' service and in local affairs. M. de Vaulx was a muster commissioner in 1525 and seems to have been inherited as *maître d'hôtel* by

---

89 Vendôme to Montmorency, 19 Oct. [1528], BN fr. 3010 fo. 36; AN KK 278ᴬ; AD Aisne, E 664 fo. 124v; sentence concerning the goods of the sieur de Hames, Aug. 1565, AM Amiens AA 5 fo. 346v. In 1549, he was repaid for a rente on Epernon by the domain of La Fère (AN KK 278ᴬ fo. 69r). His son Claude regained Hames and his daughter brought it into the Hallewin family.

90 Montmorency to la Rochepot, 17 March 1537, BN fr. 3008 fo. 10; Francis I and Breton to La Rochepot, 20 March 1537, fr. 3008 fo. 15/ fr. 3062 fo. 62; Montmorency to La Rochepot, 14 June 1537, BN n.a. fr. 10227 no. 5. For his position in 1549, see AN KK 278ᴬ. He was in Vendôme's service as early as 1522 (see letter to La Fayette, 25 Aug. 1522 fr. 2888 fo. 73). On his activities in 1545, see the *mémoire* of 21 March [1545], fr. 20521 fo. 93–4.

91 AN KK 278ᴬ; mentioned as 'conseiller et chambellan' 31 Dec. 1551 (AD Pas-de-Calais 9B 1 fo. 157–9 – protection for his property on the Artois border); Vendôme to Francis I, 12 Aug. 1544, BN fr. 20521 fo. 26–7; *Mémoire* for M. de Gennes, *ibid.*, fo. 93–4; Vendôme to Guise, 22 Sept. 1551, BN fr. 20470 fo. 65 (de Ruble, *Antoine de Bourbon*, I, 333–4); 1547 in *CAH* I, 1951; *ibid.* II, 2197 (royal grant to him of a house at Amiens, naming him as *échanson du roi*).

92 Cardinal Louis de Bourbon to Vendôme, 19 June 1553, in Blanchet, 'Recueil de lettres missives addressées à Antoine de Bourbon', 53–6.

93 Thierry, *Tiers Etat* II, 616 (29 Sept. 1524); Beauvillé, *Recueil de documents* II, 208–9 (1542). He was succeeded by his nephew, see BN fr. 28515 no. 98 (1548)

Vendôme from La Gruthuse. There was still a Hugues de Vaulx listed in the ducal household for 1549.[94] The most notable in this category, though, was Nicolas de Bossu, sieur de Longueval, who began his career in Vendôme's service as *maître d'hôtel*, active in the duke's negotiations with Tournai in 1521, and went on to a spectacular career commanding in the field, became *maître d'hôtel du roi*, *bailli* of Vermandois (June 1530) and then, through his relationship with his niece Anne de Pisseleu duchess of Etampes, one of the most influential figures at court in the later years of Francis I.[95] Another ducal *maître d'hôtel*, Jean III d'Estourmel, went on to be *général des finances de Picardie*.[96] Others listed in 1549 were Hugues de Roussy, sieur de Sissonne and François de Blécourt, sieur de Neufville.

In the dukes' more purely military suite, we find Jacques de Coucy-Vervins (later executed for surrendering Boulogne in 1544),[97] Moy and Torcy, successively lieutenants of Vendôme's gendarmerie company and close military advisers.[98] Nicolas de Moy was vassal of Marie de Luxembourg for the barony of Moy and she witnessed his son's marriage in 1538. Ties to the ducal house were therefore well established and close, while the family was also predominant in the captaincy of Saint-Quentin.[99] Torcy was particularly important in the 1520s, serving as deputy to his master and carrying out a

94 Bernieulles to Parlement, 11 April 1525, AN X[1A] 1527 fo. 367; a 'M. de Valux' was *maître d'hôtel* to La Gruthuse (*Inventaire sommaire, Abbeville*, p. 137) and, as commissaire to M. de Vendôme, he wrote to Abbeville (delib. of 8 May 1524 BM Abbeville MS 378 fo. 15r). A *panetier ordinaire* of the king of that name sent to Compiègne in 1544 (AM Compiègne BB 20 fo. 26r). He was possibly Jean de Villiers, sieur de Vaux, who wrote to announce the king's death at Beauvais in 1515 (BM Beauvais, Coll. Bucquet 57, p. 375). A 'Sieur de Vaux' was *maître d'hôtel* to cardinal Odet de Châtillon in 1557 (BM Beauvais, Coll. Bucquet 59 fo. 71). Duke Antoine of Vendôme interceded on behalf of Mlle de Vaulx for a benefice for one of her children, 'pour le recognoissance des services que je tire ordinairement de son filz aisné et que j'espère recevoir avec le temps de l'autre' (to Nantouillet, camp of Jumel, 28 Aug. 1554, BL Egerton 23 fo. 263).
95 Victualling commissioner for the Field of the Cloth of Gold (AM Péronne BB 7 fo. 105v; Floranges, *Mémoires* II 130, 136); G. Moreau (ed.), *Journal d'un bourgeois de Tournai*, 64–74 *passim*. Refs. to him in Vendôme to La Fayette, 16 June [1522] (BN fr. 2888 fo. 61) and cardinal de Bourbon to same, 17 June [1522] (*ibid.*, fo. 55); as a commander of troops, ment. in Vendôme to Péronne, 17 Feb. 1524 (AM Péronne BB 7 fo. 213–14); as *bailli* of Vermandois – CAF, 20046, 31875, 9945.
96 Cagny, *Le château de Suzanne en Santerre*, 37. Mentioned as *chambellan* to Vendôme in 1535/6 (AM Amiens CC 128 fo. 86). See below, ch. 4.
97 Vervins was also *chambellan* to the duke of Vendôme. See abbé C. Thelliez, *Marie de Luxembourg* (1970), 81; D. L. Potter, 'A Treason Trial', 603.
98 On Nicolas de Moy, sieur de Moy, sieur de Chin, see the report of 24 July 1521, BN fr. 2968 fo. 1; instructions for him to report to the king, fr. 2938 fo. 67; he was lieutenant of Vendôme's company in 1513. (*Inventaire sommaire, Abbeville*, 144; R. Rodière, *La maison de Moy*, preuves, no. 510). As for Jean de Torcy, his importance is shown in the pension of L 1,800 he received in 1532–3 (BN fr. 2997 fo. 16–17) far above the normal one for a lieutenant of a gendarmerie company.
99 R. Rodière, *La maison de Moy*, II, p. 204 (nos. 532, 533), p. 212 (no. 574).

number of special tasks.[100] François de Stavaye, lieutenant of the company of Enghien, Vendôme's brother, in 1549, was captain of the Bourbon castle of Vendeuil and recommended in 1547 for continuance in his office as a man 'nourri en nostre maison' and from a family who had served the Bourbons well in the past.[101] M. de Maretz, ducal *maréchal de logis*, was also used as an agent in liaison with Amiens.[102] The gendarmerie company, in fact, provided a pool of military men, often drawn from the lesser local nobility, upon whom the governors could rely to transmit their orders. We must now turn to a discussion of the milieu from which such men were drawn.

[100] E.g. as commissioner to oversee the restitution of property under the treaty of Madrid (Vendôme to Torcy, 21 July 1526, AD Nord, B 18903, no. 34640), to oversee the truce of 1528 (Torcy to Montmorency, 14 July [1528], MC Chantilly L XV fo. 60) and as commissioner at Cambrai (his letters to Montmorency, 12 Sept. [1528], *Ibid.*, L X fo. 232, 17 Sept. [1528], *ibid.*, L VIII fo. 211).

[101] François de Stavaye was probably the son of Philippe, the captain of Vendeuil in 1513 (AD Aisne E 663 fo. 102r) and in 1535 was governor of Marle and receiving a *rente* of L 120 on the *chatellenie* of Vendeuil (*ibid.*, E 664 fo. 124v). He represented Marie de Luxembourg at the funeral of Mlle de Varennes (AN KK 277). François became captain of Vendeuil (E 664 fo. 124v). The letter of Vendôme of 1547, BN fr. 20521 fo. 19 was probably addressed to his brother Enghien and may have concerned his appointment as lieutenant of the latter's company. By 1549 a sum of L 400 was assigned to him as such on Vendeuil (AN KK 278A). He had begun around 1530 as *guidon* of Vendôme's company (AM Chauny EE 5, 13 Oct. 1530).

[102] Vendôme to Amiens, 27 Oct. 1551, *Inventaire sommaire, Amiens* II, 386 and AM Amiens CC 157 fo. 83 (ment. as *maréchal de logis*).

4

---------------------- ✥ ----------------------

THE PICARD NOBILITY AND ROYAL
SERVICE

That the public ethos and code of honour of the nobility remained predominant
in early modern French society is now hardly open to challenge, though the
implications for regional and national power structures are still being worked
out.[1] The nobility was a vast social order accommodating enormous differences of wealth, property, ability and interest; only a small proportion played a
leading political role, though military activity continued to provide a function
and some income for many more. The relationships which bound together this
heterogeneous social group were partly expressed in terms of kinship, partly
of the much-discussed notion of *clientèle* or patronage. Kristen Neuschel, in
her study of Condé's circle in Picardy during the 1560s and her subsequent
analysis of noble culture based on it, has argued, rightly, against simplistic
notions of patronage. Individuals certainly inherited ties of loyalty to great
magnates like the Bourbons or Guises, but such ties were not unconditional
and, in a province like Picardy with many small fiefs held directly of the crown,
feudal ties could be complex and contradictory.[2]

Neuschel, however, in viewing the nobility, like Arlette Jouanna, from the
perspective of the intensely chaotic period of the Wars of Religion, has tended
to exaggerate its independence and self-sufficiency as well as its own sense of
an autonomous legitimacy outside the scope of the crown and of public

---

[1] For example in A. Jouanna, 'Recherches sur la notion d'honneur au XVIe siècle', *RHMC* 15
(1968), 597–623; Jouanna, *Ordre social* (1977), 54–72, and *L'idée de race en France au XVIe
et au début du XVIIe siècle* (abridged, 1981) I, 105–24. For discussions of the general position
of the nobility, see J. B. Wood, *The Nobility of the Election of Bayeux, 1463–1666* (1980),
3–19; Wood, 'The Decline of the Nobility in 16th and early 17th Century France: Myth or
Reality?' *Journal of Modern History* 38 (1976).

[2] K. Neuschel, 'The Prince of Condé'; Neuschel, *Word of Honor. Interpreting Noble Culture in
Sixteenth-Century France.* R. Fossier, *La terre et les hommes*, II, 732–4.

114   *War and government*

power.[3] The interdependence of the crown and the French nobility remained indissoluble until the end of the ancien régime. Viewed from the perspective of the century from 1460 to 1560, a somewhat different picture emerges in which, after the initial purchase of support by Louis XI, the legitimacy of royal government ceases to be challenged and the nobility sought employment, office and charges under the crown to reinforce its fortune and influence.

This chapter will examine the way in which the Picard nobility from the reign of Louis XI onwards was incorporated in what M. Harsgor has called the 'oligarchy', both central and local, that came to dominate the administration of the monarchy. The method adopted is a discussion of the exercise of patronage by the crown and the pursuit of civil and military functions by the nobility in that period. The overall numbers of noblemen in the province was substantial, though no precision can be obtained. Two general surveys from this period establish the spread of wealth in the *bailliage* of Amiens, though they are not easily comparable. The 1529 list of fief-holders for payment of the king's ransom gives 745 names, though comparison with the 1557 feudal levy, with around 400 nobles and 570 *roturiers* holding fiefs, indicates that about 350 on the 1529 list must have been *roturiers*. However, from the letter it is clear that the old nobility monopolised the fifteen most valuable fiefs (worth over L 500 p.a.) and all but seven of the sixty worth over L 200 p.a. Only in the small fiefs worth under L 50 p.a. were non-nobles in the majority. In terms of title, the 1557 list gives 30 *chevaliers* and 258 *écuyers* with 6 titled (mainly absentee) lords. If we assume a number of around 400 nobles for Amiens and add the 149 members of the nobility of the Boulonnais (1560), the 182 noble fief-holders of Ponthieu (1577) as well as Vermandois, the number of adult noble fief-holders in Picardy cannot have been less than around 800.[4]

Only a much smaller group, of course, enjoyed royal favour. At the very

[3] Neuschel, *Word of Honor*, esp. 17–20, 196; Jouanna, *Le devoir de révolte* (1989), 91–116 and 119–46 on the importance she ascribes to 1559–60 in the growth of aristocratic discontent.

[4] E. de Rosny (ed.), 'Liste de personnes tenant fiefs nobles au bailliage d'Amiens qui contribuèrent à la rançon du roi François Ier en 1529', *MSAP* VI, 436–9: this gives sums levied as one-tenth of declared annual revenue, the largest being at Rambures at L 250. Unfortunately, it is imprecise on status. The 1557 survey in V. Beauvillé, *Recueil*, III, 380–540, is much clearer on status but ambiguous on wealth; many on the list made no declaration and the transaction was largely fictional, since the majority of Picard nobles were exempted either because of royal service or for war losses. Even so, and with due caution concerning the reality of the figures, a wealth profile of declarations actually made indicates an increase of the top level since 1529: 10 persons with revenues of over L 1,000 *p.a.*, 17 on L 500–1,000, 64 on L 200–500 and 121 on L 100–500. Around 390 noble fief-holders were listed for levy and 39 others served in person or provided substitutes. For other areas of Picardy: see Calonne (ed.), 'Répartition entre les gentilzhommes tenant fiefs nobles en Ponthieu (1577)', *MSAP*, XXIII, 71–98 and the 'Rolle des gentilzhommes' in the Estates of Boulonnais, Oct. 1560–March 1561, AD Pas-de-Calais 9B 2 fo. 162–, 190–8.

centre of affairs were the members of the *conseil du roi* but, as has been seen, Louis XI tended to keep his Picard converts away from this centre of power and none of them can be found among the core of the council. Only after Louis's death did the Beaujeu regency, on the dying king's recommendation it must be said, bring in first Esquerdes then Louis de Hallewin, Jean de Hangest-Genlis, a sort of expert in Picard affairs on the council, and Jacques de Luxembourg-Richebourg.[5] In the next decades, Louis de Luxembourg-Ligny and Raoul de Lannoy entered the council, but changes in its functions, its specialisation and emergence of the executive *conseil privé* from the 1520s meant that thereafter only the Bourbon-Vendômes continued sporadically to hold a place and then only in the wider council.

Much more widely distributed was the title of *conseiller et chambellan*, given, of course, not to members of the royal council, but indicating those who 'gravitent dans l'orbite du roi', to use Harsgor's expression. In the last two decades of the fifteenth century it is possible to identify at least thirty in Picardy, encompassing virtually all important provincial commanders, though the significance of the title began to wane after 1515.[6] Most informative in the earlier part of this period are the lists of those holding some kind of royal pension in the province. P. S. Lewis has thoroughly analysed the means of obtaining pensions under Louis XI and concluded that their main function was to reward service to the king, with a small group gaining the lion's share.[7] In fact, pensions were much more profligately scattered in the late fifteenth century than they were in the sixteenth, when they were distinctly concentrated on the provincial elite.

In 1480–1, about L 900,000 was paid out to 760 people, with 50 per cent of the money going to 8 per cent of the recipients. In the generality of Picardy, there were forty names, to which should be added ten others (including Richebourg at 10,000) paid in different receipts, receiving L 64,174. Clearly, Picardy was not over-represented.[8] A great increase in numbers, as might be expected, came from the Beaujeu regency's need to win support. The pensions list for 1485–6 gives seventy-six names for the generality of Picardy alone, but these only received L 29,862 as a result of proliferation of small grants. Of these seventy-six, fifty-nine were nobles and of those, twenty-eight (37%) were *chevaliers* and thirty-one (41%) *écuyers*. The rest were of uncertain status. Of the *chevaliers*, thirteen were also *conseillers et chambellans* (17%). As for

[5] P. R. Gaussin, 'Les conseillers de Louis XI' in Chevalier and Contamine, *La France de la fin du XVᵉ siècle*, 105–34; M. Harsgor, *Recherches* I, 267, 280, 282, 310, 375, 429.
[6] Harsgor, *Recherches* I, 210; for names of *conseillers et chambellans* see appendix 1.
[7] P. S. Lewis, 'Les pensionnaires de Louis XI' in Chevalier and Contamine, *La France de la fin du XVᵉ siècle*, 167–81.
[8] For all the following figures, see appendix 1.

rates, *chevaliers* and *conseillers* were above the rest with an average of L 1,547; four individuals – Esquerdes, Crèvecoeur, Cardonne and La Gruthuse – were far above this with sums ranging from 2,000 to 10,000, but the plain *chevaliers* drew an average of only L 198. The list for 1497–8 is broadly similar: eighty-five names, including forty-three not on the earlier list (roughly balancing forty who had disappeared). However, while the total paid out was comparable at L 26,975, the number of those drawing sums at the higher levels increased, and include figures like François and Jean de Créquy, Rambures and Miraumont. It seems reasonable to conclude that the pension was an important supplement to the income of not only the provincial governor, but also to those of the local governors and captains of castles. Beyond that was a penumbra of payments as small rewards, with noblemen who were members of companies of gendarmerie well to the fore.

The list of pensions given in the 1523 *Etat des finances* provides a useful comparison with the general list of 1480–1.[9] The overall allocation was L 500,000 (to 250 persons) but a supplementary list of pensions amounting to L 234,833 (for at least 465 persons) remained unpaid for lack of funds. This represents a substantial contraction, though the allocation of L 25,400 for Picardy is broadly comparable with 1485. There were considerable changes, however. The actual allocation in the *recette-générale* of Picardy of 24,200 was for twelve individuals only (including three – Vendôme, Saint-Pol and Pont-Rémy – on the top level as governors). The rest were mainly town governors and captains, like Humières, Huppy, Heilly and Montmor. The full list included twenty-four Picards for whom no assignation could be made. Considering the long gap since 1498, the continuities are revealing: Heilly, Créquy, Bournonville, Monchy-Montcavrel, Belleforrière and Longueval are all families which continue on the list. The list of 1532, the evidence from the assignations of the *Epargne* of 1537–8 and a list for the early years of Henri II indicate the continuing trend for the governors' pensions to increase greatly and for the whole list to be dominated by town governors and gendarmerie captains.

In view of the fragmentary nature of pensions lists after 1523, it is important to establish another yardstick by which to judge the composition of the governing elite down to 1560. By identifying those individuals of the local nobility who occupied town captaincies and governorships, as well as court office and other royal appointments, it is possible to gain an impression of a

---

[9] It seems likely that it was on the accession of Louis XII that the inflated pension allocation of the 1480s and 1490s was retrenched (see L. Firpo (ed.), *Relazioni di Ambasciatori Veneti al Senato*, 11 vols. (1965–84) V, 38.

kind of elite within the nobility. Avenues of preferment in both the province and at court were available and sometimes combined. Appendix 2 lists, with admittedly a certain margin of the arbitrary, eighty-six individuals from local families who held combinations of these positions in Picardy roughly in the period from 1500 to 1560. They were drawn from only forty-eight families (six of which provided twenty-three individuals: Créquy, Hallewin, Hangest, Humières, Lannoy and Pisseleu). Thirty-four individuals held combinations of town captaincies and court office and roughly half of these had command of gendarmerie companies, including: Créquy, Hangest, Humières and Pisseleu, all of whom had extensive court connections during the period. Importance at court may be measured by membership of the royal household, especially as *gentilshommes de la chambre du roi* or *maîtres d'hôtel*, while the title *conseiller et chambellan* gradually fell out of use. The court posts of the new reign were some measure of the degree of intimacy with the king, or an indication of administrative importance. Picard nobles might pursue largely military careers while obtaining posts at court as rewards; they might also be primarily courtiers and administrators who were given *ad hoc* local commissions and, as courtiers, could occupy ambassadorial posts in England or the Netherlands as 'gens aisez et d'icy près', in the words of Jean du Bellay.[10] Both kinds of career will be examined in the course of this chapter. Allowance must be made, of course, for accidents of genealogy and competence. Early in this period, the houses of Moy and Esquerdes were very prominent; neither retained their importance into the mid-sixteenth century. Some families, like the Humières and Créquy, experienced something of a golden age as a result of military capacity and fortunate court connections, while others, like the Mailly, retained local influence but had little success at court.

Gouverneurs et capitaines

In the first half of the sixteenth century, the captaincy of certain towns took on a new social and political significance because of the pressures of war and the importance of certain posts. Nomenclature began to change with a shift from the simple *captaine* to *gouverneur et capitaine* and the fact that captains were exercising some powers delegated from the provincial governor.[11]

Certain town governorships were more prestigious than others. The

---

10 Scheurer, *Correspondance de Jean du Bellay* I, 67.
11 Sénarpont was 'gouverneur et capitaine' at Corbie in 1541 (see letter of Antoine de Bourbon to him, St-Quentin, 21 Mar. BN fr. 3006 fo. 40); at Abbeville, the usual title was *capitaine de la ville*, but by the 1550s often *gouverneur de la ville* or *lieutenant par le roy à ceste ville* (BM Abbeville MS 378 fo. 133r; Des Forts, *Le château de Villebon*, p. j. no. 52, letter of Villebon, 13 Oct. 1557).

governor of Boulogne was also usually *sénéchal* of the county while the governor of Péronne was *bailli-gouverneur* of Péronne, Montdidier and Roye. A distinction should also be drawn between captaincies of prime military importance because of their proximity to the frontier (Montreuil, Hesdin, Doullens) and town governorships where little more than a ceremonial role and prestige were involved (Amiens and Beauvais, for instance). Péronne was a special case; of prime military importance, it was monopolised by one family in favour at court.

In the case of the great cities like Amiens and Abbeville relations with municipal authorities would be aggravated by disputes over prerogatives which reflect the greater self-confidence of established urban oligarchies and the fact that the captains received their salaries from the towns. Captains in purely military commands were paid by the crown. There were, in addition, a number of seigneurial towns where the captains were appointed and paid by their lords (Ham, Bohain, La Fère, for instance).

In the late fifteenth century, provincial governors like Esquerdes and La Gruthuse could still hold town captaincies as well, but by the mid-sixteenth century this kind of pluralism was no longer the norm. In 1541, du Biez gave up his captaincy of Boulogne on becoming marshal of France and then provincial governor and, in 1559, the captaincy of Boulogne was declared 'vacant' by Sénarpont's 'promotion en l'estat de nostre lieutenant général au gouvernement de Picardye'.[12]

In the captaincies of greater towns, where the posts were largely honorific, there was a strong tendency towards hereditary transmission in the sixteenth century. At Amiens, three generations of the Lannoy family (Raoul, François and Louis) held the post from 1495 to 1562, though only the first combined it with the *bailliage*. In 1515, Guillaume de Montmorency was succeeded by his son François, later sieur de La Rochepot, in the captaincy of Beauvais, in view of the 'bons et agréables services'[13] the family had done to the town, and on La Rochepot's death in 1551 his brother the constable succeeded him. Abbeville was perhaps a more sensitive post in the decades after the French reoccupation, but after 1512 was held, with some breaks, by two generations of the Haucourt de Huppy family. The governorship of Saint-Quentin, still militarily important, became quasi-hereditary in the Moy family, yet was too important to be left entirely in their hands in times of crisis.[14] At Montreuil, the captaincy passed from Pont-Rémy on his death in 1525 to his brother Bernieulles, who indicated

[12] MC Chantilly L XVII fo. 24; AD Pas-de-Calais 9B 2 fo. 94–5, provisions of 28 May 1559.
[13] BM Beauvais, Coll. Bucquet 57, 19 Nov. 1515, 5 July 1515.
[14] R. Rodière, *La maison de Moy*, nos. 530, 533, 575. Du Lude was in effective command there in 1524–5, Glevetz and then Guiencourt in 1556–7.

in a letter of the period that the duke of Vendôme had more or less appointed him.[15]

Such appointments were made, of course, by *lettres d'office* from the crown, requiring *lettres d'attache* from the marshals of France,[16] and were followed by the taking of an oath, sometimes before the town assembly. At Abbeville, Jean de Torcy (Vendôme's lieutenant) did this in January 1529, as did Huppy in November 1531 with a traditional oath not to bring in a garrison.[17] Esquerdes had also agreed to do this in 1477 'combien qu'il en ait fait le serment ès mains du Roy nostred. Seigneur quant il lui avoit donné et fait expédier les lettres d'icellui office.'[18] Trouble had also arisen over the guardianship of the keys. When Esquerdes gave up the office shortly afterwards to Picart, the *général des finances de Normandie*, the town took the opportunity to reassert its rights to the keys, usurped in the Burgundian period.[19] By 1531, the captains took an oath accepting that the *maire* and *échevins* had the right to guard the keys and control the opening of the town gates.

At Amiens, the role of the magistrates in appointment may have been more significant. The city appointed its own captain in 1465 and obtained royal letters of confirmation afterwards. The Burgundian captain Saveuses died in 1467 and was replaced by Jean Le Normant the *maire*, 'parce que on a tousjours dit que, quiconque fust maire, il estoit réputé comme capitaine'.[20] This was difficult to sustain, though by 1491, when Esquerdes was captain, he had another Jean Le Normant as his lieutenant, a man who was 'pas agréable à mesdis seigneurs de la ville ne au poeuple'. It was proposed that another, La Rendu, 'homme expert, dilligent et agréable au poeuple' should replace him. Clearly, though, the appointment of a bourgeois as lieutenant was becoming established.[21]

The city claimed the right to guard itself, the wall, munitions and the keys to the gates 'à l'ouverture desquelles portes et garde d'icelles, celluy quy est en l'office de maieur et non ledit cappitaine' had the right to be present.[22] The city's case was that the captain's main function was to give the watchword and, when Lannoy de Morvillier omitted to do this in 1542 a major row exploded, which indicates long-term irritations. In February 1543, Morvillier submitted

---

[15] Philippe de Créquy to the Parlement, 8 April 1525, AN X[1A] 1527 fo. 337v: 'd'autant qu'il a pleu à monseigneur de Vendosme après le trespas de feu monsieur de Pont de Rémy mon frère que Dieu pardoint, m'en donner la charge'.

[16] E.g. Louis XI, letters-patent for Picart as captain of Abbeville, 16 Sept. 1477; Gié's *lettres d'attache*, 20 Sept. (BN Picardie 91 fo. 176–7).

[17] BM Abbeville MS 378 fo. 22v (1529), 24v (1531). His successor, Azincourt, took the same oath, 15 Oct. 1537 (MS 347 fo. 32).

[18] BN Picardie 91 fo. 176r.   [19] *Ibid.*, fo. 177r.

[20] Thierry, *Tiers Etat* II, 295–6.

[21] *Inventaire sommaire, Amiens* II, 262.   [22] *Ibid.*, 348.

a long memorandum claiming what he said were the rights of captains 'des autres villes du royaulme de France'. These were (1) control of prisoners entering the town, (2) the right to all prisoners and booty entering the town, (3) the right to make all regulations concerning gate-duty, (4) to be consulted on fortification works, (5) to issue the watchword, (6) to be present should the *maire* wish to open the gates at night, (7) to hear any communications from the enemy during war and (8) to seize any valuables from foreigners entering the towns during war. In response, the *échevins* declared that, from time immemorial, their position as royal judges gave them the guard of the town, and that the captain received his salary simply for issuing the watchword.[23]

Such quarrels were the routine stuff of relations between proud municipalities and their captains, which elsewhere, as in Languedoc, could reflect a growing battle between the crown-appointed captain and *bonnes villes* ferociously determined to preserve their traditional privileges. P. D. Solon has shown how the royal captain could be involved in multi-cornered disputes with municipalities and ecclesiastical authorities in this period. La Rochepot had similar problems at Beauvais in 1528 over cognizance of a criminal case involving theft of firearms from the town hall. His representative claimed jurisdiction; the city and the bishop's men opposed him, though in this case La Rochepot was able to use his influence at court to gain an evocation to the *conseil privé* and the bishop appealed to the Parlement. The case dragged on until 1532, because too much was at stake in terms of prestige.[24]

A captain in La Rochepot's position could use his political influence to overawe opposition, of course. In 1533, La Rochepot, by now governor of Picardy, wanted his secretary's relative, Pierre l'Heureux, made a *sergent de ville*, despite a criminal record, and his will prevailed.[25] Lesser figures might have greater difficulty in making themselves obeyed. La Capelle, one of the most sensitive new border fortresses, had little municipal independence. In 1548, however, the commander, d'Esguilly, came into conflict with local landowners and asked for further powers. The constable merely ordered him to use his existing authority 'estant ung cappitaine de La Capelle fort là, comme il est, il n'y a personne qui luy puisse reffuzer aux environs'.[26] Unlike the more honorific governors, military men appointed directly by the crown not only had the task of guarding their towns but often, like Riou at Corbie in 1551, held

---

[23] *Ibid.*, 251–2.

[24] P. D. Solon, 'War and the *bonnes villes*: the case of Narbonne, ca. 1450–1550', 65–7. BM Beauvais, Coll. Bucquet 57, pp. 494–5, 498, 497. Normal appeals from the captaincy went to the Maréchaussée at the Table de Marbre at Paris.

[25] *Ibid.*, 522, 525.

[26] Montmorency to La Rochepot, 26 May 1548, BN fr. 3116, fo. 41.

powers as *ordonnateur des réparations* to order and assign payment for work on the fortifications.[27] The pay received by captains differed to some extent. At Amiens, the captain was paid by the town out of the *deniers communs* at a rate ranging from L 120 to L 200 p.a., admittedly a paltry sum in itself without perquisites.[28] This was also the case at Beauvais. After his brother's fall from grace at court, La Rochepot was perhaps of much less use to the town and his salary as captain was paid late. In December 1544, he expressed surprise at this and obtained a commission from the *bailli* of Senlis to obtain his due for 1543. Again in 1546, his salary was two years in arrears.[29]

In posts of a more purely military nature, the salary of L 600 (raised to L 1,200 by the 1550s)[30] was paid by the crown and attracted a virtually automatic pension, subject to the vagaries of royal finance.[31] In addition, municipalities paid a range of small emoluments.[32] Crown salaries might be paid directly by the *Epargne* from the 1520s but still more usually by a *mandement portant quittance* on a local *recette*. As with all such procedures, getting the money was a minefield of obstruction, especially with the overstrain of the royal finances in the 1550s. Belleforrière at Corbie in 1558 got a *mandement* for his L 1,200 assigned on Amiens, but when he sent to find out whether it was good, 'il m'a faict responce que non' and that the king had forbidden such assignations. So, Belleforrière had to lobby the duke of Guise to overrule this.[33] In the same year, Louis d'Humières had to lobby for prompt payment of his salary as gentleman of the chamber in order to cover his expenses as governor.[34] At Roye, in October 1558, Feuquières was ten months

---

[27] BN Picardie 31, fo. 277, compte. See also the orders of Adrien de Pisseleu for works at Hesdin, AM Hesdin no. 661 (AD Pas-de-Calais). La Fayette was *ordonnateur* for works at Boulogne, 1516–17 see Francis I to La Fayette, 8 Nov. [1516] BN fr. 3057 p. 237; 17 Aug. [1517] *ibid.* p. 161.

[28] Different figures, see *Inventaire sommaire, Amiens* II, 348, 352.

[29] BM Beauvais, Coll. Bucquet 57, pp. 603, 613.

[30] Possibly L 1,350 by 1560, see Ledru, *La maison de Mailly*, II, preuves, no. 482. For receipt of Jean de Pas, sr. de Feuquières as gov. of Roye in 1557, L 1,200 BN pieces orig. 2203 no. 56. In the late fifteenth century, the captain of Corbie received only L 100 (paid by the crown), see A. Bernier (ed.), *Procès-verbal du séances conseil . . . de Charles VIII*, 9 Aug. 1484.

[31] The nominal salary was supplemented by an automatic pension, see MC Chantilly L XVII fo. 24 and the pension list for 1532, BN fr. 2997 fo. 16–17. Pensions were usually allocated on local *recettes* but were not always easy to make good, see Montmorency to La Rochepot, 7 May 1548, BN fr. 3120 fo. 54; Bernieulles to Dubourg, Thérouanne, 22 May [1537], AN J 968 no. 15/11: 'avoir mémoire de moy pour le faict de ma pension . . . ayant regard au lieue où je suis, la despence qu'il m'a convenu et convient faire et le petit payment que j'ay tousiours eu jusques à présent'.

[32] E.g. L 11 5s paid to Heilly by the town of Hesdin in 1546 'pour avoir gardé les deux frances festes'. AM Hesdin no. 661.

[33] Belleforrière to Guise, 16 March 1558, BN n.a. fr. 21698 fo. 316–17.

[34] Humières to cardinal of Lorraine, 22 May 1558, BN fr. 3123 fo. 141.

behind with his salary and had to ask for the award of an office 'dont l'homme me offre mil escus' to cover his expenses. He claimed to have engaged L 4,000 of his own in the king's service and, indeed, it was quite usual for governors to be expected to cover such emergencies out of their own resources.[35]

Like the provincial governor, the local governor or town captain needed a degree of local popularity to assure cooperation. He had to some extent to act as a patron for his town and the more prestigious the governor the greater use he would be to the town in its political affairs. Beauvais made an especially lavish gift to La Rochepot as captain in November 1534 'attendu qu'il a grand accès auprès du roy' – of course, through his brother.[36] Such popularity brought rewards for a gracious governor like La Gruthuse at Abbeville, whose 'grandz paynes et services' to the town in obtaining a *franc-marché* brought him a gift of L 300 in March 1507 and a sumptuous present from Paris. Again, in December 1509, he got L 200 for services rendered and yet to come, and in April 1511 100 *écus* 'pour le plaisir qu'il a fait à ladicte ville' in obtaining letters.[37]

Not all governors were in a position to gratify their people or use influence at court. When, in May 1516, Péronne was faced by another levy on *franc-fiefs* it naturally resorted to its governor, Philippe de Hallewin (son of the provincial governor, Piennes) for letters to court requesting exemption. However, there was a conflict of interest since Hallewin, who had spent a great deal in the king's Italian campaign, had been recompensed out of the very levy they were trying to avoid. He could only suggest they go and see the royal commissioners: 'et sur ce propos lui a esté remonstré qu'il est nostre gouverneur et que c'est celui à qui nous debvons adresser pour nous secourir et aider à noz affaires'.[38] Jean II d'Humières, his successor as governor, was a far more effective patron. His intervention certainly saved the town from contribution to the Field of the Cloth of Gold and he got the town an *évocation* to the Grand Conseil.[39] Even so, there is a hint of difficulty. Early in 1524, during his absence, the usual aggravations had occurred between the town and his lieutenant. Humières's reaction was sour: 'vous me donnez assez à cognoistre que tous les plaisirs que je vous ay fait par cydevant sont perdus et que aymez autant estre mal de moy que bien. Il fauldra que je asaye à faire aultrement que je n'ay fait.'[40] Nevertheless, the relationship was restored to an amicable

---

[35] Feuquières to Guise, 8 Oct. 1558, BN fr. 20646 fo. 125–6.
[36] BM Beauvais, Coll. Bucquet 57, p. 532.
[37] *Inventaire sommaire, Abbeville*, p. 138, 140, 141, 142 (April 1512 – L 200).
[38] AM Péronne BB 7 fo. 18 (8 May, 10 May 1516).
[39] *Ibid.*, BB 7 fo. 106v (14 June 1520); fo. 123r (6 Nov. 1520).
[40] *Ibid.*, BB 7 fo. 214v (Humières to Péronne, Feb. 1524)

one and the town continued to take advantage of the favour of Humières at court. Throughout the 1520s and 1530s, the magistrates of Beauvais were sending constantly to La Rochepot to make use of his influence at court. This could involve getting rid of garrisons, lifting the moratorium on the *deniers communs*, help in disputes with the bishop or intervention against the depredations of the new legionnaires.[41] On each visit, he received gifts 'et on luy recommanda les affaires de la ville'. In 1536, it was noted, both La Rochepot and his brother were 'promps à faire plaisir à la ville'.[42] In the same way, when the town of Montreuil wanted to get rid of its gendarmerie garrison, it applied first to the governor, Saternault, and then to La Rochepot.[43]

Such captaincies, then, could be used to build a base of supporters and augment a nobleman's prestige, but the game was a difficult one; favours must be traded carefully and influence at court not overused.

How were captains appointed by the 1550s? Traditional *capitaines et gouverneurs* were still appointed by letters-patent, usually on resignation, rarely on dismissal.[44] By the 1550s, however, many more short-term captaincies were being made informally by simple letters-missive from the king. On the death of Jean III d'Humières in March 1554, the king installed Gournay by letters-missive 'tant qu'il y avoit altrement pourveu', with the charge 'avoir l'oeil à la garde, seureté et deffence d'icelle', which was the standard phrase of appointment.[45] By June, the king formally instituted Louis d'Humières as his brother's successor.[46] By this period, more commands were being given to professional soldiers who, while not normally displacing the titular governors, replaced them in military emergencies. They did not hold their posts by *lettres d'office* but by temporary commissions. For Amiens, which was a special case, the fifteenth-century precedent of a *lieutenant du roi* for the city was revived for two periods in the 1550s.[47]

For such commands, the king simply made his choice and sent orders to the local officers to receive him. Thus, at Abbeville in November 1558, on the departure of d'Ozence, Henri II ordered captain Lanquetot to replace him:

---

[41] BM Beauvais, Coll. Bucquet 57, pp. 490, 503, 537, 542, 548, 550.
[42] *Ibid.*, pp. 556 (17 May 1536), 504.
[43] AM Montreuil CC 1 (AD Pas-de-Calais).
[44] See *lettres de capitainerie* for Saragosse and Morvilliers at Boulogne, AD Pas-de-Calais, 9B 2, fo. 94v–95r, 113–14.
[45] Henri II to Péronne, 19 March 1554, AM Péronne BB 9 fo. 322.
[46] *Ibid.*, BB 9 fo. 349r (31 July 1554). He is addressed as governor on 31 August. Letters of expedition for office of governor, 12 June 1554, with that of *maître des eaux et forêts* (BN fr. 5128 p. 343).
[47] For the cardinal de Bourbon in 1552/3 and François de Montmorency in 1557.

y résider et commander . . . chose dont j'ay bien voulu vous en advertir et par mesme moyen vous commander et ordonner bien expressement et sur tant que craignez me désobeir et desplaire . . . que vous ayez à luy . . . obéyr en tout ce qu'il vous ordonnera pour le bien de mon service et la seureté, deffence et conservation dud. Abbeville.[48]

Exactly the same procedure can be seen in the replacement of Chavigny by captain Bresse at Doullens in November 1558. This indicates that the instrument of appointment was simple letter-missive – 'vous ay choisy pour commander à Dourlens' – and letters-close to the captains and people of the town.[49]

Town governors were often in sensitive posts and not free to come and go as they chose. Even Oudart du Biez, who had remained constantly at his post in Boulogne from the summer of 1529 until July 1530 – 'je n'ay couchie une seulle nuyt hors d'icy' – had to ask for leave to go to his manor at Le Biez on private business and then to go to Paris to meet the king.[50] As the wars went on, and especially towards the end, the strain of continual service began to tell in the rapid turnover in personnel. In November 1558, the captains of Abbeville and Doullens, d'Ozence and Chavigny, had to obtain royal *lettres de congé* to take leave for their private affairs. 'J'ay bien considéré', the king wrote to Chavigny, 'le besoing que vous pouvez avoir d'aller faire ung voyage en vostre maison, qui a esté cause que je vous ay accordé congé'. The duke of Guise told him to stop at Paris to report to the king.[51] In fact, even to leave Montdidier and visit Etaples for twelve days to collect his wife and see to his property, Artus de Rubempré had to obtain permission only on condition that he would 'laisser le charge et garde de lad. ville' to a suitable person and then return as soon as possible.[52] Sometimes permission would be refused, as when Alègre wanted to leave his post at Boulogne in November 1558 (he had been promised this by Guise when the armies broke up), but the king wanted him to

---

[48] Henri II to captains of Abbeville, 19 Nov. 1558, BN fr. 23192 fo. 212, draft; Guise to Sansac, 19 Nov. 1558, *ibid.*, fo. 210–11; Henri II to people of Abbeville, 19 Nov., *ibid.*, fo. 213.

[49] Henri II and Guise to Chavigny, 27 Nov. 1558, BN fr. 23192 fo. 333, 334; to captain Bresse, fo. 335–6; to the new captains of Doullens, fo. 336. See the same procedure in the appointment of Blérancourt at Chauny, March 1558 (Henri II to Blérancourt, 26 March 1558, BN n.a. fr. 21698 fo. 438–9).

[50] Du Biez to Montmorency, 9 July 1530, BN fr. 20502 fo. 53; to Berthereau, same date, MC Chantilly L XI fo. 189.

[51] Henri II to captains of Abbeville, 19 Nov. 1558, BN fr. 23192 fo. 212: 'un congé d'aller faire ung voyaige en sa maison'; Henri II to Chavigny, 27 Nov. 1558, *ibid.*, fo. 333; Guise to Chavigny, same date, *ibid.*, fo. 333v–334r; Henri II to Sansac, 27 Nov. 1558, *ibid.*, fo. 329–30: 'estant fort pressé du sieur de Chavigny . . . de luy donner congé pour aller durant ceste yver ung tour en sa maison'.

[52] Rubempré to Guise, 22 March 1558, BN n.a. fr. 21698 fo. 108–9; Henri II to Rubempré, 27 March 1558, *ibid.*, fo. 58.

stay on for a while until the peace negotiations with Philip II should be more clear.[53]

When François de Hangest-Genlis wanted leave from Chauny in March 1558, there were difficulties which produced an outburst of anger from him. Family business, he said, was pressing since he had had no chance to deal with it:

> vous sçavez en quel estat je suis de la pluspart de mon bien. Et à ceste cause de m'arrester en charge que je n'en ay jamais désiré de pareilles, et me voyant sy peu honnoré et advantagé que je me verres campaignon de beaucoup, qu'encores que je les estime fort gens de bien, je m'asseure qu'ilz n'ont jamais pretenduz d'avoir plus hault que ce que j'avois il y a vingt ans, depuis lequel temps je ne me trouve de guerres advancé.[54]

Genlis went on to ask for a post in which he could gain more honour, but it is clear that the refusal of leave had sparked off a deep-seated grievance that he had lost our financially by his military service. Guise quickly wrote back to grant his leave so that he could the sooner get back to his post and added:

> quant à ce qui touche vostre advancement, asseurez vous que Sa Maiesté demeure en si bonne volunté de vous faire cognoistre à la première occasion ce qu'il veult faire pour vous en cela, et moy, combien que je désire vous y faire d'ayde, support et faveur, que vous ne pourrez guères tarder que vous et [*sic*] n'en recevez les fruict que vous en désirez et que méritent voz services.[55]

The extent to which Genlis (a gentleman of the chamber, after all) received further reward is not known, though he did gravitate into the Protestant camp.

Most town captains had lieutenants to represent their interests in their absence. At Beauvais, La Rochepot nominated two generations of the Boileau family to this position. The captain's choice was fairly wide and was largely up to him. In December 1557, Louis d'Humières submitted a list of three men for his lieutenancy to the king, who replied:

---

[53] Guise to Alègre (Meilhaud) 16 Nov. 1558, BN fr. 20471, pp. 187–8: 'Il m'a donné charge de vous escripre que vous luy ferez agréable service en demeurer encores pour quelques jours, et ayant veu ce que réussira de la négociacion de la paix, j'auray souvenance de vous.' Alègre wrote again to the duke for 'souvenance de moy après la négotiation de la paix' (BN fr. 23192 fo. 337). He was close to Coligny as *guidon* of his company and became a noted Protestant, though he was promoted during the Guise predominance in 1558. Though from an Augergnat family, he had connections in Normandy through his mother, an Estouteville, and, as a result of his service in Picardy, gained further connection there through his marriage to Françoise de Mailly. See P. de Vaissière, *Une famille. Les d'Alègre*, 32–9.
[54] Genlis to Guise, Chauny, 13 March 1558, BN n.a. fr. 21698 fo. 161–2.
[55] Guise to Genlis, 22 March 1558, BN n.a. fr. 21698 fo. 148–9.

J'estime tous ces trois gens de bien et de service. Pource remectz je en vous, Monsieur d'Humières, de donner la charge à celuy d'eulx que vous jugerez estre plus propre . . . et s'il a besoing de lettres de moy à ceste fin, les luy feray expédier.[56]

In December 1558, this appointee, Saint-Martin, died and Humières wrote to Estinchan to take command of Péronne 'et vous luy obéirez comme ferez à moy mesmes'.[57] Nevertheless, at certain times the presence of the titular governor was encouraged by the crown no matter how competent the lieutenant might be.[58]

Such deputies were usually drawn from the minor nobility who had made a life out of military service, though gentlemen of more prestigious lineage did not shrink from taking the position. Jacques de Coucy-Vervins had started his career in the company of the duke of Vendôme in Italy and was closely connected with the Luxembourg-Bourbon family. Both Vendôme and Montmorency recommended him to Oudart du Biez in 1528, and the latter replied that: 'Je me suis advisé que n'avoie meilleur moyen de l'avancher que de le faire mon lieutenant et aussy que monseigneur de Vendosme m'en a escript à ce propos'.[59] He also acquired a pension of L 400 with the lieutenancy of the company, went on to act as captain of Boulogne during du Biez's absence in 1536, to marry du Biez's daughter and take over the captaincy on du Biez's promotion as marshal in 1541. Unfortunately, as is well known, his career ended in disaster because of the fall of Boulogne in 1544.[60]

As more temporary commands became available in the 1550s, there was a rush to get places for friends and relatives. In such matters, speed was all, for, as La Rochepot found when he tried to get the captaincy of Beauquesne for his lieutenant in 1536, the post had been disposed of before his letter arrived.[61] Villebon knew better when, in October 1557, on simply hearing of the illness of captain Ysnard, governor of Abbeville, he wrote in favour of his nephew the baron de Montenay, 'pource que le Roy n'en sçauroit mettre ung plus homme

[56] Henri II to Humières, 14 Dec. 1557, BN fr. 3134 fo. 83.
[57] Humières to Péronne, 4 Dec. 1558, AM Péronne BB 10 fo. 124r–v.
[58] E.g. Villebon to Humières, 13 March 1558, BN fr. 3128 fo. 99.
[59] Du Biez to Montmorency, 20 March (1528), BN fr. 3004 fo. 41–2.
[60] On Vervins, see D. L. Potter, 'A Treason Trial in 16th Century France', 603. Du Biez to Montmorency, 23 Oct. [1528], BN fr. 20503 fo. 33 and the pension list of 1532, BN fr. 2997 fo. 16–17.
[61] Jean Breton to La Rochepot, 1 Oct. 1536, BN fr. 3062 fo. 120–21. This was a long-standing problem. La Fayette had sought the captaincy of Hardelot in 1516, but the king replied: 'Entendez que là vous eussé tresvoulontiers et de bon cueur donnée . . . mais j'ay trouvé que avant mon partement de Millan je l'avoye réservée et donnée au filz dud. Sr de Capres', the previous captain Jean de Bournonville. Francis I to La Fayette, Lyon, 7 March [1516] fr. 3057 p. 41. See also B. J. Thobois, *Le château de Hardelot*.

de bien, et qui me soit agréable, pour aultant que c'est la ville de Picardie où je faiz tousjours ma résidence'.[62] Towards the end of the wars, when it looked as though certain places would be restored to the king under a peace treaty, there was a rush to take advantage. A rumour went round that the *bailliage* of Hesdin, with its new Spanish fort, would be handed over to France. If so, wrote René de Mailly, and since his town of Montreuil would no longer be so important a frontier post, he would give 'aultant et meilleur service pour congnoistre le pays' in the new fortress.[63] As peace approached and Blérancourt at Chauny saw that M. de Genlis would return to his post, he cast around for a new one in one of the restored fortresses and asked the king 'm'en faire départir quelqu'une pour y faire le debvoir . . . en considération aussi, Monseigneur, que j'ay perdu tout mon bien et n'ay eu jamais estat ne recompense'.[64]

Nobles sought these governorships for a variety of reasons, of course, despite the burdens they could impose in time of war. For some, such service could gratify their sense of honour, for others provide income and employment. But, as we have seen, the town governorships went very largely to the wealthy middle rank of the nobility and it was above all for the advantages of clientage that these posts were sought. They were then able to extract special advantages, like the protection of their estates in wartime and compensation for losses.[65]

Criteria of appointment and contacts at court

The tendency towards hereditary transmission of function was deeply rooted at all levels of French society, and it should not be surprising that military governorships should have been allocated in this way. The king himself made his assumptions clear in 1537 when, on the death of Jean de Sarcus, Mme d'Etampes's cousin and captain of the newly captured town of Hesdin, he announced his concern over the loss of a good servant and appointed his son to the captaincy of Le Crotoy, 'car le père m'a trop fait de services pour n'avoir de mémoire de ses enfans'.[66]

---

[62] Des Forts, *Le château de Villebon*, p. j. no. 52.
[63] Mailly to Guise, 10 Oct. 1558, BN fr. 20471, pp. 171–4.
[64] Blérancourt to Guise, 7 Nov. 1558, BN fr. 23192, fo. 37–8.
[65] See letters for Thibault Rouault, sr. de Riou for the protection of his estates in Artois, 31 March 1553, 'Par le Roy, le duc de Montmorency present, Bourdin', AD Pas-de-Calais 9B 1 fo. 226v–337r.
[66] Francis I to Orléans, 14 Dec. 1537, Ribier, *Lettres et Mémoires d'Estat* I, 75–6. Sarcus had died on 5 Dec. In the following May his widow received his pension fully paid up to that date (at L 1,000 p.a.), see *CAF* VIII, 294, 32057. See also A. B. Houbigant, 'Notice sur le château de Sarcus, tel qu'il devait être en 1550, précédé d'une vie de Jean de Sarcus', *MSAO*, 3 (1888), 369ff.; 4 (1889), 158–220.

The other most important consideration was local influence. When, in 1521, Vendôme was appointing commissioners to visit towns and gather in grain supplies, he appointed mainly town captains, 'gentilzhommes, gens de bien . . . qui sont demourans sur lesd. lieux ou voisins pour y estre continuellement'. The assumption was that the best man for a captaincy was usually a substantial local landowner with military experience.[67] In recommending the sieur de Fresnel as captain of Compiègne in 1539–40, Antoine de Bourbon did so 'pour ce qu'il est voisin de lieu et que suys seur il vous y fera service' and in May 1558, Blérancourt was appointed at Chauny because he was 'voisin dud. Chauny et personnage pour faire bien s'acquicter en une telle charge comme celluy qui en a ja faict preuve en deux places où il a eu le pouvoir de commander.'[68] Naturally, other considerations might apply, so that a certain Montbrun became governor of Guise in 1527, partly because of his local influence, but also because he was a gentleman of the duke of Vendôme's household.[69]

Of the subsidiary governorships of the province, only two, Péronne and Boulogne, seem to have required a continuing connection between the military command and the civil/judicial authority of the *bailliage*. The holders of both posts were closely allied to Anne de Montmorency and in many ways profited from his patronage and their careers illustrate the importance of court connections in conjunction with local influence.

The *baillis* and *sénéchaux*, by the sixteenth century, were noble and titular heads of the superior royal courts, received routine royal mandates concerning government and acted as marshals of the nobility for purposes of convoking the feudal levy. In addition, as will be seen later, they presided over the allocation of certain new military levies from the 1540s, though for most purposes they were represented by legally trained lieutenants. At Péronne, this function remained institutionally linked to the governorship, but at Boulogne the fact that the military governor was also, for most of the period 1500–60, *sénéchal* of the county (equivalent of *bailli*) was the result of local military necessity.

Antoine Motier de La Fayette, an Auvergnat whose family was closely connected with the Bourbons, was the son of an *écuyer* and *maître d'hôtel* to Louis XI and Charles VIII and himself served in Italy as *maître de l'artillerie*. There he formed a connection with John, duke of Albany. He is found in Picardy first as captain of a company of fifty *gens d'armes* at Doullens in 1513 and appointed captain of Boulogne in the autumn of the same year. Called on

[67] Vendôme to Francis I, 15 July [1521], BN fr. 3059 fo. 37.
[68] Antoine de Bourbon to Montmorency, 21 Nov. [?1540] BN fr. 3006 fo. 45; Guise to Genlis, 26 March 1558, BN n.a. fr. 21698 fo. 440–1.
[69] Chabannes to Francis I, 2 July [1521], BN fr. 2968 fo. 24–5; G. Moreau (ed.), *Journal d'un bourgeois de Tournai*, 246–8.

by Francis I to continue his service at Boulogne, he was one of the few complete outsiders to hold the post in the sixteenth century.[70] Some time between June and November 1518, he exchanged the *sénéchaussée* of Ponthieu for that of Boulogne, hitherto held by François de Créquy, sieur de Dourriers (the latter was dismissed or pressed to resign) and was in command of Boulogne during the opening stages of the Habsburg–Valois Wars.[71] There he was noted by the English as 'a great mocker and a coward' and may have been locally unpopular. Certainly the Créquy family seems to have remained at odds with him.[72]

In the early summer of 1521, he fell into dispute with the duke of Vendôme, who accused him of starting to raid the Burgundians without permission. The duke's argument was that Thérouanne was in need of supply before hostilities should commence. The magistrates of Montreuil had reported La Fayette's activities to Vendôme, who wrote to him 'affin que cognoisses que n'en suys pas content', forbidding the sale of any booty. La Fayette had threatened the magistrates and Vendôme promised 'de les garder envers vous et autres de toutes molestes et oppressions'. As a result, La Fayette sent one of his *gens d'armes* to court with a memorandum which, among other things, accused the duke and marshal de Chabannes of deception: 'Je ne sçay s'ilz ont paour de perdre leurs terres par delà'; in other words, he suggested that their main preoccupation was fear of losing their Burgundian lands in the event of war. He also suggested that the duke was envious that he had already equipped three ships for raiding at his own expense. These seem wild accusations, but indicate that La Fayette was at least a touchy man and that his relations with Vendôme were distinctly volatile.[73]

Some time later in 1522, he asked to be relieved of the governorship and was replaced by a protégé of Anne de Montmorency's, Oudart du Biez, who had distinguished himself in the capture of Hesdin.[74] La Fayette was outraged,

---

[70] Louis XII to La Fayette, 6 Oct. [1513], BN fr. 2888 fo. 23 (add. as captain of fifty *gens d'armes* at Doullens); 10 Dec. [1513], fr. 2888 fo. 21 (add. as captain of Boulogne, 14 Feb. 1514, fr. 2934 fo. 3).

[71] La Fayette add. as *sénéchal* of Ponthieu by Francis I, 11 March [1516] BN fr. 3057 fo. 45 and 31 Oct. [1516], *ibid.*, fo. 225–6. Until 1519 he is usually 'gouverneur et capitaine'. The first letter add. to him as *sénéchal* of Boulonnais is 20 Oct. [1518], fr. 2934 fo. 88.

[72] Edward Hall, *Chronicle* (reprint of 1550 edn. by C. Whibley, 1904) I, 262; *L&P*, III, ii, 3229 (on the clash between La Fayette and the Créquy family). Dourriers had been *sénéchal* since 1484.

[73] Vendôme to La Fayette, La Fère, 24 Aug. [1521], BL Galba B VI fo. 86 (71). Copy of the memorandum, unsigned and somehow purloined by English agents, in BL Caligula D VIII fo. 236. Authorship and date (June–July 1521) are confirmed by internal evidence. Guillaume du Lys, the bearer, was a member of La Fayette's company in 1520 (see Rosny, *Recherches généalogiques*, IV, 255).

[74] AN X^{1A} 4872 fo. 129v: 'auquel office le Roy l'a destitué et deschargé'. In 1521, La Fayette had asked for a cavalry command (letter to Robertet, 20 Sept., BN fr. 2933 fo. 259).

however, when in January 1523 he was summarily dismissed from the *sénéchaussée* and this, too, was given to du Biez. The reasons are somewhat obscure, but probably connected with the growing suspicion on the king's part of the constable of Bourbon's treasonable dealings with the emperor; the clientage connections between Bourbon and La Fayette were close and the duke of Vendôme, as a relative of the constable's, was also under a cloud.

In April 1523, La Fayette registered opposition in the Parlement of Paris, claiming that he had obtained Boulogne in exchange for Ponthieu and in return for good service to the crown. He had not committed any of the limited number of offences for which a *sénéchal* might be removed from office.[75] The crown claimed that the king had accepted La Fayette's resignation as captain 'considérant que si led. La Fayette à regret la tenoit ne luy feroit service qui estoit nécessaire'. Furthermore, Boulogne was 'l'une des clefz principalles' and great dangers could arise should the captaincy and *sénéchaussée* be in different hands 'pour les discors que de jour en jour peuvent entre eulx survenir pour la préheminence de leurs estatz'. This had been seen between La Fayette himself and Dourriers 'lesquelz différendz pourroient estre cause d'une mutinerie entre la ville et le chasteau', especially since La Fayette might bear a grudge against his successor. The court ruled, on du Biez's oath that he had not pursued the office or paid for it, that his appointment be registered.

La Fayette certainly took all this badly and we know that the constable stayed at his family's castle of Monteil-Gelat for a night on his flight from France the following September. Whether Antoine de La Fayette was the man of the same family who was in negotiation with English envoys in Lorraine the following November to hand over Boulogne to them is not clear; it may have been a cousin or a brother. Certainly, Antoine de La Fayette was never prosecuted for treason and seems to have retained his gendarmerie company until his death in 1531.[76]

Oudart du Biez was therefore left in sole charge of Boulogne. In January, he had received a bounty of L 10,000 on the domain of Airaines and Arceuil (royal forests) by Montmorency's influence and got his patron to have this pushed through the *Chambre des Comptes*. During the litigation in the Parlement, he

---

[75] Hearings of 27 April and 5 May 1523 in AN X^{1A} 4872 fo. 79v–80r, 129v–130r. In 1521 La Fayette had called du Biez 'merveilleusement homme de bien' (letter to Francis I, 22 Oct. BN fr. 2933 fo. 299).

[76] P. Paris, *Etudes sur François Ier*, 2 vols. (1885), 151–3 says that Antoine de La Fayette was involved but that he did not approve of the constable's actions. On the negotiations with the English, see Russell to Henry VIII, 1 Nov. 1523/9 Jan. 1524, *L&P*, III, ii, 3496; R. Doucet, *Le gouvernement de François Ier*, I, 282, says that the king was aware of the plot to hand over Boulogne.

asked Montmorency 'avoir tousiours l'affaire de mon office de séneschal pour recommendé'.[77] Montmorency himself had land in the Boulonnais and was now able to rely on the governor to help his agent there collect his revenues: 'je vous supplye ordonner à voz gens et me commander ce qu'il vous plaira que je face', he wrote to his patron around the same time.[78] Du Biez probably took over Saint-Aubin, La Fayette's lieutenant, but later dismissed and seems to have carried on something of a vendetta against La Fayette's clerical son Gilbert to get him deprived of some of the benefices he had acquired in Boulogne.[79]

The career of du Biez really prospered with his participation in the Piedmont campaign of 1536, his success at the siege of Hesdin in 1537 and his appointment as gentleman of the chamber on 22 March of that year. The office of marshal of France followed in 1541.[80] Du Biez remained a reliable client of Montmorency until the latter's fall from favour in 1540–1, at which time he seems to have accommodated himself to the new régime and replaced La Rochepot as governor of Picardy. In his absence, he had one son-in-law, Jacques de Fouquesolles, appointed *sénéchal* and the other, Vervins, governor. Jacques de Coucy-Vervins was closely connected with the Bourbon-Vendôme family. Du Biez took back the *sénéchaussée* on Fouquesolles's death in February 1545 and, despite his spectacular fall in 1547, he was not removed from the office until his final condemnation for treason in 1551. The day afterwards, Jean d'Estrées was appointed *sénéchal*, while Sénarpont had been governor since the expulsion of the English from the town in 1550.[81] Du Biez's success was closely related to his patronage at court, and his fall was the result of his failure to realise that the dominant figures of the old reign could not survive the king's death.

Two families in this period prospered significantly in their own localities as a result of cultivating fortunate connections which gave them access to royal favour: the Humières and the Heilly clans.

The political fortunes of the Humières family were built upon their close

---

[77] Du Biez to Montmorency, 6 Jan. [1523], BN fr. 3004 fo. 73 and same to same, 14 March [1523], *ibid.*, fo. 44–5: 'vous avez esté cause de don qu'il a pleu au Roy me faire des terres d'Araynes et d'Argueil'. Du Biez had been recommended to the king by Chabannes in 1521 as 'fort homme de bien' who stood to lose his property in Artois because of the war and needed compensation (Chabannes to Francis I, 20 July [1521], BN fr. 2968 fo. 32; Chabannes, *Preuves*, I, ii, no. 249).

[78] Louis Pocques to Montmorency, 6 Feb. [1523], MC Chantilly L XV fo. 90 and 28 May [1523], *ibid.*, L VI fo. 107; du Biez to Montmorency, 28 May [1523], BN fr. 3004 fo. 16–18.

[79] Du Biez to Montmorency, 30 April [?1530] BN fr. 3004 fo. 28; royal letters of 15 April 1526 and Du Biez, letters of registration, 1 Sept. 1526, AD Pas-de-Calais 9B 1 fo. 64v, 64v–65r.

[80] See *CAF* VIII, 169, 30829. He was appointed marshal in June 1541. See D. L. Potter, 'A Treason Trial in 16th Century France', 598.

[81] AD Pas-de-Calais 9B 1 fo. 112–13.

relationship with the Montmorency family, consolidated by the marriage of Jean II's daughter Charlotte to La Rochepot in 1525. Humières was already *gouverneur-bailli* of Péronne, Montdidier and Roye by 1519, *conseiller du roi* and captain of fifty lances by 1522. In 1528, Vendôme made him godson to his son Enghien and the following year his gendarmerie company was increased.[82] He was already well in favour at court, having accompanied Montmorency on special embassy to England in September 1527, and by 1530 was frequently present at the *jussio* for royal letters; on taking leave of the king at Compiègne, he had held 'long propos' with him which involved some confidential business for Louise of Savoy.[83] The following year he was gentleman of the chamber by Montmorency's patronage. By the 1530s, Humières and two of his sons held posts in the household of the royal children, establishing an important link with the entourage of Henri II. By May 1528, he had become lieutenant of one of the most prestigious gendarmerie companies, the dauphin's 100 lances.[84] In 1536, he was made governor of Piedmont for a while and, in 1537, stood in for La Rochepot as governor of Picardy. After an eclipse in the later years of Francis I, the family came into its own in the new reign, since M. and Mme d'Humières were given the governorship of Henri II's children and their son, Jean III, the sieur de Béquincourt, succeeded his father at Péronne by resignation in March 1548.[85] Jean III and his brother Louis also found places in the royal household as gentlemen of the chamber in 1547 and, when old M. d'Humières died in 1550, his wife continued to look after the younger royal children.[86] From Anet, in June 1550, the constable de Montmorency wrote of:

> le grand regret et desplaisir que j'ay de la perte que vous avez faicte de feu monsieur d'Humyères . . . et à moy d'avoir perdu ung si bon parent et amy que cestuy là.[87]

[82] BN pièces orig. (fr. 28033) nos. 2 & 4 & fo. 45. Cf. M. Hémery, *Monchy-Humières*, 20–40 *passim*.

[83] Humières to Montmorency, 6 Sept. [1529/30], BN fr. 3082 fo. 64. Bourrilly and Vaissière, eds., *Ambassades en Angleterre de Jean du Bellay*, 1–2.

[84] Household list for 1531, BN fr. 21449; receipt of Feb. 1536, fr. 28033 nos. 5 and 12 (for household offices), 6, 7 and 8 (for gendarmerie). Jean II de Humières was *chambellan* to the princes, 1532–6, his son Jean *enfant d'honneur* and *pannetier* 1536 – and Louis *enfant d'honneur* 1534 – (BN fr. 7853 pp. 1728–41); T. Lhuillier (ed.), 'La maison des princes, fils de François Ier', *BPH* (1889), 212–23.

[85] For the vast correspondence of M. and Mme d'Humières as governors of the royal children, see BN fr. 3116, 3120, 3134, 3128 *passim*. Receipts by Humières as governor of the Dauphiné, fr. 28033 nos. 8, 11, 13. Provisions for Jean Sr de Becquincourt as gov. of Péronne, *CAH* II, 2479.

[86] Household list for 1547, BN fr. 21449; Henri II to Mme d'Humières, 15 March 1552, BN fr. 3120 fo. 87.

[87] Montmorency to Mme d'Humières, 22 June 1550, BN fr. 3116, p. 349.

The following year, the constable's brother La Rochepot died and he wrote
to thank Jean III for looking after him:

> J'ay receu la lectre que m'avez escripte et ne sçaurois dire l'ennuy et grand
> fascheur que je porte de la perte que j'ay faicte de mon frère, qui m'est
> autant dure à passer que fortune qui m'eust sçeu advenir . . . vous remer-
> cyant de bon cueur de la peine que j'ay entendu qu'avez prinse au près de
> luy et de la bonne compagnie que vous tenez à madicte seur.[88]

In 1552, he was writing to Louis d'Humières that, in his family's affairs,
'asseurez vous que je feray tousiours en toutes choses qui concernent vostre
avancement ce que vous pouvez esperer de vostre bon parent et amy'. In
November of that year, Jean III received his reward in the form of a commission for fifty lances, obtained from the king at the constable's request.[89]
When he died in March 1554, his brother Louis succeeded him at Péronne and
was made a captain of the king's guard by October, when the king called him
to court to take up his duties.[90]

Louis d'Humières had already made a substantial career at court under
Montmorency's patronage. Entrusted as gentleman of the chamber with
various confidential missions to Picardy in autumn of 1552, and commissions
from the king to Catherine de Medici during the 'voyage d'Allemaigne', he
was captured in Italy in late 1553, when special measures had to be taken to
obtain his release. By this time, Charles, the second son of the family, had
obtained the bishopric of Bayeux.[91]

Numerous family letters survive from the 1550s which indicate the close and
easy relationship between the Humières brothers and the constable's family,
including the new governor of Picardy, Gaspard de Coligny.[92] Louis
d'Humières was an impetuous type who found himself in Spanish captivity

[88] Montmorency to Jean III d'Humières, 23 Aug. 1551, BN fr. 3116 p. 111.
[89] Montmorency to Louis d'Humières, 23 Nov. 1552, BN fr. 3116, p. 167; same to Jean III
d'Humières, 13 Nov. 1552, BN fr. 3116, p. 161: 'J'ay eu si bonne souvenance de vous que le
Roy à ma requeste vous a donné la charge de cinquante hommes d'armes.' Act expedited the
same day – BN fr. 5128 p. 247.
[90] Montmorency to Louis d'Humières, 31 Aug. 1554, BN fr. 3116, p. 285, 289 (add. as
captain of the guard and governor of Péronne); BN fr. 5128 p. 343, captain of guards, 1554;
Henri II to same, 31 Oct. 1554, BN fr. 3134 fo. 50; request to Louis d'Humières, for
reinstatement of a man he had dismissed from the guard, by Guise, 21 Oct. 1554, fr. 3123
p. 11.
[91] Henri II to Humières, 7 Nov. 1553, BN fr. 3134, fo. 47; same to bishop of Noyon, 24 April
1553, fr. 3120 fo. 78 (for the lands of the extinct Lassigny branch of the Humières to be transferred to Louis d'Humières).
[92] Charles d'Humières, bishop of Bayeux to Charlotte d'Humières, 1 Jan. [1553], BN fr. 3038
fo. 109; same to Jean d'Humières, Creil, 8 March 1552/3, Pichon, 'correspondance des
d'Humières', no. 31 (also nos. 27, 29); Montmorency to Humières, 6 Nov. 1553, BN fr. 3116,
p. 273; Coligny to Louis d'Humières, 16 Aug. 1556, fr. 3128 fo. 92–3; same to Charlotte
d'Humières, 9 April 1557, Pichon, fo. 35.

during the winter of 1555–6.[93] He had, however, to be pressed to accept a company of fifty lances in the crisis of 1557, when the king wrote to him:

> vous ferez chose qui me sera fort agréable de l'accepter, estant asseuré que pour cela vous n'aurez diminution d'aucune chose mais augmentation d'honneur et de bienfaict estant bien délibéré de le vous faire congnoistre par effect et recompense de pensions.

This was presumably because Humières would have to relinquish his company of the household guard. The cardinal of Lorraine told him that he could have had a company of 100 lances had one been vacant.[94]

By 1560, the youngest Humières brother, Jacques, sieur de Roncquerolles, was also gentleman of the chamber and had become involved in negotiations for a marriage to strengthen his family's ties with the Montmorencys. In November 1559, the constable wrote to both Louis and Jacques of talks which had already begun between him and his sister-in-law, Charlotte d'Humières, for the marriage of Jean III's daughter and heiress, Léonore, to the constable's son, Guillaume de Thoré, mentioning 'l'antyenne alliance qui a esté entre noz maisons avec l'amytié que nous avons porté respectivement'. There might be difficulties, he added later, but he would agree to a hundred lawsuits 'pour la singullière affection que je vous porte, ensemble à toute vostre maison, car ayant vescu d'entyennetté en grande amytié avec voz prédécesseurs, vous pouvez estre certain que je désire continuer de bien en plus'. In January, he pressed both Louis and Charles to come to Chantilly to agree terms, being unwilling to go further without them, and the marriage was agreed. Unfortunately, Léonore d'Humières died young in 1563 without issue and all the family property reverted to Jacques, who also became governor of Péronne in 1560.[95] His determined Catholicism gave him a leading part in the foundation of the Catholic League in Picardy and distanced him from the court.

The Humières family exemplifies how a clan of considerable regional importance could reinforce its position by a close alliance with an all-powerful court politician. By the help of Montmorency, the Humières were almost taken into the royal family itself by holding so many posts of intimacy in the royal household, and their hold on the government of Péronne was never in doubt during this period.

In many ways, the family of Pisseleu, sieurs de Heilly, may be seen as

[93] 'vostre retour de prison' since the truce – see Coligny to Louis d'Humières, 13 May 1556 BN fr. 3128 fo. 88.
[94] Henri II to Humières, 15 Aug. 1557, BN fr. 3134 fo. 62; Lorraine to Humières, 12 Aug. 1557, fr. 3123 fo. 35; 15 Aug. 1557, fr. 3123 fo. 37 (CC Colbert, 23 fo. 109).
[95] Constable to Jacques d'Humières, Chantilly, 21 Nov. 1559, BN fr. 3116 p. 369; to Louis d'Humières, *ibid.*, p. 367; to Louis, 26 Nov. 1559, *ibid.*, p. 371; to same, 22 Jan. 1560, *ibid.*, p. 307.

complementary to the story of the Humières, for when the Humières were enjoying their greatest political fortunes, those of the Heilly were in eclipse. Guillaume de Pisseleu, sieur de Heilly, Fontaine-Lavaganne etc., came of a Beauvaisis family which had acquired important properties in Picardy by marriage in the fifteenth century.[96] It was a tough stock, for his father is supposed to have died aged 115 in 1508 and he himself married three times and had thirty children. His sisters were married into the Soyécourt, Mailly and Sarcus families. Guillaume took part in the defence of the province in 1521 and was a *maître d'hôtel du roi* in 1524.[97] The real fortunes of the family, however, were made by his daughter, a member of Louise of Savoy's household, who at the age of eighteen captivated the king on his return from Spain in 1526. Anne de Pisseleu was a young woman of remarkable intelligence and beauty – 'la plus belle des savantes et la plus savante des belles' – but had a penchant for worldly goods which led her not only to enrich herself but also her family. The king also forced Jean de Brosse-Bretaigne, comte de Penthièvre, to marry her in order to regain his confiscated property and created the county (1534) and then duchy (1536) of Etampes in their favour. From 1540 and Montmorency's decline in favour, Mme d'Etampes became all-powerful at court.[98]

Anne's eldest brother, Adrien sieur d'Heilly, joined the court as an *écuiyer d'écurie* in 1531 but, as sieur de Fontaines-Lavaganne, had already acquired a reputation for commanding infantry and became one of the captains of the Picard legion in 1536 along with his kinsman, Jean de Sarcus.[99] When Sarcus died in 1537, Orléans appointed Estrées to look after Hesdin, while the king approved, reserving his right to appoint another in due course 'tel que ie verray et connoistray estre à propos pour mon service'. This proved to be none other than Adrien de Pisseleu, whose fortunes were distinctly rising.[100] By

---

[96] E. Jumel, 'Monographie d'Heilly', *La Picardie*, 19 (1874); J. Garnier, 'Inventaire de quelques papiers provenant de château d'Heilly', *MSAP* IX, 311–55. See also D. L. Potter, 'Marriage and Cruelty among the Protestant Nobility in 16th-Century France', *Eur. Hist. Quar.* 20 (1990), 9–11.

[97] Report by Vendôme, 24 July 1521, BN fr. 2968 fo. 1: at Péronne 'monsieur de Heilly tiendra garnison avec les cinq cens hommes de pied dequoy il a charge'. Du Biez to La Fayette, 11 Sept. [1521], BN fr. 2971 fo. 25. In Feb. 1524 Heilly was told by Vendôme to assemble 100 men for guard duty at Ancre in his son's name (Vendôme to Péronne, 16 Feb. 1524, AM Péronne BB 7 fo. 213v).

[98] E. Desjardins, *Les favorites des rois. Anne de Pisseleu, duchesse d'Etampes et François Ier* (1904).

[99] See royal household list of 1531, BN fr. 21449 fo. 184v, 198v (1532), 213v (1533) and all subsequent years to 1546. M. du Bellay, *Mémoires* (Michaud et Poujoulat) p. 169 (1523); letters of Montmorency to Heilly, 26 Aug. [1536] in Friant, 'Lettres de plusieurs personnages . . . au château d'Heilly' *MSAP* II, 172–3: as commander of 1,000 Picard foot; Francis I to Heilly, 30 May 1537, BN fr. 2973 fo. 5. Jean de Sarcus was Anne de Pisseleu's first cousin. See A. Houbigant, 'Notice sur le château de Sarcus', *Mém. Soc. Acad. Archéol. de l'Oise* IV (Beauvais, 1859), 158–220.

[100] Ribier, *Lettres et Mémoires d'Estat*, I, 75–6. The first letter add. to him as *gouverneur et capitaine* of Hesdin is 23 March 1539/40, SAP MS 57 no. 27.

September 1545, he was commanding a company of gendarmerie and was employed on a number of special royal commissions in the later years of the reign.[101]

Anne's full sister, Péronne, was married to Michel de Barbançon, sieur de Canny in 1522, and the latter in turn benefited from royal favour with the lieutenancy of Vendôme's company (1523), a command of 2,000 men of the Picard legion (1536), participation in the Savoy campaign of 1535–6, the defence of Péronne in 1536 and special embassies to the court of the Netherlands. Canny, like others of his family a member of the young duke of Orléans's household, was fortifications commissioner at Ardres and, briefly, in 1541–2, deputy governor of the province, dying in 1543.[102] Mme d'Etampes watched over the fortunes of Canny's six surviving children. François, the eldest, was placed at court as gentleman of the chamber with his cousin Jean de Pisseleu in 1546, and had already become *bailli* of Senlis in 1543. Anne's other sisters were well placed by marriages into the Bretaigne-Avagour and Chabot families.

One of Mme d'Etampes's most effective forms of patronage was finding ecclesiastical posts for relatives in holy orders. Her brother Charles became an abbot of several houses, bishop of Mende then of Condom. Another brother, François, became bishop of Amiens in 1546, while her nephew Jean de Barbançon became bishop of Pamiers in 1544 (though he had difficulty in getting recognition). But it was her maternal uncle, Antoine Sanguin, who did best of all. Known as cardinal de Meudon after his castle near Paris, he was successively bishop of Orléans, archbishop of Toulouse and *Grand Aumônier of France*.

The crucial nature of court favour is revealed by the fate of the family after Francis I's death in 1547. Not only were the duchess and her uncle deprived of the best items of their landed property (in favour of the Guise family) but, almost as soon as the new reign began, Adrien de Pisseleu was stripped of his governorship of Hesdin in favour of Louis de Saint-Simon.[103] He never regained military office and in 1558 was described as 'ung veil gentil homme, homme d'honneur et fort oppiniastre, qui s'estoit retiré en sa maison depuis la mort du roy François'. He only emerged from obscurity when, during the crisis of 1557, he threw himself into Ham. There, as Villebon reported, 'les cappitaines sont gens de bien et le bon homme Monsieur de Helly qui y est

[101] SAP MS 57 no. 3 and *passim*.
[102] J. Garnier, 'Inventaire', 315–16; Peigné-Delacourt, *Histoire de l'abbaye de N-D d'Ourscamp* (1876), 59, transcribes the date as 15 April 1547, but the true date is given in BN fr. 7853 fo. 1744–51.
[103] *CAH* I, no. 600; II, no. 2182 (revenues of seigneurie of Hesdin).

entrez, qui ne parlera pas les premiers'.[104] The castle, however, fell by assault during negotiations and Heilly surrendered to the duke of Savoy, dying in captivity at Béthune in December 1558.[105] The old Heilly's heroism during his last campaign seems to have rehabilitated his family for, despite the Protestantism of Mme d'Etampes and so many of her relatives, his son Jean de Pisseleu went on to obtain the governorship of Corbie after the death of Henri II.

The attitude of Anne de Pisseleu may also have proved influential in the fortunes of another major Picard family, the Créquy. A family of ancient lineage and reputation, they had acquired a firm hold on a number of local governorships by the early sixteenth century. Jean VI's brother, Dourrier, was *sénéchal* of Boulogne down to 1518 (when he was replaced by La Fayette) and his children married into the Moreul, Saveuse, Lannoy and Humières families. His most brilliant son was Antoine, sieur de Pont-Rémy, captain of Thérouanne in 1513, *bailli* of Amiens and governor of Montreuil. As governor of the province in 1524, under Vendôme, his career was brought to a premature end by death in a skirmish, leaving a formidable reputation acquired in the Italian and Picard wars.

Pont-Rémy's daughter Anne married Guillaume du Bellay in September 1531 after two years of negotiations. The king, Montmorency and Vendôme were all persuaded to regard the match favourably and the witnesses to the marriage contract, as for an earlier one between Anne de Créquy and Jean de Mailly in 1527, reveal the close ties of familiarity between the Créquy and families like the Montmorency, Humières, Saveuse, Rambures, Sarcus and du Biez.[106] Pont-Rémy's brother, Jean VII, 'le riche', sieur de Créquy, married the heiress of the Soissons-Moreul family and inherited the principality of Poix.[107] His wife's bastard brother, Artus sieur de Fresnoy, took over the governorship of Thérouanne, while another Créquy brother Philippe, sieur de Bernieulles, was given the governorship of Montreuil on Pont-Rémy's death and transferred it to Jean VII in 1537 on his move to Thérouanne following Fresnoy's

---

[104] BN fr. 4742 fo. 8v; Villebon to Humières, 12 Sept. 1557, BN fr. 3138 fo. 130; *Mémoires de Guise*, 390.

[105] SAP MS 60.

[106] V. L. Bourrilly, *Guillaume du Bellay* (1905), 110–11; compare with the marriage contract of Anne de Créquy and Jean V. de Mailly, baron de Conty, Aug. 1527, A. Ledru, *La maison de Mailly*, ii, 275–7. On this du Biez to Montmorency (Jean's uncle), 16 Dec. (1526), BN fr. 2979 fo. 142: he had spoken to Anne's mother Jeanne de Saveuses, who had agreed 'néantmoins qu'elle en veult faire par l'advys de messeigneurs ses parens et amys. Il me semble . . . que sy vous avez envye que la choze sortisse son effect . . . ' Jean de Mailly died of plague at Naples in 1528.

[107] There is no substantial study of the Créquy family, but on the principality of Poix, see A. Delgove, 'Poix et ses seigneurs', *MSAP* XXV, esp. 439–52. See also Richoufftz, 'Les Créquy dans le Vimeu', *MSE Abbeville* ser 4, VI, 1–277, on related lines.

death.[108] The Créquy estates were concentrated on the Canche area and their interests in these positions were natural. All these men were commanders of gendarmerie companies, though Pont-Rémy's command of sixty lances (raised to eighty-five by 1524) indicates the importance of his military reputation.[109] Neither Jean VII nor Bernieulles were commanders of the same rank, though each inherited portions of their brother's company in 1525.[110]

The military abilities and political success of the family were carried on by Jean VII's son, known for most of his life as the sieur de Canaples, a great favourite with Francis I. Brantôme calls him 'le plus rude homme d'armes qui fust en toute la chrestienté', because of his prowess in jousting, and adds that he was 'grand, puissant et de haulte taille et forte corpulence'.[111] In 1525, he was considered as successor to Pont-Rémy as provincial governor, but it was decided that he was too young.[112] Canaples's career was much enhanced by his marriage in 1525 to Marie d'Acigné, a Breton lady-in-waiting to queen Claude and a second-rank mistress of Francis I, one of his 'little band' of vivacious ladies. They received the revenues of the counties of Mantes and Meulan as a wedding present (bringing in L 25,000 a year in the 1520s),[113] by October 1527 Canaples was a *gentilhomme de la chambre* and by 1532 captain of one of the bands of 100 *gentilshommes de la maison du roi*, with a pension of L 4,000 attached.[114] Marie d'Acigné was able to use her influence in 1528, when Canaples wished to resign the *bailliage* of Amiens (which he had taken over on the death of Pont-Rémy in 1525) to his relative, Saveuses.[115] Canaples became one of the leading infantry commanders in Picardy in the mid-1530s and commanded the garrison which surrendered at Montreuil in

---

[108] Bernieulles to the Parlement, Montreuil, 8 April 1626, AN X¹ᴬ 1527 fo. 337v. For mention of Jean VII de Créquy as governor of Montreuil, 21 Jan. 1537, BN p.o. Créquy no. 31. Bernieulles married Louise de Lannoy, daughter of Raoul, sieur de Morvillier, as a result of the great friendship between her father and his uncle, M. de Dourrier. See C. Bazin, 'Description historique . . . de Folleville', *MSAP* (1850), 70–3 for Raoul de Lannoy's will making this clear.

[109] Pont-Rémy was captain of eighty lances 1515–18 (BN p.o. Créquy nos. 8–10) including, by 1521, ten lances 'de creue' and in 1524 a total of eighty-five (*ibid.*, nos. 11–12).

[110] Bernieulles inherited thirty-two lances (*ibid.*, no. 15) and Jean VII de Créquy twenty-four (*ibid.*, no. 16). Jean VII was captain of fifty lances by May 1538 (*ibid.*, no. 33). See also Jean VII de Créquy to Parlement, Abbeville, 8 May 1525, AN X¹ᴬ 1528 fo. 437v.

[111] Brantôme, *Oeuvres complètes*, ed. Buchon, 2 vols. (1838) II, *Hommes Illustres*, 239–40.

[112] AN X¹ᴬ 1527 fo. 255v (see ch. 3).

[113] *CAF* I, 443, 2345; VII, 589, 27301. For receipts for revenues from Mantes, see BN p.o. Créquy, no. 20 (L 1,530–4,420), no. 21 (L 1,526–4,092), no. 28 (L. 1,533–2,529 for the *grenier à sel*).

[114] Appointed *gentilhomme de la chambre* in the year 1527–8 (BN fr. 21449) and by 20 Oct. 1527 (BN p.o. Créquy no. 19). Captain of 100 *gentilshommes de la maison du roi* by 1532 (*ibid.*, no. 26). His pension in 1532 was L 4,000 (BN fr. 2997 fo. 16–17 – his father drew L 1,200 on this list).

[115] Marie d'Acigné de Montmorency, [August 1528] MC Chantilly L XII fo. 48.

June 1537. The king then sent his father with a force to reinforce Thérouanne.[116]

The Créquy family was somewhat eclipsed in the later years of Francis I, to judge by its loss of local governorships, and it is tempting to ascribe this to court politics. Mme de Canaples was evidently on unfriendly terms with Mme d'Etampes by the later 1530s and the latter, of course, was at that stage about to enter her period of greatest influence. Letters to Montmorency indicate that difficulties were being experienced in getting to payment of pensions, always an indicator of political weight.[117] Nevertheless, Canaples retained his post at court and accompanied an embassy to England in July 1546.[118]

The death of Francis I changed the alignment of interests. Marie d'Acigné was chased from the court by the new favourite, Diane de Poitiers, but Canaples, now sieur de Créquy on his father's death (1547), repudiated her and found himself again high in favour both with the king and the Guise family. Henri II renewed his father's gift to Canaples of the confiscations judged against forgers in November 1548.[119] His relatives proceeded to advance as ecclesiastical pluralists. His brother François became bishop of Thérouanne in 1539 and another, Antoine, bishop of Nantes in 1561. His eldest son Antoine was nominated bishop of Nantes in 1553 and bishop of Amiens in 1561, though had difficulty in gaining acceptance.[120]

[116] For a narrative of these events, see BL Add. MSS 2103 fo. 57ff. Jean VII was titular governor of the place, but his son Canaples was in command there. See Jean VII de Créquy to Lisle, Montreuil, 29 and 30 April 1537 (*L&P* XII, i, 1065, 1073). Jean and Philippe de Créquy to Montmorency, 23 June 1537, BN fr. 3155 fo. 68; Francis I to Bernieulles, 19 Oct. 1537, BN fr. 3058 fo. 27.

[117] In the late 1530s Bernieulles was succeeded at Thérouanne by Villebon (possibly by May 1538, see Montmorency to La Rochepot, 13 May 1538, BN fr. 2995 p. 265–6). Jean VII was replaced at some time before 1544 as governor of Montreuil by Satenault. Mme de Canaples was an 'enemy' of Mme d'Etampes, see Brantôme, *Oeuvres complètes*, Dames Galantes, ed. Pouchon, I, 398 – she had given 'la belle Torcy' to queen Léonore as maid-of-honour. For letters concerning patronage, see Jean VII de Créquy to Montmorency, 16 March 1538/9, MC Chantilly L XVI fo. 40; Canaples to same, 14 April 1539, *Ibid.*, L XVI fo. 42.

[118] *L&P*, XXI, i, 1185, 1292, 1348. Canaples had the function of conducting ambassadors to court.

[119] R. Knecht, *Francis I*, 423; I. Cloulas, *Henri II*, 149, argues that Mme de Canaples was protected by Diane de Poitiers, though chased from court by queen Léonore. For grants to Canaples in 1548, see *CAH* II, no. 3923, 4038, Jean VIII was still referred to as 'Canaples' in 1548–9, which causes confusion. The letter signed 'Canaples' to the duke of Guise, 4 Jan. 1549/50, and complaining of gout and colic is surely by Jean VIII: 'le plus grand honneur et bien qui me peut avenir seroit d'estre jà auprès de vous pour toute ma vie vous obéir', BL Add. MS 38034 fo. 31. Rabutin describes M. de Canaples as present in the royal army of Picardy in 1553 as head of a company of the royal guard. This, too, should be Jean VIII (*Commentaires*, SHF edn, I, 222–3). He seems to have inherited his father's gendarmerie company, now forty lances, while remaining captain of the royal guard (BN p.o. Créquy no. 52, 55, 56, 59, 62), a point which Louis d'Humières was unable to carry in 1557.

[120] *DBF*, Créquy, no. 5, 6, 12. On the appointment of François de Créquy to Thérouanne in 1539 and his arrival there with a force of cavalry, see Lisle to Cromwell, 22 May 1539, *L&P*, XIV, i, 1032 (see also 1108, ii, 246).

The military traditions were continued by Canaples's son, Jean IX, who started as *guidon* of Aumale's company in 1547 and went on to become a gentleman of the royal military household and lieutenant of Sansac's company by 1553.[121] Jean IX saw service as one of the commanders of light horse in the province from the late 1540s and worked closely with Guise in 1552–3, though he was taken prisoner at Hébuterne in August 1553.[122] Jean IX's death at Saint-Quentin in 1557 dealt a blow to the fortunes of the family. His father had died in 1555 and his only surviving son, Antoine de Créquy, was a cardinal in holy orders. The family estates, one of the most substantial holdings of the province (cardinal Antoine had an income of L 60,000 p.a.) with their political influence, passed into the hands of a number of different families and the family name was subsumed into that of the Blanchefort.[123]

The lesser nobility as royal commissaires

Posts at court provided another avenue for advancement to the lesser nobility of Picardy in this period and added to the provincial elite a number of expert administrators, drawn from the ranks of the ancient nobility, whose functions were not primarily military but whose activities, in that they were often concerned with army provisioning, were closely allied to those of the military elite. It is the aim of this section to examine this route of promotion through the careers of two particularly well-documented individuals, François de Rasse and Jean d'Estourmel.[124]

At the start of his career, François de Rasse, sieur de La Hargerie, was only a modest Picard landowner. Family tradition claimed descent from the old counts of Hainault and, though the lordship of Tilloloy in the Santerre had been

[121] BN p.o. Créquy no. 46 (March 1547), 64 (July 1553). In July 1549, he received a gift of L 2,500 drawn on a fine levied on an *élu* of Amiens (BN fr. 5127 fo. 89r).

[122] See correspondence of 'Canaples' (Jean VIII or Jean IX) with Guise in the Gaignières collection BN fr. 20513–15, 20519, 20534, 20548–9, 20553–5, portions of which are printed in *Mémoires de Guise*. E.g. his protestation that Guise 'ne pouvoyr jamais avoyr ung plus fidelle serviteur que moy' (letter of August 1548, BN fr. 20534 fo. 54). On his capture in August 1553, see Jean Thieulaine's 'Livre de Raison', *MSA Morinie* XXI, 154.

[123] A. de La Morlière, *Recueil de plusieurs nobles et illustres maisons*, quoted in A. Janvier and C. Bréard, *Etude sur Domart-les-Ponthieu* (1878), 48. See also E. Allard, *Histoire généalogique des familles de Bonne, de Créquy, de Blanchefort etc.* (1572).

[124] Another such case is that of Florimond de Biencourt, sieur de Poutrincourt, of the old nobility of Vimeu, who was brought up by duke Claude de Guise and in 1526 became a member of his gendarmerie company. In 1532 one of 100 *gentilshommes de l'hôtel du roi* and in 1544 *maître d'hôtel* to the dauphin, he replaced Longueval as *bailli* of Vermandois in 1547 and became *maître d'hôtel du roi* (BN Clair. 813; fr. 3132). As such, he played an important part in army organisation in the 1550s (see, for instance, Guise to Amiens, 12 Jan. 1557/8, AM Amiens EE 323 fo. 97). See A. Huguet, 'Jean de Poutrincourt', *MSAP*, 4–5. For letters to him in victualling matters, 1560s, see BN fr. 18676 fo. 220v.

in the family for generations, strong links with the Cambrésis were still maintained.[125] Reliable records go no further back than François's grandfather, Pierre, who had been governor of Péronne for the duke of Burgundy but had been replaced in 1475, at which time he probably entered the service of Louis XI.[126] After the death of his father, Adam, around 1509, François was a prominent local landowner in the Santerre only, but later he acquired the lordship of Démuin, and his wife, Anne de Fouquesolles, brought him La Motte and Mazinghem as well as connections with the Bernieulles and Bournonville families. His only child, Antoinette, he married to Jean III de Soyécourt, whom he described as 'de bonne rasse et de bonne anchienne maison de ceste Picardie', and later she was to rebuild Tilloloy and marry one of the leading Picard noblemen, Louis d'Ognies de Chaulnes.[127] The family therefore prospered considerably in the first half of the sixteenth century and this may be explained largely by success at court.

In 1530, La Hargerie claimed to be fifty years old and that he had served several princes since the age of twenty. He had entered major service as a *gentilhomme de la maison* (military household) by 1509, at the start of a court career which was to last well into the reign of Henri II.[128] By 1513 or 1514 he had obtained the captaincy of Crèvecoeur, a castle in the Cambrésis claimed by France and much in dispute in the sixteenth century.[129] When war began in 1521, he was in command of a troop of 600 light horse at Thérouanne, and in the autumn of 1522 was in command, under Vendôme, of the Somme crossing at Bray during the unsuccessful English campaign. In the great crisis of 1525,

---

[125] For general notes on Tilloloy and its lords by A. Ledieu, see *Cabinet historique de l'Artois et de Picardie*, 1980–91, 123–6 and E. Coet, 'Tilloloy et ses seigneurs', *Le Vermandois*, i (1873), 820–75, containing numerous inaccuracies and little on François de Rasse. Also BN dossiers bleus 557 nos. 1 and 2.

[126] On Pierre, sieur de La Hargerie, see Dournel, *Histoire générale de Péronne*, 154; AM Péronne CC 3 fo. 96v. A relative may have been Jacques de Rasse, captain of Compiègne (AM Compiègne BB 5 fo. 11r). Pierre had a bastard son Guillaume, see BN dossiers bleus 557 no. 3. Baudost de Noyelles (*d.* 1461), sieur de Tilloloy, had earlier been governor of Péronne for the duke of Burgundy and also commander of the troops against Jeanne d'Arc at Compiègne. Pierre de Rasse presumably inherited Tilloloy from him. See A. Huguet, 'Aspects de la guerre de Cent Ans en Picardie Maritime' part 1, 205–6.

[127] BN fr. 8177 (Inventaire des titres de Henri de Bourbon) fo. 95v: attestation of relief for lands held of the seigneurie of Roy, 7 June 1482; fo. 105r: 5 *dénombrements* submitted by Adam de Rasse, 10 June 1482. François bought Bellincamp etc. near Roye in 1509 (*ibid.*, fo. 96r). For the purchase of Démuin in 1543, see Beauvillé, *Recueil*, IV, 409. On his wife's connections, see BN dossiers bleus 557, nos. 1 and 2. See also La Hargerie to Montmorency 11 Aug. [1530] MC Chantilly L VIII fo. 351, and 'Messire Adam de la Hargerie' in 'Estat d'aucuns gentils-hommes de l'ostel du Roy de la nacion de Picardie', October 1481, BN fr. 2906 fo. 14–15.

[128] *Ibid.*, MC L VIII fo. 351 'J'ay porté le harnas et servy les prinches et eu plusieurs petites cerges'. See also Louis XII to La Hargerie, Feb. 1509, in Deloffre, *Mém. de la Soc. d'Emulation de Cambrai*, 1888. *Registres de Paris*, III, 85. *Rôle* for 100 *gentilshommes de la maison*, BN fr. 2933 fo. 22v (L 390 p.a.).

[129] La Hargerie to Montmorency, 28 Aug. [1529], MC Chantilly L VI fo. 1.

he was sent by the Parlement as muster commissioner to Picardy in the absence of any other responsible officials.[130]

The mission of 1525 is the first recorded instance of La Hargerie's appointment to the post of military administration and foreshadows a career as an adaptable administrative agent. In 1530, he claimed to have entered the service of Anne de Montmorency in 1524 and, in view of the importance of this move, his words should be quoted:

> Depuis six ans entièrement me suis retyrer soubz la protection de vos elles, désirant sur toutes choses vous fayre agréable service affin de vous fayre entendre que mon principal désir estoyt qu'il vous plut moy tenyr du nombre de vos bons et léaulx serviteurs. Par tout oue il vous a plut moy commander à vous suyvre, je l'ay faict sans avoyr regret.[131]

La Hargerie had entered into the clientage of Montmorency, though not, it seems, into his household. His service meant that he received various commissions and in turn expected favours from the man who was, from 1526, *Grand Maître de France* and thus in a position to appoint him, in 1528, a *maître d'hôtel du roi*.[132]

The correspondence, most of it in La Hargerie's own hand and showing traces of Picard dialect, which survives between La Hargerie and his patron for the years 1528 to 1531 is a precious source for the activities of a figure who was at once a local notable, a minor courtier and an administrative expert.[133] It reveals that his chief task was to keep his master informed about what is going on, both in Picardy and on the other side of the Netherlands frontier, transmitting both rumours and solid information.[134] The first extraordinary commission to come La Hargerie's way in 1528 was to arrest and examine some men accused of getting Burgundian prisoners out of France with the

---

[130] Report by Vendôme, 24 July [1521], BN fr. 2968 fo. 1: 600 horse under Picquigny and La Hargerie at Thérouanne; La Hargerie to Francis I, 24 Nov. [1521], Tilloloy, BN fr. 2933 fo. 285; Vendôme to Montmorency, 31 Sept. [1522], BN fr. 6637 fo. 4; La Hargerie to Montmorency, Bray, 4 Oct. [1522] MC Chantilly L I fo. 43–4; order of Parlement, 15 April 1525, AN X¹ᴬ 1527 fo. 370r; De La Forge to Parlement, 19 April 1525, *ibid.*, fo. 379r–v.

[131] La Hargerie to Montmorency, 11 Aug. [1529] MC Chantilly L VIII fo. 351.

[132] BN fr. 21449 fo. 143 (first mention as *maître d'hôtel du roi*).

[133] There are thirty letters from La Hargerie to Montmorency and his secretary for 1528–30, an unusually large number for a person of his standing. The letters from La Hargerie in the former Montmorency archives at Chantilly and the BN cover the periods 1522, 1528–31, and 1542, as do those of all the other correspondence. This is a matter simply of archival survival characteristic of the Montmorency archive, evidently, from an early period. The papers were kept by Nicolas Berthereau, the secretary.

[134] For example, La Hargerie to Montmorency, 13 Feb. [1528], MC Chantilly L XII fo. 24–5 with enclosure: 'propos tenus d'entre le vischancelier de Flandres et ung gentilhome espaignol' sent to La Hargerie, *Ibid.*, L XII fo. 58–60.

connivance of local officials. After the truce of 1528, he was sent on a mission to Malines for discussions with the regent Margaret on the question of the restoration of Marie de Luxembourg's property in the Low Countries and, incidentally, to buy tapestries for Montmorency at Antwerp.[135] Then came a commission to discuss infractions of the truce at Cambrai. This he tried to withdraw from on grounds of ill health – 'ne vouldroes presser vos serviteurs à choses impossibles', he wrote – and also because he was not enough of a lawyer for the task. He suggested instead his friend and neighbour Pierre de Belleforrière, also a *maître d'hôtel*, but on recovery he was pressed into service again.[136]

La Hargerie married his daughter to Jean de Soyécourt in January 1529 and was unable to go to court to serve his quarter because of the festivities.[137] However, he was one of those, along with Jean d'Humières and Oudart du Biez, appointed to look after the practical arrangements for the peace conference of Cambrai in June, taking pains over minute details concerning furnishings and lodgings.[138] The peace left the status of Crèvecoeur uncertain and, as its captain, La Hargerie was bound to be concerned. The seigneurie, he pointed out, was not worth very much but he had to defend the position against the pretensions of the titular lord, M. de Bèvres. He was there in October 1529 to press the people to remain loyal to France, but an arbitration commission which met in December 1529 failed to agree and the status of the place remained in doubt until 1559.[139]

La Hargerie's next major task was to join Montmorency for the journey

---

[135] La Hargerie to Montmorency, Malines, 24 July [1528], MC Chantilly L VII, fo. 55: 'J'ay esté en Anvers pour voyr des tapisseries pour vous. J'en ay achepté . . . Aussy j'ay trouvé ugne belle tapisserye et fort excellente pour ugne grand salle qui est parcelle à celle de l'Enpereur don m'aves parlé qui sont les temples de honneur oue sont les vices et vertux est en hystoyre . . . elle est triumphante et croy este cells que désires à recouvrer.' On this mission, see also *CAF* IX, 49, and Dumont, IV, 517–18. Bourrilly, ed., *Ambassades . . . de Jean du Bellay*, 356–7, 365–6, 372–3; AD Nord B 18985 no. 38182 etc.

[136] La Hargerie to Montmorency, 1 Oct. [1528], MC Chantilly, L X fo. 78: 'car la commission est honeste et près de luy', Belleforrière to Montmorency, Yttre, 9 Oct. [1528], L VI fo. 32 (Belleforrière was *maître d'hôtel* in 1526). La Hargerie recovered and by Jan. 1529 was at Cambrai with Ymbert de Saveuses, see La Hargerie to Montmorency, Cambrai, 11 Jan. [1529], L XV fo. 61. On this mission see AD Nord, B 382.

[137] *Ibid.*, and La Hargerie to Berthereau, 23 Jan. [1529], MC Chantilly L XV fo. 328. Ledieu gives the wrong date, 1524, for this marriage. La Hargerie to Montmorency, 14 Feb. [1529], L XIV fo. 326.

[138] La Hargerie to Montmorency, Cambrai, 19 June [1529], MC Chantilly L XIV fo. 21; 27 June [1529], L III fo. 289; L VIII fo. 175; 20 June [1529] L V fo. 235; 30 June [1529], L III fo. 287. Guarantees for security were negotiated by La Hargerie and du Biez together.

[139] La Hargerie to Montmorency, 28 Aug. [1529], Tilloloy, MC Chantilly L VI fo. 1. He advised that commissioners well versed in the local custom be appointed. La Hargerie to Montmorency, Péronne, 16 Oct. [1529], L VIII fo. 296–7 and to Berthereau, 8 Dec. [1529] L VI fo. 275; 16 Jan. [1530] L IV fo. 307.

south to negotiate the release of the king's children.[140] He stayed with the *Grand Maître* until the entry of queen Léonore into Paris and was back at Tilloloy in June, when rioting broke out in Picardy over grain shortages. He was called on by Vendôme to visit the grain stores of the province and was also involved in suppression of the disturbances: 'et ay donné tieulles terreurs et courses à plusieurs suyvant ladicte commission que espère cesseront désobeyr le Roy'.[141]

La Hargerie had been told to be back at court to serve his quarter at the end of June 1530, but his main task seems to have been to escort the marquise de Genette, one of queen Léonore's suite, to the Low Countries, keeping an eye on her and also on Louis de Praet, the envoy who was with her. Praet was an unsympathetic travelling companion and the mission was an awkward one, but La Hargerie managed to extract some useful information and, when the marquise left France on 8 August, she gave him a handsome present.[142]

The difficulties of this mission coincided with a dangerous moment in La Hargerie's relations with Montmorency and it is worth for a moment considering how these had developed. La Hargerie is first found inscribed in the list of *maîtres d'hôtel* in the royal household in 1528 and his appointment must have been made on Montmorency's recommendation. Inclusion on the active household list was a coveted honour, and we find La Hargerie thanking his patron in fulsome terms for his instructions to serve his quarter in October 1529: 'Je me tiens à james tenu et oblegié vous fayre service se que renderay paine fayre tous les jours de ma vye. Je suis touiours prest fayre service au Roy de toute ma petite puissanche'.[143] From his correspondence, it seems that, for help at court, La Hargerie relied on Montmorency's secretary Nicolas Berthereau, asking him to bring his business to his master's attention on entering the council chamber, for instance.[144] Other friends seem to have included La Pommeraye, Bochetel and marshal Maigny. There were also connections with a major Picard aristocrat with court office,

---

[140] The order mentioned in La Hargerie to Montmorency, 14 Feb. [1530], MC Chantilly L XII fo. 26. La Hargerie was to be at Bordeaux by 15 March.

[141] La Hargerie to Montmorency, Tilloloy, 4 June [1530], MC Chantilly L VII fo. 118–19.

[142] La Hargerie to Berthereau, 4 June [1530], MC Chantilly, L XV fo. 354. While he was at Bayonne his daughter had fallen ill (L VIII fo. 351). Letters on the mission with Mme de Genette: to Montmorency, 22 July [1530] L VI fo. 51–2.

[143] La Hargerie to Montmorency, 16 Oct. [1530], MC Chantilly L VIII fo. 296–7.

[144] 'Je vous prie présenter à mondict seigneur mesdictes lettres et de bouche luy recommander l'affayre don luy escripts quant il enterra au conseil.' La Hargerie to Berthereau, 1 Oct. [1528] MC Chantilly L XV fo. 265. 'Vous m'aves tant de foys obligié à vous fayre service plus le grand plaisirs que piecha m'aves faict sans vers vous l'avoyr mérité ny encore satisfaict', same to same, 1 Jan. [?1531] L VI fo. 271–2.

Charles de Roye, whose wife Madeleine de Mailly was Montmorency's niece.[145]

For some reason, it was during La Hargerie's service with Montmorency at Bayonne that a cloud passed over the *Grand Maître*'s good will towards him. We find his own version of this in a letter of complaint that he addressed to Montmorency in August 1530, at the end of his mission with the marquise de Genette:

> Monseigneur, quelques temps avant que partissies de Bayonne, il m'a semble que me feistes plus froide et maigre chière que n'avyes acoustumé, don j'ay ew plusieurs mele'celyées et de laquelle chose me suit descouvert secrètement de vos bons et pryvés serviteurs . . . je ne puis pensser d'oy peut venyr que vous ussies aultre extyme de moy que de vostre léal serviteur. Je sçay bien que les grands vens d'envye aus cours des prinches font aussi bien branler les petits clochiers comme les grands . . .

He hinted that perhaps his zeal for Montmorency's service had led to the jealousy of others who had determined to poison the *Grand Maître*'s mind against him. As it was, being neither poor nor rich, he was content with his lot. However, – and here we come to the point – his son-in-law Soyécourt, a young man of nineteen or twenty, had been placed in the service of Montmorency's great rival at court, the admiral Chabot.[146] La Hargerie had hoped for him to be placed with the new queen and the marquise de Genette had written in his favour. Clearly, La Hargerie was asking for the appointment as a sign of Montmorency's renewed trust. Whether he got it is unknown but, though there is no reason to suppose that La Hargerie suffered from any ill favour later, there is little sign of his close relations with Montmorency after 1530 (though this may be archival accident). For the rest of the year and until the end of the surviving correspondence, La Hargerie seems to have continued his regular reports on the Low Countries.[147]

Though La Hargerie's regular surviving correspondence ceases after 1530, other evidence indicates that, if anything, his employment in administrative affairs became even more important. He had been recommended by Jean du Bellay in August 1530, along with two other Picard lords, Antoine Lameth and Ymbert de Saveuses, as a possible successor as resident ambassador in England, 'qui seroyt bien, comme il me semble, pour faire ce mestier', especially as negotiation in French rather than Latin had become the norm in

---

[145] La Hargerie to Berthereau, Pentecost (4 June) 1530, MC Chantilly L XV fo. 354: 'Je prie estre recommandé à la bone grace de monsieur de La Pomeroye, greffier Bouchetel et mareschal Maigny.' La Hargerie to Berthereau, 1 Jan. [?1531].

[146] La Hargerie to Montmorency, Tilloloy, 11 Aug. [1530], MC Chantilly L VIII fo. 351.

[147] E.g. La Hargerie to Montmorency, 29 Aug. [1530] MC Chantilly L VIII fo. 57.

that post. Nothing came of it.[148] At court, he continued as *maître d' hôtel* and, with Jean de La Barre, was commissioned to make the arrangements for Louise of Savoy's funeral in 1531. In December 1532, he was commissioned to investigate fraud among accounting officials in Picardy and in January 1533 to oversee the collection of domain revenues there. He was still acting in this capacity during March of the following year, when he visited Saint-Quentin to collect certain revenues.[149]

La Hargerie continued to act as captain of Crèvecoeur (even though its status had been left unsettled in 1529) and, just after the recommencement of war in 1536, he held a dramatic meeting at the castle with the estates of Cambrésis, 'fort effroiez et estonnez', in which he demanded that they undertake the food supply of the French troops. Pointing out that they were beholden to the king for his recognising their neutrality, he threatened them that the supplies would be taken by force if not freely given and added:

> Sire, ma harengue leur fist venir la sueur au front et non sans cause. Et me
> firent responce que la fureur d'un prince de telle puissance que vous l'avez
> est à craindre à si povre chose comme eulx.

The deputies withdrew to consider and it seems likely that they agreed not to affront the king.[150] La Hargerie retained the governorship and, in 1538, obtained the *survivance* for his new son-in-law, Chaulnes.[151]

The beginning of war in 1536 saw the assignation of numerous missions to La Hargerie. In April, he was at Montreuil to assist in the revictualling of Thérouanne and in July at Amiens to organise provisions.[152] By this time, he must have received the commission of *commissaire des vivres* which was henceforth to occupy much of his time. Early in August, he was present at a meeting of the high command under Vendôme[153] and in the spring of the following year he was helping La Rochepot organise provisions for troops at Montreuil.[154] In May, the king gave him the task of helping suppress 'vaccabons et autres gens sand adveu tenans les champs', which echoes

---

[148] Scheurer, *Correspondance de Jean du Bellay*, II, 67, 74.

[149] Order to pay his salary for 1531, Aug. 1540 (*CAF* IV, 131, 11598) *Ordonnances, François Ier* VI, no. 608 (28 Dec. 1532); commission of Jan. 1533, *CAF* II, 299, 5294; AM Saint-Quentin liasse 138 no. 18, fos. 9–23.

[150] La Hargerie to Francis I, Crèvecoeur, 15 Oct. [?1536, poss. 1543] BN fr. 3085 fo. 80–2.

[151] *CAF* III, 637, 10428. Ledieu, 'Notice sur Tilloloy' gives 1543 as the date of the Chaulnes marriage, which must be wrong.

[152] Vendôme to La Rochepot, 19 July 1536, BN fr. 3069 fo. 98; Bernieulles to Vendôme, 20 April 1536, MC Chantilly L XV fo. 42. He is clearly named as *commissaire des vivres* in 1543 by M. du Bellay, *Mémoires* (Michaud et Poujoulat), 512.

[153] Vendôme to La Rochepot, 11 Aug. 1536, BN fr. 3069 fo. 22.

[154] Du Biez to Montmorency, 18 April [?1537], Montreuil, BN fr. 3004 fo. 30.

the action he had taken against the unruly peasantry of the province in 1530.[155]

The truce of Bomy required negotiations for clarification and, as in 1528, La Hargerie was considered the man for the job. With Imbert de Saveuses, he joined the commission at Cambrai which met to negotiate in September–November 1537 and the final conclusions, bearing La Hargerie's name, were finalised on 3 November.[156] In February 1538, he is found with Jean d'Estourmel advising La Rochepot on the procurement of food for the garrisons, and in July he transmitted the king's angry command to the abbé of Saint-Riquier to stop delaying his resignation in favour of the Imperial ambassador.[157]

Between 1538 and 1542, there is a dearth of information about La Hargerie's life, but it seems that he continued to be a *commissaire des vivres*, especially during the war with the emperor which began again in 1542. One of his first tasks was to join his old colleague Saveuses in evaluating the property lost by the king's subjects in the Netherlands and that of the emperor's subjects in France.[158] The fact that he was active in Antoine de Bourbon's service at this time, however, meant that his work was delayed on this commission, which in any case was an enormous undertaking and unlikely to be a source of profit. The nature of the relationship with Antoine de Bourbon is unclear, but we know that La Hargerie lent the duke 1,000 *écus* on his marriage in 1548, in itself a testament to his wealth and status.[159]

Other tasks in the period included a visit to Compiègne to inspect the fortifications,[160] but undoubtedly the most difficult commission on which La

[155] Francis I to La Rochepot, 26 May 1537, BN fr. 3058 fo. 33. See also the appeal of the victualling commissioners to the chanceller occasioned by the absence of Estourmel and that 'monsieur de La Hargerie est aussi ailleurs empesché' (Dodieu and La Rochepozay to Dubourg, Abbeville, 21 July 1537, AN J 968 no. 81).
[156] On these negotiations, see Francis I to La Rochepot, 4 Oct. 1537, BN fr. 3044; 13 Oct. 1537, fr. 3035 fo. 69; 19 Oct. 1537, fr. 3035 fo. 72; 7 Nov. 1537, fr. 3044 fo. 8; Mary of Hungary to La Rochepot, 5 Oct. 1537, MC Chantilly L II fo. 293; same to Montmorency, 2 Oct. 1537, BM Carpentras, MS 490 fo. 226. The final act, signed 'De Revsse', in Ribier, *Lettres et Mémoires d'Estat*, I, 58–9, 59–62; Francis I to La Rochepot, 20 Nov. 1537, fr. 3058 fo. 3.
[157] Francis I to La Rochepot, 13 Feb. 1538, BN fr. 3044 fo. 14–25; Francis I to La Hargerie, 24 July 1538, fr. 3000 fo. 83–4 (file copy, crs. Breton).
[158] La Hargerie and Saveuses to Francis I, Amiens, 29 Aug. 1542, BN fr. 6616 fo. 42–3, *CAF* VII, 333, 24803: order of 6 Sept. 1542 to seize goods of the emperor's subjects; La Hargerie to Tournon, 25 Sept. 1542, fr. 6614 fo. 233–4: 'soudainement monseigneur de Vendosme m'a envoyé requérir à cause d'aucuns amas de viij mille hommes que on luy avoyt rapporté estre ensanble . . . '
[159] AN KK 278^A fo. 72 – the sum was repaid in 1549.
[160] AM Compiègne BB 20 fo. 13r. On 1 May 1543 he was appointed one of the 'commissaires généraux des vivres de l'armée de Hainault', *CAF* IV, 433, 13076, 13168. Named as 'commissaire du roi pour faire la munition de pain pour le camp', letter to Amiens, May 1545 (AM Amiens, BB 25 fo. 139).

Hargerie served was the one that met at Cambrai between December 1544 and January 1545 in order to clarify the treaty of Crépy and put an end to the long-standing disputes. It failed, of course, but not before generating a mountain of paper. The final act settled some matters but left others, including Crèvecoeur, still in dispute.[161]

Appropriately enough, La Hargerie's last service to Francis I was as his *maître d'hôtel* when, with La Rochepozay, Poton and Babou, he organised the dead king's lying in state, notably the service of the funeral effigy and, on 3 May 1547, its removal and the installation of full mourning. In this capacity, he had to decide on the esoteric matter of whether to continue the service of the royal table after the effigy had been removed from the royal bed.[162] With the new reign, he continued as at least titular *maître d'hôtel* in the royal household, but there is now no sign of the former close relations with the restored Montmorency. There is also some evidence that La Hargerie was seeking to ingratiate himself with the Guise who were, after all, his feudal superiors at Démuin. In 1550, he arranged for his grandson, François de Soyécourt, to enter the service of the duke of Guise and in his letter of thanks he pointed out that:

> il est jeune et souvent que la jeunesse ne poize point les fais que prente aus jeunes personnes mais le plus grand remède et qui plus dompte les premiers maniemens d'une jeusne personne c'est de leur bailler crainte, exercisse et honnestes compaignons. Pourquoy tréshumblement je vous supplie luy faire commander . . . ne partir continuellement de vostre présence . . . Je sçay bien que vostre estat est fort cergé pour recoeuillir les bons et anciens serviteurs de feu monsigneur vostre père . . . mais mon intention est qu'il despende son bien à vous faire service.

It seems that this important move had been arranged by Jean de Biencourt-Potrincourt, a Guise agent in Picardy described by La Hargerie as 'l'un de mes espéciaux amis'.[163]

La Hargerie continued as *commissaire des vivres* in the new reign for we find him in May 1553 instructed to prepare stores for the king's field army in Picardy. In each of the towns he visited, he was to call the *échevins* together

---

[161] Documents on these negotiations are in BN fr. 17889. See particularly La Hargerie to Jacques Mesnage, 21 Feb. 1545, fr. 17889 fo. 232–3.

[162] La Rochepozay, Fr. de Raisse, Poton and Babou to the constable, Saint-Cloud, 2 May (1547), BN fr. 20648 fo. 70: 'nous sommes tumbez en une difficulté, qui est de sçavoir si l'on continuera le service de la table royalle . . . après que lad. effigie sera osté, le lict de parement abbatu'.

[163] La Hargerie to François de Guise, Tilloloy, 8 June 1550, BN fr. 20543 fo. 140. François de Soyécourt was *guidon* of Humières's company in 1553, see Fleury Vindry, *Dictionnaire de l'Etat major français au XVIe siècle. Première parti. Gendarmerie* (1901). See also A. Ledieu, 'Un grand seigneur Picard au XVIe siècle', *Bull. de la Confér. scientifique d'Abbeville*, III (Paris, 1892), which indicates that he accompanied the cardinal of Lorraine to Rome in 1550 (p. 14).

and give them the king's instructions on the amount of food they were to assemble. A *procès-verbal* at Péronne on 1 July makes the difficulties he faced clear.[164] His last-known public act was involvement in a commission of January 1555 to assemble local landowners in order to suppress the pillaging being carried out by French, English and Scots light horse in the king's service.[165] This was hardly an enviable job for an old man, but it does sharply illustrate an important aspect of his career throughout: his role as servant of the king in the province, a member both of the royal household and one of the established local notables upon whom both the court and the governors relied repeatedly in both routine matters of government and difficult problems. In 1555, La Hargerie must have been about seventy-five. Clearly a man of intelligence, though no stranger to the battlefield, it seems that he preferred administrative tasks, despite his own admitted lack of legal training.

La Hargerie died in 1558, having founded a mass at Notre-Dame de Boulogne for his soul and passed on Tilloloy to his grandson Soyécourt. Démuin went to his daughter Antoinette and on her death in 1566 to his other grandson, the later comte de Chaulnes, who was required to take his name. Another grandchild married Jacques II de Coucy-Vervins.[166] La Hargerie had failed to found a local dynasty, but did his best to preserve his name and establish his descendants among the most substantial families of the province.

Jean d'Estourmel may properly be considered, with La Hargerie, an example of a member of the long-established lesser nobility involved deeply in local royal administration. The known origins of Estourmel's family go back much further than La Hargerie's – to the eleventh-century crusader Reimbold Creton, in fact. Its original home, Estourmel, was in the Cambrésis and its fiefs depended on Crèvecoeur (in the early fourteenth century, another branch, the Estourmel-Vandeville, appeared and are to be found in the emperor's service in the sixteenth century). In the fourteenth century, the main line of the family came to fix its residence at Templeux-la-Fosse near Péronne and allied itself with the Bazincourt and Soyécourt families.[167]

The fortunes of the family were firmly reestablished by Gilles Reimbold Creton, who was governor of Saint-Quentin in 1473. In 1479, he was in a

---

[164] Henri II to La Hargerie, 22 May 1553, crs. Bourdin, AM Péronne BB 9 fo. 284–5 and BN Picardie 174 fo. 64.

[165] Henri II to La Hargerie, 18 Jan. 1554/5, BN Cangé 14 fo. 177.

[166] La Hargerie was selling his grain on the Amiens market in August 1557 (AM Amiens EE 323 no. 90) but was dead in 1558 (see Ledieu, 'Notice sur Tilloloy' and homage by Antoinette de Rasse for Démuin, 11 June 1558, Beauvillé, *Recueil*, IV, 410). For the mass 'dicte de la Hargerie', *MSAB* XXVIII (1917), 131.

[167] P. de Cagny, *Notice historique sur le château de Suzanne en Santerre et sur le maison et marquisat d'Estourmel*, 1–5, 27–32.

position to receive from Louis XI confiscations of land from Maximilian's supporters in the Cambrésis and Picardy. The family also acquired Guyencourt and Marquaix around this time. Gilles died in 1522 and passed on this inheritance to Jean III d'Estourmel. The latter's wife, Madeleine d'Aumale, was the daughter of Jean de Rasse and therefore a relative of La Hargerie, and their marriage contract was witnessed by the lords of Hangest, Davenscourt, Longueval and Mametz. The earliest public act surviving in the family archives was a council *arrêt* of October 1529 giving him the *droit de guet* at Templeux.[168]

By February 1531, Jean d'Estourmel was a *commissaire de l'ordinaire des guerres* (that is, responsible for payments to the gendarmerie) and by 1535 he was *chambellan* to the duke of Orléans, the future Henri II. In March 1535, he was a witness to James V's abortive betrothal to Marie de Bourbon as *maître d'hôtel* to the duke of Vendôme.[169] In the latter position, of course, he played an important part in the entourage of the provincial governor, as we have seen. Thus, by the mid-1530s, Estourmel was established in a position of trust with the king and the governor and was already involved in practical military administration. After the start of war in 1536, he rapidly became a confidential agent for La Rochepot and Vendôme[170] but his reputation was immensely enhanced by his famous participation in the siege of Péronne when, in August–September 1536, by bringing his family and property into the town, he strengthened the will of the inhabitants to resist the Imperial army. More than this, he brought in the harvest from his estate and used it to feed the garrison. In all, it was a textbook case of how a landowner in royal favour should behave as the neighbour of a town under attack, and Estourmel undoubtedly reaped great rewards for his action.[171]

Immediately after the siege of Péronne, Estourmel went to court and it may be that he received his appointment as *maître d'hôtel du roi*.[172] There is no doubt that he was well in favour with the king and with Montmorency when the latter wrote to La Rochepot:

[168] *Ibid.*, pp. 36–7; *CAF* I, 673, 7520.
[169] Cagny, *Château de Suzanne*, pp. 36–7. In 1530–1 he received a gift of L 912 from royal revenues in the seigneurie of Hangest. For Estourmel as *maître d'hôtel* to the duke of Vendôme in 1536, see AM Amiens CC 128 (ment. as *chambellan*) and *L&P* XI, 916, Penven to Douglas, 29 Oct. 1536: 'Estourmail' is 'steward' of Vendôme's household.
[170] Vendôme to La Rochepot, 10 July 1536, BN fr. 3069 fo. 75; *Registres Paris*, III, 235–6.
[171] Du Bellay, *Mémoires* (Michaud et Poulloulat) 426; P. Fenier, *Relation du siège memorable de la ville de Péronne* (repr. 1872), 16.
[172] Cagny, *Château de Suzanne*, 39; the household lists for 1537–39 are missing but that for 1540 (BN fr. 21449 fo. 98r) lists 'Antoine d'Estourmel' – this is a mistake and it is changed to 'Jean' in 1546. The 1550 list (BN Clair. 813) and that for 1551 (BN fr. 3132) lists Jean d'Estourmel as *maître d'hôtel*.

pource que je l'ay trouvé fort affectionné à faire à vous et a moy service, je vous prie, mon frère, le retenir auprès de vous et vous servir et aider de luy, car je suis seur qu'il s'i employera en tel soing et dilligence que nous en demeurerons tenuz à luy.[173]

This is an early example, already noted, of the attachment of a professional administrator to the governor's staff. In October 1538, while serving his quarter as *maître d'hôtel du roi*, he was commissioned, with Pommeraye and Morette, to go to Compiègne in order to make preparations for the queen of Hungary's reception there.[174]

Estourmel seems to have been a *commissaire des guerres* as early as 1531,[175] but during the war of 1536–7 was active as *commissaire des vivres* in arranging food supplies for fortresses like Thérouanne, Saint-Pol and Hesdin and employing one Pierre Durant as his deputy to receive and disburse the supplies he had assembled.[176] He carried out the same duties in the wars of 1541–45, though a brevet of September 1541 indicates a concurrent appointment as *maître des fortifications*.[177]

The year 1543, however, saw him involved in curious diplomatic dealings with the governor of Artois, du Roeulx, on behalf of his patron, the duke of Vendôme. Du Roeulx reported in March that Estourmel had sent him 'ung propre homme de Cambray' to tell him:

qu'il désiroit fort parler à moy pour aulcunes choses grandement touchans le bien de la Chrestienté et que je ne sçauroye faire meilleure pasques que d'entendre à ce qu'il me diroit; et combien que plusieurs estimoyent que j'estoys en partie cause de la guerre, le duc d'Orléans, de Vendosme et luy comme mon serviteur sçavoient le contraire et qu'il failloit que je servisse mon maistre.

Roeulx replied that he would inform the regent and let him know, clearly suspicious that Estourmel was only interested in spying out the land. It is unlikely, in the circumstances, that he was attempting to initiate peace talks,

173 Montmorency to La Rochepot, 6 June [1537], BN n.a. fr. 10227 no. 2.
174 AM Compiègne BB 19, 2 Oct. 1538.
175 BN pièces orig. 1081 nos. 4 and 5 (receipts for salary as *commissaire des guerres*, 1531, 1533 at a rate of L 400; *CAF* VII, 756, 28847.
176 Dubourg to La Rochepot, 13 June 1537, BN n.a. fr. 23168 no. 27. He was probably appointed *commissaire des avitaillements* on 1 Sept. 1537, as he was paid from that date (*CAF* VIII, 262, 31724).
177 Entitled 'commissaire general sur le faict des advitaillements des places de frontière de Picardie et Artois' (*CAF* III, 9408, ment. of 6 Nov. 1537) for which he received L 1,200 p.a. (rec. of 10 April 1541, Beauvillé, *Recueil*, II, 204–5). *Brevet* of Sept. 1541 – Cagny, *Château de Suzanne*, 39. On his activities in 1541–5, see du Bellay, *Mémoires* (Michaud et Poujoulat) 512; Vendôme to Francis I, 5 May 1541, BN fr. 20521 fo. 10–11; du Biez to Francis I, 1 Jan./ 3 Feb. 1545, fr. 20521, fo. 78–9, 80–1.

but may have been trying to lull Imperial suspicions.[178] Estourmel was also a member of the commission sent to Ardres (with Heilly and du Biez) in December 1546 to negotiate with the English about the frontier and the implementation of the Anglo-French peace treaty. A preliminary series of meetings in October–November had simply stated positions, and the further meetings in December proved abortive. Heilly and Estourmel received their letters of congé at Ardres in mid-December and it was left to La Garde to negotiate a further treaty with England.[179]

In September 1541, Estourmel had entered into what might seem a surprising new function when he was appointed to replace Antoine de Lameth as *général des finances de Picardie et Outre-Seine*. As a non-robe official, he was thus called upon to preside over the apparatus of royal direct taxation in the province (to be discussed in chapter 7) and, as such, in 1544–5 we find him active in the commission to collect *tailles* and sell royal lands in his generality. It should not be assumed that the high levels of royal finance always employed men of distinct financial training, but Estourmel did bring to his new job wide practical experience in disbursing funds, if not in collecting them.[180]

Though, on the accession of Henri II, Estourmel seems to have continued in his household post, he resigned the office of *général des finances* to Jean de La Chesnaye in return for the very substantial pension of L 2,000.[181] The exact significance of this transaction is difficult to clarify, since he had again become *général des finances* by the early 1550s. Presumably, his reinstatement as *général* was part of the reorganisation in the *généralités* which took place during those years, for he emerges later as *tresorier-général des finances* in Picardy.[182] During the same period, he remained a provisioning commissioner and in June 1553 was, with Saveuses, responsible for the victualling of the king's army in Artois.[183] His activities both in this field and in finance are well

[178] Adrien de Croy, sieur de Roeulx to Mary of Hungary, 11 March 1542/3, Vienna HHuStA Frankreich, Varia, fasz. 5 fo. 167.

[179] Cagny, *Château de Suzanne*, 53; erroneously gives Estourmel a rôle in the Anglo-French peace treaty of 1546 based on these negotiations; 'Mémoire de ce que Guesdon aura a dire au Roy' S.A. Picardie MS 59 no. 53, draft (Guesdon was du Biez's secretary); Francis I to Heilly and Estourmel, 8 Dec. 1546, BN n.a. fr. 23167 fo. 11; Léonard, *Recueil des Traitez de Paix*, 6 vols. (1893) II, pp. 465–8.

[180] Cagny, *Château de Suzanne*, 39; *CAF* IV, 240, 12113 (provisions, 19 Sept. 1541); IV, 628, 13940–41; 646, 14022; 787, 14667–8.

[181] *CAH* I, 1920, 1847. La Chesnaye was still *général* of Outre-Seine in Dec. 1552 (AM Compiègne BB 21 fo. 72v). Presumably, the generality had been split by this time (see ch. 7).

[182] E.g. as 'Conseiller et maître d'hôtel ordinaire du roi, trésorier de France et général de ses finances au pays et province de Picardie', recepisse for sums owed by Amiens for munitions (AM Amiens EE 323 no. 53 – dated 1553 or 1554).

[183] In 1550, he is noted as formerly having had commission to revictual Thérouanne (AM Amiens BB 26 fo. 54v); Henri II to Abbeville, 11 June 1553, *Inventaire sommaire, Abbeville*, AA 72 no. 5 (destroyed); Saint-André to Amiens, 10 March 1554, AM Amiens EE 323 no. 45.

documented, for these are years in which there survive many instructions from him to local authorities. Moreover, in October 1551, he received a present of wine from the city of Amiens 'en considération du plaisir qu'il faict à lad. ville en ayant advancé pour elle la somme de deux mille'.[184]

By 1554, Jean d'Estourmel's health was beginning to fail. So, already in March 1554, we find a meeting of the échevinage of Amiens:

> où estoyent le sieur d'Estourmel le jeune, filz de messire Jehan d'Estourmel chevalier, sieur dud. lieu conseiller du Roy nostre Seigneur et général de ses finances au pays de Picardie . . . led. sieur d'Estourmel le jeune pour la maladie dud. sieur d'Estourmel son père.[185]

From this point, he seems gradually to have handed over his financial office to his son Antoine, though he did not make his will until August 1557.

Jean d'Estourmel had two sons. Jean IV, the eldest, sieur de Guyencourt, was lieutenant to Jean d'Humières at Péronne for a while in 1553 and was also in command at Saint-Quentin for a while before 1557. Guyencourt was an essentially military man; his career had started as lieutenant of Vieilleville's company and he had already obtained a post at court as *échanson ordinaire du roi* by 1548.[186] In 1555, he and his wife fell into dispute with François de Barbançon-Canny over some property at Péronne, where the governor's lieutenant had given sentence in Canny's favour. Jean d'Estourmel wrote to the town on his son's behalf asserting that the decision would prejudice local custom and asking that the magistrates oppose it: 'Je vous prie, messieurs, ne me voulloir reffuzer ceste requeste, ayant esgard que j'ay tousiours esté, comme encores suis, l'un de vos meilleurs amys et voisins.' Not surprisingly, the town agreed to oppose Canny on behalf of its old protector.[187]

Antoine, who succeeded as *trésorier-général des finances*, was active during the crisis of 1557, when the state's financial resources were being strained to breaking-point.[188] Based at Saint-Quentin in the months before its

---

[184] AM Amiens BB 27 fo. 75r.
[185] AM Amiens BB 28 fo. 159r (7 March 1554). Antoine d'Estourmel was exercising the office in March 1555 (Llhomel, *Nouvel recueil*, 164).
[186] BN pièces orig. 1081 no. 6 (*echanson du roi* at L 400 p.a.), nos. 7 and 8 (as lieutenant of a company, 1554–5, at L 142 per quarter). Montmorency to Jean d'Humières, 11 Sept. 1553, BN fr. 3116, p. 267. He was captain of Saint-Quentin from 1556 until just before the siege (AM Saint-Quentin, liasse 138 no. 19 – called 'Jacques d'Estourmel, sieur de Guiencourt') and Cagny, *Château de Suzanne*, 42–3. Guiencourt is also listed as a gentleman of Vendôme's household in 1549 (AN 278ᴬ). He died shortly after his father in 1557 or 1558.
[187] Estourmel to Péronne, Amiens, 9 Dec. 1555, AM Péronne BB 9 fo. 409r–v and deliberation of 10 Dec.
[188] 'conseiller du roi, trésorier de France et général de ses finances du pais et province de Picardie' in April 1558 (BN pièces orig. 1081 no. 9). Antoine was present 'comme habitant' at an Amiens échevinage of 26 Sept. 1557 on how to raise money for the fortifications: 'Surquoy monsieur le général d'Estourmel a dict et remonstré qu'il y avoit petite assemblée pour faire telle délibération . . . ' (AM Amiens BB 30 fo. 137r).

fall, he set new rates for gold coins in circulation, received instructions to visit
the towns and make a forced levy on municipal and royal officials and
transmitted the routine royal edicts.[189] In the months following the fall of Saint-
Quentin, he worked closely with the duke of Guise and treasurer Raconis in
scouring up all available funds, raising money on his own credit and visiting
Amiens in December 1557 in order to press the municipality into contributing
to the duke's war-chest. Guise was fulsome in his praise:

> m'avez faict bien grant plaisir de la dilligence dont vous avez usé au
> recouvrement des vj^m livres que vous avez emprunctez à Amyens soubz
> vostre obligacion et promesse . . . lesquelles et le présent je vous promet
> vous en faire rembourser dedans le temps que vous l'avez promis à ceulx
> qui vous ont presté lad. partie.[190]

In December 1562, Estourmel formally succeeded Louis de Lannoy as
captain of Amiens (a post which he had held as substitute during the first civil
war) and continued to issue *lettres d'attache* as *général des finances* throughout the 1560s. By 1568 he had become a *gentilhomme de la chambre du roi* and
a close assistant to Charles de Hallewin as governor of Picardy in the Catholic
interest.[191]

The activities of men like La Hargerie and Estourmel will be further
amplified in a discussion of army organisation and supply in the following
chapter. At this point it may be stressed that the long-established nobility at all
levels remained exceptionally vigorous in its grasp of administrative positions
within the province during the late fifteenth and early sixteenth centuries, but
that a complex interaction between local influence, traditional loyalties and
ability to sustain contacts at court through a wide range of patrons was vital in
the maintenance of a preeminent position. Local affairs are impossible to
understand without a grasp of the interaction of traditional links of loyalty and
court politics.

---

[189] Estourmel to *sénéchaussée* of Boulogne, Amiens, 4 April 1447, AD Pas-de-Calais, 9B 2
fo. 28r–v; May 1557, *Ibid.*, fo. 22–3; Saint-Quentin, 19 June 1557, *ibid.*, fo. 27r–v.

[190] See D. L. Potter, 'The duc de Guise and the Fall of Calais', *EHR* (July 1983) 498–500; Guise
to Estourmel, 2 Jan. 1558, BN fr. 23191 fo. 29; AM Amiens BB 30 fo. 137r. In July 1558, he
transmitted orders for the convocation of the *ban et arrière-ban* (Estourmel to *sénéchaussée* of
Boulogne, 16 July 1558, AD Pas-de-Calais 9B 2 fo. 72).

[191] For the captaincy of Amiens, see AM Amiens AA 5 fo. 338v, resignation *ibid.*, EE 155. *Lettres d'attache*, BN pièces orig. 1081 nos. 10, 11 ('Antoine d'Estourmel, chevalier, conseiller
du Roy, trésorier de France et général de ses finances au pais de Picardye, Boulogne et Artois,
pais nouvellement reconquis et capitaine de la ville et cité d'Amyens' 5 Dec. 1563) and no. 13
('Messire Anthoine d'Estourmel, sire et Baron de Massi et gentilhomme ordinaire de la
chambre' – 1568).

5

✠

MILITARY ORGANISATION IN PICARDY
DURING THE HABSBURG–VALOIS WARS

The Habsburg–Valois Wars outside Italy have failed to attract the attention of modern historians, in contrast to the formidable analysis brought to bear on the Religious Wars of the later sixteenth century or the Thirty Years War.[1] It may be surmised that this results from the suspicion that conflicts generated essentially by dynastic rivalry are more trivial than those with some kind of ideological or economic impulse behind them. The Habsburg–Valois conflict, much of it inconclusive, might easily have attracted Veronica Wedgwood's verdict on the Thirty Years War as 'the supreme example of meaningless conflict'. Yet it would be difficult to imagine the genesis of modern warfare without the lessons taught in tactics and fortification during the first half of the sixteenth century; nor would the instruments of Absolute Monarchy have been so substantially developed.[2]

For some regions of western Europe, this was the most devastating experience for centuries. Picardy was, during the first half of the sixteenth

---

[1] Among more recent studies, J. R. Hale, *War and Society in Renaissance Europe* (1985), 13–15 gives a brief overview as an introduction to a general analytical study. J. Black (ed.), *The Origins of War in Early Modern Europe* (1988) *passim*. On the Habsburg–Valois Wars, F. Mignet, *La rivalité de François Ier et de Charles-Quint*, 2 vols. (1875), is largely a diplomatic narrative down to 1529. On thought about war in this period, see J. A. Fernandez-Santamaria, *The State, War and Peace: Spanish Political Thought in the Renaissance 1516–1559* (1977), 120–60; M. J. Rodriguez-Salgado, *The Changing Face of Empire: Charles V, Philip II and Habsburg Authority, 1551–1559* (1988), 25–33, 169–205, gives a stimulating reconsideration of the wars in the 1550s.

[2] C. Oman, *A History of the Art of War in the Sixteenth Century* (1937) concentrates on set-piece battles. More recently, C. Duffy, *Siege Warfare: the Fortress in the Early Modern War 1494–1660* (1979), 43–59; M. E. Mallet and J. R. Hale, *The Military Organization of a Renaissance State: Venice, c. 1400–1617* (1984) on Venice, and S. Pepper and A. Adams, *Firearms and Fortifications* (1986) on Sienna in the 1550s. P. Anderson, *Lineages of the Absolute State*, 32–3.

century, the most consistently fought-over region of France, and its history in that period is inseparable from war. After the generation of uneasy peace that followed the definitive restoration of royal government in the later fifteenth century, the forty-seven years from 1521 to 1559 saw twenty-eight years of war, all of which involved fighting of some kind and fifteen of which witnessed the mounting of major campaigns. The king appeared in person at the head of his armies in 1521, 1524, 1537, 1543, 1549, 1553, 1554 and 1558.[3]

The English invasion of 1513, though serious in that it led to the capture of Thérouanne and Tournai, left most of the province relatively unscathed by direct conflict.[4] The opening of war between Francis I and Charles V in 1521, however, signalled the start of a generation of war. The immediate causes of a conflict both dynastic and geopolitical in origin were French aid to Henri d'Albret in Navarre and Robert de La Marck's defiance of the emperor at Sedan. Small-scale fighting began both in the Pyrenees and Luxembourg in the spring of 1521. Renewal of conflict in Italy over the vital control of Lombardy was now also inevitable.

Though the causes of war lay far from the Somme, however, the border area between France and the emperor's patrimonial lands in the Netherlands was bound to become a theatre of conflict in view of the opportunities for gain and the renewal of old claims. Moreover, no 'natural frontier' existed which might seriously impede the movements of soldiers, the land offered rich pickings for looters and the walls of the towns and cities were, as yet, inadequately strengthened by the standards of the new 'Italian' style. The succeeding decades of conflict therefore witnessed almost constant operations of armies and war bands across the arc of land from Boulogne in the west to Guise and Mézières in the east.

Both Picardy and Artois remained debatable land, especially in view of the remaining tenurial links between Artois, Flanders and the French crown, as well as the anomalous position of the county of Saint-Pol between them (all to be discussed in chapter 8). The continued existence of important French enclaves like Thérouanne and Tournai (regained from England in 1518) and the complex series of smaller enclaves along the border of Picardy and Artois all gave ample scope for hostilities.

The aims of the participants in this increasingly bitter struggle naturally

[3] The 'Guerres de Picardie' are often covered in general works only on the basis of the major printed memoirs of Florange, Martin du Bellay, and Rabutin. There are numerous studies by local historians like La Fons Mélicocq, F. Le Sergent de Monnecove and an important collection of documents in E. Lemaire and E. Fleury, *La guerre de 1557 en Picardie* (1896).
[4] A. Hocquet, *Tournai de l'occupation anglaise* (1901), 167–70; G. Cruickshank, *Army Royal* (1969) and Cruickshank, *The English Occupation of Tournai* (1971).

shifted from decade to decade. In the earlier period, Francis I was determined to defend his remaining territories in the Low Countries and, if possible, to extend them. In the 1520s and even more so in the 1530s this involved ambitious campaigns into the emperor's lands, at first for the defence of the Tournaisis, in 1537 for the reconquest of Hesdin, lost by the treaty of 1529. In fact, the conventional view that it was the 1550s that saw the reorientation of French policy away from Italy towards the north-east frontier should be revised. The royal campaign of 1537 and its cost represents a significant move towards the north. For his part, Charles V sought to defend his territory and take advantage of his victories in Italy to break the tenurial link with France between 1525 and 1529. The emperor's advisers, however, were realistic about the prospect of acquiring further territory in France, though the course of war dictated large-scale invasions in 1536, 1544 and 1557. Despite the bombastic claims of Henry VIII, the English were similarly realistic, though this did not prevent their campaigns of 1522–3 and 1544 (in the Boulonnais) from being devastating.[5] The climax of the wars came with the great campaigns, sieges, sackings and battles of the 1550s. For the French, this meant the final destruction of Thérouanne and Hesdin, the burning of Chauny and Noyon and the fall of Saint-Quentin.

Warfare became more static in this period. The English march beyond the Somme in 1523 was increasingly difficult to emulate and, though the French commander of that time, La Trémoille, explained the English failure in his own terms – 'est une povre nation que ces gens-là' – the real reason was the increasing military emphasis in sieges and the inability of armies to move rapidly with their supply and artillery trains without high risk.[6] Towns were starting to see their fortifications transformed in the 1520s and military thinking saw sieges as central to strategy. Towns and castles, once captured, were also difficult to hold against a determined opponent. The main alternative to such warfare was the devastating raid designed to enfeeble the enemy's base of operations. One offshoot of the period was the drive to attain a clearer definition of the frontier, itself linked with the demands of the state but also partly produced by the need to define territory for military operations.

The organisation of armies, with their pay, billeting and supply problems, tended, therefore, to occupy an important position in the public life of Picardy during this period. The French army in the sixteenth century was a complex and unwieldy body, with both archaic and innovatory features. It has never been

---

[5] S. Gunn, 'The French Wars of Henry VIII' in J. Black (ed.), *The Origins of War in Early Modern Europe*, 28–51.
[6] La Trémoille to Montmorency, 8 Nov. (1523), BL Egerton 22 fo. 125. On the 1523 campaign, see S. Gunn, 'The Duke of Suffolk's March on Paris in 1523', *EHR* 101 (1986), 596–634.

studied with the same depth and richness of documentation exemplified by Contamine's work on the mediaeval French armies. Gaston Zeller, however, paved the way and various aspects of its organisation have been studied more recently.[7] The aim of this chapter is mainly to analyse the army as it affected Picardy, but some points may extend to French military organisation in general.

The increase in the scale and complexity of French military operations on several fronts after 1521 imposed a severe strain on instruments of control. In Picardy, it brought a permanent augmentation of garrison troops. It also revealed the absence of any consistent and workable arrangements for the supply and billeting of the troops, despite previous attempts. There were no barracks and only a confused system of victualling, which had to be adapted to circumstances. Pay was irregular and medical provision rudimentary. The periodic assembly of full royal armies in the province revealed that French armies could be as destructive to their own population as those of the enemy. The first section of this chapter will examine the development of the different *corps* of the French army, both traditional and new. The second will analyse the supply control system.

The cavalry: compagnies d'ordonnance and light horse

Established in the fifteenth century as the main royal force of heavily armed cavalry, the *gens d'armes*, in *compagnies d'ordonnance* (named after the royal *ordonnance* by which they had been created) were often regarded as 'la principalle foulle de povre peuple' through much of this period.[8] The main problems arose from irregularities of pay and chaotic billeting. Francis I, in the first month of his reign, had issued an *ordonnance* to suppress their disorders and attempted to tighten up control, but the succeeding series of regulations modifying the rules and attempting further controls indicates the problems involved. Indeed, so confused had the situation become by 1541 that the constable de Montmorency called on the *Chambre des Comptes* for its records,

---

[7] P. Contamine, *Guerre, état et société à la fin du moyen âge* (1972); G. Zeller, *Le siège de Metz par Charles-Quint* (1942); R. de Beccarie de Pavie, sr. de Fourquevaux, *Instructions sur le faict de la guerre* ed. with a useful introduction on the French army by G. Dickinson (1954); Pierre d'Espezel in a thesis summarised in the *Positions des thèses de l'Ecole des Chartes*, 1916, argued that the keynote of this period was the professionalisation of the French army. F. Lot, *Recherches sur les effectifs des armées françaises* suffers from its fragmentary nature. Recent important studies include: A. Corvisier, 'Armées, état et administration dans les temps modernes' in *Francia*, Beihefte, band 9 (1980); H. Michaud, 'Les institutions militaires des guerres d'Italie aux guerres de religion', *RH*, 1977, 29–43; J. E. Iung, 'L'organisation du service des vivres aux armées de 1550 a 1650' *BEC*, 1983, ii, 269–306.

[8] Vendôme to Parlement, 9 April 1525, AN X/1A 1527 fo. 366–7.

since so many regulations had been issued that 'les aucunes d'icelles ne se treuvent accorder et convenir avec les autres'. This had bred disputes between the men and the army administrators.[9]

The sources for the history of the gendarmerie have traditionally been the *ordonnances* and muster-rolls. However, in order to understand the full story, it is also important to sift through correspondence and financial records. The *gens d'armes* operated in companies, but inherited from the past the idea of the small active unit of the 'lance'. Originally, there were two archers – men slightly less well accoutred – for every *homme d'armes* and each 'lance' consisted of four combatants (including the *coutillier*). By the reign of Francis I, only the *gens d'armes* and archers need be considered, since by then the 'lance' had become a fiction. A standard company consisted of forty lances, and by the 1530s this meant forty *gens d'armes* and sixty archers. The ratio of 1:1.5 was promulgated by edict in 1534 and this effectively ended the 'lance' as a fighting unit. A garrison of 400 *gens d'armes* in the 1540s therefore entailed around 1,000 men. In addition, each lance would have two pages (usually young noblemen in training). Military innovation began to impinge in the 1550s, when most companies began to have fifty mounted *arquebusiers* attached to them.[10]

The gendarmerie had attained its largest numbers in the later years of Louis XI, with around 4,000 lances. The Estates-General of 1484 reduced this to 2,200, including 600 in Picardy, and thereafter numbers would be increased by about 1,000 in wartime. There were usually between five and eight companies in Picardy during peacetime, though in July 1521, the province had been stripped of men for other fronts, like Italy, and there were only 2 left (those of Vendôme and Theligny). Even by 1523, there were only 327 lances in the province out of a national total of 3,752.[11]

At the end of wars, it was usual to reduce the numbers of companies or their

9 *Ordonnances, François Ier* I, 61–2; Francis I to La Fayette, 31 Oct. (1516) BN fr. 3057, p. 225–6. Montmorency to Chambre des Comptes, 8 Feb. 1541, BL Egerton 23 fo. 262.
10 F. Lot, *Recherches sur les effectifs* 16–18, 62. R. Doucet, *Les institutions de la France au XVIe siècle* 2 vols. (1948), 622ff. For proportions of *hommes d'armes* to archers in Picard companies: Louis de Graville, 1496, 60:120 (Beauvillé, *Recueil*, II, 182–92); La Gruthuse, 1500, 30:60; Dauphin-Humières, 1538, 100: 148 (*ibid.* I, 223–8); du Biez, 1539, 40:60 (BN fr. 21518 no. 1370); Villebon, 1540, 40:50 (*ibid.*, no. 1376); du Biez, 1542, 60:90 (*ibid.*, no. 1384); La Rochepot, 1549, 39:59, '40 lances' (BN fr. 21520 no. 1457); Vendôme, 1551, 78:119 '80 lances' (*ibid.*, no. 1481). But note Coligny, 1557, 66:81 '81 lances' – reduced by battle loss?; Sansac, 1557, 49:74 (*ibid.*, no. 1687). The edict of Nov. 1549 seeking the restore the old relationship was thus inoperative in practice. On mounted *arquebusiers*, see BL Add. 38032 fo. 284–5.
11 P. Contamine, *Guerre, état et société*, 278ff.; lists of companies in Picardy: 1525: AN X/1A 1527 fo. 369v; 1530, 'Estat de la gendarmerie' BN fr. 4050 fo. 98r; Vendôme to Francis I, 23 July 1521, BN fr. 3059 fo. 59–60; *Journal d'un bourgeois de Paris sous la règne de François Ier*, ed. V.-L. Bourrilly (1910), 117–21.

complement. In late 1525, the regent decided to reduce the companies (that of Bernieulles, for instance, from thirty-two to twenty-four lances; twenty-four men lost their pay) 'pour dyminuer la despense et soullager le povre peuple'.[12] The general scale of such reductions is indicated by the national figure of 2,152 lances in 1530, when there were eleven companies (478 lances) in Picardy. By 1534 these had been reduced to nine and there were eight during the truce of 1538–41. In September 1538, 300 *hommes d'armes* 'qui avoient de coustume d'y estre en garnison' were removed from the province. In February of that year, the king had already, on the death of Sarcus, disbanded his company 'pour autant me descharger de despence'. A reduction by one-third was effected in Picardy as late as June 1541.[13]

Conversely, the opening of wars, especially from the 1540s onwards, demonstrated that the gendarmerie continued to be regarded as vital. In November 1543, the crown ordered 800 lances for Picardy and the Ile-de-France and in March 1547 there were still 720. In 1549, there were 480 lances in ten companies in Picardy and part of the Ile-de-France.[14] Thus, the startling fluctuations in the size of the gendarmerie noted by Contamine for the fifteenth century, with all their attendant social, economic and psychological problems for the militarily active nobility, continued throughout the Habsburg–Valois Wars. The national total of 2,400 lances was increased by 340 in November 1552 by the augmentation of all companies and grew in the following years. By the end of 1559, the total was back to 2,610 lances. Though 360 had been allotted to Picardy, its war-ravaged state only permitted 120 to be stationed in the province proper; the rest had to find their lodgings in towns just over the boundaries of neighbouring provinces.[15]

Most companies were stationed in particular towns for lengthy periods but in practice would not remain in their entirety. A regular system of leave was prescribed by *ordonnance* for a quarter of the company at any time. In peace-time or at times of 'reduction', many, if not most, of the men retired to their homes. These were moments of much potential disorder and discontent.[16] Conversely, when wars were declared, the governor would order the captains to get their men to the colours in two weeks. The responsibility fell on the

---

[12] Receipt of Bernieulles as capt. of gendarmerie, 28 Jan. 1526, BN p.o. Créquy, no. 15.
[13] BN fr. 4050 fo. 98–9; *CAF* VII, 615, 27632; 721, 28608; VIII, 232, 31416–449; Francis I to La Rochepot, 16 Feb. 1538, BN fr. 3058 fo. 29. Vendôme to Francis I, 7 June 1541, BN fr. 20521 fo. 35.
[14] Vendôme to Francis I, 27 March 1543, BN fr. 20521 fo. 50–54; same to same, 27 March 1547, *ibid.*, fo. 98. List of 1549, BL Add. 38035 fo. 228. List of 1554, signed by constable, *ibid.*, 38032, fo. 284–5, showing withdrawals for the Ardennes army.
[15] *Arrêt* of *conseil privé*, 17 Nov. 1552, BN fr. 18153 fo. 340r; L. Paris (ed.), *Négociations . . . de François II*, 347–8.
[16] Montmorency to La Rochepot, 3 Sept. 1538, BN fr. 2995 fo. 299.

captains. Pressure of space in the garrison towns was always acute. At the start of war in 1551, for instance, the dauphin's company, usually stationed at Péronne, took up residence in a convent.[17]

Even in wartime, the winter was a slack period and many of the men went off on their own business. Keeping track of them was a perennial problem. Francis I made attempts to ensure that the companies remained up to strength and even in July 1545 found that, of 500 lances supposed to be in Picardy, there were only 100 available. He angrily ordered all the captains to muster their men and the report of one, Heilly, has survived. Twelve *gens d'armes* and eighteen archers were absent from his company of forty lances and, though a few were dead, the rest provided various excuses. One had lost his mother through plague and his household was infested, another was under medical treatment, another on his deathbed.[18] The crown always suspected fraud in the muster rolls, and in 1552 a royal *ordonnance* declared that captains must keep at least a quarter of their men in winter quarters. Though men could be cashiered for failure to appear at the musters, favouritism could always undermine the rules. Thus, when an archer of Aumale's company (then at Hardelot) was dismissed for being seven or eight hours late, the duke of Guise wrote to his son for the man's reinstatement as he was 'homme de service'.[19]

Companies had strong connections with particular towns during peacetime, especially those where their captain was also governor. Heilly's company occupied Hesdin, those of La Fayette and du Biez Boulogne, Villebon's Thérouanne and the dauphin's 100 lances (in practice commanded by Humières) was at Péronne. The prestigious companies of the provincial governors would be stationed at Abbeville, Doullens or Saint-Quentin.[20] Some of the companies were remarkably stable in composition, being passed from one captain to another or sometimes inherited. When Moyencourt's company was badly cut up at Saint-Pol in 1537, La Rochepot was asked to take on the

---

[17] Orders for muster: Francis I to La Rochepot, 9 April 1538, BN fr. 3035 fo. 13: captains to make 'extreme dilligence de faire retirer les hommes d'armes et archiers'; proclamation by Vendôme, 19 April 1540, AM Amiens AA 12 fo. 195v: on punishment of defaulters as 'vaccabons' and letters to Amiens 24 Jan. and 15 April 1542 *ibid.*, fo. 202v, 206. Vendôme to Humières, 13 Nov. 1551, BN fr. 3131 fo. 66.

[18] Francis I to Matignon, 3 March 1545, L. H. Labande (ed.), *Correspondance de Joachim de Matignon, lieutenant-général en Normandie* (1914), 114–15; Francis I to Vendôme, 2 July 1545, A. de Rosny, 'Documents inédits ou rarissimes concernant les sièges de Boulogne, 1544–49', *MSAB* 27 (1912), 379–420, no. 15. SAP, Chartrier d'Heilly 57 no. 3.

[19] La Marck to Humières, April–June 1552, *passim*, BN fr. 3128, esp. 48–9; Claude, duke of Guise to Aumale, 28 Feb. 1548, BL Add. 38033 fo. 160, in favour of Antoine d'Obigny, archer.

[20] The company of Vendôme, transferred to Boulogne in 1541, asked for a change because they 'sont à Boullongne estrangers', Vendôme to the king, 18 Feb. BN fr. 20521 fo. 17.

survivors.[21] Command of a company was sought after as a source of prestige and it conferred considerable powers of patronage. Captains were drawn from the middle and upper ranks of the provincial nobility and from men who could be relied on to form a good complement as a result of their reputation. Marshal de Chabannes recommended Humières for a company in 1521, since he was already governor of Péronne and 'homme pour vous y faire service autant que homme que je congnoisse'. Of the eight companies stationed in the province in 1539, seven were commanded by local noblemen: Créquy, du Biez, Brienne, Piennes, the dauphin (effectively Humières) and Vendôme (raised in 1537). The one outsider was the duke of Etampes.[22]

A major concern of the captains was to keep their companies up to strength and resist the desire of the crown to reduce numbers in peacetime. For this, contacts at court were essential. At the start of 1528, du Biez regained ten men who had been discharged because of the truce 'adfin que je n'abuse les gentilzhommes quy se délibèrent de mectre en ordre pour faire service au Roy soubz ma charge', while further talk of reductions in the summer of 1529 had du Biez again invoking the intervention of his patron, Montmorency. Consequently, his company was maintained at fifty lances.[23] A captain had, therefore, to be a good recruiter and to have effective contacts at court.

Recruitment took place through the network of personal acquaintance and connections, not by royal intervention. Men sought positions in companies stationed within their province if possible, but had to be prepared to go further afield. There was, however, only a limited pool of likely men. When, in the aftermath of Saint-Quentin, new companies had to be raised, Louis d'Humières found it impossible to raise a full complement of fifty lances 'sans pratiques et retirer plusieurs hommes d'armes et archers des autres compaignyes anciennes'.[24] Promotion depended on a judicious use of patronage. Recommendations for places form a commonplace of administrative correspondence. A few examples will serve as illustration. Around 1520, we find the constable of Bourbon recommending a 'gentil homme . . . qui est de mes pais' (an

---

[21] C. de Vendôme's company was passed on in part to his lieutenant, Torcy, in 1537 (Breton to Du Bourg, 28 March 1537, AN J 968 no. 12/18); his son Antoine received a new company, BN fr. 3044 fo. 93–109; Jean d'Humières got his company after his father's death (Montmorency to Humières, 13 Nov. 1552, BN fr. 3116 p. 161). Montmorency to La Rochepot, 28 June 1537, BN nafr. 10227 no. 17.

[22] Chabannes to Francis I, 23 July 1521, Chabannes, *Preuves*, I, ii, no. 251. List of 1539, BN fr. 6637 fo. 296.

[23] Du Biez to Montmorency, 25 Feb. (1528) BN fr. 3004 fo. 64; same to same, 1 Dec. (1528) fr. 20503 fo. 20.

[24] Henri II to Louis d'Humières, 17 Oct. 1557 BN fr. 3134 fo. 79. See Sansac to Guise, 16 Nov. 1558, BN fr. 23192 fo. 152–3.

Auvergnat) for a place in the company of his client, La Fayette, at Boulogne. Louis de Brézé recommended another man to the same captain as 'homme de bien' (the standard phrase) who had served well in Italy as an *arbalestrier* in Brézé's company. In 1521, the duke of Vendôme noted that one Jehan Lestrelée 'lequel depuis son jeune aage a esté nourry au service de monseigneur le Roy en ses ordonnances' had come to him, sought and obtained a position in his company but 'principallement mon service'. A few decades later, we find the young Antoine Duprat, son of the *prévôt* of Paris, on campaign in the Cambrésis in August 1554, taking the opportunity to press the duke of Guise on his cousin's part for a place in the duke's company. This Guise did as a favour to Duprat's father.[25]

Patronage was even more carefully exercised in the promotion to the coveted post of lieutenant of a company, often a step to full command. Oudart du Biez probably started as a client of the Créquy family and became lieutenant of Pont-Rémy's company around 1520. When he acquired his own, in 1521 or 1523, he appointed a relative, Senlis, as his lieutenant and in 1528 Jacques de Coucy-Vervins on the recommendation of Anne de Montmorency and the duke of Vendôme. Lieutenants sometimes had royal pensions, as did Vervins. When du Fresnoy's company was disbanded in 1537, the officers were assigned royal pensions until they could find new positions.[26]

Contacts at court were essential for captains in confronting the endemic problems of delay and failure of payment, themselves a spur to absenteeism and fraud. Desertion was as much a problem among the gendarmerie as with the notorious foreign mercenaries. The correspondence of La Fayette at Boulogne between 1515 and 1520 is full of appeals from the court for him to appease his men until the delayed musters could be held. In September 1518, for instance, musters were put off from May to September and then only one payment made out of the three quarters due.[27] In April 1525, the pay of the gendarmerie in Picardy was thirteen months in arrears: the governor of Champagne, Guise, would not allow money to be diverted from his men, themselves owed nineteen months pay, to Picardy. Brienne reported 'maulx et pilleries' by the troops in his charge. Such arrears had consequences. In 1521, Vendôme reported that it would be impossible to transfer Theligny's company

[25] Bourbon to La Fayette, 10 March BN fr. 2934 fo. 52; Brézé to same, 3 Sept. (1516) *ibid.*, fo. 96; Vendôme to Péronne, 25 April 1521, AM Péronne BB 7 fo. 132r; Antoine IV Duprat to Antoine III Duprat, 1 Aug. 1554, BN fr. 4052 fo. 23; Montmorency to Antoine III, 30 Aug. (1554), BL Egerton 23 fo. 270.
[26] Du Biez to Montmorency, 20 March (1528) BN fr. 3004 fo. 41–2. *CAF* VIII, 31290.
[27] Louise of Savoy to La Fayette, Oct. 1515, BN fr. 2934 fo. 20; Francis I to same, 24 March (1518), BN fr. 3057 fo. 69; same to same, June (1518), *ibid.*, fo. 149.

from Picardy to Guienne as planned, since the men had no money to pay their debts and their creditors would lose.[28]

In 1450, the standard pay of the *homme d'armes* was L 15 per month and of the archer L 7.10s. This, astonishingly, remained the same until 1549, a fact partly explained by the institution of a selective 'nouvelle paye' in the 1530s, L 20 and L 10, for a proportion of the men, roughly a quarter of the *gens d'armes* and two-thirds of the archers. This was a palliative response to inflation.[29] In fact, until 1548, the main burden of the disparity between pay and prices was borne by local communities in the form of contributions, which became the main source of aggravation between the military and civil populations in garrison towns.

The years 1545 and 1546 were ones of great shortages of food supplies in northern France, which were reflected in protests from both civil and military. Marshal du Biez thought that the large new draft of gendarmerie of March 1545 would be unlikely to serve well, since they each needed an *écu* a day to live on in the prevailing shortages. The assignment of garrisons by the duke of Vendôme was met by deputations to court from the towns affected. Companies were shifted from place to place as the towns proved unwilling or unable to support them. Temporary price-fixing had never worked and the result was that the gendarmerie resorted to self-help by scouring the country-side.[30]

La Rochepot's correspondence in 1548 to 1549 is full of such problems: the inability of Montreuil to go on supporting a garrison, the discontent of the men themselves as expressed by Sansac, lieutenant of the duke of Guise's company at Hardelot:

> Je vous asseure qu'ils ont bon besoin vue la depense chère et qu'elle est icy, car vous assure que le moindre qui soit icy ne sçauroit etre quitté pour quinze écus le mois avec un cheval et un valet tant seulement et tant qu'ils auront moyen ils ne se ennuyeront point de y demorer . . . Il n'est jour

---

[28] Du Biez to Parlement, 17 April 1525, AN X/1A 1527 fo. 376; Guise to same, *ibid.*, fo. 393–4, 404; Brienne to same, 25 April, 15 May 1525, *ibid.*, fo. 397–8; X/1A 1528 fo. 470–1. Vendôme to Francis I, 23 July 1521, BN fr. 3059 fo. 59–60. Péronne, Nov. 1523: with Montmor's company unpaid, Humières demanded supplies. The mayor replied that there were royal *ordonn.* to deal with this but that meanwhile the soldiers offered insults, blows 'prenant leurs biens' (AM BB 7 fo. 205v).

[29] Contamine, *Guerre, état et société*, annexe VI, D. The *grande paye* and *petite paye* are present in the account of *trésorier des guerres* Poncher in 1520–21, BN fr. 2933 fo. 1–7: 50 lances equivalent to 33⅓ at *grande paye*. The musters of 1538–43 (see note 10) show that the *grande paye* was meant to advantage the archers in the main. In 1521, officers were still paid by *places mortes* (Vendôme to Francis I, 27 Sept. 1521, BN fr. 3060 fo. 92), but later by a fixed salary scale.

[30] Du Biez to Francis I, 30 March 1545, BN fr. 20521 fo. 95–6. AM Chauny BB 6 fo. 10v (23 July 1545), fo. 12r (25 July).

qu'ils ne montent trois ou quatre fois à cheval pour aller et venir au fort [Oultreau], de sorte que le chemin y est seur tout ainsy que de Paris à St Denis et ne s'y perd un seul vivandier, sinon ceux qui se veulent perdre.[31]

In November 1547, a royal *ordonnance* for the supply of the garrison in Picardy had been promulgated. This had the effect of formalising existing arrangements by calling for local provision of specific quantities of wood, vinegar, salt and candles at fixed prices. The response to this is well documented at Péronne, where the magistrates were particularly concerned at the scale of the demands for Humières's company. The *maire* and some other counsellors organised a deputation to court, despite the opposition of the *receveur*, who was all for temporising and fearful of incurring Humières's wrath. Henry II was aware of the discontent, writing to La Rochepot in late January that 'Il m'est venu icy beaucoup de plainctes tant des gens de guerre que du peuple ou sont establies les garnisons de mon pays de Picardye de l'imposibilité que ung a y vivre et les autres à contribuer.' The *maire* of Péronne went to see marshal La Marck and learned that there was no way out; the town would have to contribute. It did so by levying a duty on wine. Even so, the town was still not complying fully in August, when La Rochepot threatened them, even though he had himself been lobbying at court to get the gendarmerie reduced. Conferences between the magistrates and captains were acrimonious, but an agreement was eventually reached that a merchant would take on the supply problem.[32]

The continuation of complaints from garrison towns partly explains the promulgation of the *taillon*, a new tax to support the gendarmerie, in 1549. News that the *conseil privé* was about to continue the régime of provision in January 1549 brought consultations between Péronne and Saint-Quentin and plans to petition for its abolition. In February the king wrote to La Rochepot asking him, in view of all the complaints about pillaging, to order the towns to calculate the cost of supplies for 100 *gens d'armes* for one month. When the magistrates of Péronne met to discuss the problem on 12 February, they opted for an augmentation of gendarmerie pay, to be met out of an increased *taille*. The advantage of this was the spreading of the cost throughout the kingdom and onto the less privileged.[33]

---

[31] Henri II to La Rochepot, 4 Jan., 12 Jan., 26 May 1548, BN fr. 3035 fo. 85, fr. 3120 fo. 58. Sansac to Guise, 29 March 1548, BL Add. 38030, fo. 27r–29r (orig. BN fr. 20511 fo. 16).

[32] *CAH* I, no. 1481 (15 Nov. 1547). AM Péronne BB 9 fo. 56: 'suyvant les ordonnances du Roy faicte pour la fourniture de sa gendarmerye . . . ès villes de Picardye'. *Ibid.*, fo. 60r (7 Jan. 1548), fo. 61r (18 Jan.); Henri II to La Rochepot, 31 Jan. 1548 BN fr. 3035 fo. 88. AM Péronne BB 9 fo. 62v (23 Jan. 1548); fo. 71v, 73v (8 June); fo. 85v (7 Aug.).

[33] AM Péronne BB 9 fo. 95r (24 Jan. 1549). La Rochepot to the *élus* of Péronne, 24 Feb. 1549, *ibid.*, fo. 95v–96r. *Ibid.*, fo. 100v–101v (12 March 1549).

The *taillon* emerged through a process of consultation with all the provinces where the companies were stationed, starting in May 1549. The garrison towns of Picardy sent deputies to Amiens in June in order to elect five or six deputies to go to court, where, early in July, they made their remonstrances before the *conseil privé* and were promised a response.[34] The old system of provision continued through 1549, but consultations went on throughout the year and resulted in the *ordonnance* of 12 November 1549. This raised the pay for an *homme d'armes* from L 180 to L 400 p.a. and for the captain from 1,000 to 1,800. The preamble explained that, after consultation, the king's subjects had declared that a financial commutation would be 'beaucoup plus grande soulagement et descharge' than a continuation of the present system. Letters-close went out on 26 November fixing the next muster for the five companies in Picardy on 2 January and specifying that the *gens d'armes* were to pay fully for all provisions. They were also forbidden to forage. The *taillon*, which will be discussed in chapter 7, was the price for all this. The extent to which the new system of supply coped with the strains of the 1550s will be discussed later in this chapter.[35]

The gendarmerie was by the mid-sixteenth century complemented by the light horse. This was an arm of warfare increasingly significant since the 1520s. During the spring campaign in Picardy of 1537, there had been ten companies commanded by admiral d'Annebault amounting to 874 men, though reduced by half in December. In December 1550, there were eight companies of gendarmerie, amounting to 400 lances (about 1,000 men). Companies at Beauvais and Noyon brought the total to 480. In addition to this there were 280 light horse commanded by Entragues, Sipierre and Pelloux. Their standard pay was L 10 per month, bringing the monthly pay bill for 100 men, with officers, to L 1,288. In 1557, there were 750 in eleven companies stationed at Péronne, Guise, Bray, Coucy and Assy, four of them commanded by Scotsmen. By the summer of 1558, there were 1,600 (600 of them Scots).[36]

As a more recent creation than the gendarmerie, they were in some ways more flexible and often used for skirmishing. Entragues asserted in September

[34] *CAH* III, no. 4674, 4676, 4678, 4682, 4848, 4849, 4921, 5024; AM Péronne BB 9 fo. 104r (17 June 1549); fo. 106–7 (21 June); fo. 116r (10 July).
[35] AM Péronne BB 9 fo. 120 (23 Aug.); Isambert, *Anciennes lois* XIII, no. 102; Henri II to governor of Péronne, 26 Nov. 1549, BN fr. 3134 fo. 26–7; same to muster commissioners for Picardy, 2 Dec., BN fr. 20543 fo. 52 (*CAH* III, 5763, 5767); Instructions of Aumale, 10 Dec. 1549, *Mémoires de Guise*, 21–2; Aumale to Jean d'Humières-Becquincourt, 11/24 Dec. 1549, BN fr. 3123 fo. 3–4. M. Wolfe, *The Fiscal System of Renaissance France* (1972), 305.
[36] Vendôme to Regent, 30 Jan. 1525, BN fr. 20648 fo. 9; Francis I to Duprat, 14 April 1528, BN Dupuy 486 fo. 27. For figures in the 1530s: *CAF* VIII, 3, 29824; 301, 32141; 14, 29374; 144, 30596. Muster of Haraucourt's 100 in Nov. 1536, BN fr. 25790, no. 335. In 1550: BN fr. 20543 fo. 55v. 1557: 'Département des chevaux légiers . . . en Picardie' BL Add. 38030 fo. 290.

1549 that they 'gagnent bien leurs dis francs par mois', a pay augmented in the general rise to L 200 p.a., disbursed by their own corps of *commissaires des chevaux-légers*. Methods of recruitment were much the same as for the gendarmerie. When Thibault Rouault, governor of Corbie, asked for a command of light horse, he claimed to have the 'gens de bien' ready to serve and that 'en ce lieu j'en tirerois beaucoup plus de service pour le Roy, que je ne puis faire des autres'.[37] By 1557, they were receiving L 312. Their growing importance is indicated by the willingness of great aristocrats to command them. The duke of Vendôme himself requested a company of his own in 1551–2 in a letter which suggests that recruitment took place much along the lines of the gendarmerie: 'J'ay desjà retenuz beaucoup de gentz, vous supplyant que je ne recoipve ceste honte de les avois abusez.' In 1553, his brother Condé was commanding a company of them, as was Montmorency's son, Damville. By November of that year, Saint-André reported that there were twelve companies in the province.[38]

There seems to have been some circulation between the light horse and the gendarmerie. In 1553, two light horsemen took their pay and then went off to the musters of Humières's company at Péronne, 'expressement prohibé et grandement pugnisable', according to La Marck, who ordered exemplary punishment. Nevertheless, there was a conventional distinction observed between the functions of the two corps, especially in routine skirmishing. Marshal du Biez in 1545 wanted to withdraw the *chevaux-légers* and replace them by *gens d'armes* because of the 'maulx et pilleryes' committed by the former. The governor of Guise wanted to form a troop of thirty light horse out of sixty new 'compagnons' in 1551, 'car vous sçavez que les gens d'armes ne serviront de chevaux légiers'.[39]

Another new formation was that of the *arquebusiers à cheval*, originally attached to the gendarmerie. Rabutin relates that just before the campaign of August 1553 in Picardy, the king authorised captains of 100 and 50 lances to raise fifty and twenty-five *arquebusiers* respectively. He explained that they were meant to increase the flexibility of the gendarmerie and be commanded by experienced *gens d'armes*. They were still grouped with the gendarmerie in

---

[37] Entragues to Aumale, 28 Sept. 1549, BN fr. 20457 fo. 201; Henri II, *lettres-closes*, 26 Nov. 1549, fr. 3134 fo. 26–7. In the 1520s, they were paid by the *ordinaire des guerres*, see Francis I to Duprat, 14 April 1528 (note 36). Rouault to Guise, 25 Feb. 1553, BL Add. 38032 fo. 153–4.
[38] Coligny to Humières, 15 May 1557, BN fr. 3148 p. 95; Vendôme to Montmorency, 23 Dec. 1551, MC Chantilly L XVII fo. 63–4; Villebon to Humières, 19 April 1553, BN fr. 3128 fo. 46; Montmorency to same, 19 April 1553, fr. 3116, p. 193; Saint-André to same, 3/5 Nov. 1553 BN fr. 3128 fo. 61/2.
[39] Le Marck to Humières, 27 April 1553, BN fr. 3128 fo. 51–2; Du Biez to Francis I, 26 Feb./ 6 Mar. 1545, *Mémoire*, 21 March, BN fr. 20521 fo. 90, 92, 93. Croizy to Guise, 20 Nov. 1551, BL Add. 38030 fo. 407–8.

the constable's *département* of April–June 1554, but by 1557 were in part attached to the light horse companies. In 1559, a company of *arquebusiers* were operating separately under the baron de Bournazel.[40]

The closing stages of the Habsburg–Valois Wars saw the introduction of a new arm of cavalry warfare, that of the *pistoliers*, known sometimes as *reîtres*. As yet, their tactics of advancing *en caracole* and discharging their firearms were unperfected and they were notoriously undisciplined. The Rhingrave Johann Philipp was the first military entrepreneur to be commissioned to raise a troop of them for France in Germany, in March 1552. Special regulations were issued for their control in 1557 and 1558, since they had caused such disturbance in their relations with the civil population.[41]

The infantry

By far the largest number of men in the garrison were infantry of various kinds. The wartime garrison seldom rose about 15,000 foot. In 1545 14,000 were ordered for the province, but by March only 11,720 were available.[42] In the December–January musters of 1550, there were 12,476 foot. The field army prepared for the final royal campaign in Picardy during the summer of 1558, however, assembled 11,420 horse and 37,360 foot (see appendix 3).

Such numbers conceal a great complexity and imprecision. Of the 12,476 foot in December 1550 there were 4,521 *lansquenets* (most of them commanded by the Rhingrave) and 7,235 French, Gascons and Picards of the 'old' and 'new' bands, allocated into thirteen garrisons. A typical French 'band' stood at around 300 men (in contrast to 400 for the Germans) but this was only notional. Where comparisons can be made between estimates and active troops, there was much variation. In April 1552, while on the Metz campaign, the king left in Picardy 500 lances, 600 light horse and 12 ensigns of French foot (? 3,600 men) with 6,000 Swiss mercenaries. The survey taken of the garrison in January–February 1558 indicates 480 lances and 600 *pistoliers* and 15,274 foot of the old and new bands with 8,400 *lansquenets*. There was also an important and highly paid complement of 1,600 infantry *arquebusiers*. The 37,360 foot listed for the summer of 1558 included 60 ensigns of *lansquenets*

---

[40] Rabutin, *Commentaires* (SHF edn) I, 222–3; 'Département des compagnies' 1554, BL Add. 38032 fo. 284–5; 'Département des bandes des chevaux légiers' 1557, *ibid.*, 38030 fo. 290 (750 light horse included 150 *arquebusiers à cheval*). Sansac to Guise, 11 Nov. 1558, BN fr. 23192 fo. 98.

[41] The Rhingrave to Montmorency, 11 March 1552, BM Reims, Coll. Tarbé IX, no. 42; J. D. Pariset, *Les relations entre la France et l'Allemagne au milieu du XVIe siècle* (1981), p. 157 n. 35, p. 159 n. 84. G. Zeller, *Le siège de Metz*, 81. 'Réglement pour donner ung ordre . . . à la nourriture des chevaulx pistoliers' Nov. 1557, BN Cangé 15 fo. 63.

[42] Du Biez to Francis I, 30 March 1545, BN fr. 20521 fo. 95–6; BN fr. 20543 fo. 54–5.

(in six regiments), 20 ensigns of Swiss and 55 French 'sans compter une seulle enseigne de légionnaires de la nation françoise'.[43] Clearly, both peacetime and wartime garrisons included substantial numbers of mercenaries.

Besides all these, there were the permanent garrison troops called the *mortespaies*, by the sixteenth century much reduced in significance and perhaps only of local importance. Essentially a creation of the mid-fifteenth century designed to defend territories newly won from the English and Burgundians, they had been transformed from cavalry to pikemen under Louis XI and had risen to their greatest numbers between 1480 and 1484, when 6,000 were envisaged for the whole kingdom. They first appeared in Picardy at Le Crotoy in 1470. At the estates of 1484, 2,900 were allocated for the defence of the northern frontier, to be stationed at Boulogne, Ardres, Thérouanne, Aire, Arras, Béthune and Péronne. Between 1485 and 1490, there seem to have been about 1,000 in Picardy and Artois, but the treaty of 1493 removed the garrisons from Artois and the late fifteenth century saw a general decline in numbers. By the 1539s, the number fluctuated between 370 and 380.[44] Apart from local concessions of supplies of a customary nature, their standard rate of pay was only L 5 per month in the 1530s (the original rate in the fifteenth century had been L 10). In September 1537, their yearly pay came to L 24,300. A muster roll for Le Crotoy in 1542 shows that the fourteen men there had a captain responsible to the town captain.[45]

The duke of Vendôme, at the time of mobilisation in 1528, indicated that the *mortespaies* were no more reliable than the rest of the infantry under his command. None of them had been paid and 'la plus part tiennent les champs et ce qui est demouré aux villes petit nombre et ne sçay de quelle volunté'. In September 1529, the captain of Abbeville reported that his *mortespaies*, unusually, were far in arrears of pay, 'pourquoy ilz sont en grosse suspycyon' and had been forced to sell their 'habillemens' to live.[46] Payment seems to have been more regular in the 1530s, though in April 1537 Montmorency reported those at Doullens well in arrears. In 1557, Henri II decided to replace them by 'bandes de gens de pied que j'entretiens ordinairement tant en temps de paix et de guerre' in Picardy, possibly the 1,170 men recorded in 1550 as 'longtemps entretenuz es garnisons dud. province'. The garrison infantry were

---

[43] 1552: *CSPF Edward VI*, misdated; 1558: BN Clair. 346 fo. 73–92; BN fr. 20470 fo. 167.

[44] Contamine, *Guerre, état et société*, 290–4. For the 1530s: *CAF* VIII, 102, 30182; 262, 31734. In 1542, there were 520, see *CAF* IV, 322, 12511.

[45] *CAF* VII, 667, 27531; 663, 28111; VIII, 5, 29295; 51, 29702; 102, 30182; 231, 31411; 291, 32022. On Le Crotoy, the captain there in 1525 had 13 *mortespaies*, insufficient for guard duty (AN X/1A 1527 fo. 376–7). In 1542 there were 14, see Beauvillé, *Recueil* II, 208–9.

[46] Vendôme to Francis I, 6 Feb. (1528) BN fr. 3016 fo. 24–5; Huppy to Montmorency, 11 Sept. (1529) MC Chantilly, L III, fo. 32–3.

not much advantaged by the new pay rates and still had to be bailed out by supplies from the town councils while awaiting their pay in the 1550s.[47]

By the mid-sixteenth century, the main French infantry were the so-called 'old' and 'new' bands (of 300 each), the latter sometimes called *aventuriers*. The date of their emergence is obscured by the repeated unsuccessful attempts to create a reliable French infantry. The *francs-archers* of 1448, little used to collective training and exposed badly at the battle of Guinegatte in 1479, had been suppressed in 1480 when Louis XI sought to create a force of 10,000 permanent infantry armed with bows, pikes and halberds and paid L 9 per month. Esquerdes played a leading role in the organisation in *camps de manoeuvres* for them in Picardy, with units mobilised in bands of 4,000 as with the *francs-archers*.[48] It is at this time that the *bandes picardes* appear. In 1485, however, the *franc-archer* system, with one man to be raised per eighty hearths, was reintroduced and the force taken to Ghent in 1488 by Esquerdes consisted of 12,000 of them paid at the old rate of L 5 per month. Their quality was poor and the failure of Gié's attempt in 1504 to raise another infantry force of 20,000 shows that the *vielles bandes* were still not in being.[49] The latter probably emerged in the 1520s, recruited in the province, commanded by men of local prestige and kept on permanent footing. These were possibly the men whom Admiral Bonnivet told Vendôme that the king 'veult estre retenuz à sa soulde et le demourant cassez . . . pour le bien du pouvre peuple' in October 1522. Elsewhere it was in Italy that the 'vieilles bandes de Piedmont' emerge much more clearly from the 1530s.[50]

The new bands, or *aventuriers*, were temporary formations and, like the *francs-archers* before them, prone to disorder and crime. The fact that six *ordonnances* were issued between 1518 and 1543 for putting down discharged *aventuriers* who had turned to robbery indicates the nature of the men. Picardy was regarded as a fruitful area for their recruitment. In the 1480s, 2,000 men were 'nouvellement mis sus au pays de Picardie' for the Breton war and in 1552 there was a report of '17,000 Gascons and Picards, footmen well

---

[47] Montmorency to Dubourg, 3 April 1537, AN J 968 no. 1/10. Henri II to Guise, 15 Nov. 1557, BN Cangé 15 fo. 60. List of 1550, BN fr. 4552 fo. 15v. AM Boulogne 1013 fo. 36v (22 April 1556) – there were only 30 foot then at Boulogne; fo. 26r (30 Sept. 1553).

[48] See the powers to Esquerdes, 9 Oct. 1480, A. Collet, 'Philippe de Crèvecoeur', 445–6; muster of 7,000 archers under Esquerdes, Amiens, 5 May 1480, Ledru, *Histoire de la maison de Mailly*, preuves, no. 403; of 4,000 archers, Amiens, capt. bât. de Longueval under Esquerdes, 21 Jan. 1483, AN K 72 no. 73.

[49] G. Zeller, *Le siège de Metz*, 51. P. Contamine, *Guerre, état et société*, 304ff., 337–51. A Spont, 'La milice des francs archers 1448–1550', *Revue des questions historiques*, 1897; General Susanne, *Histoire de l'infanterie française* (1876), 54ff.; H. Sée, *Louis XI et les villes*, 83–99.

[50] Bonnivet to Vendôme, 16 Oct. (1522), BN fr. 3028 fo. 61–2.

exercised in the wars in the name of Venturers'.[51] In fact, Gaston Zeller showed conclusively that *aventurier* was a name used for all types of infantry during the reign of Francis I, but that under Henri II it became increasingly confined to 'new bands' recruited for a specific campaign.[52] It was in the mid-1540s that we see the effective emergence of 'regiments' under colonels, like Thibault Rouault's command of ten companies of Picard *aventuriers* in 1545 or de Thaix's companies of old bands of Piedmont. The command was moving towards the development under Henri II of the posts of *colonel-général de l'infanterie* on both sides of the Alps.[53]

The pay of L 5 per month for infantry established in 1485 remained stable until the mid-sixteenth century. However, there was provision for selective double pay, as for the gendarmerie. Out of a band of 500 *aventuriers* at Beaurains under Jean de Castille in 1522, 50 received double pay. The officers-captains, *caps d'escoadre* etc., of course received at least double pay but in 1543, a company of 250 men at Péronne included 59 *corselletz*, armed more heavily, receiving an extra 50s. A band of 82 *aventuriers* at Rue were receiving basic pay of L 6. In fact, an informal two-tier pay structure prevailed into the 1540s, garrison troops paid at the simple pay rate of L 5, other infantry companies and mercenaries at L 6.

Firearms were introduced only slowly. A band of Corsicans at Nouvion in 1525 were almost entirely men with firearms, but were paid very little more than the basic pay. The proportion of infantry with firearms in 1550 seems to have been 32–34%. Other than the large increases necessary in times of emergency, a force of 1,300–1,450 *aventuriers* were thought essential by the 1530s for garrison duty. In 1537–8, 1,450 men drew monthly pay in Picardy which averaged L 6 per man with extra pay for firearms. The proportion of men with firearms seems to have increased very significantly in the 1540s.[54]

As far as the purchasing power of this pay hierarchy is concerned, rates prevailing in the 1550s indicate that, while the basic infantry pay of 3s 9d per

---

[51] BN fr. 21501 fo. 430–2; *CSPF Edward VI*, 84. For measures taken in 1529 to deliver the Beauvais area from the devastations of the *aventuriers*, see BM Beauvais, Coll. Bucquet LVII, p. 500.

[52] G. Zeller, 'De quelques institutions mal connues du XVIe siècle', *RH*, 194 (1944), 'Des aventuriers', 210–18. See musters of *aventuriers des vieilles bandes de Piedmont*, BN fr. 25792 no. 509, 513 (1545), or *aventuriers françoys et gascons*, fr. 25793 no. 554 (1547).

[53] Musters of companies in 1545 under Rouault as *colonel*: BN fr. 25792 no. 517, 519, 520; under Thaix: fr. 25793 no. 518.

[54] For 1485: Contamine, *Guerre, état et société*, 343–7; other figures: muster roll in Beauvillé, *Recueil* I, 166–8, 266, 243–4, 244–6, 210–12. 1530s: *CAF* VIII, 5, 29301; 14, 29375; 41, 29610; 231, 31409; 80, 29971; 83, 29992. Types of pay structure: basic pay of L 5 with L 6 for *arquebusiers* and 7 for *corselets*, BN fr. 25792 no. 448 (Boulogne garr. troops, 1543); no. 463 (Le Câtelet garr., 1544). L 6 with L 7 for *arquebusiers* and L 9 for *corselets*: fr. 25793 no. 460 (old bands, Montreuil, 1543).

day compared well with that of the simple pioneer hod-carrier at 15d, it was rather less than the 4s earned by the skilled artillery pioneer. At rates established for food munitions in the late 1540s, the unskilled pioneer earned daily 5 12-ounce loaves or 1¼ *pintes* of wine, and the simple pikeman 15 loaves or 3¾ *pintes*. The captain earned 266 loaves. The daily bread requirement for a soldier has been established as 1 k for the seventeenth century, so in theory the pay was adequate when available and when the munition system worked.[55]

Processes of recruitment remain obscure. When men were needed, blank commissions were sent to governors for issue to reliable captains. In February 1528, Vendôme reported that he had 'incontinent dépesché pour faire tenir prestz six mil hommes que s'il vous vient affaire en bien peu de jours les mectray ensemble et les tiendra l'on prestz sans rien lever de peur de la foulle de peuple'.[56] These were undoubtedly *aventuriers*, but how they could be mobilised so fast is unclear. Some evidence emerges from another period when Vendôme was authorised to recruit men in Picardy and the Ile-de-France during the summer of 1536. Maître Legay, a Parisian lawyer with a wry sense of humour, observed that:

> le tambour sonne fort en ceste ville et sont partis plus de iij ou iiij mil hommes, et j'entends tant hommes que garçons, car je vous promets que j'en ay vue beaucoup qui auroient bien affaire à seulement porter leur picque et s'ils se deffendent ce sera beaucoup, car de battre je ne leur en voy grand monstre, aussi sont ilz bon filz et cuyde bien que si on ne leur demande rien aussi ne feront ils pas eulx.

In September, Legay wrote again of the 6,000 men raised by Vendôme from the unwilling Parisians that they were 'la plus grande pitié de canaille que vous veistes jamais', a sentiment echoed by Vendôme in calling them 'les paillardz que vistes jamais les plus subjectz à mutinerie'.[57] Later still, La Rochepot, then commander at Ardres in 1544, wrote that the captains of infantry had been 'bien empeschez de faire leurs bandes pour la peine qu'ilz avoient de recouvrer

55 Musters in Picardy of pioneers (*hottiers*), at 15d p.d. BN fr. 25797 no. 292 and at 4s p.d. fr. 25796 no. 279. Prices of bread and wine fixed, 16 Nov. 1547, *conseil privé*, BN fr. 18153 fo. 17–20. For an important study of the food needs of armies, see G. Perjes, 'Army Provisioning, Logistics and Strategy in the Second Half of the 17th Century', *Acta Historica* XVI (1970), esp. 5–6.

56 Vendôme to Francis I, 6 Feb. (1528) BN fr. 3016 fo. 24–5; same to Montmorency, 18 July (1528) BN fr. 6635 fo. 161.

57 Legay to Jacques Brunet, secr. to the bishop of Lavaur, 3 July, 9 Sept. (1536) BL Add. 38033 fo. 126, 138. Vendôme to La Rochepot, 19 June 1536, BN fr. 3069 fo. 40; same to Jean du Bellay, 10 Aug., Scheurer, *Correspondance de Jean du Bellay*, II, p. 424. For other evidence on infantry recruitment at the time: BN Dupuy 486 fo. 89, Vendôme's patent of 28 Aug., and AM Senlis BB 5 fo. 309 (3 Sept. 1536).

gens'; this shortage of supply made it even more essential to pay them promptly if they were not to desert.[58]

Part of the infantry formations in the province consisted of the Picard Legion, created by Francis I in 1534 with a view to obtaining a reliable French infantry. In fact, similar attempts had been made before. The principles upon which they were based are similar to those for the bands of foot raised in Picardy from 1521 onwards, which themselves continued the tradition of the fifteenth-century *francs archers* and the *bandes de Picardie* of 1481. Louis XII's *ordonnance* of 1512 had also tried to raise an infantry on a territorial basis. Such earlier formations had been commanded by local noblemen like Heilly, his cousin Sarcus and La Hargerie. They, too, were called *aventuriers* and sometimes even *légionnaires*. In 1525, the crown decided to raise 15,000 men in each frontier province for local service. They may have been the nucleus of the legions formally created in 1534.[59]

The Boulonnais, in particular, was an area where the practice was already established of raising local infantry by commission to the *sénéchal*, du Biez. In 1528, the crown wanted to raise 1,000 foot in order to intimidate the Burgundians and du Biez was instructed to nominate 'cappitaines pour lever huit cens hommes de pié'. He asked to be their captain himself, and these were to be the 1,000 Boulonnais foot eventually commanded by du Biez with Montcavrel and Framezelles as deputies.[60]

It was around this time that a *mémoire* was drawn up outlining how the crown could raise a permanent force of 50,000 foot at minimal cost. This involved suppressing the *francs-archers*, as unlikely to attract men of high enough calibre as captains, but the same parish system of recruitment was retained. In each *élection*, there would be captains, 'gens de bien et gentils-hommes, qu'ils ayent de quoy et qu'ils soyent cogneus et que autrefois ont mené gens'. They would command 500 men and have four gentlemen – *centeniers* – under them. These would be paid permanently, but the infantry recruits would only be paid a minimal L 15 retainer for livery and conduct to the musters (in place of the L 50 for *francs-archers*, paid for harness which was usually defective). In peace, there would be yearly musters and the parishes would pay the men directly their L 8 a month. It was an attempt to get a

---

[58] La Rochepot to Vendôme, Ardres, 25 July 1544, Vienna, HHuStA, P.A. 55 fo. 445–6, in cipher.

[59] Martin du Bellay, *Mémoires* (Michaud et Poujoulat), 377, 143. B. Quilliet, *Louis XII* (1986), 388–9. Spy report of Sept. 1522(?), PRO SP1/26 fo. 192 (*L&P* III, ii, 2706) 'les légionnaires de Normandye et les légionairz de Bretaigne sont demourés chacun en leur pays'. Date conjectural but could fit early 1520s or mid-1530s, the former more likely. Vendôme to Parlement, 29 March 1525, AN X/1A 1527 fo. 333. Jean de Sarcus, 'cappitaine général de tous les gens de pied de Picardie', receipt of 26 July 1526, BM Reims, Tarbé VIII, no. 76.

[60] Du Biez to Montmorency, 9 Feb., 9 July (1528), BN fr. 3004 fo. 52; fr. 20507 fo. 67.

permanent infantry on the cheap, but attention was paid to equipment and each band of 500 was to include 150 *arquebusiers* and 50 *halbardiers*. Like the *francs-archers*, the men were to be exempt from the *taille*.[61]

The ideas behind the legions had thus been under consideration for some time, besides any possible echoes of Machiavelli's *Arte della Guerra*. Once the legions were formed, the practice was retained of appointing local noblemen to command them. The *ordonnance* of 24 July 1534 specified a legion of 6,000 men under six gentlemen, each with two lieutenants commanding ensigns of 500. Montmorency shortly afterwards wrote to individual captains issuing commissions to raise the men. All were to be enrolled by name and address for a rapid call to the colours, and the king himself inspected the Picard legion near Amiens on 20 June 1535 in a spectacular ceremony. By this time the six captains were Antoine de Mailly-Auchy, Jean de Sarcus, Michel de Barbançon-Canny, Jean de Senicourt-Saisseval, Adrien de Pisseleu-Heilly and Oudart du Biez. Most were local noblemen with court connections.[62]

Though much was expected of the legions they proved ineffective. The reasons are not clear. Fourquevaux explained the problem in terms of reliance on volunteers rather than conscripts. Only the riff-raff would join up. Brantôme, however, praised these 'jeunes gens . . . des villages, des boutiques, des escoles . . . des forges, des escuries', who could rapidly be shaped into good fighters. Claude de Seyssel had suggested that it was inexpedient to have the 'menu peuple' 'exercité généralement aux armes'. Later in the century, Jean Bodin claimed, on what authority is unclear, that Francis I had reduced the legions, thinking that it was dangerous to 'aguerrir tous les sujets d'une république'. The argument, often based on the reports of Venetian ambassadors, that the French nobility feared the peasantry and were thus distrustful of any attempts to raise a French infantry, reflects a certain contemporary social prejudice but hardly serious thought. It may be that suspicions from some quarters ultimately undermined their effectiveness. On the other hand, as we have seen, the local nobility were eager to command them as well as to enlist as officers.[63]

---

[61] 'Mémoire pour ung estat des gens de pied' BL Add. 38028 fo. 68–71, copy.

[62] Procacci, 'La Fortuna del Arte della Guerra de Macchiavelli nella Francia del secolo XVI', *Rivista Storica Italiana* 67 (1955), 495. Martin du Bellay, *Mémoires* (SHF edn) II, 289–91; *Ordonnances, François Ier* VII, 133–49; Montmorency to Heilly, 20 Aug. 1534, in Friant. 'Lettres . . . trouvées au chateau de Heilly' *MSAP* XI, 72–3. Legionary captains like du Biez were paid L 50 per month in peacetime and 100 in war (*CAF* VIII, 216, 31253; BN fr. 25790 no. 334, muster of 300 legion, under du Biez, Nov. 1536). Ledru, *Maison de Mailly* I, 383–4.

[63] Fourquevaux, *Instructions sur le faict de la guerre*, introduction by G. Dickinson, xxxii–iii; C. de Seyssel, *La Monarchie de France* (ed. Poujol), XVI, 'Du Peuple Menu'; Jean Bodin, *Siz Livres de la Republique* (edn 1578), 569. Tavannes, *Mémoires* (Michaud et Poujoulat), 267, says that the French were not well equipped in infantry before the civil wars 'soit leurs roys les

One of the earliest complaints about the legions was lack of discipline. There were signs of this as early as 1536–7, when they were much used. In July 1536, an officer was sent to punish them for 'meschanceté'. Vendôme even threatened to cut them to pieces for refusing to obey orders, though it is possible that the reason for this was the usual slowness of pay.[64] The *légionnaires* were paid separately from the *aventuriers* but at the same rate: L 5 p.m. with an extra livre for the *arquebusiers*, established at 20% of effectives (other provinces had more or less). The chief difference was that the *légionnaires* were permanent troops, mustered twice a year, whereas the *aventuriers* were paid only during campaigns. Most officers' pay was the same except that the *caps d'esquadre* of the *aventuriers* received an extra L 5 and those of the legions L 10. In the 1530s, they remained organised in bands of 1,000, though this pattern tended to break down into the more traditional smaller bands in the 1540s. In 1543, Heilly was ordered to assemble three companies of 300 men, but in the event it was the legion of Champagne, commanded by the count of Brienne as 'colonel', which contributed most; musters of seven companies of 500, most complete, survive for Landrecies in June 1543. In the same period the legions of Normandy and Picardy were commanded by Lorges, with nine musters surviving showing rather smaller companies.[65] For the campaign of the summer of 1545, 6,000 Picard legionnaires were raised in companies of 500 under Genlis as captain-general. The lists for 2,000 have survived, and what is striking is not only the participation of 6 'gentlemen' in each company, as well as the officers, but also the strong fire-power involved. In 1536, du Biez's company of 300 included only 60 *arquebusiers*; in 1545, the companies of 500 included only 160–80 simple pikemen. The rest were *arquebusiers* with or without *corseletz*. In this respect, the *aventuriers picards* of the time were virtually indistinguishable.[66]

Methods of recruitment were supposed to be systematic, but it seems clear

---

craignissent, ou que les combats ne fussent si fréquent que depuis'. On social attitudes, see for instance H. Heller, *Iron and Blood*, 24, based on Giustiniani's and Suriano's *relazioni* (M. N. Tommaseo (ed.), *Relations des ambassadeurs vénitiens sur les affaires de France au XVIe siècle* 2 vols. (1838) I, 185–7, 495–7); see the lists of *gentilshommes* in the musters of the Picard legion, 1545, BN fr. 25793 no. 526, 527, 528 (e.g. Le Vasseur, La Motte, Saisseval etc.).

[64] At Beauvais, 1536, 'il y a plusieurs légionnaires qui sans charge ne capitaine vont aux villages et les mangent'. BM Beauvais, Coll. Bucquet LVII, p. 550; Vendôme to La Rochepot, 19 June, 17 July, 22 Sept. 1536, BN fr. 3069 fo. 40, 94, 122; Henri II to La Rochepot, 3, 17 Sept. 1548, BN fr. 3124 fo. 14, 17.

[65] Orders for the muster of the Picard legion under Sarcus, Saisseval, Heilly: Vendôme to Heilly, 5 June 1543, SAP 57 no. 44. Musters for 1543: Champagne: BN fr. 25791: no. 394, 395, 397, 399, 411, 479, 485; Picardy: fr. 25791, no. 412 (La Lande), 413 (Dyville), 414 (La Lande), fr. 25792 no. 453 (Montcavrel); Normandy: fr. 25791, no. 393, 417, 418, 419, 432, 433.

[66] Musters of the Picard legion, 1545: fr. 25792 no. 526 (Bouchavannes), 527 (Varennes), 528 (Chaulmont), 529 (Marigny); 1536: fr. 25790 no. 334 (du Biez, 300).

that they gradually fell into the traditional patterns. One very obvious incentive to enlist was exemption from the *taille*; legion captains provided certificates for their men to produce for tax officials.[67] In 1549, for the Boulonnais campaign, the king commissioned the captain of the Norman legion, Armenonville, 'de vous asseurer jusques au nombre de trois cens des meilleurs de voz gens que vous tiendrez prestz'. Four ensigns were raised in Normandy and four in Picardy, while La Rochepot was given blank commissions to issue to suitable captains 's'asseurer de leurs gens pour en faire la levée'. It would seem, therefore, that by this time a pool of likely men was drawn on by the captains to reinforce the royal army. The Picard legion was not restricted to the province for recruitment, since some men were certainly drawn from the Ile-de-France and the legion was even sometimes known as 'de Picardie et l'Ile-de-France'.[68]

Though use of the legions was only sporadic in the 1540s and early 1550s, the regulations for them were fully recast in March 1558 and their structure was modified. At that time, Flour d'Ardres, sieur de Crésèques, was commissioned as 'colonel' of the Picard legion and immediately submitted a list of captains for secretary Bourdin to get approved in the *conseil des affaires*. The list contained the names of twenty men, mostly young and the sons of experienced chiefs. They were to be appointed by districts. At the head of the list came Jean Pocques, captain of Monthulin for the Boulonnais. At Amiens, there was Saisseval, formerly his father's lieutenant as captain of Ardres and at Compiègne the sieur de Moutiers, who had fought in Piedmont. Of the young sieur de Belleforrière at Vervins, Crésèques noted: 'je ne voys point qui arreste d'en prendre. A esté cappitaine en chef.' There were also two former *gens d'armes* of Vendôme's company. The commissions were despatched in April, though one man was reluctant and was replaced by an 'honeste gentilhomme et de bonne part'. Pocques was also replaced. In May the king decided on a new levy of eleven ensigns of légionnaires, five earmarked for garrison duty and five for Paul de Termes's disastrous expedition from Calais.[69]

At Calais in November 1558, the légionnaires consisted of 964 men in six companies. The vidame de Chartres estimated that just over 11 per cent were out of action, mainly through illness. They were badly in arrears of pay and had

[67] See certificates signed by Blerencourt in AM Senlis BB 5 fo. 348v (1542); fo. 109r (1552).

[68] Henri II to Armenonville, 11 Dec. 1549, BN fr. 20534 fo. 118; *Mémoire* of the king to La Rochepot, 4 March 1548, BN fr. 3088 fo. 9–12. AM Senlis BB 6 fo. 231v, certificate by a captain of 'la légion de Picardie et Isle de France'.

[69] Commission to Crésèques, AD Pas-de-Calais 9B 2 fo. 82; his list of captains, BN fr. 23191 fo. 107–8. Crésèques to Guise, 2 April 1558, BN Clair. 350 fo. 102. Aumale to Humières, 29 May, 10 June 1558, BN fr. 3123 p. 151, 171. See also Crésquès to Guise, 16 April 1558, BL Add. 38034 fo. 206v, in favour of M. de Pierrepont, 'noury' in the infantry, who wanted a captaincy of legionnaires.

to be given money to return to their homes without committing 'violences sur leur chemin'. The same was the case with other companies at La Fère and Chauny.[70] The legions had indeed proved a repeated disappointment, though it is not clear that their discipline problems were unique to them. The initial classicism of their organisation was abandoned early and they came to resemble the rest of the French infantry, which was widely condemned for its poor quality. The development of the legions and the old bands into recognisable regiments took place, of course, shortly after the end of the Habsburg–Valois Wars on the initiative of the duke of Guise.[71]

For crack troops, the French crown relied on recruitment abroad. Theorists repeatedly deplored this, but the facts of military life dictated it; the mercenaries were the professionals and it was this rather than fear of the French peasantry that dictated their employment.[72] There were usually formations of foreign troops in Picardy during the Habsburg–Valois Wars, Swiss and Italian in the earlier phases, German *lansquenets* and *pistoliers* later on. *Lansquenets* had been employed by Louis XI, and extensively in the war of 1512. In 1523–4, the de la Pole duke of Suffolk had led 2,000 of them on the northern frontier, and in 1529 the duke of Guise had been commissioned to raise 6,000, commanded by Felter von Keuringen. In the 1530s, Wilhelm von Fürstenberg was the chief commander of *lansquenets* in the king's armies.[73] Expected numbers were 7,000 for service in Picardy in June 1536, though fewer actually turned up. In March 1537, Fürstenberg's twenty ensigns (about 6,000 men) were present in the royal army in Picardy and paid at the rate of L 6 per month.[74] This remained the standard rate, though there were selective supplements. Of an ensign of 300 men in 1548, 40 received double pay and 30 an extra L 2 per month as *arquebusiers*. Their overall pay was greater than the

---

[70] Vidame de Chartres to Henri II, 24 Nov. 1558, BN fr. 23192 fo. 262–5; Henri II to Sansac, 17 Nov. 1558, BN fr. 23192 fo. 149; Ledru, *La maison de Mailly* II, 286.

[71] The origins of the historic regiments is to be found in the duke of Guise's division of all French troops 'de deçà les monts' under three *maîtres de camp* on the Spanish model in 1560–2. See Marchand, *Brissac*, 522.

[72] For all this, see D. L. Potter, 'Les Allemands et les armées françaises au XVIᵉ siècle', *Francia* 21, ii (forthcoming), introduction. Brantôme, *Oeuvres complètes* (SHF edn) VI, 220–7; Tavannes, *Mémoires* (Michaud et Poujoulat), 267; A. Rozet and J. F. Lembey, *L'invasion de France en 1544* (1910), 684; L. Firpo (ed.), *Relazione di Ambasciatori Veneti* II, 471–2; G. Zeller, *Le siège de Metz*, 171.

[73] Richard de la Pole to Francis I, 8 May (1524), BL Cotton, Calig. D VIII fo. 299; AM Senlis BB 5 fo. 210r (12 Feb. 1524); AM Laon EE 5 (letter of Vendôme, 9 April (1524)). R. Peter, 'Les lansquenets dans les armées du roi' in *Charles-Quint, le Rhin et la France* (Société Savante d'Alsace, XVII).

[74] Vendôme to La Rochepot, 24 June 1536, BN fr. 3069 fo. 53; Guise to same, 20 Aug., *ibid.*, fo. 34. For 1537: *CAF* VIII, 29649; Francis I to La Rochepot, 20 March 1537, BN fr. 3008 fo. 15; Martin de Troyes to same, 7 June, nafr. 23168 nos. 39, 63. On Württemberg's troops, see *Ordonnances, François Ier* VIII, 237–42.

French bands, since in January 1550, 1523 *lansquenets* received L 15,092 per month (including officers' pay) and 3,300 French L 28,022. They were paid by the *trésorier de l'extraordinaire des guerres* and, in the 1540s, had their own *prévôt général de la justice* in Picardy in the person of Ludwig von Salzburg. Though it has usually been assumed that German ensigns were larger than the French (400 rather than 300), in French service *lansquenets* seem usually to have been organised in ensigns of 300 and expanded to 350 or 400 on active campaign.[75]

Fürstenberg quarrelled with the constable and others and left French service in 1538. His place was gradually taken by a new generation of military entrepreneurs, mostly Protestants, including Ludovic von Deben and Georg von Reckerodt, both of whom commanded 'regiments' of eight ensigns in the Hainault campaign of 1543, and later Friedrich von Reiffenberg and Christoff von Roggendorff.[76] As far as Picardy is concerned, the most prominent of them was the Rhingrave Johann Philipp, a Lutheran prince from the borders of Lorraine and the Rhineland who had entered service with the French crown in 1538 and, unusually, never thereafter changed his allegiance, serving in the Boulonnais in 1545–6 and 1549, in Picardy throughout 1553 and 1554 and again in 1557, and finally in the Normandy campaign of 1562–3.

His rôle was important in the 1550s, since the 'regiment' of which he was regarded as the 'colonel' at a pay of L 1,036 per month was one of the most reliable infantry formations in the northern theatre of war. Moreover, a considerable portion of his correspondence has survived to throw light on his relations with the crown and the management of his men.[77] He was commissioned to raise 12,000 men in twenty-four ensigns in the Hesse region in January 1552, 5,500 of them (in eleven ensigns) to be his own 'regiment' and the rest commanded by Reckerodt and Schertlin. In fact, Henri II had 13,500 *lansquenets* for the campaign of 1552. In August 1555, he had twelve ensigns, about 6,000 men, at Montcornet and, even after his capture at the battle of Saint-Quentin, his regiment continued to serve in Picardy under his lieutenant, Sterne, with 4,000 men.[78]

---

[75] BN fr. 4552 fos. 8 and 12. On Salzburg, see Beauvillé, *Recueil* II, 209; AM Chauny, BB 6 fo. 7v.

[76] On this period, see D. L. Potter, 'England and France 1536–50' (Cambridge Ph.D. thesis, 1973), ch. 3; 'Foreign Policy in the Age of the Reformation: French Involvement in the Schmalkaldic War', *Historical Journal* 20 (1977), 525–44.

[77] D. L. Potter, 'Les Allemands et les armées françaises', introduction. The correspondence received by the Rhingrave in this period, partly in MC Chantilly, J II, will there be published.

[78] J. D. Pariset, *Les relations*, 118; Pariset, 'La France et les princes allemands', *Francia* X, no. 38, 50. Schirrmacher, *Johann Albrecht I Herzog von Mecklenburg* (1885) II, no. 33, 40. On the Rhingrave's regiment: BN fr. 2965 fo. 2–3; G. Zeller, *La réunion* I, 329; Rhingrave to Montmorency, 11 March 1552, BM Reims, Tarbé IX, 42.

At the end of January 1558, the strength of the *lansquenets* was recorded as twenty-eight ensigns of 300 men each (8,400) divided into three regiments under Sterne, Reckerodt and Wilhelm von Reiffenberg. The *estat* of the royal army assembled in Picardy during the summer of 1558 included 16,000 Germans in six regiments and 6,000 Swiss out of the total of 37,360 foot, as clear a testimony as is needed to demonstrate the overwhelming dominance of the mercenaries on the battlefield.[79]

The war commissariat

One of the most direct ways in which the demands of war influenced the forms of early modern state organisation was in the elaboration of the corps of bureaucrats charged with the task of paying, moving and feeding the augmented armies of the sixteenth century and constructing the fortifications which were increasingly at the centre of military operations. In many cases, they built on procedures already established, but were operating on a more complex basis. In essence, this meant the development of the war *commissaires*, appointees charged with specific duties at the king's pleasure without the prerogatives of office-holders. They were responsible for the receipt and disbursement of funds on the grand scale and there was often considerable interchange between the various 'departments' of administration. For much of the time, these administrators also had to reside in the province and had considerable knowledge of its problems.

Departments of administration were customarily staffed by a *trésorier* as the chief accountant, a *contrôleur* to keep the records and a staff of *commis* to effect payments. They received funds by *mandements* to various local revenue officials or, occasionally, directly from the central *trésorerie de l'Epargne*.[80] Occasionally orders for payment could be made by the provincial governor. The *trésorier de l'ordinaire des guerres* received *mandements* on the *taille* by quarters to pay the gendarmerie. At times this would be difficult to extract from local *réceveurs*, as *trésorier* Grolier found in 1525 when desperate to find funds in Normandy to pay the Picard gendarmerie.[81]

In principle, military administration was divided into the *ordinaire* for the gendarmerie and the *extraordinaire* for the infantry and light horse (though the

[79] BN Clair. 346 fo. 77–92; Sterne to Guise, 15 Jan. (recte Feb.); 1558, BN Cangé 62 fo. 31–3; BN fr. 20470 fo. 167 (*état* of the royal army of August 1558).
[80] E.g. Martin de Troyes in 1536 (the king to Vendôme, 27 June 1536, BN fr. 3008 fo. 85).
[81] Payment by Moreau on La Rochepot's orders, BN fr. 26132 no. 290 and list for 1537, Beauvillé, *Recueil*, 276–80; by Baillon on La Rochepot's orders, 30 May 1550, BN fr. 26133 no. 455. Vendôme to Parlement, 19 April 1525, AN X/1A 1527 fo. 390v–391r and *séances* of 13, 19 and 24 May 1525, *ibid.*, fo. 393 and 1528 fo. 446–9, 491–2.

latter had their own *trésoriers* by the 1550s). The increase in business is reflected by the rise in the number of *trésoriers de l'ordinaire* from eight to fifteen under Francis I and the establishment in 1534 of a systematic appointment of a *commis* to each gendarmerie company.[82] As for the *extraordinaire*, a *trésorier* became attached to the staffs of the provincial governors and by 1547, Raoul Moreau was entitled *trésorier de l'extraordinaire des guerres de Picardie et Artois*. The pattern observed by M. Antoine for the attachment of proto-intendants to provincial governors' staffs in the 1550s and noted above in chapter 3 was thus already in the making.[83]

Such administrators were often interrelated. Guillaume de Bours, *commis de l'ordinaire des guerres* in Picardy in 1542, was succeeded by his nephew Louis in 1548. Martin de Troyes, *trésorier de l'extraordinaire* in the 1530s had a relative, Nicolas de Troyes, in the *ordinaire* department in 1544. Raoul Moreau was related to Jean Moreau *contrôleur de l'extraordinaire* in 1550, while Jacques Veau, *trésorier de l'extraordinaire* had an Alain Veau as his *commis*. Posts could sometimes be accumulated, as by Gaspard de Lanzeray, Vendôme's secretary, who was *contrôleur de l'extraordinaire* and *contrôleur des réparations de Picardie*. François Durel, sieur de La Parnelière, was both *commissaire de l'ordinaire* and *commissaire* of victualling. Whatever their titles, life could be dangerous for these men at times.[84] Money was often in short supply and they could be detained or assaulted by enraged unpaid soldiers.[85]

Fortification and victualling each had their complement of administrators, many of them locally based. Fortifications had a *contrôleur-général des réparations de Picardie*, a *maître des ouvrages* and a staff of *commis*. The earliest known *contrôleur-général* was Gaspard de Lanzeray by 1534.[86] By then Pierre Favre, *receveur-général* of Picardy, was *commis* in the office, but by August 1537 had been replaced by Pierre de La Grange. By 1549,

[82] G. Dickinson, introduction to Fourquevaux, *Instructions sur le faict de la guerre*, p. lviii; *CAF* V, 683, 18190; VII, 756, 22847.

[83] For the residence of a *trésorier* in the province in 1525, cf. AN X/1A 1527 fo. 333 and Francis I to La Rochepot, 28 April 1538, BN fr. 3088 fo. 1–2: 'résident auprès de vous'. On Moreau, *CAH* I, 31 Dec. 1547.

[84] Beauvillé, *Recueil* II, 208–9; BN fr. 28515 no. 98 (Bours). BN fr. 28515 no. 88; Beauvillé, *Recueil*, II, 210–12; BN fr. 28515 no. 93 (Moreau). Vendôme, 16 June 1531, Beauvillé, *Recueil* I, 232–3, 243–4; Du Biez to King, 27 Aug. 1545 BN fr. 20521 fo. 97.

[85] For such an attack, see Sansac to Guise, 11/16 Nov. 1558, BN fr. 23192 fo. 98–9, 154–5.

[86] See Iung, 'L'organisation du service des vivres de 1550 à 1650' *BEC* 1983, where he argues that the earliest appearance in legislation was 1557. For an early example of a *commissaire* for supplies, Thierry de Licques, AM Péronne BB 6 fo. 133 (1491). (He was also lieutenant in the *sénéchaussée* of Ponthieu, see BM Abbeville MS 807.) On Lanzeray, see Beauvillé, *Recueil* I, 232–3 and Vendôme to La Rochepot, 16 June 1536, BN fr. 3069 fo. 32. A certificate by him, 20 June 1544 as *contrôleur extraordinaire de la guerre*, for payment for spy reports on Vendôme's orders, BL Add. Charter 164.

coordination had been attempted by creating a *contrôleur des réparations, fortifications et advitaillements* (Jacques Adam) and a *trésorier*, Jean Phrizon.[87] The various *commis* for fortifications typically disbursed money on the orders of local governors empowered as *commissaires et ordonnateurs* of such expenditure. The *trésorier* also disbursed money ordered by the crown to be deducted from the war taxes known as *soldes*. By the 1550s, fortification *commissaires* were able to order individuals or communities to make contributions.[88]

Technical work on fortifications was dominated by Italian engineers. As early as April 1524, Francis I was being advised on plans for the Montrécu Bastion at Amiens by a sieur Franseque. In the 1530s, the most prominent engineer was Antonio Castello, who devised the plan for the new fort of La Capelle in 1536 and worked to refortify Saint-Pol and Hesdin after their capture in 1537. He was receiving a pension of L 1,000 p.a. Captured in the Habsburg revanche at Saint-Pol, he was ransomed by the king and sent in the spring of 1538 to survey the border as far as Thérouanne, and was probably the Italian who came to Amiens about the construction of the Vidame platform and the Hotoie bastion. By May 1539, he was *maître des ouvrages de Picardie*. In 1541, he was in dispute with the commander of Péronne, Feuquières, over plans for the reconstruction of the walls damaged in the siege of 1536. Antoine de Bourbon ordered them to agree on joint plans.[89]

Another Italian engineer, Girolamo Marini, or da Modena, was a relative of Ippolito, a mercenary in French service. Marini was a political exile who had entered French service by 1537 and who, until the early 1540s, was employed mainly in Piedmont. His brilliant work in the defence of Saint-Dizier in 1544 signalled a move northwards and in 1545 he is found inspecting the Champagne frontier. Despite close relations with the fallen royal favourite, Mme d'Etampes, he continued to be employed by Henri II at Mézières in December 1547 and in 1548 on the plans for the new fort 'Châtillon' opposite Boulogne. The constable described him as 'personnaige grandement entendu

---

87 Lanzeray was succeeded by Claude d'Asnières. Favre is 'former *commis*' in 1539, see *CAF* III, 723, 10818. On La Grange, see *CAF* VIII, 120, 30363 and in 1549 BN p.o. 2031 no. 102–5; on Adam see fr. 26132 no. 300 and AM Amiens EE 323 (*Inventaire sommaire, Amiens*, 606 (1554)).

88 Beauvillé, *Recueil* I, 248–9 (1553) and BN Picardie 31 fo. 277 (Jan. 1552). Payments from soldes: AM Péronne BB 10 fo. 5r, 8r, 27r, 29r, 33r. On orders to individuals: Francis I to La Rochepot, 15 May 1538, BN fr. 3008 fo. 179, AM Senlis BB 6 fo. 10r (1544); AM Compiègne BB 20 fo. 6v (1544).

89 *Inventaire sommaire, Amiens* II, 327 (12 May 1524). On Castello: *CAF* VIII, 24, 29449; 40, 29606; 81, 29974; 220, 31296; Francis I to La Rochepot, 9 April 1538, BN fr. 3035 fo. 13; AM Amiens BB 23 fo. 127v; E. Picot, 'Chants historiques français du XVIe siècle', *Revue d'histoire littéraire de la France* 7 (1900), 427. Feuquières to Francis I, 14 June 1541, BN fr. 20521 fo. 37; Vendôme to same, 17 June, 19 July, *ibid.*, fo. 39, 45.

en telles choses'. This was after another Italian, Antonio Mellone of Cremona, had been employed to devise the earlier, and ineffective, fort at Oultreau.[90]

In fact, both Mellone and Ippolito Marini were potential traitors. Mellone, 'chief engineer of the French king' had already approached the English in 1546. He and Marini were suborned by the Imperial ambassador Renard in 1549 and Marini had already delivered documents to the English ambassador Nicholas Wotton, promising to get French attack plans against the English fort of Boulogneberg. Ippolito's eventual flight brought his kinsman Girolamo into disgrace, since he was reported held in prison in 1552.[91] The crisis of 1553 brought his release, however, and he was sent to Amiens to survey the walls with a local draftsman, Zacarie de Cellers, and Jean Bullant; he was killed helping the defence of Thérouanne in May 1553. At the same time, another Italian, Megliorin, 'maistre ingénieur pour le roi', was at work on Corbie.[92] Such men were the designers of works. Actual operations were in the hands of local men with the title of *maître des ouvrages de Picardie*, like Flourent Planchon, Laurent Journel, originally *maître de charpenterie* of Amiens, and Jean de Thérouanne.[93]

Army finance

That the various *commissaires* in the provinces were handling formidable sums of liquid cash is suggested by the bare pay figures. The minimal complement of eight gendarmerie companies stationed in Picardy in 1538 cost L 235,201, 5 sols p.a. At the new rates of pay prevailing in 1550, a company of eighty lances cost L 61,350 p.a. and the yearly cost of the entire gendarmerie was L 336,800. These were only a part, if an expensive one, of the full garrison. In November 1521, the cost of the royal troops in Picardy, Burgundy

---

[90] Rozet and Lembey, *Siège de Saint-Dizier par Charles-Quint*, 35–6, 62, 80–90. *CAH* II, no. 3816, 4105–7; Montmorency to La Rochepot, 13 May 1548, BN fr. 3116 fo. 31; *Inventaire sommaire, Amiens* IV, 488; Alvarotti to duke of Ferrara, 3 and 16 June 1548, AS Modena, Francia B 25 fasc. 6 p. 104.

[91] L. R. Shelby, *John Rogers, Tudor Military Engineer* (1967), 67; Hertford to Henry VIII, 2 June 1546, PRO SP1/219 fo. 282–3 (*L&P* XXI, i, 981). Arras to Renard, 29 June 1549, C. Weiss, *Papiers d'état du cardinal de Granvelle* (9 vols., 1842–52) III, 91; Wotton to Somerset, 23 July 1549, BL Cotton, Caligula E IV fo. 227v; Marillac to Montmorency, Aug. 1550, BL Add. 30663 fo. 37; Rozet et Lembey, *L'invasion*, 90.

[92] AM Amiens CC 160 fo. 34 (*Inventaire sommaire* IV, 501); BB 28 fo. 57 (4 May 1553). On Megliorin, see Beauvillé, *Recueil* I, 248–9. On his 'experience' and 'bon jugement' working at Le Câtelet, see Guise to Saint-André, 5 June 1555, BN Clair. 348 p. 138.

[93] On Planchon: AM Amiens CC 115 (1529) (*Inventaire sommaire* IV, 430–1). On Journel: CC 123 (1533) (*ibid.* IV, 442); BB 23 (1536) (*ibid.* II, 331). On Thérouanne: BN p.o. 2031 no. 102 (1549).

and Champagne was L 382,700 per month. The assignation for the entire garrison and field army in Picardy alone in February 1558 was L 378,781 per month.[94]

The quantities of cash involved explain why pay was so often in arrears, even in quiet years. In 1528, the pay of the garrison in the Boulonnais was twelve months in arrears and Oudart du Biez had to make prodigious efforts to obtain the release of L 1,200 assignation on the *trésorier* of the Boulonnais. He was reduced to borrowing 60 *écus* from his governor, Brienne, in order to keep the men satisfied. In years of crisis, matters were worse. When Vendôme received L 18,000 to pay his infantry and light horse in January 1525, he pointed out that it would scarcely last a month and, after that 'crieront à l'argent et sortiront de leurs garnisons, les places mal gardées et le peuple mangé'. The problem remained. In April 1555 a captain of Scottish horse stationed at Montreuil complained that his men were two months in arrears at a time when the expenses of a man and one horse were 20s a day. As a result they 'tiennent les champs' of the French peasants, since the enemy were so devastated they could offer no pickings. Only hand-outs from the governor, René de Mailly, kept them going.[95]

Obtaining funds usually required improvised expedients and anguished appeals especially in a period like 1522–3 when royal finances were near to collapse. During the English invasion of 1522, the crown had to borrow where it could to pay the Picard gendarmerie and admiral Bonnivet said he would rather be 'passé par les picques' than have to do with the lying 'messieurs des finances'.[96] The *état des finances* of 1522–3 reveals the extent of the failure to cope with mounting military expenditure; the deficit registered did not even take account of pay for the infantry. It was partly for this reason that the *trésorie de l'épargne* was created to centralise revenue but, as was shown by Gaston Zeller and Roger Doucet, it never fully measured up to the hopes of 1523. At best, it could provide a reserve war chest to begin a campaign but, beyond that, the old system of assignations on local *recettes* always surfaced in emergencies. The only clear case in Picardy of disbursement from the famous coffers of the Louvre was in June 1536, when Vendôme was authorised to

---

[94] 1538: *CAF* VIII, 232, 31416–31449. 1550: muster rolls: six companies of forty lances and two of eighty. 1521, Nov.: assignation – BN fr. 3002 fo. 80; 1558: BN Clair. 346 fo. 77–92.

[95] Du Biez to Montmorency, 7 Feb., 14 Feb., 25 Feb., 25 March 1528, BN fr. 3004 fo. 54, 49, 64, 41–2 and 11 April, 2 May, 6 June 1528, *ibid.*, fo. 32–3, 26, 11. Vendôme to Louise of Savoy, 30 Jan. (1525), BN fr. 20648 fo. 9–10. Captain Cokoren to Montmorency, 5 April 1555, BN nafr. 23162 fo. 55 bis.

[96] Francis I to Vendôme, 21 Oct. (1522), BN fr. 3007 pp. 98–9; Bonnivet to Montmorency, 20 Oct. (1522) BN fr. 3028 fo. 64.

recruit 2,000 foot and L 18,000 was made available to the *trésorier de l'extraordinaire*.[97]

The workings of the financial system are usefully revealed in 1525 when the Parlement of Paris briefly took charge of coordinating frontier defence. Two hundred new lances were authorised for Picardy and promised muster by 8 May. Vendôme promised their pay from the *taille* due in at the start of April but no money appeared. The *trésoriers des guerres* Grolier and Ruzé had to borrow L 20,000 on their own account and failed to divert money from the *extraordinaires*. A plan formed by Grolier to divert L 22,000 due to the gendarmerie in Champagne on the assumption that, since they were nineteen months in arrears they would not accept a quarter only, was turned down by the governor there, the duke of Guise. On 13 May, it became known that Spifame, the *receveur-général* of Normandy, had L 80,000 available, but his clerk refused to release any money without the permission of his master, who was at Lyon. By 19 May, Grolier had found L 32,000 from an assignation on Outre-Seine and reported that he had just received an assignation for L 35,000 on Normandy and hoped to get the money in two days. In Picardy Brienne, by now desperate, resorted to threats. However, the money from Spifame's account was still difficult to get at and Grolier hinted that the clerk, probably crooked, was delaying the money from the local receivers by excessive conviviality.[98]

This hand-to-mouth 'system' of finance was also apparent during the crisis of 1536, when it was compounded by reliance on forced loans from Paris. The duke of Vendôme had secured a loan of L 40,000 from that city guaranteed on the first two quarters of the *taille* for 1537 (later converted into a *rente*). However, the city first delayed payment and then only sent him L 20,000 on the king's instant order (the rest going to Guise). Repeated demands for the rest by Vendôme and La Rochepot eventually persuaded the king to allow cardinal du Bellay to raise new loans. Vendôme accused the city of 'dissimulation et délay', his exasperation only increased by the diversion of part of the new loan for city fortifications. He bitterly pointed out late in July that, should his army break up for lack of pay, none of their fortifications would be of any use. To La Rochepot, du Bellay tartly pointed out that 'je ne suys pas pour faire les

[97] R. Doucet (ed.), *L'état des finances de 1523* (1923), introduction, and his *Institutions de la France au XVIᵉ siècle*. Francis I to Vendôme, 27 June 1536, BN fr. 3008 fo. 85: Martin de Troyes was to send a *commis* to Paris 'affin de recouvrer de mes coffres du Louvre la somme de dix huit mil livres'.

[98] AN X/1A 1527 fo. 390–91, 397–8, 388v, 380, 379r–v, 393–4, 404r (letters to and *séances* of the Parlement, April 1525), X/1A 1528 fo. 448v–449v, 474, 491–2, 492–4, 499–500, 541 (same for May 1525).

miracles', and implied that Vendôme was making his job more difficult by his strident demands.[99]

On active campaign, as in 1536, an army was racked by payment crises every fifteen days, as money came in only in small amounts and L 30,000 were needed for that period. At the end of August another greater one loomed, since the men would then demand a month's pay to provide themselves for the cold season, 'autrement ne les pouray retenir et faire couscher dehors'. As each pay-day approached, Vendôme's demands became more shrill. He told the Parisians that soldiers in wartime required prompt payment, since they could threaten to surrender or go over to the enemy. By 6 August, he adopted the tactic of adding to his demands another L 35,000 on top of the original L 20,000. This would, he said, pay his infantry for two weeks. The bid paid off, for when his secretary saw the magistrates on 8 August they decided to send another L 20,000.[100]

Though the duke had written uncivilly to du Bellay, the latter in fact worked hard to help him. Maître Legay wrote to a friend at court that he had so done his duty that 'il y en a a beaucoup qui voudroient par aventure qu'il fust ailleurs'. In mid-August, L 13,000 went off from the Louvre war-chests and then another L 30,000 as part of the extra loan of L 60,000 raised by the cardinal in the city. On top of this, the rest of the L 60,000 was set aside for Vendôme, as well as L 50,000 that had been earmarked for royal buildings. All this came just in time, since the duke had been near to losing many of his infantry had they not been paid for a month on 30 August; they were stationed in towns 'lesquelles ne fauldront habandonner si leur payement fault d'ung jour'.[101]

One stratagem used successfully by the duke in September 1536 was to 'assume' a promise on behalf of Paris to pay for 6,000 men that he had been authorised to raise. Though the *prévôt des marchands* protested that he knew nothing of the promise, he was placed in an awkward position when Vendôme threatened to inform the king, and eventually the city had to agree to offer the money on condition that it was used to pay frontier troops. The crisis at Péronne had passed before the 6,000 men had been mustered, but Vendôme was still short of cash to pay them and suspected the Parisians of deliberately delaying the money. In fact, the soldiers eventually rioted and besieged du Bellay in his

[99] R. Scheurer (ed.), *Correspondance de Jean du Bellay* II, p. 398n, 391, 422. *Registres, Paris* II, 261, 246, 247. See also R. J. Knecht, 'Francis I and Paris', *History* 66 (1981).

[100] Scheurer, *Correspondance de Jean du Bellay* II, 483–4, 440, 422–3, 449, 419; *Registres, Paris* II, 264–5.

[101] Maître Legay to Jacques Brunet, 20 Aug. 1536, BL Add. 38033 fo. 133r; Scheurer, *Correspondance de Jean du Bellay* II, 412, 416, 443–4.

palace and, later, three ringleaders were hanged. Such was the desperation to which men and their commanders would be reduced.[102]

Another set of problems is revealed by unusually complete documentation for financial allocations during the royal campaign in Picardy of 1537. As in 1536, the crown was bailed out by a substantial loan from Paris, this time of L 200,000, needed, according to the king, 'par ce qu'il est seullement besoing d'accélération de quelque somme', not because his resources were inadequate. Direct royal involvement probably led to smoother operations.[103] From the records of the *acquits sur l'épargne*, it is clear that pay for the infantry, light horse, the camp and unexpected expenses were allocated by the Epargne to the *trésorier de l'extraordinaire* Martin de Troyes. Appendix 4 lists all surviving recorded sums, amounting to over L 1.5 million for Picardy during March 1537–April 1538.

The ultimate authority for allocations in the period was chancellor Dubourg, as head of the finance council. His vast correspondence indicates that Montmorency and secretary Breton wrote to him every day detailing the needs of the army and requesting despatch of funds to Martin de Troyes, whose clerks had to get special permits to enter the war zone to ensure the security of the money. Montmorency wrote to the chancellor on 23 April for 10,000 *écus* to pay the garrison newly installed at Saint-Pol.[104] One well-documented case arises at the end of May. La Rochepot then sent his man Marivaulx to Dubourg for his men's monthly pay. The chancellor dictated a *mémoire* to Troyes stipulating the reasons for sending L 21,000 and Troyes then wrote to La Rochepot on 7 June enclosing the *mémoire* and asking for quittances for the money. Troyes went off with his clerk, while on 9 June Dubourg asked for signed muster rolls. The money was actually allocated as L 5,000 on the *parties casuelles* and the rest on the *Epargne*. Other allocations, such as the L 32,000 assigned to La Rochepot in July 1538, were on the *recette* of Normandy.[105] In fact, in January 1538, La Rochepot had 'si bien employé son crédit' as to be able to lend the garrison infantry pay which was two and a half months in arrears. The duke of Orléans put the blame on Martin de Troyes's

---

[102] *Registres, Paris* II, 286–7, 288–9, 291–3, 294; Scheurer, *Correspondance de Jean du Bellay* II, 419, 461n, 438, 477, 436, 472–3. *Chronique du Roy Francoys Premier de ce nom*, ed. G. Guiffrey (1860), 175–6.

[103] *Registres, Paris* II, 326; *CAF* VIII, 121, 30372: L 62,475 sent from the Epargne to Martin de Troyes for Montmorency's army out of the Paris loan, Aug. 1537.

[104] Montmorency to Dubourg, 25 March 1537, AN J 968 no. 1/5; 27 March, *ibid.*, no. 1/6; 29 March, *ibid.*, no. 1/9; 23 April, *ibid.*, no. 1/15.

[105] Martin de Troyes to La Rochepot, 7 June 1537, BN nafr. 23168 no. 39 and 63 (*mémoire*). Dubourg to La Rochepot, 9 June 1537, *ibid.*, no. 26. *CAF* VIII, 139, 30548; 142, 30569. Montmorency to La Rochepot, 7 July 1538, BN fr. 2995 fo. 285; Francis I to same, 8 July, BN fr. 3088 fo. 49.

Table 5.1. *Payment of the 'extraordinaire des guerres'*

	Total for Picardie	German mercenaries
January 1550	108,597	43,726
May 1550	60,577.10.0	23,762
June 1550	40,135.8.0	—

Source: BN fr. 4553 fo. 12–16, 38–47

clerks in the *extraordinaires*, since the *général de Normandie* claimed to have given them 'bonne et prompte' assignation. Infantry were drifting away, leaving only 'gentlemen' in garrison.[106]

The well-preserved accounts for the *extraordinaire des guerres* in the late 1540s and early 1550s indicate both the scale of operations and the impact on Picardy of active war finance.[107] Though a long series of *états des assignations*, in effect the receipts, for the *trésoriers de l'extraordinaire* have survived from the late fifteenth century in a summary copy, only from the late 1540s is it possible to isolate regional expenditure within the global sums. Even then, there are complications. The *état des assignations* for 1549 gives L 861,184 for Piedmont and 1,821,275 for Picardy, yet a contemporary *état par estimation* of royal expenses gives the figures for the infantry of 391,452 for Picardy and 600,000 for Piedmont, and a total of extraordinary expenditure, including fortifications, war in Scotland and the *lansquenets* in Guyenne, of L 6,820,740.[108] This may reflect an estimate before the start of the year. Clearly, the surviving summaries have to be treated with caution, though it should be pointed out that the figure of L 5,274,655 for 1537 corresponds closely with a monthly receipt recorded at the time of L 432,739.

The monthly estimate projected for infantry in Picardy in 1549 was L 32,621 at the start of the year. The demands of 1549–50 are reflected in the detailed accounts of Bénoit Le Grand, *trésorier de l'extraordinaire*, see table 5.1.

Table 5.2 reveals the steady increase in *extraordinaire* expenditure during the 1550s. By the time of the Calais campaign of 1557–8, the difficulties had

[106] Charles duc d'Orléans to the king, 19, 21 Jan. 1538, AN J 964 no. 41, 42.
[107] BN fr. 4523 fo. 49 (*Estat des assignacions*, 1498–1556); BN fr. 4553 fo. 8–10 (*Estat de paiement*, 1549); fo. 12–16 (*Estat de despence*, Picardie, Jan. 1550); fo. 20ff. (fragments of *extraits des comptes* of Raoul Moreau, 1549–50); fo. 38 (*Estat de despence*, Benoist Le Grand, May 1550); fo. 44 (*ibid.*, June 1550); fo. 48 (*ibid.*, May–Aug. 1550, Scotland); fo. 70 (*Estat de l'assignacion*, artillery, Nov. 1557); fo. 72 (*Estat des forces* summer 1558). BL Clair. 346 (*Estat de l'assignacion*, Pierre Bertrand, Jan.–Feb. 1558).
[108] BN fr. 3127 fo. 91 ('Estat par estimacion de la recepte et despense des finances, Despences estraordinaires'). The sum includes L 387,764.10.0 interest on loans at Lyons and 2,421,846 repayment of loans.

mounted. The sum of L 300,000 had been granted by Paris in August 1557, but there was delay in assessment and the city finally had recourse to *rentes*. In addition, the duke of Guise demanded L 550,000 for the Calais expedition, to be drawn from a series of provincial tax receipts. By the end of December, though, only L 265,000 had been secured and the shortfall had to be made up by loans from towns, notably Amiens, where on 28 December Estourmel, *général des finances*, appeared to demand a loan of L 15,000 at two days' notice. Though the duke was only L 80,000 short of his original assignation by 7 January, new funds were now needed to refortify Calais and by the end of the month another L 260,000 had been channelled through the *extraordinaires* for building work. The costs of the Calais campaign were prodigious, as is revealed by the plangent tone of the financial officials responsible for raising the money. The duke was lucky that the campaign was so short, for the operation reveals how dangerously dependent the crown had become on large loans.[109]

In March 1558, L 200,000 were sent off by the *trésoriers de l'extraordinaire* to start the payment of the Picard garrison for the month. This sum, though, was dwarfed by the estimated expenditure for the great army of 50,000 men assembled in the province for the summer campaign. This was L 780,866, including L 218,866 for the cavalry, L 392,000 for the infantry, L 32,800 for the horses and L 80,000 for the artillery.[110]

The provisioning of the army

Armies have to be fed and housed and this was one of the principal problems handled by the royal *commissaires*.[111] As with army finance, the strains of war after 1521 saw the slow development of devices out of the chaotic and *ad hoc* methods inherited from the fifteenth century. *Munitions royales* were built up as emergency stores for sieges or campaigns and individual merchants or entrepreneurs employed. No great degree of systematisation was attained and there were periodic disastrous breakdowns, since operations were on a much greater scale than in the past. There were also physical problems; the duke of Orléans remarked to his father in 1538: 'vous entendez, monseigneur, combien tous vivres peuent estre chers en ce pays-là'.[112]

[109] D. L. Potter, 'The duke of Guise and the Fall of Calais' *EHR*, 98 (1983), 481–512, esp. 498–500. 'Estat des parties deues au trésorier Raconis', BN fr. 23192 fo. 48. Raconis to Guise, 5 Jan. 1558, *ibid.*, fo. 63–4; Bertrand to cardinal de Lorraine, 24 Jan. *ibid.*, fo. 193.
[110] Guise to Villebon, 13 March 1558, BN nafr. 21698 fo. 100. 'Estat des forces de gens de cheval et de pied', BN fr. 4553 fo. 72.
[111] See J. E. Iung, 'L'organisation du service des vivres aux armées', on the subsequent period.
[112] Charles duc d'Orléans to the king, 19 Jan. 1538 AN J 964 no. 41.

Table 5.2. *'Etats des assignations de l'extraordinaire des guerres'*

(Based on BN fr. 4523 fo. 49)

Period of receipt	Amount	
1499	649,518	
1500	792,913	
1 May 1502–31 Oct. 1503 (Naples expedition)	678,113	
23 Nov. 1509–31 June 1511	668,936	
1 March 1511–31 Dec. 1512	1,104,453	
1 July 1511–31 July 1512 (retreat to France)	1,392,919	
1 Jan. 1512–31Sept. 1513	1,952,665	
13 Sept. 1513–31 Dec. 1514 (on land and sea)	2,266,844	
1515	2,673,000	
1 Jan. 1516 'until 1517'	2,483,625	
1 Oct. 1516–30 Sept. 1517	605,130	
1 Oct. 1517–30 Sept. 1518	728,953	
1 Oct. 1518–30 Sept. 1519	1,351,229	
1520	572,833	
1 Oct. 1520–Feb. 1522	5,009,271[a]	
17 Jan. 1523–25 June 1525	4,281,285	
25 May 1525–31 Dec. 1525	717,675	
1 Aug. 1528–31 Dec. 1528	731,486	
1529	1,367,247	
1 Jan. 1529/30–31 July 1531	688,806	
11 May 1531–14 May 1534	363,506	
1536	4,439,890	
1537	5,274,655[b]	
1538	2,113,617	
24 Aug. 1539–31 Dec. 1540	410,389	
1542	3,441,651	
1 July 1542–31 Dec. 1542 (Perpignan campaign)	1,283,317	
1543	5,937,940	
1544	6,249,926	
1545	2,894,637	
1546	1,581,091	
	Picardy	Piedmont
1547	—	344,589
1548	1,427,134	930,229
1549	1,821,275	861,184[c]
1550	1,198,097	701,951
1551	660,902	2,828,569
1552	4,496,066	3,057,025
1553	4,564,592	6,016,040[d]
1554	4,312,948	6,742,129
1555	4,018,798	8,083,366

[a] Detailed acc. of Nov. 1521: BN fr. 3002 fo. 80: L 382,700 (inc. Champagne and Burgundy).
[b] Detailed accounts: July 1537, AN J 967 no. 8/10, 226,946 receipt; August, 1537, AN J 967 no. 8/6, 432,738 receipt.
[c] Detailed accounts of Benoist Le Grand, Jan.–May 1550, see table 5.1.
[d] Detailed account, September 1553, BN Clair. 347 fo. 67, 700,000.

The custom of drawing on the facilities of the towns for provisioning frontier armies was well established in the fifteenth century.[113] From 1521, provincial governors had similar recourse in order to to cope with the problem. As early as August 1521, the duke of Vendôme directed the towns of the province to ensure there were adequate provisions and demanded extra wine and grain in October. Beauvais received a demand for 50,000 loaves and 40 muids of wine in September, while at Abbeville the three estates agreed to supply the duke's camp with grain for 10,000 loaves per day until further notice. Suppliers were to be repaid by a general levy on the community. Chauny was also called on for contributions and Péronne, the market for the grain land of the Santerre, received frequent assessment for supply.[114] In March 1522, it was estimated that the troops in the province needed 1,200 muids (of Paris), Boulogne, Thérouanne and Hesdin alone needing 200. Attempts to negotiate by Péronne at Abbeville met with a rebuke from Vendôme and Humières, governor of Péronne, was threatened with a further levy as punishment for unauthorised grain shipments from his estates. All excuses 'n'ont riens valu ne servy'.[115]

Armies, of course, generated trade. The scope of provisions needed is illustrated by Vendôme's actions when his army was encamped between Péronne and Saint-Quentin in April–May 1524. The duke then ordered several towns to arrange for their butchers to have beef and lamb ready by a certain date at fair prices. This was done by persuasion. More problems were encountered in finding the necessary grain. Chauny protested that, should its limited grain supplies be taken, the people would have none for themselves. At Abbeville, it was decided to levy the grain demanded on 100 notables of the town, including all the officials.[116]

As with finance, the Parlement of Paris took charge of supply problems during the crisis of 1525. In conjunction with this the towns had to take measures themselves for their defence. Montreuil, Hesdin and Thérouanne were all under threat and affected by severe shortages as a result of regional dearth. In response to pleas from Amiens, the Parlement commissioned François d'Isque to ship grain at Pontoise and transport it to the threatened

[113] E.g. AM Compiègne BB 5 fo. 67v, 68r–v (Sept. 1479) on the demand for 10 cattle and 50 sheep and 80 flitches of bacon for Esquerdes's army, supplied by town butchers.
[114] Letters of Vendôme, copies and deliberations in BM Abbeville MS 378 fo. 11v, 12; AM Péronne BB 7 fo. 141; AM Chauny BB 3 fo. 6r, 7v; BM Beauvais, Coll. Bucquet 57, p. 433 (20 Sept. 1521). Beauvais later bought grain at Péronne for its stocks (6 April 1522, *ibid.*, p. 440). Chauny sent 10 muids of grain to Montreuil in June 1522 (AM Chauny BB 3 fo. 22r).
[115] La Forge to Humières, 24, 28 March 1522, AM Péronne BB 7 fo. 152v–53r.
[116] Letters of Vendôme, Coucy, 18 April 1524: AM Péronne BB 7 fo. 217v; AM Compiègne BB 17 fo. 11r; AM Chauny BB 4 fo. 25v and fo. 26r (22 April). For despatch of sixty sheep to Thérouanne for only 16 *écus*, see *ibid.*, fo. 29v. BM Abbeville MS 378 fo. 15r (8 May).

areas, while Amiens itself sent grain to Montreuil by boat in March. The contributions from Paris were then inventoried and placed in the town's own stores. The following month, more was sent off to Doullens.[117]

In the 1530s, by contrast, the towns of Picardy had to be harried by Vendôme and La Rochepot for the necessary supplies; those of Ile-de-France, already under pressure in the early 1520s, even more so. In July 1536, Vendôme wrote to Laon for supplies to be prepared by suitable merchants for up to 20,000 men (in effect 20,000 loaves a day and 20 *poinçons* of wine) 'combien que ne soyez de mon gouvernement'. On 3 July, he sent to Chauny to order it to prepare baking capacity for 4,000 loaves a day. Despite the duke's willingness to have accounts kept for repayment, the demand was unpopular, since the town had just been levied at L 200 for a *solde*. Requests for moderation were met by a ducal order to have 3,000 loaves a day and five pieces of wine ready for the camp of Assis-sur-Serre. Further delays brought another rebuke from Vendôme that 'ne vous en estes acquictz comme devyez', and he raised his demand to 4,000 loaves. However, by his return to the camp at Assis at the end of July, he had still received nothing from Chauny. Only when the local governor, François de Laonnois, came to report the duke's displeasure on 11 August did supplies take the road north.[118]

With the magistrates of Laon, the duke had compromised at 8,000 loaves a day and 30 pieces of wine but still accused them of failing in their duty. With his camp on the move, however, he could not expect merchants to follow him around, so he ordered the town to send supplies first to the garrison at La Fère and then to Saint-Quentin. The accounts survive in the municipal archives for the daily supply of the duke's marching camp in July and August, and then large quantities transferred on his orders to the *munition* at Saint-Quentin. On each transaction, a loss was recorded on the agreed purchase price and the total loss to the town was just over L 2,000.[119]

Meanwhile, Vendôme had also sent to Senlis for 12,000 loaves a day and 12 pieces of wine for Saint-Quentin. In this pre-harvest period, supplies were short so the town was only willing to commit itself to 3,000 loaves and 3 muids of wine, with the city coffers bearing one-third of any losses on the operation,

[117] AN X/1A 1527 fo. 212v, 285, 314v–15r, 377r–78r, 378v–79r. G. de Lhomel, *Nouveau recueil* pp. 98–113.

[118] AM Senlis BB 5 fo. 192v (15 June 1522): demand by Saint-Pol for the supply of his brother Vendôme's men in Picardy. Vendôme to Laon, 20 June, 1 July 1536, AM Laon EE 6, unnumbered. Same to Chauny, 3 July, AM Chauny BB 5 fo. 172v. Orders by Vendôme, 13 July, Chauny BB 5 fo. 176v, 177r; similar letters to Laon, AM Laon EE 6. Vendôme to Chauny, 25 July, AM Chauny BB 5 fo. 181; Laonnois to same, 12 Aug., *ibid.*, fo. 187v.

[119] Vendôme to Laon, 30 July, 4, 14, 19 Aug., 1536, AM Laon EE 6. 'Compte et estat de la munition', *ibid.*, EE 6: 'pertes' of L 2,055 resulted from the difference between supply costs and the fixed price for the soldiers. See also another such account, AM Péronne BB 10 fo. 81ff.

computed the following year at L 213 and levied on the community. It was customary for towns to keep detailed accounts of losses in these transactions. When Abbeville and Amiens made their contributions to the Artois campaign of spring 1537, they solicited repayment through La Rochepot.[120]

For the royal campaign of 1537, there were five *commissaires des vivres* (including La Hargerie) appointed to arrange supplies from Normandy by sea to Etaples with powers to overrule opposition. Another avenue for contributions to be levied was the *élection*. Through this channel, in 1537, Senlis was levied at 12,000 loaves, 6 *muids* of oats and 16 of wine per day to be sent to Amiens. Again in 1543, the same *élection* was levied at a weekly contribution of 22 *muids* of flour by a tax on the whole community. Compiègne in 1544 was required, through the same machinery, to send 15 *muids* of flour to the castle of Guise. It did this through a contract with Louis Varlet, grain merchant and town treasurer of Saint-Quentin, who had acted as entrepreneur for Laon in 1536. In an extreme case, the supply for 25,000 men at Le Havre in June 1545 was levied directly on the Norman *élections*.[121]

The obstructions encountered in the 1530s were more apparent in the 1550s, when the demands were greater. In 1552, the king sent the *commissaires généraux des vivres* Veau and Fontaine to arrange provisions for the army he intended to assemble in Picardy. Amiens agreed to furnish 20,000 loaves a day or the equivalent in flour. Duke Antoine de Vendôme found this quantity 'assez petite' and sent Veau back with the words: 'j'ai prins peine de vous soullager à ce que j'ay pensse raisonnable et me semble que ce ne vous est foullerye'. As Abbeville had offered 25,000 loaves, Amiens was pressured into 30,000 at a price to be fixed by the constable. The accounts for this (in effect bread supplied to the royal camp in Hesdin in January–February 1553) have survived. In April 1553, the royal council ordered the repayment of L 5,949 for flour supplied with the residue to be stored for a royal army to be assembled which, in the constable's words, 'sera telle que peut-estre ne s'est poinct veue si grosse de longtemps'.[122]

---

[120] AM Senlis BB 5 fo. 306v (6 Aug. 1536). Pichon, 'Correspondance des d'Humières' no. 13; *Mémoire* of the king for La Rochepot, 15 Aug. 1536, BN fr. 3055 fo. 43.

[121] For Varlet's contract with Laon in 1536, see 'Compte et estat de la munition' AM Laon EE 6. The five *commissaires* to the chancellor, 24, 25 Feb. 1537, AN J 967 no. 12/1&4. AM Senlis BB 5 fo. 313 (15 March 1537); BB 6 fo. 35v (23 May 1543). AM Compiègne BB 20 fo. 12r (13 July 1544), fo. 31r, 54r (13 Feb. 1545); fo. 154v: supplies in June–July 1545 for 6,000 Germans on their way to Boulogne, again through Varlet. Letters-patent to Matignon, 13 June 1545, L. H. Labande (ed.), *Correspondance de Joachim de Matignon*, 118–19n. Royal letters, Mar. 1546, to Abbeville for supply of 12,000 pioneers at Etaples for one month, see Louandre, *Histoire d'Abbeville* II, 33–4.

[122] Royal letters, 17 Nov. 1552, AM Amiens BB 28 fo. 13t. Vendôme to Amiens, 26 Nov., *ibid.*, fo. 19–20; accounts of Jan.–Feb. 1553, EE 323 no. 1. Montmorency to Amiens, 14 May 1553, EE 323 no. 2. Letters from court, 24 April, BB 28 fo. 52v.

The royal *commissaires* Estourmel and Saveuses revealed on 22 May that this massive force would need 120–140,000 (12 *once*) loaves a day over two to three months. Amiens and Abbeville were required to ship grain to Montreuil, Amiens alone offering 20,000 4d. loaves a day over two months. Elsewhere, at Péronne *commissaire* La Hargerie demanded contributions with a promise to the townsmen of an 'honneste prouffict'. The magistrates agreed to provide 3,000 loaves a day for two months and make six bakeries available if further contributions of oats and cartage could be waived. Abbeville offered 25,000 loaves for three months. The obvious shortfall in these contributions led to demands from Vendôme for further supplies for Montreuil in June that met a ready response in July at Abbeville, but stiff resistance at Péronne, where 15,000 loaves a day were demanded.[123]

Payment for supplies contributed by Amiens in 1553 was not authorised by the *conseil privé* until 24 January 1554, with L 3,277 assigned on the *trésorier des avitaillemens de Picardie*. Abbeville obtained repayment in September. In December 1553, Villebon released a proportion of the stocks sent to Montreuil by Amiens but Abbeville was still having problems in recovery and individuals were preparing to distrain on the municipality by virtue of its legal obligations. As money had been raised by *rentes*, a financial burden would accumulate if the grain could not be recovered and sold off. When remaining stocks were sold, the proceeds were transferred by Estourmel to Phrizon, *trésorier des avitaillemens*; thus, it seems that supplies, once conceded, had to be consumed by the army in 1553 or used to pay for new supplies in 1554.[124]

In March 1554, Saint-André ordered an inventory of all grain supplies at Amiens and then made a demand for 300 *muids*. The town promised 200 at first, and then made arrangements with merchants to find another 50. Saint-André promised to report their goodwill to the king so they would not lose. Eventually, 150 *muids* were sent to Montreuil and 100 to Doullens through its *munitionnaire*.[125] These were the two heaviest years of the early 1550s. The years 1555 and 1556 were comparatively easy as far as royal demands were concerned.

The renewal of war in 1557 brought the climax of military contributions at

[123] AM Amiens BB 28 fo. 63v–65v. Henri II to La Hargerie, 22 May 1553, AM Péronne BB 9 fo. 284v–285r; delib. of 2 June, *ibid.*, fo. 285–6; BM Abbeville MS 378 fo. 135r (30 Dec. 1553). Vendôme to Amiens, 29 July, AM Amiens EE 323 no. 6; survey of food stocks, 1 July, *ibid.*, no. 8 and 29, vi; cert. of delivery, *ibid.*, no. 9, 10, 14. AM Péronne BB 9 fo. 300r, 301–2 (2 July 1553). Montmorency to Humières, 22 Aug., BN fr. 3116 fo. 253.

[124] *Procès-verbal*, AM Amiens EE 323 no. 44; Villebon to Amiens, 19 Dec. 1553, *ibid.*, no. 44; Saint-André, *ibid.*, no. 38–42; BM Abbeville MS 378 fo. 133r–v (4 Sept./2 Oct. 1553), 134r (2 Nov.). AM Amiens EE 323 no. 53 (1559).

[125] Saint-André to Amiens, 3 March 1554, AM Amiens AA 14 fo. 37; 10, 26, 30 March and 4 May, EE 323 no. 45, 48, 49, 62.

a time when the state was increasingly unable to reimburse suppliers and the harvests were poor. Even before the disaster of Saint-Quentin, Coligny had to fix the price of fodder for the cavalry and in November 1557, the duke of Guise promulgated a detailed price-list for supplies which made provision for reimbursement by the captains after the arrival of their pay.[126] This was only a palliative. At Montreuil in March 1558 there was little grain to be had because the villages around had been pillaged by the enemy. At La Fère, the garrison was in difficulties because the rich had fled the town and the poor could not feed them. Similar problems were reported at Bray and Ardres. Faithful repayment of contributions was essential if the civil population were to trust the military and make contributions; this was why Guise recorded that the king 'ne veult pas qu'ilz perdent ung seul denier'.[127] A typical working arrangement was settled between the town and garrison at Péronne in May 1558 and an account kept by the town treasurer. In June Guise reinforced this by an order for the *lansquenets* to be paid at the agreed rate on promise of deduction from their next pay.[128]

The army for the Calais campaign involved special arrangements. On 20 December Guise demanded from Amiens 100 *muids* of wheat and 1,200 pieces of wine. Volunteers among the magistrates offered grain at L 28 per *muid*, but wine was more of a problem. Merchants would only supply it on advance of one-third of the cost and *commissaire* Coiffier was unwilling to agree to this. Though the town was already owed L 16,000 by the crown, it agreed to stand surety. By the end of the month, however, the duke's demands had risen to 200 *muids*, to be levied on the whole population. The magistrates, as usual, feared that this would cause rioting and opted to find merchants; the latter would only supply the grain at L 40. Eventually, merchants in the *échevinage* offered to supply the grain at L 36; they were in a better position to negotiate their own repayment.[129] The effects of these dealings left a legacy of problems for city finances. The supplies of December 1557 cost L 9,730 in addition to the L 16,000 already owed for 1557. Despite frequent petitions, the crown still owed the city L 39,961 in 1576, including interest paid out on *rentes*

[126] *Ordonnance* of Coligny, 18 July 1557, AM Amiens, AA 14 fo. 100–1. Patent of Borran and Veau to Chauny for the supply of 6,000 loaves for troops near Laon, 17 July (AM Chauny EE 12); D. L. Potter, 'The Duke of Guise and the Fall of Calais', 500–1.

[127] Villebon to Guise, 4 March 1558, BN nafr. 21698 fo. 267–8; Montpezat to same, 7 March, *ibid.*, fo. 26–8; Henri II to Walon, 22 March, *ibid.*, fo. 152–3; Walon to Guise, 28 March, *ibid.*, fo. 407–8; Jenonville to same, 15 Feb., *ibid.*, fo. 356–7; Cauroy to same, 26 Feb., BN Cangé 62 fo. 42. Guise to Humières, 26 March, BN fr. 3149 fo. 41.

[128] AM Péronne, BB 10 fo. 85–6; order by Aumale, 19 July 1558, *ibid.*, fo. 91.

[129] *Ordonnance* of Guise, 22 Dec. 1557, AM Amiens AA 14 fo. 126; BB 31 fo. 30–2. *Ordonnance* of 30 Dec., EE 323 no. 91 and letters, no. 92. Delib. 30 Dec. 1557, BB 31 fo. 35r–v, 36v, 39r, 40r.

raised in July 1556 in case of a grain shortage. Even an order by Henri II to the *trésorier* at Amiens to pay the town 800 *écus* out of the leasings at Calais in March 1558 had still not been made good by January 1560.[130]

L. Perjes has pointed out that even when they could live off the land, early modern armies almost always operated with magazines. In sixteenth-century France, the most effective were *étapes*, the supply depots for marching troops. Towns not on the frontier itself were increasingly under pressure to set these up. When a company of *lansquenets* arrived at Nouvion in July 1523, Pont-Rémy asked Abbeville to send them bread and beer. In 1536, Laon, as part of its contributions, had to send supplies to nearby Vaulx for a band of *lansquenets*.

Royal instructions for *étapes* to be established in Normandy during May 1545 indicate further details. Troops marching to join the fleet for the summer campaign against England had red meat prepared for them, but were likely to raid the villages unless the local governor added supplies of 100 fowl and 200 lb of bacon for each company of 1,000 men. This would alleviate the lot of the peasants and avoid disorder. The soldiers paid for their provisions at reasonable rates, the costs either borne by the local towns or, as in Normandy in 1545, advanced by the crown to the governor.[131]

At Senlis in September 1544, the avant-garde of the royal army marching from the Marne to Picardy arrived and lodged outside the walls, receiving bread and wine 'dont ilz payèrent partie et l'autre aux despens de lad. ville'. Others, passing by Creil and Beauvais, were supplied from Compiègne.[132] Senlis, in fact, became an important *étape* on the road to Picardy. When the king dismissed his Swiss troops in October 1544, Senlis and Pont-Sainte-Maxence were established as *étapes*; the sieur de Bourran was *commissaire* for movement and orders came through the *élus*. The town had already suffered losses in September and Bourran advised them to send to the chief conductor of the Swiss, La Vaulx, the king's *valet de chambre*. The latter told them at the Swiss camp near Saint-Riquier that the king had signed the list of *étapes* and that could not be changed. Another deputation to see cardinal de Tournon and

[130] AM Amiens EE 323 no. 148 and 90; statement of debt, 1576, *ibid.*, no. 93; requests to *conseil privé*, 4 Jan./28 Jan. 1567, *ibid.*, no. 163, 170. Letters of Henri II, 28 March 1558, Thierry, *Tiers Etat* II, 656–7; Francis II, 4 Jan. 1560, *ibid.*, 666.

[131] On *étapes*: G. Dickinson, introduction to Fourquevaux, *Instructions*, p. lxiv. BM Amiens MS 1707 fo. 255v (delib. of Abbeville, 11 July 1522). *Compte de la munition* 1536, AM Laon EE 6. Labande, *Correspondance de Joachim de Matignon*, 117, 119, 120–1. Royal threats to Abbeville, Aug. 1545, unless it sets up an *étape* for 12,000 Gascons, Louandre, *Histoire d'Abbeville* II, 33.

[132] AM Senlis BB 6 fo. 13r (7 Sept. 1544); AM Compiègne BB 20 fo. 26v; royal letter, 9 Sept. 1544, *ibid.*, fo. 26r.

secretary Bayard at Saint-Germain met the same result and royal missives ordered compliance. Thirty ensigns of Swiss duly arrived on 31 October and, to the surprise of the town, lodged 'le plus amyablement qu'il seroit possible', paying for everything.[133]

In November 1545, marshal du Biez ordered at a day's notice an *étape* at Senlis for 8–10,000 Italians on the march to Champagne: 1,000 loaves, 20 *muids* of wine, 60 sheep, 6 cattle and feed for horses. There was some grumbling about whether to obey the marshal's *lettre de cachet* but, kept outside the walls and with only part of the supplies demanded, they marched on without trouble. Further *étapes* are recorded at Senlis for troops on their way to Boulogne in 1549 and on several occasions in 1558, always with debates on whether to meet the cost by the auction of *fermes* or a direct levy. In July 1560, when 3,000 troops returned from Scotland via Boulogne, an *étape* was prepared there. As the men had not been paid, the food had to be supplied, on the governor's orders, from the *deniers communs*, on promise of deduction from their pay when available. The council agreed in order to avoid the oppression of the people and because 'aultrement lesd. gens de guerre se eussent peu eserciter par les villaiges et y faire ung dégast insupportable'.[134]

The duke of Guise's *règlement* for the German *pistoliers* in November 1557 declared that, when in garrison, 'leur sera faict une estappe et monition en certain lieu commode et prez d'eulx' to stop them pillaging the countryside.[135] What form did these frequently mentioned *munitions* take? By the 1530s, if not earlier, the practice of storing food – bread, bacon, salt etc. – in a royal *munition* in every major town was well established. In these, it was usual to sell off stocks before deterioration reduced their value. When *commissaire* Estourmel surveyed the *munitions* at Thérouanne and Hesdin in May 1537, Montmorency directed his brother La Rochepot to sell off stocks on the point of mouldiness, 'car je pense . . . que la vente en sera maintenant bonne et que pour un septier qui s'en vendra à ceste heure l'on pourra achepter deux après l'aoust et que le Roy y pourra gaigner la moitié'.[136]

Lines of responsibility between military and civil authorities are not clear at this stage, but the *généraux des finances* often transmitted royal letters-patent concerning the *munitions*. Renewal of stocks was obligatory and in September 1555 the cathedral chapter of Amiens, which had appealed against this

---

[133] AM Senlis BB 6 fo. 15r, 17, 18v, 28v.
[134] AM Senlis BB 6 fo. 28v (1545); fo. 61v (1 Aug. 1549); fo. 222v, 227r (1558); AM Boulogne 1013 fo. 47–48 (31 July 1560).
[135] *Règlement* of Nov. 1557, BN Cangé 15 fo. 63.
[136] Montmorency to La Rochepot, 3 May (1539), BL Add. 38033 fo. 29; Francis I to same, 11 Aug. 1538, BN fr. 3088 fo. 67; same to same, 30 April, fr. 3008 fo. 181. For protests of the wine merchants of Boulogne, forced to buy munition stocks while already encumbered with old wine, AM Boulogne 1013 fo. 17v (22 Sept. 1552); fo. 19v (4 Oct.).

obligation, was told by the *conseil privé* that it must buy a certain quantity of *munition* flour from the town. At the end of the wars, the Guise-dominated government ordered the towns of Picardy to take charge of the *munitions du roi* under terms of a contract drafted by *commissaire-général* Serres. Péronne was firmly rebuked for raising objections, since all other towns had agreed.[137]

At Amiens, the municipality administered the *munitions*, though increasing demands were being made on them in the 1550s. In January 1550, the *échevinage* agreed with the *conseil privé* to supply and transport a large proportion of the grain for the Boulogne campaign at a profit of L 10,000, while meat was provided by the city butchers on a profitable basis.[138] Private entrepreneurship always played a vital part in the transport of grain and other supplies. By the 1520s, the use of *marchands munitionnaires* who undertook to supply garrisons or field armies was well established. At Boulogne in 1516, the merchants contracted to supply grain for the garrison for L 3,000.[139] In November 1524, Jacques Favier and Jean Boursault contracted to supply the frontier towns, and on 28 March 1525 concluded a further agreement with the regent in the face of the crisis. Favier, however, had failed to make good his agreement by 8 May as a result of bureaucratic delays and the obstruction of the duke of Guise in Champagne, and his consignment did not reach Abbeville by sea until early June.[140]

In May 1544, royal letters ordered Senlis to find merchants to accept a draft contract for the supply of the king's army on the same conditions as that made by the échevinage of Amiens in 1536. In this case, the proposed syndicate refused the offer because of the shortage of grain and wine in the region.[141] What form did such contracts take? The earliest to survive is one agreed not by merchants but by Villebon, governor of Thérouanne, and Jean d'Estourmel, *commissaire des avitaillemens* for the *munition* of Thérouanne in 1540, and it establishes the pattern, while the involvement of military men and nobles at this stage is not uncommon. The contractors undertook to maintain the munitions of the town for ten years, accepting a certain proportion of existing royal stocks, in return for a yearly payment of L 6,000. They were allowed to

---

[137] Estourmel to Compiègne, 23 May 1545, AM Compiègne BB 20 fo. 88r, sending royal letters on munitions of 7 May, fo. 88v–89v. Ruling by *conseil privé*, 30 Sept. 1555, AM Amiens AA 5 fo. 291. Francis II to Humières, 3 Feb. 1560, BL Egerton 5 fo. 36.

[138] Contracts in *conseil privé*, 1550, BN fr. 18153 fo. 142r–43v, 135v.

[139] In 1513, the king had sent a *commis* to requisition supplies at Boulogne, not 'pour estre perduz aux povres gens, mais pour faire leur proufit' (Louis XII to La Fayette, 6 Oct., BN fr. 2888 fo. 23). Francis I to La Fayette, 12 April (1516), BN fr. 3057 fo. 1.

[140] Vendôme to Parlement, 27 April 1525, AN X/1A 1528 fo. 412; Amiens to same, 18 April, *ibid.*, fo. 378r–79r; *séances* of 15 April, 14 May, *ibid.*, fo. 370v–371r and 1528 fo. 422r; letters of Brienne, 24 May, 4 June, *ibid.*, 1528 fo. 491, 529v.

[141] AM Senlis BB 5 fo. 377v (25 May 1544); fo. 38vv (5 June).

sell off the perishable supplies at specified times each year and insurance was provided by the crown against losses in transit, as a result of war or natural calamity. The range of items to be stored varied, but all contracts included the staple bread grains, though not always grain for brewing beer. In 1540 Villebon was supposed to set up a brewery in the bishop's palace at Thérouanne. There was provision for wine and most cooking materials, but only the contracts of the later 1540s specified bacon, butter, cheese and fish. Storage was, of course, the major problem there. Other meats are nowhere included. Villebon's contract also specifies a wide range of medical supplies and tools, not always found in the contracts.[142]

In February 1545, the *conseil privé* made a contract with a syndicate headed by a merchant of Dieppe, Jean de Montpelle, for the supply of Montreuil over ten years, on the same basis as Villebon's but for L 4,000 p.a. In January 1549, he sold the contract, though later in the year he took on the contract for the supply of the forts recaptured from the English in the Boulonnais. It was Pierre de Salcedo, captain of Hardelot and a military entrepreneur who already had contracts for Oultreau and Hardelot, who took over Montreuil and at the same time signed a contract to supply Coligny's new fort Châtillon opposite Boulogne. The accounts show that the *munitions* in these places were treated as supply depots for field armies at the direction of royal commanders, supplies being credited to Salcedo's account. The auditing of these accounts, completed by June 1551, was carried out in order to show what items had been drawn on by successive royal governors – La Rochepot, du Bellay, Guise – and were claimed by Saledo to his credit. The tendency was for the *Chambre des Comptes* to interpret the contract harshly and strike out claims by Salcedo when they did not match the exact terms of the contract. Even Salcedo's agreement with La Rochepot in July 1549 to supply the royal army at fixed prices for two months in return for L 6,750 was scrutinised harshly.[143] All this gives reason to suppose that the crown suspected irregularities. However, where victuals were supplied to the contractors by royal *commissaires*, as was sometimes specified, these could be old and of low value. Nevertheless, the advantages of *marchés* with contractors were great in terms of flexibility, and in 1558 the duke of Guise contracted with a syndicate for the supply of Calais in return for L 30,000.[144]

[142] P. Des Forts, *Le château de Villebon*, 228-31.
[143] On Montpelle's second contract, see *CAH* III, no. 5526; Salcedo Register audited, BN fr. 2959; fo. 1–17 are pub. in G. de Lhomel, *Nouvel recueil*, 125–44. The rest is unpublished, e.g. *marché* of 18 Jan. 1549 (fo. 19r) and 16 Nov. 1547 (fo. 28). Terms of agreement, 31 July 1549 BN fr. 26132 no. 336, 337. Contract for supply of wine from Bordeaux by Salcedo's brother, 10 Mar. 1550, B. Thobois, *Le château de Hardelot*, 88–92.
[144] Henri II to Guise, 6 Feb. 1558, Cangé 1 fo. 21.

Besides the *marchands munitionnaires*, there were the *marchands voluntaires*, who undertook to supply armies and garrisons on specific occasions and sometimes under formal contract. Governors were anxious to promise them good payment, freedom from dues and military escorts when necessary.[145] La Rochepot in August 1549 had made a number of subsidiary agreements with merchants of Amiens or court purveyors to supply items not contracted for by Salcedo.[146] In autumn 1558, the still-active Louis Varlet of Saint-Quentin and Joseph Chevalier undertook to supply thirty-five ensigns of French infantry along the Somme and to take on existing supplies in the royal *munitions* at Péronne, Compiègne and La Fère. Their main problem turned out to be the high cost of transport to Doullens caused by the massive inflation of fodder prices.[147] *Commissaire-général* Serres eventually recommended a subvention of L 700 and the transfer of half the garrison to Péronne, though this was delayed by diplomatic uncertainties. That Chevalier refused to renew the old flour stocks and to take on a contract for Champagne is readily explicable. He felt abandoned by his partner Varlet and had agreed to take on the feeding of the *lansquenets*.[148] Serres argued that the conditions for the Champagne contract must be better than for a 'Picardie ruyné ... où ilz ne peuvent fournir ne recouvrer la moictié de ce qui leur fault avec double payement et force d'argent.'[149] Chevalier, though, would not budge. By the end of the wars, the prospects of profit for even enterprising merchants were limited.

---

[145] Procl. by Vendôme, 19 May 1552, AM Amiens AA 14 fo. 17; by La Roche-sur-Yon, 18 July 1554, *ibid.*, fo. 40v; by Guise, 22 Dec. 1557, *ibid.*, fo. 146.

[146] The full set of agreements and accounts for the army of 1549 is BN fr. 3122 fo. 91–8: with Salcedo, Mocquet and Warviller, merchants of Amiens, a syndicate of butchers, court purveyors, and accounts of contributions from the royal *munitions*.

[147] *Mémoire* of Sansac, BN fr. 23192 fo. 199–202; contracts, 26/28 Oct. 1558, BN Cangé 15 fo. 69. Serres to Guise, 9 Nov. 1558, *ibid.*, fo. 70–1; Inventory by him of the Doullens munitions, *ibid.*, fo. 190: 7 ensigns consume 3,319 15-*once* loaves and 1,659 pieces of wine per day. Six pieces of flour are needed, each yielding 592 loaves. Transport costs – L 225 per month.

[148] Henri II's reply to Sansac's *mémoire*, 19 Nov. 1558, BN fr. 23192 fo. 199–202; Guise to Sansac, 16 Nov., *ibid.*, fo. 154–5; same to Serres, 16 Nov., *ibid.*, fo. 165–6.

[149] Serres to Guise, 21 Nov. 1558, BN fr. 23192 fo. 234–5.

6

✥

'LES FRUICTZ QUE LA GUERRE RAPPORTE': THE EFFECTS OF WAR ON THE PICARD COUNTRYSIDE, 1521–1560

Picardy was the frontier province *par excellence* in sixteenth-century France and had come into being as a *gouvernement* essentially for purposes of defence. As a result, it suffered more systematic military operations than any other region of France in this period. Provence was invaded in 1523 and 1536 but was not a route amenable for invading armies; nor were the passes through the Alps into Dauphiné. Charles V's thrust into France via Saint-Dizier in 1544 was a dangerous but isolated campaign that illustrated the limitations of the war of movement in this period. Champagne was certainly a fortified frontier to the east but did not experience the intensity of operations or the scale on which Picardy was dominated by the actions of French and enemy forces.

Picardy was the most obvious route of invasion into France and consequently its most fortified area. It was a region, therefore, in which, during the forty years between 1520 and 1560, the impact of war on the peasantry and townsmen made normal life at times virtually impossible. Yet it was possible to survive. The aim of this chapter is to discuss the extent of the impact of war on the countryside in the different stages of the Habsburg–Valois conflict and to trace the increasing ferocity of destruction over the decades. An attempt will then be made to explain how it was possible to survive and live with the problems brought by continuous military operations.

Study of the impact of war in early sixteenth-century France is much less developed than that of the Hundred Years War and the Wars of Religion. War taxation and rebellion have become major themes in the analysis of seventeenth-century French society.[1] In the sixteenth century, little has been

---

[1] Notably in R. Boutruche, *La crise d'une société: seigneurs et paysans du bordelais pendant la Guerre de Cent Ans* (1963), and 'The Devastation of Rural Areas during the Hundred Years War', in P. S. Lewis (ed.), *The Recovery of France in the Fifteenth Century* (1971); G. Bois,

said of the social and economic impact of the Habsburg–Valois Wars, though some recent work has begun to show that the first half of the century was far from a period of social peace, while royal letters of remission for acts of violence continue to tell their story. Studies of the impact of billeting problems, disorderly troop movements and their consequences in Languedoc during this period indicate their importance in that province for the genesis of devices for the management and absorption of organised violence.[2] On the northern frontier, the context of military devastation is one of a society in some senses adjusted to routine violence, such as low-level 'baronial disputes' or urban disorder exemplified, for instance, by the grain riots at Péronne in 1512. Such features are all present in the Picardy of the early sixteenth century, though it is also clear that the mechanisms for the control of civil violence were well developed.[3]

The conventions of war, allowing soldiers to live off enemy territory and to subject it to requisitions for supply when necessary, were regarded as the legal state of 'guerre guerroyable'.[4] Custom also assumed a certain amount of wanton destruction, but this did not become widespread until the Habsburg–Valois Wars were under way. Martin du Bellay, in fact, identified the sack of Aubenton (Thiérache) by the Burgundians in 1521 as the origin of

---

La crise du féodalisme and the work of C. Allmand, P. S. Lewis and P. Contamine; on the effects of the Wars of Religion on French society, see J. B. Wood, 'The Impact of the Wars of Religion: a View of France in 1581', *Sixteenth-Century Journal*, 15 (1984), 131–68; H. Michaud, 'Finances et guerres de religion', *RHMC* (1981), 572–96. On the seventeenth century, see the work of R. Mousnier, R. Bonney, D. Parker. For a case study of the impact of war in the lower Meuse region during the seventeenth century, see M. P. Gutmann, *War and Rural Life in the Early Modern Low Countries* (1980).

[2] H. Heller, *Blood and Iron*, ch. 1, esp. 23–7, has some useful suggestions on the effects of war on social turbulence before 1560. On letters of remission, see R. Muchembled, *La violence au village*, and N. Z. Davis, *Fiction in the Archives. Pardon Tales and their Tellers in 16th-century France* (1987). For Languedoc, see J. E. Brink, 'The King's Army and the People of Languedoc, 1500–156-', *PWSFH* 14 (1986), 1–9; P. D. Solon, 'Le rôle des forces armées en Comminges avant les guerres de Religion', *Annales du Midi* 103 (1991).

[3] On the repression of 'baronial' violence, see the disputes of the Mailly and Belleforrière families, A. Ledru, *La maison de Mailly* I, 179–81, II, 270–5; and for the sombre conditions in Vimeu *c.* 1470 in relations within the du Bos family, see Marsy, 'L'exécution d'un arrêt de Parlement', *MSAP* 26 (1880), 153: the *sergent* of the *bailliage* needed an armed escort for fear of the seigneur, 'aultrement je n'y eusse osé aller'. For endemic urban violence, see AM Péronne BB 7, fo. 37v (May 1517), 52r (Jan. 1518), 77v (April 1518), 84v (July 1519), 91v, 92v (Sept. Nov. 1519); for grain riots in time of dearth BB 6 fo. 303r–306v (October 1512), all matters dealt with effectively by urban justice.

[4] J. Russell, *Peacemaking in the Renaissance* (1986), 190, translates the term 'potential war' and Huguet, *Dictionnaire de la langue française au XVIᵉ siècle*, as 'Guerre régulière, conforme aux usages'. Du Bellay always uses in the sense of 'skirmishing': 'guerre guerroyable, un jour à l'avantage de l'un, autre fois de l'autre' (*Mémoires* (SHF edn) I, 335 and 206). See also Jean du Bellay in Bourrilly, *Ambassades de Jean du Bellay*, 172: 'durant ces praticques, il ne fault obmettre la guerre guerroyable bonne et royde'.

'les grandes crautez qui ont esté faictes aux guerres trente ans après'.[5] This is clearly a contrived explanation since the acceleration of military devastation has numerous complex reasons related to the size, organisation and supply of armies in the period discussed in the previous chapter. However, it might have seemed reasonable in the 1550s to look back to a particularly savage event in order to seek what could have been the origins of a departure from the 'normal' rules of war.

Other similar events at the start of the wars were just as drastic as the sack of Aubenton: for instance, the 'fire and sword' devastation of the Boulonnais wrought by the earl of Surrey in September 1522, opposed by the emperor's council but effected because the land had been spared from fighting for a generation and the pickings were expected to be great.[6] A pall of smoke over the region was observed after the English had done their work and Anne de Montmorency's revenue agent in the region reported in the following February that no rents were forthcoming, since the peasants were afraid to return and 'ne se y osent plus tenir'. There was thought to be something unfamiliar about the extent of this destruction when the duke of Vendôme called it 'foul war', and sixty years later it was still recalled as 'l'année des grands feux'. Similarly, the pillage of villages around Saint-Quentin and Guise in September 1522 had to be accepted when the enemy was present in strength, and Vendôme's lieutenant, Torcy, reported that 'le peuple y aura grant dommaige'.[7]

Given such experiences, the duke of Suffolk's proclamation in 1523 to the peasants around Ancre, inviting them to come in with supplies under safe conduct, had a positive effect. Ellis Gruffydd reports that in no time markets were set up in the English host selling bread and cheese. Shortly before, with pay short and plague rife in Péronne, the French garrison troops had got out of hand – Jean d'Humières speaks of 'renchonnemens et pillaiges' by the infantry in the Santerre – so the English may not have seemed much worse. Indeed, the reliance of the English upon the local peasantry for supplies was to be repeated in 1544.[8]

[5] Martin du Bellay, *Mémoires* (SHF edn) I, 150–2.
[6] Surrey to Henry VIII, 7 Sept. 1522, *L&P* III, ii, 2517; Sandys, 10 Sept. 1522, *L&P* III, ii, 2530; Surrey to Wolsey, 12 Sept. 1522, *L&P* III, ii, 2540; Sandys, 12 Sept. 1522, *L&P* III, ii, 2541. In October Surrey offered to stop the burning if La Fayette gave a similar undertaking. The latter was unwilling to accept: 'byen toust que j'avoys deulz cens chevaulx je brusleroys Guynes avant que fust troys jours' (to Montmorency, 20 Oct. (1521), MC Chantilly L I fo. 175).
[7] Louis Pocques to Montmorency, 6 Feb. 1523, MC Chantilly L XV, fo. 90; *L&P* III, ii, 2541; A. de Rosny, 'Enquête faite en 1578 par le maître particulier des Eaux et Forêts du Boulonnais', *MSAB* 17 (1912), 364; Torcy to Montmorency, Saint-Quentin, 2 Sept. (1522) MC L I, fo. 182.
[8] Ellis Gruffydd, *Chronicle*, ed. by M. B. Davies as 'Suffolk's Expedition to Montdidier', *Bulletin of the Faculty of Arts of Fouad I University, Cairo*, VII (1944), 4. Humières to La

If the English march to Montdidier was the most spectacular military effort against the province in the 1520s, it was not the most destructive. In March 1525, news of the disaster of Pavia was followed by a successful Burgundian attack on Rue and the summoning of Montreuil. The Somme was crossed and the Santerre pillaged, while the land around Abbeville was also scoured.[9] The war of 1528, though brief, was marked by a great deal of looting on both sides, with the governor of Montreuil, Bernieulles, under orders to 'faire le pis qu'il me seroit possible' against the emperor's subjects and capturing prisoners before the formal declaration of war. A raiding party crossed the Somme and swept towards Arras, while a revenge raid took the reverse direction and by April the *gendarmerie* at Péronne and Corbie had already taken L 3,000 in booty.[10]

Of course, the effects of war in the 1520s were not entirely grim, since the operation of armies in this theatre of war may well have made some positive contributions to the local economy. Large quantities of bullion were brought into the province for the pay of troops, as was seen in the previous chapter, and a proportion must have been spent there. Most of the profits, it must be supposed, were gathered by the entrepreneurs who engaged to supply the armies rather than by the peasants, whose surplus was too precarious to allow of extensive profiteering. Yet even urban magistracies usually recoiled from the stationing of troops, since the destructive effects of billeting probably outweighed any profits to the local economy, and what has already been seen of the administration of supply by volunteer merchants would seem to indicate that profits in that field were precarious. In the countryside, the overall effects of military operations were uniformly destructive.

One serious development had also become apparent by the 1520s: the devastation of their own countryside by unpaid troops, largely the consequence of the grotesque arrears of pay that accumulated from the 1520s onwards. In the crisis of 1525, the Parlement noted the effects of 'gens vaccabonds qui tiennent les champs et font grosses assemblées' in calling for the appointment of local gentlemen in the frontier region to put them down.[11] After the truce of 1528, the duke of Vendôme reported the ravages of the infantry caused by lack of pay and his displeasure 'de veoir faire si près de moy une telle

Trémoille, 11 Sept. (1523) AN 1AP 626, printed in Marchegay, *Lettres missives du XVIᵉ siècle*, no. 38. Norfolk to Henry VIII, 14 June 1544, *LP* XIX, i, 70.
9   Montreuil to Parlement, 2 April 1525, AN X/1A 1527 fo. 191–2; Amiens to same, 26 March, *ibid.*, fo. 271: the enemy have crossed the Somme 'délibérez de piller ce qu'ilz pourront au pays de Sangters'. Abbeville to Parlement, 20 Mar. 1525, *ibid.*, fo. 285.
10   Bernieulles to Montmorency, Montreuil, 23 Aug. (1528), MC Chantilly L VII, fo. 82; same to Berthereau, *ibid.*, fo. 241; Humières to Montmorency, Compiègne (April, 1528), BN fr. 3155 fo. 51–2. AM St-Omer, Corr. 5 no. 1610.
11   AN X/1A 1527 fo. 388v (22 Apr. 1525).

pillerye'.[12] Such exactions after the peace of 1529, coinciding as they did with a period of severe dearth and economic crisis in northern France, provoked an explosion of discontent in the form of a local *jacquerie*. La Hargerie, by then a royal agent for such matters, reported that, as a result of the high price of grain in the region 'casi commencheront eslèvement de peuples et monopoles en ce pais'. Vendôme ordered him to put this down and make an example of the leaders.[13]

The continuation of war in the province turned the land north of the Somme and as far as Calais into a sort of a no man's land, open to pillage in wartime, which had laboriously to be brought back into use after each campaign. The French peace commissioners of 1559, observing the loss of local records to prove rights, reported that:

> il n'y a quasi ville, village, chasteau ne maison qui n'ont esté sacagée, bruslée, prinse de force ou pillée . . . et cela est plus que notoire et se void à l'oeil à commancer aux portes de la ville de Péronne jusques aux villes de Boulloigne et Ardres.[14]

The worst-hit territory lay north of the Somme between Amiens and Péronne and beyond the border of Artois as far as Arras, though eastern Picardy was also devastated several times.

The effects of war would be felt from the start in measures taken by government to secure the food supply and the harvest from enemy attack or 'friendly' requisitioning from 'les laboureurs et gens du plat pays'.[15] Measures were usually taken at the start of a campaign to break the crossings of the Somme,[16] secure at Amiens and Abbeville but vulnerable at places like Bray: failure of defence there in 1523 allowed the English to flood into the Santerre. Food supplies north of the river were vulnerable, especially after the harvest, so that orders usually went out to gather them in 'réservé ce qui sera nécessaire pour

[12] Vendôme to Montmorency, 18, 29 July (1528), BN fr. 6635 fo. 161, fr. 3070 fo. 71.
[13] La Hargerie to Montmorency, Pentecost (1531), MC Chantilly L VII, fo. 118–19. *Ordonnance* of Vendôme on grain shortages, 25 Apr. 1531, AM Amiens AA 12 fo. 165v.
[14] AN J 788 no. 1, unpag. Adrien Le Clerc, sieur de Bussy (near Amiens) *trésorier* of the *arrière-ban* of Amiens in 1557 failed to submit his account to the *chambre de comptes* for twenty years 'd'aultant qu'il a esté deux fois bruslé, de sorte que tous ses papiers, tiltres et acquiz ont esté bruslez', Beauvillé, *Recueil* III, 538.
[15] *Ordonnances* of dukes of Vendôme, 5 Mar. 1537, AM Amiens AA 12 fo. 185v; 10 May 1543, AA 12 fo. 214v. King to the governor, 2 Sept. 1543, SAP 57 no. 29: owners of the grain collected in towns 'pourront vendre, conserver ou autrement en exposer à leur prouffit'.
[16] La Trémoille to Montmorency, 6 Oct. (1522), BN fr. 3039 fo. 45: 'si les ennemys ne vont vers nous, que nous nous debvons mectre tous à long de [la] rivière en grosse troupe et rompre tous les chaussées, non pas jusques à l'eaue de paour qu'elle s'appetissast mais en grandes bresches et avant qu'ilz eussent refaict leur chaussée, nous nous rendrons tous au lieu à ce seront'.

vivre et nourir le povre peuple'.[17] Through the campaigns of the 1550s, landowners with property north of the river were required to bring their stocks south of the Somme for protection,[18] while local military commanders, as at La Fère in 1558, were able to force the villagers to bring in all their supplies except enough to last them ten days, on pain of having them burned. Not surprisingly, the town governor reported shortly afterwards that:

> Le pauvre peuple est prest à abandonner leurs maisons. Quant au labeur, il commance à cesser en beaucoups d'endroicts icy allentour pour ce que quant ung pauvre homme a achepté quelque avaine pour semer, on luy a osté aux champs et luy prent l'on ses chevaulx pour aller quérir boys et aultres provisions.[19]

Such military interference compounded disruptions caused by enemy activity and the routine depredations of badly paid garrisons, despite a consciousness on the part of the crown and its officials that the protection of the 'povre peuple' was its responsibility.[20]

H. Neveux, in his study of the Cambrésis, has offered a brief but useful model for assessing the impact of armies on the harvest, distinguishing between the passage of troops and their encampment in a locality for an extensive period. At its worst, destruction took place between the harvest, while grain was still in the barns, and transport to local fortified places.[21] To all this should be added the effects of requisition by army *vivandiers* and the removal, at any time in the campaigning season, of significant numbers of livestock.

For a French villager near Ardres recalling the past in 1560, his married life

---

[17] *Ordonnance* of Vendôme, 24 Feb. 1543, AM Amiens AA 12 fo. 214r. Similar orders went out at Boulogne for fear of an English invasion in 1516: 'toutesfoiz de travailler le peuple de ceste chose sinon que l'on veist que le besoing y feust, ce seroit mal fait et ne l'entends pas' (Francis I to La Fayette, Lyon, 12 Apr. (1516) BN fr. 3057, pp. 1–2. In April 1541, John Wallop, English commander at Guînes reported: 'commaundment is given all Boulenoise over, and also this low countrey ioynyng to Arde, every man to bring in his corne saving that which will suffice them for ther owne store.' PRO SP1/165 fo. 73–4 (*L&P* XVI, 718).

[18] *Ordonnance* of Vendôme, 15 Sept. 1552, AM Amiens AA 14 fo. 9 and BB 28 fo. 9, 13; *ordonnance* of Amiens, 30 Sept. 1554, AA 14 fo. 51, 31 July 1557, AA 14 fo. 101.

[19] Montpezat to Guise, 7 Mar. 1558, BN nafr. 21698 fo. 26–8; Walon to Guise, 28 Mar. 1558, *ibid.*, fo. 407–8. Similar situation at Roye: Feuquières to Guise, 8 Oct. 1558, BN fr. 20646 fo. 125–6.

[20] Examples of such assumptions: Vendôme's reluctance to raise too many troops 'de peur de la foulle du peuple' (to Francis I, 6 Feb. 1528, BN fr. 3016 fo. 24–5); Humières on desertion of troops through lack of pay 'et sont tenans les champs à la grant confusion du paouvre peuple' (to Montmorency, 15 Dec. 1536, BN fr. 20502 fo. 141); Francis I calls for the disbanding of Sarcus's company 'à la moindre charge et foulle de mon peuple que faire se pourra' (to La Rochepot, 16 Feb. 1539, fr. 3058 fo. 29); Henri II forbids soldiers to take food without paying 'combien que nostre pauvre peuple a souffert et enduré durant les guerres' (to *bailli* of Amiens, 5 Apr. 1559, AD Somme B 1 fo. 20).

[21] H. Neveux, *Vie et déclin d'une structure économique*, 118-21.

of thirty-two years had seen three occasions when his village had been burned out.[22] How general was this experience and how serious were the losses sustained? Generally, the only guides for this period are the demands made for tax remission by the villagers concerned. Those records kept by the Imperial authorities for territories adjoining France are on the whole more systematic than their French equivalents and can be used to characterise the sort of war losses which were apt to occur on both sides. Surveys made in 1538 and 1545, though they must be handled with caution in view of the incentive to exaggerate losses in order to gain tax remission, nevertheless reveal a convincing picture, indeed confirmed by the willingness of government to accede to demands for remission.[23]

The survey of 1538, more systematic in its quantitative evaluations of losses in grain and livestock, reveals the full effects of Francis I's campaigns in the county of Saint-Pol during the spring and summer of 1538. A sample of thirty villages covered in the first hundred folios shows an average loss in livestock (most commonly *blanches bestes*) of 86.7 per cent, including ten villages where losses were total (see table 6.1). Comparison of the harvest before the war and that of August 1538, a year after the truce of Bomy had put an end to fighting in the region, indicates that the yield was estimated on average at 18.6 per cent of that before the war, including five villages where there was still no harvest at all (table 6.2).

The explanations offered for these losses indicate that the worst devastation had been wrought by the *vivandiers* of the French host charged with keeping the king's camp supplied on its way to Saint-Pol, while *lansquenets* and French troops, encamping on fields – 'les terres advestues de bled vers' – in the early summer, effectively trampled the crop down in many places.[24] In some areas, both the French and the emperor's men pillaged and foraged the same places. The practical problems were vividly described by the villagers of Benneville in Saint-Pol: there the fields were restored after the upheavals of the summer of 1536, but in 1538 were still not cultivated and 'labourées de toutes leurs royées' left over from 1537.[25]

Horror stories abounded in the accounts given in the course of these surveys. In one village, Rebreviettes, the people were put to ransom and those unable to

---

[22] AN J 788 no. 3/6, fo. 10v (François Quenal of La Cauchie on the village of Alquines near Ardres).

[23] AN J 1016 and 1017, both of approximately 500 folios. They were used as evidence in the border negotiations of 1559–60 since they showed which villages paid the *aide ordinaire* of Artois (see ch. 8). Some extracts were printed in Louis Brésin, *Chroniques de Flandre et d'Artois. Analyse et extraits . . . 1482–1560*, ed. E. Mannier (1880), appendix.

[24] AN J 1016 fo. 29v, 33r, 56r, 66r.

[25] AN J 1016 fo. 77r.

Table 6.1. *Losses in livestock, Artois 1536–9 (numbers of 'blanches bestes')*

Village	Before 1536	1538	Percentage loss
Hébuterne	1,500	80	94.67
Douchy			100
Burbures			
Puisieux			100
Saulty	1,400	400	71.43
Fouquevilliers			
Gomecourt			100
Boiry-Saint-Martin	400	140	65
Rullecourt-lez-Avesnes	1,400	350	75
Peumiers			
Houvin			
Pas-en-Artois			100
Mondricourt			
Baudricourt	400	200	50
Gréna			100
Sussainct Leger	1,400	200	85.72
Ivregny	1,200	200	83.34
Rebreviettes			
Lignereulles			
Frévent			
Humbercamp	400	80	80
Pénin			100
Ambrines			
Berlencourt	1,200	300	75
Beaufort			100
Blavincourt	700	200	71.43
Dauphine			
Averdoing	1,000	80	92
Bourech	800	40	95
Mazières	1,100	150	86.37
Filescamp	300	80	73.34
Tilloy	600	0	100
Rebroeuves	1,200	0	100
Souatre	1,200	130	88.34
Oppy	220	0	100
Estrées-sur-Canche	500	100	80
Sarton			100
Fosseux	800	150	81.25
Benneville	700	250	64.29
Orville	3,000	300	90
Average loss in villages that made declarations			86.73%

Source: AN J 1016 fo. 1–79, all villages covered.

Table 6.2. *Decline in grain yield, Artois 1536–8 (in 'gerbes' of wheat)*

Village	Before 1536	1538	Percentage of pre-war harvest
Douchy			50
Busquoy			50
Saulty	30,.000	1,000	3.33
Fouquevillers			10
Boiry-Saint-Martin	8,000	5,000	62.5
Aubigny			
Rullencourt			
Peumiers	20,000	3,000	15
Houvin	30,000	2,000	6.66
Pas-en-Artois			0
Mondricourt			20
Baudricourt			33.33
Gréna			0
Sussainct Leger	28,000	0	0
Ivregny	30,000	0	0
Rebreviettes	10,000	2,000	20
Frévent			50
Berlencourt	40,000	0	0
Beaufort	18,000	2,000	11.11
Averdoing	28,000	3,000	10.71
Bourech	12,000	300	2.5
Mazières	27,000	400	1.48
Filescamp			33.33
Thilloy	12,000	2,000	16.66
Benneville	24,000	2,000	8.33
Orville	36,000	4,000	11.11
Mingoval			50
Average harvest of 1538 as percentage of that before 1536:			18.64

Source: AN J 1016 fos. 6–81, all villages covered.

flee beaten, while an old man had his ears cut off to force him to pay up. Between 120 and 140 people died and only one-third of the village survived. In another, Hubercamp, when the church was burned, a girl was killed in the churchyard and her mother shot. There, twenty-two people were taken for ransom.[26]

Such treatment naturally prompted the villagers to seek refuge in fortified towns, though even there they could suffer since they might be caught up in a siege, encounter epidemics and at all events run into debt in order to survive.[27] On returning, they could, like the people of Averdoing, be hit by diseases caused by malnutrition. In fact much of the mortality recorded occurred at this

[26] AN J 1016 fo. 35r, 41r.
[27] AN J 1016 fo. 31r, 35r, 28r. See also fo. 40 and 50 (deaths of two-thirds of the population); fo. 35r, 38r, 44r (Ambrines), fo. 52v (Averdoing), fo. 58 (Mazières).

Table 6.3. *War damage, 1542–4*

Bailliage etc.	No. of villages surveyed for losses
Arras	78
Lilliers	24 + the town
Bapaume	39
Lens	2
Béthune (*avouerie*)	3
County of Saint-Pol	144
Enclaves in Ponthieu	8
Aire	13
Régale of Thérouanne	27
Saint-Omer	34

Source: AN J 1017

stage.[28] Economic problems were aggravated by the need to sell livestock 'à vil pris' in order to escape looting,[29] incurring debt and high costs of replacement after campaigns. In 1538, many villages had to buy grain and livestock from merchants in order to 'réediffier et remettre leurs terres' and work for little gain during the first year.[30] Indebtedness to grain and livestock merchants seems to have been a common result of the wars of the 1530s.

The surveys conducted in 1545 of damage during the war of 1542–4, though lacking in substantial detail, contain further background information, especially about the situation of the villages. Around 373 villages and small towns in Artois claimed losses, as shown in table 6.3. It is clear that, once again, the county of Saint-Pol had suffered heavily, along with villages on the border near the vicious French garrisons of Doullens, Thérouanne, Hesdin and Ardres; the *bailliage* of Arras was also damaged as well as the Imperial enclaves near the coast subjected to English depredations during the period 1543–5. Some villages claimed to have been burned out several times, the worst moments coming in the north during the French siege of Tournehem in August 1542 and for Bapaume during Vendôme's campaign of the summer of 1543. When compared with the number of villages in Artois surveyed for the duke of Croy later in the sixteenth century,[31] it

---

[28] AN J 1016 fo. 52v (Averdoing), 79r (Orville), 33r (Ivregny), fo. 66v (Zouattre, death of 9–12 people).

[29] AN J 1016 fo. 33r (Ivregny): stock worth 30s was sold off for 3s. See also fo. 68v (Oppy), 78r (Fosseux).

[30] An J 10916 fo. 41r (Humbercamp), 42v (Pénin), 17 (Beaufort), 48r (Rullencourt), fo. 58r (Mezières).

[31] Charles de Croy, *Quatre cents vues des villages d'Artois* (Mémoires de la Commission Départementale du Pas-de-Calais, t. 10, part 2), more recently covered in the great series of *Albums de Croy*, ed. J.-M. Duvosquel, 8 vols. so far (1985–).

becomes clear that well over half had suffered serious damage in the war of 1542–4.

This impression is confirmed by the reports of the Imperial commanders in the period. In September 1542, the count du Roeulx, governor of Artois, reported that the French, in pillaging Saint-Pol and all those refusing to 'porter la croix blanche', were raping women and taking children for ransom 'et est leur guerre en ce fort oultrageuse et cruelle, telle qu'ilz ont accoustumé de faire quant ilz sont les plus forts'. Aerschot reported at the same time that in Artois, Hainault and Flanders, 'tout est ruiné'.[32]

Comparisons of reports from the 1530s, the 1540s and 1550s (the latter based on the detailed accounts of Jean Thieulaine, bourgeois of Arras)[33] present numerous examples of villages devastated in all three periods. Examples like Pas-en-Artois, in the county of Saint-Pol but on the border south of Arras, Boiry-Saint-Martin, in the *bailliage* of Bapaume, Saulty, in the *bailliage* of Arras, all share the same features of material losses, loss of population and poverty inflicted in all these periods. For one, Beaufort in the *bailliage* of Arras, the torment began with damage in 1521 from which it had still not fully recovered when the war of 1536–7 inflicted loss of all livestock and the burning of all but five houses 'et en effect ledict village a esté entière-ment destruict et ruyné'. The war of 1542–4 saw the village pillaged several times, while in August 1542 it sustained a French camp of 15,000 men for two days, leaving it in ashes and half the land still out of use in 1545. Finally, late in 1553, it was burned again by the duke of Vendôme's army.[34]

Much of the material concerning losses in Artois is of a fiscal nature, designed to effect remissions of taxation. That the French crown conducted such surveys on its side seems likely for, though they have not survived, numerous instances of tax remission exist in various sources. Indeed, there was an enquiry conducted at Péronne in 1533 concerning a border village, Villers-au-Flos, where the inhabitants had fled to Péronne from Burgundian raiders during the wars of the 1520s. As elsewhere in the region, the village church tower had been used as a stronghold, but this had been taken, along with L 500 of property, and the richer farmers forced to pay ransoms like 64 *écus*.[35] At the

---

[32] Roeulx to Mary of Hungary, 7 Sept. 1542; Aerschot to Charles V, 9 Sept. 1542, A. Henne, *Histoire du règne de Charles-Quint en Belgique* (1858–60), VIII, 45n.

[33] X. de Gorguette d'Argoeuves, 'Un livre de raison en Artois (XVIᵉ siècle)' (Jean Thieulaine, 1549–54) *MSA Morinie* XXI (1888), 139–99, hereafter Gorguette, 'Thieulaine', discussed at length below. The edition is a good one with an index, but omits personal passages and the original MS has not yet been traced. The author moved mainly in legal circles.

[34] Pas-en-Artois: AN J 1016 fo. 24v; J 1017 fo. 86v; Gorguette, 'Thieulaine', 154–6. Saulty: J 1016 fo. 13, J 1017 fo. 49r, Gorguette, 'Thieulaine', 154, 156, 163. Beaufort: J 1016 fo. 48r, J 1017 fo. 41r, Gorguette, 'Thieulaine', 162.

[35] AN J 805 no. 31, discussed at greater length in ch. 8.

end of the wars, another survey, conducted of the village of Baillon near Ardres, found that, with a *terroir* of 72 *mesures* of plougland and 20 of gardens, it had sixty hearths before the wars but by 1560 only three or four 'bonnes maisons' and thirty-one 'petites maisons occupées par pauvres gens et manoeuvriers'.[36]

Several arrangements for tax reductions were made in this area after 1529. In 1530, a reduction of L 797 for ninety villages in the *élection* of Saint-Quentin north of the Somme was continued, and the whole *élection* of Péronne was similarly treated. Taxes were remitted entirely for villages north of the Somme and a one-year reduction of L 1,600 for the Santerre conceded. In November 1531, villages north of the Somme saw their assessments reduced from L 4,977 to L 1,200 and in 1536 those of the *élection* of Doullens were allowed to compose their taxes for L 2,000.[37] An *arrêt* of the *conseil privé* in December 1553 remitted L 4,771 due in the *élection* of Ponthieu (about one-third of its *taille*) because of enemy invasions and 'bruslemens de partie des villaiges', and went on to decree exemption from all taxes in the *élection* for the duration of the war and for three years afterwards 'pour leur donner meilleur moien de se retirer et prandre peyne de réediffier leurs maisons, cultiver et labourer leurs terres'.[38]

In the *élection* of Doullens, Saint-Riquier had been exempted from all taxes for four years by the *conseil privé* from January 1551 in terms which suggest it had already been exempted for several years on the grounds of the disastrous fire of April 1544, and 'saccaigemens, pertes et dommaiges' during the wars with the English in 1543–6. Sacked again in the summer of 1554, the town received a further three-year exemption in March 1555.[39] In the same *élection*, the *décimes* owed by the abbé of Saint-Riquier (Bochetel, bishop of Rennes) were remitted in October 1554 because of losses to the abbey properties, 'qui ont esté bruslées et saccagées par les ennemys'.[40] Such remissions of *décimes* were issued in January 1553 for the clergy of Péronne north of the Somme, those 'pillez et bruslez des ennemys' for ten years, those simply 'pillez' for three. In June of 1553, the clergy of the diocese of Amiens were remitted half (L 12,670) of the *décimes* demanded because of losses since the start of the war.[41]

[36] Frontier enquiries of 14 Mar. 1560, BL Add. 30705 fo. 29v, copy.
[37] *CAF* VII, 644, 27944, 27964; III, 95, 4319; VII, 5, 26889.
[38] BN fr. 5128, p. 206, 11 Dec. 1553, signed *rôle*, 17 Dec., *rapporteur* d'Avanson.
[39] BN fr. 5127 fo. 77v, council *arrêt*, 21 Mar. 1551, *rapporteur* Sceaulx; fr. 5128 p. 377, 4 Mar. 1555.
[40] BN fr. 5128 p. 346, *rôle*, 6 Oct. 1554.
[41] BN fr. 5128 p. 368; letters-patent of Henri II, 20 June 1553, crs. Bourdin, Beauvillé, *Recueil* I, 246–7, repeated 25 Mar. 1558, *ibid.*, IV, 294–5.

The areas particularly subject to war losses in the 1540s were, as has already been noted, those most exposed to direct enemy activity on the frontier. What form did this take? Villages within range of hungry garrisons were especially exposed, so that in 1542 Charles V proclaimed that no peasants were to work the land within a league of Thérouanne. When Vendôme besieged Bapaume in the same year, twenty villages around it were destroyed[42] as were another twenty during his siege and capture of Lillers in May 1543, which left the town completely burned and the entire population ransomed. By 1545, only one-tenth of the houses had been repaired.[43]

During the same phase of the war, the coastal areas between Abbeville and Boulogne suffered repeated raids from both the English and the Burgundians. The Welsh soldier-chronicler Ellis Gruffydd, describing his travels between Montreuil and Boulogne, paints a vivid picture of the accumulated horrors of the previous two years: 'young and old people at two or three points along the road . . . cried piteously in God's name for help or a piece of bread to keep alive some of the little ones who were dying for want of food'. One woman, offered money, said it was no use; only bread could help and to eat immediately, since any stored food was at the mercy of 'the wild men', probably Irish in English service. Their appearance, he commented:

> would have made the hardest heart melt into tears from pity at seeing as many as one hundred people, old and young, with not one healthy man among them, but all shivering with ague and death in their faces from the scarcity and lack of bread to strengthen them.

For exactly the same period, the Saint-Omer monk Louis Brésin recorded that the 'povre misérable peuple' of this area, in fleeing to the towns like Abbeville and Amiens 'fut tant persécuté de famine, peste et povreté, que l'on estima le nombre des mors, en moins de six mois, monter à plus de cinquante mille personnes'.[44]

Such rhetoric may be conventional, but is substantially confirmed by the enquiries of the Imperial commissioners already discussed. Villagers of the *châtellenie* of Beaurain, an Imperial enclave in the area, suffered badly in every year between 1542 and 1544, especially during the English siege of

[42] AN J 1017 fo. 394v, 396v; *bailliage* of Bapaume: fo. 131–77.

[43] AN J 1017 fo. 94–130 (*bailliage* of Lillers), fo. 310v (Bours-lez-Pernes).

[44] Ellis Gruffydd, ed. M. B. Davies, 'The Enterprises of Paris and Boulogne', *Bulletin . . . of Fouad I University, Cairo* XI, i (1949), 35–6. Louis Brésin, *Chroniques de Flandres et Artois*, 190 (1544–5). Bresin adds that the price of the *rasière* of wheat at Saint-Omer at this time rose to 6 or 7 florins because of shortages in Artois and Picardy. Brésin's information is repeated by François de Belleforest, *Grandes Annales et Histoire générale de France* (1579) II, fo. 1530r: 50,000 dead in Picardy in six months 'de famine, peste et autres misères'.

Montreuil.[45] Another Imperial enclave, the seaside villages of Berck, Verton and Merlimont, were abandoned for much of 1544 because of the English and the Irish 'wild men'; at Berck 200 houses and many of the fishing boats on which the people depended were destroyed. Then French armies marching to Boulogne in 1544 and 1545 wrought further havoc, so that in the end only 250 out of 1,800 inhabitants remained, with 20 out of 300 houses still intact. At Verton, 270 houses out of 300 had been burned by the Irish, many inhabitants killed or dead of plague and the rest reduced to poverty. At Merlimont, the story was much the same, with half of the taxable houses destroyed, while enquiries made at Montreuil in 1547 indicate that much of the damage there had been caused by the breaking of the dykes which kept the sea out of the village fields.[46] The dauphin's relief army of 1544 was generally held, as du Biez admitted, to have been as bad as the Irish; at Groffliers it had forced the villagers to live in the woods 'comme bestes sauvaiges'. Elsewhere, in villages near Saint-Omer this army looted villages that had already suffered the ravages of Vendôme's army in 1544 and raids earlier in 1544.[47]

The war was prolonged until June 1546 by Francis I's unwillingness to come to terms with the English; operations, however, were increasingly hampered by the severe dearth caused by major harvest failure across much of northern France in 1545, similar to the calamities caused by the agricultural crisis that followed the conclusion of the Treaty of Cambrai in 1529.[48] By the end of the fighting, large areas of the frontier region were obviously uninhabitable or impossible for normal life. The worst was yet to come, however. The wars from 1521 onwards had lasted for no more than two or three seasons before

---

[45] AN J 1017 fo. 335v.
[46] AN J 1017 fo. 381r (Berck); fo. 384r (Verton); fo. 386r (Merlimont). G. de Lhomel, *Nouveau recueil*, 151–2. One witness strikingly confirms the Burgundian enquiry by mentioning damage since 1544 'par les Allemans, Pyemontois, Espaignolz, Ytalliens et aultres, lesquelz ont logié et campé par diverses et diverses foys en ladicte terre de Saint-Josse'.
[47] AN J 1017 fo. 387v (Groffliers), 192r (Sarton), 458 (Coupelles), 475r (Fasques and Verchocq), 494v (Fauquembergues). Du Biez, 1 Jan. 1545, BN fr. 20521 fo. 78–9: request for supplies from Normandy 'pour la carence de grains quy est en ce pays au moien des armées quy y ont passé l'année dernière'.
[48] Francis I to Amiens 17 Feb. 1547, AM Amiens BB 25 fo. 250, specifying new arrangements to avoid the disasters of the previous bad harvests. For other comments on this difficult period, see the spy report, April 1546, Vienna, HHuStA, P.A. 62 fo. 113–14, on scarcity of food in the frontier. See also AM Senlis BB 6 fo. 38r: 'Fault notter que en ce temps la carence du blé estoit si grande par tout le pais que la myne de blé mesure de Senlis faist vendre l'espace de deux mois et plus cent solz tournois et estoit par ce moyen la famyne si grande que le menu peuple mengeoit de pain de son et d'avoine et alloit led. menu peuple par bandes en la forest de Hallette copper et abattre boys . . . qu'ilz vendoient à la ville pour avoir pain' (May 1546). After the war of 1536–7, there was another grain shortage and Montmorency issued instructions to reopen the *traites* for grain importation with the Low Countries before the conclusion of peace to 'obvier à la nécessité qui en pourroit avoir le peuple' (to La Rochepot, 3 May (1538), BL Add. 38033 fo. 294, copy).

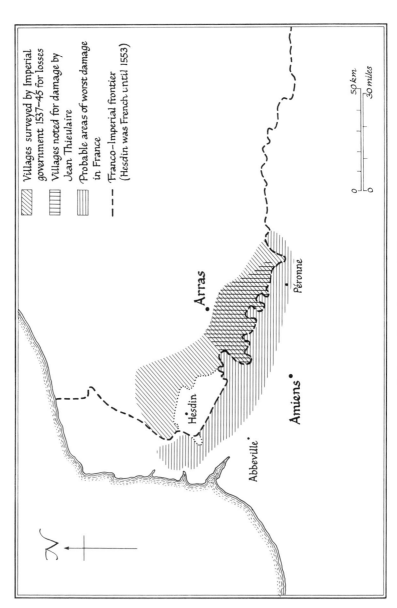

Villages surveyed by Imperial government 1537–45 for losses

Villages noted for damage by Jean Thieulaire

Probable areas of worst damage in France

Franco-Imperial frontier (Hesdin was French until 1553)

Arras

Hesdin

Péronne

Abbeville

Amiens

50 km.
30 miles

3 Areas of war damage, 1550s

exhaustion of resources forced a truce. During the 1550s, however, campaigns were sustained from 1551 to 1558 with only a brief pause during the Truce of Vaucelles in 1555–6. The 1550s, therefore, saw the most sustained levels of destruction as well as the great development of armies discussed in the previous chapter.

The first really destructive raid made by the Burgundians, ravaging the villages of the duchy of Guise and Vendôme's county of Marle in June 1552, was reported by the duke with the words in this chapter title.[49] In revenge, the French visited the area round Thérouanne.[50] In their turn, the Imperial army under the count du Roeulx mounted a massive revenge operation in October to burn Chauny, Noyon and many lesser places, a 'triste et misérable estat de guerre', recorded by the magistrates of Compiègne, 'long temps paravant incognu aux habitans'.[51] The duke of Guise was content that, since this only involved burning, 'il n'y aura que le peuple qui en patira',[52] though in fact it was at this time that the king's castle of Folembray was sacked, an act to be revenged by the French at Binche and Mariemont in 1554.

The papal nuncio, Santa Croce, who was following the fighting closely, reported the devastations he had heard of on both sides of the frontier and apportioned the blame equally: 'non si combatte più per vincer et acquister della terre, ma per abbrusarli et per disfar il paese con homicidii et crudeltà infinite, com'hanno fatto da un anno in qua l'una parte et l'altra et fanno tuttavia'. When the nuncio returned to the frontier region in 1553, it was still in ruins, with 130 villages burned out.[53] This impression is confirmed by a request from the city of Amiens for reduction of its war contributions in May 1553 because of the ruin of the country and the large number of refugees, 'qui n'ont aultre secours pour vivre que ès bledz qui sont en ladicte ville'.[54] At Péronne, the magistrates reported in June that land north of the Somme was out of cultivation and that even revenues from the Santerre were down because of burnings the previous year.[55]

Revenge raids were now the norm. For the Imperial campaign of 1553, the

---

[49] Vendôme to Guise, 23 June 1552, Ruble, *Antoine de Bourbon et Jeanne d'Albret* I, 337. Genlis to Guise, 27 June 1552, BL Add. 38031 fo. 236–7, copy: 'votre pauvre duché et la comté de Marle ont esté gastés, de sorte qu'il n'est demeuré un seul vilage en tour les deux qui n'aye été bruslé'.

[50] Gorguette, 'Thieulaine', 144.

[51] *Ibid.*, 145; AM Compiègne BB 21 fo. 56v. See also BM Beauvais, Coll. Bucquet LVII, delib. of 16 and 18 Oct. 1552: 'Les Bourguignons sont dans Chauny et qu'ils ruinent et brulent tout le pays.'

[52] *Mémoires de Guise*, ed. Michaud et Poujoulat, 110: Guise to Henri II, 17 Oct. 1552.

[53] *ANG* IX, 25 (17 Oct. 1552), 109. See also J. Lestocquoy, 'Les sièges de Thérouanne et de Vieil-Hesdin', *Revue du Nord* (1955), 115–24.

[54] *Inventaire sommaire, Amiens* II, 390.

[55] AM Péronne BB 9, fo. 285–6, reply to La Hargerie by the three estates.

constable and Saint-André planned systematic vengeance: Humières was told
to raid around Bapaume 'le plus vifvement qu'il vous sera possible sans
espargner', while the Imperial army was at work in the Boulonnais.[56] In late
summer a great force of 42,000 men was assembled by the king and constable
to avenge the loss of Thérouanne and Hesdin. This devastated the area of
Bapaume, failed to take Cambrai but did as much damage as possible.[57] The
papal nuncio, on campaign with the constable, urged him to have mercy, but
was told that revenge was necessary. He described how the night turned to day
in the light of 2,000 burning villages. Enquiries made by the abbey of Saint-
Sepulcre at Cambrai after the event confirm the scale of losses.[58] Saint-André
spread the destruction to Saint-Pol and Hesdin with what Rabutin called
'admirable furie', though in the end without 'autre chose de grand effect,
mais plustost mouvante à pitié'.[59] During November and December, the
Burgundians in turn raided Boulonnais and Ponthieu in the west and the duke
of Vendôme's lands in the east, already scoured in June 1552.[60]

The journal kept by Jean Thieulaine, bourgeois of Arras, provides a vivid
narrative of all these raids covering the same areas surveyed for damage in the
1530s and 1540s (see map 3). He mentions sixty-five villages by name burned
by French or Imperial troops. August 1553 emerges as a particularly harsh time
for the peasants all along the frontier, with newly gathered crops lost at a time
when stocks were already low from the previous year, and the emperor's
Spanish troops, no better than the French, removing livestock and raping the
village girls in their camp. Fear of famine spread as prices soared to 50 patards
per *mencaud*. The town of Lens and its suburbs were full of refugees from the
countryside, with what miserable belongings they could carry, 'couchans
misérablement ès rues et soubz les couvertures des maisons sans lictz, et de
jour bien empeschez trouver leurs repas'.[61]

Thieulaine's is the most vivid account in the period, not only of this problem

[56] Montmorency to Humières, 26 Apr. 1553, BN fr. 3116 p. 198; Villebon to same, 16 Apr. 1553,
fr. 3128 fo. 44.
[57] L. Romier, *Saint-André*, 100; Rabutin, *Commentaires* (SHF edn) I, 236–7; Montmorency to
Humières, 22 Aug. 1553, BN fr. 3116 p. 249.
[58] *ANG* IX, p. 109 (13, 22 Sept. 1553), p. 112 (28 Sept.). H. Neveux, *Vie et déclin d'une
structure economique*, 120.
[59] L. Romier, *Saint-André*, 102–4; Rabutin, *Commentaires* (SHF edn) I, 248.
[60] 'Ilz estimoient avoir brusle bien iiiic villages dont une bonne partie estoient de la [*sic*] conté de
Marle, appartenant au duc de Vendosme' (Gorguette, 'Thieulaine', 164); Saint-André to
Humières, 3 Nov. 1553, BN fr. 3128 fo. 61: 'les ennemys ont bruslé Beaurevoir, Bohain et
quelques villaiges autour et qu'ilz actendent encores quelzques renfort pour brusler jusques à
Ham'; same to same, 8 Nov., *ibid.*, fo. 63: adding that the pickings must have been few 'veu
qu'il n'y avoit guyères de villaiges qui n'eussent esté en partye ou le tout bruslé par les
premiers feuz que feit faire il y a ung an passé la Royne de Hongrie et Monsieur du Ru'.
[61] Gorguette, 'Thieulaine', 154–6, 157, 158. The price of wheat by this time was 66 *patards* the
mencaud.

of refugees in the towns but of all the other evils of 'guerre guerroyable': 'tous actes exécrables de tuer femmes vieilles, ravir josnes filles et religieuses'.[62] Though there may be an element of exaggeration, the diary is a private one with no axe to grind and Thieulaine seems to have gone out of his way to check the veracity of these reports. By the winter of 1553–4, the border region was largely ruined, with no winter feed for livestock, the worst weather for years causing more suffering and the peasants raiding the forest with impunity for fuel and rebuilding materials.[63]

So impossible had conditions become by early 1554 that the commander of Cambrai was approached by Louis d'Humières from Péronne with a proposal to halt the burnings. Mary of Hungary agreed 'affin que le povre peuple puisse estre à recours et demeure couvert', the French constable confirmed it and a public exchange of letters seems to have proved efficacious.[64] Pious concern for the 'povre peuple', however, seldom prevailed for long against the clamour of an unpaid and underfed soldiery. Burnings started again in the Boulonnais and around Ardres in April and Arras in July. Thieulaine was convinced that the French aim was now 'de tout ruyner le plat pays d'Arthois' and in July he visited ruined villages 'où je trouvay la ruyne et destructions plus grande que je n'eusse aulcunement cru'.[65] Thieulaine died in August 1554 with Burgundian cattle raids in the duchy of Guise in full swing.[66]

By the mid-1550s, not only was the destruction more savage and systematic than in previous decades but the depredations of 'friendly' troops seem, from Thieulaine's descriptions of the behaviour of Spanish soldiers, to have been as vexatious as those of the 'enemy'. The French were as burdensome to their own population: even during the truce of 1555, Coligny had to excuse the people of Bray-sur-Somme from labour dues on the fortress because of the damage wrought the previous year during the passage of French troops.[67] From 1552, a new scourge in the already largely mercenary French army appeared: the dreaded *reîtres*, mounted German *pistoliers* whose oppressions became notorious during the 1550s. The cardinal of Lorraine's property was one of the early casualties, when one of his farms near Laon was looted by them in 1555

---

[62] Gorguette, 'Thieulaine', 160–1. At this time, 300 villages burned betweenn Saint-Omer and Aire.

[63] Gorguette, 'Thieulaine', 165, 167, 165.

[64] Boufflers to Humières, Cambrai, 1 Jan. 1554, BN fr. 3128 fo. 39; Montmorency to same, 7, 19 Jan. 1554, BN fr. 3116 p. 177, 181: 'pour la pitié qu'il a du pauvre peuple qui ne peult mais de leurs querelles'.

[65] Gorguette, 'Thieulaine', 179, 186–7, 188, 189.

[66] De Murs to Guise, 6, 30 July 1554, BN Clair. 347 fo. 245, 287: 'ce jourd'huy les Bourguignons sont venus jusques au barrière de vostred. ville d'Aubenton et ont admenez toutes les vaches' (fo. 245).

[67] Coligny to Humières, 6 Aug. 1555, BN fr. 3128 fo. 79.

with 1,000 *écus* of damage reported to their commander, the Rhingrave. One of the *censiers* was taken for 325 *écus* ransom and others assaulted, the constable wrote, and it was an outrage that men whom the king 'entretient pour la conservacion de ses pauvres subgectz feussent les premiers à leur courir sus ne faisans aucune distinction nc différence de l'amy à l'ennemy'. Other *reîtres* at Péronne were indicted in 1558 similarly for making 'aucune distinction de l'amy à l'ennemy'.[68]

In addition to this savagery, climatic and economic conditions worsened generally from 1556 onwards. During the winter of 1556–7, a period of truce, restrictions on grain movement were imposed as the previous summer, a very dry one, had produced a poor harvest. On local pressure, Coligny imposed border patrols to impede movement of grain out of the land beyond the Somme and issued a stern *ordonnance* against profiteers aiming to sell grain over the frontier. The magistrates of Boulogne were empowered to seek grain supplies all over France.[69] This winter was also a harsh one and, like that of 1553, drove increasing numbers of peasants into the towns. At Amiens, the *échevinage* was forced to act over numbers 'que de longtemps ne fut veu' and the three estates were convoked to deal with the problem.[70]

When war began again in January 1557, local commanders were under orders to refrain from burnings, though there is plenty of evidence that such rules were ignored, and in March Villebon reiterated that burnings should only take place when the peasants defended themselves.[71] Looting of livestock remained the norm until the end of the wars.[72] In fact, from the ruthless French sack of Lens and its region in June 1557, depredations became more destructive, as victualling systems on both sides began to give way and foraging 'friendly' villages became more necessary. In Picardy, this was aggravated by the scorched-earth policy adopted by the commanders after the defeat of Saint-Quentin, designed to deny the victorious enemy troops access

---

[68] Montmorency to Rhingrave, 17 Sept. 1555, MC Chantilly J II no. 39; Instruction to young Reckerodt, 15 Mar. 1558, BN Res. impr. Cangé 15 fo. 28.

[69] AM Amiens BB 30 fo. 14 (12 Nov. 1556); *Ordonnance* of Coligny, 12 Dec. *ibid.*, AA 14 fo. 81v; AM Boulogne no. 1013 fo. 38r (29 Nov. 1556). On the harvest and plague in Artois at this time, see A. Genel, 'Les mémoires de Jacques Genelle, bourgeois d'Arras', *Revue du Nord* 51 (1969), 97.

[70] AM Amiens BB 30 fo. 23 (7 Dec. 1556), *Inventaire sommaire, Amiens* II, 405f. The figures for the 'poor', were 2,000, many of them weavers whose trade had been disrupted.

[71] Montmorency to Humières, 24 Jan. 1557, BN fr. 3148 p. 1–2; Sipierre to Guise, 30 Nov. 1557, BN fr. 20465 p. 47–52: 'Si n'eust esté question que de bruler villages, douze Escossois départez en deux trouppes avec deux bons guides sçauroient faire aussi bien ceste office que cent hommes d'armes', exculpating himself from the accusation of burning villages.

[72] Rabutin, *Commentaires* (SHF edn) II, 235: the garrison of Renty were surprised when they came 'pour voller la vache et piller le pauvre peusan, selon qu'ilz ont accustumé par toute ceste frontière' (Sept. 1558).

to local crops and the mills.[73] Peasants were also subject to draft as temporary soldiers and building labourers on military projects.[74]

During 1557 and 1558, the armies had increasingly to live off their own peasantry. Complaints grew in the duchy of Guise towards the end of 1557 about foraging by French soldiers who had no food.[75] In November the garrison of Boulogne was foraging systematically and its captain was involved in an ugly quarrel with the royal governor, who charged the garrison with 'meutres de femme et de fille et des exactions et pilleries'; it was only defused by accident.[76] At La Fère and Péronne similarly, the fields were scoured by the garrison light horse.[77] The worst were the *reîtres*, who, without food or pay and disdainful of garrison duty, had to be allotted villages near to the frontier so that their depredations should spill over it as much as possible. It was hardly a practicable solution.[78]

By 1558, large areas of Picardy, especially north of the Somme, southern Artois and Boulonnais had become impossible to live and work in. Even in August 1558, with news of a truce in the offing but also a royal army poised to move, a local governor reported that the peasants of the Authie valley would not be sowing crops 'doubtant la venue dud. camp'.[79] Normal life would not resume until peace talks were well under way.

If fiscal documents, correspondence and journals all agree on the general scope and time-scale of the damage, it is more difficult to assess the exact effects of war on the local economy, since the sources are more fragmentary for the French side of the frontier. Such as they are, though, they seem to confirm the general picture. Pierre Deyon demonstrated a general tendency for rents in kind to rise in Picardy during the period 1530–60.[80] However, notarial records at Montreuil for the 1550s indicate a tendency for rents to fall in that area. New

[73] Sack of Lens: A. Genel, 'Mémoires de Jacques Genelle, bourgeois d'Arras', 100–2. Villebon to Humières, 12 Sept. 1557, BN fr. 3128 fo. 130: order to destroy all millwheels around Péronne; Sipierre to Guise, 30 Nov. 1557, BN fr. 20465 p. 49–52: need to burn the mill at St-Quentin: Robertet de Fresne memoirs, BN fr. 4742 fo. 12v.
[74] Henri II to Humières, 31 Aug. 1557, BN fr. 3134 fo. 66–7; Mailly to Guise, 28 Nov. 1558, BN nafr. 21698 fo. 132–3; La Mothe Rouge to Guise, 28 Mar. 1558, *ibid.*, fo. 159-60 (on *corvées*).
[75] Lechelle to Guise, 7 Oct. 1558, BN fr. 20536 fo. 63–4; Tranchelyon to Guise, 24 Nov. 1558, BN fr. 23192 fo. 286–7.
[76] Allègre to Guise, 7, 11 Nov. 1558, BN fr. 20471 p. 183–6, fr. 23192 fo. 105–6; Boulogne to Guise, 13 Nov. 1558, *ibid.*, fo. 122–3.
[77] Humières to Guise, 23 Nov. 1558, BN fr. 23192 fo. 280–1; Guise to Humières, 25 Nov., fr. 3123 p. 373. Sansac to Guise, 29 Nov., fr. 23192 fo. 360–1: three villages allotted 'pour faire vivre' two companies.
[78] Wallon to Guise, 20 Nov. 1558, BN fr. 23192 fo. 220; Feuquières to Guise, 26 Feb. 1558 BN Cangé 62 fo. 38; Henri II to Feuquières, 3 Mar. 1558, fr. 20460 fo. 149; same to Humières, 15 Mar., BN nafr. 21698 fo. 252.
[79] Mailly to Henri II, 29 Aug. 1559, BN fr. 20434 p. 71 (fo. 35).
[80] P. Deyon, *Contribution à l'étude des revenues fonciers en Picardie*, chs. i–iv; 'Quelques remarques sur l'évolution du régime seigneurial en Picardie', *RHMC* 8 (1961), 270–80.

leases of *censes* agreed in 1550 and 1551 refer frequently to war damage as explanations for reductions of rent or agreement on the deduction of rebuilding costs from rents.[81] In 1553, foraging by the local French garrison was attested as the reason for the low stocks of hay and grain in one village near the town.[82]

Seigneurial accounts, though often fragmentary, reveal some of the impact of fighting on revenues and the use of land. The properties of the Bourbons, inherited from the Luxembourgs, retained their value during this difficult period as a result of careful management,[83] though the effects of war could have sharply adverse consequences. The fairly complete series of accounts for Lucheux, near Doullens (inherited from Marie de Luxembourg by her grand-daughter Marie de Bourbon, countess of Saint-Pol, in 1546) tell the story of a small town near the Artois border.[84] Though the series is not complete between 1520 and 1546, there is enough to show that revenues dropped sharply during the war of 1536–7. In the same period, at Vendeuil, another property of Marie de Luxembourg, the receiver sold grain stocks cheaply for fear of war and the miller suffered losses during the stay of the French army in the vicinity.[85] At Lucheux in 1541–2, rents were not paid and remissions given to forest lessees. The auditors cancelled these and the receiver ended up in debt to the tune of L 2,500, which he had to recoup by forcing the payment of arrears. The profits of the mill had also fallen.[86] When the accounts become available in an almost complete series after 1546, it is clear that seigneurial income, mainly from forest profits, plummeted sharply during the 1550s (see table 6.4). Here, even before the fighting of 1553–4, revenue was declining. Seigneurial fines were difficult to levy and dues for grazing fell because of general uncertainty. In early August 1553, the Imperial army, having just captured Hesdin, camped in the town for over a week, during which time the Spaniards plundered both French and Imperial territory. When the receiver rendered his account in September, L 668 of rents for farms had to be remitted, most of the timber contractors lost profits and even in the following year rents were halved. The enemy had also wrecked the mill and taken the millwheels. Further disaster struck when the French army camped at Lucheux in August 1554.[87] In fact,

---

[81] AD Pas-de-Calais, 12 J 196 fo. 26v no. 38 (2 Sept. 1550), no. 8 (20 Oct. 1550), p. 75 no. 115 (21 Nov. 1551).
[82] *Ibid.*, p. 107 (3 Sept. 1553), p. 111 (13 Feb. 1552).
[83] D. L. Potter, 'The Luxembourg Inheritance: the House of Bourbon and its Lands in Northern France during the Sixteenth Century', *French History*, 6 (1992).
[84] AC Lucheux nos. 199–220.
[85] AC Lucheux, no. 211/c, fo. 7, 23v; AD Aisne E 664 fo. 118v, 151r.
[86] AC Lucheux, no. 211/a fo. 78: fall in mill profits.
[87] Gorguette, 'Thieulaine', 154–6; AC Lucheux, no. 216 fo. 19, no. 217 fo. 70r, 73r; 'Thieulaine', 191.

Table 6.4. *Clear revenues of the seigneurie of Lucheux (in 'livres tournois')*

Year	Receipt	Clear revenue
1545–6	2,819	?
1546–7	5,452	4,347
1550–1	5,037	3,273
1551–2	1,608	1,233
1552–3	2,357	546
1553–4	1,058	400
1554–5	missing	
1555–6	missing	
1556–7	948	1,702
1560–1	3,003	1,607
1561–2	3,581	2,213

Source: AC Lucheux nos. 213–20

all money rents for 1551–4 were remitted because it was impossible to find officers to bring people to Péronne for justice, and in fact the countess of Saint-Pol remitted them for the rest of the war. This was only a small item in revenues; however, the fall in forest profits severely affected seigneurial income in these years.[88]

Inaccessibility of border villages to seigneurial receivers may have been a major problem. At Mézerolles, part of the countess of Gavre's confiscated estate of Auxi-le-château, the inhabitants simply refused to pay arrears after her reinstatement in 1545.[89] The receiver had fled to Lille in the war of 1536–7 but, stopping off at Saint-Pol, had lost most of his movables in the sack of that town by the French.[90] From the Imperial surveys of 1538 and 1545, it appears that some landowners were prepared to remit rents and others not. Where estates were held as confiscations during wartime, there was a tendency for the inhabitants to refuse to pay any rents to the temporary lord, though it would seem that the latter were often more determined to milk their temporary holdings for revenues, a cause of considerable resentment.[91]

88 AC Lucheux no. 217 fo. 71v; 210 fo. 1v, fo. 5v (Charles d'Arras, forest lease).
89 AC Lucheux no. 174 (account for *seigneurie* of Mézerolles, 1546–7) fo. 50, 44v.
90 H. Dusevel, *Etude sur les archives du château de Lucheux* (1857), 15 (this account of 1541 has since been lost).
91 AN J 1016 fo. 27v (Gréna, bel. to sieur de Humbercourt); J 1017 fo. 8r, 63r (Warluzel), fo. 9r (Aiette), 65r (Betonsart), 25r (Noyelles), 26v (Noyelles-Wion), 40r, 43r (Bavaincourt, Gouy), fo. 68v (Villers Broulin). The villages of Saint-Pol so severely damaged seem sometimes to have paid rents (e.g. AN J 1017 fo. 185r) to their owners by confiscation. Azincourt had not paid rents to its temporary owner (it belonged to the French Rouault family by the 1530s), *ibid.*, fo. 267r. At Bours, some properties had their rents reduced, others not, *ibid.*, fo. 310v.

Such circumstances might seem to have made life all but impossible on the frontier. That some sort of life continued and that cultivation proved resilient in the worst conditions might be explained by devices for self-protection and avoidance. Castles only occasionally provided places of refuge in this period.[92] Though the area around Ardres was scattered with fortified manor houses, these were a prey to fairly small detachments of raiders.[93] By the 1550s, the construction of improvised village strongholds for the protection of livestock and people was usual. In addition, the military established a string of small garrisons to encourage the peasants to stay on their land; thus, when the forts along the Authie were threatened by lack of pay in 1558, it became likely that the peasants would evacuate the land and take refuge beyond the Somme at Abbeville, where they had been before.[94]

One solution to the problem of security was a makeshift fort. Villagers in Artois in the 1540s had to leave in 'grand misère et perplexité' for lack of forts.[95] In February 1557, Coligny actually authorised funds for their restoration; they would prove a first line of defence and the only way of keeping the peasants on the land.[96] Thus, when the French burned the village forts of the Cambrésis in 1551 and others in Artois at the end of 1553, Jean Thieulaine was sure that the land would go to waste 'par faulte que les paisans n'auront retraicte ne fourages pour leurs bestes'.[97] Villebon's destruction in July 1554 of a whole swathe of village forts, along with the peasants, women and monks inside them, testifies to their importance.[98]

Some of these forts could be substantial, so that Montmorency was able to use one built by the peasants for a garrison in 1554. The most common, however, was the church tower strong enough to resist a casual assault, used much as it had been in the fourteenth century.[99] Some were able to resist during the 1540s, but it was evidently impossible to hold out against artillery

---

[92] AN J 1017 fo. 45v (Bailloeul – 'par le moyen duquel (château) les villaiges allenvirons ont esté conservez en partie').

[93] Humières-Bequincourt to Aumale, 26 Feb. 1550, BL Add. 38030 fo. 42–4.

[94] Villebon to Guise, 22, 29 Mar. 1558, BN nafr. 21638 fo. 490–1, 525–7. At the start of the war in Sept. 1551, captain du Breuil had expected the enemy to come to 'Uchy et Dampierre ruyner les forts' along the Authie as their first move to find supplies (to Guise, 9 Sept. 1551, BL Add. 38030 fo. 213–14, copy).

[95] AN J 1017 fo. 21r (Noyelles): forced to leave 'au moyen qu'il n'y a aucun fort'; fo. 36r (Villeroye); fo. 157r (Beaulaincourt); fo. 407v (around Thérouanne), fo. 214v (Rebecque, Thiremonde).

[96] Coligny to Humières, 5 Feb. 1557, BN fr. 3135 p. 125–6.

[97] Gorguette, 'Thieulaine', 159 (Lesdaing, 1551), p. 163 (1553).

[98] *Ibid.*, p. 187.

[99] Montmorency to Henri II, 21 June 1554, Pierpoint Morgan Lib. MF. On the fourteenth-century equivalent, see *The Chronicle of Jean de Venette*, ed. R. A. Newhall, trans. J. Birdsall (1953), 85, 99–100.

and the appearance of a full-scale army was the signal to flee. When resistance was offered, as at Rollencourt near Avesnes in 1537 or Fauquembergues in 1544, the tower was set on fire. At Vélu, near Bapaume, in 1543, several villagers were burned to death in the tower and a young woman cast herself to her death from the roof. The people of Riencourt held out in 1542 but were caught by the French in 1543.[100]

Forts could take other forms: either quarries or underground caves like the one discovered by Ellis Gruffydd near Desvres (Boulonnais) in 1544. This had been used as long ago as the war of 1513 and the inhabitants were sworn to secrecy on its entrance and construction. When the Cornish miners had failed to smoke them out, they capitulated under the threat of annihilation; inside there were found twenty-one men armed with firearms led by a captain, with ample food supplies and the valuables of the village.[101] The only alternative to such places of refuge was either flight or concealment in the forest. The people of Fosseux (Arras) lived through the war of 1542–4 in the nearby woods in 'povretez et misères', but woods also posed a danger. When a village was surrounded by them, the French could descend without warning.[102]

Villagers were not only subject to assault; the better-off could easily be selected for ransom and it is surprising that so many less wealthy individuals could be so treated. In 1552, the troops of Auvringhen, the governor of Montreuil, had taken a number of prisoners in a nearby Imperial village but they escaped in the night, leaving a merchant who had been in charge of them out of pocket.[103] In May 1554, a *laboureur* near Montreuil was taken off while tending his flocks to Aire and only then released on caution for his ransom.[104] The Imperial survey of 1545 gives the numbers of people taken off for ransom: thirty at Puisieux, eight at Aiette, twenty at Berlencourt etc. Few villages went without experience of ransom demands. The sums demanded varied from a few livres to the 24 *écus d'or* demanded of the 65-year-old curé of Locquin by the Burgundians.[105]

Other than flight or retreat into refuges of one kind or another, there was little else for the peasants to do. Instances of attacks on organised bands of

[100] AN J 1017 fo. 20v, 21r (Diéval), fo. 18r (Fouquevilliers), fo. 161r (Havraincourt), fo, 17–18 (Rullencourt), fo, 494r (Fauquembergues), fo. 153v (Vélu), fo. 259v (Riencourt).

[101] AN J 1017, fo. 148v (Avesnes-lez-Novain), fo. 149v (Fremiécourt), fo. 152r (Favreuil); Ellis Gruffydd, ed. M. B. Davies, 'Enterprise of Calais and Boulogne', 12–15.

[102] AN J 1017 fo. 15r (Fosseux), fo. 12r (Busquoy). At Foufflin and Ricamez the French were constantly lurking in the neighbouring woods (fo. 190r).

[103] AD Pas-de-Calais, 12 J 196, p. 100. R. Rodière, 'Acte relatif à la rançon d'un paysan (1552)', *Cab. hist.* (1891–2), 157.

[104] AD Pas-de-Calais, 12 J 199, p. 2783.

[105] AN J 1017 fo. 8r etc.: all examples from the *bailliage* of Arras. J 788 no. 3/6 fo. 10v, evidence of Clippel. In 1537 at Puisieux, 17–18 men had been taken and the village had only 27 houses (J 1017 fo. 10v).

soldiers are relatively unusual. There was a story recounted in 1521 of a brave woman of the Boulonnais who, when a party of Burgundians under Adrien de Croy came raiding at Nyeurre, dragged their leader off his horse and mortally wounded him in a melée which took the life of six others.[106] In 1546, nine villagers from Luseul crossed into Artois and slaughtered Burgundian soldiers at Sainte-Margriete, claiming they were 'Anglois sauvaiges'.[107] In 1523, a fight broke out in the village of Bonneuil-en-Valois near Clermont, belonging to the constable of Bourbon, when a captain of *aventuriers* was refused lodging. His men assembled, according to the villagers, crying: 'les Bourguignons et Hennuyers, il les fault mectre à sacq tous, thuer et n'espargner femmes ny enffans'. However, in this case, the villagers, who had taken refuge in the cemetery, found their numbers were greater 'et dechassèrent iceulx aventuriers hors du village; et en y eust tant d'un costé que d'aultre de bastez'.[108]

Such cases may have been reported for their rarity. On the other hand, instances of conflict between individual peasants and soldiers were probably common. Robert Muchembled, in his study of rural violence in Artois during this period, characterises the relations between the peasantry and soldiery as 'constamment et systématiquement conflictuelles'. The records of letters of remission for homicide which he uses are exceptionally numerous for this period and often involve quarrels between villagers and soldiers. Both were ready with their daggers at a moment's notice, especially if, as in 1554 at Annay, a villager called a soldier a 'bougre et jendarme de la Vièrge Marie'.[109]

The most common solution to the problem of raiding was, as has been seen, flight to a stronghold or town. It seems most likely that the prosperous farmers

---

[106] La Fayette to Francis I, 4 Oct. 1521, BN fr. 2933 fo. 160. The peasants of the Boulonnais were hardy. When an English raiding party came to Audinghem in May 1523, two archers of du Biez's company assembled 100 'compaignons du pays' and defeated them (Du Biez to Montmorency, 28 May (1523), BN fr. 3004 fo. 16–18).

[107] Vienna HHuStA Frankreich, Varia 6 fo. 20–4.

[108] The case emerges from a petition (1523) for protection to Louis de La Trémoille as governor of Picardy, AN 1AP 220: the captain under the overall command of Morvilliers was one 'Radingan' (possibly connected with the Senlis, sieurs de Radinghen near Montreuil, relatives of du Biez) and his men were 'revenant de Picardie'. He had used the excuse that the constable 's'estoit rendu Bourguignon' and that the villagers were Hainaulters. Radingan claimed in turn that the villagers had robbed him in the fight and wrote to them and to Bourbon's *receveur* a letter signed 'par tout votre annemy mortel' threatening that 'vanres courir les brandons de feux par my votre village' unless they returned his belongings (*ibid.* 221, 223). The latter two documents were printed by P. Marchegay in *Revue des Sociétés savantes* ser. 5, i (1871), 80–1, though the context is only clear from the petition.

[109] R. Muchembled, *La violence au village*, esp. 111–15. For his discussion of the high level of remissions for violence, 1515–60, see p. 20–1, arguing that the explanation is to be found in the growth in the authority of the Habsburg state. The disorders of war should surely be added as a major contributor. Fear of royal soldiers was given as the excuse for resistance by villagers (mainly women) near Coucy to tax collectors in 1539, see N. Z. Davis, *Fiction in the Archives*, 28.

usually left first with their movables.[110] Consequently, it was often the case that only the poor were left in the villages. At Sars (Bapaume), Martinpuich and Warluzel in the 1540s, most of the men had gone, leaving only women 'qui vivoient illecq en grand misère'.[111] It is more than likely that, in the frontier zone, most of the villages stood virtually empty for several months, at least during the campaigning.

In some cases, it was possible to pay 'composition', essentially blackmail or protection money, to the local garrisons. Burnings were only partly carried out for revenge or for economic reasons; they also served to terrorise enemy villages into giving up supplies and money to garrisons left unpaid by their own governments. A rich *censier* at Filescamp tried this in 1542, though without much added security.[112] Villagers collectively tried to assuage local garrisons in the form of 'fournitures', usually under some kind of threat.[113] Those of Pénin paid up when Thibault Rouault appeared with a party of 'boutefeux' in 1543 and were forced to contribute supplies to the garrison of Doullens in the following year. Imperial villages round Hesdin had to buy their security from the garrison there, one at the cost of 300 florins.[114] Imperial letters of remission for two villages in the county of Saint-Pol, issued in 1552, indicate further problems. Most of the men had fled to the towns but, as was commonly the case, could not survive there because of the cost; they therefore went home. The French governor of Hesdin 'adverti que la plus grande partie des poures gens dudict conté se seroient retirez en leurs maisons' threatened to repeat the pillages they had already suffered – houses burned, women and children ransomed, clerics tortured for extortion – unless they signed the oath of loyalty to France and placed themselves in his safeguard. Having decided to do this, they then repented and had to obtain letters of grace from the emperor.[115]

The impact of war is to some extent revealed by the fortunes of traditional arrangements for making life more bearable. From the beginning of the wars,

---

[110] AN J 1016 fo. 60v, J 1017 fo. 34r (Robert de Cocquel, *censier* of Filescamp). Examples of flight to towns, 1537: J 1016 fo. 23r. AN 1017 fo. 38r (Berlencourt), fo. 37r (Barly).

[111] AN J 1017 fo. 136r (Sars), fo. 139v (Martinpuich), fo. 161–2 (Lechelle): 'aucuns povres femmes se hazardoient pour gaigner sur vie', fo. 165r (Lenvacque): most had left 'sauf les femmes', fo. 163r (Warluzel).

[112] AN J 1016 fo. 60v, J 1017 fo. 34r (on Robert de Cocquel).

[113] AN J 1017 fo. 25r (Noyelles), fo. 35r (Yser), fo. 54r (Zouattre): contributions to the French garrisons at Mailly and Aulty, fo. 190r (Foufflin-Ricametz): main *censier* had to pay 300 florins to the Hesdin garrison.

[114] AN J 1017 fo. 195r (Pénin): payments to Doullens garrison; fo. 199r (Yvregny): 300 florins *fournitures* to Hesdin garrison.

[115] R. Muchembled, *La violence au village*, 107–8, case of the villages of Foufflin-Ricametz and Roellecourt. Muchembled stresses the impossible position of the county of Saint-Pol, caught between the two powers.

the device of 'safeguarding' villages was practised by commanders on both sides. In essence, this involved the establishment of protection for a village or group of villages in return for reciprocal arrangements on the other side. Some safeguards were issued simply to register agreements made on the ground between neighbouring villages; a patent of the regent Catherine de Medici in 1552 did this for villages near the frontier of the Boulonnais.[116] More frequently, a village sought such protection by petitioning a governor on its own side to 'safeguard' an enemy village in return for similar protection for itself.

There is evidence for such petitions as early as 1521, when the curé of a village near Doullens asked the Imperial commander Buren for a safeguard in return for reciprocal arrangements on the French side.[117] In the same year Charles V placed Ardres, Fiennes, Fouquesolles and Courtebourne under his protection on condition that the peasants there brought their harvest into Guînes rather than Boulogne.[118] Lack of trust led to retaliatory revocations of safeguards at regular intervals, especially if it became difficult to provision armies without allowing scope for pillage. As early as April 1523, Vendôme had, on the king's orders, to revoke all except royal safeguards, and only a few days' notice was given.[119] Again, in February 1537, the duke revoked, on the king's command and with four days notice, all the safeguards he had issued since the start of the war except for those covering Saint-Pol and the *régale* of Thérouanne (soon to be infringed in practice anyway). In 1542 duke Antoine issued a general revocation, because the emperor's equivalents had lasted only six weeks.[120]

One peculiarity of the region was the special privilege accorded to the administrators, mainly *censiers*, of the property of three religious confraternities, of Saint-Antoine-en-Vienois, Saint-Hubert-en-Ardennes (patron of lepers) and Saine-Barbe-en-Auge (known casually as Antoniers, Hubertiers and Barbariers).[121] Despite his general revocation in 1537, Vendôme confirmed their privileges, which were still in force at the start of the war in 1542.[122] However, in May 1543 they were finally revoked on the king's order,

[116] AD Pas-de-Calais, 9B 1 fo. 187–90, letters of 21 May 1552.
[117] P. Le Riole to Montmorency, 6 Oct. 1521/22, MC Chantilly L I fo. 50.
[118] *L&P* III, ii, 2511; IV, i, 380.
[119] Vendôme to governor of Arras, AD Nord B 18898 no. 34204. *Ordonnance* of Vendôme revoking all non-royal safeguards, 20 Apr. 1524, add. to *bailliage* of Amiens, BN Picardie 112 bis fo. 4r, summary.
[120] *Ordonnance* of Vendôme, 4 Feb. 1537, AM Amiens, AA 12 fo. 184v: 'pour certaines bonnes et raisonnables causes' and of duke Antoine, 22 Sept. 1542, *ibid.*, AA 12 fo. 209.
[121] Properties held of these orders were widely scattered in northern France and the Low Countries.
[122] *Ordonnance* of Vendôme, 18 Feb. 1537, AM Amiens AA 12 fo. 185; AN J 1017 fo. 18r; J 788 no. 2; *ordonnance* of Vendôme, 28 Sept. 1542, AM Amiens AA 12 fo. 209.

'a cause que par aucuns d'iceulx soubz coulleur de leursd. previllièges ont esté comys aucuns abbus'. Thereafter farms of these orders suffered the same fate as those of their neighbours in 1543.[123] The importance of such exemptions for the habitability of the frontier is illustrated by the fact that in some areas where they had been used as cover and refuge for neighbours, the revocation caused rapid abandonment of the countryside.[124] This seems to have been the reason why the privilege was revoked.

Proximity to the frontier made the acquisition of safeguards urgent. Saulty, near the border and on the road from Doullens to Arras, was raided no less than twenty times between 1542 and 1544 and only managed to get a safeguard six months before the peace of Crépy. At Pas-en-Artois, by the time a safeguard was in force in May 1543, the village was in ruins.[125] Nor was it always possible to make safeguards effective; they were often violated.[126] Such break-downs, however, were much more common during the wars of the 1550s. Despite being safeguarded by Saint-André in December 1553, Ognies in Cambrésis was looted and burned by the French in December, and the same happened to the unfortunate Saulty.[127]

Other territories were regarded as 'neutral' by convention, much in the same way as Tournai had been in the fifteenth century. The county of Saint-Pol and bishopric of Cambrai fell into this category. However, though French governors frequently repeated letters of neutrality for Cambrai its territory was open to exploitation by both sides and the *échevins* were open to bullying.[128] Neutrality finally broke down when Charles V managed to install a garrison there in 1543. The status of Saint-Pol was more ambiguous, as will be seen in chapter 8. As the patrimony of the house of Luxembourg and then of the Bourbon-Vendômes, it was confiscated at the start of every war. However, the French respected its safeguard until 1537, when Francis I launched his campaign to conquer it on the pretext that he had effected an exchange with Marie de Luxembourg and her son Saint-Pol for the duchy of Estouteville. The 1538 survey reveals that the villages of the county had trusted to the French safeguard only to be deceived, since it was 'déclarée nulle' and the peasants

---

[123] *Ordonnance* of Vendôme, 3 May 1543, AM Amiens AA 12 fo. 294v; AN 1017 fo. 43v, fo. 145.
[124] AN 1017 fo. 134r (Warlincourt), fo. 492r (Helfaut).
[125] AN 1017 fo. 186v (Pas-en-Artois); fo. 49r (Saulty); fo. 15–16 (Fosseux); fo. 57v (Bailleuelle-mont).
[126] AN 1017 fo. 54v (Zouattre); fo. 136r (Sars); fo. 193r (Famechon).
[127] Boufflers to Humières, Cambrai, 1 Jan. 1554, BN fr. 3128 fo. 39; Gorguette, 'Thieulaine', 163.
[128] La Hargerie to Francis I, 15 Oct. (1542/3), BN fr. 3081 fo. 80–1. L. Trénard, *Histoire de Cambrai* (1982); *Inventaire sommaire, Cambrai*, AA 60 no. 1, concerning infringements of Cambrai's neutrality (25 Nov. 1527). See also *ordonnance* of Vendôme, 21 Jan. 1528 on the same subject (AM Saint-Quentin, liasse 182, C no. 1). Bandits based in Cambrai raided France and brought its neutrality into question (Humières to *échevinage* of Cambrai, 28 July (1528), AD Nord B 18905, no. 34811).

found their goods looted. The same happened in 1542–4 and again in 1551.[129] Farmers who had traditionally marked their livestock with the symbol of Saint-Pol if they held their lands of the county, wherever they happened to be, had been spared up to 1537 and were still claiming special status in 1560.[130]

Provincial governors were in a strong position, since the concession of such safeguards involved great advantages to their own property and much scope for patronage. The text of one sort of safeguard survives in the papers of the duke of Guise for 1558 as a draft order 'De par le duc etc.' to all military commanders not to 'loger, fourraiger ou prendre . . . aucuns vivres ne autres choses' in a particular village.[131] A more systematic estimation of the process of safeguarding becomes possible in the 1550s, when a group of fourteen texts issued by the duke of Vendôme for villages in the Boulonnais and registered in the *sénéchaussée* there, have survived.[132] These were issued as ducal *ordonnances* and involved a brief summary of the exchange and protection intended. Villages taken into royal protection were to be spared pillage or requisitions and, as a sign of their status, they were entitled to put up the duke's arms at the entry to the village. Proclamation would be made by a trumpeteer in the appropriate local town.[133]

What emerges from these texts is that such protection not infrequently involved the gratification of ducal dependants, *chambellans*, financial officials, or members of the middle-ranking nobility, like the Crequy and Humières families, whom it was advisable to help.[134] Provincial governors were also willing to protect the property of certain religious orders: the *soeurs grises* and *soeurs noires* at Saint-Pol, the poor Claires of Hesdin, even all the clergy in the frontier zone, protected by order of Saint-André so that divine service could be maintained.[135]

In 1528, Jean du Bellay argued that Habsburg envoys had opposed the clause

[129] AN J 1017 fo. 52v (Averdoing), fo. 64r (Rebroeuves), fo. 29r (Orville); Gorguette, 'Thieulaine', 147.
[130] AD Pas-de-Calais, 12J 196, p. 46 no. 70; border enquiries of 2 April 1560, BL Add. 30705 fo. 67v, copy.
[131] BN Moreau 266 fo. 9.
[132] Registered at the *sénéchaussée* of Boulogne, AD Pas-de-Calais, 9B 1, between folios 130 and 354. Dec. 1551–Dec. 1553, *passim*.
[133] *Ibid.*, fo. 157–9, 31 Dec. 1551, for property of the sieur de Tremblay in return for that of M. de Gennes.
[134] AD Pas-de-Calais, fo. 157, 166–8, 28 Feb. 1552, for La Cressonière, a castle near Ardres (M. de Cressonière, retained in royal service in 1516, see Francis I to La Fayette, 17 Oct., BN fr. 3057 p. 209); fo. 174–5, 4 Mar. 1552: Embry protected in return for the Emperor's safeguard of Bonelles's property (Embry also protected in 1536, see Vendôme to La Rochepot, 15 June 1536, BN fr. 3069 fo. 28); fo. 192–7, 1 Jan. 1552: for Fressin and Créquy; fo. 226–7, 31 Mar. 1553: for Rouault's lands in Artois.
[135] AD Pas-de-Calais 9B 1 fo. 130–1, 159–60, 4 Feb. 1552: Vendôme's prohibition of pillage in the county of Saint-Pol; fo. 346–7: 1555, for the poor Claires; fo. 354: Saint-André, 155.

for complete restitution of confiscated property under the terms of the truce because officials in the council of Brussels had, before war broke out, got compensations for their friends out of such property before the 'pouvres gentilzhommes' of the frontier 'qui estoyent suz le pays et sans crédit' could obtain anything.[136] It was the extent of this sort of patronage in the concession of safeguards which the crown was not slow to challenge by demanding their partial or complete revocation, especially in the later stages of the war. Auxi-le-château, the property of the Luxembourg-Fiennes family, may serve as an example. Usually confiscated in wartime, since it lay partly within France, it was taken by the French in 1536 and in 1542, on both occasions to be held by the dukes of Vendôme as confiscation.[137] In 1544, Heilly, as governor of Hesdin, complained that Vendôme and du Biez had safeguarded at least forty villages around Auxi, thus making it difficult for him to requisition food. Denying this, the duke remarked that he wished he had so many villages at his disposal, 'car tant plus y en avoit et mieulx seroit mon prouffict pour me rescompenser des pertes que je foys à l'occasion de ceste guerre'.[138] In 1553, though Humières got his property in Artois protected, he had already been told that the king did not want villages beyond the Canché covered, since they would be likely to afford supplies to the enemy.[139]

The revocations of safeguards are a sign that all was not well with the system of supply and revictualment. Though in their negotiations for a mutual pact against looting in 1553–4, the governors of Guise and Landrecies talked of 'le soullaigement du peuple' as a meritorious act in the eyes of God,[140] excessive extension of safeguards severely limited the ability of soldiers to live off the land at a time when their pay was increasingly delayed. As a result, Gaspard de Coligny as governor after 1556 was far more circumspect, advising against a plan by Louis d'Humières to protect a border village and asking for information on 'la commodité ou incommodité qui en peult advenyr . . . sy la chose portoit prouffict ou prejudice au royaulme' when Humières asked for safeguards for abbeys in Artois in order to protect that of Mont-Saint-Quentin near Péronne. When asked to arrange a pact for the safeguard of Mme d'Humières's land across the frontier, he passed it on to the king for a decision.[141] The renewal of war in January 1557 brought a revocation of

---

[136] Bourrilly and Vaissière, *Ambassades de Jean du Bellay*, p. 305. AM St-Omer, Corr. 5 no. 1709.

[137] Jacques de Luxembourg to Saint-Omer, 8 Apr., 19 Mar. 1528 and certif. of 9 Mar., AM Saint-Omer, Corresp. du Magistrat, 5A, 1602, 1604, 1606. Francis I to La Rochepot, 25 July 1538, BN fr. 3088 fo. 59; order for restitution of Auxi, Contes and Caumont.

[138] Vendôme to Heilly, 22 May 1544, BM Amiens MS 1150, no. 25.

[139] Villebon to Humières, 28 Jan. 1553, BN fr. 3128, fo. 28.

[140] Governor of Guise to governor of Landrecies, 20 Feb. 1554, BN fr. 20530 fo. 71.

[141] Coligny to Humières, 27 Feb., 12, 21 Mar. 1557, BN fr. 3148 p. 47, 83, 105.

safeguards at forty-eight hours' notice and this was to remain in force until the end of the war.[142]

If the traditional arrangements for maintaining the habitability of the frontier region were increasingly under strain, the emergence of a new device at the start of war indicates the growing incompatibility of divided loyalties and the demands of governments on both sides of the frontier for obedience. The problems of sorting out the frontier will be examined in chapter 8, but at this point it should be noted that the procedures against 'aliens' living in border territory seem to have become more rigorous. Given the shared cultural and social characteristics of the region, it is not surprising that there was movement from one village to another which, in effect, now meant the crossing of an international frontier.

The series of naturalisation patents registered at the *sénéchaussée* of Boulogne in 1551–2 shows how this was developing.[143] In September 1551, procedures for naturalisation began in the *bailliages* and *sénéchaussées* and Vendôme issued an *ordonnance* expelling from his *gouvernement* all women whose husbands were in the emperor's service at eight days notice and on pain of having their houses demolished. The chief consideration was security. At the same time, all aliens were ordered to take the oath to the king or leave.[144]

For the Boulonnais, we have documents concerning sixty-one individuals who provided full information for those administering the oath. Of these, twenty-seven came from Artois, twenty-three from the county of Saint-Pol, two from Flanders, one from Lille and one from Hesdin. Of these, twenty-four had settled in the Hucqueliers area and thirteen others in places south of the Liane. Only fourteen had settled in the northern part of the county. Twenty-four had wives and family with them, five had married in the Boulonnais, two were unmarried and there was one soldier and one servant. Most had come to rent tenancies in the Boulonnais (nineteen cases mention property but only three had bought houses) and their average stay in the Boulonnais had been just over three years. While there were a few cases of well-off farmers, employers of labour, inheriting or marrying into property,[145] most were probably middling tenants who had found the county of Saint-Pol unsafe and were eager to move. It is therefore not easy to infer from these examples the extent of general movement across an increasingly dangerous frontier. All had to provide a certificate of good conduct from the local governor or captain and received

---

[142] Coligny to Humières, 30 Mar. 1557, BN fr. 3148 p. 119.
[143] AD Pas-de-Calais, 9B 1 fo. 97–150, *passim*.
[144] *Ordonnance* of Vendôme, Doullens, 16 Sept. 1552 (? recte 1553), AM Amiens AA 14 fo. 8–9.
[145] AD Pas-de-Calais, 9B 1 fo. 97–8 (19 Sept. 1551), fo. 102v (La Tueur, from Marcq-St-Liévin), fo. 141–5 (Pasquier Troaquel, 20 Jan. 1552).

their letters on condition that they notified local authorities of their movements.[146]

When all the evidence discussed in this chapter is considered, the sheer dogged persistence of peasant society when faced by the operation of increasingly destructive war machines leaps into the foreground. To some extent, the resilience of village life must be explained by the essentially renewable nature of the basic equipment; houses were of timber and, though easily burned, could quickly be rebuilt (though at a cost). The devastation at Montreuil in 1537 was total, but the master of the Hôtel-Dieu recorded how much of the buildings and *censes* had been reconstructed by 1541, only to suffer again in 1544.[147] The Arras chronicler, Jacques Genelle, like Thieulaine an avid observer of war, noted that even after the thorough destruction of the little town of Saint-Pol in 1555, the inhabitants 'se reboutèrent audict lieu . . . faisant huttes et petites retraictes pour eulx bouter'. During the truce of 1556, 'le plat pays se commenca à rabatailler. Chacun rédifia sa maison au moins mal quilz peuvent.'[148] Above all, the harvest could be ruined several years in succession but the land brought back into cultivation by the contracting of obligations and debts. As the constable of Saint-Pol had put it during an earlier time of tribulations in 1472, 'la terre ne se peut emporter'.[149] The extent of population loss is impossible to define, though in the areas along the frontier itself the combinations of slaughter, poverty and disease must have inflicted losses that took a generation to restore. The physical environment could be replaced far more rapidly, as the drawings made for the duke of Croy later in the century attest.

Perhaps the most surprising result of this appraisal is that there was not more evidence of rebelliousness on the part of a population which was the most heavily affected by war in France during the first half of the sixteenth century. In part, this may be a result of the obvious fact that a community preoccupied by the problems of sheer survival does not necessarily resort to rebellion in order to solve its problems. It may, however, also be connected with the devices that have been noted for coping with the inordinate demands of war. Moreover, as will be seen in the next chapter, Picardy, though it had no estates to protect its tax régime from the demands of the crown, was not the most

---

[146] *Ibid.*, fo. 137–8 (30 Nov./Dec. 1551).
[147] A Bracquehay, *L'Hôtel-Dieu de Montreuil* (1882), 89–94; memoir by frère Jean Dumont of the events of 1537 and his reparations. See also the enquiries leading to a royal concession of a small perpetual *rente* to the *Hôtel-Dieu, ibid.* 99–106 and Lhomel, *Nouveau recueil*, 146–53.
[148] A. Genel (ed.), 'Les mémoires de Jacques Genelle bourgeois d'Arras', 94, 97.
[149] Louis de Luxembourg to Dammartin, Ham, 25 Oct. 1472, H. de Chabannes, *Preuves* II, 363.

heavily taxed area of the kingdom by any means. The measures taken by the crown to alleviate problems by tax reduction undoubtedly played their part in this and should raise a question over the view of Absolute Monarchies as blindly predatory power machines.

7

WAR, TAXATION AND THE TOWNS

The towns of Picardy were confronted in a markedly direct way by the demands of the state and its military administration in the sixteenth century. The high levels of direct royal taxation which prevailed later in the reign of Louis XI were relaxed under his successors, but began to rise again in the semi-permanent war conditions after 1521, though not steeply until the 1550s. In the course of this, the balance of taxation shifted from direct to indirect, and the exemptions of the towns were gradually abridged by new sorts of taxes and special loans. Picardy, though it had no estates to protect its interests, was relatively lightly burdened by direct taxes as a result first, of the need to conciliate interests, and then to offset the effects of war. The newer urban levies of the 1540s and 1550s, however, contributed to debts which aggravated the economic effects of war in the form of demands for military supplies. To explain the complex nature of these developments, it will be useful to examine the framework within which they were shaped.

The administrative structures

Though there has been much debate about the extent to which administrative frontiers in early modern France were clearly defined, there is no doubt about the massive complexity of the layers of administration which existed by the middle of the sixteenth century. Above all, this is the case in financial districts, which were bedevilled by arcane procedures and bewildering enclaves. Without estates which participated regularly in the raising of taxes, Picardy was taxed through *élections* which had begun to form in the fourteenth century.

Table 7.1

	1497	1498
Taille	20,083.15 (*restes*)	41,333.15
Domain	10,000	10,000
Terres de Mortagne	2,000	2,000
Aides	10,000	10,000
Greniers à sel	4,460	4,460

Source: 'Etat des finances' of 1497–8 in *Ann.-bul. SHF* (1866), 185–92.

These were groups of parishes, assessed by crown appointees who were predominantly local men.[1]

The reign of Francis I saw determined attempts on the part of the royal council to gain control of finances by centralisation of some revenues and a degree of local systematisation. The latter process took the form of a much more effective organisation of provincial taxation *généralités*. In Picardy, the *recette-générale* of Amiens was not formally defined until 1542. Louis XI had created a *généralité de Picardie* out of the lands recovered from Burgundy in 1477 – Boulonnais, Ponthieu, Péronne, Artois – but left those acquired in 1470–1, notably Amiens and its district, Vimeu and Saint-Quentin, in the department of Outre-Seine. The deputies to the Estates-General of 1484 bemoaned this state of affairs and called for the annexation of the whole province to Outre-Seine as they felt over-burdened.[2] However, no changes took place until the 1490s and the situation was not finally modified until the reorganisation of 1542.

The officials of the interlinked *généralité* of Picardy and Outre-Seine were closely connected to the conciliar oligarchy identified by M. Harsgor. Louis XI's *général* in the province, Baudoin Bucquel, was a figure of considerable influence and importance both locally and at the centre.[3] His successor, Jean de Moncheaux, owed his position to the marshal d'Esquerdes, as did the *receveur-général* Jean de La Forge (from 1494), whose son held the same office down

---

[1] G. Dupont-Ferrier, 'Essai sur la géographie administrative des élections financières en France', *Annuaire-Bulletin de SHF* 1928–9. B. Guénée, 'La géographie administrative de la France à la fin du Moyen Age: élections et bailliages', *Le Moyen Age*, 67 (1961), 293ff., for a more positive analysis of boundaries. On the evolution of the *élections*, see G. Dupont-Ferrier, *Etudes sur les institutions financières de la France à la fin du moyen âge*, 2 vols. (1930).

[2] Dupont-Ferrier, *Etudes* I, 240; Bernier, ed., *Journal des Etats-généraux de 1484*, 469.

[3] Dupont-Ferrier, *Etudes* I, 240, says he was dead by 1486. For evidence of his subsequent activity down to 1489: AM Péronne BB 6 fo. 47r, 86r, 93r, 105r, 108v, 117r and *Inventaire sommaire, Amiens* II, 251, 253, 266. Doc. of 1490 headed 'les généraux conseillers du Roy sur le fait . . . de ses finances ès pays de Picardie et Artois', AM Péronne BB 6 fo. 128v.

Table 7.2

Taille	46,234
Crue de taille	11,556
Domain	11,718.12.0
Aides	12,600
Greniers à sel	10,045.10.0
Fortification levies	4,824

Source: L'Etat des finances de 1523, ed. R. Doucet (1923).

to the 1520s.[4] The removal of Artois from French control in 1493 so reduced the *généralité* of Picardy, however, that it lost its separate *général* some time around 1500, though the acts of the *généralité* were still promulgated by 'les généraulx conseillers du Roy sur le gouvernement de ses finances ès pays de Picardye'. In effect, from then until 1542 part of Picardy was a subsidiary *recette-générale* of Outre-Seine.[5]

The revenues of the *généralité* of this part of Picardy were, therefore, among the smallest in the kingdom. The regular income registered for the two years 1497–8 was L 114,338, divided as in table 7.1. In the *Etat* for the year 1522–3, total revenues had risen to L 97,978.2.0, this largely resulting from direct taxes: see table 7.2. The slump in revenues during war is reflected in a quarterly *état* for January–March 1537 which, yielding just over L 16,000, would produce a yearly revenue of L 64,000.[6]

After the establishment of the *recette-générale* of Picardy in 1542, which included the *élections* of Amiens, Doullens, Saint-Quentin, Ponthieu, Péronne and Noyon, the scale of direct taxation can be deduced from the levy of the *taillon*, the tax for the augmentation of the gendarmerie pay agreed in 1549. (The detailed figures are shown in appendix 5.) By chance, the records of the *conseil privé* also preserve the *taille* assessment for Picardy out of a basic levy of L 4,600,000 (including *crue*); it then stood at L 123,222 (2.7% of the whole),

[4] On Moncheaux: in office by 1493 – AM Amiens BB 16 fo. 262v (*Inventaire sommaire* II, 270); L. Pihan, 'Les anciennes maisons d'Hauvoile', *Mémoires de la Société Academique de l'Oise* 21 (1910), 239–73. On La Forge: AM Amiens BB 16 fo. 137v (1491, *Inventaire sommaire* II, 262); BM Abbeville MS 807 (CC 1488–9, fo. 92v).
[5] G. Jacqueton, *Documents relatifs à l'administration financière en France de Charles VII à François Ier* (1891), appendix, gives a Denis Le Mercier as Moncheaux's successor, *c.* 1498–1502. For documents headed by the *généraux de Picardye* after that, AM Péronne BB 7 fo. 33r (1517), fo. 311v (1527), AA 8 no. 12 (1527), BM Abbeville MS 378 fo. 12r (1523). For G. Spifame as *général de Picardie* as well as Outre-Seine in 1534 see AM Saint-Quentin, liasse 138 no. 18. One consequence of the absorption of Picardy into Outre-Seine was probably that it ceased to benefit from the exemption of territories outside the 'quatre grandes généralités' from *crues de tailles*. See P. Dognon, 'La taille en Languedoc', *Annales du Midi* 3 (1891), 347–8.
[6] *Etat* for the generality of Picardy, Jan.–Mar. 1537, AN J 967 no. 8/5.

a figure difficult to compare with the taille assessments of the earlier sixteenth century because of the addition of Amiens and Noyon to the *recette*. Without these two *élections*, the figure would be L 88,749, clearly a rise but not a sharp one. For other comparative purposes, the assessment of L 39,279 for the *taillon* itself is a little over half that for Normandy. The *élection* of Péronne is obviously the most important, reflecting its 426 parishes, and that of Amiens is certainly under-assessed. It seems likely that assessments were drawn up by counts of parishes rather than by any hearth surveys.[7]

Of the total crown revenues of L 4,555,322 recorded in an account of 1528, Picardy accounted for 75,176, though only 9,277 went to the centralised *trésorie de l'Epargne*. The rest was distributed locally by *mandements portant quittance* for local military and civil expenditure.[8] This pattern continued one in which most revenues were disbursed locally. This may be seen in the comparisons of expenditure from earlier accounts shown in table 7.3. Even in 1522–3, much of the increased military expenditure is accounted for by payments to gendarmerie companies in the province.

In December 1542, Amiens became one of the sixteen *recettes-générales* created by the Edict of Cognac. This clarified changes already under way in the 1530s. In stressing the procedures for supervision, the edict sought to create a centralised accounting mechanism for each area.[9] Jean d'Estourmel, the nobleman renowned for the defence of Péronne in 1536, was appointed as *général* of Outre-Seine and Picardy in September 1541, thus maintaining the overall link with Outre-Seine. His successor from 1547, Jean de La Chesnaye, an active member of the *conseil privé*, was in post during the further changes introduced by the Edict of Blois (January 1552). These proved definitive in that they united the posts of *trésorier de France* and *général* in that of a *trésorier-général* in seventeen *recettes* responsible for both taxes and domain revenues. Each new *trésorier-général* was required to choose a seat, and in September 1553 La Chesnaye relinquished that of Amiens to Jean d'Estourmel (who was replaced by his son Antoine in 1554).[10] Henceforth, the *généralité* of Amiens was to be a separate district embracing most of Picardy.

[7] BN fr. 18153 fo. 118–19, 126v–130r. The *taillon* for 1550–1 decreased slightly to L 1,146,236, the assessment of Outre-Seine and Picardy remaining much the same, while the proportion paid by Normandy increased by an extra L 17,936 granted by its estates: BN fr. 18153 fo. 255r.

[8] See Jacqueton, 'Le Trésor de l'Epargne sous François Ier' part 1, *RH* 55, p. 34. Outre-Seine accounted for L 696,201; 502,215 were disbursed by local *mandements*.

[9] Isambert, *Anciennes lois* XII, no. 356; M. Wolfe, *The Fiscal System of Renaissance France*, 261–3. On procedures, see A. d'Estourmel to Humières, 6 Aug. 1558, AM Péronne BB 10 fo. 144.

[10] *CAF* IV, 240, 12113. La Chesnaye: AD Pas-de-Calais 9B 1 fo. 3v (1550), fo. 253–3 (1553). Isambert, *Anciennes lois*, XIII, no. 179. Estourmel, père et fils: AD Pas-de-Calais 9B 1 fo. 289r (1553); AM Amiens EE 323 no. 53, BB 28 fo. 159r (meeting, March 1554); Lhomel, *Nouveau Recueil*, p. 104 (March 1555).

Table 7.3

	1485–6	1497–8	1502–3	1522–3
Military	30,729.18.0	24,380	7,657	38,045
Pensions	33,682	27,812	29,885	26,714
Salaries	4,440	4,140	—	—
Gifts	3,950	—	3,000	—
Remission of *taille*	—	3,617	3,567	4,768
Remission of *aides*	—	980	1,719	2,565
Remission for war losses	—	—	—	20,000

Source: for 1485–6s, BN fr. 20685 fo. 742–6; 1502–3, fr. 2930 fo. 100–12.

The aim of these changes from 1542 to 1552 was greater royal supervision and the control of fraud. The *trésorier-général* was to visit his district regularly and also report regularly to the *conseil privé*. In addition, he became an important agent in the transmission of a wide range of administrative orders to the *baillis* and *sénéchaux*. As before, his *lettres d'attache* were required for all sorts of royal gifts and financial appointments.[11]

The staff of the *recette-général* throughout the first half of the sixteenth century remained much the same, with a *receveur-général*, *contrôleur* and clerks. These men were frequently dependants of provincial governors. Jean de Moncheaux (1483–93) was a servant of Esquerdes and Jean de La Forge (1493–1517) had been his secretary. After La Forge the younger's death around 1526, his post passed to Pierre Fabvre.[12] The *receveur* collected the *taille* but also carried out a wide range of other duties and could be an influential figure. The magistrates of Péronne were lobbying La Forge frequently in the years 1517–19 for help in obtaining exemptions. In December 1518, he refused help and threatened enquiries into the use of *octrois*, claiming that the town had not helped in his private affairs and that 'l'on ne luy faisoit point de plaisir et n'estoit point tenu d'en faire à la ville'. La Forge the younger played a leading part in raising emergency funds for Vendôme in 1525 by

11 Art. 8–13 of edict of 1552. Procedures: AD Pas-de-Calais 9B 2 fo. 23, 27, 28 (1557), fo. 105v (1559). *Attaches: ibid.*, 9B 1 fo. 289r, 253–4 (1551).
12 Dates of succession: L. Mirot, *Dom Bévy et les comptes des trésoriers des guerres* (1925), 113. See note 4 above. The first *contrôleur-général* identified in Pierre de Rouville, 1530 (*Inventiare sommaire, Amiens* IV, 434). Subsequent succession of *receveurs*: La Forge, l'aisné, 1519 (BN fr. 3057 fo. 231–4); 'feu monsr. Day', 1522, AM Amiens CC fo. 88; 'feu monsr. Jehan de La Forge', Dec. 1526 (AM Péronne BB 7 fo. 310r); Pierre Favre, 1534 (Beauvillé, *Recueil* I, 232–3 – possibly still in office in 1547 AM Péronne BB 9 fo. 24v). 'Commis à l'exercice': J. Robineau, N. Saimbault, *CAF* IX, p. 250. Canteleu, *receveur, c.* 1550–3, AM Amiens BB 26, 7 Nov. 1550, BM Abbeville MS 378 fo. 133v. Jean Lefevre, 1554, AM Amiens EE 323 no. 53.

guaranteeing loans from the towns on his own property, a device which caused problems for his executors after his death.[13]

The edict of 1542 specified that the local *receveurs* should transfer funds to the *receveur-général* every quarter at their own expense.[14] It seems likely that, in view of the modest sums involved in Picardy, and the continuation of local disbursement, funds were seldom transferred from the province to the central treasuries; quite the reverse. Military emergencies and fortifications required, as has been seen, the transfer of large sums from Paris or Rouen to Picardy. The *généralité* did, though, take a leading part in the assessment of special levies, the convocation of the feudal levy, sales of royal lands, forced loans and war provisioning, which latter probably explains the doubling of Jean d'Estourmel as *général* and victualling commissioner in the 1540s and 1550s. Both Jean and his son Antoine were local noblemen deeply enmeshed in the society of the province.[15]

By the start of the sixteenth century, Picardy was divided into seven *élections* for purposes of assessing the direct taxes, the *taille royale*. They should not be envisaged as distinct geographical areas, since there were so many enclaves and anomalies. Nor did the existence of *élus*, as at Boulogne, determine whether an area was subject to *taille*, though that was usually the case in Picardy.[16] Though the archives of the *élections* have not survived for this period,[17] enough of their brevets exist to indicate how they worked. Each

---

[13]   AM Péronne BB 7 fo. 48r, 60v, 72r, 132v; Vendôme to Regent, 30 Jan. (1525), BN fr. 20648 fo. 9–10; Lhomel, *Nouveau recueil*, 109; AN X/1A 1527 fo. 332r, 367v, 379r–v; AM Péronne BB 7 fo. 310r, 327v, 329v.

[14]   Isambert, *Anciennes lois*, XII no. 356; BM Abbeville MS 378 fo. 133v (1553), 137r (1554). On the *estat de Picardie*, the yearly list of regular assignments, see AM Péronne BB 7 fo. 152–3. Orders of the *généralité* to local *receveurs*: AD Pas-de-Calais 9B 2 fo. 2; Vendôme to Laon, 11 April (1521) AM Laon EE 5, ment. Assignments on the *recette* of Amiens: AM Amiens BB 26, 3 Oct. 1550; BN fr. 3072 fo. 13, BN nafr. 21698 fo. 316.

[15]   Levies of the *soldes* and on the *octrois*: AM Compiègne BB 20 fo. 164 (1547); AM Péronne BB 9 fo. 411v (1555). Feudal levy, Amiens, 1558: AD Pas-de-Calais 9B 1 fo. 345–6; AD Somme B 1 fo. 8–9. Commissions on royal lands and loans: *CAF* IV, 628, 13940–1; 646, 14022; 787, 14667–8. Provisioning: activities of R. Hurault, 1552–3 – MC Chantilly L I fo. 240; BN fr. 3058 fo. 15; AM Péronne BB 7 fo. 152r–v; Pierre Favre, 1536: AM Chauny BB 5 fo. 192r; commission to Estourmel, 23 May 1545; AM Compiègne BB 20 fo. 88. Present to Estourmel from Amiens 'en considération du plaisir qu'il a fait à lad. ville', AM Amiens BB 27 fo. 75r (15 Oct. 1551).

[16]   Guénée, 'Le géographie administrative', 305; Dupont-Ferrier, 'Essai sur la géographie administrative': *Elections* – Amiens, from which were detached Abbeville (by 1478), Doullens (by 1477); Saint-Quentin (sep. from Noyon by 1439); Péronne, Montdidier and Roye (from deaneries of Amiens and Noyon, by 1439–40); Montdidier, sep. in 1537 (*CAF* VIII, p. 13); Boulogne, *c.* 1477 – see AN X/1A 69 fo. 52v (appeal of 1483); ment. in SAP 60, will of J. de Bournonville, 1507; renewal of royal exemption from *élus*, 1552, AD Pas-de-Calais 9B 2 fo. 183–5.

[17]   The first register of the *élection* of Amiens from which Dom Grenier made copies began in January 1570, the second in March 1583. Neither originals have survived (BN Picardie 112 bis fo. 47–54). No other registers of *élections* for the province are known for the sixteenth century.

élection centred on a town of greater or lesser importance and dealt with 100–300 bourgs and villages. The *élus* themselves were members of the urban legal or commercial oligarchies and, since many towns were exempted, the interests of the countryside were scarcely defended in the apportionment, though the brevets always required levies 'le fort portant le foible'. Much of the work consisted in transmitting routine demands, assessment being received from the royal council in the autumn before the tax year starting on 1 January, and local demands being sent out by the *élus* in October and November. Payments were due in quarters and, by the mid-sixteenth century, automatically incorporated *crues* or supplementary demands as well as, from 1549, the *taillon*. The assessment on local communities was always contentious, the struggle to obtain individual exemption (through proofs of nobility) or communal exemption (through royal letters) strenuous. Corruption was frequently suspected.[18]

The apportionment of the *taille*, however, was only one of the functions of the *élus*. In the sixteenth century, extensive military administrative duties persisted and were extended under the stress of war. In the 1490s, the *élus* were active in the supply of Esquerdes's armies and in the 1520s and 1530s we see the *élus* as special commissioners for the collection of emergency levies to pay Vendôme's troops as well as to ensure their supply. Thus the cumulation of office between *élus* and war *commissaires* was not uncommon in this period.[19] The most regular military function was the levying of transport costs for all sorts of war *materiel*, including artillery and the regular levy of horses and carts, either by a levy supplementary to the *taille* or direct levies of horses in the *élections*.[20] Once in receipt of an *ordonnance* from the governor, the *élus* drew up *rôles* for each parish which were executed by *sergens*.[21] There could be resistance or defence of local interests, as when in 1543 the *élus* at Abbeville protested that the governor's transport levies could not be met because of war devastation and the smallness of the

---

18 Examples of contention: AM Péronne BB 6 fo. 50v (1487); fo. 20, 145r, 156r, 157r, docs. on Haussy, collector of *tailles*.
19 AM Compiègne BB 13 fo. 38v, 48r (1492). AM Chauny BB 5 fo. 191r; BB 3 fo. 35v; BB 4 fo. 8v (docs. on *élus*, 1522–3). *Elus* and selection of *francs-archers*: *ibid.*, AM Chauny BB 3 fo. 12r (1523); BB 4 fo. 23v (1524). Alain Veau, *élu* of Beauvais also *commissaire ord. des guerres*, BN fr. 28515 no. 88.
20 *Brevets*, 1478: AM Compiègne BB 5 fo. 4; 1487: AM Péronne BB 6 fo. 53r; direct fiscal levies: 22 May 1523 for artillery horses, AM Chauny BB 3; April 1543, for horses and *pioniers*: AM Compiègne BB 20 fo. 72r. Admin. of horses raised by *élus*: AM Chauny BB 4 fo. 24v, 25v (1524); MC Chantilly L XIII fo. 19 (1529); BN fr. 36133 no. 392 (1549).
21 AM Chauny BB 5 fo. 179r, ord. of 14 July 1536 by the *élus* of Noyon 'commissaires en ceste partie par Monsr. le duc de Vendosmois'. *Rôles* for muster, 1523, Beauvillé, *Recueil* I, 224–6; Aug. 1562 – see Brandt de Galametz, 'Lettres de Jean d'Estrées' *BSEA*, 1888–90, 330–2.

élection.[22] There were, of course, great disparities in the resources of the *élections* even within Picardy.

The *élections* also supervised the recruitment of labour – *pioniers* – for military works such as fortifications, sieges or camp construction. The usual method was for the governor to commission the *élus* to despatch men to the appropriate places by assessing their districts and towns with precise numbers. How they were found is not clear. Vendôme's order to Amiens in June 1553 was to supply 300 *pioniers* 'des plus jeunes, plus fors et de la meilleure volonté' for the work at Montreuil. The *élus* protested that they did not have enough money, had to borrow L 150 from the *échevins* and then only 250 men could be found.[23] In this case the cost per man was 10s a day but the usual rate of pay, 4s a day for a *pionier*, was not unreasonable when money was available. Where *rôles* of *pioniers* survive they indicate that each company included a small number of skilled carpenters at 6s a day for the service of artillery trains, for instance in the Calais campaign of 1557–8.[24]

As local men, the *élus* could defend local interests against the crown, for example by lobbying for the reduction of special military demands, but at Amiens local politics were racked by disputes between the *échevinage* and the *gens du roi* who were close to the *élus*.[25] In 1505, a violent dispute broke out between the *élus* of Amiens and the town council over jurisdiction which led to the arrest of an *élu*, Jean du Caurel, who was closely related to members of the royal *bailliage*.[26] This was part of a long-running battle that came to a head in 1506, but it should be stressed that this was not so much a dispute between the city and the crown as between two rival local interest groups, which were eventually to fuse in the course of the sixteenth century. Maugis argued that the spread of venality of office was the key to this process, and it is certainly the case that the *élections* were increasingly subject to sale. In 1538, La Rochepot pressed for the office of *élu* at Compiègne for a servant of his father-in-law Humières, to be paid for at the rate of one year's emoluments.[27]

---

[22] *Elus* of Ponthieu to Heilly, 29 Sept. 1543, SAP, Chartrier Heilly 57 no. 46.

[23] La Hargerie to Montmorency, 4 Oct. (1522), MC Chantilly L I fo. 43–4; levies at Compiègne and Senlis for work at Montreuil, 1545, AM Compiègne BB 20 fo. 56v, 83r; AM Senlis BB 6 fo. 20v. Henri II to Humières, 10 July 1553, BN fr. 3120 fo. 82. Vendôme in 1553; AM Amiens EE 323 no. 29; BB 28 fo. 81r.

[24] Muster rolls of *pioniers*: Corbie, 1553, SAP 132 no. 3; Rue, 1557, Beauvillé, *Recueil* I, 251–2. Rate in 1538 1s. 8d p.d., *ibid.*, I, 238–9. BN fr. 25796 no. 279 (1553) 25797 no. 292 (1552), no. 334–7 (1553); fr. 25799 no. 516–558 *passim* (1557–8).

[25] Unpopularity of *élus* at Péronne in 1522, AM Péronne BB 7 fo. 199r, but see their obstruction of Hurault's demands in that year, *ibid.*, fo. 152r. Defence by them of local interests at Compiègne, 1545, AM Compiègne BB 20 fo. 13r, 142r, 169r. *Elu* of Ponthieu also *procureur* for lady Jeanne de Hallewin-Piennes, 1553, BM Abbeville MS 378 fo. 136.

[26] *Inventaire sommaire, Amiens* I, 229, 302.

[27] E. Maugis, *Essai sur le régime financier*, 22ff.; Montmorency to La Rochepot, 8 May 1538, BN fr. 2995 fo. 259.

The scale of taxation: taille royale

The *généralité* of Picardy was relatively lightly taxed, though only after negotiations. Outre-Seine as a whole bore only 8 per cent of the kingdom's burden in 1461, but an average of 12 per cent in 1461–1514 and 18 per cent after that. Within this, Picardy contributed 1.4 per cent of the total in 1483 but 3.6 per cent of the total planned at the estates of 1484 (because its share of 55,000 remained the same). It had dropped to 1.6 per cent in 1498, after the transfer of part of the burden of Outre-Seine-Picardie to Languedoil. It was 2.7 per cent in 1549–50, by which time the *généralité* included the whole province.[28] The reason was the size of Picardy and the fact that problems of war required measures to maintain the loyalty of a frontier province by lower rates and exemptions. The *crues de taille* of 1487 were remitted in Picardy and again in 1488, though at the same time special levies for army support were made.[29] There was a decided increase in the global burden of the basic *taille* after 1521, on Clamageran's figures from L 2.4 million to L 5.3 million in 1559 (though not out of line with population increases until the 1540s and 1550s – see appendix 6). In Dauphiné, a territory seriously undertaxed until this period, L. van Doren has shown the traditional exemptions being overborne by massive emergency taxes from the 1530s, while in Languedoc the estates and *bonnes villes* struggled to maintain their position by bargaining over military supplies and contributions. Narbonne, as Paul Solon has shown, aimed to 'protest everything, demand everything, concede nothing'.[30] In Picardy, many towns continued exempt to some extent and villages were periodically remitted their taxes because of war damage (see chapter 6).

Town exemption is best seen in the concessions made to Amiens by Louis XI in 1471. The town was not to pay *taille* and was given the right to set aside part of the *aides* for fortifications. These concessions were confirmed by Charles VIII, Louis XII and Francis I.[31] Lists of tax exemptions for 1498 and 1522–3 indicate their continuation elsewhere: see table 7.4. The assessment remained stable and at a modest level. The only basic tax assessment to change

[28] G. Dupont-Ferrier, *Etudes sur les institutions financières* III, 48–50. See also A. Spont, 'La taille en Languedoc de 1450 à 1515', *Annales du Midi* 2 (1890), 368–9; 3 (1981), 487–9; on complaints about the apportionment between provinces, Spont, 'Une recherche générale des feux à la fin du XVe siècle', *Annuaire bulletin de la SHF* (1892), 222-36.
[29] Louis XI's early levies on Picardy: La Fons Mélicocq, 'Tailles et impositions diverses acquittées par la ville de Péronne', *La Picardie* XII (1866), 471. Remissions of 1487–8: AM Péronne BB 6 fo. 49r, fo. 53r, 68v (*brevets*) and 1490, fo. 108v.
[30] L. van Doren, 'Institutional Change and Social Conflict in Provincial France – The Royal *Taille* in Dauphiné, 1494–1559', *Proceedings of the American Philosophical Society* 121 (1977), 70–96; P. D. Solon, 'War and the *Bonnes Villes*', *PWSFH* 17 (1990), 69.
[31] A. Thierry, *Tiers Etat* II, 321, 386, 411, 480.

in the period was that of Péronne and that was, in fact, remitted, as will be shown. Curiously, the *etat général des finances* of 1523, though surveying the kingdom as a whole, only lists tax exemptions in Picardy. Amiens, in Outre-Seine, was certainly free of *taille*. However, there is reason to suppose that the actual tax assessments after the 1520s exceeded the exemption level, while the establishment of forced loans from the late fifteenth century and the emergence of the *octrois* on sales as the main form of local taxation certainly circumvented the privileged status of the towns.

Nevertheless, all this did not reduce the anxiety of town councils to pursue exemptions with determination. This applied to the smaller towns in particular. Péronne only managed to obtain a ten-year exemption from Louis XI in 1477 after the *taille* had been levied in October of that year and had to continue to pay its part in special army levies. At the arrival of the *brevet de taille* in January 1486, the exemption had expired and missions to court were unsuccessful, though concessions for *octrois* to pay for fortifications were obtained by October 1488. In December 1489, there were approaches to Esquerdes and the *général* for six-year exemption from a *taille* that had crept up from L 360 to L 750 between 1477 and the mid-1490s.[32] By 1498, exemption had been obtained again, though it was limited, since in March 1515 a deputation was sent to the new king for renewal. A number of missions to court in 1517–22 failed,[33] though the *Etat général* of 1523 shows an exemption from the *taille* of L 1,134. It would seem this had only been made on a yearly basis, since the town was lobbying again in January 1524, when Vendôme intervened to secure a five-year exemption from April 1524, prolonged for a further ten years in 1526 after a visit of the mayor to court and further help from the duke.[34] Only after the siege of 1536, with physical damage estimated by the *échevinage* at 300,000 *écus*, did the crown, in February 1537, concede perpetual exemption from the *taille*, 'pour attirer le peuple du pais et leur circonvoisins à venir fréquenter, demeurer et résider en icelle'. Representations to Antoine de Bourbon at court in 1548 procured confirmation and it was renewed by all succeeding sovereigns.[35]

---

[32] R. Dournel, *Histoire générale de Péronne*, 448–53; Mélicocq, 'Tailles et impositions', 471–3; AM Péronne BB 6 fo. 29r, 42r, 47r, 106r.

[33] AM Péronne BB 6 fo. 337v (16 March 1515); BB 7 fo. 27r; BB 7 fo. 33r (cert. of quittance of L 1,134 *tailles* and 684 *aides*); BB 7 fo. 60v, 67v, 132v, 168r, 152r (*Gén.* Hureault to *rec.* of *tailles* at Péronne, 15 Mar. 1522).

[34] *Taille* of 1523 exceeded exemption: AM Péronne BB 7 fo. 199r. Negotiations with Vendôme and the court, *ibid.*, fo. 208r, 214v; exemption for five years, *ibid.*, fo. 218v, 231r; for 10 years, Dec. 1526: *ibid.*, fo. 310r, 311r.

[35] Orig. letters,. Chantilly Feb. 1537, AM Péronne AA 44 no. 2, copy BN Picardie 174 fo. 37–8. Renewal, Saint-Germain Jan. 1548, AM Péronne AA 44 no. 3, BB 9 fo. 81–2, copy BN Picardie 174.

Table 7.4. *Tax exemptions of the Picard towns*

	1497	1502–3	1522–3
Montreuil	600	600	600 + 150 *crue*
Doullens	250	250	250 + 62.10.0 *crue*
Péronne	375	375	1,134 + 283.10.10 *crue*
Abbeville	800	800	800 + 200 *crue*
banlieue of Le Crotoy	42.5.0	42.4.6	42 + 10.0.0 *crue*
Saint-Quentin	300	300	300 + 75 *crue*
Boulogne	1,250	1,200	?
Corbie	—	—	574 + 143.10.0 *crue*
Saint-Riquier	—	—	42.10.0 + 11.10.0 *crue*

Sources: 1498: *Ann.-bull. SHF* (1866); 1502: fr. 2930 f. 100–9; 1523: R. Doucet (ed.), *L'Etat des finances.*

Renewals of exemption, both periodic and at the start of a new reign, were used by the crown to maintain the principle of its control and to enable officials to profit from the process. Otherwise, the *élus* proceeded readily to levy the *taille*. Even after its disastrous sack in 1537, Montreuil only obtained a moratorium on arrears and a ten-year exemption, prolonged in 1548 for five years.[36] All this cost expensive lobbying. Abbeville, not seriously damaged directly by war, was forced to make heavy supplementary payments on top of its standard L 800 assessment (L 1,500 in 1484 for instance). It obtained exemption in 1493-1503 but had to pay again after that, until Louis XII suspended the *crue* of L 1,500 in 1513. Though the main *taille* was remitted in 1522–3, an exceptionally heavy demand of 5,000 was made in 1524.[37] Lacunae in local records render it unclear when the town gained exemptions thereafter, but renewal was again being pursued with marshal Saint-André in 1554 in the context of heavy costs for fortification. The local estates of 1560 complained of subjection to both *taille* and *soldes* for the army. Its success was therefore limited, since the town was concerned to pursue its prized exemption from the salt-tax and all too readily resorted to municipal loans to pay for the *taille*. Moreover, it was a major supply depot for the armies.[38]

Like Abbeville, Saint-Quentin chose to avoid general assessments but, in its case, paid the *taille* out of indirect taxes on wine and salt, principally the *quatrième des vins* conceded by the crown for this purpose (it produced L 1,200

[36] Lhomel, *Nouveau recueil*, 116–17, 156–7; lobbying at court: AM Montreuil-sur-Mer (AD Pas-de-Calais, dep.) CC 2, accounts, 1555–6.

[37] *Inventaire sommaire, Abbeville*, 127 (15 May 1484), 136, 144 (13 Aug. 1513), 147 (6 Oct. 1514), 157 (7 Feb. 1526); BM Abbeville MS 378 fo. 15v–16r (19 Aug. 1524).

[38] BM Abbeville MS 378 fo. 136r (5 May 1554); *cahiers* of estates, 1560, 1561: *ibid.*, fo. 113r, 117r. Louandre, *Histoire d'Abbeville* II, 33–9. AD Somme, inventaire ms. des archives d'Abbeville, ser. EE 43–75.

in 1533–4). A special war levy of L 3,570 in 1543 was paid by contracting loans.[39] As with other towns in the province, exemptions were only short-term. One for eight years and limited to L 300 was obtained in April 1524, but in the 1530s, the tax demand stood at L 1,254, reduced to 945. Confirmation of the L 300 exemption was still being pursued in 1556, though in fact the crown remitted the entire demand of L 1,847 and 551 *crue* for two years from March 1555. The disaster of 1557 and the French reoccupation in 1559 led to new letters of exemption, confirmed by Charles IX in 1561, but by 1564 a *taille* of L 5,065 was again being levied.[40]

The costly pursuit of these exemptions stemmed not only from the quest for limited financial advantages, but also from the demands of municipal prestige and dislike of divisive *impôts de répartition*. A shift of the tax burden to indirect levies was more welcome to the mercantile and legal oligarchies.

The exact allocation of the *taille* throughout the *généralité* of Picardy is very difficult to establish, but the general assessment of 1550 already discussed (appendix 5) and the survival of *brevets de taille* gives some information, which is summarised in appendix 7. Within that picture, the proportion of taxes paid by the villages and their impact on the countryside is difficult to establish. In the *élection* of Péronne, the villages beyond the Somme had their assessment reduced from L 4,977 to L 1,200 in 1531 because of war damage.[41] The chance survival of *taille rôles* for three neighbouring villages in the *élection* near the frontier makes it possible to get some idea of the relative obligations and rate of increase (see table 7.5).

Lest it be assumed that the increases of the 1530s were catastrophic, it should be remembered that the area benefited from partial tax exemption because of war damage. In the *élection* of Doullens also, all villages received temporary exemption in return for L 2,000.[42] One set of *taille rôles* for a village there, Souich,[43] survives but only for the period 1550–9: see table 7.6. On the base of 1520–1, possibly an aberrant year, the tax burden at Athies multiplied ten times; taking 1521–2, it doubled. This one village stood at 11.4 per cent of the tax assessment for the town of Péronne. The *taille* did increase substantially, but the special conditions applying in Picardy should caution against the assumption that this was as great as in other provinces.

[39] AM Saint-Quentin liasse 138 no. 18, account of 1533; no. 19, account of 1556, fo. 18–21.
[40] AM Saint-Quentin liasse 134. A. Lemaire, *Procès-verbaux des séances de la chambre du conseil des maire, échevins et jurés de Saint-Quentin* (1902) I, xxv–vi. AM Saint-Quentin liasse 4, royal letters, 18 Sept. 1560, exemption for five years, renewal 29 June 1561; levy of *taille* 1564 – all unnumbered.
[41] *CAF* III, 95, 4319.   [42] *CAF* VII, 5, 26889.
[43] AN J 805 no. 36/ 1 and 2 gives the *gabelle rôles* for the same village, 1539–40: 4 *minots*; 1541–2: 1 *minot*; 1558–9: not levied 'pour raison de la guerre lors ayant cours en ce pays et que lad. e village est des plus frontières dud. magazin'; 1559–60: 1 *minot*.

Table 7.5. *'Taille': villages in the 'élection' of Péronne*

	Athies	Villiers	*cense* de Cappy
1494–5		6	46
1496–6		6	50
1496–7		6	50
1497–8		6	50
1498–9		6	50.10.0
1499–1500		6	43
1500–1		6	43
1501–2		6	43
1502–3		6	43
1503–4		7.10.0	50
1520–21	28	1.14.0	
1521–2	28	10	
1522–3	130	10	
1523–4	130	10	
1524–5	122	10	
1525–6	133	10	
1526–7	133	10.13.0	
1527–8	133	10.18.0	
1528–9	163.4.6	13. 7.0	
1529–30	163.4.6	13. 7.0	
1530–1	163.4.6	13. 7.0	
1531–2	163.4.6	13. 7.0	
1532–3	163.4.6	13. 0.0	
1533–4	164	13	
1534–5	164	13	
1535–6	180	14	
1536–7	220	17	
1537–8	221	17	
1538–9	227	17	
1539–40	211	16	

Sources: AN J 805 no. 28; no. 35/2; J 794 no. 25/10.

Table 7.6. *'Rôles des tailles' for Souich*

1550–1	32
1551–2	32
1552–3	32
1553–4	33
1554–5	34.16.4
1555–6	34.16.4
1556–7	34.16.4
1557–8	34.16.4
1558–9	38.15.0

Source: AN J 805 no. 36/1.

Military taxes: the solde des gens de pied

The pattern of *taille* contributions is reflected in that of military taxes on the towns. In reality the tax exemption of towns like Amiens and Abbeville had been circumvented from the late fifteenth century by the imposition of special occasional military levies.[44] Though immune from the *taillon* of 1549, all the towns faced the imposition of levies known as the *soldes des gens de pied* from the early 1520s,[45] which became much more systematic in the late 1530s; notably from the royal council's imposition, in February 1538, of a tax on the walled towns of the kingdom for the support of 20,000 foot. Though all the towns of Picardy and Outre-Seine were exempted from this (with the exception of Saint-Valéry) because of war losses, there were widespread fears that it would become a permanent tax.[46] It was indeed established as such by the mid-1540s. At first levied through the machinery of the *receveurs des tailles*, by 1543 it had become the practice to collect the levy through *bailliage* assemblies which were responsible for apportioning it between the towns. The cash collected then went to the *receveurs* of the *généralités*. The advantage to the crown lay in circumventing urban tax immunities and the linkage of the tax to the prevailing rate of infantry pay, though L 6 per month remained the basis of calculation into the 1550s.

The tax was levied first on the community of the walled town as the pay of a specific number of men: Beauvais paid L 2,400 for its share of 20,000 men in 1538 and L 8,000 for the 50,000 of 1544.[47] In 1549, L 400,000 was levied on the towns for the Boulogne campaign; the demand on the *gouvernement* of Péronne for this was L 320, to be divided between its three walled towns. Where, as in the *bailliage* of Senlis, some small towns had only recently been walled, there was much debate as to whether they were obliged to pay the tax.[48] In any case, periodic adjustments indicate a degree of negotiation between towns. The most common device was for the obligation to be met out of the

[44] AM Amiens BB 16, 10 Dec. 1492 (*Inventaire sommaire* II, 266): loan of L 300. Mélicocq, 'Tailles et impositions', 471: levies for artillery, 1478.

[45] M. Wolfe, *Fiscal System of Renaissance France*, 305; AM Péronne BB 9 fo. 259r: request for exemption from *taillon*, 1553; AM Montreuil CC 2: ass. of *taillon*, 1555. Jacqueton, 'Le Trésor de l'Epargne', part 1, *RH* 55 (1894), 7. Infantry levies, 1522: BM Beauvais, Coll. Bucquet 57, p. 443–5, 455; *Inventaire sommaire, Amiens* II, 325; AM Amiens EE 268, BB 22 fo. 72v (levies and exemptions, 1522–3).

[46] *Ordonnances, François Ier* IX, no. 843; AM Senlis BB 5 fo. 322r (28 Mar. 1538); *Registres, Paris* II, 355–6. Letters of Lameth, AN J 966 no. 29/19; no. 27/21.

[47] BM Beauvais, Coll. Bucquet 57, p. 589 (5 June 1544); p. 82 (27 Dec. 1557).

[48] Letters to *baillis*, 31 Dec. 1549, A. Teulet (ed.), *Relations politiques de la France et de l'Espagne avec l'Ecosse au XVIe siècle*, 5 vols. (1862) II, 235–6; AM Péronne BB 8 fo. 134r. AM Senlis BB 6 fo. 81v.

octrois or by loans.[49] In reality, temporary reductions or exemptions were made in times of hardship. Montreuil was totally exempted in 1544–6 and, in 1547, the contribution of Saint-Quentin was reduced from L 1,646 to 823. Though Amiens paid the *solde* of 1543, it only contributed L 1,200 out of the total of 2,400 for its *bailliage*, a derisory sum. There is no further evidence that it paid until the levies of L 1,200 in 1552, 1554 and 1558.[50] The comprehensive list of *solde* assessments issued at Blois in 1577 reveals that, until 1559, Picardy was very lightly burdened by this tax (see appendix 9).

Sales taxes: octrois et deniers communs

The gradual appropriation since the fourteenth century of royal sales taxes had stabilised town budgets. Edouard Maugis argued that the concession of these *octrois*, particularly for fortification costs, in the sixteenth century constituted a new form of subordination at a time when the crown was abandoning the *taille* in the towns, since the crown could revoke them or control the audit of the taxes.[51] It did this by keeping the *octrois* temporary, forcing regular missions to court for renewal and periodically demanding inspection of the accounts under the suspicion that the levies were not being use for the military/fortification purposes for which they were intended.[52] Louis XII and Francis I both issued *ordonnances* for the audit of the *octrois*, the latter before royal officials by a *contrôleur des deniers communs*. Yearly enquiries were conducted from 1516 to 1520, despite local opposition to the appointment of *contrôleurs*. There were serious arguments at Péronne over the demand of the *receveur-général* La Forge for a full audit of the accounts over thirty years, and in 1524 the crown ordered that the local governor conduct the audit.[53]

By this period, *octrois* had become by far the most important form of urban taxation. For Amiens, one of the great achievements of the agreement with Louis XI in 1471 was royal concession of the right to vote *aides* without special royal *lettres d'octroi* and the abandonment of the *aides royales*. Most

[49] Letters for the *solde* in Ponthieu, 8 Jan. 1552, BN Picardie 301 fo. 13; BM Abbeville MS 378 fo. 134r, 137r. AM Péronne BB 9 fo. 372r, 379r: *soldes* paid out of 'deniers patrimoniaux' and loans.
[50] Lhomel, *Nouveau recueil*, 160. AM Saint-Quentin liasse 127 (royal letters, 21 July 1547). AM Amiens BB 24 fo. 245 (*Inventaire sommaire* II, 353); BB 27 fo. 143v (*ibid.*, II, 384); CC 162 fo. 18. E. Maugis, *Essai sur le régime financier*, 460–2: list of *soldes* payments by Amiens.
[51] E. Maugis, *Essai sur le régime financier*, 441. B. Chevalier, *Les bonnes villes de France*, 210.
[52] Docs. on renewal of *octrois*: AM Amiens AA 5 fo. 304v; AM Péronne BB 9 fo. 69v; on royal enquiries: AM Péronne BB 7 fo. 8v, 72r (1518).
[53] BM Abbeville MS 378 fo. 8v, 9r (orders of Louis XII, 1513). Francis I to sen. of Ponthieu, 6 Mar. (1516), BN fr. 3057 fo. 45; to gov. of Péronne, 15 July 1520, AM Péronne BB 7 fo. 130; to sen. of Boulogne, 21 Dec. (1518), BN fr. 3057 fo. 287. AM Amiens AA 5 fo. 245, 254. AM Péronne BB 7 fo. 72r (1 Dec. 1518), fo. 149r (4 Feb. 1522), fo. 224v, 229v, 310r, 311v.

levies were on alcoholic drinks or salt; a city like Amiens drew its income from a complex set of duties on cloth and other manufactures as well. These *octrois* or *aides* were levied on goods as they entered the towns or at the point of sale and were invariably farmed out to a member of the municipality.[54] At Amiens, the budget for public works was drafted on Saint-Rémy's day and the scale of duties on which goods agreed and proclaimed by the *gens du roi* in the *bailliage*. War expenditure and discord between the *échevinage* and the people were the catalyst for the inception of a régime of royal *octrois*. Until 1518, the town was prepared to forego the *aide* on wine during the *franc-fête* but, with the commencement of a new programme of refortification in that year, it began to levy the due and provoked a law case with the tavern-keepers that was only settled definitively by decree of the Parlement in 1536, which required the *échevinage* to solicit yearly *lettres d'octroi*. In effect this meant that royal control over the *aides* had been reestablished.[55] The duties were bringing in around L 10,000 a year in the 1530s, when public discontent led the Parlement, in February 1539, to provide for wider participation in the budget meetings, as part of its drive to maintain the principle of devoting the *aides* to fortification. As a result, the subsequent assembly reduced the levies to L 6,000, crippled the works programme and provoked the restoration of oligarchical control under a régime of a royal *octroi*.[56] The dependence of the town on royal *octrois* for fortifications was reinforced by Henri II's creation in 1552 of the *aide* of 4s per minot of salt, used to guarantee massive loans floated by the municipality in the 1550s for fortifications, and the complete abandonment of the *aides royales* to the town in 1557 for the same purposes.[57]

The main effect of war on this system was to place it under strain. From early in the reign of Francis I the crown tried to lay hands on part of the *octrois* to defray its local expenditure. La Fayette at Boulogne, for instance, was authorised to take L 2,000 from the *octrois* for use in the fortifications.[58] In 1527, 1528, 1533–5, the crown actually demanded half of these *deniers communs* for transfer to the *Epargne*.[59] The difficulty was that, as at Péronne

---

[54] *Inventaire sommaire, Amiens* II, 297: 'aides de la ville', 1504. BM Abbeville MS 378 fo. 9r, 10v: *aides*, 1516. Henri II to Amiens, 8 Oct. 1556, AM AA 14 fo. 76v: on the farm of the *aides*. Maugis, *Essai sur le régime financier*, 400; AM Chauny BB 5 fo. 16v: farm of the *aides* for L 330 in 1532.

[55] Maugis, *Essai sur régime financier*, 422–6. Thierry, *Tiers Etat* II, 561.

[56] Thierry, *Tiers Etat* II, 561–2, 602–3; Amiens to chancellor, 23 Sept. (? 1526) BN Dupuy 486, fo. 112–13.

[57] Maugis, *Essai sur régime financier*, 443, 459: loans of L 12,000 and L 60,000 (AM Amiens AA 15 fo. 50–2).

[58] Louise of Savoy to gov. of Boulogne, n.d. BN fr. 2934 fo. 22, 42. AM Chauny BB 2 fo. 11v.

[59] C. Jacqueton, 'Le Trésor de l'Epargne sous François Ier', part 2, *RH* 56 (1894), 14; *Ordonnances, François Ier* VI, p. 301–3; VII, p. 227–9; *Inventaire sommaire, Amiens* IV, 446 (1534–5).

in 1528, there were insufficient funds to hand and the magistrates had to borrow to cover the gap. The demand of 1535 exempted frontier towns, but others like Chauny had to contribute.[60] The conviction grew in court circles that the *octrois* were being misappropriated and, in June 1539, the crown ordered the presentation of accounts for the previous ten years. In June 1541, the entire *deniers communs* were seized. Another such demand went out in December of that year, at which point the towns of Picardy asked Vendôme to intervene on their behalf, arguing that all money should be kept in the province for local works. In fact, he forbade the movement of any cash.[61]

The increased demands of war in the 1550s introduced further tensions: an attempt by the crown in 1550 to compel the privileged orders at Soissons to contribute to the fortifications, a demand by the crown for a detailed audit of the accounts of Compiègne in 1554 and a general demand in November 1554 for L 100,000 from the *octrois* to be used in fortifications. The year 1555 saw pressures on Abbeville and Amiens for the use of their *octrois*.[62] Where new *octrois* were conceded, as to Boulogne in 1550, this was only with the proviso for the direct transfer of L 400 to royal officials, though the economic misfortunes of those years forced the crown to forego this by 1563.[63] By the end of the 1550s, exceptions were being widely made to the new regulations requiring transfer of funds direct to the *Epargne*.[64]

B. Chevalier's argument that the *bonnes villes* were increasingly dependent on *aides* and *octrois* in the fifteenth and sixteenth centuries[65] is partially borne out by the example of the medium-sized town of Saint-Quentin. Throughout the first half of the sixteenth century, transfers from the *octrois* to the municipal budget remained static at L 400 and, though the latter was maximised from the exploitation of non-tax revenue, the main municipal account was always in deficit.[66] This was because income from the *octrois* was kept in a separate

---

[60] AM Péronne BB 7 fo. 343r; AM Chauny BB 5 fo. 26r (29 Jan. 1533); fo. 144r (1535). *Aides* inadequate for fortifications, 1524, *ibid.*, BB 4 fo. 27v.

[61] Royal letters to Compiègne, 28 Jan. 1539, AM Compiègne BB 19 fo. 40v; to Soissons, 16 June 1541, BN Picardie 89 fo. 375. Vendôme to Chabot, 2 Jan. 1542, BN fr. 20521 fo. 49–50; *Inventaire sommaire, Amiens* II, 346; IV, 464.

[62] Royal letters to Soissons, 26 Aug. 1550, BN Picardie 89, fo. 377–8; AM Compiègne BB 22 fo. 32v, 49r; AM Péronne BB 9 fo. 410–11, 418–19 (royal letters to Coligny, 20 Aug. 1555). AM Amiens BB 29 fo. 65, 167r. BM Abbeville MS 378 fo. 135v (letters, 10 Feb. 1554).

[63] AD Pas-de-Calais 9B 1 fo. 253–4.

[64] AM Péronne BB 10 fo. 75r (letters, 5 Mar. 1558). Henri II to F. de Montmorency, 21 June 1558, BN Picardie 89 fo. 37–9.

[65] B. Chevalier, *Les bonnes villes de France*, 216–17.

[66] The revenue of 1553–4 was boosted by a war loan of L 1,800, constituted on the town domain (which required a large repayment to Louis Varlet the former mayor and royal victualling commissioner) and a windfall sale of offices, L 401. Renewal of the right to pay rents out of the *aides*, 1551, AM Saint-Quentin, liasse 4 no. 9: justified in terms of the commitments of the town as a frontier fortress.

Table 7.7. *Accounts of the argentiers, Saint-Quentin (in 'livres tournois')*

	1516–17	1526–7	1541–2	1553–4	1555–6
Fines			192	167	185
Rents, houses	101		197	207	271
Rents, domain			74	74	74
Rights, domain			162	199	172
Total normal revenue	831	1,153	1,474	3,632	2,413
Transfers from *aides*	311	400	400	400	400
Expenditure	1,028	?	1,480	?	2,843

Sources: AM Saint-Quentin, liasse 69 nos. 51–55.

account. From the accounts of 1533–4 and 1556–7, it is clear that revenues were buoyant and always in surplus, the main profit coming from the *quatrième* on beer and wine sold retail (L 4,400 in 1556, half going to the town and half to the crown).[67] The main charges on the *octrois* remaining to the town were fortifications (L 660 in 1533, L 2,000 in 1556), salaries and pensions of the military governor and the payment of the *taille*. In 1556 this had been remitted, but the *solde* still had to be found from the *deniers communs*. Even after these commitments, a surplus remained for emergencies (tables 7.7 and 7.8).

The evidence therefore seems to confirm the overwhelming importance of the *octrois* both for municipal finance and as a measure of the relations between the crown and the urban centres in this period of war.

Forced loans and special levies

Exemptions from the *taille* were also circumvented from the late fifteenth century by royal demands for loans from the greater towns, despite Louis XI's concessions over direct taxes. Louis levied 9,600 *écus* in this form on the towns of Outre-Seine for his campaign of 1477. Abbeville was paying 600 *écus* annually in this form from 1479 to 1483 and Péronne 500 *écus* in 1479 and 400 in 1480–3. There could be resistance. Amiens had been leniently treated by Louis XI over demands for special subsidies, but these started in 1486 and went on until 1496. The town contributed L 3,500 in 1491, and agreed to turn this into a gift of L 3,000 in May 1492 when confronted by another demand for L 4,000. Annual demands culminated in one of L 6,000 for the king's Italian

---

[67] Renewals of the *quatrième*: 1524, AM Saint-Quentin, liasse 134; 1555, liasse 4 no. 11. Three months of the *quatrième* had been anticipated in 1555–6 and this left L 1,600 to carry over.

Table 7.8. *Farm of the 'aides', Saint-Quentin*

	1533–4	1556–7
4s per barrel of wine, wholesale	376	315
2d per lot of wine, retail	790	1,017
1d per lot of beer	90	96
16d per minot of salt	496	638
½ the *quatrième des vins* +		
½ the *quatrième des cervoises*	1,231	1,600
Total (incl. surplus from prev. year)	3,222	4,753

Source: AM Saint-Quentin, liasse 130 nos. 18–19.

expedition in 1494, reduced to 2,000 after a deputation to Paris followed threats of distraint on individuals.[68]

In addition to this, when money was not forthcoming from royal treasurers, provincial governors were moved to require loans guaranteed on their own property. Esquerdes did this several times, notably in 1486 for his Thérouanne siege; in June he demanded L 2,000 each from Abbeville and Amiens. In August 1487 he demanded the return of his pledged plate from Amiens, and in 1488 Abbeville agreed to the deferral of repayments that left the marshal's heirs still owing it L 500 in 1512.[69]

The return to war in 1521 brought both greater chaos in the royal finances and more frequent demands for loans. Having used 1,000 *écus* of his own funds to complete fortifications in 1521, Vendôme launched a credit operation in 1524 which involved high demands on all the towns of Picardy and some of the Ile-de-France. The total amounted to L 35,000. At Amiens, L 8,000 was demanded and L 4,000 agreed. The demand of L 4,000 from Péronne met with extreme reluctance and plans to concert opposition with other towns; in the event the magistrates made a firm offer of L 1,000 when La Forge made guarantees of repayment to wealthy bourgeois. Abbeville received a demand for L 6–7,000 against a pledge of the duke's gold chain and silver plate. The local estates made a show of opposition and a reduction was agreed.[70]

---

68 *Vidimus* of royal letters, 19 Jan. 1477, for levy on towns of Outre-Seine 'pour cette fois par manière de prest', BN Picardie 89 fo. 322–3 (Paris, 6,000, the rest 4–600); *Inventaire sommaire, Abbeville*, 124–6; Mélicocq, 'Tailles et impositions', 462; *Inventaire sommaire, Amiens* I, 266, 272. Maugis, *Essai sur le régime financier*, 454.

69 *Inventaire sommaire, Amiens* I, 247, 251; A. Janvier, *Les Clabault*, 176; *Inventaire sommaire, Abbeville*, 127–8, 142–3. Direct to Esquerdes via the *élus*: AM Péronne BB 6 fo. 52r (June 1487).

70 Vendôme to king, 3, 19 July (1521), BN Fr. 3059 fo. 24, fr. 3082 fo. 5. *Inventaire sommaire, Amiens* II, 327; AM Péronne BB 7 fo. 272v, 259, 261r, 262r; BM Abbeville MS 378 fo. 15v–16r; BM Beauvais, Bucquet 57, p. 473–5.

The loans launched by Vendôme at Paris in January 1525 were complicated by the obligations he had directly contracted. He told the regent that he had begun to repay the loans of the previous year from the *recette-générale* of Picardy, 'par ce que je craignoye de perdre mon crédit et estre descryé de n'avoir tenu me promesse'. In fact, the Péronne loans had still not been repaid by the autumn of 1526.[71]

Amiens was particularly subject to forced loan demands in this period. In 1519 L 6,000 were lent, in 1521 L 2,000, in 1524 L 4,000, in 1526–7 L 3,000 were demanded; in 1535–6 2,000 *écus* were required for the pay of infantry; in 1536–7 L 6,000 went in further loans. A massive L 30,000 loan was floated in January–March 1545, repaid by October. Up to August 1549, the crown's debt to Amiens still stood at L 3,500, settled in October but back to L 3,751 for the Boulogne campaign.[72] The 1550s saw another expansion in loan demands, building up to a royal debt of L 16,690 by September 1558. This was a period which also saw the device of forced loans from individual royal officials, lawyers and merchants, a device bemoaned by Montreuil in 1557 because of its poverty and war losses.[73]

The special circumstances arising from the collection of Francis I's ransom in 1529–30 may be considered under the heading of 'windfall revenue'. The demands affected both the nobility and townsmen holding fiefs. By the terms of the Treaty of Cambrai, Francis I had to pay 2,000,000 *écus*, 1,200,000 in cash and the rest in transfers of property like that of Marie de Luxembourg in the Low Countries. This was the equivalent of 4,200 k of fine gold from the kingdom as a whole.[74] Preparations began before the treaty and the money was found by contributions of the nobility under their feudal obligations, the towns, the *taille*, the *décimes, parties casuelles* and loans.

Records of *bailliage* and *sénéchaussée* meetings convoked in October 1529 indicate the course of negotiations with provincial nobilities. When the nobility of Péronne met in December, there were refusals to accept the demand for a tenth of revenue and the governor, Humières, had to ask for instructions.[75] In the Boulonnais, du Biez convoked the assembly while warning the court that

[71] Vendôme to regent, 30 Jan. (1525), BN fr. 20648 fo. 9–10. AM Péronne BB 7 fo. 307v, 310r.
[72] *Inventaire sommaire, Amiens* IV, 422, 450, 454, 361, 363, 332, 379, 373. Maugis, *Essai sur le régime financier*, 457.
[73] *Inventaire sommaire, Amiens* IV, 401; ii, 414, 415, 419. AM Péronne BB 10 fo. 32r. AM Montreuil-sur-Mer, CC 3.
[74] M. François, *Le cardinal François de Tournon* (1951), 80–1; *Ordonnances François Ier* V, p. 224.
[75] Royal letters of convocation, 5 Oct. 1529, for Péronne, BN fr. 3068 fr. 23; for Beauvais, BN Picardie 155 fo. 17v. Humières to Montmorency, 2 Nov., fr. 6635 fo. 95; Montmorency to Humières, 11 Nov., fr. 2995, p. 221; Humières to Berthereau, 9 Jan. (1530), MC Chantilly L IX fo. 130.

the country was ruined by war. In December, the gentlemen of the county voted to offer only a twentieth of their wealth and were backed up by the governor. Montmorency was certainly unwilling to place this offer before the king and told du Biez to put on further pressure, whether successfully is not known.[76]

The 745 gentlemen and fief-holders of the *bailliage* of Amiens contributed L 5,603 as a tenth of their revenues, quite obviously a shameless underestimate. With this may be compared some of the heavy demands made on the *bonnes villes*. Beauvais discussed its levy of L 12,000 in January 1529; the municipality piled up a mountain of excuses, reminding the crown of its great services in the past and the recent economic problems of the town. Negotiations throughout 1529 and into 1530 eventually brought a reduction to L 8,000, though only after much exertion.[77] Amiens was also assessed at L 12,000, as early as November 1528. The magistrates immediately remonstrated to Vendôme that recent military expenses, the royal visit and the loss of the *ressort* of Artois had impoverished the town; while a deputation went to court with a recommendation from him, a commission started to assess property for contributions and a long process of negotiations brought a compromise of 3,000 *écus*. To this was added late in 1529 the levy of one-tenth on fief-holders in the town. The latter were reluctant to pay this as they claimed they had already contributed. The *bailli* supported them, saying that most nobles lived in the country 'et ceux desd. habitans qui tiennent fiefz sont pour la pluspart practiciens de ce siège qui sont pauvres', lawyers who had suffered from the loss of the Artois *ressort* as well as from the wars. This was a recurrent theme played by the lawyers of Amiens in these years.[78]

The raising of the king's ransom was a single unrepeated operation, but it neatly illustrates, in its scope and complexity, most of the problems of raising revenue in the period; in particular, the requirement of negotiation and some form of compromise in the process.

---

[76] Du Biez to Montmorency, 8 Nov., 10 Dec. (1529), BN fr. 20503 fo. 25r, 166; to the king, 11 Dec., fo. 12. Montmorency to du Biez, 17 Dec., *ibid.*, fo. 5; Du Biez to Montmorency, 18 Jan. (1530), fr. 3004 fo. 69; to Berthereau, 18 Jan., MC Chantilly L XIII fo. 180; to Villeroy, 23 Jan., BN fr. 3004 fo. 67; to Montmorency, 23 Jan., 12 Feb., BN fr. 3004 fo. 71, fr. 3038 fo. 61.

[77] 'Liste des personnes tenant fiefs nobles du bailliage d'Amiens . . . 1529' *MSAP* VI, 436–49. BM Beauvais, Bucquet 57, p. 499 (14, 15 Jan., 13 Feb. 1529), p. 504 (27 Oct.), p. 505 (6 Jan., 21 March 1530), p. 506 (18 May 1530). The agreed sum for Paris was L 50,000, see *Ordonnances, François Ier* V, p. 265.

[78] Vendôme to Montmorency, 7 Nov. (1529), BN fr. 3072 p. 61; *Inventaire sommaire, Amiens* IV, 431–2, 434; Amiens to Montmorency, 12 Nov. (1528); 24 Jan. (1530) MC Chantilly L X fo. 285; L XI fo. 237; Vendôme to same, 12 Jan. (1529), BN fr. 20648 fo. 12. Louvencourt and Castellet to Berthereau, 25 Jan. (1530), MC L IV fo. 306. Saveuse to chancellor, 2 May 1530, BN Dupuy 573 fo. 15. Maugis, *Essai sur le régime financier*, 457 n. 3.

Political negotiations and patronage

The growing presence of the crown in local affairs demanded enhanced skills of political negotiation linked to court patronage. Louis XI's reign in particular saw frequent deputations from the *bonnes villes* to the royal court engaged in negotiations over privileges and money necessary for military works. These missions were laborious, frustrating and costly, but thought essential if a town aimed to minimise taxation and gain control of the local sales taxes. Municipal archives often preserve detailed accounts of these missions. Those at Amiens indicate a notable decline in their frequency after 1487 and a sharp drop after 1500, which may be a measure of the extent to which the provincial governor was being built up as the crucial intermediary between the province and the court. The other side of this is the marked reduction in preserved letters-missive from the crown to town corporations and the growth in the importance of royal correspondence with the provincial governor. Therefore, fewer large-scale deputations were necessary, though every major town continued to maintain a *conseiller* at Paris to conduct legal business with the Parlement.

The earlier phase may be illustrated by the series of missions carried out for Amiens by Antoine Clabault, mayor for much of the 1470s. One *compte-rendu* of 1471 refers to the envoys as 'ambaxadeurs', as in a sense they were. This case, a mission to caution against any plan to restore the town to Burgundian control, was reported at a meeting of 'le peuple . . . en bien grant nombre'. The most usual cause of missions was the preparation of royal letters of privilege. One, sent in September 1472 about the *octrois*, resulted in a royal patent dated the following 30 March.[79]

The delicacy of the negotiations is not always apparent from the documents, but one mission in 1477 neatly illustrates the *modus operandi*. The cause was the pressure from Arras on the king to remove Artois from the appellate jurisdiction of the *bailliage* of Amiens; this had produced royal letters in their favour. A *conseiller* of Amiens and a lieutenant in the *bailliage* were sent to court and found the king at Melun, where, as was his custom, he gave them a benign welcome, but passed them on to the chancellor and the judicial counsellors at Paris since the case involved conflicting interests. Meanwhile, he promised to send his own opinion via the bishop of Mende. A meeting with the chancellor at Paris obtained his promise to do what he could and the bishop reported that the king wished that 'on feist pour lad. ville au mieulx que faire se pouroit'. The chancellor asked for submissions and the envoys went back to

---

[79] A. Janvier, *Les Clabault*, 89–91, 103–8.

Amiens to report, only to be sent back to see the king at Montilz-les-Tours. The audience, in the chancellor's presence, saw the king speak against the manoeuvres of Arras, and the next stage was a meeting of all parties before the council in the chancellor's lodgings. In the event, it was announced that the royal patent would specify that Arras would have the same status as under the last French king to possess the county, a compromise leaving the matter in suspense. Finally, in January 1478, the king suspended his letters in favour of Arras.[80]

The frustrations of such missions are conveyed by a report of a deputation from Compiègne in 1475 to get a nine-year exemption from the *taille*. Presented to the king at Notre-Dame de La Victoire by Guy Pot, then high in favour, they were received with his usual bonhomie by the king, who commanded the bishop of Evreux to attend to the matter in council the next day. Having obtained their letters, however, they failed at first to get a meeting with the *général des finances* Beauvarlet in Paris and, in fact, he refused his *attache* for any privilege longer than for five years 'disant que led. octroy faisoit à la charge du play pays à l'environ'. One of the envoys was a friend of his, however, and he agreed to extend it to six years after negotiations.[81]

There were many deputations from Compiègne in these years in pursuit of privileges. One of the most vexatious came in July 1478, for exemption from a garrison. This involved following a fast-moving king to Amiens, Beauvais and then on to Creil in order to catch the king at his *lever*. Though the king received their request, he passed it on to Picart, the *général* of Normandy and governor of Abbeville, who held on to it and then went off to Paris without acting. Another audience had to be sought and this time the king passed the matter to Bouchage, who promised expedition when a *secrétaire des finances* should be available. They were advised to go home and wait. Where a deputation could make use of a patron at court, expedition could be faster. The envoys of Laon, who made the journey to Tours in September 1473 to obtain renewal of their *octrois*, gained their objectives in three days by the intervention of their patron, Guérin de Groing, 'sans lequel eussions longuement séiourné avant nostred. despesche'.[82] Failure to obtain the intervention of a patron is illustrated by the mission sent by Péronne to court in August 1517 for a one-year exemption from *taille* and the concession of royal domain dues in order to finance a new

---

[80]　AM Amiens BB 12 fo. 115r (22 Oct. 1477), fo. 126r (7 Dec.); BB 13 fo. 3v (15 Feb. 1478). M. Fleury, 'Le bailliage d'Amiens, son ressort et le problème des limites administratives au moyen âge', *BEC*, 1956, esp. 52–9.

[81]　AM Compiègne BB 4 fo. 131v.

[82]　AM Compiègne BB 5 fo. 11r. AM Laon EE 2, letter of 24 Sept. 1473; royal letters, 21 Sept. 1473.

town hall. The court was then at Amiens, the *grand maître* was benevolent but did little – he said, 'il n'en sçauroit que faire' – and *général* Hurault was uncooperative.[83]

Money was crucial to success in these missions. The accounts kept by the municipalities from the mid-fifteenth to the mid-sixteenth centuries of disbursements for court lobbying indicate a continuity of tactics and relative stability of costs. Payments to the officials and servants of the *grande chancellerie*, as well as the costs of the seals, formed a major part in this. In addition, there were the costs of lobbying at court, such as payments to ushers for entry into the royal apartments and to the *gens des finances* and their servants, in money or presents, for the necessary documents of *attache* or *contrôle*. These were all additional to travel and accommodation costs.

Deputations to court for Péronne cost, in payments to officials, L 50 in 1477 and L 229 in 1517; one for Compiègne in 1484 cost L 102; Beauvais paid out 50 *écus* in 1515 and Amiens L 249 in 1498.[84] Costs had risen only slightly by the middle of the sixteenth century, when Montreuil paid out L 189 for confirmation of its privileges in 1548, including L 82 for documents. Saint-Quentin spent L 170 in 1556 for confirmation of the *octrois* and diminution of the *tailles*, including payments to a *maître des requêtes* and to Le Gras, Coligny's secretary, for drawing up a missive from his master to cardinal de Châtillon in order to get a hearing for him, 'dont il n'avoit peu estre expédié'.[85]

The role of a provincial governor like Coligny by the mid-sixteenth century was by now well established, increasing both his field of patronage and local reputation, though his effectiveness was dependent on conditions at court.[86] Deputations to court still took place occasionally, but the provincial governor increasingly took on the role of mediator. This was a sort of commerce of favours envisaged by the count of Dammartin in 1471 in his promise to the Amiénois to help them 'et leur fera tout le plaisir qu'il leur pourra faire' in return for their cooperation.[87] It was a pattern confirmed by the vice-regal behaviour of marshal d'Esquerdes for periods of his governorship. Records survive of seventy-six separate missions in the form of letters and deputations

[83] AM Péronne BB 7 fo. 43–4.
[84] AM Compiègne BB 7 fo. 99r (1 May 1484); BM Beauvais, Bucquet 57, p. 376; AM Amiens BB 18 fo. 49v (17 July 1498); AM Péronne CC 3 fo. 93r (1477); *ibid.*, BB 6 fo. 277v, 278–9 (1517).
[85] AD Pas-de-Calais, AM Montreuil, CC 1; AM Saint-Quentin, liasse 138 no. 19, fo. 16–17.
[86] 'ay faict ce qu'il m'a esté possible pour faire oyr vestre député au conseil privé, mais les empeschemens ont esté sy grands . . . il ne m'a esté possible de moienner que vous eussiez l'expédition' (Coligny to Amiens, 6 June 1559, AM AA 14 fo. 59).
[87] AM Amiens BB 11 fo. 8 (April 1471). For a deputation to court from Amiens in 1522 to obtain exemption from a military levy, see *ibid.*, BB 22 fo. 76v (1 June).

from Abbeville to the marshal in the years 1477–92, with the greatest concentration in the 1480s and concerning war problems.[88]

The most typical was a mission simply to 'recommend' the affairs of the town. In the summer of 1477, he ensured by his 'entremise' that the king would accede to the town's request for exemption from a new due on salt. He received L 120 for this. An attempt to set up a *grenier à sel* in the town in 1480 was countered with a mission to Esquerdes at Hesdin to get his advice. A threat by the *élus* to conduct a hearth survey in May 1486 brought a promise by Esquerdes to do what he could to counter it. His help in obtaining exemption from the *taille* and approval of the use of the *octrois* to pay its arrears was obtained in 1487 by the surrender of the marshal's pledge of his plate against the loans raised by him in the previous year. Esquerdes consistently helped the town in the matter until he arranged for the king to grant a ten-year exemption in the course of his formal visit in June 1493.[89]

La Gruthuse in the earlier years of the sixteenth century was an active promoter of the towns' interests at court, as is seen by the prominent part he played in organising the provincial deputation to the estates of Tours in June 1506 and in his handling of a deputation from Amiens in February 1507 about a conflict of jurisdiction between the town and the *bailliage*. On that occasion, he presented the deputation to Louis XII and was charged, with other councillors, with the investigation of the matter.[90] The high regard in which he was held at Abbeville has already been discussed in chapter 2.

The dukes of Vendôme, as princes of the blood, were undoubtedly regarded as more effective personal representatives of the king. In fact, when the consuls of Tournai tried to bypass him and go directly to the king in 1521, duke Charles let it be known that he was 'très mal content pour ce que il luy sembloit que lesdis de la ville se deffioient de luy'. The 1520s saw many deputations to him from Amiens on the perennially difficult problems of the separation of Artois from the *bailliage* and the payment of the king's ransom.[91] As nominal *chef du conseil* in 1525, he was in an even stronger position to recommend suits, and a plea from Péronne for *taille* exemption progressed well, 'par ce que

---

[88] BM Abbeville MS 807, copies by A. Lediu of the now destroyed argentier's accounts relating to Esquerdes.
[89] BM Abbeville MS 807: Arg. 1477–8 fo. 121v; 1479–80 fo. 51; 1485–6 fo. 42v; 1486–7 fo. 101v; 1488–9 fo. 100v: 'pour lui rendre sa lettre du prest qui lui avoit esté fait par ladicte ville de la somme de mille livres, laquelle somme icelle ville lui donnoit et quictoit avecq pour lui requerre que son plaisir feust de aidier à faire descharger et tenir quicte ladicte ville ... de taille'. See also *Inventaire sommaire, Abbeville*, 131.
[90] AM Amiens BB 20 fo. 125v (16 June 1506); fo. 154 (5 March 1507): 'ilz avoient communicqué leur affaire et lui supplié estre leur médiateur vers le Roy'.
[91] G. Moreau (ed.), *Journal d'un bourgeois de Tournai*, 64, 74. *Inventaire sommaire, Amiens* II, 306.

monsr. de Vendosme a la chose en recommandation'.[92] His son Antoine was
receiving frequent town deputations after taking up active duties in 1541,
handling requests for the renewal of the privileges of Amiens; in January 1542
he received a deputation on the town's fortifications, in March over a dispute
with the cathedral chapter, in August over quarrels involving the captain's
powers and in October over procedures for the mayoral election.[93] In the late
fifteenth century, some of these matters would have gone to court.

Whether or not the crown consciously willed all this, there were obvious
advantages in allowing provincial governors to screen petitions. Such was
the change that, by 1561–2, the prince of Condé regarded the decision of the
échevinage of Amiens to seek its address at court without his intervention as a
serious affront.[94]

The crown and municipal office

The battles between the crown and the towns over finance were mirrored by
the changes which were taking place in municipal constitutions, notably in
the contraction in popular participation. Here the crown played a by no means
consistent part. Its main concern was order in peacetime and security in war;
otherwise it preferred to leave procedures to local notables. When quarrels
broke out, it was prepared to exploit them, as Maugis pointed out,[95] but its
intervention was often sought by one local faction or another. The crown had
no fixed determination at this stage to limit municipal independence.

One major determinant of royal policy, as has been seen, was hostility to
misuse of the *deniers communs*. The general edict of March 1515 which
created the office of *contrôleur des deniers communs* cited the 'brigues et
menées' of urban magistrates seeking their 'singulier profit'. This was a
constant source of conflict that was reflected, for instance, in the accusations
brought by the lieutenant of the *bailliage* of Saint-Quentin in 1539 that the
magistrates 'faisoient coutumièrement leurs brigues' to have their cronies
elected in order to cover up their misuse of the *octrois*. The subsequent case in
the Parlement, however, only conceded to the lieutenant the right to be present
at the audits of the accounts as a citizen, not as a supervisor.[96]

[92] AM Péronne BB 7 fo. 310r. See also AM Amiens BB 22 fo. 171v–172r (26 Sept. 1526);
Vendôme to Montmorency, 7 Nov. (1528), BN fr. 3072, p. 61.
[93] *Inventaire sommaire, Amiens* II, 346, 348. Vendôme to Amiens, 4 Mar. 1542, 14 Oct. 1542,
AM BB 24 fo. 167–9, 201v–202r.
[94] AM Amiens BB 35 fo. 44 (see ch. 2 for discussion of this episode).
[95] E. Maugis, *Essai sur le régime financier*, 428ff.
[96] Isambert, *Anciennes lois*, XII, 26ff. See also the edict of Henri II, June 1555, *ibid.*, XIII,
p. 488ff. E. Lemaire and E. Bouchot, eds., *Le Livre-rouge de l'Hôtel de Ville de Saint-Quentin*
(1881), 235ff., *arrêt* of Parlement, Dec. 1539.

The reoccupation of Picardy by Louis XI naturally saw a surge of royal intervention in town elections, if only to ensure initial loyalty to the French crown. At Montreuil in 1477, the king reserved the nomination of twelve councillors to watch over the town for three years. At Abbeville, where the Burgundian duke's interference had cost him much support, Louis XI laid a firm hand on municipal independence. The mayor for 1478 was chosen 'selon le plaisir du Roi' and, for the rest of the reign, that official was chosen by the king from a list of nominees by the *échevins*. Only in 1484 did the regency government concede the right for elections of the mayor and two of the new *échevins* in the old style by the sixty-four *mayeurs des bannières*.[97]

Louis XI claimed specifically to be acting in the interests of order,[98] but it is clear that the *mayeurs des bannières* themselves had begun to distrust wide participation of the trade corporations in their own elections. They therefore sought to avoid 'grans assemblez du peuple'. By 1515, they were offering 20s each for automatic reelection on the argument that large assemblies were inconvenient and that by drawing in country people there was a danger of plague. In 1522, there were complaints of the presence of enemy aliens in the assemblies and the cost of elections was denounced. The years 1533 and 1535 saw denunciations of canvassing for support in the taverns.[99] The consequence was that for practically every year between 1506 and 1532 there were automatic continuations of the *mayeurs des bannières*. Only later in that period did a rift open up between this group and the *échevinage*, which denied in 1525 its status as a distinct 'corps' in the way that the sixty-four *jurés* at Saint-Quentin were regarded as one with the *échevins*.[100]

Amiens proved to be most robust in its response to Louis XI's interference. The town refused to accept the king's nominee for mayor in 1481 and elected Antoine Clabault instead, though in 1495 letters from admiral de Graville asking for continuation of the magistrature were accepted 'sans préjudice des privilèges'.[101] The complication was that pressure for automatic continuation sometimes came from within the town itself. Thus in 1508, the existing mayor was accused of 'grande trahison' in obtaining royal letters 'de surprinse' to this effect, without the real knowledge of the king or of the governor. The affair was

[97] *Ordonnances* XVI, 234, 241ff. Louandre, *Histoire d'Abbeville* II, 58. Richard, 'Louis XI et l'échevinage d'Abbeville' *MSEA* 27 (1960), 32–4. *Inventaire sommaire, Abbeville*, 57 (1484), 183. Royal missives, 15 Sept. 1481, 1 Aug. 1482, Vaesen, *Lettres de Louis XI*, IX, p. 76.
[98] *Inventaire sommaire, Abbeville*, 56 (BB 58 fo. 76v).
[99] Louandre, *Histoire d'Abbeville* II, 248–9; *Inventaire sommaire, Abbeville*, 141 (25 Aug. 1511), 149 (1515); 59 (1521–2), 61 (1533).
[100] BM Abbeville MS 378 fo. 18r (12 Dec. 1525). E. Lemaire, *Procès-verbaux*, p. xii.
[101] *Inventaire sommaire, Amiens* II, 262–3, 275; Janvier, *Les Clabault*, 222–3.

partly a personal one, in which the sitting mayor had most of the *échevinage* behind him; when the governor, La Gruthuse, was brought in, his main aim was to maintain tranquillity, but it proved impossible to bring the leader of the minority faction to heel and the elections of the following two years turned to farce and disorder.[102]

The electoral process at Amiens involved the participation of a large town assembly, including all bourgeois, in a choice from three candidates nominated by the *échevinage*. Disturbances in 1519 resulting from a failure to agree on three candidates produced a royal commission and an *ordonnance* of 23 October 1520, which restricted the nomination to an inner group of six electors instead of the twenty-four *échevins*. The town assembly was to be selected rather than inclusive, though deemed to represent the 'commun populaire'. The disorders had produced a more narrowly oligarchical system not unwelcome to those in place.[103] The emergency of war provoked the continuation of the magistrature on the initiative of the crown or the governor in 1525, 1551–3 and 1557. By 1559, the *procureur du roi* in the presidial court protested that some of the town's financial officers had been in place for twelve years. The next phase was the remodelling of the magistrature after the religious crisis of 1562. In October, the *échevinage* agreed to break up the assembly into three parts and that the election of the mayor should precede that of the *échevins* by the assemblies; only good Catholics were to be accepted. These changes, confirmed by the Parlement in 1563, spelled the doom of any non-oligarchical element in the constitution.[104]

Behind many of the disturbances which racked the urban body politic was the relationship between magistrates and the *officiers du roi* within the towns. Both were increasingly drawn from a homogeneous social group, but the first half of the sixteenth century saw a series of crises. Town statutes in Picardy generally prohibited the simultaneous holding of royal and municipal office. In September 1503, Louis XII issued an edict at the request of the Amiens magistrature reaffirming this prohibition. At this stage, both crown and magistrates saw advantages in blocking the path to fusion, the *échevins* in

---

[102] *Inventaire sommaire, Amiens* II, 307 (29 Oct., 3 Nov. 1508), 308–9 (14 Dec.); 308 (La Gruthuse to Amiens, 8 Nov. 1508), 310 (1 July 1509), 311 (28 Oct.), 314 (28 Oct. 1510).

[103] *Ibid.*, II, 320–2 (28 Oct. 1518). A. Thierry, *Tiers Etat* II, 564–5, 565–7.

[104] Louise of Savoy to Amiens, 6 Oct. 1525, AM Amiens BB 22 fo. 157; Brienne to Amiens, 17 Oct., *ibid.*, fo. 157. Vendôme to Amiens, 27 Oct. 1551, *ibid.*, BB 27 fo. 99v–100r; same to same, 27 Oct., BB 28 fo. 1r; same to same, 13 Oct. 1553, BB 28 fo. 127v; Condé to same, 26 Oct. 1553, BB 28 fo. 127–8; Henri II to Amiens, 14 Oct. 1557, *Inventaire sommaire* II, 412. Thierry, *Tiers Etat* II, 665.

defence of their autonomy, the crown in order to ensure its control over its judicial bureaucracy.[105] The problem was that there was a continuing pressure to elect *bailliage* officials to municipal office until the modification of the law in the 1550s. When the *procureur du roi* at Amiens intervened in the elections of 1538, he did so in a way which indicates that the pressure was coming from the *bailliage* for the election of royal officials. At Abbeville in 1531, however, when the *procureur du roi* intervened to prevent the election as *échevin* of a *greffier des eaux et forêts*, the magistrature agreed.[106]

At Amiens in 1541, royal letters-missive ordered the maintenance of the rules of 1503 and twenty-three out of twenty-four *échevins* voted to obey, noting, however, that the several mayors since 1503 had, to the 'bien de la chose publique', been royal officials. The one opponent took the view that only letters-patent could enforce the rules. The ground for the elections of 1542 was thus well prepared by several warnings from the duke of Vendôme that the royal edicts must be observed, saving the privileges of the town. When, however, the electoral assembly broke into a tumult for the election of Vilain, *procureur du roi* in the *bailliage*, the duke fined five of the *échevins* as ringleaders of the tumult.[107]

Henri II issued a general prohibition on the election of *officiers* in 1547, but by now there was considerable momentum at Amiens behind the argument that merchants alone lacked the skills for justice and administration. A document of 1566 suggests the pressure came from those excluded by the rules.[108] In March 1552, the crown issued a special dispensation for Amiens from the edicts of 1542 and 1547, responding to arguments that those of the 'robe courte' were unequal to the knowledge of justice and conduct 'des grandes affaires concernans la république d'une telle ville, qui est limitrophe et frontière'. When generally known in January 1553, these letters were found insulting by

---

105 *Inventaire sommaire, Abbeville*, 123 (20 Aug., 9 Sept. 1477). Thierry, *Tiers Etat* II, 495. E. Maugis, *Essai sur le régime financier*. The royal letters of 23 April 1529 for Saint-Quentin recognised the endemic hostility of *échevinage* and *bailliage*, see AM St-Q. liasse 37/A, no. 30.

106 Thierry, *Tiers Etat* II, 601; *Inventaire sommaire, Amiens* II, 334 (28 Oct. 1538). BM Abbeville MS 378 fo. 24r–v (24 Aug. 1531). On a protest of an *élu* against his election in 1535, *ibid.*, fo. 30v–31r (30 Aug. 1535).

107 *Inventaire sommaire, Amiens* II, 344 (royal letters, 9 Oct. 1541); 349 (same of 24 Sept. 1542); Vendôme to Amiens, 29 Sept. 1542, AM BB 24 fo. 199 (Thierry, *Tiers Etat* II, 615–16), referring to a royal edict of 9 Oct. 1542 (BB 114). Vendôme to Amiens, 14 Oct. 1542, BB 24 fo. 210vff.; to the lieut. of *bailli*, 23 Oct., BB 24 fo. 207v; to Amiens, 18 Nov., BB 24 fo. 220v (Thierry, *Tiers Etat* II 615–16); Vendôme's judgement, 15 Nov., BB 24 fo. 220v–221v (Thierry, *Tiers Etat* II, 615–16).

108 Edict of 28 Oct. 1547, *CAH* I, no. 1384 (AM Amiens AA 38 no. 11). Thierry, *Tiers Etat* II, 763.

some merchants.[109] In fact, in 1551 Vendôme had already proposed as mayor François de Canteleu, *receveur-général des finances*, on the grounds that the prohibition only concerned judicial officers and that, in the impending military emergency:

> il est très nécessaire que la police et gouvernement de vostre ville, qui est la capitale de la province, soyent administrez par personnaiges de qualité, auctorité, riches, bien apparentez et de sy bonne réputation envers le poeuple commun que par leur moyen on puisse . . . tirer . . . non seullement obéissance mais aussy une prompte et forte secours.

Such terms clearly anticipate the royal edict of the following year.[110]

When Vendôme called for Canteleu's reelection in 1552, the *échevinage* was split between those who saw it as a threat to the town's privileges and those who had gone behind their backs to get the duke's missive, a device increasingly used by a faction of the council to get their way. There were those who argued that letters from the governor should only be sought after open discussion. The election of Canteleu went ahead. Similarly, the election of Adrien Vilain, *procureur-général*, proceeded on Vendôme's request in the following year, though the *bailliage* itself seemed split, in raising objections that the royal letters of exception could not supersede the general edicts prohibiting the election of officers. There was an appeal in the Parlement that involved the arrest in March 1554, for trespass on the town's jurisdiction, of the *lieutenant-civil*, Jean de Thérouanne, an enemy of Vilain and a devoted Catholic ever on the watch for signs of heresy. From the Parlement the case went to the *conseil privé*, which ruled in April to annul the election, fine the *échevinage* for its treatment of Thérouanne and forbid the election of royal officers in future. After some resistance, the *échevinage* agreed to elect Firmin Lecat, sieur de Fontaines, as mayor without calling an assembly.[111]

The *bailliage* continued to act against infringement of the edicts. So when, during the emergency of 1557, the king again required the continuation of Dainval the current mayor, though the *échevinage* agreed, the *bailliage* opposed this, since Dainval had in the previous year acquired the office of *garde du sceau royal*. The *bailli* struck out his name and put in that of Antoine Louvel, and the case went via the Parlement to the *conseil privé*, which in November 1557 ratified Louvel's election, while remitting the fine imposed by the *bailliage*. At the same time, it repeated the exception to the 1547 edict

---

[109] Thierry, *Tiers Etat* II, 631–2 (AM Amiens AA 38, BB 135); *ibid.*, 631, n. 3 (13 Jan. 1553).
[110] Vendôme to Amiens, 27 Oct. 1551, AM Amiens BB 27 fo. 99v–100v.
[111] AM Amiens BB 28 fo. 1r (27 Oct. 1551 – Thierry, *Tiers Etat*, II, 639, no. 1). Vendôme to Amiens, 13 Oct. 1553, AM BB 28 fo. 127v; *Inventaire sommaire* II, 395 (Feb. 1554); Thierry, *Tiers Etat* II, 638–41 (AM BB 145); *Inventaire sommaire* II, 383–4 (21 Jan. 1552).

issued by the crown in 1552.[112] The elections of 1558 saw the *bailliage* again trying to interfere, this time to prevent the election of Adrien Vilain on the grounds that he was a notorious heretic. The *échevinage* stood its ground, claiming that Vilain's reputation was the result of Jean de Thérouanne's enmity.[113] The original dispute on electoral procedure had clearly become hopelessly entangled with growing religious antagonisms in a town increasingly polarised over religion.

In fact, it was to prove impossible to exclude officers from municipal administration. In 1562–3, the *bailliage* obtained modifications of the electoral process which effectively excluded Protestants, but by 1566 half the *échevinage* were royal officers and the royal council's attempts in the late 1560s to restrict the number of officers on the *échevinage* to two proved impossible to enforce.[114]

In Picardy, these confrontations were by no means confined to Amiens; in the smaller towns, the rivalries were just as intense. In 1548, the *échevinage* of Péronne obtained royal letters reducing the number of magistrates from fifteen to eight on the grounds that the town was diminished and that the 1503 edict restricted the choice of suitable candidates. In the elections of June 1553, when the twelve *prud' hommes* opposed the nomination of officers as *échevins* as contrary to the edict of 1547, a meeting of the old council in Humières's presence decided that, as theirs was a frontier town with only few merchants and because matters of importance had to be dealt with:

> non obstant led. édict que le Roy n'entendoit avoir lieu en si petite ville que ceste, et affin que le bien de lad. ville feust myeulz administré par personnes expertz, de procedder à l'eslection de gens de bien, officiers royaux, practiciens et aultres.

Vendôme's permission was obtained by Humières, so illustrating the ineffectiveness of the edict in the fact of necessity, especially in a frontier town where strategic considerations applied.[115]

In June 1558 Péronne petitioned the *conseil privé* that the town's merchants were unable to cope alone with the administration and the council gave permission to elect *officiers* on this one occasion. When this was translated into royal letters-patent the following year, the crown noted that, while the edict might 'apporter commodité' in other towns, it had damaged the interests of

---

112 Thierry, *Tiers Etat* II, 652–3, council *arrêt*, 4 Nov. 1557.
113 *Inventaire sommaire, Amiens* II, 421 (29 Oct. 1558).
114 Royal Council order, 12 Oct. and Nov. 1566, Thierry, *Tiers Etat* II, 762–5; delib. 24 Oct. and 20 Nov. 1566, *ibid.*, 768. *Ibid.*, 779–82, 898–900, 950–1 (injunction for observance of 1566 edict). This remained in force until Henri IV reorganised municipal government; even then the limit of two officers was maintained, *ibid.*, 1088.
115 2 June 1548, AM Péronne AA 47 no. 1; BB 9 fo. 297r–v (24 June 1553).

Péronne. There 'si peu de marchans qu'il y a' were too often away on business and were unsuited to judicial work.[116]

One other example, that of Boulogne, illustrates the difficulties of a frontier town where the merchants were weak, in this case after the French restoration of 1550. François Framéry, one of the first *échevins* of the new municipality, was renewed in October 1550 but also given the office of *prévôt de la vicomté*. By 1554 he was *procureur* in the *sénéchaussée* and also, despite clear knowledge that this was contrary to the edicts, *procureur de la ville*. Another *échevin*, Jacques Rieu, *greffier* in the *sénéchaussée*, was censured for ignoring the interests of the town in a conflict with the latter, and it debated whether to remove him, 'actendu qu'il est officier du Roy'. He remained until his replacement as *greffier* by the sieur du Biez in 1555.[117] In the 1550s, it was clearly the royal judicial officers who took the lead in the reestablishment of municipal life and conflict over office would in practice be ignored until one side or another chose to make an issue of it.

The conclusion to emerge from these constant disputes is far from the simple one that the crown consistently exploited the internal divisions of the towns in its own interests in order to weaken them. Insofar as it had any clear abiding interests, these were the maintenance of the security of the frontier in wartime. Confronted by disputes between the *échevinage* and *bailliage* at Saint-Quentin in 1539, the crown condemned the 'grans inconvéniens pour la chose publicque, mesmement en ville de frontière, comme celle de Sainct-Quentin'.[118] Otherwise, the pronouncements of the king's representatives lacked any consistent line and were, rather, manipulated by the configurations of local politics, especially by the judicial circles which considered themselves the king's chief representatives in the towns.

---

[116] Minute of *arrêt* at foot of petition, 2 June 1558, AM Péronne AA 49 no. 2; royal letters of 1559, AA 49 no. 1, BB 10 fo. 142–4.

[117] AM Boulogne 1013 fo. 7r, 21v (5 May 1553), 31r (16 Sept. 1554), 26v (23 Oct. 1554), 28v (March 1554); AD Pas-de-Calais 9B 1 fo. 371 (provisions for sieur du Biez, 20 July 1555).

[118] *Livre rouge de Saint-Quentin*, ed. E. Lemaire, 235ff.

8

✤

PEACE NEGOTIATIONS AND THE FORMATION OF THE FRONTIER IN PICARDY, 1521–60

On 3 April 1559, the long intermittent war which had begun in 1521 was finally terminated by the treaty signed at Le Cateau-en-Cambrésis. The significance of this peace has long been understood, somewhat simplistically, as a sort of 'hinge' between the Habsburg–Valois Wars and the epoch of the Wars of Religion. The details of the negotiations are well known, though the classic work of de Ruble largely ignores the problems of implementation insofar as they concern the north. On the surface, of course, there was no reason to suppose that the treaty would be any more durable than its predecessors; it had been the exhaustion of the great monarchies that had motivated a substantial effort at settlement and the continuation of that exhaustion, coupled with the descent of France into civil war after 1562, froze the agreements that were reached in 1559. It is also easy to forget that the political imperatives behind war dictated that fighting should be accompanied by frequent, even long-lasting, negotiations for the conditions which would be conducive to 'une bonne paix', or stable settlement. What this meant for both sides, of course, was distinctly divergent, but both sides faced similar problems: how to achieve a stable relationship.[1] This in turn meant agreement on the conflicting territorial and jurisdictional claims of the Valois and Habsburg monarchies,

---

[1] For the most recent general examination of Franco-Habsburg diplomacy in the period, see J. C. Russell, *Peacemaking in the Renaissance*, 3–20, 81–9. The first major study of the Treaty of 1559 was baron A. de Ruble, *Le traité de Cateau-Cambrésis* (1889), which concentrates on implications for Italy and Navarre, but is rather limited. See also L. Romier, 'Les guerres de Henri II et le traité de Cateau-Cambrésis' *Mélanges d'archéologie et d'Histoire* 30 (1910), 1–50, on the role of the duke of Savoy; C. R. Romano, 'La pace di Cateau-Cambrésis et l'equilibrio europeo a meta del secolo XVI', *Rivista Storica Italiana*, 1949, advances a tendentious thesis. The most useful insights are in J. Lestocquoy, 'De la prise de Calais au traité du Cateau-Cambrésis', *Revue du Nord* (1958), 39–47, and especially M. J. Rodriguez-Salgado, *The Changing Face of Empire*, 1–2, 305–37.

including Navarre, Savoy-Piedmont, French claims in Italy and, of course, the frontier between France and the Low Countries.

That the 1559 treaty should have been signed on the borders of Picardy was both appropriate and significant, since it indicates the centrality of the conflict in the north during the 1550s and marks the culmination of a series of negotiations, which had been undertaken in the area since the 1520s in order to settle the many disputes on the nature of the frontier of Picardy. The latter, it should by now be abundantly clear, was not only the most fought over but also the least juridically determined frontier of the French kingdom in the sixteenth century. There were problems in the east with the chronically unresolved position of the border between the *Barrois mouvant* and the Clermontois, along the frontier between the kingdom and the duchy of Lorraine and between Burgundy and the Franche-Comté, but nowhere had the uncertainty of frontier status become so interwoven with the course of endemic warfare as in Picardy.[2] The region may be classified among the quintessentially 'hot' or 'active' frontiers of Europe, ever likely to arouse hostilities.[3]

The old notion of the kingdom bounded on the east by the rivers Rhône, Saône, Meuse and Escaut – still present in the work of Charles Estienne – had only ever been a vague approximation. From the 1540s, it is possible, as Daniel Nordman has shown, to document the impact of the revival of the notion of 'Gallic' frontiers very different from those actually in place. Cosmographers from Sebastian Munster onwards were highly conscious of the Rhine as a frontier, though they also seem to have understood the significance of language in marking a division. Nordman has argued that while such ideas were seeping into general consciousness in the sixteenth century, courts and governments were more cautious. For them, attention to the actual *limites* of the kingdom was the priority.[4]

---

[2] F. Schrader, *Atlas de géographie historique* (1896); L. Mirot, *Manuel de géographie historique de la France* (1929), 148–62; R. Dion, *Les frontières de la France* (1947). The main area of debate on the nature of internal frontiers is to be found in Dupont-Ferrier, 'Essai sur la géographie administrative', *Annuaire-bulletin de la Société de l'histoire de France*, 1928, 1929; B. Guénée, 'La géographie administrative de la France à la fin du Moyen Age' *Le Moyen Age* 67 (1961) and Guénée, 'Espace et état en France médiévale', *Annales*, 1968, 744–58. On external frontiers, see Guénée, 'Des limites féodales aux frontières politiques', in P. Nora (ed.), *Les lieux de mémoire* II, *La Nation* (1986), part ii, 11–33.

[3] The classification is discussed most recently by P. Sahlins, *Boundaries: the Making of France and Spain in the Pyrenees*, 1–24, but see also M. Foucher, *L'invention des frontières* (1987) and R. Gross, 'Registering and Ranking of Tension Areas', in *Confini e Regioni: Il potenziale di sviluppo e di pace della periferie* (1973), 317–28.

[4] D. Nordman, 'Des limites d'Etat aux frontières nationales', in P. Nora, *Lieux de mémoire* II, 2, 35–60, esp. 35–8: Munster (1544): 'mais aujourd'huy les languages et seigneuries divisent une région de l'autre'. The attitude of the French crown to natural frontiers seems to have been dictated by advantage of the moment. In the east, its purpose was served by arguing that the Meuse was the frontier in the disputes with Lorraine. In this it was more concerned with a

In military terms, a frontier could be controlled for defence by the creation of a cordon of great new fortifications, but these in themselves could not define territory. We should remember that the opening of the sixteenth century saw the perpetuation of a frontier arrangement in the north that was the outcome of an uneasy compromise in 1493 confirming Picardy as a province of France. This had left the juridical frontier of France where it had been since early mediaeval times, including Flanders and Artois and rendering the ruler of the Netherlands, from 1506 Charles V, a French vassal.[5] The frontier was more of a *marche* or zone, a fact reflected in the fifteenth-century titularies of governors. This in a sense concealed the problem of the juris-dictional intermingling of French and Netherlands communities along the frontier between French Picardy and the Habsburg lands, but rendered the relations between the dynasties endemically unstable, since major French outposts and claims remained in Burgundian territory. The preoccupation of the French crown with the question of Italy only delayed a confron-tation.

The renewal of the conflict in 1521 immediately reopened the problem when in that year France lost Tournai, the emperor Hesdin; even old Burgundian claims to the Somme could now be scoured up. All certainty about the position of the frontier began to dissolve and in the treaties of 1525 and 1529 Artois and Flanders were decisively removed from the suzerainty of the French crown. Henceforth, the frontier in Picardy was also that between France and the Empire and the demands of rival sovereignties began to be felt in border villages of contested jurisdiction. The importance of this jurisdictional change should be stressed; the French crown had been determined until 1521 to main-tain some effectiveness in its suzerainty of Flanders and Artois.[6] Its concession was the first major retreat of the French crown from the historic frontier of 843 and it generated enormous problems, not least because royal lawyers would not necessarily accept that such treaties could abrogate age-old regalian rights.

No clear continuously delineated boundary existed on the ground with frontier posts. The distinction noted by Lucien Febvre between *limite* (clear boundary line) and *frontière* (frontier zone, with military connotations), which

---

reading of chroniclers like Gaguin and Gilles. See H. Stein and L. Le Grand, *La frontière d'Argonne (843–1659). Proces de Claude de La Vallee (1535–61)* (1905), 128; J. Rigault, 'La frontière de la Meuse. L'utilisation des sources historiques dans un procès devant le Parlement de Paris en 1535', *BEC*, 106 (1945–6), 80–99.

[5] On this problem, see W. P. Blockmans, 'La position du comté de Flandre dans le royaume à la fin du XVe siècle' in B. Chevalier and P. Contamine, *La France de la fin du XVᵉ siècle*, 78–9.

[6] *Ibid.*, 85–7. In 1594 royal *lettres de naturalité* for a native of Artois declared that, though 'le comté d'Artois soit à présent hors de ses mains, il a toujours réputé les habitans d'iceluy comme régnicoles et ses naturels sujets' (AN U 616 fo. 313).

increasingly overlapped in the early modern period, may be observed in this region.[7] The former is observable in one stretch of the frontier, between France and the Cambrésis and Hainault, which was of an extraordinary antiquity, its origins going back to the boundary of the Gallo-Roman *civitas*, later the bishopric of Cambrai, then of France and the Empire under the Treaty of Verdun and still serving as the boundary of the modern *départements* of the Nord and Aisne.[8]

Elsewhere, however, the line was a more indistinct *frontière*, though this did not mean that it was impossible to define or that the *limites* of France and the Low Countries were no more than a vague penumbra of jurisdiction, as is sometimes supposed. As with internal administrative boundaries, so many enclaves existed in the region of the frontier that it should be imagined as a bewildering patchwork of territories subject to various feudal tenures. It was a frontier of the type described by Guénée as 'des limites précises ensore, mais complexes . . . issues des conflict féodaux'.[9] So, one mainly Burgundian village on the Artois border could declare itself in 1545 to be 'contigu au terroir de France, tellement que partie dud. villaige est pays de France, meismes l'église et paroisse dudict lieu est scitué en France'. Another near Doullens could declare that 'il y a plusieurs terres de France enclavées aud. terroir', while at others French *laboureurs* came to work the fields in Burgundian territory.[10] A 'border' existed, therefore, but one which was quite alien to subsequent conceptions of what a border should be, and the negotiations of the sixteenth century represent the tension between this existing idea and the demands of international politics during the emergence of quasi-national states. The point emerges clearly from the response of a small landowner on the borders of the Calais Pale to the challenge of some English commissioners in 1541; he answered that he was neutral between princes and that he must please both the French and the English.[11] In the same way, villages on the eastern border in the Argonne were able to play off the jurisdictions of

[7] L. Febvre, '*Frontière*: the Word and the Concept', in L. Febvre, *A New Kind of History from the Writings of Febvre*, ed. P. Burke (1973), 208–18; D. Nordman, 'Des limites d'Etat aux frontières nationales' in Nora, *Lieux de mémoire* II, ii, 50–9.

[8] L. Trénard (ed.), *Histoire des Pays-Bas français* (1972), 89.

[9] For an example of internal enclaves, see J. Richard, 'Royal "Enclaves" and Provincial Boundaries: the Burdundian *Elections*', in P. S. Lewis (ed.), *The Recovery of France in the Fifteenth Century*. The argument that linear frontiers were impossible is found in G. Dupont-Ferrier, 'L'incertitude des limites territoriales en France du XIIIᵉ au XVIᵉ siècle', *Académie des inscriptions et belles lettres: Comptes rendus* (Paris, 1942), 62–7. But see Guénée, 'Des limites féodales aux frontières politiques', 12.

[10] AN J 1017 fo. 7v (Puisieux), 192r (Sarton), 185r (Orville).

[11] Hertford and others to Henry VIII, 29 Jan. 1541, Historical Manuscripts Commission, *Calendar of the Manuscripts of . . . the Marquess of Bath, preserved at Longleat* IV, Seymour Papers (1968), (hereafter HMC *Bath MSS* IV), 16–18.

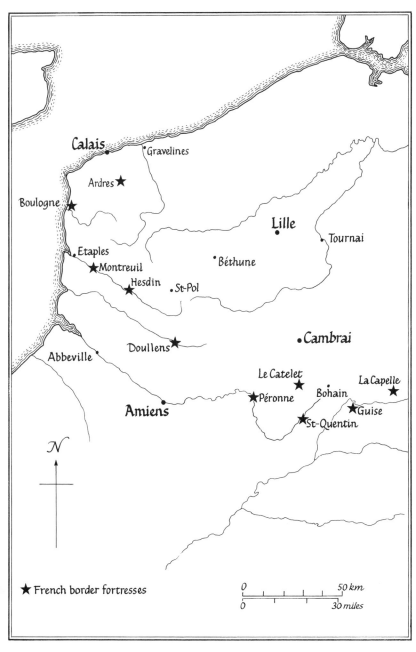

★ French border fortresses

0   50 km

0   30 miles

4   The frontier region

the kingdom and the Empire against each other in the lawsuits before the Parlement of Paris in the 1530s and 1540s.[12]

Modern negotiations for the delimitation of frontiers inherit the device of recourse to joint commissions of arbitration which were in existence by the sixteenth century,[13] but whereas most modern frontier disputes – in Africa, South America or the Middle East – concern areas where frontiers have seldom been clearly defined on the ground, the Franco-Netherlandish disputes of the sixteenth century involved frontiers which had existed for centuries, but over which the principal disputes had been in terms of feudal tenures. The latter were bound to affect the terms devised in treaties for frontier definition. This is an act of sovereignty *par excellence*; indeed, it is impossible to imagine the solidification of the early modern state without a drive to define its territory.[14] However, in sixteenth-century western Europe this had to take place within the context of an immensely complex feudal tradition which could not be ignored. The general tenor of negotiations was created by the military decisions which shaped the peace treaties, but the details could only be supplied by the interpretation in the light of feudal tenure.

The military decisions of the wars after 1521 imposed some clarification by ripping into the traditional tenurial relationships which had always accepted enclaves, and which had allowed the county of Saint-Pol, for instance, to be held of the Habsburgs by a French aristocratic family, the Luxembourgs (and their Bourbon successors). The period after 1521 saw a growing tension between the continuing respect for ancestral rights on the part of aristocratic landowners and a consciousness on the part of officials that these were incompatible with strategic necessity. Hence the long and often fruitless arbitration conferences about private suits. The French *procureur* at the border conferences of 1560 accused owners of property on the border who were subjects of the king of Spain of having always 'tasché à joindre lesd. fiefz nouvellement acquis à leurs terres principales et anciennes . . . et au moyen des guerres qui ont esté entre les deux princes ont changé de seigneur à leur appétit'.[15] The treaties of 1525 and 1529 forced new attempts to come to terms with this but, by breaking the ties between Artois and Flanders and the French

[12] H. Stein and L. Le Grand, *La frontière d'Argonne*, 1–5. See here the argument in terms of enclaves during the 1537 enquiry, 134–46.
[13] See neutral arbitration by Britain in the Argentina–Chile dispute of 1965 (see *Award of Her Majesty Queen Elizabeth II for Arbitration of a Controversy between the Argentine Republic and the Republic of Chile* (HMSO, 1966). The same principle of neutral arbitration was at work when Henry VIII was briefly arbitrator between France and the emperor over Crèvecoeur in the 1530s.
[14] Point made admirably in P. Sahlins, *Boundaries*, 2–3, 93–102, following the formulation of E. de Vattel in 1758.
[15] AN J 788 no. 1, unpag.

crown, they created new problems which were repeatedly addressed in the negotiations which accompanied the main treaties.

The *bailliage* of Hesdin is a characteristic problem in that many of its seigneurs were French or had interests in France. Garrisoned by Burgundian troops after 1492, it was already in danger by 1513 and fell into French hands in 1521, only to be snatched back by the peace of Cambrai in 1529. The 1530s saw attempts to upset this and in 1537 the French reoccupied Hesdin, though failing to hang on to Saint-Pol. The status quo was accepted in 1538 and 1544, but the Treaty of Cateau-Cambrésis finally determined the matter in Habsburg interests after the sack and destruction of the town and its replacement by a new fortress on a different site in 1553.

The impact of diplomacy on all this requires some understanding of the provisions made by the main treaties and the arbitration conferences that accompanied them. The Treaties of Madrid, Cambrai and Crépy were formulated along the same lines, sometimes word for word, and dealt, as far as we are concerned, essentially with the transfer of suzerainty over Artois from France to the emperor. There were, however, important differences which reflected differing agendas in each negotiation.

The French chancellor François Olivier noted in 1555 that the Treaty of Madrid 'est comme le pivot et fundement des deux autres traitez, qui ont esté pris et tirez mot à mot dudict traité de Madrid'.[16] It had, of course, registered the significant shift in power stemming from the French defeat at Pavia and forced concessions, for instance over Burgundy, which were unacceptable to France in the long run. A number of articles had specified the renunciation by Francis I of certain claims so as to remove future disagreements: article IX abandoned those to the *cité* of Arras, Tournai, Lille and Hesdin; V quitted the sovereignty of Artois. In XI the emperor in his turn abandoned claims to Péronne, the Somme towns, Ponthieu and the Boulonnais. Article XXXII restored property confiscated during the war and a number of special clauses (like XLI) enshrined the rights of the emperor's individual supporters. The preponderance of Imperial power was thus indicated, for the Somme towns were easily abandoned and only the interests of Imperial subjects were specifically mentioned.[17] The treaty attempted to clear up old quarrels, then, but could not last in the political circumstances of the 1520s.

---

[16] F. Léonard, *Recueil des Traitez de Paix* (6 vols., 1693) II, 591–2, 'Mémoire des differendz' for the conference at Marcq, 1555.

[17] Text in J. Dumont, *Corps universel diplomatique du droit des gens*, 8 vols. (Amsterdam, 1726–8) IV, i, 400–9. In the negotiations of 1525, Francis I argued that the emperor was giving up nothing since he held Lille-Douai-Orchies instead of Péronne and because Louis XI had paid for the Somme towns, see C. Weiss, *Papiers d'état du cardinal de Granvelle* I, 270–3.

There was scarcely time for the Treaty of Madrid to be put into full effect. Individuals pursued the restoration of their confiscated property, but war started again in 1528, to be terminated by a truce in July which applied to the northern frontier only. This was followed by a conference at Cambrai between local officials for the settlement of infractions and the restoration of confiscated property.[18]

The Treaty of Cambrai in August 1529 sought to establish a more permanent peace which could be acceptable to the French king by providing for the return of his sons and setting aside the Habsburg claim to Burgundy.[19] The frontier agreements were more precise: by article V, France specifically agreed to hand over Hesdin and its *bailliage* fifteen days after ratification of the treaty. Article VI introduced careful delimitations on the clauses concerning Artois and Flanders 'd'autant que par la généralité de ladite quittance et délaissement, se pourroient ci après trouver diverses difficultez'. In particular, VIII abandoned any French claims to a *droit de rachat* over the *châtellenie* of Lille (mentioned in the Franco-Burgundian treaty of 1498), IX definitively abandoned Tournai and its *droit de régalle* and X confirmed the abandonment of all rights to Arras except to the property of its bishopric in France. Most importantly, articles XI and XII carefully delimited the French abandonment of sovereignty over Artois: by XI France abandoned the goods of the Artois churches held in France, patronage of ecclesiastical foundations 'jaçoit qu'elles soient de fondation des Roys de France', of all those enclaved in Artois except Thérouanne and the homage of all fief-holders of the county and its enclaves where 'l'aide ordinaire a eu cours', a fateful and definitive phrase, including a number of villages in the Boulonnais which had formerly paid this:[20] (see map 5). Article XII then abandoned all claims to the *aide ordinaire*, formerly called the *composition d'Artois* levied at L 14,000. Article XIV confirmed the emperor's abandonment of the Somme towns, the Boulonnais and Guînes, but XV exempted from this the rights of the emperor over Tournehem, Andruicq and Bredenarde, as dependencies of Artois. Articles XVII and XVIII confirmed the judicial separation by transferring all personal cases involving the emperor's subjects in the *bailliages* of Amiens, Vermandois and Péronne to

---

[18] Margaret of Austria to Brienne, Ghent, 24 May 1526, AD Nord B 18903, no. 34638, on the restitution of his property and release of a monk of Mont-St-Jean. For the 1528 conference at Cambrai, see Torcy to Montmorency, 17 Sept. (1528), MC Chantilly L VIII fo. 211; Saveuse to same, 20 Sept., L X fo. 233: 'vous advisant toutesfoys ad ce qu'il me semble n'y ferons plus grant chose'; Belleforrière to same, 9 Oct., 7 Dec. L VI fo. 32, 64.

[19] Dumont, *Corps universel* IV, ii, 7–13.

[20] Ligny, Nédonchel, Aloste, Saint-Michel-en-Artois, Helly, Arguy, Avesnes, Estrailles, Marles, Sempy, Reques, Clenleu, Thiembronne, Neufville and Estrées. Attention should be drawn to the dual meaning of the word *enclave* in the sixteenth century: a detached piece of territory or simply land 'enclosed' in a jurisdiction. Much confusion arises otherwise.

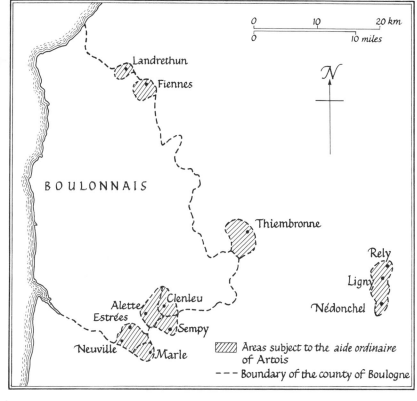

5 Villages and territories of the County of Boulogne subject to
the *aide ordinaire* of Artois. (Bocquet, pp. 126–7)

courts in the Low Countries. As for private matters, article XXXIX again
restored the Luxembourg-Fiennes family to Auxy and XLII provided for
arbitration of the claims to Crèvecoeur by another Imperial subject, the sieur de
Bèvres.

The Treaty of Cambrai is a document of prime importance for understanding
subsequent border negotiations, since it is the first major treaty to detail the
fundamental problems. Madrid had created the new frontier, but Cambrai
sought to implement it in detail and spelled out the limitations to French
concessions. As such, it gave French negotiators a basis from which to argue
their optimum case in the subsequent disputes, notably over the enclaves.
Neither side conceived of a clear linear frontier; they simply wished to
establish rights over as many enclaves as possible.

Crèvecoeur, a castle and lordship held of the bishopric of Cambrai, provides a useful point of departure for examining how the thinking of both sides developed. Its status posed the first major problem to be solved by interpreting the treaties after 1529, as it had been expressly mentioned. Although the hereditary claims of the house of Bèvres were strong, the French crown was reluctant to give it up. Technically in the Empire, France had acquired it in the fifteenth century by alienating part of the royal domain in a transaction by which Louis XI had rewarded the Grand Bastard of Burgundy for helping him at Péronne in 1468.[21] The Grand Bastard's son, Adolphe de Bèvres, had claimed it on his death but the French council confiscated it, because the transaction had involved the royal domain, and it was presented, as a fief of Cambrai, to the then governor of Picardy, La Gruthuse, and on his death in 1512 to Francis I, with first Gonnelieu and then La Hargerie as captains. The archbishops of Cambrai maintained their rights and the claim of Bèvres was registered in the Treaty of Madrid.

La Hargerie remained as captain into the 1530s. During the wars of the 1520s, he had twice to recapture Crèvecoeur from M. de Bèvres and reported to the court that its revenues, L 1,200–1,300 in peacetime, were wiped out by the costs of its garrison; he thought it could well be handed back during the negotiations of 1529.[22] However, it seems that the French crown continued to regard it as of potential strategic importance and, during the commission, including La Hargerie, which met at Cambrai at the end of 1529 the French refused to admit Bèvres's rights.[23] As late as 1543, La Hargerie was sent to harangue the three estates of the Cambresis at the castle of Crèvecoeur, threatening them should they refuse to supply the king's army at Landrecies.[24] Francis I's withdrawal finally gave Charles V the opportunity to garrison both Cambrai and Crèvecoeur and revenues henceforth went to Bèvres, now a powerful general in the emperor's service.[25] For France, rights to the town had been passed to the dauphin and then to Catherine de Medici as part of her dower,[26] and the treaty of 1559 finally specified that Henri II should have it, without prejudice to the residual rights of Bèvres's heirs.

---

[21] The history of the dispute over Crèvecoeur is given in AN J 794 no. 25/16, a summary dating from 1544–50.
[22] La Hargerie to Montmorency, 28 Aug. 1529, MC Chantilly L VI fo. 1. La Hargerie to Montmorency, 16 Oct. 1529, MC Chantilly L VIII fo. 296–7.
[23] La Hargerie to Berthereau, Crèvecoeur, 8 Dec. 1529, MC Chantilly L VI, fo. 275; same to same, 11 Jan. 1530, *ibid.*, L IV fo. 307.
[24] La Hargerie to Francis I, 15 Oct. (1543), BN fr. 3081 fo. 80–2.
[25] *L&P* XVIII, ii, 345, 384. AN J 794 no. 25/16. See also a *mémoire* on procedure for the settlement of the Crèvecoeur dispute, 25 Jan. 1545, BN fr. 17889 fo. 47–8: on appointment, unagreed, of an arbitrator; Francis I to commissioners at Cambrai, 30 Jan. 1545, *ibid.*, fo. 49–50: transferring the matter to ambassadorial level.
[26] Rabutin, *Commentaires* (SHF edn) I, 231.

The case of Crèvecoeur illustrates the predicament of a range of castles and major houses held in the border area – Autingues and Estrembecques in the Boulonnais, Auxi, Caumont and Contes along the Picard frontier – held by individuals whose loyalty to one side or another made their possession untenable; they would usually be seized at the outbreak of war and returned at the peace.

The county of Saint-Pol posed even more substantial and insoluble problems. Neither the treaty of 1525 nor that of 1529 mentioned it specifically, but Marie de Luxembourg was supposed to regain all her properties in the Low Countries, a case pressed by La Hargerie in 1528–9. It was the richest group of fiefs in Artois and of considerable strategic significance for the frontier. Could the Brussels government give it up? In 1529, it promised to do so, but Marie's properties in the Low Countries were engaged by Francis I as part of a deal to pay part of his ransom in landed revenues.[27] Though she got the rest of her lands back in 1531, Saint-Pol remained unredeemed.

Saint-Pol was covered by a safeguard from the French crown, but in 1537 the king took over the claim to the county from Marie's son François de Bourbon (in return for the duchy of Estouteville) and proceeded to invade the county, capturing and sacking Saint-Pol as well as Hesdin.[28] The French were driven out of Saint-Pol and the Truce of Bomy (30 July) provided for the withdrawal of French forces in return for the raising of the siege of Thérouanne and French agreement not to fortify any place in the county, while 'néantmoins y sera la Justice administrée comme il appartiendra'. This was a deliberately vague formulation to preserve rival claims, as was apparent in the subsequent conference at Cambrai (September–November).[29] It is clear that the French king continued to regard himself as legal possessor.[30]

The conference at La Fère in October 1538 for the working out of the Truce of Nice in the north simply provided for Marie de Luxembourg's restoration to

---

[27] See D. L. Potter, 'The Luxembourg Inheritance: the House of Bourbon and its lands in Northern France During the Sixteenth Century', *French History* 6 (1992), p. 32.
[28] Act of exchange between the king and the count of Saint-Pol, who had been created duke of Estouteville in 1534 on the occasion of his marriage to Adrienne d'Estouteville (père Ansèlme, *Histoire généalogique et chronologique de la maison de France, des pairs, grands officiers de la couronne et de la maison du roy* 9 vols. (1726–33) V, 549–66). The crown annexed the county in 1537 but lost control of it militarily. In 1538, it was paying François de Bourbon L 7,153 p.a., its estimated revenue (*CAF* VIII, 210, 31212). In 1541, there were plans for Saint-Pol's formal compensation (*ibid.*, VII, 307, 24754) and this was effected on 23 Oct. 1543 in the form of the county of Chaumont-en-Vexin and Sezanne (*ibid.*, IV, 520, 13443). This was for his lifetime only.
[29] Dumont, *Corps universel* IV, ii, 153; G. Ribier, *Lettres et mémoires d'estat* I, 58–9, 59–62; BN fr. 3044 fo. 59, 25 July 1537.
[30] Reply to articles sent by Dampont, 15 Aug. 1537, BN fr. 3035 fo. 43; Francis I to La Rochepot, 27 Aug. 1537, BN fr. 3035 fo. 59–60.

Enghien and for wartime compensation.[31] The issue of Saint-Pol had to be thrashed out at ambassadorial level, a way of putting it off until the Greek Calends, Francis I claiming that he had omitted to appoint revenue officials in the county simply to allow time for post-war restorations, Mary of Hungary denying his claims completely.[32] When France returned to the case in 1541, it was to press the need to work out the claims of Marie de Luxembourg's heirs, Saint-Pol and the duke of Vendôme, since the original exchange agreement had specified that the county should return to the family, and to argue that it was held of Boulogne rather than of Artois.[33] Shortly afterwards, the outbreak of war shelved the question.

Other border problems were raised after the war of 1536–7. Thérouanne was incontrovertibly French by all the treaties, but the extent of its *régalle*, or surrounding jurisdiction, was a matter of argument. Imperial authorities tried to prevent local peasants taking supplies there and issued wartime briefs infringing the bishop's jurisdiction. Allied to this was the question of whether the strategically placed abbey of Mont-Saint-Jean should be considered part of the *régalle*. All the peace treaties after 1537 wrestled with this without success; a conference in January 1539 referred it to ambassadorial level. These problems remained unsolved until the destruction of the city in 1553.[34] Difficulties over isolated enclaves in French or Imperial territory also come to the fore after 1537, particularly those of the county of Saint-Pol on the coast like Berck and Merlimont, increasingly subject to demands from French jurisdiction.[35]

The Treaty of Crépy (1544) more or less reiterated that of Cambrai, adding

---

[31] Truce of Nice: Dumont, *Corps universel* IV, ii, 169–70; F. Léonard, *Recueil des Traitez* II, 407; Capitulations of La Fère: BN fr. 17889, fo. 55–8, copy; *Ordonnances, François Ier* IX, no. 869; Dumont, *Corps universel* IV, ii. Francis I to Vendôme, 16 Dec. 1538, AM Amiens AA 12 fo. 192.

[32] Instructions to Castelnau, BN fr. 3916 fo. 238–9, 242–4, 258–69; Castelnau to Montmorency, Toledo, 6 Feb. 1539, BL Add. 18741 fo. 20–22, orig.: 'Touteffoys si lors que la tresve fust faicte les souldars de l'Empereur estoient dedans la ville de Saint-Pol, qu'il semble par lad. tresve chacun devroit demourer en la jouyssance et possession etc.' (passage omitted in Ribier's printed version). Francis I to Hellin, 22 Jan. 1539, BN fr. 3913, fo. 6–7: 'pour autant que considérant la paouvreté et désolacion dud. conté . . . '; Montmorency to same, 7 Feb., *ibid.*, fo. 11.

[33] 'Pour saitisfaire a l'escript puis naguères baillé par l'ambassadeur de l'empereur', Vienna, HHuStA, Frankreich, Varia 4, fo. 248–51: 'ne peut estre trouvé tropt estrange que l'on prétende led. conté de Sainct Pol estre tenu du conté d'Arthoys, veu qu'il a esté offert de monstrer promptement . . . qu'il est tenu du conté de Boullongne.'

[34] See *ibid.*, fo. 249: 'L'on a empesché les subgectz de ladicte Régalle de respondre et obéyr en lad. ville et cité de Thérouanne.'

[35] *Ibid.*, fo. 250 and Vienna, Frankreich, Varia 6 nachtrag fo. 26–9: the French claim that the dependencies of Saint-Pol were not held of Artois 'quant à la féodalité' and had always answered to the courts of France. For example of property at Verton, see AD Pas-de-Calais 12 J 190 no. 2 and for Waben, no. 56, fo. 39.

6 The county of Saint-Pol and its enclaves

the agreement for the marriage of the duke of Orléans as a means of settling the
problem of Milan.[36] All places taken since the Truce of Nice were to be
restored; full renunciation of French claims to Artois, Flanders, Lille and
Tournai were repeated and all obligations due from Artois (with the exception
of the *régalle* of Thérouanne and the Boulonnais villages paying the *aide
ordinaire*) again renounced. For his part, the emperor reiterated his renunciation of claims to Péronne, Boulogne, Ponthieu and the Somme towns (with the
exception of Tournhem and the Pays de l'Angle). All subjects were again to be
restored to their property; Marie de Luxembourg was now to regain Saint-Pol

---

[36] Léonard, *Recueil des Traitez* II, 430–48; Dumont, *Corps universel* IV, ii, 280–7.

as a fief held of the emperor and Hesdin was to remain French until a full agreement could be reached on compensation for it.

The now usual conference to flesh out the details of the treaty for frontier purposes was held at Cambrai at the end of the year and is the first to leave substantial records. All the problems already noted were raised and what emerges clearly is that the discussions were still largely concerned with feudal tenures and the difficulties faced by lords in obtaining *main levée* after the peace.[37] Only the major enclave difficulties were dealt with; the rest were impeded by destruction of records during the war and the final resolution of the envoys was to report back to their governments. The final act of 16 January 1545 failed to produce a settlement for Mont-Saint-Jean, referred the claims to Crèvecoeur to arbitration (that of Henry VIII had become unacceptable) and remitted the rest to ambassadorial level.[38] The one major settlement was that of Saint-Pol. In July 1545, the children of the now deceased François de Bourbon were put in possession under Imperial suzerainty and French claims reserved. A bill of L 200,000 for compensation of losses during Francis I's 'tenure' was drawn up, but the royal officials sought to minimise the destruction.[39]

Though the subject of the border enclaves was not directly addressed in 1544–5, it quickly became the major problem of border definition in the years down to 1560. By July 1546, Imperial officials were attempting to assert their jurisdiction in the dependencies of Ardres enclaved in Artois, and du Biez was ordered to defend them.[40] Only those villages subject to the *aide ordinaire* should obey the emperor; the numbers are indicated in table 8.1. There were at least twenty-eight enclaved wholly or in part in France and subject to the *aide*; those like Baillon-lez-Warloy, 4 leagues into France and near Corbie, were subject to constant French harassment.[41]

It seems unlikely that the blandishments of the Imperial authorities around Ardres in 1546 were a new departure. Rather, they seem to have brought to a

---

[37] Papers of this negotiation preserved in those of Jacques Mesnage, ambassador to the emperor, BN fr. 17889–90. On *mainlevée*, see fr. 17889, fo. 62–7, 6 Jan. 1545 and Léonard II, 450–5 (final articles, 16 Jan.).

[38] Léonard, *Recueil des Traitez* II, 450–5; Dumont, *Corps universel* IV, ii, 294. Complaints of the Imperial ambassador, Vienna HHuStA, Frankreich, Varia 6 fo. 23–9; Francis I to his commissioners, 30 Jan. 1545, BN fr. 17889 fo. 49–50.

[39] BN fr. 17889 fo. 245–6: case for *mainlevée* of county of Saint-Pol; Francis I to N. Brulart, 31 July, 10 Aug. 1545, AN J 795 no. 5 and 6; Du Mortier and the chancellor thought that the countess of Saint-Pol's men 'facent quelque menée pour trouver moyen de faire estimer à quelque pris excessif la démolicion . . . ', *ibid.*, no. 7. In the *conseil privé* in 1551 it was noted that the king's commissioners had reported L 53,000 damages (BN fr. 18153 fo. 249v).

[40] Francis I to du Biez, 24 July 1546, AN J 794 no. 25/34. The Burgundians had been trying to acquire this area since 1521 (La Fayette to Robertet, 16 Sept. (1521), BN fr. 2963 fo. 109–10).

[41] AN J 1017, fo. 89–90.

Table 8.1. *Border villages, 1545*

Bailliage etc.	No. of villages	No. 'limitrophe'	Encl. in France	Part encl.
Arras	78	15	2	2
Bapaume	39	9	3	5
Saint-Pol	144	12	10	3
Aire	1			1
Thérouanne, reg.	27			
Saint-Omer	34	6		2

Source: AN J 1017.

head a problem which had always been implicit in the treaties and had caused skirmishes since at least 1530. The Treaty of Cambrai had introduced the limitation of the definition of 'enclaves' by the stipulation concerning the *aide ordinaire*, and the Treaty of Crépy had tacitly accepted this.[42] The Imperial side tried to argue that, by silence, it had lapsed; the French relied on Crépy for claims to villages in the Boulonnais specifically abandoned by the emperor. In any case, as the border negotiators after the 1559 treaty realised, the tendency of villages on the Imperial side to pay slightly lower taxes and to enjoy marginally greater protection, especially in the late 1550s, produced an impulse for border villages to slip out of the French sphere where there was a debate.[43]

Attempts made by French taxation officials in 1532–3 to levy the *taille* on Imperial enclaves in France near Amiens and Péronne led to protests by the Imperial ambassador to Francis I and the latter's concession of an enquiry. This took place at Péronne in April 1533 and established the pattern whereby the taking of 'evidence' from local *laboureurs* and other substantial individuals provided the material for bolstering the government's case; in this instance, claims that the villages concerned were indeed subject to the French *taille*, even though surrounded by Artois villages not subject to it. One of them, Villers-au-Flos, was subject to a Burgundian lord who held his *seigneurie* of the French county of Néelle, but there were a few houses not part of the French kingdom and it was made out to be an isolated pocket of French territory subject to Imperial harassment in wartime.[44] In fact, the officials at Péronne continued in their pretensions, calling village representatives to hear about the assessment of the *taillon* in 1549; this led to another Imperial protest and, as

[42] Remon to Bochetel, 8 Nov. '1547' (*recte* 1546?), AN J 794 no. 25/34.
[43] AN J 788 no. 1: argument on Grandcourt – 'pource qu'elle n'estoit beaucoup si grande que celle qu'ilz paioient auparavant en France'.
[44] AN J 806 no. 13/16, copy of full transaction; Imperial protest, royal response, no. 31. J 806 no. 13/5.

was seen in the previous chapter, the French negotiators in 1560 sought to produce the tax rolls for the village as evidence.[45]

Diplomatic bargaining took the form of raising counter-claims, in this case over a village, Combles in the *bailliage* of Bapaume, where, even though the emperor was feudal lord of half the land, the French claimed that it was totally enclaved in French territory. The peasants had, since 1521, refused to pay taxes at Péronne and in 1545 the *procureur du roi* at Péronne told the border commissioners that they 'se disent estre Bourguignons' and no evidence was available that they had ever paid the French *taille*.[46] That the village was indeed subject to the *aide ordinaire* is confirmed by its claim for damages in 1545 and consequent remission of taxes by Brussels on the grounds that it was 'partie d'Artois et partie de France' and the villagers had had to abandon their homes.[47]

Even more complicated was the position of the *bailliage* of Hesdin, lost to the emperor and recaptured in 1537, consisting of 100 bourgs, villages, *censes* and hamlets in 52 parishes, as well as fiefs. Here, the problem by the 1540s was the enclaved villages of Artois within the *bailliage*. Consulted in 1546, Pierre Rémon, president of the Parlement of Paris, argued that the agreement of 1537 and Treaty of Crépy had placed all enclaved villages here in French jurisdiction.[48] In 1547 and 1548, the Imperial ambassador in France complained of attempts made by French officials to exercise authority in villages where jurisdiction was debatable. The French governor, Rasse, listed forty villages of ambiguous status, some where he admitted that Hesdin had no rights and others where land was held of the *bailliage* or of the priory of Saint-Georges near Hesdin, and could therefore be argued to be within its jurisdiction.[49] From this survey it becomes clear why the French possession of Hesdin introduced such a degree of instability into border arrangements, since it was virtually impossible to establish a clear tenurial separation from Artois in law. The Imperial recapture and destruction of Hesdin in 1553, therefore, removed a major obstacle to an agreed frontier.

Similarly, the position of the group of villages south of Ardres posed a problem of jurisdiction that was a constant irritant. The emperor claimed them as part of the *châtellenie* of Tournehem, totally enclaved in his territory, the French as part of the county of Guînes. In 1547, the French *conseil privé*

---

[45] AN J 806 no. 13/15, complaints of Imperial ambassador, 1549; AN J 788 no. 1, fo. 13v. In 1557 Coligny decided to treat Villers as an enemy village since the Burgundians were using it 'pour en tirer toute la commodité' (to Humières, 27 Feb. 1557, BN fr. 3148 fo. 55–8).

[46] AN J 806 no. 13/11, reports of royal officials; J 794 no. 25/22, two letters of 29 Nov., 11 Dec. 1545.

[47] AN J 1017 fo. 169v.

[48] Remon to Bochetel, 8 Nov. 1546/7, AN J 794 no. 25/34.

[49] AN J 806 no. 13/14 and 15.

asserted that they had never paid the *aide ordinaire* and that the emperor's men should keep out,[50] but Henri II wrote to the governor of Ardres in 1550 of 'entreprinses, usurpations, tors et domages' committed by Imperial agents there because of the ill-defined frontier.[51] These had included pretensions in the barony of Zelthun and attempts to prevent French officials from making use of forests in the county of Guînes.[52] This was to be a stretch of the frontier closely examined by the commissioners of 1559–60.

One further area of dispute along the frontier may illustrate the kind of difficulties likely to emerge: that between France and the English territories in Calais. While the latter had a fairly clearly defined water-course frontier with Flanders to the east, with France the frontier was formed by the many water-channels between Guînes and Ardres and the Saint-Inglevert hills. The most acrimonious problems concerned the disputes over the stretch of soggy pasture roughly triangular in shape called 'la Cauchoire' or 'the Cowswade' to the north of Ardres. The deterioration of relations between England and France in the early 1540s and the decision by the French crown substantially to refortify Ardres in 1541–2 forced the issue into high relief. The consequent well-documented negotiations between Oudart du Biez and the earl of Hertford are instructive on attitudes to the frontier during the period.[53]

The Anglo-French Treaty of 1360 had conceded the county of Guînes to England but, after a period of rule by the Grand Bastard of Burgundy in the mid-fifteenth century, it had in practice been divided between France and England. In 1541, the French claimed that the river which formed the frontier and thus determined possession of the Cowswade had changed course and that over it, some years before and on English sufferance, they had built a bridge. Now the English wished to demolish or block it. Old documents were examined and an expedition to view the site was mounted in which the French showed where they claimed the old course ran and the English denied the case. Maps were drawn up and the French offered to produce witnesses from elderly residents or neutral Burgundians. The English, however, warily refused to accept such witnesses 'specially whenn the proufit of the thinges in contention redoundith to them selfes' and knew that one Burgundian witness had told

---

[50] Act of *conseil privé*, Fontainebleau, 8 Nov. 1546/7, AN J 794 no. 25/34. In reply to a letter of du Roeulx to La Rochepot, 8 Oct. 1547, BN fr. 18153 fo. 15 claiming, after 'oculaire inspection' that Zelthun, Recq and Leulinghen 'sont evidentement enclavemens dud. Arthois non accessibles de quelque part que ce soit de France'.

[51] R. Dary to La Rochepot, 12 Feb. 1550, Vienna, HHuStA, Frankreich, Varia 7, *nachtrag* fo. 10; Henri II to Blérancourt, 29 Nov. 1550, AN J 794 no. 25/34.

[52] AN J 795 no. 25/36; J 795 no. 30.

[53] For main documentation, see PRO SP1/164 fo. 156–222 *passim* (*L&P*, XVI, 465, 500, 502, 512, 517, 518, 532, 538, 543, 547, 562) and SP1/165 fo. 36–41 (*L&P*, XVI, 637), *procès-verbal* and HMC *Bath MSS*, IV, 16-25.

marshal du Biez 'the Cowswade is so necessarie for Ardre that ye may not forbere it and therefore in any wise stike to it'. The conference broke up without agreement and the issue remained unresolved until the fall of Calais.[54] Similarly, the 1546–7 surveys by Estrées and Coligny of the course of the river Liane, frontier between the French and the English at Boulogne, proved fruitless, since they depended on rival quite valid interpretations of the Anglo-French Treaty of that year, some giving the French access to Ardres, others not. In practice, the line of demarcation had to remain undefined.[55] In general, these border surveys and negotiations all recall the attempts, for instance by French and Burgundian officials, to agree the course of the Escaut frontier in 1464 (there were unresolved disputes over which were tributaries and which the true source) and between French and Lorraine commissioners over border villages in the first half of the sixteenth century, again unresolved.[56] They look forward to the massively detailed negotiations of 1559–60.

During the negotiations which took place during the truce of 1555–6, the French sought to reopen the whole border issue by denouncing the previous treaties based on Madrid as 'inique', since the French king had been forced to alienate parts of his kingdom.[57] The course of the conflict in its final phase, however, did not allow the French to maintain such high claims. The final terms agreed at Cateau-Cambrésis in April 1559, while maintaining the basic provisions of 1525–44, sought to put an end to a generation of accumulated frontier disputes.[58] Henri II was to regain Crèvecoeur but Hesdin (now rebuilt on a new site) was to remain with the Habsburgs in perpetuity. Thérouanne remained a desolate ruin, in practice within Imperial territory but with French claims left open, its bishopric divided between Saint-Omer and Boulogne. The issue of Mont-Saint-Jean was referred to arbitrators. As far as property claims were concerned, they were nearly all settled in the interests of the hereditary owners; Marie de Bourbon regained Saint-Pol and the count of Egmont the French lands of the Luxembourg-Fiennes family.

In general terms, then, Cateau-Cambrésis provided a viable solution to frontier problems, but it must be stressed that it could not define the frontier in

---

[54] Hertford and Carne to Henry VIII, 13 Feb. 1541, SP1/164 fo. 218–22 (*L&P* XVI, 538).

[55] BN fr. 6637 fo. 293–4. For other documents on this, see SAP Amiens, 59 II, no. 52 and 53, draft; Du Biez's report that the river source claimed by the English would be 'trèsgrand préjudice du Roy, tant pour la perte du pais que pour l'incommodité de radvitailler et aller à Ardre sans passer sur les terres de l'Empereur ou du Roy d'Angleterre' (13 Nov. 1546).

[56] Points made by R. Mousnier in *La France de 1492 a 1559* (Cours de Sorbonne, n.d.) I, p. 5–7. See in particular E. Duvernoy, 'Un règlement de frontière entre la France et la Barrois en 1500', *Annales de l'Est*, 1888, 543–65; H. Stein and L. Le Grand, *La frontière d'Argonne*, 149–79.

[57] 'Mémoire de differendz', 1555, in Léonard, *Recueil des Traitez* II, 491–2.

[58] Léonard, *Recueil des Traitez* II, 537–55; BL Add. 20851, copy. J. Russell, *Peacemaking in the Renaissance*, 133–223.

detail. Disputes which had arisen since 1544 and the endemic problems of claims and counter-claims to villages were referred to a conference scheduled to meet at Cambrai in September. Meanwhile, violent incidents continued to aggravate relations and show how difficult it was to bring a war to a definitive end.

The two negotiating teams were led by Sénarpont for France and Molembaix for the Burgundians, but in practice the work was done by less exalted lawyers, Noircarmes and, for France, Jacques de Mesmes, sieur de Roissy, a bad-tempered and ailing septuagenarian.[59] The French immediately refused to discuss Mont-Saint-Jean and went on to table all the accumulated disputes over the enclaves. The French *procureur du roi* launched a massive position paper outlining the French case.[60] There were two categories of dispute: (1) the supposed Artois villages enclaved in French territory, and (2) villages along the frontier which were claimed as held mediately or immediately of the king of Spain. For their part, the Habsburg representatives wanted, in effect, a wider definition of the status of enclaves and pressed for an interpretation of the terms of the series of treaties since 1529 mentioning the *aide ordinaire* of Artois, which would give them most of the places in dispute.[61] In other words, all enclaves should be ironed out except those where the *aide ordinaire* clause privileged the Habsburg case (arguably most of them). There could be little hope of compromise, but the necessity of trying to reach an agreement initiated full enquiries and generated massive documentation, which gives an extra-ordinary insight into the state of the frontier and attitudes towards it.

Both sides agreed on 20 September 1559 to go out, take evidence and view the land. Mesmes for the French and Pierre Grenet for the Burgundians led the parties.[62] The *procès-verbaux* of both sides, with drafts and copies of title deeds, have survived[63] and, with their attached maps, constitute one of the

---

59 C. Thelliez, 'Après la paix de Cateau-Cambrésis de 1559: négotiations pour fixer les limites', *Standen en Landen* 48 (1969), 77–91, esp. 89, based on the Habsburg copy of the *procès-verbal*, BM Cambrai MSS 1423, 1423 bis (1254 pp.), the most complete to survive. Thelliez's study is a brief sketch of the document. For a comparison with the Franco-Spanish frontier negotiations of 1659–60, see P. Stahlin, *Boundaries*, 25–60.
60 Two copies: AN J 788 no. 1; J 789 no. 15.
61 Thelliez, 'Après la paix de Cateau-Cambrésis', 84–5. The French *procureur* said that the problem 'deppend premièrement de la deffinition et intelligence de ce mot enclavement' (J 788 no. 1).
62 'Acte passé entre Messieurs les députez' AN J 794 no. 25/13; J 788 no. 1.
63 The Habsburg *procès-verbal* BM Cambrai MS 1423 bis. There are original depositions in AN J 788 no. 3/4–12 and a fair copy of them in J 788 no. 2. The French *procès-verbal*, of the border survey only, is preserved in a copy in the Brienne collection, now BL Add. 30705. Add. 30707 is a copy of an inventory of documents submitted by the French. These seventeenth-century copies have, for convenience, been used here. Examples of topographical description: description of the little valley of the Warnelle that falls into the Authie near Raye. There are three or four houses 'estant sur le haut par diamettre vis à vis de lad. forest (de Raye) qu'il a

earliest substantial topographical and descriptive surveys of any area of France.[64] While seeking to establish the right to as much territory as possible, it is clear that the French were thinking not so much in terms of blocks of territory as of rights to seigneuries and villages. As we have already seen, seigneurial claims did not always correspond to the demands of royal policy and this created a certain ambiguity of attitude. The evidence can hardly be described as impartial, since those who were asking the questions were seeking to establish a case, as the English had pointed out in an earlier attempt to do this on a smaller scale in 1541. As in the enquiries of 1533, testimony was shaped and the royal officials and wealthy farmers interrogated were to some extent stage-managed. They do, however, reveal much about life on the frontier.

The perambulation of the frontier began at Villers-au-Flos on 3 March 1560 and took about six weeks.[65] It seems to have been the mid-sixteenth century when the crown began to realise the value of map-making in the prosecution of policy. The map of France by Orance Fine of 1525 and the earliest diocesan map, of Le Mans in 1539, paved the way. Special survey maps had been drawn up for enquiries into the îles de Saintonge in 1543 and the 1552 investigations into the productivity and boundaries of Rouergue, but have not survived.[66] During the 1559–60 survey, twelve detailed maps were drawn for the French side by the Amiens painter-architect Zacharie de Cellers.[67] This was despite the argument of the Burgundians that, since the investigation was to be by 'inspection occulaire et information verballe', maps were unnecessary. The maps, among the earliest of their type to survive, ranged from surveys of large areas to detailed plans of individual villages in dispute and show both a surprising degree of detail and reasonable accuracy. That of Terremesnil

---

dit estre le village de Fondeval tenu de l'abbaie de Dammartin, distant dud. lieu de La Broie de trois quartz de lieues demonstrans aucuns bois estans un peu plus loing sur led. haut. Outre disoit que le village de La Chapelle, Guinchy and Regnaville estoient au delà asses près de lad. forest par la situation desquels lieux entendoit démontrer lesd. village du Ray, Rapaissy et Dompierre estre enclavées dedans le bailliage dud. Hesdin' (BL Add. 30705 fo. 56r).

[64] For a slightly earlier case of a survey, of productive resources, in the province of Rouergue, see J. Bousquet, *Enquête sur les commodités du Rouergue en 1552*, especially the analogous survey of *limites*, 222-4.

[65] AN J 789 no. 2.

[66] F. de Dainville, *Cartes anciennes de l'église de France* (1956); de Dainville, *Le langage des géographes* (1964); A. Libaut, *Histoire de la cartographie* (1964); R. Mousnier, *Les institutions de la France sous la monarchie absolue* I, 533; D. Buisseret, 'The Cartographic Definition of France's Eastern Boundary in the Early Seventeenth Century', *Imago Mundi* 36 (1984), 72–80. J. Bousquet, *Enquête sur les commodités du Rouergue*, 22–4, 27.

[67] These maps, signed, are in AN J 789 no. 1–14. Cellers was a draughtsman, especially on works like the building of the great new Guyencourt bastion (e.g. AM Amiens BB 27, fo. 73–9, 15 Oct. 1551). The Habsburg draughtsman was Hugues le Febvre of Arras (BL Add. 30705 fo. 6v).

reveals the problem vividly, with practically every plot labelled 'France' or 'Saint-Pol' and the village main street going in and out of France several times.[68] Surveying techniques involved essentially riding to suitable high ground to view the villages and woods claimed by one side or another. Distances were estimated visually in 'lieues' (approx. 3 miles) or, occasionally for places closer together, in 'traits d'arbaleste'.[69]

Only two or three stretches of the frontier will be considered in detail in order to illustrate the assumptions of the participants. Taking those supposedly in the *bailliage* of Bapaume first, business started on 5 March, when the commissioners rode out from Bapaume to Villers-au-Flos. It seemed encircled by Burgundian villages, but this could not be verified by available surveying techniques and the French claimed that it could be reached directly from French territory across ploughed fields.[70] The case of Grandcourt was different, involving tenure. Here, the Burgundians claimed that most of the sixty hearths and the church were subject to an abbey in Artois; the French claimed that most of the property was owned by the French sieur de Miraumont and that proclamations for the king of France took place at the church portal.[71] Yet another variant existed at Baillon, near Warloy, well inside French territory, where the Burgundians tried to find witnesses that this place, no more than an extension of Warloy, was free of French taxes, while the French denied the distinction.[72]

Moving on to the Doullens area, we find that the village of Souich was in contention, with the French producing its tax rolls and claiming that its houses were held of both France and Saint-Pol. A witness was available to swear that one could walk from a nearby French village across the fields to a 'manoir' held of France at the entry to the village. The pillory, church and cemetery were on French ground and French proclamations read there, though one witness revealed that 'aucuns habitans tenans le party dudict comte murmuroient, soustenu au contraire par ceulz qui sont du party de France'. So divided, in fact, was the village that the house of the *lieutenant* was half French, half Saint-Pol. The Burgundians argued that the French properties were isolated from French ground.[73]

[68] Terremesnil was the '4ᵉ figure', now AN J 789 no. 5 (signed and dated 17 March 1560).
[69] E.g. at Villers 'avons esté conduits et menez sur la main gauche et en montant quelque peu contre mont nous sommes arrestez sur un petit tertre. Nous a esté montré le village de Baucourt sur la main gauche ... distant ... d'environ demye lieue ...' (BL Add. 30705 fo. 8r).
[70] BL Add. 30705 fo. 6v–16v (5–8 March 1560).
[71] BL Add. 30705 fo. 24.　[72] BL Add. 30705 fo. 28v–31r.
[73] AN J 788 no. 2; 'avons trouvé une potence en laquelle avoit un homme pendu depuis deux mois, laquelle potence le procureur du Roy Catholicque nous a dit estre planté sur les limites du conté de Saint-Paul' (BL Add. 30705 fo. 37r). 'Un pays qui est du comté de Saint Paul et illec sur le milieu du chemin où il y a un arbre et un poteau en forme de pillory qu'on a dit estre assis en terre de France' (*ibid.*, fo. 38r).

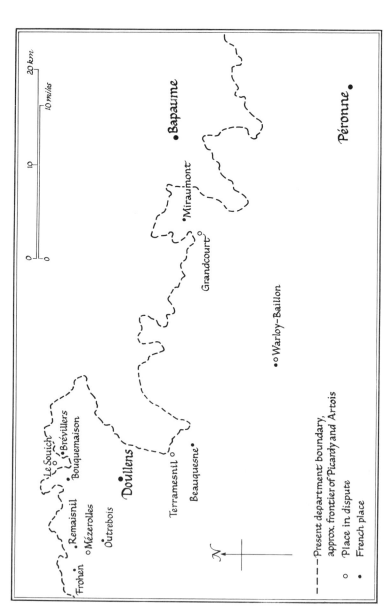

7 Border survey, 5–22 March 1560

Places on map:
Frohen
Remaisnil
Mézerolles
Outrebois
Le Souich
Brévillers
Bouquemaison
Doullens
Terramesnil
Beauquesne
Warloy-Baillon
Grandcourt
Miraumont
Bapaume
Péronne

20 km
10 miles
10
0

N

– – – – – Present department boundary,
approx. frontier of Picardy and Artois
o Place in dispute
• French place

Further west still, in the valley of the Authie, villages in dispute like La Broie, Waulx, Haravesnes, Dompierre and Rapessy, local witnesses were found who claimed in a straightforward way that they were French, while the Burgundians claimed them as enclaves of the new Burgundian *bailliage* of Hesdin. Elsewhere, the position of Berck and Merlimont, already discussed, still proved insoluble. They were undoubtedly detached enclaves of the county of Saint-Pol, but had also paid dues to Montreuil.[74] Other places like Vron and Argoules were no longer isolated enclaves since the Burgundian recapture of Hesdin and were ostensibly simple problems, though even at Vron the village was divided down the middle.[75]

In fact, the area with the largest number of villages in dispute was the land between Ardres and Tournehem already discussed. Evidence was taken there between 9 and 17 April 1560. The French had claimed Tournehem as a *châtellenie* of Guines throughout the Wars and in 1521 and 1542 had tried to take it.[76] All the places on map 9 marked with a broken cross or encircled dot were claimed by the Burgundian side, but the latter as enclaves of Artois in French territory. The French case was to try to show that as many of these places as possible came within the *ressort* of French courts at Ardres, had contributed to the French war supply or, if they were enclaves, had not paid the *aide ordinaire*. As in most of these places, documentation was in short supply. The seigneur at Eclemy swore that he had done homage to the 'most Christian king', but unfortunately his papers had been lost in the wars.[77]

In the same area, the French claimed Alquines, a village strategically placed between the Boulonnais and Ardres, by finding local witnesses to the existence of a road over the *fosse Boulonnaise* common to both sides where all comers could gather wood and where French, English and Burgundians could take prisoners in time of war.[78] The priest of Locquin claimed to know the road and

[74] BL Add. 30705 fo. 55–60; J 788 no. 2.

[75] BL Add. 30705 fo. 63r–v, 67r.

[76] Chabannes to capt. of Tournehem, 17 Aug. 1521, BN fr. 3059 fo. 80. It belonged to descendants of the Grand Bastard of Burgundy, see J. de Pas, 'Notes pour servir à la statistique féodale dans l'estendue de l'ancien bailliage de Saint-Omer', *MSA Morinie* 34 (1926), 769, n. 1; A. Courtois, 'Rapports, declarations et reliefs . . . mouvans des chasteau et chastellenie de Tournehem', *BSA Morinie* 1852, 2nd fasc., 58–64. In 1559–60, thirty villages were claimed by the Burgundians as having been given up at Cambrai and Crépy (denied by the French). Twenty-six of them were on the borders of Ardres, Boulonnais and Tournehem. The Burgundians also claimed here thirteen places enclaved in France that they said were held of Philip II mediately or immediately. See AN J 788 no. 2 for list. For disputes on the barony of Zelthun, see J 795 no. 25/35 and 36.

[77] AN J 788 no. 3/6 fo. 2v, orig. dep. of Julien de Beauvais, *garde des munitions* at Ardres re: Landrethun. *Ibid.*, fo. 4r, orig. dep. of Jacques de La Caurrye, sieur d'Eclemy aged 33: 'dict qu'il est né et natif du villaige de Crézecq près Loche'.

[78] AN J 788 no. 3/6 fo. 5, 9v, 17v.

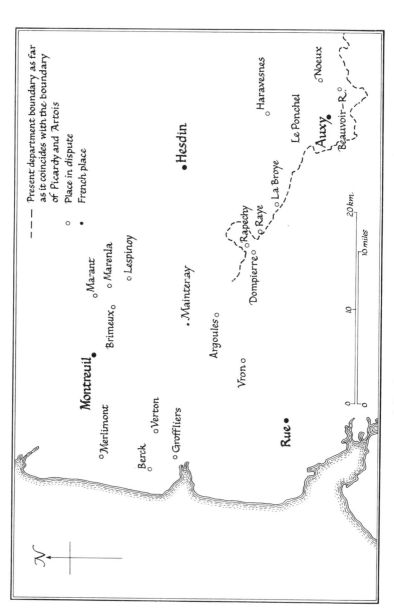

8 Border survey, 23 March–6 April 1560

Map legend:
- - - Present department boundary as far as it coincides with the boundary of Picardy and Artois
○ Place in dispute
● French place

N

Places shown on map:
Merlimont, Berck, Verton, Groffliers, Montreuil, Brimeux, Marant, Marenla, Lespinoy, Mainteray, Hesdin, Argoules, Vron, Rue, Dompierre, Rapechy, Raye, La Broye, Haravesnes, Le Ponchel, Auxy, Beauvoir-R., Noeux

Scale: 0, 10, 20 km; 10 miles

the place 'like his Ave Maria'.[79] The point of all the effort was to establish that Alquines could not be an enclave of Artois. For France, it was important to maintain communications between Montreuil and Ardres that way. The witnesses also reveal incidentally that they knew, or thought they knew, exactly when they were on French or Burgundian territory, thus confirming Guénée's characterisation of mediaeval boundaries.

There were many other villages around Ardres where the French orchestrated their evidence to show that they could not be reached from Artois without crossing French territory. Those around Yeuse and Polincove are cases in point.[80] In the case of the latter, mention was made many times of access by a great road running from Ardres to Thérouanne and descriptions of it reveal a curious state of affairs on the border. This road attracted much attention during the enquiries. It had been of prime importance when Thérouanne was an isolated outpost which had to be supplied from Montreuil or Ardres. Curiously, though, even in 1560, years after the annihilation of Thérouanne, the French sought to vindicate their rights to the road; presumably it was thought to be of potential value. Usually called by witnesses the 'chemin réal', it had always been freely available to the French – soldiers and civilians alike – during war and peace and eventually joined the 'chaussée Brunehault', the old Roman road from Boulogne. Deemed to be 40 feet wide, it provided, according to the French, a zone of safe haven for them, and the emperor's subjects were liable to capture on it during war. One witness claimed even to remember officials taking provisions to Thérouanne in 1536, untouched by the emperor's men lying in wait to capture those who strayed from the path.[81] That the road always enjoyed this degree of protection in time of war is difficult to believe, though it was certainly privileged in peacetime. The Burgundian representatives claimed that it was used equally by the emperor's subjects even in time of 'trève non communicative', as after the Truce of Bomy in 1537.[82]

The border commissioners got to the end of their travels at Boulogne late in April and on 3 May 1560 the French declared they had finished taking evidence; all that remained was the collation of title deeds. Little time remained as a deadline of three months had been set for business and there were last-minute quibbles raised about what had actually been seen. No more could be agreed and it was decided to meet at Péronne on 25 June to hand over the inventories of documents.[83] It seems as though the participants had wearily decided simply to acquit their duty and leave decisions for further talks. A final

---

[79] AN J 788 no. 3/6 fo. 10v.
[80] AN J 788 no. 3/6 fo. 2r (J. de Beauvais), 11r (C. Plevault, *greffier* of Ardres), 22r (Ancel).
[81] AN J 788 no. 3/6 fo. 1 (J. de Beauvais on activities of A. Le Vadre, *bailli* of Ardres).
[82] AN J 787 no. 8 (26 April 1560).
[83] AN J 787 no. 3; BL Add. 30705 fo. 119–26.

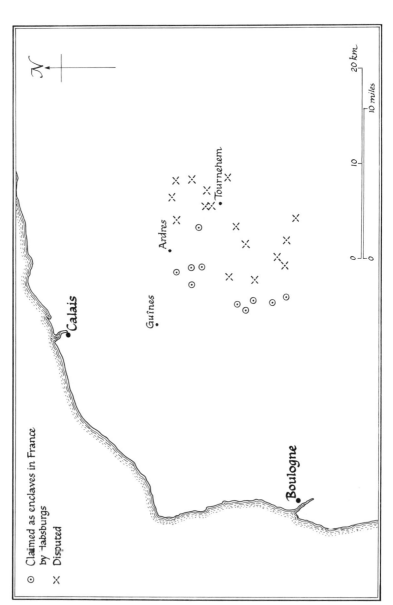

9 Border survey, 9 April–5 May 1560

procès-verbal drawn up at the end of 1561 left all matters 'en la discretion de ceux qui auront charge de continuer les communications encommenchées'.[84] Thereafter, the state of affairs existing in 1559 remained frozen, somewhat forgotten during the strife of the following decades.

The disputes of the first half of the sixteenth century and their culmination in the great survey of 1560 reveal certain assumptions about the nature of the frontier. First, the negotiations of 1559–60 stemmed from an agreement in principle, followed by the drawing of maps and the identification of the frontier physically on the ground, where possible. It was assumed that such a frontier did indeed exist, though it may have been difficult to elucidate. Most of the complications were caused by the complexities introduced by the continued acceptance of feudal jurisdictions. Even so, both sides sought to show how man-made or natural features could mark the frontier and in doing so indicate that the conventions, noted by Bernard Guénée in the twelfth century for marking boundaries, were still in force. At Bainghen in the Boulonnais, a witness claimed that the line between the counties of Boulogne and Guînes could be identified 'à coup d'oeil' in 'deux bornes plantées et regardans à droicte ligne l'une et l'autre de la haulteur de la ceinture d'un homme faisans séparation des contez'.[85] Near Villers-au-Flos, the Burgundians pointed out 'un petit hurt' called 'le trou béranger' near the main road and a wooden cross set in a stone block all marking the 'separation' between France and Artois. At Souich, two border stones facing each other marked the line between Saint-Pol and the 'terres de France'. The abbé Thelliez actually identified a hexagonal stone erected in 1578 to mark the border at Crèvecoeur.[86] Sometimes, pillories and gallows were held as valid symbols of jurisdiction and appeared on maps. The territory of Maizerolles was held by the French to extend 'jusqu'à une hauld ou borne', and by the Burgundians at 'quelqu'autre chemin'. Elsewhere, main roads could be used to mark the border. At Grandcourt, the French claimed that the 'chemin des mallades' marked the frontier of France.[87] Identifiable frontier markers also served the purpose of providing neutral ground. The cross at Villers was called 'la pièce du Mesnil' and provided a place 'la où les subiets d'une parte et d'autre s'assemblent pour communiquer tant pour le fait de leurs marchandises

[84] C. Thelliez, 'Après la paix de Cateau-Cambrésis', 90. On further talks in 1563, which produced no result, concerning the border between Calais and Gravelines, see *procès-verbal*, BL Add. 30702.

[85] B. Guénée, 'Des limites féodales aux frontières politiques', in Nora, *Lieux de Mémoire* II, ii, 15; P. Turpin, 'La survivance dans les noms de lieux de la notion de limite', *Revue du Nord*, 17 (1932); AN J 788 no. 2, fo. 140r–v.

[86] BL Add. 30705 fo. 9v (Villers); fo. 38v–39r (Souich); Thelliez, 'Après la paix de Cateau-Cambrésis', 87.

[87] BL Add. 30705 fo. 43r–44r (Maizerolles); fo. 21v (Grandcourt).

comme pour contracter entre eux chacun en temps de tresve communi-
catives'.[88]

Such assumptions, however, were undermined by a determination to use the
evidence of feudal tenures to prove cases and also by the sheer impossibility,
with the map-making techniques then available, of reaching an agreement
when both sides naturally sought to maximise their holdings. As for published
maps showing frontiers, from Orance Fine in 1525 to Ortelius's *Theatrum
Orbis Terrarum* of 1570 (including one map of the whole of Picardy), the line
was drawn only crudely. The argument of contiguity – that where a place in
dispute abutted or was near by a village in one's own jurisdiction, its valid
possession was proved – stemmed naturally from the problem of enclaves and
was too imprecise to allow a clear linear frontier. Nevertheless, the attempt at
detailed map-making in 1560, however flawed it may have been, marks an
important advance. The attempt at a survey was a genuine one and constituted
the earliest attempt to define, or perhaps even discover, a frontier of France
with a degree of clarity. Daniel Nordman has argued from the different
perspective that in terms of image, 'vers 1550–1560, la longue et lente genèse
des limites, pour la France, est à peu près achevée'.[89] It is perhaps easier to
argue that it was just beginning.

That this attempt was made on the Picard frontier seems above all to be a
response to the demands of the nascent state structures of the sixteenth century,
however rudimentary they may have been. Forged in the course of war and
military change, such structures demanded a much higher degree of clarity
in the definition of national territory than had been possible before. The
ambiguity of the situation stemmed from the legal framework in which
negotiations took place and the absence of a suitably developed structure of
international law. Frontier definition still in the end came down to the exchange
of title deeds and the plotting of *mouvances*, an art in which the property
lawyers were consummate but which could not provide answers for international relations. In essence, this was because, as Peter Sahlins has pointed
out, the ancien régime state, especially in the sixteenth century, was 'something
less than a territorial one', in other words its concept of the linear frontier was
permeated by a notion of sovereignty over subjects rather than over territory.[90]
In the north on the frontier with Artois, the problem was further compounded
by the fact that, whereas in other frontier disputes the crown usually confronted

---

[88] BL ADD. 30705 fo. 9v (Villers). Other examples: 'La justice à quatre pilliers' at La
Broie (fo. 55v); 'la justice estant sur un montagne' at Brimeu (fo. 71v); pillory at Souich
(fo. 38r).
[89] D. Nordman, 'Des limites d'Etat aux frontières nationales', in Nora, *Lieux de mémoire* II, ii,
35.
[90] P. Sahlins, *Boundaries*, 6.

the appeal to *mouvance* with its own *souveraineté*,[91] the peculiar international situation stemming from the treaties of 1525–59 forced it to rely on *mouvance* and *enclavemens* for its case.

Some major issues of the region, like Saint-Pol and Crèvecoeur, could be settled by time and usage, but the terms of reference provided by the peace treaties did not as yet provide a structure for understanding or constructing a mutually agreed linear frontier, though as far as international law was concerned, the principles of 1559 remained the definitive settlement of the Picard frontier until the outbreak of war with Spain in 1635. Anomalies were therefore bound to continue and could be settled only by slow adjustment during the succeeding generations. It took the rest of the history of the ancien régime for the two conflicting notions of the frontier, linear and jurisdictional, to evolve into a line on the map.

---

[91] B. Guénée, 'Des limites féodales aux frontières politiques', in Nora, *Lieux de Mémoire*, II, ii, 26–7.

CONCLUSION

The general peace treaty was signed and proclaimed at Le Cateau on 3 April 1559. The day before, Sansac, the governor of Picardy, announced the news to Amiens and on 7 April a great service in the cathedral was followed by a general procession. On 5 April the king had issued from Coucy a manifesto against the robberies and exactions of his soldiers, committed to his 'trèsgrand regret', in terms that echoed the denunciations of military abuses throughout the wars.[1] The demobilisation of forces was not markedly different from that following earlier treaties: reductions in garrisons took place only in stages and work on fortifications was slowed down over the course of 1559. In April 1559, there could have been little to indicate that this was any more than another pause in the seemingly endless dynastic wars.[2]

Two factors in reality turned the treaty of 1559 into something different: first, the financial exhaustion which had pushed both sides to the conference table remained a determinant; secondly, the far-reaching political upheavals in France stemming from the sudden death of Henri II froze the international compromise. That monarch had made known as soon as the treaty was sealed his desire to deal conclusively with heresy, but similar plans had been

---

[1] Sansac to Amiens, 2 April 1559, AM Amiens AA 14 fo. 158; Henri II to *bailli* of Amiens, 5 April 1559, AD Somme B 1 fo. 20; Sénarpont to same, 6 May 1559, *ibid.*, fo. 23r (on provisions to report infractions of the proclamation).
[2] Coligny to Amiens, 6 June 1559, AM Amiens AA 14 fo. 163; Francis II to *bailli* of Amiens, 10 Dec. 1559, AD Somme B 1 fo. 34r; to *sénéchal* of Boulogne, 10 Dec., AD Pas-de-Calais 9B 2 fo. 114r; to Sénarpont, 8 Aug. 1560, *ibid.*, fo. 147r. In the summer of 1560, with war in Scotland still a possibility, troops were still being levied in Picardy, see Chantonnay to Philip II, 8 Sept., *Archivo Documental* I, p. 371, though 'algunos piensan que es solamente par atemorizar los rebeldes con esta fama'.

envisaged in 1544–5 and had come to nothing.[3] The preparation of an anti-heresy campaign was more dangerous, of course, in the context of 1559 and gave rise to extreme reactions, but it was the king's death that released a naked struggle for power.

It is not the aim here to embark on an analysis of the origins of the Wars of Religion either in France generally or Picardy in particular, especially since their most destructive phase there came much later, in the 1580s and 1590s; but it will be useful to point up the connections between the state of the province at the end of the Habsburg–Valois Wars and the development of the religious–political crisis in the early 1560s. This can be done usefully by some discussion of the furious activity launched directly as a result of the crisis by the local estates, in this *pays d'élections*.

One of the ways for contemporaries to understand the civil wars was that used by Jean du Tillet when he wrote of the 'grande superfluité des mauvaises humeurs' stemming from the 'continuation des guerres estrangeres' under Francis I and Henri II, which 'auroient peu à peu disposé le corps de cest estat à recevoir & endurer le changement & alteration'.[4] The wars left a fairly obvious immediate legacy of physical destruction on the land and interruption of trade but they had also, especially on the frontier, created a populace more than usually armed to the teeth, with plenty of firearms in circulation. Royal orders throughout 1559 and 1560 tried, without much effect, to get this under control and became more urgent in the context of the Conspiracy of Amboise, with royal orders to convoke local assemblies and inducements to inform on malefactors.[5] The wars, in the course of emergency action and fiscal pressure, also created a reservoir of discontent which was to be expressed in the assemblies of 1560–1.

Picardy was not to become a stronghold of Protestantism, though this could not have been clear around 1560, when the prospects of the Reformed faith were generally bright. As in other regions, seigneurial patronage of a vague 'heresy' was important in the early stages: Louis de Berquin was arrested in Picardy in 1526, Lutheran works were found at Rambures at the same time, and, while heresy was being preached at the castle of Sénarpont, 1529 saw Francis I's famous remark to the pope that 'la secte luthérienne commence à

---

[3] Henri II to *sénéchal* of Boulogne, 2 June 1559, AD Pas-de-Calais 9B 2 fo. 104v–105v. On the effects of the fiscal squeeze of the 1550s, see C. Michaud, 'Finances et guerres de religion en France', *RHMC*, 1981, 572–96.

[4] Jean du Tillet, *Advertissement envoyé à la noblesse de France* (1574), fo. Aijr.

[5] Francis II to *bailli* of Amiens, 23 July/6 and 17 Dec. 1559, AD Somme B 1 fo. 27v, 38r, 38–9; to city of Amiens, 1 Sept. 1559, AM Amiens AA 14 fo. 175; to *sénéchal* of Boulogne, 31 May 1560, AD Pas-de-Calais 9B 2 fo. 140–1; on response to the Conspiracy: Francis II to *bailli* of Amiens, 14 March 1560, AD Somme B 1 fo. 45v; to *sén.* of Boulogne, AD Pas-de-Calais 9B 2 fo. 122.

pulluler en Picardie'. Isolated cases of heresy were pursued at Amiens in 1534 and 1539 and Noyon, the home of Calvin, in 1534, but systematic action was not taken until the time of the *Chambre ardente* in 1548–9.[6] Despite the work of humanist reformers of Picard origins, there was little sign until the eve of the Wars of Religion of any notable renewal within the church. The upper reaches of the hierarchy remained the preserve of prodigiously worldly clerics drawn mainly from the families who dominated the government of the province: Hallewin, Créquy, Hangest, Pisseleu, many of whom were on bad terms with their cathedral chapters. François de Créquy of Thérouanne was a frankly military figure cast in the mould of a Julius II; Jean de Hangest of Noyon was a courtier, diplomat and patron of scholars whose determined attachment to his beard precluded entry into his cathedral from 1532 to 1547; cardinal Antoine de Créquy of Amiens, another courtier and maecenas, long found it virtually impossible to gain the acceptance of his chapter.[7]

It is clear that, by the 1550s, reformed ideas had gained a decided hold at Amiens among all sectors but particularly among the poorer and, unusually, the less literate sections of the textile workers; the years 1540–60 had been ones of deep war-engendered depression in the industry of *saieterie* and this had caused much discontent. An episcopal official thought there were about 500 heretics in 1558; by the early 1560s, there may have been around 3,700.[8] A number of *échevins* had already been accused of reformist sympathies, as has been seen, though the overall result of this was a thoroughly divided magistrature. May 1559 saw orders against riotous assemblies and March 1560 against 'presches, lectures et chants de psaulmes contre le commun usaige de l'Eglise'. It proved impossible to control them since the *échevinage* was hopelessly divided about how far to prosecute them.[9] Ultimately, it was to be an effective *coup* against the Protestant magistrates that ensured the loyalty of

[6] On early reform in Picardy, see Imbart de la Tour, *Origines de la Réforme* 4 vols. (1904–) III, 376–8; O. Douen, 'La réforme en Picardie' *Bulletin de la Société de l'Histoire du Protestantisme français* 7 (1859), 392–3 and on the early stages in general, D. Nicholls, 'The Nature of Popular Heresy in France, 1520–45', *Historical Journal* 26 (1983). Interestingly, the investigations of the parlement at Sénarpont and Rambures seem to have brought no great danger to their owners.

[7] On J. de Hangest, see L. P. Colliette, *Mémoires . . . du Vermandois* III, 161–3; on F. de Créquy, see ch. 3, n. 118; on A. de Créquy, see Secousse (ed.), *Mémoires de Condé* V, 66–79: 'Consultation de Paris, pour la noblesse de Picardie, contre N. Cardinal de Créquy, évesque d'Amiens': 'sans le sçeu, autorité, consentement ou élection des Estats, mesmement des Nobles du pays' (1564). The opposition was led by Louis d'Ailly, vidame of Amiens.

[8] L. Rossier, *Histoire des Protestants de Picardie* (1861), 8–17, but now replaced by D. Rosenberg, 'Social Experience and Religious Choice' (Yale thesis, 1978). See also M.-L. Pelus, 'Amiens au XVIe siècle: de l'expansion à la rebellion' in Hubscher (ed.), *Histoire d'Amiens*, 101–32.

[9] Thierry, *Tiers Etat* II, 683 n. 1, 684; 684–5 (March 1561), 686 (17 March), 687 (June 1561).

the city. The magistrature at Abbeville was more decisive; in September 1560, when a night-time riot led to the tearing down of a crucifix, stern measures were taken and a general procession ordered to thank God for the maintenance of the Catholic faith.[10] Elsewhere, Protestantism was feeble in the early stages. A Calvinist preacher named Pierre Le Sueur stirred up trouble at Boulogne at the end of 1561 but, despite the protection afforded by a new local governor sympathetic to them in 1559, Morvilliers, the Protestants were not strong enough to make a bid for power there until 1567. At Péronne, there was little sign of Protestantism in a town where Jacques d'Humières was to take the lead in forming the first of the Catholic leagues.[11] With the exception of Boulogne, after the peace of 1563, Reformed worship was only to be tolerated in the suburbs of lesser places like Pont-Rémy (for Ponthieu), Picquigny (for Amiens) and Montdidier (for Péronne).[12]

Amongst the nobility, the picture is a complex one and has been thoroughly discussed by Kristen Neuschel. What should be emphasised is that though many of the nobles who were ultimately to follow the prince of Condé were drawn from the military clientage networks of the Bourbon family, the latter did not guarantee support. Protestant sympathies were declared late, as generally among the nobility, but the milieu of educated aristocratic women played its part in Picardy, as elsewhere, from the 1540s, not only in the person of Eléonore de Roye at the highest level, but also among figures like Péronne de Pisseleu, sister of a duchess of Etampes who was to be regarded by the 1560s as one of the pillars of the Reformed church. The sisters made of the Pisseleu and Barbançon families staunch Protestants. Elsewhere, Jeanne de Saveuses, the widow of Pont-Rémy and later wife of Thibault Rouault, governor of Corbie, ensured that the castle of Pont-Rémy would be a place of refuge for Protestants in Ponthieu at the start of the civil wars.[13]

[10] BM Abbeville MS 378 fo. 111v (21 Sept. 1560); *ordonnance* of Sénarpont, 12 Oct. 1560, *ibid.*, fo. 112r; Francis II to Abbeville, 8 Oct. 1560, *ibid.*, fo. 112v.
[11] F. Lefebvre, *Les huguenots et la Ligue au diocèse de Boulogne. Esquisse historique* (1855); first mention of troubles in the town archives concerning the impending baptism of a child of P. Pascal, *commis* of the *trésorier du Boulonnais*. Morvilliers himself drew attention to this as 'chose publicque et assemblée que par l'ordonnance ne se devoit . . . au dedans de ceste petite ville frontière de telle importance'. F. de La Planche, *avocat de la ville* and deputy to the Estates-General, was also accused of Protestant sympathies.
[12] Secousse (ed.), *Mémoires de Conde* IV, 536: 'Rolle des villes, aux Faulxbourgs desquelles l'exercice de la nouvelle Religion a esté ordonné-Gouvernement de Picardie'. For Vermandois, the list gives 'Quincy' (? Coucy).
[13] K. Neuschel, *Word of Honor*, 30–7. Condé had gone to his brother's estates in Picardy in December 1560 'porque estará más cerca de las suyas y se podrá mejor valer de lo que tiene', Chantonnay, 28 Dec. 1560, *Archivo Documental* I, p. 518. J. Delaborde, *Eléonore de Roye, princesse de Condé (1535–64)* (1876); N. K. Roelker, 'The Appeal to French Noblewomen in the 16th Century' *Jour. Interdisciplinary Hist.* 2 (1971–2), 391–418. D. L. Potter, 'Marriage and Cruelty Among the Protestant Nobility', 10–11, 37 n. 109.

The convocation of the Estates-General for the end of 1560, on the advice of an Assembly of Notables, gave an impetus in Picardy to the further development of representative bodies that had not, until recently, played an important part in the life of the province. Russell Major has argued that, after their late start, the estates in Picardy gained a certain impetus from the meetings of 1482, 1484, 1506–7 and 1545.[14] The county of Boulogne in any case had local estates meetings on a far more regular basis (for example in 1529, 1550 and 1552), while at Abbeville and Péronne meetings of the town estates were a regular part of urban politics.[15] At Amiens, they became more frequent in the 1550s to deal with poor relief and defence matters, that of 1556 actually leading to an *ordonnance* by Coligny based on 'les plainctes et doléances . . . des estatz de cedict gouvernement'.[16]

The preliminary meetings for the Estates-General were held in October 1560 in the *bailliages* and in March 1561 in the estates of the *gouvernement* at Amiens, the latter following the precedent of 1545. *Procès-verbaux* or *doléances* have survived for the meetings of October 1560 in Boulonnais, Ponthieu and Péronne, and from these we can judge the state of opinion in the aftermath of the great wars and on the eve of the civil conflict.[17] In all of them, the clergy were very much on the defensive, attacked by the other estates for their failings: by the nobility for their attempts to deprive them of their tithes and by the third estate for the 'inicquité' which was 'la source principalle de tant de scismes, abbus et erreurs en l'église catholicque', a phrase echoed

[14] J. Russell Major, *Deputies to the Estates-General in Renaissance France* (1960), 13–22; on three estates of Amiens, 1482: *procès-verbal* 2 Jan., Thierry, *Tiers Etat* II, 402–6; prelim. meeting 1484: *Inventaire sommaire, Amiens* II, 240; report from the Estates-General, 6 April: AM Amiens BB 14 fo. 132v (*Mélanges historiques* (CDI) II, 473–5 and Thierry, *Tiers Etat* II, 418–22); 1494: *ibid.*, 477–9. On estates of Ponthieu, 1482: BN Picardie 91 fo. 178; 1506: BM Amiens, coll. Prarond 1707 no. 17–18, BM Abbeville 378 fo. 7; estates of Amiens, 1506: Thierry, *Tiers Etat* II, 506, AM Amiens BB 20 fo. 125–6; estates of Picardy, 1524 (BM Beauvais, Bucquet 57, p. 470); 1545: AM Amiens BB 25 fo. 114; E. de Sachy, *Essais sur l'histoire de Péronne* (1866), 181.

[15] Estates of Boulonnais, 1529: BN fr. 20503 fo. 25; 1550: AD Pas-de-Calais 9B 1 fo. 43; 1552: *ibid.*, fo. 199r; D. L. Potter, 'A Treason Trial', 618–19. Estates of Abbeville: BN Picardie 91 fo. 179r (Aug. 1482); estates of Péronne: AM Péronne BB 6 fo. 317–19 (1513) and BB 11 fo. 402r (Sept. 1555) and *passim*.

[16] *Inventaire sommaire, Amiens* II, 406, 409, 411; *ordonnance* of Coligny, 12 Dec. 1556, AM Amiens AA 14 fo. 81.

[17] Boulonnais, 1560: letters of convocation, Aug. AD Pas-de-Calais 9B 2 fo. 156–7; *procès-verbal*, Oct., *ibid.*, fo. 158–60; remonstrances of clergy, *ibid.*, fo. 168v–70v; of nobility, *ibid.*, fo. 170v; of third estate, *ibid.*, fo. 172–85; 1561: convocation, *ibid.*, fo. 185–6, *procès-verbal*, 6 Mar. *ibid.*, fo. 199–202 (no remonstrances). Ponthieu, 1560: *procès-verbal* and remonstrances, 11 Oct., BM Abbeville 378 fo. 112v–115r; letter of deputies, Jan. 1561, *ibid.*, fo. 119r; *procès-verbal*, 8 Mar. 1561, fo. 119r; remonstrances for estates of Picardy, *ibid.*, fo. 119–121v (part pub. in Thierry, *Tiers Etat* IV, 404–6). Péronne, remonstrances Oct. 1560: AM Péronne BB 10 fo. 208–13. Amiens: no *cahier* survives but see incidental docs. in Thierry, *Tiers Etat* II, 668–70.

almost exactly in the *cahier* of the estates of Péronne and Abbeville. At Boulogne, where separate *cahiers* have survived, the clergy admitted their shortcomings (which, they claimed, they had been unable to remedy because of the state of warfare over the previous twenty years), but pointed out that all estates were to blame and this should be used as an excuse to attack the clergy. Their main grievance was maltreatment at the hands of the military and of the nobility.[18]

Though the agenda of debate in 1560 placed religion first, there were obviously other grievances to be dealt with. The burden of the military was always stressed. The German captain Georg Reckerodt may have bemoaned the 'grande poeuvreté' his men were suffering in the spring of 1559,[19] but the civilian population were unlikely to sympathise. The third estate at Boulogne attacked the outrages committed by soldiers going to and from Calais and those of nobles unpunished for crimes who hunted over cultivated land, demanded excessive inheritance dues and used the new weights and measures of Paris being encouraged by the crown to deceive their more simple-minded tenants. Both here and at Abbeville there were attacks on false claims to noble status.[20]

The estates of Péronne framed the most comprehensive indictment of military administration. They claimed that the garrison had continued to refuse payment for supplies, despite the introduction of the *taillon*, and continued to damage property. Despite the powers held by magistrates to allot billets, they continued to impose themselves by force, break open locks and steal furniture. They had 'ruyné et desmoly tous les villaiges et lieux voisins de la ville jusques à deux lieues', stealing transport, ruining the peasants and making farm work impossible, 'à raison desquelles pilleryes, oppressions et pertes ne sera les pays remys ne reduict en tel estate qu'estoit auparavant lesd. guerres et pilleries qu'il ne soict plus de vingt ans'. In fact, it was claimed that the population of the *gouvernement* of Péronne had fallen by half. It was, of course, part of the aim of the estates to press for reduced taxes: the growth of the burden of the *taille* on the *élection* was aggravated by a certain over-assessment in view of population fall and only that part of it north of the Somme had been exempted. The end of wartime tax exemptions would, in these conditions, render the *taille* excessive and provoke the migration of peasants in areas bordering other *élections*. Péronne, which had to pay its *solde* at L 300–400 was about to have to renew its *taille* exemption. Moreover, increases in the *gabelle* due to the

---

[18] AD Pas-de-Calais 9B 2 fo. 168–70; AM Péronne BB 10 fo. 211r–v; BM Abbeville 378 fo. 112r.
[19] Reckerodt to Guise, 7 Mar. 1559, BN fr. 20536 fo. 141–2.
[20] AD Pas-de-Calais 9B 2 fo. 173–85; BM Abbeville MS 378.

grenier at Laon were prompting the peasants to fraud by seeking their salt in Artois.[21]

It is possible that grievances at Péronne were aggravated by an issue which only came to the fore in 1559–60, when the Guise-dominated government had ordered the towns of Picardy to enter contracts to take over the grain and wine in the royal munitions now that the war was over. In February 1560, the *échevinage* at Péronne was alleging 'quelques difficultez et incommoditez' and the governor, Louis d'Humières, was told to overrule them. In November, they were still being ordered to comply on the grounds that other towns had done their duty.[22]

The estates of Abbeville also advanced claims about excessive *taille* assessment in comparison with Amiens and complained about rises in the salt tax, in fact farmed by the estates of Ponthieu under Francis I. The impossibility of farming the *gabelle* at a profit was ascribed to a list of problems going back nearly fifty years. The rise in the price of salt had proved impossible to sustain and, above all, the burning of the *pays* four or five times since 1513 had caused population loss and made restoration of the land so difficult that the end of *taille* exemption would lead to flight by the peasants to other elections 'qui ne seront tant surchargé de tailles'. Abbeville itself had incurred debts generating annual interest payments of L 1,700 stemming from the costs of supplying the royal armies from 1543 onwards.[23]

Failing to obtain financial supply, the crown called another Estates-General for Melun in March 1561, prorogued to May when the deputies made 'observations désagréables'. The third estate of Péronne, in its recommendations for the preliminary meeting of the estates of Picardy at Amiens on 20 March, had been willing to concede a levy on salt and a *vingtième* on wholesale wine for four years,[24] but those of Ponthieu for the same meeting were even more marked in their lamentation of past and present miseries:

> led. pais, principallement de la ryvière de Somme proche et contigu de conté d'Arthois, a esté bruslé, la plus grande partie des habitans prisonniers et le reste déceddez ou expatriez, cherchans et mendians les vies de eulx, leurs femmes et enfans.

[21] AM Péronne BB 10 fo. 209v, 210r–v. The estates of Péronne incidentally added a complaint about gypsies: 'par les Bohémiens ou Egyptiens passans de trois moys en troys mois en grand nombre et soubz umbre desquelz se joignent en leur troppe plusieurs gens cherchans oisifveté vaccabons et vivans de pilleryes et larcins . . . ' an interesting insight into the permeability of frontiers for gypsies even during wars (*ibid.*, fo. 211r).
[22] Francis II to Louis d'Humières, 3 Feb. 1560, BL Egerton 5 fo. 36; to Péronne, 10 Nov. 1560, AM Péronne BB 10 fo. 220–21; resolution, 1 Dec. 1560, *ibid.*, fo. 215v–18v.
[23] BM Abbeville, MS 378 fo. 114r–v.
[24] AM Péronne BB 10 fo. 233v–234r (4 March 1561).

The point was to make clear that the third estate could not possibly help the crown out of its financial problems. Existing indirect taxes, it was claimed, were already crippling and assigned to pay the *soldes*; the exemption of the county from the worst of the *gabelle* was because of its high assessment for the *taille*. The only advice offered, therefore, was to make a levy on all ecclesiastical benefices worth more than L 1,000 a year, annates, vacancies and forest profits of monastic estates, sparing only benefices in frontier districts where timber was needed for rebuilding churches. Coupled with this was a strongly worded demand for the expulsion of all heretics from the kingdom.[25]

Were it not for the evidence considered in chapter 7, it would be tempting to see in this no more than the conventional invocation of anti-military and anti-fiscal rhetoric. What has been seen of the effects of war, the tendency of towns like Abbeville to increase municipal debt rather than make general levies for war contributions and the slowness of the crown to repay loans indicate that Picardy on the eve of the Wars of Religion was indeed in a thoroughly exhausted state and that, in view of population loss and dislocation, even the considerable tax remissions of the 1550s had failed to sustain the stability of the region.

The uncertain tone of royal policy during 1561 that opened the way for the widening rather than pacification of antagonisms generally was perhaps most notable for the headway made by Protestants at court at the time of the Edict of Romorantin and the Colloquy of Poissy. Early in 1561, local officials in Picardy as elsewhere received orders for the release of religious prisoners and the pacification of religious quarrels; in May Sénarpont was told to oppose the molestation of Protestants and house searches, while making it clear that they must cease their armed assemblies. In November, the governor was told: 'cloyez les yeux aux aultres choses qu'ils feront avec la doulceur et modestie pour la seule observation de lad. Religion' if the Protestants refrained from iconoclasm and acts of violence.[26] Sénarpont, effective governor in Brissac's absence and still described by the king in October 1560 as among 'des gens fidelles et expérimentés' in command of the frontier, was widely suspected of Protestant sympathies as a result of Knox's preaching at Dieppe in 1559. Though close to the prince of Condé he remained ultimately loyal to the crown.[27]

---

[25] BM Abbeville MS 378 fo. 119r–122v.

[26] Charles IX to *sénéchal* of Boulogne, 28 Jan./15 Feb./20 May/19 Apr. 1561, AD Pas-de-Calais 9B 2 fo. 149r, 153r, 237r, 240–41; to Sénarpont, 12 May 1561, fo. 236r; Charles IX to Condé, 3 Nov. 1561, AN 1AP 24 no. 96 and AM Amiens AA 14 fo. 187v (letter to all governors, forwarded by Sénarpont on 8 Nov., *ibid.*, fo. 187v).

[27] T. de Bèze, *Histoire ecclésiastique des églises réformées au royaume de France*, ed. Baum and Cunitz, 3 vols. (1883–9), II, 432. L. Paris, *Négociations . . . François II*, p. 672.

On the other hand, the sieur de Chaulnes, also governor in Brissac's absence for part of 1560, was strongly Catholic and determined to resist heresy. The triumph of Condé in making good his claim to the governorship in October 1561, though it brought joy to his friends and supporters, was a signal to action for the Catholics.[28]

The *cahiers de doléances* of 1560–1 have already made clear what the attitude of the civilian urban population was to the military; in 1559–61 they came to view them also as carriers of the infection of heresy. The presence of so many German Lutherans in the royal armies during the 1550s could only have confirmed this view. So, it was the presence of the military entourage of the Protestant governor of largely Catholic Abbeville, Robert de Saint-Delis, sieur de Haucourt, in June 1562 that sparked off the appalling riot in which he was killed.[29]

The nobility of the province was, it should be clear, thoroughly divided by 1561. Though Sansac, a noted Catholic, had been appointed governor under the aegis of Guise in 1558, the duke had also allowed or promoted the appointment to local governorships of men like Antoine d'Alègre (Meilhaud) and the vidame de Chartres, both shortly to avow their Protestantism. Many of the local town governors – Morvilliers at Amiens and Boulogne, Genlis at Chauny, Bouchavannes at Doullens, Belleforrière at Corbie – were sympathetic to Protestantism by 1561. Others, like Mailly at Montreuil and Jacques d'Humières at Péronne, were opposed.[30] That some nobles should have declared openly for the Reform at this stage is not surprising, but it should still be registered more as a measure of central disintegration than of true religious antagonism that an order which had come to regard service to the crown as part of its life-blood and *raison-d'être* should have been so compelled. At least one-

---

[28] Letters of Chaulnes, 20 Sept. 1560 and Sénarpont, 12 Oct./22 Nov. 1560, BM Abbeville 378 fo. 111r, 112r, 112v–113r. On suspicions at Amiens of Sénarpont's intentions, see Catherine de Medici to Antoine de Créquy, bp. of Amiens, 30 Dec. 1562, AM Amiens AA 5 fo. 328 (not in La Ferrière); in fact he remained trusted, despite his son's joining Condé at Orléans, see K. Neuschel, 'The Prince of Condé', 52, Catherine to Sénarpont, 23 Aug. 1562, H. de La Ferriere, *Lettres de Catherine de Médicis* I, 383. When he was ordered to suppress Protestant preachings in May 1562 (*ibid.*, I, 289) this was backed up by a commission to Antoine de Créquy to oversee the process (see Charles IX to Péronne, 13 May 1562, AM Péronne BB 10 fo. 278–9).

[29] Louandre, *Histoire d'Abbeville* II, 48–50; T. de Bèze, *Histoire ecclésiastique* II, 435–7.

[30] For the town governors on the eve of the Wars of Religion, see 'Les cappitaines qui sont en toutes les places de Picardye . . . ' BN fr. 15872 fo. 65. See also 'Liste des gentilshommes de l'armée protestante à Orleans en 1562', 72 names (BL Lansdowne 5 fo. 181) pub. in H. Meylan and F. Aubert (eds.), *Correspondance de Théodore de Bèze* 9 vols. (1960–), IV, 266–71 and discussed in Neuschel, 'The Prince of Condé', ch. 1. To be compared with the much fuller list of 226 names: 'Estat du partie des princes . . . de l'association du prince de Condé', September 1562, PRO SP 70/41 no. 436.

third of the noble fief-holders of the *bailliage* of Amiens in 1557 were in royal service at court or in the army.[31]

One example may serve for many others of the complexity of motivation and interest involved. Jean de Pas, known as 'le jeune Feuquières' after his family's principal fief, was not listed as present with Condé at Orléans, but was certainly a Protestant and in Condé's following by September 1562; he was, moreover, implicated by Poltrot de Méré's confession in the assassination of the duke of Guise. He died of fever during the siege of La Charité in 1569. His grandfather had been a *panetier du roi* and the latter's brother Philippe had been captain of Beauquesne. His father, Jacques (*d.* 1566) governor of Corbie, spent much of his military career in the gendarmerie company of Jean II d'Humières and commanded at Péronne in Humières's absence from 1536 to the 1550s. In 1539, he became a *maître d'hôtel* and *conseiller* to the dauphin Henri. He had two sons: the eldest, Louis, later sieur de Feuquières, and Jean, born 1530, who was to inherit the seigneurie of Martinsart. Jean followed his father's path of service in the royal household: by 1557, he was *écuyer d'écurie* to the dauphin François, when he received a royal gift of 200 *écus* 'tant en la faveur de mons. sr. le daulphin' and for his expenses in commanding a company of light horse, and by 1560 was *écuyer d'écurie du roi*. At the same time, he was governor of Roye, though it is worth noting that he was not paid his salary for the year ending May 1557 (L 1,200) until October 1560. He seems to have been a close adherent of the admiral in Picardy.

Feuquières had also served with the duke of Guise in Italy in 1555 and been well treated by him. Monluc observed that 'despuis, à ce que j'ay entendu, a tourné le visage a la maison de Guise, combien que ledict seigneur luy faizoict tant d'honneur ou plus, qu'à gentilhomme que feust près de luy'. Thus, with close connections to two Catholic families, Humières and Guise, 'le jeune Feuquières' chose instead to follow Coligny and the Protestant cause, while his family, too, became Protestants. His redoubtable wife Charlotte d'Arbaleste, who married him in 1567, left a brief but telling outline of his predicament. On the one hand 'il se voyoit avancé en une court, et sur le poinct de recevoir des biens et honneurs, lesquelz il ne pouvoit avoir ny espérer s'il faisoit profession de la vérité'. The need to choose made him ill, but in the end he decided to 'quitter la messe et les abus', at first staying at court and hearing sermons in the queen's chamber while she was at mass until involvement in the Conspiracy of

---

[31] See Beauvillé, *Recueil*, III, 'Arrièreban d'Amyens' (1557), discussed in ch. 4: 'Premier rolle ... exemptz ... pour ce qu'ilz ont charge du Roy en ses guerres, ou sont de la maison de sa majesté ... ' (pp. 386–409); in 1557 only 39 nobles served personally – compare with the 'Rôle des Gentilshommes qui se sont offerts à servir personellement pour le ban et arrière-ban du bailliage d'Amiens', 11 Oct. 1575 (*BSAP* 12 (1904)), 82–99, when 169 nobles were exempted for various reasons.

Amboise forced him to be more careful. It was the death of Francis II 'qui le délivra de beaucoup de peines, aussy bien que plusieurs aultres' and he was able to join Condé.[32]

At Amiens by early 1562, Protestants had a 17–18 majority in the *échevinage*. The opening of the crisis saw a rapid move by the crown to remodel it first by replacing the *maire* Firmin Lecat and the *prévôt* Guillaume Legrand on 5 May and then on 3 June by creating ten new Catholic magistrates, thus paving the way for the following elections to exclude Protestants.[33] At the same time the crown replaced not only Condé (formally at any rate claimed to be in detention) but also Morvilliers by the cardinal de Bourbon and Estourmel respectively.

The opening of the war by Condé's seizure of Orléans and the flocking to him there of a number of Picard nobles sympathetic to his cause was one decisive moment for the region in that it simplified the determination of the crown to ensure the security of the province.[34] In July it was reported that 'Monsr de Sénarpont dothe begin to awake in Picardy, whether the cardinal of Burbon shalbe governour to empeache Senarpontz purposes', but, in fact, though both Sénarpont and his son were listed among Condé's followers, both seem to have abandoned his service as a result of English intervention and 'ce sont retirez d'Orléans estans en leurs maisons'.[35] At least ten out of the thirty or so *chevaliers* resident in the *bailliage* of Amiens had Protestant sympathies, but by no means all fought on the Protestant side in the first civil war. François d'Ailly, the vidame of Amiens, had inherited the Reform sympathies of his

[32] On the family of Pas: BN dossiers bleus 512 fo. 1–18. Philippe de Pas, letters, AN Péronne BB 6 fo. 213v. Jacques de Pas: BN p.o. 2203 no. 52, 53, 54, 57–62 (will, 1566); Montmorency to La Rochepot, 14 June 1537, BN nafr. 10227 no. 5; Beauvillé, *Recueil* I, 243–4; correspondence in BN fr. 20521 fo. 58 (etc. (1542); AM Péronne BB 9 fo. 38 (Aug. 1547), fo. 239v (1552). Jean de Pas: BN p.o. 2203 no. 55, 56, 57, B. de Monluc, *Commentaires* (SHF edn) II, 146; 'Ce que le jeune Feuquières a rapporté au Roy de la part de monsr l'admiral touchant la prinse de Lens' (Jan. 1557), BL Add. 24206 fo. 23–4; quarrel with St-Luc at Roye, Jan. 1558: BN fr. 23191 fo. 81; corresp. as capt. at Roye, Feb.–Mar. 1558: BN Cangé 62 fo. 38–9, fr. 20460 fo. 149–51, 153–4, nafr. 21698 fo. 156; Coligny's reply to Poltrot's confession, *Mémoires de Condé*, ed. Secousse, IV, 285–304, esp. 287. For Charlotte d'Arbaleste's biography, see *Mémoires et correspondance de Duplessis-Mornay* 12 vols. (1824–5) I, 50–8. See also N. M. Sutherland, 'The Assassination of François, duc de Guise, February 1563', in her *Princes, Politics and Religion, 1547–1589* (1984), esp. 152.
[33] Thierry, *Tiers Etat* II, 711–16; A. de Calonne, *Histoire de la ville d'Amiens* II, 27–32.
[34] T. de Bèze, *Histoire ecclésiastique*, II, 432–3. By September, Condé's Picard supporters included (their followings in brackets) Sénarpont (150), Genlis (150), Piennes (50) and Morvillier (50) among the *chevaliers de l'ordre* and, among the gentlemen and captains, Bouchavannes, gov. of Doullens, Charles de Barbançon, Seychelles, Louis d'Orbec, Gamaches (his stepson), Haplaincourt, Bayencourt, Feuquières, Coucy, Pitton, Rubempré d'Isques and Fouquesolles (PRO SP 70/41 no. 436).
[35] Throckmorton to council, 23 July 1562, PRO SP 70/39 no. 252, fo. 153r; 'Intelligences from France', 5 Sept. 1562, SP 70/41 no. 431, fo. 39v.

mother Marguerite de Melun, but died in England in 1560 and his successor Louis, though a decided Protestant and bitter enemy of the new bishop of Amiens, cardinal de Créquy, is not listed as active in the first civil war. Their younger brother Charles, though also a Protestant, had good cause to be grateful to the duke of Guise for protection against the baron des Adrets.[36] Other major figures, like Morvilliers and Genlis, joined Sénarpont in abandoning Condé's party before the end of the fighting, having followed the prince out of personal regard but unable to accept his dealings with the English; others, like Bouchavannes, the prince's lieutenant, and Feuquières, stayed on. The analysis of clientage developed in recent years should caution against simplistic notions and it is certainly the case that the house of Bourbon proved unable to carry the province with it.[37] In part, this resulted from the division between the king of Navarre and his brother in 1562 and also from the fact that, as has been argued here, magnate clientage formed only one aspect of the public life of a nobility deeply enmeshed in royal patronage and service.

The Habsburg–Valois Wars had important repercussions not only in the field of military organisation and strategy, but also in terms of the balance of political structures which were characteristic of the sort of Absolute Monarchy which developed in sixteenth-century France. The wars had built up the resources at the disposal of both the central apparatus and of the provincial governors but, latterly, in placing insupportable stresses on the finances of the state, had called into question the distribution of patronage through pensions and offices that had been such an element of success from the late fifteenth century.

In Picardy, as we have seen, the incorporation of the newly organised province, hitherto a confused *mêlée* of *pays* and jurisdictions with little

---

[36] Louis d'Ailly to Cecil, Picquigny, 16 April '1561'. PRO SP 70/25 no. 89: 'mon feu frère, lequel est décéddé en vostra pais'. It is interesting that the Ailly family, so ancient and connected in this period to the Crèvecoeur, Montmorency, Warty, Batarnay families held so few posts of importance in the sixteenth century: no governorships, a few *ad hoc* military commands and royal grants. It held some court posts: Antoine d'Ailly may have been a *gentilhomme de la chambre* 1547–8 (*CAH* I, no. 940, though not listed on the *rôles*) François d'Ailly was *pannetier du roi* in 1549 (BN fr. 21450 fo. 191v). See also F. J. Darsy, *Picquigny et ses seigneurs. vidames d'Amiens* (1860). The battle of Saint-Denis in 1567 wiped out three male members of the family, the vidame Louis, his son and brother. The physical setting of the château of Picquigny has been considered in K. Neuschel, 'Noble Households in the Sixteenth Century: Material Settings and Human Communities', *French Historical Studies* 15 (1988), 600–3.
[37] For a recent summary of the debates over the significance of clientage during the later sixteenth century, see S. Kettering, 'Clientage during the French Wars of Religion', *Sixteenth-Century Journal* 20 (1989), 222–39.

coherence, into the kingdom was the response of Louis XI and his successors to the collapse of the Burgundian state and the growing challenge of its Habsburg successor. An essential part in this was played by the absorption of its leading elements into the orbit of royal patronage and favour which may be viewed as a vast 'affinity', involving both court and military posts. To this, the technical aspects of the administration generated by military needs were closely allied. Service at court, in the army or its administration was vital to the interests of a ruling order still engaged in recovering from the setbacks of the fifteenth century as well as from the blows dealt out by war in the sixteenth. But the benefits stemming from such patronage were dangerously exposed to the vicissitudes of expansion and contraction in the resources of the monarchy, as well as the political dangers most apparent in the period of factionalised government and then royal minority which opened in 1559, and which itself was to be profoundly marked by the effects of aristocratic clientage. To this extent, the monarchy of the later Valois continued to depend on the deployment of decidedly traditional modes of political action, though on a grandiose scale and in the context of a significant increase in the scope and sophistication of state activity generated by the Habsburg–Valois Wars. It was this above all that gave the monarchy of the Renaissance period a certain transitional quality within the development of modern state structures and, for instance, failed to reconcile the different attitudes to the definition of territory which we have seen in chapter 8.

Picardy had become part of France as perhaps its most profoundly militarised province. Despite all efforts, chaos – or 'la confusion et désordre que la guerre traine' as Henri II put it – remained characteristic of military organisation in the sixteenth century.[38] The struggle to keep the military machine going had been exhausting. It is perhaps not surprising that, on the eve of the civil wars, it was the potential threat from outside that still seemed greatest in Picardy. Jacques d'Humières was told in 1562 that it was likely that Spain and England, though they had thought to live in peace for a while as a result of the Treaty of Cateau-Cambrésis, 'ne veullent laisser perdre le moien qui se penseront ouvert parmy tant de troubles de France, quelques entreprinses sur aucunes de mes places'. Security on the frontier was more than ever needed. This was also the view of a *Discours* of 1562, arguing that Spain was only awaiting an excuse to attack in Picardy, 'l'endroict le plus foible de la France'. On the other hand, the king could easily defend it as it was now the only province threatened: 'c'est à sa porte, là où il fera venir au son du Tabourin tant de gens qu'il voudra'. Though the princes

[38] Henri II to *bailli* of Amiens, 5 April 1559, AD Somme B 1 fo. 20v.

of Christendom had leagued together against France in the past 'toutesfois,
ils n'ont peu faire mal qu'en un seul endroit de ce Royaume, qui est la
Picardie'.[39]

---

[39] Charles IX to Jacques d'Humières, 4 April 1562, AM Péronne BB 10 fo. 276v–77r. Secousse
(ed.), *Mémoires de Condé* III, 159–68: 'Discours du bruict qui court que nous avons la guerre
à cause de la religion' an example of the sort of thinking current in circles which preferred
not to see the troubles in terms of religion but rather in those of foreign intervention or, as with
the Spanish envoy Chantonnay, 'plus fondé en rebellion qu'en religion', *ibid.*, II, 39 (May
1562).

APPENDICES

Appendix 1. *Holders of royal pensions in Picardy*

	1480–1[1]	1485–6[2]	1497–8[3]	1522–3[4]	Posts held
Ph. de Crèvecoeur†*	12,000	10,000			gov. Picardy, Abbeville, etc.
Antoine de Crèvecoeur†*	4,000	2,000			*sénéchal*, Artois
G. de Bisches†*	6,000	1,200			gov. Péronne
Ph. Bat de Longueval†	1,200	120	800		cap. 4,000 archers, 1482
Pierre de Rasse†	1,200				
Drieux de Humières	500	90			
Pierre de Monchy†*	600	300	750		lieut. to Esquerdes
Robert de Miraumont†	1,200	100	850		*gent. maison*
P. de Ranchicourt*	2,000	160	300		bp. of Arras
C. de Viefville-Frestoy†*	800	160	400		gov. Namur
Morlet de Saveuzes*	500	160	240		
Guillaume Le Bien*	200	50	200		
Jean de Monceaulx	1,200				*rec. gen.* Picardy
Jean de Saveuzes†	500	240	240		
Jacques Le Marchant*	300	50	50		
Jac. Le Marchant filz	600				
Gaimaing de Bailleul†	300				
Laurens Caignart	500	300			
Charles de Courteville	240				
Jean de Luxembourg	1,200				
Pierre Caignet	200				*contr. gen.* Picardy
Honnerot Adaim	300				
Anthoine d'Estrées	100		300		
Jean Tassart	50				
Hutin de Miraumont	600	100			
Jean de Meleun†*	900	300	800		
Dme Jacqueline de Néele	800				

* *conseiller et chambellan*
† *chevalier*
** *payments cited in* CAF VIII
na not assigned

	1480–1	1485–6	1497–8	1522-3	Posts held
Jean de Sailly†	200				
Jean de May	200				
Pierre de Sachy	100				
Martin 'le bon'de Rely†	200	110	70		
Jean de Bournonville*	164	120			cap. 50 1, '91, g. Hardelot
Jean du Boys-Esquerdes†*	1,200	200	2,000		lieut. gov. Picardy, 1490
Guillaume de Fretin	400				
Chantre d'Abbeville	120				
Jacques de St Benoist	600				
Anthoine de Bernaige	800				
Jean Compaignon	900				
Mr. de Parenties	500				
Jean de Courteville*	600	50	50		
M. de Richebourg†*	10,000				conseiller du roi
Guy Pot	2,900				bailli, Vermandois
Hugues d'Ailly†	300				
Jean III de Hangest	2,000				conseiller du roi
Bourlens de Luxembourg	1,600				
Charles sr de Contay*†	1,000				gov. Corbie
Philippe de Contay*	600	300	300		
Waleran d'Ognies†	1,200	240	500		bailli, Hesdin
Mme. de Richebourg†*	2,000				
Bat. de Saveuzes	1,200				capt. Amiens
Mr. de Bours	1,200				
Mr. de Longueval*	600	240			
Raoul de Lannoy*		1,000	2,000		bailli, capt., Amiens
Philippe de Hallwin†*		1,200	2,000		cap. gov., Béthune
Pierre-Loys de Valtan		300			
Jean Bat. de Cardonne†*		1,200	2,100		capt. Boulogne
Louis Brunetel*		150			
Nicolas de Longvilliers		120			bailli, Etaples (Blondel)
Waleran de Bailleul†*		200	500		
Adrien Bat. d'Aveluz		50	400		hd'armes. co. Ligny, 1495
Philippe de Habart		160	160		
Alardin Bournel		100			
Jean, sr. de Lannoy†		300	700		gov. Montreuil
Anthoine sr. de Gapannes†*		160	240		muster comm. 1499 p, gent. m.
Jean de Roye†*		240			
Andrieu de Rambures†*		480	1,400		gov. St-Valéry, sen. Ponth.
François de Créquy†		240	2,000		sén. Ponthieu
Anthoine Bat. d'Auxy		160	400		hd'armes. co. Framezelles
Jean de Longueval-Vaux†*		200	300		capt. Bapaume, bail. Hesdin
Jacques de Bussu		120			
Jean de Sailly†		60	180		
Anthoine d'Avelus†		90	300		
Jean d'Yaucourt†*		240	300		
Emond de Monchy†		240			
Drieu d'Azincourt†		160			
Charles sr. de Rubempré		120	600		capt. 311 men, 1491
Olivier de Kesele		60			
Jean de La Forge		120			rec. gen. Picardy
Sauvaige de Pronville		90	400		
Jacques de Quesnoy		90			gent. maison
Ant. d'Ailly-Varennes		160			gent. maison

	1480–1	1485–6	1497–8	1522-3	Posts held
Jean de Sainte-Audegonde		50			
Pierrequin de Souych	50	180			
J. de Bournonville-Le Veau	160	700	300		
Thierry de Licques	50	50			*comm, vivres*, lt. Ponthieu
Olivier de Coesman*	440				gov. Auxerre, *capt.* Arras
Jean de La Cavrye	200	400			prem. prés. Parlement
Jacques de Bailleul	50	100			*gent. maison*
Jacques de Fillièvres	90				*gent. maison*
Jean de Poix	50				
Jean Le Fevre	120				
Dimenche de Requier	240				
Raymonnet de Cleriadus	110				
Jean sr. de Mailly†*	300				*capt.* infantry, 1480
Jean Delphant	240				
Jean de La Gruthuse†*	2,000	1,200			*gov.* Abbev. Béthune Picardy
Jean d'Auffay	600				*conseiller du roi*
Theodore Guinnier	120				*médecin du roi*
Jean sr. de Créquy†*	270	1,600			
Jean Caudel	110	100			
Jacques de Hangest*	220	300			(*d.* 1519)
Guillaume Balard	36				
Jean Colo	36				
Nicolas de Vauxelles	120				
Jean Bournel	180				
L. de Luxembourg-Ligny		1,500			gov. Picardy
Gapannes, fils		600	300na		
M. de Dompmart		300			
Guillaume Caubart		320			*capt.* castle, Péronne
Baugeois Wicardel		90			
M. de Rayneval (Ailly)†		1,200			
Gratien de Saint Martin		200			
Antoine de Fontaines		800			
Bat. de Saint-Pol		400			
Philippe de Pas		400			*hd'armes*, co. La Gruthuse
Roussecap		400			
Jacques de Fousquesolles		800			
M. de Cohain		600			
M. de Hulliz		300			
Jacques de Rivery		400			gov. Thérouanne
M. Dinguessant		600			
M. de Rebecourt		400			
M. de Boullain		240			
René de Broutières		240			
M. de Sarcus		600			
M. de Ruguessant		240			
Despert de Bournoville		400			
M. de Himbercourt		800			
M. de Hames		400			
Antoine Lorgest		120			
Ponthieu Hérault		180			
Jacques Roussel		400			
Watequin Grant		400			
Mess. M. Destrac		100			

	1480–1	1485–6	1497–8	1522–3	Other posts
Lancelot de la Mare			200		
Pierre de Broutières			400		
Athiot de Bournoville†			600		*gov.* Aire 1497
Porus de Launoy			500	250na	
Antoine de Moyencourt			400		
Jean de Rely			400		
Jacques de Mauchevalier†*			500		*homme d'armes*, c. J. de Moy *mh*
Lancelot de Maunay			100		
Nicolas Rendu			250		
M. de La Vallée†			600		gov. Brunemberg, *m.d'hôtel*
Jeune Cardonne			400		
G. de Pisseleu-Heilly†			400	400	
Michel de Belleforrière*†			400		
Pierre de Belleforrière†			600	400na	

	1522–3	1525[5]	1532–3[6]	1536–8[7]	1547–9[8]
Oudart du Biez (incl. captaincy)	2,000		?**		
Jean de Sarcus (incl. captaincy)	1,000		1,000**	1,000	
C. de Bourbon-Vendôme	10,000	14,000	24,000		
F. de Bourbon-Vendôme	10,000	10,000	12,000	20,000	
A. de Sarrebruch, c. de Roucy	1,200				
A. de Créquy, Pont-Rémy*	6,000				
L. de Hangest-Montmor*	1,700	12,000			
N. de Moy-Chin*	500	500			
G. d'Humières-Lassigny	400	400			
J. d'Humières*	2,000		2,000**		8,000
M. d'Olhain	1,000				
M. de Hubecy	400				
Sr. d'Espoy	800	300			
M. de Huppy	400	400	400		
M. de Nyelle	500	300			
A. Rouault-Gamaches*	1,000na	1,000			
A. de Hangest-Genlis	1,000na	1,000			
M. de Lameth	6,000na	600			
Saint-Aulbin	200na	200			
M. de Colambert	300na				
Governor of Marle	300na				
M. de Redeval, picard	400na				
Marie de Luxembourg	1,700na	1,700	2,400		
Lieut. of Thérouanne	300na				
Jean de Créquy-Canaples	300na	?	4,000	4,000	4,000
Gamaches, *mh* to Pont-Rémy	400na				
J. de Bournonville-Auvringhen	240na	240			
Louis de Rabodanges	400na	300			
A. de Hallwin-Esclebecq	400na	400			
M. de Varennes	400na				
M. de Lygnon	400na	400			
P. de Créquy-Bernieulles	300na	2,000			
Loys d'Isque	300na	300			
Myraulmont	200na				
N. de Monchy-Montcavrel	240na				
Gapannes	300na	300			
Veau de Bournonville (d.)	300na	300			

	1522–3	1525	1532–3	1536–8	1547–9
G. de Pisseleu	400	400			
s. of *bailli* of Amiens	240na				
Picardie Hérault	60na				
J. Roussel	120na				
J. de Monchy-Sénarpont	300na				600
M. de Longueval	300na	600	800**		
A. de Pisseleu-Heilly	240na	240			
M. de Torcy	1,000na	1,000	1,800		
F. de Montmorency			4,000	6,000	6,000
J. d'Estouteville			1,200	?	
J. d'Estrées			1,200		
M. du Fresnoy			1,400		
J. sr. de Créquy			1,200	1,200	1,200
M. de Bouchavannes			400	400	
M. de Foudras			600		
J. de Coucy-Vervins			400	400	
J. d'Humières			2,000**		8,000
A. de Bourbon-Vendôme			.	12,000	24,000
A. de Hallum-Piennes				1,200	
M. de Stavaye				900	
L. de Bourbon-Condé					4,000

Sources:
1. BN fr. 2900 fo. 7–16. Other pensions recorded in the same period but not on this list: Colart and Jacques de Moy, 1479 (Rodière, *La maison de Moy*, ii preuves, no. 407, 408).
2. BN fr. 20685 pp. 742–6, copy of the *rôle* of moneys ordered to be paid by the *receveur-général* of Picardy for year beginning Oct. 1485.
3. 'Estat des finances du Roy nostre sire tant ordinaires que extraordinaires des pais de Picardie', *Annuaire-bulletin de la SHF*, 1866, pp. 185–92. Similar list, 1502–3, BN fr. 2930 fo. 101–8.
4. R. Doucet, *L'Etat des finances de 1523* (1923), 110–43. L 26,713 were assigned on the *recette-générale* of Picardy but only L 25,400 were listed as definite (including L 16,000 to Vendôme and Saint-Pol).
5. AN J 964 no. 55.
6. BN fr. 2997 fo. 16 17 (total: L 419,560, 'le contenu duquel sera paié ou appoincté selon les acquits que le Roy expediera'). See also J 966 no. 66, undated, for this period.
7. Evidence from the *acquits sur l'epargne* 1536–8, *CAF* VIII, *passim*.
8. BN fr. 4523 list for the reign of Henri II dated on internal evidence, 1547–9.

Appendix 2. *The main holders of local governorships in Picardy, 1490–1560*

Name	Governorship	Court post	Gendarmerie	Other
Antoine d'Alègre, bar. de Meilhaud	Boulogne, 1558–9	*gc*, 1561		ens. Coligny 1560
Flour d'Ardres, sr. de Crésecques	Abbeville, 1545–55 Ardres, 1558	*gm* 1549–52–		*légion, capt.*
Pierre de Belleforrière, d. 14 Oct. 1530	Bohain, 1528 deputy, Ile-de-France, 1523	*mh* 1523–4		pension, 1523 *commis, frontier,* 1528
Charles de Belleforrière	Corbie, 1558 Doullens, 1553	*p* 1551		
Michel de Barbançon, sr. de Canny	Picardy, 1541	*p.e.f.* 1534–		*légion, capt.*
François de Barbançon, Canny		*gc* 1546–7		*bailli, Senlis,* 1543
Florimond de Biencourt, sr. de Potrincourt		*mh,* 1547		*bailli Vermandois* 1547
Jean de Biencourt, sr. de Potrincourt		*mh,* 1547–51		*comm. des vivres,* 1558
Oudart du Biez	Boulogne, 1523 Picardy, 1542	*mh,* Fr. I, 1512–15 *gc,* 1537–47	50 lances	*sén.* Boulonn. marshal, 1541
Jean du Biez, sr. de Cauroy	Ardres 1558–9			
Claude de Lanvin, sr. de Blérancourt	Chauny, 1538 Ardres, –1547			*légion, captain,* 1541

Abbreviations
chamb.   *chambellan ordinaire*
ec.ec.   *écuier d'ecurie du roi*
ech.   *échanson du roi*
e.h.   *enfant d'honneur*
e.f.   *la maison des enfants de France* (until 1538)
ec.t.   *écuier tranchant*
g   *gentilhomme*
gc   *gentilhomme de la chambre*
gm   *un des cent gentilhommes de la maison du roi*
l.   lieutenant of a company of gendarmerie
la.   *lances des ordonnances*
MEF   *maître des eaux et forêts*
mh   *maître d'hôtel ordinaire du roi*
mr   *maître des requêtes de l'hôtel du roi*
Orléans household of duke Charles of Orléans, king's second son (1540–5)
p   *pannetier du roi*
qu.   queen's household
v.tr.   *valet tranchant du roi*

Name	Governorship	Court post	Gendarmerie	Other
Jacques Blondel, sr. de Bellebrune		*vt* 1521–42		*sén.* Ponthieu *bail.* Etaples
Ant. dc Bayencourt, sr. de Bouchavannes	Doullens 1528–57 Coucy in 1558			pension, 1532
Louis Bournel, sr. de Thiembronne				*bailli*, Ams. 1537–50
Martin de Bournonville, sr. de Saternault	Montreuil 1544–50		guidon, Bernieulles 1535	
Jean de Bournonville, sr. d'Auvringhen	Montreuil 1551–*c*. 54			pension 1532–5
Nicolas de Bossut, sr. de Longueval		*mh* 1528–43 *chamb.* Orléans 1528–43	Vendôme's co.	*bailli* of Vermandois pension, 1523
François du Brueil dit Bretagne	Abbeville, 1556 St-Quentin, 1557 Rue, 1560			
Jean de Bruges sr. de La Gruthuse	Abbeville 1494–1512		35 l. 1491, 80 l. 1510	*maître des arbalestriers*
Louis de Bruges sr. de La Gruthuse	Abbeville castle, 1522	*eh* 1518–23 *gc* 1524d.		
François de Coligny sr. d'Andelot	Le Crotoy Jan. 1551	*e.h. e.f.* 1532–8		*Col. gén. infanterie*
François de Créqui sr. de Dourrier	Boulogne, 1484–			*Sén.* of Boulonnais, pension
Antoine de Créqui sr. de Pont-Rémy	Thérouanne, 1513; Montreuil,	*e.h.* 1499– *gm* 1502–4	60 l. 1515 co. 1525	*bailli* of Amiens
Philippe de Créqui sr. de Bernieulles	Montreuil, 1525 Thérouanne, 1537		co. 1535	pension, 1522
Jean VII, sr. de Créqui			co. 1525–44	
Jean VIII de Créqui sr. de Canaples	Montreuil, 1537–42	*gc* 1527–55 Capt. 100 G		pension, 1532 *bailli* of Amiens 1525–8
Jean III d'Estourmel d. 1557		*mh* 1540–57 *Ch.* to Orléans		*gén. fin.* pension
Jean d'Estourmel, sr. de Guyencourt, d. 1557	St-Quentin	*ech.* 1547–	l. co. Vielleville	*gén. fin.*
Antoine d'Estourmel d. 1569	Amiens, 1562	*gc* by 1568		*gén. fin.*
Jean d'Estrées (1486–1567)	Hesdin, 1537 Le Câtelet, 1541 Folembray, 1556		co. in 1559	*maître de l'artillerie Sén.* Boulonn.

Name	Governorship	Court post	Gendarmerie	Other
Antoine IV d'Estrées bar. de Doudeauville	Boulogne La Fère, Ile-de-France			*Sén.* of Boulonnais
Jean d'Estouteville sr. de Villebon	Thérouanne, 1537–50 Picardy, 1550	*ec.ec.* 1526–7 *gc* 1528–	40 l. 1540 36 l. 1549	
Jean du Bois d'Esquerdes, sr. de Tenques	Picardy, 1490		30 l. 1475–1509	
Quentin Gourlé, sr. d'Azincourt	Abbeville 1537–*c.* 41			
François Gouffier sr. de Crèvecoeur	Doullens, 1555–60	*gc*, 1544		
Louis de Hallewin sr. de Piennes	Péronne, 1496 Picardy, 1512		co. 1501–19	*MEF*, Péronne
Philippe de Hallewin sr. de Bughenault	Péronne, –1517	*ech.* 1499–1516		*MEF*, Péronne 1513
Jean de Hallewin sr. d'Esclebecq	Le Crotoy, 1519	*ech.* 1509–12		
Antoine de Hallewin sr. de Piennes		*e.h.* 1521–2 *gc*, 1540–3		
Louis de Hangest sr. de Montmor	Corbie, 1524 Mouzon	Cons. Ch. Grand Ec., qu., 1523	10 l. 1520	pension, 1522
Adrien de Hangest sr. de Genlis d. 1532		*e.h.* 1484–90 *ech.* 1520–2 Grand Echanson		*Capt.* Louvre pension, 1522
François de Hangest sr. de Genlis	Chauny, 1558	*ec.ec.* 1547–51 *gc* 1551		*Capt.* Louvre col. legion, 1545
Jean de Haucourt sr. de Huppy	Abbeville, 1513–27			pension, 1532
Jean de Haucourt sr. de Huppy, fils?	Abbeville *c.* 1531–37			
Jean II d'Humières	Péronne 1519–49	*gc* 1531–49 *gov.ch.e.f.* 1532–7	*comm.* 1522–3 25 l. 1522 *lieut.* Dauphin 1534	
Jean III d'Humières sr. de Becquincourt	Péronne 1549–54	*e.h. e.f.* 1532–6; *e.f.* 34–8 *gc* 1547–54	50 l. 1552	
Louis d'Humières sr. de Contay	Péronne 1554–59	*e.h. e.f.* 1543–8 *gc* 1548–49 *cap. gardes* –54		
Jacques d'Humières	Péronne, 1560–	*g* Orléans, 1540–5		

Name	Governorship	Court post	Gendarmerie	Other
Jacques de Lameth	Corbie, 1522			
Antoine de Lameth sr. du Plessis		*mh* 1519–40		*gén. fin.* Picardy
Jean, sr de Lannoy	Montreuil, 1490s			
Raoul de Lannoy sr. de Morvillier	Amiens, 1495– 1513; Picardy, 1490			*bailli,* Amiens
François de Lannoy sr. de Morvilliers	Amiens, 1513–48 Chauny –1548			
Louis de Lannoy sr. de Morvilliers	Amiens Boulogne, 1558– Lt. at Amiens	*ec.ec.* 1550		
Philippe de Longueval sr. de Haraucourt, d. 37	La Capelle 1536–7			*Chamb.* to Vendôme
Philippe III de Longueval sr. de Haraucourt	Coucy	*mh* 1544–7		*Chamb.* to Vendôme
Robinet de Mailly sr. de Rumesnil	Doullens *c.* 1522–6			
Jean de Mailly sr. de Rumesnil	Doullens, 1526–			
René de Mailly	Montreuil, 1555	*e.h. e.f.* 1532–8; *ec.t.e.f*, 1532–8; *gc* by 1560		
Jean de Monchy sr. de Sénarpont	Corbie, 1540s Boulogne, 1550–9 Picardy, 1559–		50 l. 1554	*bailli,* Amiens, 1550–1
Jean de Monchy, sr. de Montcavrel		*mh*, 1508	*h d'a,* Gruthuse	
Colart de Moy bar. de Chin	Tournai St-Quentin to 1489	cons. chamb.		
Jacques de Moy bar. de Chin	St-Quentin 1489–1520	cons. chamb. capt.		*MEF* Normandy & Picardy
Nicolas de Moy bar. de Chin	St-Quentin to *c.* 1539	cons. chamb. L Vendôme		pension, 1522 *MEF* Nor. Pic.
Louis d'Ognies sr. de Chaulnes	Corbie, 1553 St-Quentin, 1560; Picardy	*ec.ec.* Orléans 1540–5; in qu. 1532–8; to K. 1551		

Name	Governorship	Court post	Gendarmerie	Other
Jean, sr. d'Oultreleau	Le Crotoy –1551			*lieut.* infantry, 1525
Jacques de Pas sr. de Feuquières	Corbie	*mh.* 1539 *mh* Orléans 1540–5	ens. dauph. by 34	*Lieut.* Péronne, 1541–
Louis de Pas sr. de Feuquières		*mh,* 1533		
Jean de Pas 'le jeune Feuquières'	Roye, 1557–60	*ec.ec.* Dauphin, 1557		
Artus de Moreul sr. du Fresnoy	Thérouanne 1525–36		50 l. 1525	pension, 1532
Guillaume de Pisseleu sr. de Heilly		*mh,* 1524		pension, 1522 infantry, 1521
Adrien de Pisseleu sr. de Heilly	Hesdin, 1537–47	*ec.ec.* 1530–44 *p.* in qu. 47–	*hd' armes,* du Biez, 1519 capt. 1545	*légion*
Jean de Pisseleu sr. de Heilly	Corbie, 1559–	*gc* 1544–7		
Francois de Rasse sr. de La Hargerie	Crèvecoeur 1520s	*gm* 1519–20 *mh* 1528–55		*commis.* vict. frontier
Charles de Roye c. de Roucy		*e.h.* 1524; *gc* 1529–47		royal gift L 3,000
Artus de Rubempré	Etaples, 1558			
Thibault Rouault sr. de Riou	Oultreau, 1548 Corbie, 1551 Hesdin, 1552–3	*eh* 1518 *gc,* 1551–	ens. Const. l. du Biez	*commis.* repar. 1551
Jean, sr. de Rambures		*ech.* 1517–44		*MEF,* Ponthieu
Jean de Sarcus	Hesdin, 1521–9, 1537	*p* 1527–8; *mh* in qu. 32–7; *mh* 1531–6	capt. 50 la.	*capt.* Legion Picardy
. . . de Sarcus (son)	Le Crotoy, 1537			
Robert de Saint-Delis sr. de Heucourt	Abbeville after 1560			
Imbert de Saveuses		*mr,* Fr. I–H.II		*bailli,* Amiens
Jean de Sénicourt sr. de Saisseval d. 29 July 1546	Ardres, 1540s	*mh* 1540–6		
François, sr. de Stavaye	Ribemont –1552	*ec.ec.* 1951–49+		*chamb.* to Vendôme

Name	Governorship	Court post	Gendarmerie	Other
Jean, de Torcy	Abbeville, 1529–31		l. Vendôme	
Jacques, sr. de Wallon	Ribemont 1552–			*chamb.* to Vendôme

Sources:
For court posts: copies of the *rôles* of the *officiers domestiques de l'hôtel du roi*, 1460–1560 BN fr. 21449–50; copies of the *rôles* of the *officiers* of the military household, BN fr. 21448. For town captaincies, numerous mentions in general correspondence.

Appendix 3A. *The military establishment in Picardy, 1521–59*

(*Etats*, assignations for payment and estimates)

1521

(1) accounts of the *ordinaires des guerres* for gendarmerie, 1520–21 (BN fr. 2933 fo. 1–7): account for Jan.–Mar. 1521 (in *livres t.*)

40 lances (Pont-Rémy)	3,720
20 lances, Boulogne (La Fayette)	1,800 (= 30 lances at *petit paye*)
100 lances, Tournai (Loges)	7,800
33.3 lances, Thérouanne (Fresnoy)	3,100 (paid only Jan.–Aug. 1520)
Total: 193.3 lances	16,420 per quar. at *grand paye*
Total for kingdom, 1,233.3 lances	*18,935.8.8*

(2) Levies ordered in April 1521 (Du Bellay, I, 125–6)
Under duke of Vendôme:

Cavalry:	Infantry: (each with 400 men)
C. de Luxembourg, c. of Brienne	Jean de Sarcus
A. de Sarrebruck, c. of Brayne	Jean d'Estrées
Jean d'Humières	Sr de Bournonville
Antoine d'Ailly, vid. of Amiens	G. de Pisseleu-Heilly
Jean de Haplaincourt	Louis de Mailly, sr de Lalleu
F. de Rasse, sr de La Hargerie	N. de Montmorency, sr de Bours
Philippe de Croy, sr de Renty	Sr de Bellegarde
	G. sr de Preteval 'et autres'

(3) Estimates for an army for the relief of Tournai, July 1521 (BN fr. 2968 fo. 26)

Horse for the guard of Picardy	2,000 (1,000–1,200 allowed)
Picard foot	7,000
Swiss	3,000
Aventuriers under Saint-Pol	3,000

(4) 'Estat de l'extraordinaire pour Picardie, Champaigne et Bourgogne', Nov. 1521 (BN fr. 3002 fo. 80) (in *livres tournois*)

Swiss	100,000
10,000 men under the constable	60,000
6,000 *aventuriers* under Saint-Pol	37,000
8,400 men under Vendôme	48,000
2,000 men at Dijon	11,000
1,000 men at Tournai	5,000
1,000 men at Mouzon and Mézières	5,000
2,000 men under Beauvaux etc.	11,000
2,000 horse under the constable	16,000
2,000 horse under Vendôme	16,000
500 horse under Brienne	3,700
Artillery	20,000
cas inopinez, supplies	50,000
Total	*382,700*

(5) Winter quarters in Picardy, 1521–2 (Du Bellay, I, 169–70, 208–9)

Abbeville	2,000 Swiss
Hesdin	1,000 foot (Hutin de Mailly, La Barre)
Boulogne	75 *gens d'armes* (La Fayette, Rochebaron)
Thérouanne	50 *gens d'armes* (Fresnoy)
	Dammartin (25)

Listenay (25)
Vauguion (25)

Bray-sur-Somme	25 *gens d'armes* (Lavedan)
Montreuil	Theligny's company
Doullens	Vendôme's company
Corbie	Saint-Pol's company
Péronne	Humières's company
Saint-Quentin	Chabannes's company
Guise	Guise's and Brienne's companies
Vervins	Count of Brayne's company

1522

Garrisons ordered by Vendôme in Picardy, summer 1522 (Du Bellay, I, 244–5)

Boulogne	50 *gens d'armes* (La Fayette)
	100 (Alençon)
	25 *hs. d'armes* (Rochebaron)
	1,000 foot (Bourbarré)
Thérouanne	Chabot de Brion (lieut. gen.) part co.
	50 *hs. d'armes* (Fresnoy)
	Dammartin (25)
	Listenay (25)
	Turenne (25)
	1,000 foot (capt. Saulseuze, Norman)
	1,000 foot (capt. Montbrun)
Hesdin	30 *hs. d'armes* + 20 *mortespaies* (du Biez)
	1,000 foot (Sarcus)
	500 foot (La Lande-Longueval's command)
Montreuil	400 *hs. d'armes* (Saint-Pol)
	6,000 foot (Guise – commanded by Lorges)
Abbeville	2,000 Swiss + gendarmerie + French foot
	(Vendôme and La Trémoille)
Total: Gendarmerie	*705+*
Infantry	*12,700+*

1523

Army of Vendôme, May 1523 (Du Bellay, I, 254–5)

'Blancherose' duke of Suffolk	4,000 Germans
Jean de Sarcus	
Bournonville	
La Hargerie	
A. de Pisseleu	4,000 Picards
	500 *hommes d'armes*
Chabot-Brion	400 archers of the royal guard
La Fayette	*maître de l'artillerie*

1530–4

Estat de le gendarierie, 1530 (BN fr. 4050 fo. 98–9), compared with companies paid from the Louvres coffers in 1534 (*CAF* VIII.721, 28608)

Companies in Picardy

1530		*1534*
Vendôme	80	100
Montmorency	80	100
Humières	40	100 (the Dauphin)
La Rochepot	40	40
Du Biez	40	40

Du Lude	40	—
De Fresnoy	40	40/50
La Roche-du-Mayne	40	40/50
La Meilleraye	30	—
Créquy	24	40/50
Bernieulles	24	40/50
Total	*478 lances*	

1536
Infantry dispositions in June, of 2,000 paid (BN fr. 3069 fo. 28, 32; fr. 3008 fo. 85)

Montreuil, Sarcus	300
Rue, Sarcus	100
Thérouanne	300 (incl. 100 of Boulonn. legion)
Saint-Riquier, Saisseval	100
Guise, Vervins, under Heilly	400
Infantry at L 12,000	*2,000*

August:
'Compaignons de guerre' *6,000* (raised in Picardy and Ile-de-France, Dupuy 486 fo. 89)

1537
(1) The royal army of invasion of Artois (Lot, p. 65)

Lansquenets, Fürstemberg	10,000
Lansquenets, Würtemberg	10,000
	25,000–30,000 foot and 6–7,000 horse

(2) Army of the Dauphin and Montmorency, June 1537 (Lot, p. 66)

Gendarmerie	1,600
Light horse	2,000
Lansquenets	12,000
French infantry	14,000

(see also 'L'ordre de l'armée', BN fr. 20502 fo. 69 and *role* of payments fr. 3044 fo. 39–109)

(3) Garrison troops in 1537–8 (*CAF* VIII)

Mortespaies	370 (30,182)
Garrison infantry	3,000 (29,301)
aventuriers, reinforcements	1,300–1,450 (29,301, 29,610, 29,735, 29,801)
Légion under Heilly	500 (30,596)

1538
(1) Payments to gendarmerie in Picardy, April quarter (*CAF* VIII, p. 232–)

Dauphin/Humières	100 (31,416)
Vendôme	70 (31,425)
La Rochepot	100 (31,423)
Brienne	50 (31,343)
Du Biez	50 (31,440)
Torcy	50 (31,444)
Villebon	50 (31,449)
Total	*470 lances*

(2) 'Mémoire des choses dont M. de Piennes aura à advertir M. de La Rochepot' signed by the king 4 May 1538 (BN fr. 3088 fo. 9–12)
Dispositions of troops if peace not concluded:

Legion of Picardy	6,000 ?
Part of Normandy and Champagne	4,000
Thérouanne	50 lances (Villebon)

	50 lances (La Rochepot)
	600 foot + Saisseval's band
Guise	80 lances (*bailli* de Vitry)
	70 lances (Vendôme)
	1,000 foot of Lalande
Boulogne	50 lances (Du Biez)
	1,000 fuut
Hesdin	50 lances
	1,000 foot under Heilly
Doullens	1,000 foot under Bouchavannes

1539

Rôle of gendarmerie dat. Compiegne, 11 Oct. 1539 (BN fr. 20502 fo. 10)

Lances in the kingdom	2,400
In Picardy	610 (in 12 companies)

1543

(1) Estimate of forces needed in maritime Picardy (letter of du Biez, 9 July, in Rosny 'Documents inédits' pp. 389–90)

Infantry	4,000 (3,000 present)
Gendarmerie	400 lances (350 present: Du Biez, Créqui, Villebun, Espinac, La Rochcpot)

(2) Royal army at Maroilles, July 1543 (Lot, pp. 69–70)

Cavalry	1,600–1,800 *hommes d'armes*
	1,800 light horse
Infantry	12,000 *légionnaires*
	4,000 *lansquenets* (Rognac)
	4,000 *lansquenets* (Fresnoy of Lorraine)
	4,000 *lansquenets* (L. Wondoven)

1544

Defensive troops in Picardy under Vendôme in summer (Lot, p. 116n)

Present	10–12,000 foot from Picardy, Normandy, Beauvaisis
Expected	8,000 Italians
	3,000 *lansquenets*

1545

Expedition of du Biez to the terre d'Oye (du Bellay, IV, 307–8)

Cavalry	1,000–1,200 *hommes d'armes*
	700–800 light horse
Infantry	12,000 *lansquenets*
	12,000 French
	6,000 Italians
	4,000 *Légionnaires*

1547

Estat de la gendarmerie (Lot, pp. 231–2)

For the whole kingdom	51 companies
For Picardy/Ile-de-France	14 (? 12 in Picardy)

1549

'Estat abrégé du nombre des gens de guerre à pied estans en Picardye et Boullonoys', Nov. 1549 (BN fr. 20543 fo. 54–5, 60)

Lansquenets:

Rhingrave's 4 ensigns	1,540
Wondoven's 8 ensigns	2,701
French and Gascons:	
10 old bands	2,887
11 new bands	3,208
7 garrison ensigns	1,480
Others	990
Total infantry	*12,476*

Light horse:

Entragues	100
Sipierre	100
Pelloux	50
At Outreau	30
Total light horse	*280*

Gendarmerie:

Péronne, Dauphin	80 lances
Abbeville, La Rochepot	40
Boulonnais, Du Biez	80
Hesdin, Crequi	40
Doullens, Langey	40
Saint-Quentin, Enghien	40
Laon, La Roche-sur-Yon	40
Thérouanne, Villebon	40
Beauvais, Coligny	40
Noyon, La Meilleraye	40
Total gendarmerie	*480 lances (1,200 men ?)*

Legions:

Normandy, 4 ensigns	1,200
Picardy, 4 ensigns	1,200
Total legionnaires	2,400
Grand total	*16,356*

1550

Estat de despense in Picardy of B. Le Grand, *trés. de l'extraordinaire des guerres*, Jan. 1550 (BN fr. 4552 fo. 12)

Lansquenets:

Rhingrave, 4 ensigns	1,523 men	15,092 *livres*
L. Wondoven, 8 ensigns	2,730 men	28,634
French infantry:		
Old bands, 11 ensigns	3,300 men	28,022
New bands, 10 ensigns	3,000 men	32,412
Garrison	1,170 men	9,900

1554

The royal army at Corbie, August (Rabutin, I, 221–4)
Avant-garde:

Gendarmerie, 6 cos. of 200 lances	1,200 *hommes d'armes* + 1,800 archers
French infantry, Coligny	10–12,000 (49 ensigns)
Lansquenets, Rhingrave	10–12,000 (20 ensigns)
Scots and English	1,200–1,500 (8 ensigns)
Light horse, Sansac	200
Arrière-ban, Jaille	3,000
Battle:	
King and three princes	4 regiments of *hommes d'armes*
Royal household	2 companies
Gentlemen in king's service	?
Artillery, Estrées	
Total	9,200–9,500 horse and 35,200–39,000 foot

1554

(1) 'Estat de l'armée du Roy où il sera ceste année' (BN fr. 3090 fo. 12; Lot, p. j. x)

Royal household	200 gentlemen
	400 archers
	1,800 *hommes d'armes*
Mounted *arquebusiers*	1,000
Light horse	3,000
Arrière-ban, cavalry	2,000
French infantry	15,000 (50 ens., incl 40 old Piedmont)
Lansquenets	11,000 (32 ens. in 4 reg.)
Swiss	7,000
Scots	1,800 (6 ens)
Total	34,800 foot and 8,400 horse

(2) Picard garrison in June 1554 under La Roche-sur-Yon (Rabutin, pp. 255–7)

Hommes d'armes	300
Infantry, mostly Picards	9–10,000 (rest old bands)
Light horse/mounted *arqu.*	5–6,000

1557

(1) 'Departement des bandes des chevaux-légiers . . . en Picardie', Jan. 1557 (copy, BL Add. 38030 fo. 290)

5 bands of 50	250
4 bands of 100	400
2 bands of 50 mounted arqu.	100
Total	*750*

(2) *Rôle* of gendarmerie, July 1557 (BN fr. 20532 fo. 46–7)

Number for the kingdom	3,320 lances
Boulogne	50
Saint-Quentin	320
For the army to be assembled	960 + 480

(3) Estat abrégé des gens de pied en Picardie' (1557) (*Ibid.*)

Arquebusiers à pied	2 bands
4 bands of 270	1,080
14 bands of 200	2,800
8 bands of 80 horse/150 foot	1,200 foot + 640 horse
20 bands of 280	5,600
7 bands of 280 (Nevers)	1,960

4 bands of 200	800
8 bands of 200	1,600
Total	*15,400 + arqu. à pied + 640* horse

Light horse:

9 cornettes of 100	900
15 cornettes of 50 + 10 *arqu.*	900
1 cornette of 80 + 10	90
1 cornette of 60 + 10	70
3 cornettes of 25	75
Total	*2,035*

(4) The constable's army for the relief of Saint-Quentin (Lot, p. 169; Rabutin)

Cavalry:

Hommes d'armes	900–1,000
Light horse	1,000
Pistoliers	700–800
Total	2,800 max.

Infantry:

Lansquenets	11,000 (22 ens. of 500)
French	4,500–4,800 (15/16 ens. of 300)
Total	*15,500–15,800*

1558

(1) 'Estat de l'assignation' for Picardy, Jan. 1558 (BN Clair. 346, pp. 77–92)

Garrison:

Arquebusiers à pied	2,400
Horse	480
Old bands	3,600
New bands	7,500
Garrison infantry	3,364
Lansquenets	8,400
Pistoliers	600
Total	*26,344*

(2) 'Estats des forces' of the royal army for Summer

	BN fr. 4552	BN fr. 20470 fo. 167
Hommes d'armes	2,320	2,300
Light horse	1,000 French	
	600 Scots	2,000
	500 mounted *arqu.*	
Pistoliers	7,000	8,300
Royal guards	?	?
Gentlemen of the household	200	200
King's personal cornette	?	?
Duke of Guise, same	?	?
Lansquenets	16,000	18,000 (60 ens. 300)
Swiss	6,000	6,000
French infantry	12,000 (30 ens. 400)	22,000 (55 ens. 400)
French *arquebusiers*	2,800 (14 ens. 240)	
Totals	*48,420*	*58,800*

(3) Review of the royal army at Pierrepont, 8 Aug. (Lot, pp. 179–85)

	BN fr. 3081	Rabutin
Light cavalry	1,500.	1,400
Gendarmerie	1,550 lances (2,325)	1,750 lances (2,625)
Pistoliers	8,000	8,100
French infantry	5,400 (18 ens. 300)	5,400
Swiss	1,800 (6 ens. 300)	1,800
Lansquenets	19,200 (64 ens. 300)	18,900
Pioniers	3,000	3,000
Royal household	200	?
Totals	*41,425*	*41,225*

Appendix 3B. *Infantry bands in Picardy, November 1549 – as planned and as mustered*

(Notes detail musters of companies surviving separately during 1540–50, for comparison)

Garrison	Captain	Plan[1]	Muster[2]	
Ambleteuse	Coligny	300	299	old
	Villefranche[3]	300	300	old
	Baron	300	291	old
	Favas[4]	300	278	old
	Cleve	?	286	old
Blaquenez	Sainte-Marye	300	285	old
Montlambert	Auvringen	300	300	new
	Bonaventure	300	300	new
La Mothe Rouge	Cressonières	300	300	new
Oultreau	Riou[5]	300	296	old
	Riou	300	298	new
	Salcedo[6]	300	299	old
	Gordes	300	260	old
	Hamel	300	296	new
	Coligny[7]	?	300	new
Portel	Serf	300	300	new
	Lignières	300	298	new
	Villaines	300	267	new
	Santrisse	300	259	new
Fort Châtillon	Soleil	300	293	old
	Briquemault	300	290	new
Desvres, Monthulin	Pocques[8]	240	260	garrison
Montreuil	Saternault[9]	100	100	garrison
Ardres	Blerencourt[10]	300	300	garrison
	Dampont[11]	200 (*arquebus*)	200	garrison
Thérouanne	Villebon[12]	100	100	garrison
Le Câtelet	Estrées[13]	80	400	garrison
La Capelle	Esguilly	120	120	garrison

[1] 'Estat de despence' of Benoist Le Grand, *trésorier de l'extraordinaire* in Picardy, January 1549, BN fr. 4552 fo. 12–15.
[2] 'Estat abrégé du nombre de gens de guerre à pied estans en Picardye et Boullonoys', mustered November 1549, BN fr. 20543 fo. 54–5.
[3] Muster at Oultreau, 13 April 1549, 288 French and Gascon *aventuriers* under Villefranche, captain Breuil lieut., BN fr. 25974 no. 59.
[4] Muster at Oultreau, 1 Feb. 1550, 289 French and Gascon foot under sr. de Favas, lieut. La Basca, BN fr. 25794 no. 91. Jean d'Auberard, sr. de Favas, capt. of the old bands, acq. of a castle in Albigeois, 1552, BN fr. 5128, p. 107.
[5] Muster at Oultreau of 200 Picard foot under Thibault Rouault, sr. de Riou, conducted by his lieut. the sr. de Heucourt, BN fr. 25794 no. 71.
[6] Muster at Oultreau of 299 French and Gascon foot under Pierre de Salcedo, 1 Feb. 1550, capt. Breuil lieut., BN fr. 25794 no. 92.
[7] Coligny was colonel of all 8 ensigns in the Boulonnais but also captain of 288 *aventuriers* and Gascons mustered at Oultreau 10 May 1549, conducted by the sr. de Blecquin his lieut., BN fr. 25794 no. 69.
[8] Muster of 200 French and Picard *aventuriers* at Monthulin, 14 April 1548, under Jean Pocques, the sr. Decluzes lieut., BN fr. 25794 no. 29.

9 Muster of 100 French and Picard *aventuriers* at Montreuil under the sr. de Saternault, 10 May 1549, BN fr. 25794 no. 70.

10 Muster at Ardres, 18 May 1549 of 200 French and Picard foot under sr. de Blerencourt, François de Brisse lieut., BN fr. 25794 no. 75.

11 Muster at Ardres, 18 May 1549 of 200 French and Picard foot under Adrien de Dampont, BN fr. 25794 no. 76 (also infantry muster *commissaire* – promoted to *commissaire ordinaire des guerres*, 20 April 1552, BN fr. 5128, p. 123).

12 Muster at Thérouanne, 14 May 1549, of 100 French and Picard foot under Villebon, BN fr. 25794 no. 73.

13 Musters at Le Câtelet of 80 French and Picard *aventuriers* under Estrées, 14 April, 16 May 1549, capt. Benard lieut., BN fr. 25794 no. 61, 74.

Appendix 3C. *Lansquenet companies in Picardy, 1548–50*

Captain	1548 June[1]	Nov.[2]	Nov. 1549[3]	Jan. 1550[4]
Under Lodovich Wondoven:				
Felix de Joinville	300	300	321	340
Engelard von Mallin	300	298	342	353[9]
Jheronime Franch[5]	300	300	353	343
Baptiste Jacob	300	300	338	352
Philipp de Auberk	300	298	352	336
Jacob Munich	300	296	331	333
Michel Schercheymer	300	300	326	328[10]
P. Herschof/Georges Dondreval	300	298	338	345
Under the Rhingrave:				
Jacques de Nieuvylle	300		?	?
Nicholas Wilstein	300		395	388[11]
Achatius Sterne	300		356	349[12]
Tantonville	in Scotland		398	395[13]
Count von Kastel	in Scotland		391	391

Other ensigns of the Rhingrave in Scotland throughout:[6]

	1547–8	1549
Conrad von Rothouzen	300[7]	300
Hans Muret		300
Claud Ruik		300
Hans Danguestain	494[8]	300
Capt. Froch		300

[1] BN fr. 4552 fo. 8– 'Estat de paiement' to start 7 June (1548).
[2] Monstre des lansquenets à Blanzac sous Ludovic, 10 Dec. 1548, Angoulême, BN fr. 3036 fo. 44, pub. by F. Lot, *Recherches sur les effectifs*, 232–3.
[3] BN fr. 20543 fo. 54–5 – 'Estat abrégé des gens de guerre à pied estans en Picardye . . . pour le mois de novembre derrenier.'
[4] BN fr. 4552 fo. 12 – 'Estat de despence' of Benoit Le Grand, Jan. 1550.
[5] Original muster at Abbeville, 11 April 1548, 300 men, Peter Fresvic lieut., BN fr. 25794 no. 27.
[6] 'Estat de la despense que le Roy veult à present estre faicte en Escosse' BN fr. 18153 fo. 69v, 20 Apr. 1549.
[7] Original muster at Montivilliers on point of embarkation, BN fr. 25794 no. 67.
[8] Original muster at Vaux sous Laon, 10 Aug. 1547 'nouvellement descenduz en France', BN fr. 25794 no. 14.
[9] Original muster of 317, Mont d'Aumalle (Lambert), nr. Boulogne, 1- Jan. 1550, BN fr. 25794 no. 87, Adolf Reuth, lieut.
[10] Original muster of 291 at Mont Lambert, 1 Feb. 1550, BN fr. 25795 no. 96.
[11] Original muster of 329 at Mont Lambert, 1 Mar. 1550, BN fr. 25795 no. 98.
[12] Original muster of 200 at Auxi-le-château, 30 April 1550, BN fr. 25795 no. 100. lieut. Melchior Genfalph.
[13] Original muster of 355 at Mont Lambert, 1 Mar. 1550, BN fr. 25795 no. 99, lieut. Gaspar de Munthe.

Appendix 4. *Financial allocation for Picardy, 1537–8*

Period	Sum (*livres t.*)	Source (*CAF*)
Mar.–Apr. 1537	400	29277
	158,679	29284
	8,869. 7.6	29301
	13,000	29326
	5,481	29337
	45,539. 9.0	29371
	20,000 *écus*	29373
	12,775. 6.9	29376
	90,000	29382
	19,316.15.0	29399
	41,560	29401
	13,369	29402
	43,100. 2.6	29403
	3,000	29424
	3,000	29435
	270	29454
Total: 557,653.16.5	99,393.16.8.	29469
20,000 *écus*		
Apr.–May–June 37	1,692	30541
	1,200	30542
	7,014 (4,000 paid)	30544
	4,000	30546
	6,015	30547
	21,000 (5,000 paid)	30548
Total: 48,641	7,720	30522
June 1537	22,500	30430/4*
	3,000	30568
	4,000	30569
	77,927.16.8 decharge	30596
	16,657. 5.0	30598
	12,000	30668
	18,000	30683
	1,245	30156
Total: 157,580.1.8	2,250	30529
July 1537	30,000	30482
	4,500	30483
	7,500	30484
	5,000	30485
	12,000	30486
	8,000	30511
Total: 70,000	3,000	30200
Aug. 1537	9,000	30379*
	50,000	30427
	19,653	30428*
	15,000	30429
	22,500	30430
	71,229. 6.7	30431
	115,222	30290

Period	Sum (*livres t.*)	Source (*CAF*)
	2,741	30291
	53,369.10.0 decharge	30316
	10,386. 9.5	30325
	1,406. 5.0	30334
	15,000	30369
	2,271	30371
	12,062. 2.6	30375
	3,000	30377
	44,155	30778
	9,000	30779
Total: 469,176.4.3	13,180. 1.9	30421
Sept. 1537	84,461.11.9	30175
Total: 105,996.11.9	21,535	30181
Oct./Nov. 1537	?	?
Dec. 1537	9.097.10.0	29921
	6,000	29922
	9,097	29971
Total: 31,194.10.0	7,000	29992
Jan. 1538	10,167.10.0	29801
Feb. 1538	4,000	29689
Total: 58,000	54,000	29701
Mar. 1538	35,896	29600
Total: 48,663.10.0	12,767.10.0	29610
Apr. 1538	19,535	31409
June 1538	1,500	31572
July 1538	32,000	BN fr. 2995 fo. 285

•Loans to the king in cash or plate by Anne de Montmorency.

Appendix 5. *Assessment of the 'taillon' on the 'généralité' of Outre-Seine, 1550*

The first 'Estat de la creue et augmentation de la soulde de la gendarmerie' was fixed by the *conseil privé* on 12 Nov. 1549 at L 1,195,720, the principal *taille* then standing at 4,000,000 plus *crue* of 600,000. The apportionment by *généralités* was based on a notional number of lances:[1] (totals as given in manuscript)

Généralité	Apportionment	Lances
Normandy	71,743. 4.3	150
Outre-Seine	286,972.10.0	600
Burgundy	71,743. 4.0	150
Languedoil	310,887. 4.0	450
Guyenne	133,920.12.0	280
Languedoc	71,743. 4.0	150
Lyonnais etc.	47,828.16.0	100
Dauphiné	23,914. 8.0	50
Provence	23,914. 8.0	50
Piedmont	57,394. 6.2	120
Savoy	23,914. 8.0	50
Bresse	23,914. 8.0	50[2]

The *estat de l'assiette* within each *généralité* was fixed by the council on 20 November, that of Outre-Seine uniquely juxtaposing this with the *assiette* of the main *taille* of 4,600,000 in each *élection*:[3]

Election	main *taille*	*taillon*
recette-gén. Paris:		
Beauvais	22,155.18. 0	8,000
Compiègne	10,174. 1. 0	4,000
Clermont	12,837. 9. 0	5,000
Senlis	15,012.17. 4	5,000
Soissons	49,174. 7. 8	18,000
Mante	12,873.13. 6	5,000
Montford l'Amaury	5,773.19. 2	2,000
Chartres	53,478. 1. 4	22,000
Paris	68.434	22,000
Etampes	8,776. 4. 6	3,000
Meaux	43,414. 8. 4	18,000
Melun	28,410. 7. 4	9,000
Montargis	10,513.18. 0	4,000
Nemours	35,223.18. 6	12,000
Provins	15,726.16. 6	5,000
Château-Thierry	15,128.12. 8	5,000
Sens	26,920. 5. 8	10,000
Tonnere	11,177.11. 6	4,200
Vézelay	9,190.16. 0	3,000
Total	*454,409. 3.12*	*164,200*

Election	main *taille*	*taillon*	
recette-gén. of Châlons:			
Châlons	53,471. 3. 0	13,400	
Laon	21,801. 8. 4	8,000	
Langres	42,747.12. 2	10,680	
Reims	45,534.12. 8	15,000	
Rethelois	8,776. 4. 6	3,000	
Troyes	49,326.13. 4	18,000	
Sezanne	16,975. 1. 0	6,000	
Total	*238,632.16.10*	*74,080*	
recette-gén. of Amiens:			no. of par.[4]
Amiens	11,251. 4. 4	4,129. 1.0	300
Doullens	24,676. 6. 4	6,157	335
Saint-Quentin	5,804. 1.10	1,450.15.0	93
Ponthieu	18,167. 9. 4	4,543	191
Péronne, Mon. & Roye	39,948.16. 6	14,000	426
Noyon	23,104.13. 0	9,000	133
Total	*123,222.11. 4*	*39,279.15.0*	
recette part. Gien	*18,607.19. 2*	*8,000*	
Grand total	*834,782.10. 6*	*286,972.16.0*[5]	
		+	
		*4,810.17.*6 costs, collection	

[1] BN fr. 18153 fo. 118–19.
[2] The actual sums received are listed as the 'Estat des sommes' accorded by 'Le peuple des provinces' for 1550 as L 1,146,235.16.0. In the *généralité* of Outre-Seine the *recette-générale* of Paris recorded L 165,600, but the rest remained as assessed, BN fr. 18153.
[3] BN fr. 18153 fo. 126v–130r.
[4] As fixed by royal letters, 27 Oct. 1587, reg. at the *élection* of Amiens, BN Pic. 112 bis, fo. 51r, extract.
[5] The *taillon* for 1551 was again fixed at L 1,195,720 but with a supplement of L 180,000 for 'utencilles et meubles' formerly supplied to the gendarmerie. The portion of Outre-Seine was therefore L 288,972.15.0 + 43,200 (BN fr. 18153 fo. 283v). No apportionment by *élections* survives for this.

Appendix 6A. *The global assessment of the 'taille royale', 1461–1559*

Year of payment	Basic *taille* + *crues* (*livres t.*)	Source
1461	1,220,000	Clamageran for years 1461–1514
1483	4,440,000	
1484	1,220,000 + 300,000	
1485	1,500,000 + 463,000 *cr*	
1486	1,500,000	
1487	1,500,000 + 350,000 & 265,000 *cr* (2,115,000)	
1488	2,115,000	
1489	2,115,000	
1490	2,115,000 + 355,000 *cr*	
1491	?	
1492	2,115,000 + 800,000 *cr*	
1493	2,115,000	
1494	2,115,000	
1495	2,115,000	
1496	2,115,000 + 400,000 *cr*	
1497	2,115,000	
1498	2,155,000 + 300,000 *cr*	
1499	1,811,000	
1500	1,811,000	
1501	1,811,000	
1502	1,811,000 + 288,000 *cr*	
1503	1,811,000 + 400,000 *cr*	
1504	?	
1505	1,681,000	
1506	1,681,000	
1507	1,389,000	
1508	1,389,000 + 714,000 *cr*	
1509	1,389,000 + 300,000 *cr*	
1510	1,200,000	
1511	1,200,000 + 300,000 *cr*	
1512	2,000,000	
1513	2,800,000	
1514	3,300,000 (incl. *crues*)	

Date of levy		
Sept. 1514	3,000,000	*Ord.* I, no. 67
April 1516	600,000 *cr*	*Ord.* I, no. 46–7
Aug. 1515	2,900,000	*Ord.* I, no. 67–8
March 1516	6000,000 *cr*	*Ord.* I, no. 82
July 1516	2,900,000	*Ord.* I, no. 85
Aug. 1517	2,900,000	
Sept. 1518	500,000 *cr*	
Oct. 1518	2,400,000	*Ord.* II, no. 161
Feb. 1519	600,000 *cr*	*Ord.* II, no. 186
Sept. 1519	2,400,000	*Ord.* II, no. 226
Aug. 1520	2,400,000	*Ord.* II, no. 265
Dec. 1520	400,000 *cr*	*Ord.* II, no. 274 (*CAF*, 17336)
1521	2,400,000	Clamageran
Feb. 1522	600,000 *cr*	*CAF* I, 277, 1500

Date of levy	Basic *taille* + *crues* (*livres t.*)	Source
Aug. 1522	2,400,000	Clamageran
Dec. 1522	600,000 *cr*	*CAF* I, 315, 1700
Jan. 1523	861,000 *cr*	*CAF* I, 321, 1732
June 1523	2,400,000 *cr* excep.	*CAF* I, 343, 1837; 369, 1938
Jan. 1524	600,000 *cr*	Clamageran
Sept. 1524	2,400,000	*CAF* I, 388, 2074
Sept. 1525	2,661,000	*CAF* I, 418, 2219
Jan. 1526	600,000 *cr*	*CAF* I, 431, 2280
Aug. 1526	2,561,000	*Ord.* V, no. 445
Feb. 1527	600,000 *cr*	*Ord.* V, no. 445
	5,061,000 tot.	Clamageran
July 1527	600,000 *cr*. antic.	*CAF* I, 513, 2706
	5,061,000 tot.	Clamageran
Sept. 1528	3,261,000 incl. *cr.*	*CAF* I, 602, 3159
	5,.661,000	Clamageran
Sept. 1529	3,261,000 incl. *c.r*	*CAF* I, 663, 3469
Oct. 1530	3,061,000 incl. *cr.*	*CAF* I, 723, 3786
Oct. 1531	3,061,000 incl. *cr.*	*CAF* II, 84, 4267
1532	3,051,000 incl. *cr.*	AM Chauny
1533	3,051,000 incl. *cr.*	
1534	?	
1535	4,100,000	Clamageran
Oct. 1536	4,000,000	*CAF* III, 245, 8653
1537	4,280,000	Clamageran
1538	4,280,000	
1539	3,700,000 (300,000 rem.)	*CAF* IV, 118, 11537
1540	3,600,000	Clamageran
Aug. 1541	2,400,000	*CAF* IV, 233, 12077
	+ crues = 4,000,000	Clamageran
Sept. 1542	2,000,000 + 600,000 *cr.*	*CAF* IV, 369, 12735
Aug. 1543	2,000,000 + 600,000 *cr.*	*CAF* IV, 485, 13283–4
Sept. 1544	4,000,000	*CAF* VIII, 34159
1545	4,000,000	Clamageran
Sept. 1546	4,000,000 + 600,000 *cr.*	*CAF* V, 131, 15538, 132, 15361
Sept. 1547	4,000,000 (5,325,000 tot.)	*CAH* I, no. 989; Clamageran
Sept. 1548	4,000,000 + 600,000 *cr.*	*CAH* II, no. 3572
1549	4,000,000 (5,200,000 tot.)	Clamageran[1]
1550	4,000,000 (5,920,000 tot.)	
1551	4,000,000 (6,030,000 tot.)	
1552	4,000,000 (6,030,000 tot.)	
1553	4,000,000 (6,030,000 tot.)	
1554	4,000,000 (6,030,000 tot.)	
1555	4,000,000 (6,030,000 tot.)	
1556	4,000,000 (6,030,000 tot.)	
1557	4,000,000 (6,755,000 tot.)	
1558	4,000,000 (5,840,000 tot.)	

[1] Under Henri II the total figure includes the *soldes*.

Appendices

Appendix 6B. *Proportions of the 'taille'*

Year	Kingdom	Outre-Seine	Picardy	Percentage/Picardy
1461[1]	1,055,000	⎯⎯⎯ 85,000 ⎯⎯⎯		
1483[2]	3,837,313.12	604,975.14	55,000	1.4
1484[3]	1,500,000	208,800	55,000	3.6
1497[4]	2,305,000	270,000	40,084	1.7
1498[5]	2,555,000	?	41,333.15	1.6
1511[6]	1,499,899. 5	243,260. 3	28,898. 5	1.9
1514[7]	2,891,900	519,700	47,600	1.6
1522–3[8]	3,566,942	527,243	63,614	1.8
1550[9]	4,600,000	711,650	123,222	2.6

[1] Spont, 'La Taille en Languedoc', 1890, p. 367.
[2] *Ibid.*, 1891, p. 489.
[3] *Ibid.*, 1891, p. 487. *Généralité* includes Artois. Percentage is high but Picard contrib. was then adjusted to 20,000.
[4] *Ibid.*, 1890, p. 369 (MS Arsenal 4545) reduced to 20,084.
[5] Clamageran and *Ann. bull. SHF* 1866, 185–92.
[6] Spont, 'La taille en Languedoc' (1891), 487.
[7] *Ibid.*, 1890, p. 369. Made up: 23,100 + 24,500 'restes'.
[8] Excl. the *crue exceptionnel* of June 1523; Doucet, *L'Etat des finances*, 47. The proportion of Picardy for the cost of the gendarmerie was 1.4%,. *Ibid.*, 72–3.
[9] See appendix 5. *Généralité* now includes the whole of Picardy.

Appendix 6C. *Total contributions to the crown*

Type	1461[1]	1483	1497	1498	1514	1523
Domain	?	?	10,000	10,000	7,900	11,719
Mortagne			2,000	2,000	?	alienated
Aides	130,000	10,000	10,000	10,000	11,900	12,600[2]
Gabelle	35,000		4,460	4,460	6,400	7,033 (+ 3,012 *cr.*)
Taille	85,000	55,000	20,084	41,334	23,100	26,698 (+ 11,556)
Restes					24,500	
Anticipations						20,536
Special levies			⎯⎯⎯	⎯⎯⎯		4,824
Total	250,000	64,084[3]		114,338	73,800	97,978

[1] Includes Outre-Seine
[2] Includes L 800 for 'impositions et Péronne'.
[3] Actually paid, Spont, 'La taille en Languedoc' (1890), 368.

Note: the *généralité* of Picardy excluded Amiens (which was accounted for in Outre-Seine) but included Arthois until 1493. The *composition d'Artois*, *aides* voted by the Estates of Artois was fixed at L 14,000. After 1493, it was still accounted for fictionally in the receipt of the *généralité* of Picardy but balanced under *charges* as granted by the king to the archduke. (It was still accounted for in 1523 as conceded to Charles V under the terms of the 1515 treaty). The difference between the L 55,000 *taille* of 1483–4 and the 40–41,000 usually levied in the 1490s–1500s is therefore accounted for by the subtraction of the *composition d'Artois*.

Appendix 7. The 'taille royale' in the 'élections' of Picardy

(A) Recette-générale Picardy

(1) Election of Péronne, Montdidier and Roye

Date of brevet	Kingdom	Election	Péronne	
1477			330	LFM, 471
May 1478			140	LFM, 471
Jan. 1479			400	LFM, 472
May 1484		15,078.10.0	360	LFM, 473
Nov. 1484		14,084.10.0 + 214	460	LFM, 473
Nov. 85/Jan. 1486	1,500,000	14,710.10.0 + 324	460	AM BB 6 fo. 29r
Jan. 1487	1,500,000	14,880.10.0 + 324	480	AM BB 6 fo. 49r
Sept. 1487/Jan. 88	1,500,000	14,710 + 323	480	AM BB 6 fo. 68v
Nov. 1488			640	LFM, 474
May 1489, *crue*			220	"
Sept./Nov. 1489	2,400,000	14,804 + 274	570	AM BB 6 fo. 102v
Mar. 1490 *cr.*	(10,000, Pic.)	2,566	91.10	AM BB 6 fo. 108v
Oct./Nov. 1490		16,540 + 324	650	AM BB 6 fo. 125v
June 1491 *crue*			60	AM BB 6 fo. 139r
Nov. 1491			711	AM BB 6 fo. 156r
Mar. 1492 *crue*			311	AM BB 6 fo. 170r
May 1517			1134 (exempted)	AM BB fo. 33r
Apr. 1521			800+	AM BB 7 fo. 132v
Sept. 1522			318	AM BB 7 fo. 168r
1522–3			1134 (exempted)	
1524, antic (quit)			968	AM BB 7 fo. 231r
1550	4,600,000	39,948.16.6	exempted	(see app. 5)
1550, *taillon*	1,195,720	14,000	?	
Dec. 1560, *taillon*		?	300	AM BB 10 fo. 224v

(2) Election of Noyon

Date of brevet	Kingdom	Election	Chauny	
Oct. 1491	2,300,000	11,440	840	AM BB 1 fo. 4r
Mar. 1492 *crue*	800,000	?	246	AM BB 1 fo. 7v
Nov. 1492			852	AM BB 1 fo. 10r
Aug. 1517, antic.	500,000		225	AM BB 2, at f. 13 or
Oct. 1517	2,400,000	12,573	1040	AM BB 2, orig.
Mar. 1518, *crue*	600,000	3,054.5.0	270	AM CC 292
Nov. 1518			1034	AM BB 2 fo. 26r
Mar. 1519 *crue*	600,000		252	AM BB 2
Nov. 1519	2,400,000	12,573.18.0	1034	AM CC 292
Aug. 1521 *crue*		4,000	160	AM BB 3 fo. 5v
Oct. 1521	2,400,000	12,573	1050	AM BB 3 fo. 8, or.
Mar. 1522 *crue*	600,000	?	260	AM BB 3 fo. 14r
Sept. 1522	2,400,000	?	1050	AM BB 3 fo. 1r (nf)
Dec. 1522 *crue ant.*	600,000	?	260	AM BB 3 fo. 12r

Abbreviation
LFM Le Fons Mélicocq, 'Tailles et impositions'.

Date of brevet	Kingdom	Election		Chauny	
Feb. 1523 *crue*	361,000	?	112		AM BB 3 fo. 16r
July 1523			1050		AM BB 3 fo. 8r (nf)
Nov. 12/Jan. 1524			1042		AM BB 3 fo. 15v
June 1524 *crue*			371 ı 53		AM BB fo. 32r
Dec. 1531	3,061,000	15,887	1393		AM BB 4
Dec. 1532	3,051,000	16,653.8.11	1480		AM EE 1/BB 4 fo. 23
Dec. 1533	3,051,000	15,887.4.1	1354		AM BB 4 fo. 63, orig.
1550	4,600,000	23,104.13.0			see app. 5
1550 *taillon*	1,195,720	9,000			see app. 5

(B) Généralité of Outre-Seine

(1) Election of Compiègne

Date of brevet	Kingdom	Election		Compiègne	
June 1478 *crue*		410, artillery	140		AM BB 5 fo 4
Jan. 1478		full taille	1300		" (less 247)
June 1479 *crue*		artillery	220		AM BB 5
Jan. 1481			800		AM BB 5
Jan. 1482			2400		AM BB 7
Jan. 1483			2150		AM BB 7
Aug./Nov. 1484	1,500,000	3,103.9.4	780		AM BB 8 fo. 6v
Nov. 1486			950		AM BB 10
Nov. 1489			1240		AM BB 12
Nov. 1490			1183		AM BB 12
Nov. 1492			1283		AM BB 13 fo. 46v
Nov. 1493			1200		AM BB 13 fo. 75r
May 1494 *crue*			313		AM BB 13
Nov. 1494			1160		AM BB 13 fo. 90v
Nov. 1495			1152		AM BB 13 fo. 124r
July 1518	2,400,000	5,308	1135		AM BB 15 fo. 49r
Mar. 1519 *crue*	600,000	1,347	346		AM BB 15 fo. 65v
1537			2216		
Dec. 1538			2216		AM BB 19 fo. 20r
Dec. 1539		8,386.16.2	2072		AM BB 19 fo. 46v
Dec. 1544			2480 + 27		AM BB 20 fo. 41v
Mar. 1545 *crue*		1,349	369		AM BB 20 fo. 64r
Dec. 1545		9,060	2480		AM BB 20 fo. 111v
Dec. 1546		9,060.6.8	2450		AM BB 20 fo. 154v
1550	4,600,000	10,174.1.0			see app. 5
1550 *taillon*	1,195,720	4,000			see app. 5

(2) Election of Senlis

Date of brevet	Kingdom	Election		Senlis	
Mar. 1519 *crue*		1,958.4.0	230		AM BB 5 fo. 166r
Nov. 1519	2,400,000	7,832.6.0	940		AM BB 5 fo. 171v
Nov. 1520	2,400,000	7,832.16.0	930		AM BB 5 fo. 174r
Feb. 1521 *crue*		1,305 + 26	150		AM BB 5 fo. 175v
Aug. 1521 2nd *cr.*		1,305.9.0.	150		AM BB 5 fo. 181r

Date of brevet	Kingdom	Election	Senlis	
Oct. 1521		7,832.6.0	930	AM BB 5 fo. 186r
Mar. 1522 *crue*		1,958.4.0 + 26	225	AM BB 5 fo. 187v
July 1522		7,832	930	AM BB 5 fo. 195r
Dec. 1522 *crue*		?	225	AM BB 5 fo. 197v
Feb. 1523 2nd *cr.*		?	92	AM BB 5 fo. 198v
July 1523		7,832	900	AM BB 5 fo. 201v
Jan. 1524		8,046	930	AM BB 5 fo. 209r
June 1524 *crue*	261,000	819 ⎱	325.10	
June 2nd *crue*	600,000	1,963 ⎰		AM BB 5 fo. 211r
Oct. 1524		7,832	960	AM BB 5 fo. 214r
Feb. 1525 *crue*		?	336	AM BB 5 fo. 215v
Oct. 1525		8,652.4.4	1052	AM BB 5 fo. 224v
Mar. 1526 *crue*		1,994.17.0	234	AM BB 5 fo. 229v
Sept. 1526		9,160.12.5	1100	AM BB 5 fo. 236v
Mar. 1527 *crue*		1,963.4.0	247	AM BB 5 fo. 238v
Aug. 1527, antic.		6,694	853	AM BB 5 fo. 244v
		(1963 by antic.	244)	
Dec. 1527 *crue*		1,958.4.0	246	AM BB 5 fo. 249r
April 1528 *crue*		1,958	246	AM BB 5 fo. 253v
Dec. 1528		10,610.8.4	1400	AM BB 5 fo. 258r
Dec. 1529		10,610.8.4	1450	AM BB 5 fo. 258v
Dec. 1531		9,957.3.8	1317	AM BB 5 fo. 285r
Dec. 1532		9,957.13.8	1317	AM BB 5 fo. 291r
Dec. 1533		?	1350	AM BB 5 fo. 294v
Dec. 1534		?	1300	AM BB 5 fo. 297r
Dec. 1535		?	1402	AM BB 5 fo. 301r
Dec. 1536		?	1850	AM BB 5 fo. 311r
Dec. 1537		?	2072	AM BB 5 fo. 320r
Dec. 1538		?	?	AM BB 5 fo. 328r
Nov. 1541 *crue*			131	AM BB 5 fo. 341v
Oct. 1542 *crue*		?	320	AM BB 5 fo. 349v
Dec. 1542		?	2075	AM BB 5 fo. 351v
Oct. 1543		?	2201	AM BB 5 fo. 366r
Dec. 1545		13,054.13.4	322	AM BB 6 fo. 30r
Dec. *crue*		1,958	322	AM BB 6 fo. 30r
Dec. 1546		?	1950	AM BB 6 fo. 40r
Dec. 1548		13,054.13.4	1900	AM BB 6 fo. 52v
Dec. *crue*		1,958	270	AM BB 6 fo. 52v
Dec. 1549	4,000,000 ⎱	13,054.13.4	2000	AM BB 6 fo. 76v
Dec. *crue*	600,000 ⎰	1,958	270	AM BB 6 fo. 76v
Nov. 1549 *taillon*	1,195,720	5,490	805	AM BB 6 fo. 76v
Dec. 1551	4,000,000 ⎱	13,554.13.4 ⎱	1953	AM BB 6
Dec. *crue*	600,000 ⎰	1,958.4.0 ⎰	271	AM BB 6
Dec. *taillon*		6,324	897	AM BB 6
Oct. 1552, antic.			504	AM BB 6 fo. 113r

Appendices

Appendix 8. *The 'soldes des gens de pied'*

(1) Relative assessment of the 'soldes'

Généralité	1540s – typical levy	List of 1577
Paris + Ile-de-France	180,000	300,000
Senlis	18,000	17,200
Champagne	?	79,500
Vermandois	22,800/25,000	36,800
Picardy:		24,900
Amiens	2,400	14,000
Ponthieu	1,200	600
Boulogne	?	300
Péronne	900	5,100
Normandy:		
Rouen	85,000 (1548)	80,000
Caux	21,600	13,900
Caen	?	24,050

(2) Apportionment of the 'soldes'

(a) *'Bailliage' of Senlis*

Date	Purpose	Bailliage	Senlis	Compiègne	Beauvais
Mar. 1538	20,000 foot		1,200		
Mar. 1543	?	18,000	3,000		
Mar. 1544	50,000 foot	18,000		3,000	8,000
Mar. 1545	50,000 foot	12,000	?		
Mar. 1546	25,000 foot	9,000		1,200	2,500
Mar. 1547	25,000 foot	9,000	?	1,200	2,500
Mar. 1548	50,000 foot	18,000			5,310
Mar. 1549	?				
Mar. 1550	Boulogne camp.	6,000			
Mar. 1551	50,000 foot	?			6,000
Mar. 1552	50,000 foot	18,000			6,752
Jan. 1553	50,000 foot	18,000			
Dec. 1554	50,000 foot	18,000			

(b) *'Gouvernement' of Péronne, Montdidier and Roye*

Date	Purpose	*Gouvernement*	Péronne
Mar. 1547	25,000 foot	400	210.13.7
Feb. 1548	50,000 foot		450
Jan. 1550	Boul. Camp.	320	?
Mar. 1552	50,000 foot		450
Mar. 1553	50,000 foot		450
1560			300–400

(c) *'Bailliage' of Amiens*

Date	Purpose	Bailliage	Amiens	Montreuil
Mar. 1544	50,000 foot			300
Mar. 1545	25,000 foot		1,600	150
Mar. 1546	20,000 foot	1,200		112
Dec. 1547	(L 1,200,000)	2,400		
1552	50,000	2,400	1,200	
1553	50,000	2,400	1,300	
1554	50,000	2,400	1,200	
1555	50,000	2,400	1,200	
1556	50,000	2,400	1,200	
1557	50,000	2,400	1,200	
1558	50,000	2,400	1,200	
—				
1569			5,000	
1570			5,000	
1574		9,200	8,000	
1575		?	1,200	
1576		26,400 (*gén.*)	8,800	
1577		14,000	12,500 (red. to 10,000)	
1578		8,300	8,000 (red. to 4,000)	

(d) *'Bailliage' of Vermandois*

Date	Purpose	Bailliage	St-Quentin
Mar. 1547	25,000 foot	22,800	1,646 (reduced to L 823 in July)
1557			727.9.10

(3) *'Soldes' assessments of 1577 (Folger Library V.a. 146, fo. 55v–)*

Généralité of Picardy:

Bailliage of Amiens:	Amiens	12,500	
	Doullens	100	
	Corbie	400	
	Picquigny	150	
	St-Valéry	500	
	St-Riquier	150	
	Montreuil	200	Total: 14,000
Sénéchaussée of Ponthieu:	Abbeville	500	
	Le Crotoy	100	Total: 600
Sén. of Boulonnais	Boulogne	300	Total: 300
Gouvernement of Péronne:	Péronne	2,000	
	Montdidier	1,800	
	Roye	300	
	Ancre	200	
	Bray-s-Somme	100	Total: 4,400

Généralité of Champagne:

Bailliage of Vermandois	Reims	15,000	
	Chalons	7,000	
	Laon	2,500	
	Soissons	2,500	
	Noyon	1,500	
	St-Quentin	600	
	Ribemont	300	
	Chaveny	600	
	Coucy	500	
	Beaumont	300	
	Ham	200	
	Nesle	400	
	La Fère-s-O	500	
	Veilly?	300	
	Guise	800	
	Bohain	150	
	Aubenton	150	
	Marle	300	
	Bumeres?	100	
	Crépy-en-L	150	
	Dochery?	200	
	Cormissy	400	
	Vervins	500	
	Breme	600	
	Fère-en-T	800	
	Visuresme?	100	Total: 36,900
			Total for Champagne: 79,500

BIBLIOGRAPHY

MANUSCRIPT SOURCES

FRANCE
Paris
Bibliothèque Nationale
fonds français (grouped according to provenance):
Papers of Florimond Robertet: 2930, 2931, 2933, 2963, 2968, 2985, 2971, 2991, 3030, 3052, 3059, 3060, 3082.
Papers of La Fayette: 2888, 2933, 2934, 2968, 2971, 3030, 3057.
Papers of Anne de Montmorency: 2915, 2973, 2974, 2979, 2976, 2977, 2987, 2986, 2995, 2997, 3000, 3004, 3055, 3006, 3007, 3012, 3016, 3022, 3021, 3019, 3028, 3027, 3032, 3038, 3039, 3046, 3047, 3046, 3049, 3052, 3047, 3054, 3058, 3070, 3072, 3082, 3150, 3511, 4050, 4051, 6620, 6637, 6635, 18741, 20460, 20461, (former Gaignières coll.): 20500–503, 20505, 20507–8.
Papers of Jean Breton de Villandry: 2977, 3000, 3016, 3081, 3088.
Papers of the Guise family: 6632, 20457, 20461, 20463, 20465, 20468, 20471–2, 20511, 20420–3, 20529–30, 20535–7, 20549, 20554–5, 20553, 20645–6.
Papers of Jacques Bourdin: 23191–3.
Papers of the Humières family: 2985–6, 3116, 3120, 3123, 3128, 3131, 3134, 3135, 3144, 3148, 3149, 3150, 3155.
Papers of La Rochepot (originally deposited at Monchy-Humières): 2915, 2978, 2979, 2982, 2995, 2997, 3077, 2008, 3029, 3035, 3041, 3044, 3052, 3055, 3056, 3058, 3062, 3068, 3069, 3071, 3081, 3082, 3088, 3110, 3116, 3119, 3124, 3120, 3127, 3134, 6635, 6639, 20500, 20504, 20510, 20507.
L'Aubespine Papers: 6604–6621.
Galland Collection (on domain of La Fère): 16832, 16831, 18959, 18962–4.
Papers of Duprat family: 4052.

Miscellaneous
2846   Coligny's negotiations, 1556
2900   Pensions list of Louis XI (Bouchage papers)
2930   *role* of Jean de La Forge, 1502–3
2959   commissaires de vivres, Picardy 1547–51
2968   negs. at Cambrai, 1528

3002	extraordinaire des guerres
3006	letter to Sénarpont
3044	Gendarmerie, 1537
3154	rôles des commandements, Henri II, 1551
3897	La Trémoille to Louis of Savoy, 1523
3913	Hellin correspondence, 1539–40
4050	état de la gendarmerie, 1530
4523	extraordinaire des guerres
4552	extraordinaire des guerres
4742	mémoires of Robertet de Fresne
5086	chancellery formulary
5127	reg des commandements, 1544–50
5128	reg. des commandements, Clausse, 1551–5
6343	Hallewin to Louis XI
8177	Inventaire des titres, Henri, prince de Condé
8546	Documents on Hallewin family
7856	Royal household
15540–41	Esquerdes et al. to the royal council, 1480s
17889–90	Mesnage papers, negotiations at Cambrai, 1545
15872	captains in Picardy, 1559
18153	register of conseil privé 1546–54
20440	La Rochepot to d'Inteville
20470	état de l'armée, 1558–9
20483–99	papers of Jean Bourrée, sec. to Louis XI
20502	rôles of gendarmerie, 1530s
20521	chancellery of Antoine de Bourbon, 1541–7
20532	état of army, 1557
20543	gens de guerre Picardie, 1549; La Hargerie
20648	Vendôme letters
20685	compte for Picardy, 1485 etc.
20991	Bassefontaine correspondence, 1556
21448–50	lists of royal household
21512–41	gendarmerie musters, 1522–60 (Gaignières)
25764–8000	infantry musters, 1521–63
26103	quittances
26132–3	quittances from chambre des comptes
32511	accounts, Picardy

Nouvelles acquisitions françaises:
8617–8624	Musters, 1520–62
9179	household of Marie de Luxembourg
10227	La Rochepot papers
23162	Bliss collection
23168	Humières papers
21698	Bourdin papers
23167	Heilly papers

Clairambault:
Guise papers: 339, 345–6, 347, 250, 351, 352 (including copies, Bourdin papers)
Other: 961   patents for governors

Dupuy:
263, 269   Jean du Bellay correspondence
273   Formulary
474   Trial of du Biez
486   letters to chancellor Duprat
726   correspondence of du Biez and d'Inteville

genealogical collections:
pièces originales: Estourmel (1081)
                      Feuquières (Pas) (2203)
                      du Biez (340)
                      Créquy (926–7)
                      Hallewin (1468)
                      Pisseleu (2291) fr. 28775
                      Montmorency (2031) fr. 28515
Dossiers bleus: Feuquières (512)
                   Rasse (557)

Collection de Picardie/dom Grenier:
8   population survey of 1772
26   plans
31   letter of Vendôme
89   originals and copies from archives of Laon and Saint-Quentin
98   documents on Soissons, Saint-Quentin
91   extracts from Abbeville archives to 1493
108   extracts from Péronne archives to 1547
112 bis   extracts from registers of bailliage of Amiens, 1505– ; of *élection* of Amiens,
           1570–
155   provisions for governors
174   royal letters from Péronne archives
300–1   documents from Abbeville archives
301   letters-patent of Henri II, 1552 on *soldes*; fortific. etc.

Reserve imprimés:
Chatre de Cangé Collection: (drawn from the Bourdin papers):
F 159   (Cangé 1)
F 164   (Cangé 6)
F 165   (Cangé 7)
F 172   (Cangé 14)
F 173   (Cangé 15)
F 220   (Cangé 62)

F 227   (Cangé 69)
F 230   (Cangé 72)

Bibliothèque de l'Institut de France
Coll. Godefroy 255 letters of Louis de Hallewin.

Archives Nationales
1 AP	La Trémoille papers
4 AP	Brienne papers
300 AP I	330, 333, 920 (archives of the house of Orléans: Bray, Ancre, etc.)
AB XIX 781	états de l'armée 1552–3 (Moreau Nelaton coll.)
AB XIX 3622–28	Coppet collection of autographs
J 964	
J 965	
J 967	Papers of chancellor Dubourg, mainly 1530s
J 968	
J 787–9	enclaves in Artois, frontier maps
J 786	disputes over Crèvecoeur
J 790	Saint-Pol
J 788	border negotiations
J 794	border negotiations
J 795	Saint-Pol
J 805	
J 806	documents on border negotiations
J 807	
J 1003	
J 1016	losses in Artois villages, 1542–4
J 1017	
K 71–75	Documents of 1470–97
K 560	Dénombrement, Ancre, 1532
KK 230	
KK 278ᴬ	account for lands of duke of Vendôme, 1549
KK 277	argenterie of Marie de Luxembourg, 1534–5
K 501	Election of Amiens, 1446–7
K 560	dénombrement of Châtellenie of Ancre, 1531
K 1097–8	register of pays reconquis
R⁴ 37*	Soissons, account 1544, 1568–9
R⁴ 73	La Fère, account 1531–3
*Q¹ 10¹	La Fère, recette 1585
*Q¹ 10²	register of leases, La Fère, 1585
Q¹ 917*	Orville, account 1518–19
Xᴵᴬ 1495	Conseil, Parlement, 1487
Xᴵᴬ 1527–8	Conseil, 1525
Xᴵᴬ 4829	Luxembourg succession, 1501
Xᴵᴬ 4823	

X¹ᴬ 4872   case between Oudart du Biez and La Fayette, 1523
X¹ᴬ 8624 ⎫
X¹ᴬ 8627 ⎬ letters-patent
X¹ᴬ 9319 ⎭
Z² 1   registre de plaids, Ancre 1477–85

Somme
Archives Départementales, Amiens
B 1   register of Bailliage, 1558
E 740–43   accounts of Falvy-sur-Somme
J 2555   accounts of Lucheux, 1429–1501
Typescript inventories: for destroyed archives of Abbeville
                        for archives of Lucheux

Archives municipales and communales
Amiens (at Bibliothèque Municipale)
AA 5, 12, 14   registers of charters and letters
BB 11–31   registers of échevinage, 1471–1558
CC 132, 137   accounts
EE 323   army supplies, orig. documents

Péronne (at Bibliothèque Municipale)
AA 8, 8, 20, 37, 40, 41, 42, 44, 45, 47, 49 original letters-patent
BB 6–10   registers of *échevinage* 1485–92, 1515–29, 1546–56, 1556–64
CC 1–4   comptes 1472–89, 1471–91, 1492–1500

Lucheux (in the town beffroi)
198–220   accounts for seigneurie 1502–1562
222–3   auditoire de justice 1517–20, 1551–71
118   accounts for Auxi-le-château, 1536–7
174   accounts for Mézerolles 1546–7

Bibliothèques:
Bibliothèque Municipale, Amiens
1150   Letters of Francis I, Vendôme
1157   Letter of du Biez
1189–91   Devauchelle Coll.
1707–9   Prarond Coll.
1785   Extracts from Abbeville archives

Bibliothèque de la Société des Antiquaires de Picardie
Chartrier of Heilly:
53, 54, 57, 58, 59i, 59ii, 60
129   letters to La Rochepot, 1537
136–7   documents on Picardy, 1456–1614

Bibliothèque Municipale, Abbeville
347   copies of register of *échevinage* 1426–1600 (by Le Ver)
378   copies of register of *échevinage*, 1493–1561
405   *registre aux plaids*, 1557–61
409i   comptes of Saint-Vulfran, 1515–17
410   building accounts, Saint-Vulfran, 1531–2, 1539–46
408   Courteville de Hodicq papers
441   Happeglenne papers
Livre rouge de l'échevinage – orig.
Livre blanc de l'échevinage – orig.
806–7   copies made by A. Ledieu

Pas-de-Calais
Archives départementales
9B 1   *Sénéchaussée* of Boulogne, register, 1550–6
9B 2   *ibid.*, 1556–61
12 J 196 Collection Rodière: Montreuil – notaires
12 J 199 *Ibid.*, Montreuil – acts before échevinage

Archives communales déposées
Hesdin: CC no. 3 661   comptes de l'argentier 1546–7
                            660   comptes de l'argentier 1550–51
                    GG 718, 742   table des pauvres, 1492, 1547
Montreuil-sur-Mer: CC no. 2   comptes de l'argentier 1547–8, 155–6, 1556–7,
                                  1557–8, 1561–2

Archives municipales et communales
Boulogne-sur-Mer
1   comptes de l'argentier 1563–4
705   contrerolle des vins 1551–2
706   contrerolle des vins 1552–3
707   extraits des comptes 1558–62
970   renouvellement des privileges par Henri II, 1551
1013   registre de *l'échevinage* 1550–1618

Saint-Omer
Correspondance du Magistrat: 4A (1521–5)
                              4B (1521–5)
                              5A (1525–49)
                              5B (1525–49)
Délibérations municipales: 3 Reg. H 1544–50

Aisne
Archives Départementales
Bailliage royale of La Fère:
B 662   doc. of 1555

B 671	audience, 1561
B 672	audience, 1562–3
B 673	*ibid.*, 1563–4
B 810	docs. of 1523
B 875	inventaires après décès. 1556–
B 1217	domaine of La Fère, 1542
E 657–644	comptes, châtellenie of Vendeuil, 1451–1536

Archives Municipales déposées
Chauny

AA 6	letters of Vendôme, 1545
AA 12	octrois
BB 1–6	délibérations, 1491–2, 1517–38, 1545
CC 4	comptes 1540–41
CC 929	brevets de taille, 1518–19, visitation des comptes, 1488–1523
EE 1	petition on status of Chauny, 1586, brevet de taille, 1532
EE 12	patent of commissaires de vivres in Picardy, 1557
EE 5	certificate for billeting, 1530
FF 26–8	audiencier 1486–1547

Laon

EE 2	correspondence, military affairs, 1472–4, 1479
EE 3	*ibid.*, 1475
EE 4	*ibid.*, 1479–95
EE 5	*ibid.*, 1518–25
EE 6	*ibid.*, 1536–42

Archives Municipales et communales
Saint-Quentin (at Bibliothèque Municipale)

liasses	4	letters patent, 1518
	30B	*ibid.*
	37A	arrêts of Parlement
	52	ordonnances of Vendôme
	69	comptes 1526–7, 1541–2, 1553–4, 1555–6
	116	comptes, chaussées et travaux
	127	letters-patent
	134	*ibid.*
	138	comptes des aides et octrois, 1533–4, 1556–7
	160G	correspondence
	150O	correspondence
	150H	correspondence
	151C	correspondence
	151L	correspondence
	181L	correspondence
	182B	correspondence
	182B	correspondence

275   comptes, *béguinage*, 1523–4, 1544–7
280   *ibid.*, 1525–8
292   comptes, biens de pauvres, 1536–7, 1539–40
Collection of Le Serrurrier (deposited at Bibliothèque)

Oise
Archives Municipales
Compiègne
AA1   royal letters
AA 4   *ibid.*, 1552
BB 3–22 délibérations, 1472–1500, 1507–13, 1517–19, 1524–56
CC 1   letters on tailles
CC 36   comptes, 1514–17
CC 40   comptes, 1541–3
CC 43   comptes, 1550–59

Senlis
BB 5   registres de l'assemblée 1495–1544
BB 6   registres de l'assemblée 1544 1610

Bibliothèques Municipales
Beauvais
Collection Bucquet aux Cousteaux:
57 copies of registers of *échevinage* 1472–1553
59 *ibid.*, 1553–8

Château de Chantilly – Musée Condé
J II   letters of Anne de Montmorency
L I   correspondence of Montmorency, 1521–2
L II–X   *ibid.*, 1526–31
L XVI   Papers of Montmorency's secretary, Du Thiers, 1538–40
L XVII   Miscellaneous Montmorency papers, 1540–59
GE 1   seigneurie of Offémont
GE 2   seigneurie of Offémont
D 2   county of Guise (1443–1512)

Nord
Archives Départementales
B 195–7 Surveys of hearths, 1469
B 3616   confiscation accounts, 1542–4
B 3665   Marie de Luxembourg, 1529–30
B 18897, 18905, 18906, 18907, 18986, 18991, 19259, 19260, 19265, 19266, 19267
         Collection of lettres missives, 1515–30

Archives Municipales, Douai
BB 1

Other collections
Bibliothèque Municipale, Reims
Collection Tarbé
Collection des autographes

Bibliothèque Municipale, Rouen
Collection Léber
Collection des autographes

Château de Villebon, Eure-et-Loire
L'Aubespine archives (private archives)

Bibliothèque Inguimbertine, Carpentras
MS 409

UNITED KINGDOM
Public Record Office, London
SP 1   State papers of the reign of Henry VIII
SP 3   Lisle Papers
SP 70   State papers foreign, Elizabeth
PRO 31/3   Paris transcripts
PRO 31/18   Vienna transcripts

British Library
Cotton Manuscripts, E I & II, D X & XI
Harleian Manuscripts 288 – Cobham corresp.
Copies of manuscripts in the Gaignières Coll. (BN): Egerton 2 & 3, Add. MSS 38028–38035
Original French correspondence: Egerton 5–26
Add. MS 18741, papers from Ribier's collection (Castelnau etc.)
      24180, Anon Milanese travel journal

AUSTRIA
Haus-, Hof und Staatsarchiv, Vienna
PA 54 & 55 intercepts of French military commanders in Picardy, 1544–5
Frankreich, Varia fasz. 6–7

ITALY
Archivio di Stato, Modena
Carteggio ambasciatori: Francia, B 20 (1544–5)
      B 21 (1545)
      B 25 (547–8)

UNITED STATES
Pierpoint Morgan Library, New York
Letters of French kings and leading ministers and commanders, sixteenth century. MF
etc. (from the L'Aubespine and Rhingrave archives).

Edward Laurence Doheny Library (St John's Seminary, Camarillo, California)
Letter of Francis I to Heilly, 1543

Library of the Chicago Historical Society
New France Papers: Documents signed by Antoine de Bourbon, 1553

PRIMARY WORKS

INVENTORIES AND ARCHIVES
Abbeville, ville d', *Inventaire sommaire des archives municipales antérieures à 1790*
    ed. A. Ledieu (Abbeville, 1902).
Aisne, département de l', *Inventaire sommaire des archives départementales
    antérieures à 1790*, ed. A. Matton, J. Souchon, series A–E, 6 vols. (Laon, 1874–
    1936).
Amiens, ville d', *Inventaire sommaire des archives communales antérieures à 1790* ed.
    G. Durand, 7 vols. (Amiens, 1891–1925).
Beauvais, ville de, *Inventaire sommaire des archives communales antérieures à 1790*
    ed. R. Rose (Beauvais, 1887).
Boulogne-sur-Mer, ville de, *Inventaire sommaire des archives communales antérieures
    à 1790* ed. D. Haigneré and E. Deseille (Boulogne-sur-Mer, 1884).
Cambrai, ville de, *Inventaire sommaire des archives communales antérieures à 1790*
    ed. E. Sautier, A. Lesort (Cambrai, 1907).
Chauny, ville de, *Inventaire sommaire des archives communales antérieures à 1790* ed.
    J. Souchon (Laon, 1926).
Diegerick, I. L. A., *Inventaire analytique et chronologique des chartes et documents
    appartenant à la ville d'Ypres* 4 vols. (Ypres, 1853–9).
Douai, ville de, *Inventaire sommaire des archives communales antérieures à 1790* ed.
    C. Dehaisnes and J. Lepreux (Douai, 1862).
Dusevel, H. and baron de La Fons Mélicocq, *Archives de Picardie* 2 vols. (Amiens,
    1841).
Dusevel, H. *Etude sur les archives du château de Lucheux* (Amiens, 1857; *La Picardie*
    III, *passim*).
Gravelines, ville de, *Inventaire sommaire des archives communales antérieures à 1790*
    ed. J. Finot (1900).
Guesnon, A., *Inventaire chronologique des chartes de la ville d'Arras* (no date or
    place).
Hocquet, A., *Inventaire analytique des archives de la ville de Tournai* (Brussels, 1910).
Laon, ville de, *Inventaire sommaire des archives communales antérieures à 1790* ed.
    A. Matton, V. Dessein (Laon, 1885).
Lemaire, E., *Archives anciennes de la ville de Saint-Quentin* 2 vols. (Saint-Quentin,
    1898–1910) (Third vol. set but not published, see AM).

Nord, département du, *Répertoire numérique, série B (Chambre des comptes de Lille)*, *B 1–20216* ed. M. Bruchet (Lille, 1921).
Inventaire sommaire des archives départementales antérieures à 1790 8 vols., ed. abbé C. Dehaisnes, A. Desplanque, J. Finot (Lille, 1877–1906).
Pas-de-Calais, département du, *Inventaire sommaire des archives départementales antérieures à 1790* ed. Richard, Godin, Cottell, Haigneré *et al.* series A–H, 8 vols. (Arras, 1878–1911).
Seillière, G., *Inventaire des titres de la baronnie de Mello, 1300–1600* (Aurillac, 1932).
Somme, département de la, *Inventaire sommaire des archives départementales antérieures à 1790* ed. G. Durand, *et al.* 7 vols. (Amiens, 1883–1920).

DOCUMENTS

Anon., 'Attaque de la ville de Saint-Quentin par Frédéric de Horne (1485) et lettre inédite de Charles VIII', *Le Vermandois* 3 (1875), 595–7.
Anon., 'Lettre de Charles le Téméraire aux habitans de Saint-Quentin (1475)', *Le Vermandois*, I, 428–32.
Anon., 'La prise et réduction de la ville et cité d'Arras en l'an 1492', *Archives hist. et litt. du Nord de la France et du midi de la Belgique* (Valenciennes, 1833) 1st ser., 3, 401–122.
Anon., 'Lettre de M. d'Estourmel aux élus et au contrôleur des aides et tailles en l'élection de Ponthieu', *BSEA* 4 (1891–3), 94– .
Anon., 'Lettre de Charles IX à Sénarpont, 22 juin 1563', *Cab. hist.*, 1889–90.
Anon., 'Briefwechsel zwischen Herzog Christophen zu Würtemberg und den berünten Französichen Feldhern Johann Philippen wild-und Rheingrafen', *Patriotisches Archiv für Deutschland* (Frankfurt), 10, 157–344.
Archivio Documental Español: Negociacions con Francia 1559–67, 9 vols., Madrid, Real Academia de la Historia, 1950–4.
Beaurain, G., 'Testament de Bernard Bigant (1482)', *BSAP* 27 (1915–16), 209–20.
'Picardie. Etudes et documents historiques', *BSEA* (1922–24; 1925–8).
Beauvillé, V. de, *Recueil de documents inédits pour servir à l'histoire de la Picardie*, 4 vols. (Paris, 1865–90).
Bénard, L., 'Analyse sommaire des principaux documents dans les registres du roy de la sénéchaussée du Boulonnais', *MSAB*, 20 (1900).
Berger, R. and Dubois, R., *Quatre cents vues des villages d'Artois* (Mémoires de la Commission Départementale du Pas-de-Calais, vol. 10, part 2, Arras, 1960).
Berger de Xivrey, J. and Guadet, J., *Recueil de lettres missives de Henri IV*, 9 vols. (Paris, CDI, 1843–96).
Bernier, A. (ed.), *Journal des Etats Généraux de France tenus à Tours en 1484 sous le règne de Charles VIII rédigée en latin par Jehan Masselin* (Paris, CDI, 1835).
(ed.), *Procès-verbaux des séances du Conseil de Régence du roi Charles VIII* (Paris, CDI, 1836).
Blanchet, J. P. G. (ed.), 'Recueil de lettres missives addressées à Antoine de Bourbon, 1553–62', *Bulletin et Mémoires de la Société archéologique de la Charente*, ser. 7, 4 (1903–4), 29–185.
Bled, abbé O., *Regestes des évêques de Thérouanne 1500–1513*, 3 vols. (Paris, 1903–5).

Boom, G. de, 'Documents concernant les relations d'Antoine de Ligne avec Philippe le Beau, Marguerite d'Autriche, Charles V et Henry VIII', *Bull. de la Commission Royale d'Histoire*, 1950.

Bourilly, V.-L., and P. de Vaissière, *Ambassades en Angleterre de Jean du Bellay: la première ambassade (septembre 1527–fevrier 1529)* (Archives de l'histoire religieuse de la France, Paris, 1905).

Bouthors, A., *Coutumes locales du bailliage d'Amiens, rédigées en 1507* (*MSAP* in 4º, I & II, 1840–5, 1853).

Brewer, J. S., Gairdner, J. and Brodie, R. H., *Letters and Papers, Foreign and Domestic, of the Reign of Henry VIII*, 21 vols. (London, 1862–1932).

Calonne, baron A. de, 'Répartition entre les gentilshommes tenant fiefs nobles en Ponthieu de l'indempnité allouée à messire André de Bourbon Rubempré (1577)', *MSAP*, 23, pp. 71– , and *Amiens Glorieux* (1873).

'Jean et Raoul de Pocques, seigneurs d'Alincthun, en Boulonnais (1516–1600) d'après des lettres inédites', *MSAP*, 28, 505–36.

Catalogue des actes de François Ier (Académie des Sciences Morales et Politiques, ed. P. Marichal *et al.*), 10 vols. (Paris, 1887–1908).

Catalogue des actes de Henri II, ed. M. L. Baudouin-Matuszck and A. Merlin-Chazelas, Académie de Sciences Morales et Politiques, 3 vols. so far (Paris, 1979–1990).

Chabannes, comte Henri de, *Preuves pour servir à l'histoire de la maison de Chabannes*, 4 vols. (Dijon, 1872–7).

Histoire de la maison de Chabannes, 4 vols. in 9 parts (Dijon, 1892–1900).

Champollion-Figéac, A., *Captivité de François Ier* (CDI, Paris, 1847).

Champollion-Figéac, J. J., *Documents historiques inédits*, CDI, 5 vols. (1841–74).

Claude, H., 'Quelques lettres inédites de Philippe de Clèves', *Revue du Nord*, 49 (1967), 293–306.

Cocheris, H., *Notices et extraits des documents manuscrits conservés dans les dépôts publics de Paris et relatifs à l'histoire de la Picardie* (2 vols. Paris, 1854–8).

Courtois, A. (ed.), 'Rapports, déclarations et reliefs des fiefs . . . mouvans des château et chastellenie de Tournehem, 1542', *BSA Morinie*, I (1852), 2nd fas., 58–64.

'Manifestes de François Ier, de Charles-Quint et d'Henri VIII . . . 1543', *BSA Morinie*, 2 (1853), 46–55.

Dasent, J. (ed.), *Acts of the Privy Council of England*, 42 vols. (London, 1890–1938).

Des Forts, P., *Le château de Villebon, Eure-et-Loire* (Paris, 1914).

Devillers, L., 'Documents relatifs à l'arrestation de Louis de Luxembourg, comte de Saint-Pol . . . à Mons en août 1475', *Bull. Comm. Royale d'Hist.* ser. 4, vol. 17 (1890), 302–18.

Diegerick, I., 'Documents historiques concernant la ville de Tournai sous la domination anglaise et pendant le siège de 1521 par l'empereur Charles-Quint', *Mém. de la Société hist. et litt. de Tournai*, 4 (1856), 77–95.

'Quelques lettres et autres documents concernant Thérouanne et Saint-Omer (1486–1537)', *BSA Morinie*, 3, part i, 23–49.

'Correspondance des magistrats d'Ypres députés à Gand et à Bruges pendant les troubles de Flandres sous Maximilian, 1488', *Annales de la Société d'Emulation de Bruges*, 2nd ser., 9, 47–112; 10, 3–142, 311–93.

'Quelques lettres et autres documents concernant l'empereur Charles-Quint', *Annales de la Société d'Emulation de Bruges*, 2nd ser., 10, 287–326.

(Dobrée, Thomas), *Autographes. Inventaire des lettres, chartes et pieces manuscrites du Musée Dobrée à Nantes* (Nantes, 1901).

'Document sur le siège de Saint-Quentin en 1557: lettre de Philibert-Emmanuel, duc de Savoie à ses sujets', *Le Vermandois*, 3 (1875), 637–40.

Documents inédits sur l'abbaye, le comté et la ville de Corbie, 2 vols., *MSAP*, 1910–12.

Doucet, R., 'L'Etat des finances de 1523', *Bulletin Philologique et Historique*, 1920 and tirage à part, Paris, 1923.

Druffel, A., *Beitrage zur Reichsgeschichte, 1546–61*, vol. I of Briefe und Akten zur Geschichte des sechzehnten Jahrhunderts, Munich, 1873.

Dubois, R. and Weerenbeck, B. H. J., *Comptes de la seigneurie de Lucheux 1427–1474 I – Textes* (Lille, 1935).

Du Mont, J., *Corps universel diplomatique du Droit des gens*, 8 vols. (Amsterdam, 1726–8).

Duprat, marquis Antoine-Théodore, *Glanes et regains récoltés dans les archives de la maison Duprat* (Versailles, 1865).

Duthilloeuil, A. R. (ed.), *Voyage de Jacques la Saige de Douai à Rome . . . , nouvelle édition pub. d'après le texte de 1523* (Douai, 1851).

Duvosquel, J. M. (ed.), *Albums de Croy*, 8 vols. so far of 26 (Crédit communal de Belgique, Brussels, 1985–).

Espinas, G., *Recueil de documents relatifs à l'histoire du droit municipal en France . . . Artois*, 3 vols. (Paris, 1934–).

Privilèges et chartes de franchises de la Flandre. II – Flandre française, 2 vols. (Brussels, 1959–61).

'Estat des finances du Roy nostre sire tant ordinaires que extraordinaires des pais de Picardie' (1497–8), *Annuaire-bulletin de la SHF*, 1866, pp. 185–92.

Estienne, C., *Le guide des chemins de France (1553)*, ed. J. Bonnerot (Paris, 1936).

Estienne, J., 'Déclaration des feux de 1469', *BSAP*, 34 (1931–2), 96–137.

Chartes de l'hôpital et de la ville d'Albert (Ancre) (Albert, 1942).

Firpo, L. (ed.), *Relazione di Ambasciatori Veneti al Senato*, vols. 2–3 (Germania) (Turin, 1968–70), vols. 5– (Francia) (Turin, 1978).

Forbes, P., *A Full View of the Transactions in the Reign of Q. Elizabeth*, 2 vols. (London, 1740–41).

François, M. (ed.), *Correspondance de François, cardinal de Tournon, 1521–62* (Paris, 1946).

Friant, abbé, 'Lettres de plusieurs personnages célèbres, trouvées au château de Heilly', *MSAP*, 2, 171– .

Gachard, L. P., *Extraits des Registres des Consaux de Tournay 1472–90, 1559–72, 1580–81 etc.* (Brussels, 1846).

Lettres inédites de Maximilien, duc d'Autriche, Roi des Romains et Empereur sur les affaires des Pay-bas, 1478–1508, 2 vols. (Brussels, 1851–2).

Galametz, comte de Brandt de, 'Lettres de Jean d'Estrées', *BSEA*, 1888–90, 330-2.

Garnier, J., 'Inventaire de quelques papiers provenant du château de Heilly', *MSAP*, 9, 311– .

Gayangos, P. de, Mattingly, G., Tyler, R. (eds.), *Calendar of Letters, Despatches and State Papers Relating to the Negotiations Between England and Spain*, 13 vols. (London, 1862–1954).

Génin, F., *Lettres de Marguerite d'Angoulême, soeur de François Ier*, 2 vols. (Paris, 1841–2).

Godefroy, J., *Lettres du roi Louis XII et du cardinal d'Amboise*, 4 vols. (Brussels, 1712).

Goldschmidt, E. P. (ed.), 'Le voyage de Hieronimus Monetarius à travers la France, 1494–5', *Humanisme et Renaissance*, 6 (1939).

Gorguette d'Argoeuves, X. de (ed.), 'Un livre de raison en Artois (XVIe siècle)' (Jean Thieulaine, 1549–54), *MSA Morinie*, 21 (1888), 139–99.

Gosselin, J., 'Documents inédits pour servir à l'histoire de Péronne', *La Picardie*, 19 (1872–5).

Guise, François de Lorraine duc de, *Mémoires* (ed. Michaud et Poujoulat, 1st ser. vol. 6 (Paris, Lyon, 1850)).

Haigneré, D., 'Quelques chartes de l'abbaye de Samer', *MSAB*, 12 (1880), 89–252; 13, 361–412; 16, 110– .

'Cartulaire de l'Eglise abbatiale de Notre-Dame de Boulogne-sur-Mer', *MSAB*, 13 (1882–86), 89–360.

'Rapport d'un espion français en 1549', *BSAB*, 5 (1885–90), 274–8.

'Entrée solonelle de François de Créquy, évêque de Thérouanne (1539)', *Cab. hist.*, 1892–3, 123–32.

'Document inédit, concernant l'incendie de la ville de Desvres à la fin de l'année 1552', *BSA Morinie*, 8, 177–79.

Hale, J. R. (ed.), *The Travel Journal of Antonio de Beatis, Through Germany, Switzerland, the Low Countries, France and Italy, 1517–18* (London, Hakluyt Soc., 1979).

Hamy, E., 'Actes relatifs à la cession du comté de Boulogne à la couronne', *MSAB*, 19 (1899–1903), 453–98.

'Extraits de la correspondance de Maugiron relatifs à l'expulsion des Anglois du Boulonnais', *MSAB*, 7 (1904–7).

Haneffe, baron de Chrestiet de, 'Testament de Philippe de Clèves, seigneur de Ravestein', *Bull. Comm. Royale d'Hist.*, ser. 5, vol. 9 (1899), 223– .

Havard de Montagne, Mme., *Voyage du cardinal d'Aragon en Allemagne, Holland, Belgique, France et Italie, 1517–18, trad. de l'italien* (Paris, 1912).

[Henri II], 'Letters from Henri II, king of France, to his cousin Mary, Queen Dowager of Scotland, 1545–54', *Miscellany of the Maitland Club*, I, ii (Edinburgh, 1834).

Histoire générale de la ville de Paris: Registres des délibérations du bureau de la ville de Paris, vol. I (ed. F. Bonnardot), II (ed. A. Tuetey), III (ed. P. Guérin), IV, (ed. F. Bonnardot), V (ed. A. Tuetey) (Paris, 1883–92).

Historical MSS Commission, *Calendar of the Manuscripts of . . . the Marquess of Bath, preserved at Longleat, vol. IV Seymour Papers* (London, 1968).

Huguet, A., 'La clémence de Charles le Téméraire. Lettres de grâce pour crimes commis en Picardie (1473–75)', *BSEA*, 1935–7, 526–59; 20 (1957), 75–96.

Huillard-Beeholles, A. and Lecoy de La Marche, A., *Titres de la maison ducale de Bourbon*, 2 vols. (Paris, 1867–74).

Isambert, F., *Recueil général des anciennes lois françaises*, 29 vols. (Paris, 1822–33).

Jacqueton, G., *Documents relatifs à l'administration financière en France de Charles VII à François Ier* (Paris, 1891).

Jourda, P., *Correspondance de Marguerite d'Angoulême, duchesse d'Alençon, reine de Navarre (1492–1549)* (Paris, 1930).

Kaulek, J. (ed.), *Correspondance politique de MM. de Castillon et de Marillac, ambassadeurs de France en Angleterre, 1537–42* (Paris, 1885).

Knecht, R. J., *The Voyage of Sir Nicolas Carewe to the Emperor Charles V in the Year 1530* (Roxburgh Club, 1959).

Labande, L.-H., *Correspondance de Joachim de Matignon, lieutenant-général en Normandie* (Monaco, 1914).

La Ferrière, H., *Marguerite d'Angoulême . . . son livre de dépenses, 1540–49* (Paris, 1862).

Lettres de Catherine de Médicis, 10 vols. (Paris, CDI, 1880–1909).

La Fons Mélicocq, baron de, 'Documents pour servir à l'histoire du commerce des villes et les ports de mer de Picardie et de Normandie au XVIe siècle', *La Picardie*, 6 (1860), 318–24.

'Documents inédits sur le siège de Péronne en 1536', *La Picardie*, 11 (1865), 569–73.

'Documents inédits sur la prinse de Thérouanne et du Vieil Hesdin', *BSA Morinie*, 2, 595–600 etc.

La Trémoille, L. de, *Archives d'un serviteur de Louis XI (Georges de La Trémoille) . . . 1458–81* (Nantes, 1888).

Leblanc, J.-T., 'Lettres (divers): Guerre du Piemont et du Nord de la France, 1545–55', *Bull. Com. Hist. Scien.: section Hist. et Philol.*, 1893, 12–57.

'Lettres addressées à Gui de Maugiron durant les guerres du Piemont et du Nord, 1545–52', *Bull. Com. Hist. et Scientifique: section Hist. et Philol.*, 1895, 357–66.

Leblond, V. (ed.), *Documents relatifs à l'histoire économique au 16e siècle, extraits des minutes notariales. Publications de la Soc. acad. de l'Oise*, X (1925).

Ledieu, A., 'Notice et documents inédits sur le marriage de Louis XII à Abbeville', *MSEA*, 17 (1887–90), 13– .

'Entrée du roi Charles VIII à Abbeville (1493)', *Bull. Archéol. du Comité des Travaux hist. et scient.*, 1888, no. 1, 55–65.

'Réception du cardinal de York à Abbeville, 1527', *Cab. hist.*, 1889–90, 95–6, 117–25.

'Le livre de raison d'un maieur d'Abbeville, Antoine Rohault, 1548–1613', *BSEA*, 19 (ser. 4, vol. 3), 1893–7, 133.

'Entrée de la reine Eléonore d'Autriche à Abbeville le 19 dec. 1531', *BSEA*, 5 (1900–2), 15– , 53– , & *Bull. hist. et philol.*, 1899.

(ed.), *Voyages en France d'un gentilhomme lillois à la fin du XVII* (Cayeux-sur-Mer, n.d.).

Ledru, A., *Histoire de maison de Mailly*, 3 vols. (1894).

Le Glay, *Correspondance de l'empereur Maximilien Ier et de Marguerite d'Autriche . . . 1507–1519*, 2 vols. (Paris, 1839).

Legrand, A., 'Correspondance inédite des généraux de l'empereur Charles-Quint avec . . . la ville de Saint-Omer à l'occasion du siège . . . de la ville de Thérouanne', *BSA Morinie*, 2.

Lemaire, E., *La guerre de 1557 en Picardie* (Saint-Quentin, 1896).

Procès-verbaux des séances de la Chambre du Conseil des Maire, Echevins et Jurés de Saint-Quentin, vol. I (1560–4) (Saint-Quentin, 1902).

Lemaire, E. and Bouchot, E., *Le livre-rouge de l'Hôtel de Ville de Saint-Quentin* (Saint-Quentin, 1881).

Léonard, F., *Recueil des Traitez de Paix*, 6 vols. (Paris, 1693).

L'Epinois, H. de, 'Notes extraites des archives communales de Compiègne', *BEC*, 25, 124–36.

Lestocquoy, J., 'Les sièges de Thérouanne et de Vieil-Hesdin d'après les dépêches du nonce pour la paix Santa-Croce', *Revue du Nord*, 1955.

(ed.), *Correspondance des nonces en France Carpi et Ferrerio, 1535–40*. Acta Nuntiaturae Gallicae, I (Rome, 1961).

(ed.), *Correspondance des nonces en France Dandino, della Torre et Trivultio (1546–51)*. Acta Nuntiaturae Gallicae, 6 (Rome, 1966).

(ed.), *Correspondance du nonce en France Prospero Santa Croce (1552–54)*. Acta Nuntiaturae Gallicae, 9 (Rome, 1972).

(ed.), *Correspondance des nonces en France Lenzi et Gaulterio, légation du cardinal Trivultio (1557–61)*. Acta Nuntiaturae Gallicae, 14 (Rome, 1977).

Lhomel, G. de, *Nouveau recueil de documents pour servir à l'histoire de Montreuil-sur-Mer* (Compiègne, 1910).

Lhuillier, T., 'La maison des princes, fils de François Ier', *BPH* (1889), 212–29.

Louandre, M. F. C., 'Lettres et bulletins des armées de Louis XI aux officiers municipaux d'Abbeville', *MSAE*, 3 (1836–7), 129– .

Macfarlane, I. D., *The Entry into Paris of Henry II 16 June 1549* (New York, 1982).

Mandrot, B. de (ed.), *Dépêches des ambassadeurs milanais en France sous Louis XI et Francois Sforza*, 4 vols. (Paris, 1916–23).

Marchegay, P. and Imbert, H., *Lettres missives originales du XVIe siècle . . . tirées des archives du duc de La Trémoille* (Niort, 1881).

Marsy, A. de, 'Liste de personnes tenant les fiefs nobles du Vimeu dans l'Arrière Ban d'Amiens en 1557', *Revue nobiliaire*, 2.

Matton, A. (ed.), 'L'argenterie de Marie de Luxembourg' (1539), *Le Vermandois*, 3 (1875), 612–23.

'Les bois de Bohain et l'artillerie royale au XVIe siècle', *Le Vermandois*, 2 (1874), 700–1.

(ed.), 'Documents pour servir à l'histoire de La Fère au XVIe siècle', *Le Vermandois*, 2 (1874), 634–56.

(ed.), 'Estat des personnes ordonnez par Mgr. le duc de Vendosmois à manger à son ordinaire', *Revue des Sociétés Savantes*, ser. 5, vol. 4.

Maugis, E. (ed.), *Documents inédits concernant la ville et le siège du bailliage d'Amiens*, II (1402–1501), *MSDAP* in 4o, vol. 19.

Maulde-la Clavière, R. de (ed.), *Procédures politiques du règne de Louis XII* (Paris, CDI, 1885).

Meylan, H. (ed.), *Correspondance de Theodore de Bèze* 9 vols. (Geneva, 1960).

Ordonnances des Roys de France de la troisiesme race, ed. Laurière, Secousse, Vilevault, Brequigny, Pastoret, 23 vols. (Paris, 1723–1849).

Ordonnances des Rois de France: Règne de François Ier, Académie des Sciences Morales et Politiques, 9 vols. (so far) (Paris, 1902–).

Paris, A. Louis (ed.), *Négociations, lettres et pièces diverses relatives au règne de François II, tirées du portefeuille de Sébastien de l'Aubespine* (Paris, CDI, 1841).

Pariset, J. D., 'La France et les princes allemands. Documents et commentaires (1545–57)', *Francia*, 10 (1982), 229–301.

Pelicier, P. (ed.), *Lettres de Charles VIII roi de France*, SHF, 5 vols. (Paris, 1898–1905).

Pichon, J., 'Correspondance des d'Humières provenant du château de Monchy', *Bulletin de la Société historique de Compiègne*, 6, 78–140.

Pihan, L., 'Les anciennes maisons d'Hauvoile ou les archives d'un château de la Renaissance', *Mém. Soc. acad. de l'Oise*, 21 (1910).

Pollet, Dr., 'L'entrée d'Henri II à Calais en 1558', *Bull. de la Comm. des Monuments historiques du Pas-de-Calais*, 7 (part 5), 1956, 547– .

Poncelet, E., 'L'exécution de Louis de Luxembourg, comte de Saint-Pol, en 1475', *Bull. Commission Royale d'Hist.* 91 (1927), 181–98.

Potter, D. L., 'Documents concerning the negotiation of the Anglo-French Treaty of March 1550', *Camden Miscellany*, 28 (London, Royal Historical Society, 1984).

Prarond, E., 'Mistère faict à l'entrée de la très-noble et excellente dame Regne de France Madame Alyenor', *La Picardie*, 13 (1867), 351–65.

Prévôt, G. (ed.), 'Les <itinera> de Jean Second: Notice, traduction et notes', *Revue du Nord*, 9 (1923), 255–74.

Prioux, S., 'Rôle de dépense des terrassements faits sur la porte de Coucy (Laon) 1551', *S.A. Laon*, 7 (1858), 315–21.

'Monstres, rolles et revues faictes à Saint-Quentin, 3 janv. 1551', *S.A. Laon*, 12 (1862), 345–56.

'Procès-verbal et enquêtes faits en 1521 et 1522 pour constater les dommages causés à l'eglise de Notre-Dame de Nesle lors du sac de cette ville par Charles le Temeraire en 1471', *Bull. de la SHF*, I, part ii (1834), 11–17.

Quicherat, J., 'Lettres, mémoires, instructions et autres documents relatifs à la guerre du bien public', in *Mélanges historiques* (CDI), vol. 2.

'Recettes et depenses de la ville de Boulogne-sur-mer, 1415–16', *MSAB*, 7 (1882).

'Registre aux délibérations du Chauny, 1491–2', *Société académique de Chauny*, vol. 3, 308– .

'Registres des consaulx de Tournai', *Mémoires de la Société historique et littéraire de Tournai*, 2 and 3 (1856).

Ribier, G., *Lettres et Mémoires d'Estat des Roya Princes, Ambassadeurs . . . sous les règnes de François Ier, Henry II et François II*, 2 vols. (Paris, 1666).

Rochambeau, A. Lacrois de Vimeur, Marquis de, *Lettres d'Antoine de Bourbon et de Jehanne d'Albret*, SHF (Paris, 1877).

Rodière, R., 'Acte relatif à la rançon d'un paysan (1552)', *Cab. hist*, 1891–2, 157.

'Marché passé pour vivres et approvisionnement du seigneur de Langey (1553)', *Cab. hist.*, 1891–2, 94–6.

'Le livre de raison des Hibon de la Fresnoye', MSAB, 27 (1912), 2–142.

'Documents sur les guerres de religion en Ponthieu', *BSEA*, 11 (1918–21), 12–18.

Epitaphier de Picardie, Amiens, SAP, Documents inédits concernant la province, vol. 21 (1925).

La maison de Moy, 3 vols. (Le Mans, 1928).

'Rôle des gentilshommes qui se sont offerts à servir personellement pour le ban et arrière-ban du bailliage d'Amiens, octobre 1575', *BSAP* 12 (1904), 82–99.

Romier, L., 'Les guerres de Henri II', *Melanges d'archéologie et d'histoire de l'Ecole française de Rome*, 30 (1910).

Roos, J. P., *Einige Nachrichten von den wild-und Rheingrafen Philipp Franz von Dhaun* (Frankfurt, 1784).

Rosny, A. de (ed.), 'Inventaire de Mᶜ Jehan d'Oultrempuis, procureur du roi, en 1545', *MSAB*, 16 (1891–4), 290–311.

'Documents inédits ou rarissimes concernant les sièges de Boulogne, 1544–49', *MSAB*, 27 (1912), 379–420.

'Enquête faicte en 1578 par le Maître particulier des Eaux et Forêts du Boulonnais auprès des habitants d'Hesdin-l'Abbé et de Samer etc. pour savoir quels étaient les droits du Seigneur du Manoir à la couppe d'une mesure de bois en la forêt de Boulogne', *MSAB*, 17 (1912), 344–78.

Rosny, E. de, 'Liste de personnes tenant fiefs nobles du bailliage d'Amiens qui con tribuèrent à la rançon du roi François Ier en 1529', *BSAP*, 6, 436–49.

'Terrier de l'abbaye de Saint-Wulmer en Boulogne-sur-Mer (1505)', *MSAB*, 10.

Rozet, A. and Lembey, J. F., *L'invasion de France et le siège de Saint-Dizier par Charles-Quint en 1544* (Paris, 1910).

Rymer, T., *Feodera, Litterae, Conventiones* (London, 1727–32).

Scheurer, R. (ed.), *Correspondance du cardinal Jean du Bellay*, 2 vols. so far (Paris, SHF, 1969–73).

Secousse, D. F. (ed.), *Mémoires de Condé, ou Recueil pour servir à l'histoire de France*, 6 vols. (London, The Hague, 1743).

Sotheby and Co., Sale Catalogues, *Philippica, New Series*, 9th Part (London, 25–6 June 1973).

Stevenson, J. (ed.), *Calendar of State Papers, Foreign Series, of the Reign of Queen Elizabeth, 1561–2* (London, 1866).

Techener, J., *Pièces et documents relatifs au siège de Péronne en 1536* (Péronne, 1864).

Teulet, Alexandre, *Relations politiques de la France et de l'Espagne avec L'Ecosse au XVIᵉ siècle*, 5 vols. (Paris, 1862).

Thielman, M. R., 'Les Croy, conseillers des ducs de Bourgogne. Documents extraits de leurs archives familiales 1357–1487', *Bull. de la Comm. royale d'histoire* 255 (1959), 1–141.

Thierry, A., *Recueil des monuments inédits de l'histoire du Tiers-Etat, Iᵉʳᵉ série, région du Nord*, 4 vols. (Paris, CDI, 1856–70).

Tommaseo, M. N. (ed.), *Relations des ambassadeurs vénitiens sur les affaires de France au XVIe siècle* 2 vols. (Paris, 1838).

Tribout de Morembert, H., 'Chartes et documents concernant le Nord de la France aux Archives de la ville de Metz' (coll. Salis), *BSAP*, 1957, 102–54.

Turnbull, W. B., *Calendar of State Papers, Foreign Series, of the Reign of Edward VI, 1547–53* (London, 1861).

Vaesen, J. and Charavay, E. (eds.), *Lettres de Louis XI*, 12 vols. (Paris, SHF, 1883–1909).

Vaillant, V. J. (ed.), 'L'advis de la qualité de ceulx qui sont dedans Boulogne', *BSAB*, 7 (1904–7).

Weerenbeck, B. H. J., *Comptes de la ville de Doullens en 1470* (Paris, 1932).

Weiss, C. (ed.), *Papiers d'état du cardinal de Granvelle*, 9 vols. (Paris, CDI, 1842–52)

Winckelmann, O., *Politische Correspondenz der Stadt Strassburg*, vols. 3 and 4 (Strassburg, 1882–92, Urkunden und Akten der Stadt Strassburg, ser. 2).

CHRONICLES AND WRITINGS 15TH–16TH CENTURIES

Auton, J. d', *Chroniques de Louis XII*, ed. R. de Maulde de la Clavière, 4 vols. (Paris, SHF, 1889–95).

Basin, Thomas, *Histoire de Louis XI*, ed. C. Samaran, 3 vols. (Paris, 1963–72).

Beaugué, Jean, *Histoire de la guerre d'Escosse* (Paris, 1556, ed. J. Bain, Maitland Club, 1830).

Belleforest, F. de, *Grandes Annales et Histoire générale de France* (Paris, 1579).

Bèze, T. de, *Histoire ecclésiastique des églises réformées du royaume de France*, ed. G. Baum and E. Cunitz (3 vols., Paris, 1883–9).

Bodin, J., *Les Six Liures de la Republique* (Lyon, 1578).

Bourrilly, V. L. (ed.), *Journal d'un bourgeois de Paris sous le règne de François Ier, 1515–36* (Paris, Coll. des textes . . . enseignement d'histoire, 1910).

Brantôme, Pierre de Bourdeille, sieur de, *Oeuvres complètes*, ed. L. Lalanne, 11 vols. (Paris, SHF, 1864–82); ed. J. Buchon, Panthéon Litt., 2 vols. (Paris, 1838).

Brésin, L., *Chroniques de Flandres et d'Artois. Analyse et extraits pour servir à l'histoire de ces provinces de 1482 à 1560*, ed. E. Mannier (Paris, 1880).

Commynes, Philippe de, *Mémoires*, ed. B. de Mandrot, Paris, 2 vols. (1901–3), trans. A. Scoble (London, Bohn Library, 18).

Dehaussy, J., *Journal du siège de Péronne de 1536* (Péronne, 1897).

Du Bellay, Martin and Guillaume, *Mémoires*, ed. V.-L. Bourrily and F. Vindry, 4 vols. (Paris, SHF, 1908–19); ed. Michaud et Poujoulat, *Nouvelle serie*.

Du Bueil, Jean, *Le Jouvencel, suivi du commentaire de Guillaume Trigant* (ed. Favre et Lecestre), 2 vols. (Paris, 1887–9).

Du Moulin, *Consultation de Paris pour la noblesse de Picardie sur le fait de la promotion de quelqu'un en l'évêché d'Amiens sans le sceu, autorité, consentement ou élection des estats, mesmement des nobles du pays* (no place, 1564), repr. in *Mémoires de Conde*, ed. Secousse, vol. V.

Escouchy, M., *Chronique* (ed. G. du Fresne de Beaucourt, 3 vols., Paris, 1864).

Fenier, P., *Relation du siège memorable de la ville de Péronne en 1536* (repr. J. Techener, Paris, 1862).

Florange, Robert de La Marck, seigneur de, *Mémoires* (ed. R. Goubaux and P. A. Lemoisne), 2 vols. (Paris, SHF, 1913–24).

Fourquevaux, R. de Beccarie de Pavie, sieur de, *Instructions sur le faict de la guerre* (ed. with intro. by G. Dickinson, London, 1954).

'Froumenteau, N.' [J. Frotté?], *Le secret des finances de France* (1581).

Genel, A., 'Les Mémoires de Jacques de Genelle, bourgeois d'Arras', *Revue du Nord* 51 (1969), 81–104.

Gruffydd, Ellis, Chronicl. ed. and trans. by M. B. Davies as 'Suffolk's Expedition to Montdidier', *Bulletin of the Faculty of Arts of Fouad I University, Cairo*, 7 (1944); 'The Enterprises of Paris and Boulogne', *ibid.*, 11 (1949); 'Boulogne and Calais from 1545 to 1550', *ibid.*, 12 (1940).

Guiffrey, G. (ed.), *Chronique du Roy Françoys, premier de ce nom* (Paris, 1860).

Haigneré, D. (ed.), 'Récit du siège et de la prise de Boulogne par les Anglais en 1544 et de la reprise de cette ville par le roi Henri II en 1550, par Guillaume Paradin', *MSAB*, 15 (1889–90), 285–304.

Hall, Edward, *The Triumphant Reigne of Kyng Henry the VIII*, 2 vols. (reprint of 1550 ed. by C. Whibley, 1904).

La Place, P. de, *Commentaires de l'estat de religion et république*, ed. Buchon, Panthéon Litteraire, Choix de Chroniques, 16 (Paris, 1836).

La Planche, L. Regnier de, *Histoire de l'estat de France*, ed. J. Buchon, Panthéon Litteraire, Choix de Chroniques, 16 (Paris, 1836).

Le Gras, 'Véritable discours d'un logement des gens d'armes en la ville de Ham', *MSAP*, 38, 1– .

Le Prestre, Pierre, *Chronicques*, (i) ed. R. de Belleval, *MSEA*, 1877; (ii) ed. G. Vasseur in *Saint-Riquier*, II (1971).

'Les Regretz de Picardie et de Tournay en xxij couplets' (1522), in Montaiglon, *Recueil de poésies françaises*, 9 (1865), 294–305.

Le Sueur, G., 'Antiquitez de Boulogne-sur-Mer (1596)', *MSAB*, 9 (1878), 2nd part, 1–51 and notes 52–212.

Liot, E., 'Lamentation du chasteau de Hesdin (1553)', *BSA Morinie*, 6, 515–27.

Louant, A. (ed.), *Le Journal d'un bourgeois de Mons, 1505–46* (Brussels, Comm. Royale d'Hist., 1969).

Macquereau, Robert, *Traité ou recueil de la Maison de Bourgogne en forme de chronicque* (Panthéon Litteraire – Chroniques et Mémoires, ed. J. Buchon, 1838 (1500–1527); ed. J. Barrois, Paris, 1841 (1527–29).

Marsy, A. de (ed.), *Petite chronique de Doullens* (Vervins, 1852).

Molinet, Jean, *Chroniques*, ed. O. Jodogne and G. Doutrepont, 3 vols. (Brussels, 1935–7).

Faictz et Dicts, ed. N. Dupire, 3 vols. (Paris, 1936–9).

Monluc, Blaise de, *Commentaires et Lettres*, ed. A. de Ruble, 5 vols. (Paris, SHF, 1864–72).

Monnecove, F. Le Sergent de (ed.), *Brief et vray récit de la prinse de Térouane et Hedin* (Paris, 1874)

Montaiglon, A. de, *Recueil des poésies françaises des XVᵉ et XVIᵉ siècles* (Paris, 1855–78).

Moreau, G. (ed.), *Le journal d'un bourgeois de Tournai* (Brussels, Comm. Royale d'Histoire, 1975).

Mornay, P. de, sr. du Plessis-Marly, *Mémoires et correspondance de Duplessis-Mornay . . . précédée des mémoires de Madame de Mornay*, 12 vols. (Paris, 1824–5).

Nicolay, Jehan, 'Kalendrier de la Guerre de Tournai (1477–79)', *Mém. de la Société hist. et litt. de Tournai*, vol. 2 (1853) and appendices in vol. 3 (1856) (ed. F. Hannebert, 2 vols., Tournai, 1853–6).

Nicolay, N. de, sieur d'Arfeuille, *Double d'un lettre missive, envoyée à Monseigneur Du Buys . . . contenant le discours de la guerre faicte par le Roy . . . Henry deuxiesme de ce nom pour le recouvrement du pais de Boulognoys* (Lyon, 1550).

Pasquier, E., *Recherches de France* (Amsterdam, 1723).

Picot, E., 'Chants historiques français du XVIᵉ siècle', *Revue d'histoire littéraire de la France*, 1895, 1896, 1900 *passim*.

Pouy, F. (ed.), 'Récit du célèbre médecin Ambroise Paré relatif à la bataille de Saint-Quentin', *Le Vermandois*, 2, 360–7.

Quicherat, J., 'Un manuscrit interpolé de la Chronique Scandaleuse', BEC, 16 and 17, *passim*.

Rabutin, F. de, *Commentaires des guerres de la Gaule Belgique*, 2 vols., ed. G. de Taurines (Paris, SHF, 1932–42).

Roye, Jean de, *Journal de Jean de Roye connu sous le nom de Chronique Scandaleuse (1460–1483)*, ed. B. de Mandrot, 2 vols. (Paris, SHF, 1946–8), Eng. trans. Bohn edn of Commines.

Servois, G., 'Un voyage à Calais, Guignes et Boulogne en 1520', *BEC*, 1857, 453–8.

Seyssel, C. de, *La Monarchie de France*, ed. J. Poujol (Paris, 1961).

Tavannes, Gaspard de Saux, sr. de, *Mémoires* (i) ed. Michaud et Poujoulat, ser. 1, vol. 8 (1836); (ii) ed. Buchon, *Panthéon Litteraire*, 1835; (iii) ed. Petitot, *Coll. Complète*, ser. 1, vols. 23–5, 1819.

Tillet, J. du, *Avertissement envoyée à la noblesse de France tant du partye du Roy que des rebelles & coniurez* (Paris, 1574).

Villars, François de Boyvin, baron du, *Mémoires*, ed. Michaud et Poujoulat, 1st ser. 10 (Paris, Lyon, 1850).

Venette, J. de, *Chronicle*, ed. R. A. Newhall, trans. J. Birdsall (Columbia, 1953).

GENEALOGICAL WRITINGS: 16TH–18TH CENTURIES

Allard, G., *Histoire généalogique des familles de Bonne, de Créquy, et Blanchefort, d'Agout etc.* (Grenoble, 1572).

Ansèlme, père, *Histoire généalogique et chronologique de la maison de France, des pairs, grands officiers de la couronne et de la maison du roy*, 9 vols. (Paris, 1726–33).

Callier, J., *Histoire sur la généalogie de l'illustre maison de Bourbon, Vandosme et Montpensier: avec leurs alliances et origines* (Lyon, 1607).

Désormeaux, J. L. Ripault, *Histoire de la maison de Bourbon*, 5 vols. (Paris, 1772–88).

Du Bouchet, *Preuves de l'illustre maison de Coligny* (Paris, 1662).

Du Chesne, A., *Histoire de la maison de Luxembourg* (1617).

Histoire de la maison de Montmorency (Paris, 1624).

Histoire généalogique des maisons de Guisnes, d'Ardres etc. (1631).

Galland, A., *Mémoires pour l'histoire de Navarre et de Flandres* (Paris, 1648).

Ignace, Joseph, père [Jacques Sanson], *Histoire généalogique des comtes de Pontieu et maieurs d'Abbeville*.

L'Alouette, F. de, *Traité des Nobles et des vertus dont ils sons formes . . . avec une histoire de la Maison de Couci, et de ses alliances* (Paris, 1577).

La Morlière, A. de, *Recueil de plusieurs nobles et illustres maisons vivantes et esteintes, en l'estendue du diocèse d'Amiens* (Amiens, 1630).
Vigner, N., *Histoire de la maison de Luxembourg* (Paris, 1619).

SECONDARY WORKS

Abbot, P. D., *Pays et seigneuries of France* (Myrtleford, Aus., 1981).
Anderson, P., *Lineages of the Absolute State* (London, 1974).
Anon., 'Les gouverneurs de Saint-Quentin d'après les archives de la ville', *Le Vermandois* 4 (1876), 732–47.
Anon., 'Le siège de Saint-Quentin en 1557', *Le Vermandois* 1, 7–14.
Antoine, M., 'Genèse de l'institution des Intendants', *Journal des savants* (1982), 287–317.
'Institutions françaises en Italie sous le règne de Henri II: Gouverneurs et intendants', *Mélanges de l'Ecole française de Rome* 94 (1982), 759–818.
Le dur métier de roi. Etudes sur la civilisation politique de la France d'Ancien Régime, Paris, 1986.
Arnould, M. A., *Les dénombrements des foyers dans le comté de Hainault, XIVᵉ–XVIᵉ siècles* (Brussels, 1956).
Aston, T. (ed.), *Crisis in Europe* (London, 1965).
Aumale, Henri d'Orléans duc d', *Histoire des princes de Condé*, 8 vols. (Paris, 1863–9).
A.V., 'Siège et prise du château de Coucy en 1487', *BEC* 24, 79–82.
Award of Her Majesty Queen Elizabeth II for Arbitration of a Controversy between the Argentine Republic and the Republic of Chine (London, HMSO, 1966).
Barbiche, B., 'Henri IV, Sully et la première "monarchie administrative"', *PWSFH* 17 (1990), 10–23.
Basse, B., *La constitution de l'ancienne France. Principes et lois fondamentales de la royauté française* (Paris, 1986).
Baumgartner, F. J., *Henry II* (Durham, USA, 1987).
Bautier, 'Recherches sur les routes de l'Europe médiévale', *BPH*, 1960.
Bazin, C., 'Description historique de l'église et des ruines du château de Folleville', *MSAP* 10 (1850), 1–92.
Beauvillé, V. de, *Histoire de la ville de Montdidier*, 3 vols. (Paris, 1857).
Beik, W., *Absolutism and Society in Seventeenth-Century France. State Power and Provincial Aristocracy in Languedoc* (Cambridge, 1985).
Belleval, R. de, *Trésor généalogique de la Picardie*, 2 vols. (Amiens, 1859–60).
'Les capitaines d'Abbeville', *Revue nobiliaire, héraldique et biographique* 3 (1867), 104–11.
Lettres sur le Ponthieu, 1868.
Les sénéchaux de Ponthieu, Paris, 1868.
Bénard, L., 'Restitution par l'Angleterre de la ville de Boulogne en 1550', *MSAB* 4 (1884–95).
Bimbinet, E., 'La nation de Picardie à l'Université d'Orléans', *MSAP* 10 (1850).
Bittmann, K., *Ludwig XI. und Karl der Kühne*, 2 vols. (Gottingen, 1964–70).
Black, J. (ed.), *The Origins of War in Early Modern Europe* (Edinburgh, 1988).
Bled, O., 'Une ville disparue (Thérouanne)', *BPH*, 1894.

Blockmans, W. P. *et al.*, 'Tussen crisis en welwaert: sociale veranderingen 1300–1500', *Algemene Geschiedenis der Nederlanden* IV, 1980.

(ed.), *Le privilège général et les privilèges régionaux de Marie de Bourgogne pour les Pays-Bas, 1477, Standen en Landen*, 1988.

Boca, J., *La justice criminelle de l'échevinage d'Abbeville au moyen-âge (1183–1516)* (Lille, 1930).

Bocquet, A., *Recherches sur la population rurale en Artois à la fin du Moyen Age* (Arras, 1969).

Boinet, A., 'Notes sur deux lettres et un portrait d'Antoine de Créquy (évêque de Thérouanne)', *BSAP* 24 (1909–11), 257–65.

Bois, G., *Crise du féodalisme* (Paris, 1976).

Bonnault d'Houet, X. de, 'Genlis ou Jenlis. Histoire d'un fief picard', *BSAP* 23 (1904), 36–53.

Bonney, R., 'Absolutism: What's in a Name?' *French History* 1 (1987), 93–117.

Bourgeon, J. L., 'La Fronde parlementaire à la veille de la Saint-Barthélemy', *BEC* (1990), 17–89.

Bourrilly, V.-L., *Guillaume du Bellay, seigneur de Langey, 1491–1543* (Paris, 1905).

Bousquet, J., *Enquête sur les commodités du Rouergue en 1552, Procès entre l'Agenais, le Quercy et le Périgord* (Toulouse, 1969).

Boutiot, 'Louis XI et Arras', *MASA* ser. 2, I (1867), 133–206.

Boutruche, R., 'La dévastation des campagnes pendant la guerre de Cent Ans et la reconstruction agricole de la France', *Mélanges 1945* iii *Etudes historiques* (1947), 127–63.

La crise d'une société: seigneurs et paysans du bordelais pendant la Guerre de Cent Ans (Paris, 1963).

Braquehay, R., *L'Hôtel-Dieu de Montreuil* (Amiens, 1882).

Braudel, F. and E. Labrousse (eds.), *Histoire économique et sociale de la France*, vol. I, i and ii (Paris, 1977).

Bridge, J. C. S., *A History of France from the Death of Louis XI*, 5 vols. (Oxford, 1921–36).

Brink, J. E., 'Les Etats de Languedoc: une autonomie en question', *Annales du Midi* 88 (1976), 287–305.

'Royal Power Through Provincial Eyes: Languedoc 1515–1560', *PWSFH* 10 (1982), 52–9.

'The King's Army and the People of Languedoc, 1550–1560', *PWSFH* 14 (1986), 1–9.

Bryant, L., *The King and the City in the Parisian Royal Entry Ceremony: Politics, Ritual and Art in the Renaissance* (Geneva, 1986).

'The Medieval Entry Ceremony at Paris' in J. M. Bak, *Coronations. Medieval and Early Modern Monarchic Ritual* (Berkeley, Calif., 1990).

Bryois, 'Notice sur le Bailliage de l'ancien comté de Roucy', *BSA Laon* 5 (1856), 2–16.

Bueil, M. A., 'La confrérie de Notre-Dame du Puy d'Amiens', *MSAP* 13, 489–622.

Buisseret, D., 'The Cartographic Definition of France's Eastern Boundary in the Early 17th Century', *Imago Mundi* 36 (1984), 72–80.

Cagé, 'Louis de Luxembourg', *Positions des thèses de l'Ecole Nationale des Chartes* (1885), 21–49.

Cagny, P. de, *Notice historique sur le château de Suzanne-en-Santerre et sur la maison et marquisat d'Estourmel* (Péronne, 1857).
Histoire de l'arondissement de Péronne, 3 vols. (Péronne, 1867–87).
Caillet, M., *Repeuplement de la ville d'Arras sous Louis XI: le rôle de Lyon* (Arras, 1908).
Calmette, J. and G. Périnelle, *Louis XI et l'Angleterre (1461–83)* (Paris, 1930).
Calonne, A. de, *La vie municipale au XVᵉ siècle dans le Nord de la France* (Paris, 1860).
Histoire de la ville d'Amiens, 3 vols. (Amiens, 1899–1900).
Cauchie, A., 'Deux episodes de la lutte de François Ier avec Charles-Quint en 1543', *Bull. de la Commission Royale d'Histoire*, ser. 5, IV (1891), 41–56.
Cazelles, R., *La société politique sous Philippe VI* (Paris, 1958).
La société politique sous Jean le bon et Charles V (Paris, 1982).
Charbonnier, P., *Une autre France. La seigneurie rurale en Basse Auvergne au XIVᵉ au XVIᵉ siècles*, 2 vols. (Clermont-Ferrand, 1980).
Chevalier, B., 'La politique de Louis XI à l'égard des bonnes villes: le cas de Tours', *Moyen Age* 70 (1964).
'Gouverneurs et gouvernements en France entre 1450 et 1520', in *Histoire comparée de l'administration. Beihefte der Francia*, 9 (Munich, 1980), 291–307.
'The *bonnes villes* and the King's Council in Fifteenth-Century France', in J. R. L. Highfield and R. Jeffs (eds.), *The Crown and Local Communities in England and France in the Fifteenth Century* (Gloucester, 1981).
Les bonnes villes de France du XVᵉ au XVIᵉ siècle (Paris, 1982).
Chevalier, B. and P. Contamine (eds.), *La France de la fin du XVᵉ siècle – renouveau et apogée* (Paris, 1985).
Coët, E., *Tilloloy et ses seigneurs, son château et son église* (Saint-Quentin, 1873).
Histoire de la ville de Roye, 2 vols. (Paris, 1880).
Collet, A., 'Philippe de Crèvecoeur, maréchal d'Esquerdes', *MSAB* 28 (1917), 376–476.
'Biographie chronologique des barons d'Elnes', *MSAB* 28 (1917), 477ff.
Colliette, L. P., *Mémoires pour servir à l'histoire ecclésiastique, civile et militaire de la province du Vermandois*, 3 vols. Noyon/Cambrai, 1771–3.
Contamine, P., *Guerre, état et société à la fin du Moyen Age* (Paris, 1972).
(ed.), *La Noblesse au Moyen Age* (Paris, 1976).
'Guerre, fiscalité royale et économie en France (deuxième moitié du XVᵉ siècle)' in M. Flinn (ed.), *Seventh International Economic History Congress*, vol. 2 (Edinburgh, 1978).
La France au XIVᵉ et XVᵉ siècles. Hommes, mentalités, guerre et paix (London, 1981).
Corvisier, A., 'Armées, état et administration dans les temps modernes', in *Histoire comparée de l'administration. Beihefte der Francia* 9 (Munich, 1980).
Cosneau, E., *Le connétable de Richemont* (Paris, 1886).
Courteault, P., *Blaise de Monluc, historien* (Paris, 1908).
Cousin, L., 'Notice sur le château-fort du Mont-Hullin', *MSA Morinie*, 4, 237ff.
Cozzi, G. and M. Knapton, *La Repubblica di Venezia nell'età moderna* (Turin, 1986).
Crampon, M., 'Le culte de l'arbre et de la forêt en Picardie. Essai sur le folklore picard', *MSAP* 46 (1936).

Picquigny, le château fort, la collégiale (Amiens, 1963).

Crouzet, D., 'Recherches sur la crise de l'aristocratie en France au XVIᵉ siècle: les dettes de la maison de Nevers', *Histoire, économie et société* I (1982).

Croy, C. de, *Quatre cents vues des villages d'Artois* (Mémoires de la commission Départementale du Pas-de-Calais, t. 10, part 2).

Cruickshank, C., *Army Royal. Henri VIII's Invasion of France, 1513* (Oxford, 1969).

The English Occupation of Tournai, 1513–19 (Oxford, 1971).

Cuttler, S. H., *The Law of Treason and Treason Trials in Late Mediaeval France* (Cambridge, 1981).

'The Treason of Saint-Pol, 1474–5', *History Today* 37 (1987).

Dainville, F. de, *Cartes anciennes de l'église de France* (Paris, 1956).

Le langage des géographes (Paris, 1964).

Daire, L. F., *Histoire de la ville d'Amiens*, 2 vols. (Paris, 1757).

Darsy, F. J. 'Gamaches et ses seigneurs', *MSAP* 13 and 14 (and *tirage à part*, Amiens, 1857).

Picquigny et ses seigneurs, vidames d'Amiens (Abbeville, 1860).

'Notes historiques sur la ville de Rue', *La Picardie*, 1875–9.

Davis, N. Z., *The Return of Martin Guerre* (Cambridge, Mass., 1983).

Fiction in the Archives. Pardon Tales and their Tellers in Sixteenth-Century France (Stanford, Calif., 1987).

Debrie, R., *La Picardie* (Paris, 1981).

Decrue, F., *Anne de Montmorency, grand maître et connétable de France à la cour . . . de François Ier* (Paris, 1885).

Anne de Montmorency, connétable et pair de France, sous les rois Henry II, François II et Charles IX (Paris, 1889).

Delaborde, comte Louis Jules Henri, *Eléonore de Roye, princesse de Condé (1535–64)* (Paris, 1876).

Gaspard de Coligny, amiral de France, 3 vols. (Paris, 1872–82).

Delacrois, M. C., 'Les Puys d'Amiens, un fleuron original de la peinture gothique', *L'Estampille* 105 (1979), 32–9.

Delgove, abbé, *Histoire de la ville de Doullens, MSAP* in-4to, vol. 5 (1865).

'Poix et ses seigneurs', *MSAP* 15 (1876), 107ff.

Deloffre, A., 'La cité de Cambrai et le pays de Cambrésis sous les troys Croy, 1502–56', *MSEC* 43 (1888), 243–316.

Demangeon, A., *La Picardie et les regions, Artois, Cambrésis, Beauvaisis*, 3rd edn (Paris, 1925).

Deschamps, 'Précis historique sur Ardres', *MSA Morinie* 4, 379–95.

Deseille, E., 'L'année boulonnaise. Ephémerides historiques intéressant le pays boulonnais', *MSAB* 8 (1885–6).

Des Forts, P., *Le château de Villebon. Eure-et-Loire* (Paris, 1914).

'Un guet-apens à Amiens, le 23 juillet 1471', *BSEA* (1925–8), 393–8.

Desjardins, E., *Les favorites des rois. Anne de Pisseleu, duchesse d'Etampes et François Ier* (Paris, 1904).

Devraine, G., 'Le commerce de la boucherie et l'inspection des viandes à Péronne de 1349 à 1550', *BSAP* 37 (1937–8), 69ff.

Péronne, son histoire et monuments des origines à nos jours (Péronne, 1970).

Deyon, P., 'Quelques remarques sur l'évolution du régime seigneurial en Picardie (XVIᵉ–XVIIIᵉ siècles)', *RHMC* (1961), 271–80.

Contribution à l'étude des revenues fonciers en Picardie: les fermages de l'Hôtel-Dieu d'Amiens et leurs variations de 1515 à 1789 (Lille, 1967).

Amiens, capitale provinciale. Etude sur la société urbaine au 17e siècle (Lille, 1967).

Dickinson, G., *The Congress of Arras* (Oxford, 1955).

Dictionnaire archéologique et historique de la Picardie, 5 vols. pub. by SAP, 1909–31.

Dion, R., *Les frontières de France* (Paris, 1947).

Dognon, P., 'La taille en Languedoc de Charles VII à François Ier', *Annales du Midi* (1891), 340–66.

Doren, L. S. van, 'War Taxation, Institutional Change and Social Conflict in Provincial France – the Royal *Taille* in Dauphiné, 1494–1559', *PAPS* 121 (1977), 70–95.

'Military administration and Intercommunal Relations in Dauphiné, 1494–1559', *PAPS* 130 (1986), 78–99.

Doucet, R., *Etude sur le gouvernement de François Ier dans ses relations avec le Parlement de Paris*, 2 vols. (Paris/Algiers, 1921–6).

Les institutions de la France au XVIe siècle, 2 vols. (Paris, 1948).

Dournel, J., *Histoire générale de Péronne* (Péronne, 1879).

Dubois, A., *Entrées royales et princières dans Amiens pendant les 15ᵉ et 16ᵉ siècles* (Amiens, 1868).

'Aide de L 5795 10s 4d, dite aide ordonnée pour le passage de la mer', *MSAP* 26 (1880), 165–259.

'Les pestes ou contagions à Amiens pendant les XVᵉ, XVIᵉ et XVIIᵉ siècles', *MSAP* 23 (1873).

Dubois, P., 'Un voyageur allemand en Picardie à la fin du XVᵉ siècle', *BSAP* 38 (1939–40), 242–50.

Dubois, R., *Lucheux. Histoire et Monuments* (Doullens, 1954).

Dubosq, G., 'Le mariage de Charles d'Anjoy comte du Maine et le comté de Guise (1431–73)', *BEC* 96 (1935), 338–99.

Duchaussoy, H., 'La vigne en Picardie et le commerce des vins de Somme', *MSAP*, vols. 41 and 42.

Duffy, C., *Siege Warfare: the Fortress in the Early Modern World 1494–1660* (London, 1979).

Dufournet, J., *La vie de Philippe de Comines* (Paris, 1969).

Dupâquier, J. (ed.), *Histoire de la population française*, vols. 1 and 2 (Paris, 1988).

Dupont-Ferrier, G., *Les officiers royaux des bailliages et sénéchaussées et les institutions monarchiques locales en France à la fin du moyen âge*. Bib. Ecole des Hautes Etudes, fasc. 145, Paris, 1902.

'Essai sur la géographie administrative des élections financières en France', *Annuaire-bulletin de la SHF*, 1928, 1929.

Etudes sur les institutions financières de la France à la fin du moyen âge, 2 vols. (Paris, 1930).

'L'incertitude des limites territoriales en France du XIIIᵉ au XVIᵉ siècles', *Académie des inscriptions et belles lettres: comptes rendus* (1942), 62–77.

Gallia Regia, ou Etat des officiers royaux des bailliages et sénéchaussées de 1328 à 1515, 6 vols. (Paris, 1942).

Durand, G., *Chants royaux et tableaux du Puy Notre-Dame d'Amiens* (Amiens, 1902).

'Les Lannoy, Folleville et l'art italien dans le Nord de la France', *Bulletin monumental* 70 (1906), 329–404.

L'art en Picardie (Amiens, 1914).

'Peintres d'Amiens au XVIe siècle', *BSAP* 31 (1924-5), 619–728.

'Les tailleurs d'images d'Amiens du milieu du XV^c au milieu du XVI^c siècle', *Bulletin monumental*, 90 (1931), 91 (1932).

L'église de Saint-Riquier (Paris, 1933).

Dusevel, H., 'Notes sur la construction et la décoration des édifices publics dans la ville d'Amiens au XVI^c siècle', *La Picardie* 6 (1860).

'Les troupes boulonnais à Amiens au XVe siècle', *Revue des Sociétés Savantes* ser. 5, vol. IV, 151–5.

Duseval, H., baron de La Fons Mélicocq *et al.*, *Eglises, château, beffrois et hôtels de ville les plus remarquables de la Picardie et de l'Artois*, 2 vols. (Amiens, 1846–9).

Elias, N., *The Civilizing Process*, vol. II: *State Formation and Civilization*.

Ezpezel, P. d', 'L'organisation militaire de la France pendant la première partie du XVIe siècle', *Positions des thèses de l'Ecole des Chartes*, 1916.

Febvre, L., *A New Kind of History from the Writings of Febvre*, ed. P. Burke (London, 1973).

Fernandez-Santamaria, J. A., *The State, War and Peace: Spanish Political Thought in the Renaissance, 1516–1559* (Cambridge, 1977).

Fernal, 'Notice sur les limites de la Picardie et de la Normandie', *MSAP* 2, 259ff.

Flammermont, J., *Histoire des institutions municipales de Senlis* (Paris, 1881).

Fleury, M., 'Le bailliage d'Amiens, son ressort et le problème des limites administratives au moyen âge', *BEC*, 1956.

Fogel, M. *Les cérémonies d'information dans la France du XVIe au XVIIIe siècle* (Paris, 1989).

Fossier, R., *La terre et les hommes en Picardie jusques à la fin du XIIIe siècle* (Paris, 1968).

(ed.), *Histoire de la Picardie* (Paris, 1974).

Foucher, M., *L'invention des frontières* (Paris, 1987).

François, M., *Le cardinal François de Tournon: homme d'état, diplomate, mécène et humaniste, 1489–1562* (Paris, 1951).

Galametz, M., 'Montres et revues intéressant la Picardie', *BSEA* 4 (1897–9), 440–4.

Gérard, 'Ambleteuse. Un procès où se mêle l'histoire', *Année boulonnaise* 2, 189ff.

Genet, J.-P. (ed.), *Genèse de l'état moderne: bilans et perspectives* (Paris, CNRS,1990).

Germain, L., *René II, duc de Lorrain et le comté de Guise* (Nancy, 1888).

Gerrebout, J., 'Monographie d'Ambleteuse', *MSAB* 28 91917), 72–276.

Godard, J., 'Quatre exemples de réparation de dommages de guerre en Picardie au XV^c siècle', *BSAP* 40 (1943–4), 207–12.

Godard, J. *et al.*, *Visages de Picardie* (Paris, 1967; earlier edn, 1949).

Gomart, C., *Ham, son château, ses prisonniers.* Saint-Quentin, 1864.

'Les seigneurs et gouverneurs de Ham', *MSAP* 18, 325ff.

'Le Câtelet et ses sièges', *BSA Laon* 14 (1864), 25–56.

Essai historique sur la ville de Ribemont (Saint-Quentin, 1869).

Etudes Saint-Quentinoises, 5 vols. (Saint-Quentin, 1844–78).

Gosselin, J., 'Siege de Péronne en 1536', *La Picardie* 14 (1868), 15 (1869).
Mailly et ses seigneurs (Péronne, 1876).
Greengrass, M., 'Property and Politics in the Sixteenth Century: the Landed Fortune of Constable Anne de Montmorency', *French History* 2 (1988), 371–98.
Grignard, F., 'Antoine de Luxembourg, comte de Brienne', *Bull. d'histoire et d'archéologie religieuse du diocèse de Dijon* 3 (1885), 209–28.
Gross, R., 'Registering and Ranking of Tension Areas', in *Confini e Regioni: Il potentiale di sviluppo e di pace delle periferie* (Trieste, 1973).
Guénée, B., 'La géographie administrative de la France à la fin du Moyen Age: élections et bailliages', *Le Moyen Age* 67 (1961).
Tribunaux et gens de justice dans le bailliage de Senlis à la fin du Moyen Age (Strasbourg, 1963).
'L'histoire de l'état en France à la fin du Moyen Age', *RH* 232 (1964), 331-60.
'Espace et Etat en la France médiévale', *Annales* (1968), 744–58.
Guilbert, J., *Les institutions municipales du Montreuil-sur-Mer* (Lille, 1954).
Gunn, S., 'The Duke of Suffolk's March on Paris in 1523', *EHR* (1986), 496–558.
Gutmann, M. P., *War and Rural Life in the Early Modern Low Countries* (Princeton, 1980).
Guynemer, *La seigneurie d'Offémont* (Compiègne, 1912).
Haigneré, D., 'Boulogne sous l'occupation anglaise en 1549', *BSAB* I (1864–72), 432–5.
'Quelles ont esté pour le chapitre de Thérouanne les conséquences des siège et prinse de cette ville en 1553?', *MSAB* 17 (1895–6), 258–303.
Hale, J. R., *War and Society in Renaissance Europe, 1450–1620* (London, 1985).
Hallopeau, L. A., *Essai sur l'histoire des comtes et ducs de Vendôme de la maison de Bourbon*, n.d., n.p.
Harding, R., *Anatomy of a Power Elite: the Provincial Governors of Early Modern France* (New Haven and London, 1978).
Harsgor, M., 'Recherches sur le personnel du conseil du roi sous Charles VIII et Louis XII' (typescript thesis, Paris IV, atelier de Lille, 1980).
Héliot, P., *Histoire de Boulogne et du Boulonnais* (Lille, 1937).
'L'église de Hesdin et l'architecture de la Renaissance en Artois', *Bulletin monumental* 97 (1937), 5–37.
'Louis XI et le Boulonnais', *BEC* 100 (1939), 112–44.
'Les demeures seigneuriales dans la région picarde au Moyen Age. Châteaux ou manoirs?', *Recueil de travaux offerts à M. Clovis Brunel* (Paris, 1955).
'Les fortifications de Boulogne sous l'occupation anglaise (1544–50)', *Revue du Nord* 40 (1958), 5–38.
Héliot, P. and Leducque, 'Les fortifications de Montreuil au Moyen Age', *Revue du Nord* 30 (1948), 159ff.
Heller, H., *Iron and Blood. Civil Wars in Sixteenth-Century France* (Montreal, 1991).
Hémery, M., *Monchy-Humières. Histoire d'un petit village de la vallée de l'Aronde* (Société d'histoire de Compiègne, 1946).
Henne, A., *Histoire du règne de Charles-Quint en Belgique*, 10 vols. (Brussels and Leipzig, 1858–60).

Henocque, J., *Histoire de l'abbaye, de la ville de Saint-Riquier, sa commune, sa noblesse, MSAP* in-4to, 9–11 (1880–93).

Héricourt, A. d', *Les sièges d'Arras* (Arras, 1844).

Hickey, D., *The Coming of French Absolutism: The Struggle for Tax Reform in the Province of Dauphiné 1540–1640* (Toronto, 1986).

Hirschauer, C., *Les états d'Artois*, 2 vols. (Paris and Brussels, 1923).

Hocquet, A., *Tournai et l'occupation anglaise* (Tournai, 1901).

Tournai et le Tournaisis au XVIe siècle du point de vue politique et social (Mémoires de l'Academie Royale de Belgique, 1906).

Houbigant, A. G., 'Notice sur le château de Sarcus tel qu'il devait être en 1550, précédée d'une vie de Jean de Sarcus', *MSAO* 3, 369ff.; 4, 158–220.

Houriez, E., 'Les institutions communales de la ville de Chauny (1166–1565)', *Positions des thèses de l'Ecole des Chartes*, 1951.

Hubscher, R. (ed.), *Histoire d'Amiens* (Paris, 1976).

Huguet, A., 'Jean de Poutrincourt, fondateur de Port-Royal en Acadie, vice-roi du Canada', *MSAP* 44 (1932).

'Le cardinal d'Aragon à Abbeville', *BSEA* (1932–4), 447–61.

'Artillerie et munitions du château du Crotoy en 1543', *BSAP* 37 (1937–8), 117–21.

'Autour de Ronsard. Un meutre à Abbeville en 1553', *BSAP* 37 (1937–8), 101–16.

'La table du prince de La Roche-sur-Yon à Abbeville en 1554', *BSAP* 40 (1943–4), 106–13.

Aspects de la Guerre de Cent Ans en Picardie Maritime, 2 vols., *MSAP* 48 and 50.

'Mort de MM. de Ferrières (1553)', *BSEA* (1953), 344–51.

Huguet, E., *Dictionnaire de la langue française au XVIe siècle*, 7 vols. (Paris, 1925–67).

Imbart de La Tour, P., *Les Origines de la Reforme*, 4 vols. (Paris, 1905-35).

Iung, J. E., 'L'organisation du service des vivres aux armées de 1550 à 1650', *BEC* (1983), 269–306.

Jacquart, J., *La crise rurale en Ile-de-France, 1550–1670* (Paris, 1974).

François Ier (Paris, 1981).

Jacqueton, G., 'Le trésor de l'Epargne sous François Ier', *RH* 55 (1894), 1–43; 56 (1894), 1–38.

Janvier, A., 'Notice sur les anciennes corporations d'archers, de couleuvriniers et d'arbalestriers des villes de Picardie', *MSAP* 14, 61ff.

Boves et ses seigneurs (Amiens, 1877).

'Le bâtard de Saint-Pol', *MSAP* 26 (1880), 385–434.

'Les Clabault, famille municipale amiénoise (1349–1539)* (Amiens, 1889).

La Vierge du Palmier. Tableau de 1520 de la Conférie du Puy d'Amiens (Amiens, 1896).

Janvier, A. and C. Bréard, *Etude sur Domart-les-Ponthieu* (Amiens, 1878).

Josse, H., 'Histoire de la ville de Bray-sur-Somme', *MSAP* 27, 185ff.

Jouanna, A., 'Recherches sur la notion d'honneur au XVIe siècle' *RHMC* 15 (1968).

Ordre social, Mythes et hiérarchies dans la France du XVIe siècle (Paris, 1977).

L'Idée de race en France au XVIe siècle et au début du XVIIe (abridged version of 1976 thesis, Montpellier, 1981, 2 vols).

Le devoir de révolte. La noblesse française et la gestation de l'Etat moderne, 1559–1661 (Paris, 1989).

Jumel, E., 'Monographie d'Heilly', *La Picardie* 19 (1874).

Kettering, S., *Judicial Politics and Urban Revolt in 17th Century France. The Parlement of Aix 1629–59* (Princeton, 1978).

'Patronage and Kinship in Early Modern France', *French Historical Studies* 16 (1989), 408–35.

'Clientage During the French Wars of Religion', *Sixteenth-Century Journal* 20 (1989), 221–39.

Knecht, R. J., 'Francis I and Paris', *History* 66 (1981).

Francis I (Cambridge, 1982).

Labande, L. H., *Le château de Marchais* (Paris, 1927).

Labande-Mailfert, Y., *Charles VIII et son milieu. La jeunesse au pouvoir* (Paris, 1975).

Labarre, A., *Le livre dans la vie amiénoise. L'enseignement des inventaires apres décès 1503–76* (Paris and Louvain, 1971).

'Recherches sur le commerce du livre à Amiens à la fin du XVᵉ et au XVIᵉ siecles', *BSAP* 50, 11–42.

La Fons Mélicocq, baron de, *Recherches historiques sur Noyon et le Noyonais* (Noyon, 1841).

'Péronne en temps de peste, XVIᵉ siècle', *La Picardie* 2 (1856), 506-12.

'Contestation entre l'abbé et les religieux de Saint-Riquier et les habitans de Mélicocq', *La Picardie* 4 (1858), 209–15.

'Guerres de Charles le Téméraire en Picardie depuis la paix de Péronne jusqu'à la levée du siège de Beauvais, 1468–72', *La Picardie* 5 (1859), 225–30.

'Recherches sur l'administration municipale des cités picardes aux XIVᵉ, XVᵉ et XVIᵉ siècles', *La Picardie* 5 (1859), 310–22, 502–15.

'Guerres de Picardie sous François Ier et Henri II (1527–57)', *La Picardie* 6 (1860), 274–89.

'Tailles et impositions diverses acquittées par la ville de Péronne aux XVᵉ et XVIᵉ siècles', *La Picardie* 12 (1866), 468–80.

La Fons Mélicocq, baron de and M. de Lioux, 'Notice sur la ville et le château de Ham', *MSAP* 2, 273ff.

Laine, L., *Généalogie illustrée de la maison de Sarcus*. Archives généalogiques de la noblesse de France, X (1858).

Lambert, E., 'Les limites de Picardie', *Mémoires de la Société historique, archéologique et scientifique de Noyon* 34 (1972), 53–65.

La Morandière, C. de, *Histoire de la maison d'Estouteville en Normandie* (Paris, 1903).

Lamy, F., 'La Malmaison. Echevinage et bailliage d'Amiens', *BSAP* 31 (1924–5), 312–59.

La Picardie historique et monumentale, 7 vols. SAP (Amiens, 1893–1931).

Laroche, A., 'Une vengeance de Louis XI', *MASA* 37 (1865).

Lecat, L., *Deux siècles d'histoire en Picardie, 1300–1498* (Annales du Centre Régional de Documentation Pédagogique d'Amiens, 1971).

Lecocq, A.-M., 'Le Puy d'Amiens de 1518', *Revue de l'Art* 38 (1977), 64–74.

François Ier imaginaire. Symbolique et politique à l'aube de la Renaissance française (Paris, 1987).

Lecocq, G., 'Histoire de la peste à Saint-Quentin (1401–1792)', *Le Vermandois* 5 (1877), 109–90, 494ff.

Ledieu, A., 'Une seigneurie au XVᵉ siècle (Mareuil)', *La Picardie* (1883), 253–65.

'Notes tirées du voyage d'un Rochellois dans le Nord de la France au XVIᵉ siècle', *Cab. hist.* (1889–90), 349–51; (1890–1), 19–20.

'Notice sur Tilloloy', *Cab. hist.* (1890–1), 123–4.

'Les funérailles de Louis de Hallewin à Maignelay en 1519–20', *Cab. hist.* (1892–3), 48–54, 74–86.

'Creation du franc-marché d'Abbeville (1506–17)', *MSEA* 19 (1893–7), 517ff.

'Un grand seigneur picard au XVIᵉ siècle', *Bulletin de la Conférence scientifique d'Abbeville et du Ponthieu* III.

Lefebvre, F., *Les huguenots et la ligue au diocèse de Boulogne. Esquisse historique* (Boulogne, 1855).

Lefebvre, T., *Sénarpont et ses seigneurs* (Amiens, 1876).

Lefils, F., *Histoire de la ville de Rue* (Abbeville, 1860).

Legrand, A., 'Notice explicative d'un plan d'un siège de Thérouanne, decouvert aux archives de la Tour de Londres', *MSA Morinie* 5, 367–409.

Lemaître, N., *Le Rouergue flamboyant. Le clergé et les fidèles du diocèse de Rodez 1417–1563* (Paris, 1988).

Le Mené, M., *Les campagnes angevines à la fin du moyen-âge (v. 1350–v. 1530)* (Nantes, 1982).

Lennel, F., *Histoire de Calais*, 2 vols. (Calais, 1908–10).

L'Epinois, E. de B. de, *Histoire de la ville et des sires de Coucy* (1859).

Le Proux, F., 'Sorcières brulées à Chauny en 1485', *Le Vermandois* 1 (1873), 385–9.

Leroy, B., 'Autour de Charles "le mauvais". Groupes et personnalites', *RH* 553 (1985), 3–18.

Le Roy Ladurie, E., *Les paysans de Languedoc*, 2 vols. (Paris, 1966).

L'Etat royal de Louis XI à Henri IV (Paris, 1987).

The French Peasantry, 1450–1650 (English trans., Aldershot, 1987).

Lesort, A., 'Un document inédit concernant la diplomatie de Louis XI à propos de la neutralité de Tournai (1478–9)', *BEC* 62 (1901), 15-24.

'La succession de Charles le Témeraire à Cambrai (1477–82)', *MSEC* 55.

Lestocquoy, J., 'Relations artistiques entre Arras et Amiens à la fin du XVᵉ et au début du XVIᵉ siècle', *BSAP* 37 (1937–8), 325–7.

Beffrois, Halles, Hôtels de Ville dans le Nord de la France et la Belgique (Arras, 1948).

'De la prise de Calais au traité du Cateau-Cambrésis', *Revue du Nord* (1958), 39–47.

Histoire de la Picardie et du Boulonnais (Paris, 1962).

Lesure, F. (ed.), *La Renaissance dans le Nord de la France*. CNRS (Paris, 1956).

Lewis, P. S., *Later Mediaeval France: the Polity* (London, 1968).

(ed.), *The Recovery of France in the Fifteenth Century* (London, 1971).

Essays in Later Medieval French History, 1985.

Lhomel, G. de, *Le bailliage royal de Montreuil-sur-Mer, ses principaux officiers (1360–1790)* (Abbeville, 1903).

Libaut, A., *Histoire de la cartogrtaphie* (Paris, 1964).

Liot de Nortbécourt, E., 'Epitaphe du maréchal d'Esquerdes par Jean Molinet', *BSA Morinie* 8, 632–59.
'Le maréchal d'Esquerdes', *BSA Morinie* 9, 865–931.
Lloyd, H. A., *The State, France and the Sixteenth Century* (London, 1983).
Longeon, C., *Une province française à la Renaissance. La vie intellectuelle en Forez au XVIe siècle* (Sainte-Etienne, 1975).
Longnon, A., 'L'Isle-de-France, son origine, ses limites, ses gouverneurs', *Mémoires de la Société de l'Histoire de Paris et l'Ile-de-France* I (1875).
Lot, F., 'L'Etat des paroisses et des feux de 1328', *BEC* 90 (1929), 51–107, 256–316.
Recherches sur les effectifs des armées françaises des guerres d'Italie aux guerres de religion, 1494–1562 (Paris, 1962).
Louandre, F. C., *Histoire d'Abbeville et du comté de Ponthieu*, 2 vols. (Abbeville, 1884).
Louvencourt, A. de, *Les Trésoriers de France de la Généralité de Picardie* (Amiens, 1896).
Macqueron, H., *Iconographie du département de la Somme* (Abbeville, 1886).
Bibliographie du département de la Somme, MSAP in-4to, documents inédits 15 (1904).
'Essai sur l'histoire de la Confrérie de Notre-Dame de Puy d'Abbeville', *MSEA* sér, 4, VIII (1917), 289–486.
'Essai sur les portraits picards', *MSAP* 30, 245ff.
Mallett, M. E. and J. R. Hale, *The Military Organisation of a Renaissance State: Venice, c. 1400–1617* (Cambridge, 1984).
Mandrot, B. de, 'Jacques d'Armagnac, duc de Nemours 1433–77', *RH* 43 (1889), 274–316; 44 (1980), 241–312.
Maravall, J. A., 'The Origins of the Modern State', *Journal of World History* 6 (1961), 789–808.
Marchand, C., *Charles Ier de Cossé, comte de Brissac et maréchal de France, 1507–63* (Paris and Angers, 1889).
Marsy, A., *Mélanges sur le Vermandois aux XIVe et XVe siècles* (Saint-Quentin, 1874).
Marsy, comte de, 'L'exécution d'un arrêt du Parlement au XVe siècle. Adjudication du château de Raincheval et mise en possession du nouveau seigneur (1469)', *MSAP* 26 (1880), 149–64.
'La peste à Compiegne (XVe et XVIe siècles)', *La Picardie* (1878–84), 281–301.
Marsy, M. E. de, 'Note sur un miracle en déc. 1531 à Notre-Dame-de-Lorette-de-Saint-Wulfran d'Abbeville', *MSEA* 6 (1844–8), 267ff.
Matton, A., *Histoire de la ville et des environs de Guise*, 2 vols. (Laon, 1898).
Maugis, E., *Recherches sur les transformations du régime politique et sociale de la ville d'Amiens, des origines de la commune à la fin du XVIe siècle* (Paris, 1906).
Essai sur le régime financier de la ville d'Amiens, MSAP in-4to, 33.
Essai sur le recrutement et les attributions des principaux officiers du siège du bailliage d'Amiens de 1300 à 1600 (Paris, 1906).
La saieterie à Amiens, 1480–1587 (Vierteljahrschrift für Social- und Wirtschafts-geschichte, 1907).
Michaud, C., 'Finances et guerres de religion en France', *RHMC* 1981, 572–6.

Michaud, H., *La grande chancellerie et les écritures royales au XVIe siècle (1515–1589)* (Paris, 1967).

'Les institutions militaires des guerres d'Italie aux guerres de religion', *RH* 258 (1977).

Mignet, F., *La rivalité de François Ier et de Charles-Quint*, 2 vols. (Paris, 1875).

Mirot, L., *Dom Bévy et les comptes des trésoriers des guerres* (Paris, 1925).

Manuel de géographie historique de la France (Paris, 1929).

Miskimin, H., *Money and Power in Fifteenth-Century France* (1984).

Monnecove, F. Le Sergent de, 'Siège de Thérouanne et trève de Bomy en 1537', *BSA Morinie* 6, 217–58.

La Prise de Tournehem et de La Montoire (1542) (Paris and Chartres, 1873).

Morel, A., 'L'espace sociale d'un village picard', *Etudes rurales* 45 (1972), 62–80.

Mousnier, R., *Le conseil du roi de Louis XII à la Revolution* (Paris, 1970).

Les institutions de la France sous la monarchie absolue, 2 vols. (Paris, 1974–80).

'Centralisation et décentralisation', *XVIIe siècle* 155 (1987), 101–11.

La France de 1492 à 1559 (Cours de Sorbonne, n.d.).

Mousnier, R. and F. Hartung, 'Quelques problèmes concernant la monarchie absolue', *Relazione de X Congresso Internationale di Scienze Storiche* IV (Rome, 1955).

Muchembled, R., *La violence au village. Sociabilité et comportements populaires en Artois du XVe au XVIIe siècles* (Paris, 1990).

Neuschel, K., 'The Prince of Condé and the Nobility of Picardy: a Study of Noble Relationships in the Sixteenth Century' (Brown Univ. Thesis, 1982).

'The Picard Nobility in the Sixteenth Century: Autonomy and Power', *PWSFH 1981* (1982), 42–9.

'Noble Households in the Sixteenth Century: Material Settings and Human Communities', *French Historical Studies* 15 (1988), 595–622.

Word of Honor. Interpreting Noble Culture in Sixteenth-Century France (Ithaca, 1989).

Neveux, H., 'L'expansion démographique dans un village du Cambrésis: Saint-Hilaire (1450–1575)', *Annales de démographie historique* (1971), 265–98.

Vie et déclin d'une structure économique. Les grains du Cambrésis, fin du XIVe–début du XVIIe siècle (Paris and The Hague, 1980).

Nicholls, D., 'The Nature of Popular Heresy in France, 1520–42', *Historical Journal* 26 (1983).

Nora, P. (ed.), *Lieux de Mémoire. II: La Nation* (Paris, 1986).

Oman, C., *A History of the Art of War in the Sixteenth Century* (London, 1937).

Orlea, M., *La noblesse aux Etats généraux de 1576 et de 1588* (Paris, 1980).

Palys, E. de, *Le capitaine de Breil, de Bretagne, baron des Hommeaux, gouverneur d'Abbeville, Saint-Quentin et de Granville . . . 1503–83* (Rennes, 1887).

Paris, P., *Etudes sur François Ier*, 2 vols. (Paris, 1885).

Pariset, J. D., *Les relations entre la France et l'Allemagne au milieu du XVIe siècle* (Strasbourg, 1981).

Pas, J. de, 'La reddition et la démolition de Thérouanne en 1513', *BSA Morinie* 13, 312–24.

'Notes pour servir à la statistique féodale dans l'estendue de l'ancien bailliage de Saint-Omer', *MSA Morinie* 34 (1926).

Peigné-Delacourt, *Histoire de l'abbaye de Notre-Dame d'Ourscamp* (Amiens, 1876).

Les anciens monuments du département de la Somme, n.d., n.p.

Peltier, H., 'Corbie, ville frontière', *BSAP* 39 (1941–2), 100-21.

Pepper, S. and A. Adams, *Firearms and Fortifications* (Chicago, 1986).

Perjes, L., 'Army Provisioning, Logistics and Strategy and the Second Half of the Seventeenth Century', *Acta Historica* 16 (1970), 1–51.

Perret, P. M., *Notice biographique sur Louis Malet de Graville, amiral de France (144?–1516)* (Paris, 1889).

Peter, R., 'Les lansquenets dans les armées du roi', in *Charles-Quint, le Rhin et la France*. Société Savante d'Alsace, Recherches, 17 (confer. 1973).

Pimodan, marquis de, *La mère des Guises, Antoinette de Bourbon* (Paris, 1925).

Pinard, *Chronologie historique-militaire*, 8 vols. (Paris, 1760–72).

Plancher, Y., *Histoire générale et particulière de Bourgogne*, 4 vols. (Dijon, 1739–81).

Poissonier, *Notes sur la ville de La Fère* (Chauny, 1898).

Potter, D. L., 'England and France, 1536–1550', Ph.D. dissertation, Cambridge, 1973.

'International Politics and Naval Jurisdiction in the Sixteenth Century: The Case of François de Montmorency', *European Studies Review* 7 (1977), 1–27.

'Foreign Policy in the Age of the Reformation: French Involvement in the Schmalkaldic War', *Historical Journal* 20 (1977), 525–44.

'The duc de Guise and the Fall of Calais', *EHR* 98 (1983), 481–512.

'A Treason Trial in Sixteenth-Century France: the Fall of Oudart du Biez (1549–52)', *EHR* 105 (1990), 595–623.

'Marriage and Cruelty Among the French Protestant Nobility: Jean de Rohan and Diane de Barbançon, 1561–67', *European History Quarterly* 20 (1990), 3–38.

'The Luxembourg Inheritance: the House of Bourbon and its Lands in Northern France during the Sixteenth Century', *French History* 6 (1992).

'Les Allemands et les armées françaises au XVIe siècle. Jean-Philippe Rhingrave, chef de lansquenets: étude suivie de sa correspondance en France, 1548–66', *Francia* 21, ii (forthcoming).

Praet, J. B. B. van, *Recherches sur Louis de Bruges, seigneur de La Gruthuyse* (Paris, 1831).

Prarond, E., *Notice sur Rambures. La Picardie* 3 and 4, *tirage à part* (Paris, 1859).

Histoire de cinq villes III, t. i (Saint-Valéry) (Paris and Abbeville, 1863).

Histoire d'Abbeville. Abbeville aux temps de Charles VII, des ducs de Bourgogne . . . de Louis XI (1426–83) (Paris, 1899).

Les lois et les moeurs à Abbeville (Abbeville, 1906).

Prévenier, W., 'La démographie des villes de Flandre aux XIVe et XVe siècles', *Revue du Nord* 65 (1983), 255–75.

Proyat, 'Louis XI à Arras', *MASA* 35 (1862), 69–122.

Procacci, 'La Fortuna del Arte della Guerra de Macchiavelli nella Francia del secolo XVI', *Rivista Storica Italiana* 67 (1958).

Renet, *Beauvais et le Beauvaisis aux temps modernes . . . 1461–83* (Beauvais, 1898).

Richard, R., 'Louis XI et l'échevinage d'Abbeville', *MSEA* 27 (1960), 1–146.

Richoufftz, comte de, 'Les Créquy dans le Vimeu', *MSEA* ser. 4, III, 1–277.

Rigault, J., 'La frontière de la Meuse. Utilisation des sources historiques dans un procès devant le Parlement de Paris en 1535', *BEC* 106 (1945–6), 80–99.

Rodière, R., 'Notes sur les gouverneurs de Montreuil', *Cab. hist.* (1892–3).

'Un lieutenant-général à Montreuil et sa famille au XVIe siècle', *BSEA* (1899), 492–541 (*tirage à part*, Abbeville, 1900).

La pays de Montreuil, supplement to *La Picardie historique et monumentale* (Paris, 1933).

'Le château d'Olhain', *BSAP* 36 (1935–6), 659–80.

Rodière, R. and P. des Forts, *Le pays de Vimeu*, suppl. to *La Picardie historique et monumentale* (Amiens, 1938).

Rodriguez-Salgado, M. J., *The Changing Face of Empire: Charles V, Philip II and Habsburg Authority, 1551–1559* (Cambridge, 1989).

Roelker, N. L., 'The Appeal of Calvinism to French Noblewomen in the Sixteenth Century', *Journal of Interdisciplinary History* 2 (1971–2), 391–418.

Romano, C. R., 'La pace di Cateau-Cambrésis e l'equilibrio europeo a metà del secolo XVI', *Rivista Storica Italiana* (1949).

Romier, L., *La carrière d'un favori: Jacques d'Albon de Saint-André, maréchal de France, 1512–62* (Paris, 1909).

Les origines politiques des guerres de religion, 2 vols. (Paris, 1913–14).

La conjuration d'Amboise (Paris, 1923).

Rosenberg, D., 'Social Experience and Religious Choice: a Case Study. The Protestant Weavers and Woolcombers of Amiens in the Sixteenth Century' (Ph.D. thesis, Yale, 1978).

Rosenfeld, P., 'The Provincial Governors of the Netherlands from the Minority of Charles V to the Revolt', *Standen en Landen/Anciens Pays et Assemblées d'Etats* 17 (1959).

Rosny, A. de, *Album historique du Boulonnais* (Neuville-sous-Montreuil, 1892).

'Travaux exécutés à Boulogne au XVIe siècle aux fortifications et bâtiments du Roi', *BSAB* 6 (1900–3).

Rosny, H. de, *Histoire du Boulonnais*, 3 vols. (Amiens, 1868–73).

Rosny, L. E. de La Gorgue, *Recherches généalogiques sur les comtés de Ponthieu, de Boulogne, de Guînes et pays circonvoisins*, 4 vols. (Boulogne, 1874–7).

Rossier, H., *Histoire des Protestants de Picardie* (Amiens, 1861).

Ruble, baron A. de, *Le mariage de Jeanne d'Albret* (Paris, 1877).

Antoine de Bourbon et Jeanne d'Albret, 4 vols. (Paris, 1881–6).

Le traité de Cateau-Cambrésis (Paris, 1889).

Russell, J. G., *Peacemaking in the Renaissance* (London, 1986).

Russell Major, J., *Representative Institutions in Renaissance France, 1421–1559* (Madison, Wisconsin, 1960).

The Deputies to the Estates General in Renaissance France (Madison, Wisconsin, 1960).

Representative Government in Early Modern France (New Haven, Conn., 1980).

'Noble Income, Inflation and the Wars of Religion in France', *American Historical Review* 86 (1981).

Sabean, D., *Power in the Blood. Popular Culture and Village Discourse in Early Modern Germany* (Cambridge, 1984).

Sachy, E. de, *Essais sur l'histoire de Péronne* (Péronne, 1866).

Sahlins, P., *Boundaries. The Making of France and Spain in the Pyrenees* (Berkeley, Calif., 1989).

Samaran, C., *La maison d'Armagnac au XVᵉ siècle et les dernières luttes de la féodalité dans le midi de la France* (Paris, 1908).

Sartre, J., *Chateaux 'brique et pierre' en Picardie* (Paris, 1973).

Saulnier, E., *Le rôle politique du cardinal de Bourbon (Charles X) 1523–1590* (Paris, 1912).

Schelesser, N. D., 'Frontiers in Medieval French History', *International History Review* 6 (1984).

Schrader, F., *Atlas de géographie historique* (Paris, 1895, rev., 1907).

Sée, H., *Louis XI et les villes* (Paris, 1891).

Seydoux, P., *Le château de Rambures et la guerre au XVᵉ siècle en Picardie* (Paris, 1974).

Shelby, L. R., *John Rogers, Tudor Military Engineer* (Oxford, 1967).

Shimizu, J., *Conflict of Loyalties: Politics and Religion in the Career of Gaspard de Coligny, Admiral of France, 1519–72* (Geneva, 1970).

Sneller, Z. W., 'Le commerce de blé hollandais dans la région de la Somme au XVe siècle', trans. J. Godard, *BSAP* (1947), 140–60.

Solon, P. D., 'War and the *Bonnes Villes*: The Case of Narbonne, ca. 1450–1550', *PWSFH* (1990), 65–73.

'Le rôle des forces armées en Comminges avant les guerres de Religion (1502–62)', *Annales du Midi* 103 (1991), 19–40.

Spont, A., 'La taille en Languedoc de 1450 à 1515', *Annales du Midi* 2 (1890), 365–84; 478–513; 3 (1891), 482–94.

'Une recherche générale des feux à la fin du XVᵉ siècle', *Ann.-bull. de la SHF* (1892), 222–36.

'La milice des francs archers, 1448–1550', *Revue des questions historiques* (1897).

Stein, H., *La bataille de Saint-Quentin et les prisonniers français (1557–59)* (Saint-Quentin, 1889).

Stein, H. and L. Le Grand, *La frontière d'Argonne (843–1659). Procès de Claude de La Vallée (1535–61)* (Paris, 1905).

Sterling, C., 'La peinture sur panneau picarde et son rayonnement dans le Nord de la France au XVᵉ siècle', *Bulletin de la Société de l'histoire de l'art français* année 1979 (1981), 7–49.

Sutherland, N. M., *Princes, Politics and Religion 1547–1589* (London, 1984).

Suzanne, général, *Histoire de l'infanterie française* (Paris, 1876).

Thelliez, C., 'Après la paix de Cateau-Cambrésis de 1559. Négotiations engagées pour fixer les limites entre les possessions françaises au Nord et a l'Est de la France', *Standen en Landen Anciens Pays et Assemblées d'Etats* 48 (1969).

Marie de Luxembourg. Standen en Landen 52 (1970).

Thobois, E., *Le château de Hardelot* (Montreuil, 1905).

Thomas, A., 'Jean de Salazar et le guet-apens d'Amiens, 23 juillet 1471', *BEC* 86, 122–67.

Thompson, J. W., *The French Wars of Religion, 1559–76* (New York, 1957).

Thorpe, L., 'Philippe de Crèvecoeur, seigneur d'Esquerdes: two epitaphs by Jean

Molinet and Nicaise Ladam', *Bull. de la Commission Royale d'Histoire*, 119 (1954).

Tourtier, C., 'Le péage de Picquigny', *BPH* (1960), 271–94.

Traullé, L. J., *Quelques faits de l'histoire d'Abbeville tirés des registres de l'échevinage* (Abbeville, 1876).

Trénard, L. (ed.), *Histoire des Pays-Bas français* (Toulouse, 1972).

Histoire des Pays-Bas français: Documents (Toulouse, 1974).

(ed.), *Histoire de Cambrai* (Lille, 1982).

Turpin, 'La survivance dans les noms de lieux de la notion de limite', *Revue du Nord* 17 (1932), 195ff.

Vaissière, P. de, *Récits du temps des troubles (XVIe siècle). Une famille, les d'Alègre* (Paris, 1914).

Vaughan, R., *Charles the Bold* (London, 1973).

Vaux de Foletier, F. de, *Galiot de Genouillac* (Paris, 1925).

Vieux Manoirs du Boulonnais, Commission départementale des Monuments du Pas-de-Calais, 1915.

Vincent, M., 'Fondation d'Hesdinfert: conseils politiques addressées à la princesse Marie', *MSA Morinie*, 1857.

Vinchon, 'Des droits seigneuriaulx dans la coutume du Vermandois', *BSA Laon* 4 (1854), 144–57.

Vindry, Fleury, *Dictionnaire de l'Etat-major français au XVIe siècle. Première partie. Gendarmerie* (Paris and Bergerac, 1901).

Wellens, R., *Les états-generaux des Pays-Bas des origines à la fin du règne de Philippe le Beau (1464–1506). Standen en Landen/Anciens Pays et Assemblées d'Etats* (1972).

Wolfe, M., *The Fiscal System of Renaissance France* (New Haven, Conn., and London, 1972).

Wood, J. B., 'The Decline of the Nobility in 16th and early 17th Century France: Myth or Reality?' *Journal of Modern History* 38 (1976).

'The Impact of the Wars of Religion: a View of France in 1581', *Sixteenth-Century Journal* 15 (1984), 131–68.

Zanettacci, H., 'Statuaire de la façade à Saint-Vulfran d'Abbeville', *Bulletin monumental* 95 (1936), 333–68.

Les ateliers picards de sculptures à la fin du Moyen Age (Paris, 1954).

Zeller, G., *Le siège de Metz par Charles-Quint*, 2 vols. (Nancy, 1942).

'De quelques institutions mal connues au XVIe siècle', *RH* (1944).

Les institutions de la France au XVIe siècle (Paris, 1948).

Aspects de la politique française sous l'Ancien Régime (Paris, 1964).

INDEX

La Rochepot, François de Montmorency, sr.
de (d. 1551), 72–9, 100–1, 103, 105,
132–3, 147, 150, 164–5, 172, 176, 184,
186, 191, 198–9, 240, 312
captain of Beauvais, 118–23, 125
Charlotte de Humières, Mme de, 73, 132,
134
death of, 133
entry at Paris, 102
gendarmerie company of, 161–2, 320–3
letters of provision for, 99–101
La Roche-sur-Yon, Charles de Bourbon,
prince of, 80, 323
Louise de Bourbon, princess of, 72
L'Aubespine, Claude de, *secrétaire d'état*, 83,
105
Le Vaulx, *valet de chambre du roi*
commissaire, 195
Lecat, Firmin, sr. de Fontaines, mayor of
Amiens, 262, 304
Le Câtelet (Aisne, arr. Saint-Quentin), 83, 94,
314
Le Crotoy (Somme, arr. Abbeville), 169
governors of, 127, 314–15, 317
treaty of (1472), 33
Lefèbvre d'Etaples, 28
Legay, maître, Paris lawyer, 172, 185
legions, 18, 95, 173–7
of Champagne, 175
depredations of, 123, 135
of Ile-de-France, 176
of Normandy, 175–6
of Picardy, 136, 175–7
see also Canny; Heilly; Sarcus; Du Biez
Le Grand, Benoit, *trés. de l'extraord. des*
guerres, 187, 327
Le Havre, 192
Le Normant, Jean, mayor of Amiens, 119
Lens (Pas-de-Calais, arr. Béthune), 37, 216,
218
truce of (1477), 39
Le Prestre, Pierre, *abbé* of Saint-Riquier, 27,
33, 46, 60–2
Le Sueur, Guillaume, sec. to Vendôme and La
Rochepot, 106
Levain, sec. to Vendôme, 106
Liane, river, 282
Ligny, *see* Luxembourg
Lille (Nord), 38, 62, 221, 230, 271–2,
277
Lilliers (Pas-de-Calais, arr. Béthune), 40,
212
Lohéac, André de Laval, sr. de, *maréchal*
(d. 1486), 66
Longueval, family, 116
see also Haraucourt

Longueval, Nicolas de Bossu, sr. de, *mr.*
d'hôtel du roi and *bailli* of Vermandois
(d. *c.* 1548), 111, 312, 314, 210
Lorges, Jacques de Montgommery, sr. de, 175
Lorraine, dukes of, 35, 70
Lorraine, Charles, cardinal de (d. 1574), 83,
134, 217
see also Aumale; Guise
Louis XI, king of France (1461–83), 1, 4–6, 8,
13–14, 30–60 *passim*, 66, 70, 91, 96,
101, 114–15, 150, 169–70, 233, 242, 250,
254–9, 305
Louis XII, king of France (1498–1515), 8,
44–7, 49, 102, 173, 243, 257
as duke of Orléans, 94
Louise of Savoy, Regent (d. 1531), 9, 71, 132,
135, 146
Louvel, Antoine, mayor of Amiens, 262
Lucheux, *châtellenie* of (Somme, arr.
Doullens), 20–1, 220–1
Luxembourg, duchy of, 35, 156
Luxembourg, family of, 21, 47–8, 51, 66–7,
227, 270
Jean de, count of Marle (d. 1476), 48, 58
Louis de, count of Saint-Pol, constable
(ex. 1475), 13, 31–6, 45, 47, 54, 59, 70,
231
Louis de, count of Ligny (d. 1503), 67–8,
115, 310
Marie de, dowager duchess of Vendôme
(d. 1546), 48–9, 66–7, 73, 111, 143, 220,
227, 252, 275–6, 277, 311
Pierre II de, count of Saint-Pol (d. 1482),
48
see also Brienne; Richebourg

Macchiavelli, Niccolo, 174
Macquereau, chronicler, 97
Madrid, treaty of, 267, 270–4, 282
Mailly, family of, 6, 117, 135
Jean III, sr. de (d. 1505), 46, 310
Nicolas de (d. 1475), 46
René I bar. de (d. 1572), governor of
Montreuil, 127, 183, 302, 316
see also Auchy; Conty; Roye
Maine, count of, *see* Anjou
Mametz, sr. de, 150
Maretz, *mar. de logis*, comp. Vendôme, 112
Marguerite of Angoulême, queen of Navarre,
71–2, 73
Marguerite of Austria, regent of the
Netherlands (d. 1530), 40, 44, 45, 70, 143
Marini, Girolamo, engineer, 181–2
Ippolito, mercenary, 181–2
Marivaulx, Jean de Lisle, sr. de, dep. gov. Ile-
de-France, 79n, 103, 186